AMSTERDAM & THE NETHERLANDS

1st Edition

Where to Stay and Eat
for All Budgets

Must-See Sights
and Local Secrets

Ratings You Can Trust

Fodor's Travel Publications   New York, Toronto, London, Sydney, Auckland
www.fodors.com

FODOR'S AMSTERDAM & THE NETHERLANDS

Editor: Margaret Kelly

Editorial Production: Astrid deRidder
Editorial Contributors: Neil Carlson, Susan Carroll, Nicole Chabot, Madelon Evers, Karina Hof, Ann Maher, Shain Shapiro, Tim Skelton, Mark Sullivan
Maps & Illustrations: Bob Blake and Rebecca Baer, *map editors*
Design: Fabrizio LaRocca, *creative director*; Guido Caroti, Siobhan O'Hare, *art directors*; Tina Malaney, Chie Ushio, Ann McBride, *designers*; Melanie Marin, *senior picture editor;* Moon Sun Kim, *cover designer*
Cover Photo: (Keizersgracht bridge): SIME s.a.s/eStock Photo
Production/Manufacturing: Steve Slawsky

1st Edition

ISBN 978–1–4000–1917–5

ISSN 1937–8599

SPECIAL SALES

This book is available at special discounts for bulk purchases for sales promotions or premiums. Special editions, including personalized covers, excerpts of existing books, and corporate imprints, can be created in large quantities for special needs. For more information, write to Special Markets/Premium Sales, 1745 Broadway, MD 6-2, New York, New York 10019, or e-mail specialmarkets@randomhouse.com.

AN IMPORTANT TIP & AN INVITATION

Although all prices, opening times, and other details in this book are based on information supplied to us at press time, changes occur all the time in the travel world, and Fodor's cannot accept responsibility for facts that become outdated or for inadvertent errors or omissions. So **always confirm information when it matters,** especially if you're making a detour to visit a specific place. Your experiences—positive and negative—matter to us. If we have missed or misstated something, **please write to us.** We follow up on all suggestions. Contact the Amsterdam & the Netherlands editor at editors@fodors.com or c/o Fodor's at 1745 Broadway, New York, NY 10019.

PRINTED IN THE UNITED STATES OF AMERICA
10 9 8 7 6 5 4 3 2

Be a Fodor's Correspondent

Your opinion matters. It matters to us. It matters to your fellow Fodor's travelers, too. And we'd like to hear it. In fact, we need to hear it.

When you share your experiences and opinions, you become an active member of the Fodor's community. That means we'll not only use your feedback to make our books better, but we'll publish your names and comments whenever possible. Throughout our guides, look for "Word of Mouth," excerpts of your unvarnished feedback.

Here's how you can help improve Fodor's for all of us.

Tell us when we're right. We rely on local writers to give you an insider's perspective. But our writers and staff editors—who are the best in the business—depend on you. Your positive feedback is a vote to renew our recommendations for the next edition.

Tell us when we're wrong. We're proud that we update most of our guides every year. But we're not perfect. Things change. Hotels cut services. Museums change hours. Charming cafés lose charm. If our writer didn't quite capture the essence of a place, tell us how you'd do it differently. If any of our descriptions are inaccurate or inadequate, we'll incorporate your changes in the next edition and will correct factual errors at fodors.com immediately.

Tell us what to include. You probably have had fantastic travel experiences that aren't yet in Fodor's. Why not share them with a community of like-minded travelers? Maybe you chanced upon a beach or bistro or B&B that you don't want to keep to yourself. Tell us why we should include it. And share your discoveries and experiences with everyone directly at fodors.com. Your input may lead us to add a new listing or highlight a place we cover with a "Highly Recommended" star or with our highest rating, "Fodor's Choice."

Give us your opinion instantly at our feedback center at www.fodors.com/feedback. You may also e-mail editors@fodors.com with the subject line "Amsterdam & the Netherlands Editor." Or send your nominations, comments, and complaints by mail to Amsterdam & the Netherlands Editor, Fodor's, 1745 Broadway, New York, NY 10019.

You and travelers like you are the heart of the Fodor's community. Make our community richer by sharing your experiences. Be a Fodor's correspondent.

Goede reis!

Tim Jarrell, Publisher

CONTENTS

ABOUT THIS BOOK

Our Ratings

Sometimes you find terrific travel experiences and sometimes they just find you. But usually the burden is on you to select the right combination of experiences. That's where our ratings come in.

As travelers we've all discovered a place so wonderful that its worthiness is obvious. And sometimes that place is so experiential that superlatives don't do it justice: you just have to be there to know. These sights, properties, and experiences get our highest rating, **Fodor's Choice**, indicated by orange stars throughout this book.

Black stars highlight sights and properties we deem **Highly Recommended**, places that our writers, editors, and readers praise again and again for consistency and excellence.

By default, there's another category: any place we include in this book is by definition worth your time, unless we say otherwise. And we will.

Disagree with any of our choices? Care to nominate a place or suggest that we rate one more highly? Visit our feedback center at www.fodors.com/feedback.

Budget Well

Hotel and restaurant price categories from ¢ to $$$$ are defined in the opening pages of each chapter. For attractions, we always give standard adult admission fees; reductions are usually available for children, students, and senior citizens. Want to pay with plastic? **AE, D, DC, MC, V** following restaurant and hotel listings indicate if American Express, Discover, Diners Club, MasterCard, and Visa are accepted.

Restaurants

Unless we state otherwise, restaurants are open for lunch and dinner daily. We mention dress only when there's a specific requirement and reservations only when they're essential or not accepted—it's always best to book ahead.

Hotels

Hotels have private bath, phone, TV, and air-conditioning and operate on the European Plan (aka EP, meaning without meals), unless we specify that they use the Continental Plan (CP, with a Continental breakfast), Breakfast Plan (BP, with a full breakfast), or Modified American Plan (MAP, with breakfast and dinner) or are all-inclusive (including all meals and most activities). We always list facilities but not whether you'll be charged an extra fee to use them, so when pricing accommodations, find out what's included.

Many Listings
★	Fodor's Choice
★	Highly recommended
✉	Physical address
✛	Directions
⟐	Mailing address
☎	Telephone
🖷	Fax
⊕	On the Web
✉	E-mail
🎫	Admission fee
⊙	Open/closed times
Ⓜ	Metro stations
▭	Credit cards

Hotels & Restaurants
🏨	Hotel
🛏	Number of rooms
⟁	Facilities
❍	Meal plans
✕	Restaurant
⟁	Reservations
✎	Smoking
BYOB	BYOB
✕🏨	Hotel with restaurant that warrants a visit

Outdoors
⚐	Golf
⛺	Camping

Other
🕙	Family-friendly
⇨	See also
✉	Branch address
☞	Take note

WHEN TO GO

The Netherlands is at its best when the temperatures climb, and cafés and restaurants spill across sidewalks to invite leisurely alfresco meals. Unfortunately, because such weather is so transient, you may find yourself sharing your sun-dappled experience with many others. Spring is the driest time of year, and since it's also when the famous tulip fields bloom (April and May are the prime bloom-viewing months), this is the most popular time to visit Holland.

From tulip time (about mid-April) onward, it becomes increasingly difficult to book accommodation reservations. In addition, with the approach of summer, museums, galleries, and tourist sights heave with visitors. Some say that if you're making an extended tour of Europe, you should consider scheduling Holland for the beginning or end of your itinerary, saving July and August for exploring less crowded countries.

If you have to visit in high summer, be sure to take a vacation from your Amsterdam vacation with some side trips to outer towns that have historic, quaint Dutch beauty without the crush. The main cultural calendar runs from September through June, but happily there are so many festivals and open-air events scheduled during the summer that no one really notices.

Climate

Weather-wise, the best months for sightseeing are April, May, June, September, and October, when the days are long and the summer crowds have not yet filled the beaches and the museums to capacity. The maritime climate of the Netherlands is very changeable, though, and during these months expect weather ranging from cool to pleasant to wet and windy to hot and surprisingly humid. Eastern and southeastern provinces edge toward a more Continental climate, with warmer summers and colder winters than along the North Sea coast, which can itself be very cold from December through February and March.

Forecasts **Weather Channel Connection** (☎900/932–8437 95¢ per minute from a Touch-Tone phone ⊕www.weather.com).

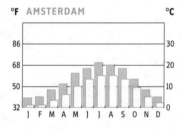

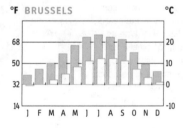

WHAT'S WHERE

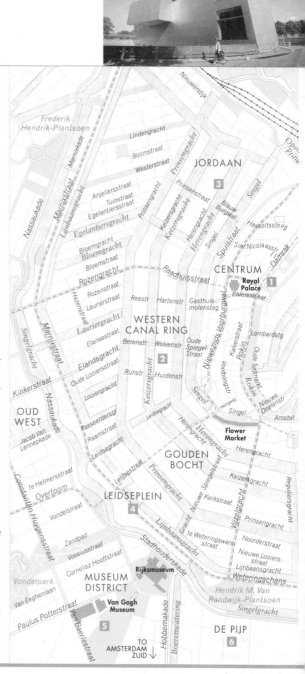

1 The Old City Center.
If only those 13th-century fishermen who decided to dam up the Amstel could see what became of this marsh, where today Gothic monuments interface with splashy billboards and Golden Age drinking holes neighbor techno-playing coffee shops.

2 The Canal Ring. Surrounding the metropolis' mushy Medieval middle is the *Grachtengordel*, or "belt of canals," which are the life-force-pumping arteries of the city's modern life. As a visitor, you'll find a sense of moderation here that Goldilocks would really dig: not too hectic, not too dull, but a just-right mix of everyday Amsterdam and touristic amusement.

3 Jordaan. This institution of a charmer wins the hearts of all walks of life. With its leafy tree-lined canals, hidden courtyards, and narrow alleyways, this neighborhood produces a postcard-perfect image of Amsterdam at any given moment.

4 Leidseplein. Eat, drink, be merry! This is the city's hub for concerts, clubs, cinemas, gambling, and ganja. Rivaled only by the Dam, Leidseplein can be a bit too much on the weekends, but the Vondelpark is just an amble away if you seek some post-thrill chill.

5 Museum District. Culture is as classic as it comes here. The Van Gogh Museum and the Rijksmuseum allure tourists, while cosmopolitan elite frequent the Concertgebouw and the late-night French-inspired brasseries. The throngs mix and match around the corner on the Madison Avenue of Amsterdam, PC Hooftstraat.

6 The Pijp. The bohemian bourgeoisie prove they can peaceably coexist with the working-class indigenous in a little grid behind the Heineken Brewery. Six days a week, Albert Cuypmarkt does its multicultural, pan-capitalist thing, uniting locals and out-of-towners in common pursuit of fresh produce, bargain fashion, and mini electronics, often to the tune of a foot tambourine-playing bassist.

7 East of the Amstel. From the opera's highest of brows to the zoo's most animalistic instincts, it's a different world on the other side of the Amstel. Wide boulevards, oddly beautiful building edifices, and high-ceilinged cafés create the streetscape while, culturally speaking, markets, parks, and houses of worship lean to the East.

WHAT'S WHERE

8 The Hague. It's the Queen's scene, yes, but also the world's legal headquarters. International tribunals, high courts, embassy rows, and diplomatic immunities make their home in The Hague, as does a burgeoning Chinatown, students of the prestigious music conservatory, and the *Girl with a Pearl Earring.*

9 The Randstad: Rotterdam, Haarlem & Delft. Compared to other Dutch municipalities, Rotterdam sticks out like a sore thumb. Bombed to the ground in World War II, this harbor town is today one of the world's busiest industrial ports, with a phenomenal skyline and a real appreciation for the cultural underground. Haarlem and Delft are wonderful, dollhouse-like cities that shouldn't be missed.

10 Belgium: Brussels, Brugge & Gent. The Continent's most underrated city will treat you to the earthly delights of Paris while encouraging you to feel as laid-back as you would in Amsterdam. A section or two of Brussels may be overrun by Babel-tongued Eurocrats in pointy shoes, but even they contribute to a unique posh-meets-pragmatic joie de vivre. Brugge and Gent are Flemish fairy-tale towns with a modern twist.

QUINTESSENTIAL
AMSTERDAM & THE NETHERLANDS

Canals

One popular explanation for why the Dutch are so frugal is that they're always preparing for a flood. Waste not, want not because the waters are always nigh. However, Amsterdam's canals are constant reminders that man—the Dutch anyway—can control nature and actually make a nice life off it. Over 60 miles' worth of canals, 400 stone bridges, and 90 islands have been created since the 17th century. Today, the *Grachtengordel* is prime real estate, and on days with even the slightest squirt of sun, cafés with canal-side seating are where it's at. Though long associated with the antiestablishment types of the 1970s, houseboats are increasingly becoming a viable option for locals, as well as visitors seeking quaint lodging (and not minding mediocre plumbing). The major canal cruise companies do a fine job of showing Amsterdam from below the banks.

Gezelligheid

If you listen carefully to local speech and detect what sounds like a mild throat clearing, no doubt you're hearing one of the most cherished words in Lowlands parlance—*gezellig*. The term is frequently translated to mean "cozy," though anyone who has had the chance to experience Dutch *gezelligheid* (coziness) will confirm that cozy doesn't quite cut it. From the word *gezel* meaning "mate," gezelligheid quite literally refers to the general companionability of a place or a person. Even if you don't have the chance to snug up on an Amsterdammer's couch, you can still witness signs of the spirit in lingering café conversations, cute cookies that come alongside your coffee, little lights along the canals at night, and cats in the window.

Tolerance

"Tolerance" has long been the buzzword of the country's live-and-let-live approach to governance. While few would disagree that the nation on the whole is progressive and left-leaning, "tolerate" may be too simplistic a translation for its Dutch parallel in the verb gedogen, which suggests something more like "turn a blind eye to." In everyday policy, this means doing damage control. Ethics that threaten consensus are zoned to their own neighborhoods (prostitutes) and widespread problems are condoned (pot). One famous Dutchman notorious for refusing to sugarcoat anything he found intolerable was filmmaker Theo van Gogh. In 2003, he was brutally murdered by a fellow Dutchman associated with a homegrown Islamic terrorist group. To many, the event marked a cataclysmic shift in the tides of tolerance.

Vices

Even though their heyday is fading, cannabis and call girls are still plentiful, professionalized, and permitted by the government. Virtuous about venality as the long-reputed nation of tolerance is, however, there's protocol. Rules apropos of both hookers and hash are as follows: buy only in controlled zones, use with caution, and leave your camera at home. Taking stoned pictures in coffeeshops and photographing live lingerie has not cool. In general, vice visitors are advised to check for updates on the changing laws, particularly regarding the legal sale of soft drugs. Recent tragedies involving tourists who have used psychedelic mushrooms have already compelled Parliamentary discussions about the possibility of altogether banning the psilocybin-laden *paddos*.

IF YOU LIKE

Bicycling

Two wheels are the preferred form of transportation, what with the land being so flat and the Dutch being so practical. If you decide to go native, be sure to ride in the bike lane, use hand signals, adhere to traffic signs, and ring your bell with prudence. The city itself makes for lovely little rides and is a superb way to avoid tram crams and pricey taxis. However, bike routes to Amsterdam's surrounding towns also make for some picturesque leisure cycling.

Broek in Waterland. Grab a ferry behind Centraal Station to Amsterdam Noord. Begin your journey to Broek in Waterland by following the signs to Durgerdam, heading toward Uitdam. Roll through 17th-century picture-book fishing villages, over dikes and polders, and stop at the region's most beloved fueling point, pancake house **De Witte Swaen** (⊠ *Dorpstraat 11/13, Broek in Waterland* ☎ *020/403–1525* ⊕ *www.dewitteswaen. nl* ☉ *Mon.–Sun. 12–9*)

Ouderkerk aan de Amstel. Follow the river out of town and pick up the well-signed path leading you to Ouderkerk aan de Amstel. In a matter of minutes, you'll come upon the Riekermolen windmill where Rembrandt sat and sketched. Cycle south along that single curvy road hugging the Amstel River, alive with rowers and fishermen, while across the way cows graze in fields behind quaint estates. Just five miles downstream, Ouderkerk is famous for a millennium-old church and the Portuguese Jewish cemetery where Spinoza is buried.

Except for the tour buses, the scenery makes it hard to believe you're just six miles from a major metropolis.

Chocolate

If you're a chocoholic, you've come to the right place. For starters, *Hagelslag* (chocolate sprinkles) is a breakfast mainstay and stocked in nearly every Dutch pantry. Other parts of the world just eat them with ice cream, but Hollanders shake them onto buttered toast, peanut butter sandwiches, and other adhesive carbohydrates. Below are some of our favorite chocolatiers and *Hagelslag* dealers.

Arti Choc. This old-school confectionary and summertime ice cream shop will fashion chocolate in any shape you like. If you can't afford Delft tile souvenirs for everyone back home, a delectable alternative are chocolate replicas painted in authentic white and blue.

Fair Trade Shop. Assuage any guilt regarding the origins of your cocoa habit by shopping at the gift kiosk of the Dutch-founded Fair Trade organization. Look for the brand Max Havelaar, so named after a fictional character who fought for the rights of coffee harvesters in the Dutch colonies.

Museum of Cocoa and Chocolate, Brussels. It's not Willy Wonka's, but this three-floor museum shows a history of the cacao bean, from early Aztec cultivation to its arrival in Europe and the Continent's subsequent fetishization of the stuff. "How to make a praline" demos are given daily.

Ron's Notenbar. Besides finding a rainbow array of nuts, dried fruits, and other poppable snacks, you can pick up some X-rated edible souvenirs at this staple of a stand on the Albert Cuyp Market. Chocolate breasts and genitalia come in black, brown, and white.

Diamonds

Though the Dutch are known for living modestly, their capital city is known for purveying the most immodest rock on earth. Diamonds first made their way to the Netherlands in 1568 when a polisher decided to call Amsterdam home, and his colleagues in the field soon followed. Jews, in particular, established successful businesses in cutting, polishing, and trading diamonds—this was one of the few industries whose inclusion was not dictated by trade guild membership, and therefore open to Jews.

Coster Diamonds. If you prefer to keep your diamond duty short and sweet, we suggest visiting this smaller homage to the stone, conveniently located on Museumplein. A replica of their most famous cut, the Koh-I-Noor diamond, is on show and jewelers patiently await your flash of plastic.

Gassan Diamonds. This company is one of the few outlets still located in Amsterdam's original diamond district. Visitors can get a free behind-the-gleams tour of the cutting room, and groups can pre-arrange an excursion that ends with a champagne toast.

Once the bubbly has been drunk, an expert's magnifying glass will inspect the small bits of bling lying at the bottom of each glass. All the zirconias will be sifted through to find the one real deal (the value of the lucky imbiber's prize will depend on the cost of the group tour).

At the on-site store, select your favorite piece for goldsmiths to inlay or stop by the Amsterdam Diamond Center near the Dam, which Gassan also owns.

Drinking from the Source

The Netherlands, Belgium, and Germany form a Bermuda Triangle of fresh brews and fine distillations known to shipwreck many a sober spirit. Enjoy the ride and fear not, deep-fried bar snacks and late-night *frites met mayonnaise* (french fries with gobs of mayo) will put you back on the radar.

Brouwerij 't IJ. What could be more Beneluxian than drinking a Trappist-inspired pilsner in the foot of a giant windmill? Each year this microbrewery produces 180,000 liters of its most beloved brews. Tours are offered from time to time.

Heineken Experience. It's the Jolly Green Giant of European beers and, unexotically universal though it may be, a Heine does taste better in Holland. This tour through the old factory (freshly renovated and reopened in June 2008) gives visitors a course in Brewing 101 and some heady facts about the company's history.

Museum van de Gueuze, Brussels. It hardly seems right to call this a museum; since 1900, this brewery, also known as the Cantillon brewery, has produced Lambik and specialty beers. Although Lambik is the quintessential Brussels beer, this is, sadly, the only Lambik brewery left in Brussels. Commercially brewed Lambiks bear scant resemblence to the real thing, so drink up while you can!

Wynard Fokking. Nestled in a tiny alleyway behind Dam Square, this bar has been pouring Dutch *jenever* (the forefather to Anglicized gin) since 1679. This is an only-in-Amsterdam experience. The distillery next door offers tours and sells jenever by the bottle.

IF YOU LIKE

Partying Outside

When it comes to having fun under the sun (or clouds and rain), the Netherlands has a lot to offer. Outdoor festivals jibe with the Dutch predilection for sharing small quarters with many people, labeling almost everything "multimedia," and letting loose within specified parameters outside the office.

A Campingflight To Lowlands. For more than four decades, the Netherlands has been hosting its own little lollapalooza of pop music. Some homegrown stars get the spotlight, but the Lowlands' real crowd-pullers are international bigwigs, à la Pink Floyd in 1968 and the Kaiser Chiefs-esque ensembles of recent modernity. This camp-happy event traditionally takes place over three days in August. ⊕*www.lowlands.nl*

Kwakoe Festival. What began in 1975 as a soccer tournament for the local Surinamese community of Southeast Amsterdam is today the biggest multicultural luau in the Lowlands, taking place weekends in July and August. The spareribs are the finest in the land. ⊕*www.kwakoe.nl*

Over het IJ festival. Every July since 1992, theater-makers, dancers, and artists have been getting into every rusty nook and corroded cranny of the NDSM wharf. Performances are given in old factories, shipping containers, submarines, and riverboats.

Parade. From late July through mid-August, this traveling theater festival makes stops in Utrecht, The Hague, and Amsterdam, putting on short, simple, and charming productions that appeal to all ages, walks of life, and levels of cynicism.

Flowers

Nowhere else in the world will you be exposed to such a dazzling diversity of flowers. Whether you're horticulturally inclined and seek some interesting species to introduce to your garden back home, or simply like being titillated by Technicolor tulips, Holland is where it's at.

Bloemenveiling, Aalsmeer. Bulbs are no longer the viable form of currency they were during the Tulip Mania that came over the Lowlands in the 1630s, but flowers remain an ever-blossoming boon to the Dutch economy. Within just microsecond intervals of time, no less than 19 million flowers and two million plants are sold every weekday in the world's largest auction house, which is also responsible for establishing the global going rate of flowers.

Bloemenmarkt, Amsterdam. Nary be there an infertile moment along the Singel canal on which the city's floating flower market is moored. Every day locals buy robust bouquets on their way to dinner parties, while travelers pick up bulbs, seeds, and green-thumbed souvenirs.

Should buds or bids be your thing, the 20-minute bus ride from Amsterdam is well worth it.

Keukenhof, Lisse. It's the largest flower garden on earth, with roots—in terms of legacy, not soil—that date back to the 15th century. And the parking is just big enough for the tour buses it must accommodate March through May. Many find the park a bit kitschy, but everyone marvels at the superbly manicured flower beds and tulips named for everyone from Lady Di to the Teletubbies.

Pottery

There are some real treasure troves for collectors of the multicolored earthenware that Delft began producing in the 17th century. Delftware was a porcelainless people's interpretation of the china that had found its way here courtesy of the Dutch East India Company. Today those blue-and-white clay-baked beauties are the most coveted of ceramics, both at design museums and on dining room tables.

De Koninklijke Porceleyne Fles, Delft. Established in 1653, this is the only remaining Delft factory of the 32 once in operation. Enjoy an awesome presentation of tableware and tiles, while, in between displays, you can observe craftspeople as they paint, kiln, and polish. Be sure to visit the bathroom, where even the toilets are touched by Delftware divination. Guided tours are given from April through October and workshops are also available.

Nederlands Tegelmuseum, Otterlo. Located in the woodlands of De Hoge Veluw national park, this museum has vast collections of Dutch wall tiles and panels. From Bible scenes to flower motifs, survey the fascinating thematic variation in tiles over time, and learn how, for centuries, Dutch houses and farms have relied on Delftware to keep their walls dry and dirt-free.

Princessehof Leeuwarden. This palace, inhabited in the 1700s by the Prince of Orange's widow, is today a royal homage to ceramics and tiles from all over the world. The permanent collection spans Chinese terra-cotta from 3,000 bc up through classic Wedgwood creations.

Quirky Theme Parks

They're known to be the tallest people in the world, but the Dutch have a taste for things diminutive and cute—Calvinistic modesty, a lack of land, and the virtue of *gezelligheid* are all contributing factors. And it shows even in their theme parks and tourist attractions, which have a family feel and an MO that's less about quantity and more about quality time.

De Eftling. Once upon a time in 1952, the well-known Dutch illustrator Anton Pieck created a life-size fairy-tale forest. The whole country loved it, and even Walt Disney paid a visit to get inspiration for his own imminent building plans. Today, high-tech rides, an 18-hole golf course, and a four-star hotel make this your best bet for some Never Neverland in The Netherlands.

Labyrint Drielandenpunt. This open-air maze winds around the area where the Netherlands, Belgium, and Germany all meet. It also happens to be the Netherlands' highest elevation, at 1,060 feet. Join the throngs of picnicking adults, birthday party-ing children, and other wandering souls. On your way out, stop by Het Drielandenpunt, a cute monument located on the exact borders. ⊕ *www.drielandenpunt.nl*

Madurodam. Call it kitschy, but this 1:25-scaled miniature recreation of a typical Dutch city is really a lot of fun. Built in 1952, Madurodam has had its own youth city council, comprised of local students and a teenage mayor. Queen Beatrix was the first mayor and is said to have worn her official chain of office until rising to the throne in 1980.

GREAT ITINERARIES

AMSTERDAM, ROTTERDAM, BRUGGE & BRUSSELS

Day 1: Welcome to Amsterdam

Begin your journey in the aorta of the city, Dam Square, a perfect example of Amsterdam's warm-blooded capacity to hold old and new altogether on one bit of earth. The Royal Palace and De Nieuwe Kerk, a 15th-century church where many a Dutch naval hero rests, peaceably coexist with big department stores and Madame Tussauds. Across the square, Hotel Krasnapolsky provides a ritzy retreat from the crowds, with one of the best tea services in town. If you're in the mood for something a little stronger, sneak down the alley next to the hotel for a nip of jenever at the Wynard Fokking. Spend the rest of your day and evening exploring the *hofjes* (hidden courtyards) in and around the Jordaan. Start off at the Begijnhof, just off the Spui.

Day 2: Culture and a Cruise

Amsterdam is home to three art behemoths—Rijksmuseum, Van Gogh Museum, and the Stedelijk. Avoid museum fatigue and don't attempt more than one per day. Afterwards, treat yourself to a little retail therapy on the fancy schmancy PC Hooftstraat. It's interesting to observe how a culture so modest and practical still manages to discreetly go glam. When the sun sets, catch an avant-garde ensemble playing at Bimhuis, listen to improv at jazz bar Alto, or find a brown café in the Jordaan for a warm brandy and a slice of *appeltaart*. From March through October, you can enjoy dinner aboard a candlelit canal cruise.

Logistics: An I amsterdam card, which can be purchased for one-, two-, and three-day validities, gives you free entrance into the city's major museums, free use of trams and buses, discounts at several restaurants, and a 25% discount on the Lovers Candlelight Cruise. See ⊕*www.iamsterdamcard.com*

Day 3: Ports and Skyscrapers in Rotterdam

As the country's second most populated city and the largest seaport in Europe, Rotterdam has a vast, high-vaulted vibe unlike any other Dutch town. Its appearance is anachronistically modern, thanks to the thorough rebuilding that took place after German bombs blasted the city to smithereens in 1940. Tragedy though it was, the destruction produced unparalleled architecture and design, not to mention an open-minded attitude toward quirky bits of infrastructure that more baroque cities would consider profane (think skate parks and a B-list celebrity-star walk of fame). Visit the Netherlands Architecture Institute for its excellent crash course in the past, present, and future of architecture. For some visual reinforcement of what you've learned, a sail along the River Maas is a prime way to take in the skyline and admire the Old Harbor's facade. If the waters aren't too choppy, venture to the less cosmetically enhanced industrial coastline, where chartered tours will take you for a behind-the-scenes peek into the ports of various multinational companies. And with such a multiethnic population, Rotterdam is your best bet for indulging in non-Continental comestibles.

Logistics: Trains depart regularly from Amsterdam to Rotterdam. To arrange a walk on Rotterdam's industrial side, contact: **Industrial Tourism** (☎*010/218–9194* ⊕*www.industrieeltoerisme.com*).

Day 4: The Abbeys and Beer of Brugges

Nothing short of fairy-tale-like, this UNESCO-declared World Heritage Site is still intact with numerous Gothic churches, abbeys, and bell towers, along with museums proudly displaying Flemish Primitive paintings. While self-indulgence is pooh-poohed by their Protestant neighbors to the north, Belgians are historically Catholic and accordingly demonstrate less resistance to earthly indulgences. Lucky for the hungry and thirsty visitor. You can't go wrong by popping into any one of the sundry bistros, cafés, and pubs that offer delicious Flemish fare and a sinful selection of Belgian beers.

Logistics: Brugges is a two-hour train ride from Rotterdam. Trains depart every half hour.

Day 5: Art Deco and Bonbons in Brussels

Not as cozy as Amsterdam, not as chic as Paris, Brussels is often overlooked by travelers who are intent on seeing the major cities of Europe. But this underappreciated metropolis has much to offer, and in even one day will provide satiety like no other. A quadrant of stately Gothic buildings form the main square known as the Grote Markt (in Flemish) or Grand Place (in French). Take it all in, perhaps with a beverage break at one of the grand cafés, but save room for plenty more consumption. The streets are paved with chocolatiers, their storybook-like windows beckoning you to come in for delicately packaged bonbons or freshly churned hot chocolate. The smell of powdered sugar ricocheting off Nutella and cream-laden Belgian waffles lingers on street corners. Build up your second appetite by taking a self-guided walking

> ### A FEW TIPS
>
> Amsterdam is safer than most cities, but you still need to be wary. Keep your belongings with you and avoid walking by yourself at night. Use extra care when visiting the Red Light District.
>
> Public transportation is excellent throughout the Netherlands, but we recommend walking. Cities are easy to navigate on foot.
>
> Take a canal tour in at least one of the cities that you visit. It's a fantastic way to see the sites.

tour of the city's famous Art Deco buildings, beginning at the Horta Museum where you can pick up a guide. On your way back into the city center, make the customary pilgrimage to Manneken Piss, the bronze fountain of a wee boy taking a wee. Mussels and *frites* are the when-in-Rome way to approach dinner in Brussels, but you could do no wrong by trying any of the French-inspired seafood-prone dishes on most menus, even in the restaurant district where maître d' practice the art of sidewalk seduction. Brussels already serves as the European Union's headquarters, though quite conceivably should be recognized as the Continent's gastronomical governing body.

Logistics: Brussels is the regional train hub. Regular high-speed train service connects you to Paris in less than 1½ hours, London in 2 hours, or you can take the two-and-a-half-hour regular train back to Amsterdam.

GREAT ITINERARIES

AMSTERDAM, HAARLEM, DE HOGE VELUWE, DELTA WORKS, THE HAGUE & SCHEVENINGEN

Day 1: Canal-crawling in Amsterdam

Make your first acquaintance with Amsterdam in everyone's favorite neighborhood, the garden-themed Jordaan, with its postcard-perfect canals, hidden little courtyards, and politely moored houseboats. Whether on foot or *fiets* (bicycle), begin your Jordaanese journey on the corner of Raadhuisstraat and Prinsengracht. If you don't mind a small cardio workout, climb to the top of the newly renovated 279-foot tower of the Westerkerk, which offers a sublime view of the city—on a clear day, of course. Continue your canal crawl northward, peeking into artists' galleries, antiques stores, and clothing boutiques. Work up your appetite for a pancake the size of a satellite dish at the Pancake Bakery. And when it's time to turn the bike lights on, make your way to the nonstop nightlife crossroads that is Leidseplein. For pop shows, rock concerts, and dancing to your favorite decade, head to Paradiso or Melkweg. Right across the street, the Sugar Factory is perfect if you're sweet on nu-jazz collectives, slam poetry, and cross-genre theatrics.

Day 2: Peddling to Haarlem

With Amsterdam's Haarlemmerplein as your starting point, hop on the bike path and forge westward to reach the bustling metropolis for which the square is named. The approximately 12-mile ride to Haarlem is chuck full of über-Dutch sights: a medieval dike, a windmill, a steam pumping station-turned-museum, an old sugar mill, sand dunes, and some unique little towns in between. By the time you spot the tower of Haarlem's Town Hall, though, get ready to dismount—a stroll is in order. The city is renowned for its elegant square, church organs played by Haydn and Mozart, the nation's oldest museum, cool boutiques, and cute cafés. If *zadelpijn* (aka sore butt) has set in, you and your bike can always take the train back to Amsterdam.

Logistics: Depending on how soon you would like to take responsibility for two wheels, you can rent a bike from several companies in Amsterdam. **Yellow Bike** (✉ *Nieuwezijds Kolk 29,* ☎ *020/620–6940* ⊕ *www.yellowbike.nl*) has economic rentals and good tours

Day 3: Cycling and Cubism in De Hoge Veluwe

Now that you've had a taste of Dutch urban life, get ready for a whiff of nature. Keep in mind, though, that most scenes of green in the Netherlands are the work of man. Years spent tweaking with dams, dikes, and polders has made the Lowlands the inhabitable, navigational landscape of today. That being said, De Hoge Veluwe, in the province of Gelderland, is the finest the country has to offer by way of a national park. And best of all, it provides free bikes for navigating modest hills and dips through 5,500 hectares (13,590 acres) of woodlands, plains, heather fields, and sand drifts. Besides the other polyglot species zooming by on shiny white two-wheelers, you might spot a wild boar or a mouflon (a wild sheep). Once you're sufficiently tuckered out, make your way to the Kröller-Müller Museum, which has a serious collection of Picassos, Mondriaans, and Seurats, as well as a superb sculpture garden to which Rodin is no stranger.

Logistics: Frequent train service can take you to one of the many park entrances. Once within the park, the distance to the museum depends on your starting point. The ride is 1½ miles from the Otterlo entrance, 2½ miles from Hoenderloo, and a little over 6 miles from Schaarsbergen.

Day 4: Cruising Along the Afsluitdijk

Trade in your bike for something motorized and take the scenic route southward to witness a sublime example of technology trumping nature. The Delta Works is a massive dam and flood barrier—24-foot-high banks stretch 20 miles along the A7 motorway. Give yourself at least a kilometer to get used to driving on the concrete tendril engulfed by blue. On your right, you'll see the North Sea's inlet, known as the Zuiderzee, while on your left, fishermen dot the freshwater banks of the Ijselmeer.

Logistics: Budget and Avis have convenient locations in Amsterdam and throughout the country. You can also join one of the many tour groups by visiting almost any tourist information center.

Day 5: Museum-hopping in The Hague

No one will try to convince you otherwise if your impression of The Hague is that of super sobriety, what with all the royalty, diplomats, international judges, and civil servants running around. But don't forget that the Count's Hedge, as the city's official Dutch name actually means, also does some serious justice to arts and culture. The Mauritshuis is visited more than ever for its recent popstar of a piece, the Girl with a Pearl Earring, while the Gemeetemuseum holds the most Mondriaans under one roof. And for when you get peckish, there's a veritable embassy

---

A FEW TIPS

Don't hesitate to bike the Hoge Veluwe. It's very safe and there are no cars.

Contact the VVV tourism office and sign up for a tour of the Delta Works. It's easier than driving yourself.

---

row's worth of eateries, from grandma-friendly Dutch cafés to posh hotel dining rooms, and one of the most prominent Chinatowns in the country. The Hague's Indonesian restaurants are said to be hemisphere-altering.

Logistics: Check the lavish-as-it-gets Hotel Des Indes for special discount rates on Friday through Sunday arrivals. ⊕*www.starwoodhotels.com*

Day 6: Sun & Fun in Scheveningen

Once you've had your fill of The Hague's manicured gardens and stately buildings, take a side trip to Scheveningen, The Netherlands' most popular seaside resort and esplanade. Restaurants, clubs, casinos, bungee jumps, ice cream stands, and trinket shops create an almost American ethos, though try testing the waters of the North Sea and you'll be quickly reminded that Atlantic City is far, far away.

Logistics: For optimum safety and security, park your car in one of Scheveningen's three public garages or two open car parks.

Exploring
Amsterdam

Updated by
Shain Shapiro
& Madelon
Evers

AMSTERDAM IS A CORNUCOPIA OF cafés, coffee shops, cozy bars, and outdoor markets. Set on 160 man-made canals (stretching 75 km [50 mi]), Amsterdam also has the largest historical inner city in Europe. The French writer J.K. Huysmans once called Amsterdam "a dream, an orgy of houses and water." It's true: when compared with other major European cities, this one is uniquely defined by its impressive gabled houses, rather than palaces, estates, and other aristocratic folderol. Most of the 7,000 registered monuments here began as residences and warehouses of humble merchants.

> **TOP REASONS TO GO**
>
> ■ Bike around the city like a local.
>
> ■ Explore Europe's largest historic city center.
>
> ■ Discover quaint, tucked-away *hofjes* (almshouse courtyards).
>
> ■ Sip jenever in a 16th-century brown bar

With a mere 730,000 friendly souls and with almost everything a scant 10-minute bike ride away, Amsterdam is actually like a village that happens to pack the cultural wallop of a megalopolis. This is an endlessly fascinating city where it's remarkably easy to relax and enjoy yourself—just take on the characteristics of the local waterways and go with the flow.

ORIENTATION

There are no straight lines in central Amsterdam, but once understood, it's an easy city to navigate—or purposely get lost in. For starters it is only about 9 square miles. Think of it as an onion whose layers come together at the stem to make a cohesive whole. With Centraal Station as the stem, the Center folds out as layers of the onion, each on a somewhat circular path under the guidance of the Canal Ring. To stay oriented, just follow each onion layer around, which will lead you east/west, while the thoroughfare streets run north/south. Amsterdam is different from most major cities as the center lies north and the suburbs are mainly south. To stay safe, always watch out for bikes and trams. Do not walk on bike paths, which are well-paved and often mistaken for sidewalks. Bikers have the right-of-way, so if you hear a bell, move quickly. Trams function similarly, and will also ring their bell (a much louder one) before they move. Just look both ways, and look both ways again before crossing streets.

PLANNING

GETTING AROUND

The best way to see Amsterdam is either by bike or on foot. The city is very, very small, and most places are easily accessible. Otherwise, the city's public transport system, GVB, is extremely reliable. It operates the buses, trams, and metro with service 24 hours a day. The *strippenkaart,* or transport pass, works on a stamping system and comes in two sizes, 15 and 40 stamps. Amsterdam is split into four zones. The driver will stamp the number of zones you are traveling, plus one for the ride. The Centrum is in zone one, so a blue *strippenkaart* with 15 stamps will last seven rides. The GVB also sells 24-, 48-, and 72-hour passes, and family passes. If you choose to take a taxi, make sure they are licensed and regulated by the city to avoid being scammed.

HOW'S THE WEATHER?

Amsterdam was built on a swamp and is only 7 feet above sea level, so the city is always a little damp. There is high humidity in the summer and a fair amount of rain, especially in the winter. But moisture aside, Amsterdam's weather is ultimately comfortable. The temperatures are rarely extreme and there are lots of balmy days, especially in June, July, and August. November to April is consistently overcast and windy, but not too cold. Rule of thumb—always wear layers to put on or take off, have sturdy shoes for walking on the cobblestones, and bring a good umbrella.

BEST TIME TO GO

Amsterdam is bustling in the summer, as travelers and locals flock to city parks for sunbathing, before and after cooling off with a few cold drinks at one of the hundreds of neighborhood outdoor cafés. In the summer, Amsterdam can be the most fascinating city in the world; a sun-bleached blend of old and new, crazy and subdued. From October to May, lines for most museums and attractions are smaller, and off-season accommodations are cheaper, but it's colder, rainier, and windier. Queens Day (April 30) and Museum night (November 4th), are worth visits in their own right.

THE OLD CITY CENTER (HET CENTRUM)

Variety really is the spice of life when you're visiting Amsterdam. This city has enjoyed a rich and turbulent history, and so much of it can be seen in the city center: the Red Light District, the oldest part of Amsterdam, is home to the city's oldest church, the most historic architecture, and of course, legal prostitution; the Old Jewish Quarter still has one of the best outdoor flea markets in Europe; and the medieval Nieuwmarkt is breathtaking. The Dam, an open square overlooked by the Royal Dam Palace, is a godsend to visitors as a landmark; when lost, even the worst student of foreign languages can easily get help by asking for "The Dam."

Numbers in the margin correspond to points of interest on the Old City Center map.

WESTERN HALF OF THE CENTER

As you walk up the Damrak from Centraal Station, you'll encounter the heart of the city—and the place where most visitors organically converge—Dam Square. Not named out of blasphemy, Dam Square is the site of the city's first dam, which was cobbled together in 1275. Home to the Royal Palace (currently under construction), the Nieuwe

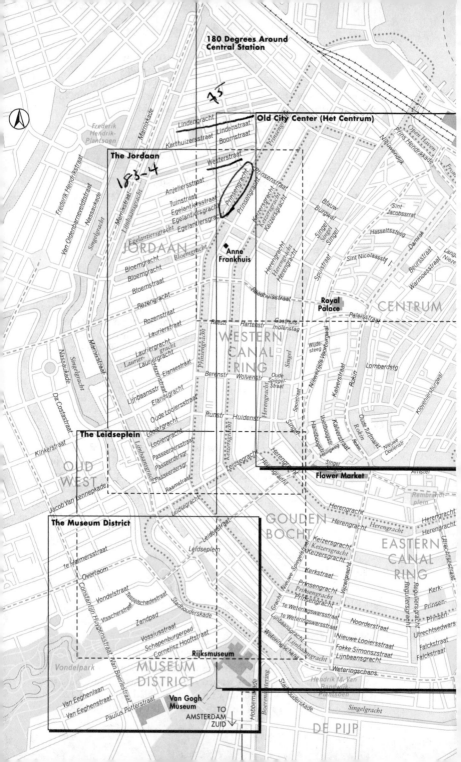

180 Degrees Around
Central Station

Old City Center (Het Centrum)

The Jordaan

73

183-4

JORDAAN

Anne
Frankhuis

WESTERN
CANAL
RING

Royal
Palace

CENTRUM

The Leidseplein

OUD
WEST

Flower Market

GOUDEN
BOCHT

EASTERN
CANAL
RING

The Museum District

Leidseplein

Rijksmuseum

MUSEUM
DISTRICT

Van Gogh
Museum

TO
AMSTERDAM
ZUID

DE PIJP

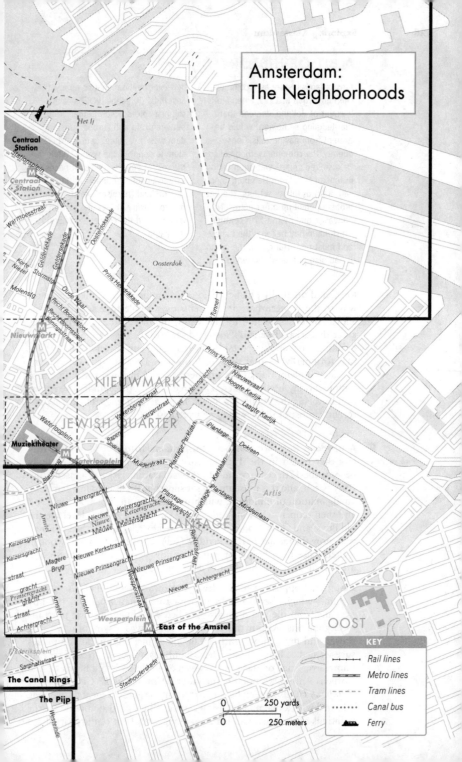

A BIT OF HISTORY

Amsterdam's history as a commercial hub began in 1275, when Floris V, count of Holland, decreed that the fledgling settlement would be exempt from paying tolls. Consequently, the community, then called "Aemstelredamme," was soon taking in tons of beer from Hamburg, along with a lot of thirsty settlers. The beer profits opened up other fields of endeavor, and by the 17th century Amsterdam had become the richest and most powerful city in the world. It had also produced the world's first-ever multinational company: the East India Company (VOC), which shipped spices, among other goods, between Asia and Europe. Amsterdam was, in Voltaire's words, "the storage depot of the world." While the rest of Europe still felt it necessary to uphold the medieval tags of "honor" and "heroism," Amsterdam had the luxury of focusing just on money—and the consequent liberty it created.

Kerk, and the oddly phallic National Monument, the Dam is the gateway to the western half of the *Centrum*. Cobblestone squares, affluent canal houses, teeny-tiny alleyways, and newer university buildings grace this area. Here you'll also find some of the best shopping, eating, drinking, and smoking establishments in the city. Stroll up the Spuistraat (originally a canal that functioned as a medieval sewer system) to the Spuiplein, one of the prettiest squares in town and home to a famous Friday book market. This area around the Spui has a reputation for being the intellectual heart of the city, since it was where, until recently, most of the newspapers were based.

MAIN ATTRACTIONS

①⑥ Fodor's Choice ★ **Amsterdams Historisch Museum** *(Amsterdam Historical Museum)*. Any city that began in the 13th century as a sinking bog to eventually become the 17th century's most powerful trading city has a fascinating story to tell, and this museum does it superbly. It's housed in a rambling amalgamation of buildings, which was used as an orphanage in 1580 and then reopened as a museum in 1975. On the ground level are the old Boys' and Girls' Courtyards, separated by a loggia. In the boys' section, now the terrace of the **David & Goliath Café**, are rows of wooden lockers once used by the orphans but now adorned with photos and artwork depicting Amsterdam's cultural life.

Exiting the opposite end will lead you toward **Schutters Gallery**. This atrium—which used to be a narrow canal that separated the boy orphans from the girl orphans—is filled with huge, historic portraits of city militias. As portrait art in the 1600s was a symbol of wealth, power and most importantly, bragging rights, the militia companies sure seemed to like to brag. These paintings, which are free to see, are impressive. Pride of place here is given to works by Dirck Barendsz and Cornelis Anthonisz, notably the latter's *Meal of the 17 Guardsmen of Company H*. Elsewhere, be sure to take in the grand Regents' Chamber, adorned with a magnificent 1656 ceiling painting. Also notable are the paintings of the great Golden Age, along with 17th-century city maps

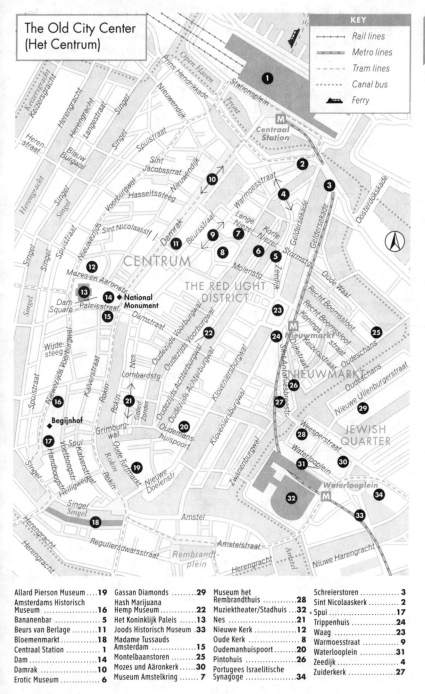

The Old City Center (Het Centrum)

KEY

┼┼┼┼	Rail lines
▭▭▭	Metro lines
– – –	Tram lines
• • • •	Canal bus
⛴	Ferry

and dour Burgomeister, or may-oral portraits, and a stirring photographic collage that captures the triumphs and tragedies of the modern-day metropolis. ⊠*Kalverstraat 92 and Nieuwezijds Voorburgwal 357, Centrum* 🕿*020/523–1822* ⊕*www.ahm.nl* ⊠*€7* ⊗ *Weekdays 10–5, weekends 11–5.*

<table>
<tr><td>UNDER CONSTRUCTION</td></tr>
<tr><td>While the city remains dedicated to preserving ancient buildings, it is fundamentally altering the Center with the construction of a new north-south subway line. The line, which is extremely over-budget, highly controversial, and not due to be completed until 2014, has turned parts of the Center, including the Rokin and Vijzelstraat into a muddy mess.</td></tr>
</table>

★ ⓫ **Beurs van Berlage** *(Berlage's Stock Exchange).* Even though some people think the Beurs looks a bit blocky, it is revered as Amsterdam's first modern building and the country's most important piece of 20th century architecture. Built in 1903 by H. P. Berlage, the building became a template for the style of a new century. Gone were all the ornamentations of the 19th-century "Neo" styles. The new Beurs, with its simple lines and the influence it had on the Amsterdam School architects who followed Berlage, earned him the reputation of being the "Father of Modern Dutch Architecture."

The building is in fact a political manifesto that preaches the oneness of capital and labor. Built upon 4,880 wooden piles, each of the Beurs van Berlage's 9 million bricks is meant to represent an individual, who together form a strong and democratic whole. Berlage showed particular respect for the labor unions by exposing their works and accenting the important structural points with natural stone.

Today, the Beurs serves as a true Palazzo Publico with concert halls (home to the Dutch Philharmonic Orchestra) and space for exhibitions of architecture and applied arts. The small museum has exhibits about the former stock exchange and its architect and offers access to the lofty clock tower, but these can be viewed only by taking part in an architecture tour organized by Artiflex (020/620–8112). Stop in at the café to admire the stunning tile tableaux over a coffee (Mon.–Sat. 10–6, Sun. 11–6). ⊠*Damrak 277, Centrum* 🕿*020/530–4141* ⊕*www.beursvanberlage.nl* ⊠ *Varies based on exhibition* ⊗ *Varies based on exhibition.*

⓲ **Bloemenmarkt** *(Flower Market).* This is the last of the city's floating markets. In days gone by, merchants would sail up the Amstel loaded down with blooms from the great tulip fields to delight patroons and housewives. Today, the flower sellers stay put, but their wares are still offered on stalls-cum-boats. ⊠*Singel (between Muntplein and Koningsplein), Centrum* ⊗*Mon.–Sat. 9:30–5.*

★ ➊ **Centraal Station** *(Central Station).* The main hub of transportation in the Netherlands, this building was designed as a major architectural statement by P. J. H. Cuypers. Although sporting many Gothic motifs (including a unique wind vane disguised as a clock in its left tower), it is now considered a landmark of Dutch Neo-Renaissance style. (Cuypers

also designed the city's other main gateway, the Rijksmuseum, whi
lies like a mirrored rival on the other side of town.) The building of the
station required the creation of three artificial islands and the ramming
of 8,600 wooden piles to support it. Completed in 1885, it represented
the psychological break with the city's seafaring past, as its erection
slowly blocked the view to the IJ river. Another controversy arose from
its Gothic detailing, which was considered by uptight Protestants as a
tad too Catholic—like Cuypers himself—and hence earned the building the nickname the "French Convent" (similarly, the Rijksmuseum
became the "Bishop's Castle"). Currently sections of Centraal Station,
both inside and outside the main entrance, are under construction with
the new North/South metro line. ⊠*Stationsplein, Centrum* ☎*0900–
9292 (public transport information).*

**NEED A
BREAK?**

A particularly stylish place to wait for a train is **1e Klas** (⊠ *Platform 2B, Centraal Station, Centrum* ☎ *020/625–0131*), whose original Art Nouveau brasserie interior, no longer restricted to first-class passengers, is perfect for
lingering over coffee, a snack, or a full-blown meal accompanied by fine
wine. Whatever the hour, it's a fine place to savor the sumptuousness of fin-
de-siècle living.

⑭ Dam *(Dam Square).* Home to the Koninklijk Paleis (Royal Palace) and
the Nieuwe Kerk, this is Amsterdam's official center. The square traces
its roots to the 12th century, when wanderers from central Europe
came floating in their canoes down the Amstel River and decided to
stop to build a dam. It became the focal point of the small settlement
and the location of the local weigh house. Folks came here to trade,
talk, protest, and be executed. Ships once sailed right up to the weigh
house, along the Damrak. But in the 19th century the Damrak was
filled in to form the street leading to Centraal Station and King Louis,
Napoléon's brother, had the weigh house demolished in 1808 because
it spoiled the view from his bedroom window in the Royal Palace.
Regardless, the Dam, with its fresh and glistening white cobblestones,
remains the city's true center.

National Monument. The towering white obelisk in the center of the
square was erected in 1956 as a memorial to the Dutch soldiers who
died in World War II. Designed by architect J.J.P. Oud (who thought
that De Stijl minimalism was in keeping with the monument's message),
it's the national focal point for Remembrance Day on May 4. Every
year, the queen walks from the Koninklijk Paleis to the monument and
lays flowers. The monument contains 12 urns: 11 are filled with earth
from all the Dutch provinces and the 12th contains earth from the former colonies (Indonesia, Suriname, and the Antilles). Oud designed the
steps to be used as seating and today it's still a favored rest spot and
a great place to watch the world go by. It is also the best place in the
city to meet people. Just schedule meetings next to the giant phallus.
⊠*Follow Damrak south from Centraal Station. Raadhuisstraat leads
from Dam to intersect main canals.*

et Koninklijk Paleis *(Royal Palace)*. From the outside, it is somewhat
rd to believe that this gray-stained building was once called the
ighth Wonder of the World." It was built between 1648 and 1665
he largest nonreligious building on the planet. From the inside, its
magnificent interior inspires another brand of disbelief: this palace was
actually built as a mere city hall. Golden age artistic greats such as Ferdinand Bol, Govert Flinck (Rembrandt's sketches were rejected), and
Jan Lievens were called in for the decorating. In the building's public
entrance hall, the **Burgerzaal,** the world was placed quite literally at
one's feet: two maps inlaid in the marble floor show Amsterdam as the
center of the world, and as the center of the universe.

The building has remained the Royal Palace ever since Napoléon's
brother squatted there in 1808. Today Queen Beatrix stays here occasionally. She required a few years to warm back up to Amsterdam
after her wedding in 1966 was disrupted by a radical student group
throwing smoke bombs at her carriage and in 1980, her coronation
was derailed by riots on the Dam. ⊠*Dam, Centrum* ☎*020/620–4060*
⊕*www.koninklijkhuis.nl* ⊠€ ⊙*The palace is closed for renovations
until sometime in 2008.*

★ ⑫ **Nieuwe Kerk** *(New Church)*. Begun in the 14th century, the Nieuwe Kerk
is a soaring Late Gothic structure whose tower was never completed
because the authorities—preoccupied with the building of Het Koninklijk Paleis—ran out of money. Whereas the Oude Kerk had the bless-
ing of the Bishop of Utrecht, the Nieuwe Kerk was supported by the
local well-to-do merchant class—the result was an endless competition
between the two parochial factions. At one point the Oude Kerk led the
race with a whopping 38 pulpits against the Nieuwe Kerk's 36. Don't
miss the Nieuwe Kerk's magnificently sculpted pulpit by Albert Vinck-
enbrinck. It took him 19 years to complete. Other features include the
unmarked grave of the poet Vondel (the "Dutch Shakespeare"), and the
extravagantly marked grave of naval hero Admiral Michiel de Ruyter,
who daringly sailed his invading fleet up the river Medway in England in
the 17th century. The Nieuwe Kerk has also been the National Church
since 1815, when it began hosting the inauguration ceremony for mon-
archs. Since this does not occur that often, the church has broadened its
appeal by serving as a venue for organ concerts and special—invariably
excellent and often cutting-edge—exhibitions, which attract a half-mil-
lion visitors a year. ⊠*Dam, Cen-
trum* ☎*020/638–6909* ⊕*www.
nieuwekerk.nl* ⊠*Admission varies
according to exhibition* ⊙*During
exhibitions open daily 10–5. In
between exhibitions hrs vary.*

⑰ **Spui** *(Spui Square)*. This beautiful
and seemingly tranquil tree-lined
square hides a lively and radical
recent past. Journalists and book-
worms have long favored its many
cafés, and the Atheneum News

BUILDING IN A SWAMP

In order to build the Royal Palace
on a blubbery former riverbed,
architect Jacob van Campen used
the standard local technique of
driving wooden piles down into
the solid subsurface to anchor
the foundation. What was less
standard was the sheer number of
piles—13,659.

Lieverdje's Radical Past

The innocent-looking statue of a woolen sock–clad boy in the middle of Spui Square, called the *Lieverdje* (Little Darling—local street slang for wild street boys), formed the focal point for the particularly wacky and inspired Amsterdam social coalition known as Provos (precursors to the hippies). Taking their name from their ultimate goal, "to provoke"—this group first rose around Robert Jasper Grootveld, who hosted absurdist anti-consumerist "happenings" off Leidseplein. In 1964, he moved his shows to the Spui around the Lieverdje statue that had just been erected there. The crowds that gathered to see the happenings had repeated clashes with the police. During the student war protest of the 1960s, the Lieverdje statue was repeatedly and symbolically set on fire. Today pranksters occasionally dress him up in silly garb just because they can.

Center (Nos. 14–16) and its adjoining bookstore are the city's best places to peruse an international array of literature, magazines, and newspapers. More cultural browsing can be enjoyed on the Spui's book market on Friday and its art market on Sunday. ⊠ *Bounded by Spuistraat and Kalverstraat, Centrum.*

NEED A BREAK?

Several of the bar-cafés and eateries on Spui square are good places to take a break. The ancient **Hoppe** (⊠ *Spui 18–20, Centrum* ☎ *020/420–4420*) has been serving drinks between woody walls and on sandy floors since 1670. For good people watching, visit the elegant **Café Luxembourg** (⊠ *Spui 24, Centrum* ☎ *020/620–6264*) but if you just want to eat and run, try **Broodje van Kootje** (⊠ *Spui 28, Centrum* ☎ *020/623–7451*) for a classic Amsterdam *broodje* (sandwich).

IF YOU HAVE TIME

🔟 **Damrak** *(Dam Port).* This unavoidable and busy street leading up to Centraal Station is now lined with a mostly tawdry assortment of shops, attractions, hotels, and greasy food dispensers. It's a shame, because behind the awful neon signs are beautiful examples of lovely Dutch architecture—they're just really hard to see. Damrak and its extension, Rokin, were once the Amstel River, bustling with activity, its piers loaded with fish and other cargo on their way to the weigh house at the Dam. Now the only open water that remains is a patch in front of the station that provides mooring for canal tour boats. Stop to admire the Beurs van Berlage and catch a canal tour, and then move on to prettier areas of the city. ⊠ *Centrum.*

🖐 ⑮ **Madame Tussauds Amsterdam.** This branch of the world-famous wax museum, above the Peek & Cloppenburg department store, depicts Holland's glitterati, including Golden Age celebrities—there's a life-size, 3-D rendering of a painting by Vermeer (alas, the lighting is dubious), and even an understandably displaced-looking Piet Mondriaan. Of course, there is also a broad selection of international superstars, including George W. Bush, who is caught in a suitably presidential pose.

Bring your own ironic distance, or skip it altogether. People watching in the Dam is much more entertaining than wax watching in Madame Tussauds. ⊠*Dam 20, Centrum* ☎*020/523–0623* ⊕*www.madame-tussauds.nl* 🎟*€23* 🕙*Sept.–June, daily 10–5:30; July and Aug., daily 9:30–7:30.*

THE RED LIGHT DISTRICT

Say "Amsterdam" and people's reflexive response is "the Red Light District." This infamous little neighborhood, sandwiched between the two oldest canals in the city (the Oudezijdesvoorburgwal and the Oudezijdesachterburgwal), employs 13,000 women of all shapes, sizes, colors, and kinks and legally generates up to half-a-billion taxable Euro per year. If you decide to take a stroll around the *wallen* (the walls—a nickname taken from the canals that surround it), be forewarned: it's the shadiest section of town, where junkies and drug dealers congregate to score, shoot up, and smoke. But don't let a little sleaze scare you away. This is also the most historic, and was at one point, the weathiest part of town.

In the 16th century, the residents of the Oudezijdesvoorburgwal were so rich that the area was nicknamed "the Velvet Canal." Edit out the garish advertising, the creepy guy on the corner, and the breasts hypnotically sandwiched against the red-neon framed windows, and you have some spectacular architecture. The Red Light District is surprisingly safe. Alongside the sex shops, bars, churches, and brothels, lives a diverse community of hardworking tradespeople, professionals, students, and families. This is also where Amsterdam's Chinatown is located.

MAIN ATTRACTIONS

❺ Bananenbar *(Banana Bar).* Since the 1970s, this super-sleazy bar has featured naked barmaids doing "now you see it, now you don't" tricks that involve fruit—this show is not for the faint of heart, nor is it something that merits landmark status. It is however, a red light institution. In the 1980s, the owner pulled a little tax dodge that was almost as sleazy as the floor show. He tried to avoid overdue taxes and a lapsed drinking license by registering as a religion—the Church of Satan. By 1988 the Banana Bar was claiming a flock of 40,000, which motivated the taxman to finally clamp down. Before legal action could be taken, the "church" disbanded and the bar returned to its secular, albeit sordid, roots. ⊠*Oudezijds Achterburgwal 137, Centrum.*

❼ Museum Amstelkring *(Our Lord in the Attic Museum).* With its elegant gray-and-white facade and spout gable, this appears to be just another lovely canal house, and on the lower floors it is. But tucked away in the attic is the only surviving *schuilkerk* (clandestine church) that dates from the Reformation, when open worship by Catholics was outlawed. The Oude Kerk was de-catholicized and stripped of its patron, St. Nicholas, so this little church was dedicated to him until the Sint Nicolaaskerk was built. The chapel itself is a triumph of Dutch classicist taste, with magnificent marble columns, gilded capitals, a colored-

Fodor's Choice ★

marble altar, and the *Baptism of Christ* (1716) painting by Jacob de Wit presiding over all. Sunday services and weddings are still offered here. The lower floors are also beautifully preserved and shouldn't be missed. ⊠ *Oudezijds Voorburgwal 40, Centrum* ☎ *020/624–6604* ⊕ *www.museumamstelkring.nl* ⊒ *€7* ⊙ *Mon.–Sat. 10–5, Sun. 1–5.*

> ### A SECOND HOME
>
> Prior to the reformation, the Oude Kerk was known as the "living room" because peddlers displayed their goods in the church and beggars slept there.

★ **8** **Oude Kerk** *(Old Church).* The Oude Kerk is Amsterdam's oldest church and its location never ceases to shock first-time visitors. It's smack-dab in the middle of a carnal circus, literally surrounded by scantily clad hookers eyeing the action in the square. It began as a wooden chapel in 1306 but was built up to a hall church and then a cross basilica between 1366 and 1566 (and fully restored between 1955 and 1979). It was violently looted during the Reformation and the church was stripped of its altars and images of saints—although the revolutionaries did leave the 14th-century paintings still visible on its wooden roof, as well as the Virgin Mary stained-glass windows that had been set in place in 1550. In the 17th century it was fitted with its famed Vater-Muller organ. Don't miss the enscription on the Bridal Chamber, which translates to: "Marry in Haste, Mourn in Leisure." Sage advice, given the neighborhood. Oude Kerk is as much exhibition space as a place of worship, hosting the annual World Press Photo competition and top-notch modern-art shows. Its carillon is played every Saturday between 4 and 5. ⊠ *Oudekerksplein 23, Centrum* ☎ *020/625-8284* ⊕ *www.oudekerk.nl* ⊒ *€5.00* ⊙ *Mon.–Sat. 11–5, Sun. 1–5.*

★ **3** **Schreierstoren.** This is Amsterdam's most distinctive fortress tower. Today it's home to a café but it began life in 1486 as the end point of the city wall. The term *schreien* suggests the Dutch word for wailing. As lore would have it, this "Weeping Tower" was where women came to cry when their sailor husbands left for sea and to cry again when they did not return. The word *schreier* actually comes from an Old Dutch word for a "sharp corner." It's also famous as the point from which Henry Hudson set sail to America. A plaque on the building tells you that he sailed on behalf of the Dutch East India Company to find a shorter route to the East Indies. In his failure, he came across Canada's Hudson Bay and later—continuing his bad-luck streak—New York harbor and the Hudson River. He eventually landed on Manhattan and named it New Amsterdam. ⊠ *Prins Hendrikkade 94–95, Centrum.*

9 **Warmoesstraat.** This touristy strip of hostels, bars, and coffee shops began life as one of the original dikes along the Amstel before evolving into the city's richest shopping street (a sharp contrast to its fallen sister, Zeedijk). It's here that the famous 17th-century poet Vondel once did business from his hosiery shop at No. 101, and where Mozart's dad tried to unload tickets for his son's concerts in the area's upscale bars. It entered a decline in the 17th century when the proprietors forsook their above-store lodgings for fancier digs on the Canal Ring; sailors

Leaning Houses

Ever wonder why all of Amsterdam's old houses lean like drunken sailors on a Saturday night? After the great fires of 1421 and 1452 swept through and destroyed nearly three quarters of the city, Emperor Charles decreed that new houses be built of brick and stone. That is why virtually no wooden buildings remain from the 15th century—a notable exception being the Houten Huis (Wooden House) at the Begijnhof. Since these brick houses were significantly heavier (and the city is still sinking into the mud at a slow and steady pace), all structures were built on wooden pilings slammed deep into the sand before construction work began. Even so, nothing could stop the lavishly built houses from tilting over after a few years. The leaning becomes especially severe when the wooden pilings begin to rot. Today, modern restoration engineers can replace rotten wooden pilings with cement ones, without tearing down the building.

(and the businesses that catered to them) started to fill in the gaps. In the 19th century, the street evolved, along with its extension **Nes,** into the city's primary debauchery zone. Karl Marx was known to set himself up regularly in a hotel here, not only to write in peace but to ask for the occasional loan from his cousin-in-law, Gerard Philips, founder of that capitalist machine Philips.

Thanks to a recent revamp, Warmoesstraat is beginning to lose some of its Sodom and Gomorrah edge. Between the sleazier tourist traps, there are such hip hangouts as the Hotel Winston (No. 123); restful oases serving stellar quiche such as De Bakkerswinkel (No. 69); and worthwhile specialty stores, such as Geels and Co. (No. 67), with its infinite selection of coffees and teas. There's even a squatted gallery, the beautifully spacious W139 (No. 139), dedicated to the very outer edges of conceptual art. ⊠*Between Dam and Nieuwe Brugsteeg, Centrum.*

NEED A BREAK?

Zeedijk offers five of the best quick snack/meal stops in town. The most revered is auspiciously placed across from the Buddhist Temple: **Nam Kee** (⊠*Zeedijk 111–113, Centrum* ☎*020/624–3470*) is a speedy and cheap Chinese spot whose steamed oysters are so sublime that they provided the title and muse for a local author's novel. Far and wide the best Chinese food in town. **Snackbar Bird** (⊠*Zeedijk 72, Centrum* ☎*020/420–6289*) offers wok-fried-in-front-of-your-eyes dishes from Thailand; for a more lingering or less cramped meal, you might want to try its restaurant across the street, offering up the best Thai food in the city. The ultimate Dutch snack, raw herring, can be enjoyed at the fresh-fish shop **Huijsmans Cock** (⊠*Zeedijk 129, Centrum* ☎*020/624–2070*), which also offers deliciously nutty whole wheat buns. A Zeedijk and students' fave, **Cafe Latei** (⊠*Zeedijk 143, Centrum* ☎*020/625–7485*) combines a dense interior of high-quality kitsch (all of it for sale) with the serving of coffee, open-faced sandwiches, and healthy snacks.

4 **Zeedijk.** Few streets have had a longer or more torrid history; until recently known as the Black Hole of Amsterdam (because of its concentration of junkies), the Zeedijk is now on the up-and-up. As the original dike created to keep the sea at bay, Zeedijk has been around since Amsterdam began life as a boggy little fishing hamlet. The building of this dike in 1380 probably represented the first twitchings of democracy as individual fishing and farming folk were united to make battle against the sea. Less noble democratic forces saw an opportunity to make a few gulden by catering to lonely, thirsty sailors—a service area businesses ended up providing for centuries. In the last 50 years, dingier dens began a lucrative sideline in heroin and by the 1970s, the only traffic Zeedijk saw was drug traffic. Tourists were advised to avoid the neighborhoood at night because of the junkies and high crime rates. A few years back, the city started cracking down and has been working hard to clean up the area. It's by no means a pristine street, but it's now much easier to accept the stray, dubious-looking character as merely part of the scenery as opposed to its definition.

There are several interesting sights along the Zeedijk. The 17th-century **Sint Olofskapel** (St. Olaf Church), named after the patron saint of dikes, sports a life-affirming sculpture: grains growing out of a supine skeleton (this used to be a positive message). Across the street at No. 1 is one of only two timbered houses left in the city. It does have stone sides—as law dictated after the great fires of 1421 and 1452. Dating from around 1550, **in't Aephen** (In the Monkeys) provided bedding to destitute sailors if they promised to return from their next voyage with a monkey. The way each floor sticks slightly more outward than the one below it accounts for the way most of Amsterdam's brick buildings lean forward: they were built aesthetically to follow this line. Café Maandje at No. 65 was the first openly gay bar. Its window maintains a shrine to its former proprietor and the spiritual forebear of lesbian biker babes everywhere: Bet van Beeren (1902–67). Although the café opens only on the rarest of occasions, a model of its interior can be viewed at the Amsterdams Historisch Museum. The rest of the street is a quirky mixture of middle-range Asian restaurants, brown cafés with carpeted tables, specialty shops, and galleries. The Chinese community is in full visual effect at the end of the street, where recently the gloriously colorful pagoda-shape **Fo Kuang Shan Buddhist Temple** (No. 118) arose. ⊠ *Oudezijde Kolk (near Centraal Station) to Nieuwmarkt, Centrum.*

IF YOU HAVE TIME

6 **Erotic Museum.** "Five floors of highly suggestive trinkets and photos" is probably a better description than "museum." Happily, it's all presented rather lightheartedly (although animal lovers should steer clear of the snapshot gallery). Beatles fans may like the original and satisfyingly suggestive sketch by John Lennon, perhaps rendered when he and Yoko did their weeklong bed-in for peace at the Hilton just down the road. ⊠ *Oudezijds Achterburgwal 54, Centrum* ☎ *020/624–7303* 🖵 €5 ☉ *Sun.–Thurs. 11* AM–1 AM; *Fri. and Sat. 11* AM–2 AM.

22 Hash Marijuana Hemp Museum. One would think that more effort could have gone into the name of this institution—lateral thinking being one of the positive effects of its subject. But regardless, here's your chance to suck back the 8,000-year history of hemp use. The use of pot as medicine was first recorded in the Netherlands in 1554 as a cure for earaches. By this time, its less potent form, hemp, had long been used—as it would until the late 19th century—as the fiber source for rope. It was fundamental to the economics of this seafaring town. Predictably, there's also an endless collection of bongs from around the world. ⊠ *Oudezijds Achterburgwal 148, Centrum* ☎ *020/623–5961* ⊕ *www.hashmuseum.com* ⊠ *€5.70* ☻ *Daily 10–10.*

2 Sint Nicolaaskerk *(St. Nicholas Church).* The architect A.C. Bleys designed this church, built in 1887, with its dark and eerie interior as a replacement to all the clandestine Catholic churches that arose during the Reformation. Following in the footsteps of first Oude Kerk and then Museum Amstelkring's "Our Lord in the Attic" chapel, this church became the third and most likely final Sint Nicolaas church. St. Nick (or Sinter Klaas as he is called here) is the patron saint of children, thieves, prostitutes, sailors, and the city of Amsterdam. The eve of his birthday on December 6 is still celebrated as a mellow family feast where everyone exchanges self-made presents and poems. Note that the church is open only when volunteer custodians are available. It hosts a Gregorian chant vesper service September to June on Sunday at 5. ⊠ *Prins Hendrikkade 76, Centrum* ☎ *020/624–8749* ⊠ *Free* ☻ *Mon.–Sat. 11–4.*

NIEUWMARKT & ENVIRONS

At the bottom of the Zeedijk and bordering the Red Light District lies Nieuwmarkt and the Magic Kingdom–like Waag gatehouse, where Rembrandt came to watch Professor Tulp in action before painting *The Anatomy Lesson.* The Nieuwmarkt has been a marketplace since the 15th century. In those days, de Waag—or Sint Antoniespoort (St. Anthony's Port) as it was then known—formed a gateway in the city defenses. Most public executions took place here as well. During WWII, the Nazis used the square as a collection point where Jews were held before being shipped off to concentration camps. The Nieuwmarkt today has evolved into an upscale local gathering place, ringed by restaurants, cafés, jazz clubs, and a microbrewery. There is also a daily farmers' market and an organic farmers' market every Saturday.

After the hustle (literally) of the Red Light District, a walk through Nieuwmarkt neighborhood provides a refreshing break. Due east are a cluster of less-touristed, quiet little canal-lined streets (the Rechtboomsloot is especially scenic). Directly south, straight up the Kloveniersburgwal is the University of Amsterdam, housed in a myriad of lovely old buildings along and between the canals.

> **NARROW HOUSES**
>
> There are a few other super skinny houses in Amsterdam besides the Little Trip House. The narrowest is at Singel No. 7 at only 1 meter wide. The building on Oude Hoogstraat 22 is only 2.02 meters (7 feet) wide and 6 meters (19 feet) deep.

NEED A BREAK?

You may want to sniff out your own favorite among the many café-restaurants that line this square. We like **In De Waag** (⊠ *Nieuwmarkt 4, Centrum* ☎ *020/422–7772*), which highlights its epic medieval roots with candlelight. An arty and studenty option is **Lokaal 't Loosje** (⊠ *Nieuwmarkt 32–34, Centrum* ☎ *020/627–2635*), which is graced with tile tableaux dating from 1912. The thematically decorated **Café Cuba** (⊠ *Nieuwmarkt 3, Centrum* ☎ *020/627–4919*) serves relatively cheap cocktails and offers a jazzy electronic dance sound track that inspires many of the hipster regulars to light up a joint in the back. Fans of more traditional jazz should check out the legendary **Cotton Club** (⊠ *Nieuwmarkt 5, Centrum* ☎ *020/626–6192*), named after its original owner, the Surinamer trumpet player Teddy Cotton.

MAIN ATTRACTIONS

⑲ Allard Pierson Museum. Once the repository of the nation's gold supply, this former National Bank with its stern Neoclassical facade is now home to other treasures. Dynamite helped remove the safes and open up the space for the archaeological collection of the University of Amsterdam in 1934, and the museum traces the early development of Western civilization, from the Egyptians to the Romans, and of the Near Eastern cultures (Anatolia, Persia, Palestine) in a series of well-documented displays. ⊠ *Oude Turfmarkt 127, Centrum* ☎ *020/525–2556* ⊕ *www.allardpiersonmuseum.nl* ☜ *€5. Children under 16 half-price* ☉ *Tues.–Fri. 10–5, weekends 1–5.*

★ ㉔ Trippenhuis (Trip House). As family home to the two Trip brothers, who made their fortune in gun dealing during the 17th-century Golden Age, this noted house's buckshot-gray exterior and various armament motifs—including a mortar-shape chimney—are easily explained. But what's most distinctive about this building is that its Corinthian-columned facade actually hides two symmetrical buildings (note the wall that bisects the middle windows), one for each brother. Be sure to look across the canal to No. 26, the door-wide white building topped with golden sphinxes and the date of 1696, which is known as both the "Little Trip House" and the "House of Mr. Trip's Coachman." The story goes that the coachman remarked that he would be happy with a house as wide as the Trippenhuis door. By way of response, Mr. Trip built just that with the leftover bricks. That may be an urban myth; the Little Trip House is actually much bigger than it looks, and its completion date was long after either brother died. ⊠ *Kloveniersburgwal 29, Centrum.*

㉓ Waag *(Weigh House).* Built in the center of the square in 1488, the Waag functioned as a city gate, Sint Antoniespoort, until the early 17th century. During those centuries, the gate would be closed at exactly 9:30 PM to keep out not only the bandits but also the poor and the diseased who built shantytowns outside the wall. When the city expanded, it began a second life as a weighing house for incoming products. The top floor of the building came to accommodate the municipal militia and several guilds, including the masons who did the evocative decorations that grace each of the towers' entrances. One of its towers housed a teaching hospital for the academy of surgeons of the Surgeons' Guild. The Theatrum Anatomicum (Anatomy Theater), with its cupola tower covered in painted coats of arms, was the first place in the Netherlands to host public autopsies. For obvious reasons, these took place only in the winter. Now the building is occupied by a café-restaurant with free Internet service and the **Society for Old and New Media** (⊕ *www.waag.org*). ⊠ *Bounded by Kloveniersburgwal, Geldersekade, and Zeedijk, Centrum.*

IF YOU HAVE TIME

㉑ Nes. Originating as a boggy walkway along the Amstel River when Amsterdam was an ever-sinking fishing village, the Nes is now a refreshingly quiet corridor filled with theaters and restaurants. At the end of the 14th century, the Nes began evolving into a long strip of monasteries and convents before the Altercation of 1578 (or Protestant takeover) when Amsterdam became more concerned with commercial pursuits on its march toward the Golden Age. The philosopher Spinoza (1623–77) moved here to escape the derision he was receiving from his own Jewish community for having fused Jewish mysticism with Descartian logic, concluding that body and soul were part of the same essence. The Frascati theater (Nos. 59–65) began life as a coffeehouse in the 18th century, but it wasn't until the 1880s that the Nes really blossomed with cafés filled with dance, song, and operetta performances; stars often represented the less uptight segment of the Jewish community. Adjacent to the southern end of the Nes is **Gebed Zonder End,** the "Prayer Without End" alleyway, which got its name because it was said you could hear prayers from behind the walls of the convents that used to line this alley. ⊠ *Between Langebrugsteeg and Dam, Centrum.*

A TASTE OF HOLLAND

The **Kruidenwinkel van Jacob Hooy & Co.** (⊠ *Kloveniersburgwal 12, on the westside of Nieuwmarkt*) is Amsterdam's oldest medicinal herb and spice shop. Try the typical Dutch *drop* (licorice) candy that comes in salty or extra salty. Beware: it's an acquired taste.

20 **Oudemanhuispoort** *(Old Man's House Alley).* Landmarked by its famous chiseled pair of spectacles (set over the Oudezijds Achterburgwal pediment)—a sweet reference to old age—this was once a pensioners' house, an "Oudemannenhuis," first built in 1754. Today, bikes, not canes, are in evidence, as this former almshouse is now part of the University of Amsterdam. One charming relic from its founding days is the covered walkway, lined with tiny shops whose rents helped subsidize the 18th-century elderly. Adorned with red shutters, the stalls now house an array of antiquarian booksellers and lead on to Kloverniersburgwal, where a statue of Mother Amsterdam protecting two elders, sculpted by Anthonie Ziessenis in 1786, stands. ✉ *Between Oudezijds Achterburgwal, and Klovniersburgwal, Centrum.*

> **REBUILDING MOKUM**
>
> The devastation of the Jewish quarter during the war, and its later (very controversial) demolition to make room for the Stadhuis/Muziektheater (City Hall/Music Theater) and the Metro architecturally marked this neighborhood like no other in the city. Today it is a hodgepodge of the old and new.

NEED A BREAK? As to be expected from a theatrical neighborhood, the Nes offers some prime drinking holes, where you can also choose to have a leisurely meal. Both the food and drink are good here, and there are several choices. Fans of Belgian beer should certainly stop at the patio of **De Brakke Grond** (✉ *Nes 43, Centrum* ☎ *020/626–0044* ⊕ *www.brakkegrond.nl*), part of the Flemish Cultural Center, to partake in one or two of the dozens of options. Coincidentally, on the "Prayer Without End" alley, which runs parallel to Nes's south end, is **Captain Zeppos** (✉ *Gebed Zonder End 5, Centrum* ☎ *020/624–2057*), which is named after a '60s Belgian TV star; this former cigar factory is soaked with jazzy old-world charm. A fun place to have a drink.

THE JEWISH QUARTER

From medieval times up to Nazi occupation, Amsterdam was considered a sort of second Jerusalem for immigrating Jews from all over Europe. The city came to be known as Mokum (the Hebrew word for "place"), as in *the* place for Jewish people.

Since the 15th century, the *Joodse Buurt* (Jewish Quarter) has traditionally been considered the district east of the Zwanenburgwal. The Quarter got its start thanks to the Inquisition, which drove Sephardic Jews from Spain after 1492. Holland's war with Spain inspired the 1597 Union of Utrecht—it was formulated to protect Protestants from the religious oppression that came with Spanish invasions, but essentially meant that all religions were tolerated. This provided a unique experience for Jewish people because unlike elsewhere in Europe, they were not forced to wear badges and live in ghettos. These and other freedoms helped attract many Yiddish-speaking Ashkenazi Jews from Eastern Europe, who were escaping pogroms. In the 17th century, only the Catholics remained barred from open worship. This explains the 17th-century synagogues in the city and the complete absence of Catholic churches from that period.

By 1938, 10% of Amsterdam's population was Jewish. They had hugely influenced the city's culture and language (the Yiddish word *mazel,* meaning "luck," is still used as a standard farewell). Today, what remains much more painfully ingrained in the city's psyche is what happened during the Nazi occupation, when the Jewish population was reduced to one-seventh of its size. There were many examples of bravery and the opening of homes to hide Jewish people, but there are many more—and less often told—stories of collabora-

> **XXX IS FOR AMSTERDAM**
>
> Those XXX symbols you see all over town are not a mark of the city's triple-x reputation. They're part of Amsterdam's official coat of arms—three St. Andrew's crosses, believed to represent the three dangers that have traditionally plagued the city: flood, fire, and pestilence. The coat's motto (valiant, determined, compassionate) was introduced in 1941 by Queen Wilhelmina in remembrance of the February Strike in Amsterdam—the first time in Europe non-Jewish people protested against the prosecution of Jews by the Nazi regime.

tion. Although the current Jewish population has risen to 20,000, the Jewish community itself exists largely beneath the surface of Amsterdam and most place Dutch identity before Judaism.

MAIN ATTRACTIONS

③③ Joods Historisch Museum *(Jewish Historical Museum).* Four Ashkenazi synagogues (or *shuls,* as they are called in Yiddish), dating from the 17th and 18th centuries were combined with glass-and-steel constructions in 1987 to create this impressive museum commemorating the four-century history of the Jewish people in Amsterdam and the Netherlands. Back in the 17th century, Ashkenazi Jews fled the pogroms in Central and Eastern Europe. They weren't exactly welcomed with open arms by the already settled Sephardic Jews (who resented the increased competition imposed by their often poorer brethren), so separate synagogues were consequently built. Four of them make up this complex: the **Neie Sjoel** (New Synagogue, 1752), traces the subject of Jewish identity; the **Grote Sjoel** (Great Synagogue, 1671), presents the tenets of Judaism; the **Obbene Sjoel** (Upstairs Synagogue, 1686), is where the bookshop and café are found; and the **Dritt Sjoel** (Third Synagogue, 1700) houses a collection that includes an 18th-century Sephardic Torah Mantle, a magnificent carved wood Holy Ark dating from 1791, and the autobiographical art of the Berlin artist Charlotte Solomon (1917–43). The museum also features a resource center and one of the city's few purely kosher cafés. Whether or not you tour the collections, check out the excellent tours of the Jewish Quarter conducted by this museum. ✉*Nieuwe Amstelstraat 1, Centrum* ☎*020/531–0310* ⊕*www.jhm.nl* 🎟*€7.50* ☉*Mon.–Wed. and Fri.—Sun. 11—5, Thurs. 11-9.*

28 **Museum het Rembrandthuis** (*Rembrandt's House*). One of Amsterdam's
Fodor's Choice more remarkable relics, this house was bought by Rembrandt, flush
★ with success, for his family and is where he lived and worked between
1639 and 1658. Rembrandt chose this house on what was once the
main street of the Jewish Quarter because he thought he could then
experience daily and firsthand the faces he would use in his Old Testa-
ment religious paintings. Later Rembrandt lost the house to bankruptcy
when he fell from popularity after the death of Saskia, his wife. When
he showed a quick recovery—and an open taste for servant girls—after
her death, his uncle-in-law, once his greatest champion, became his biggest detractor. Rembrandt's downfall was sealed: he came under attack
by the Amsterdam burghers, who refused to accept his liaison with his
amour, Hendrickje.

The house interior has been restored to its original form—complete
with one of Rembrandt's printing presses, his rarities collection, and
fully stocked studio (which is occasionally used by guest artists). The
new gallery wing, complete with shop, café, and information center,
is the only place in the world where his graphic work is on permanent
display—with 250 of the 290 prints that are known to have come
from his hand, including the magisterial *Hundred Guilder* and the
Three Crosses prints. Rembrandt was almost more revolutionary in
his prints than in his paintings, so this collection deserves respectful
homage, if not downright devotion, by printmakers today. ✉ *Jodenbreestraat 4–6, Centrum* ☎ *020/520–0400* ⊕ *www.rembrandthuis.nl*
🎫 *€8* ⊗ *Daily 10–5.*

**NEED A
BREAK?**
Just across the canal from Rembrandt's House are the designer sandwiches at Dantzig (✉ *Zwanenburgwal 15, Centrum* ☎ *020/620–9039*),
to be enjoyed either on its patio looking over Waterlooplein or within its
modern interior of mosaics.Soup Enzo (✉ *Jodenbreestraat 94A, Centrum*
☎ *020/422–4243*), has the best soup in Amsterdam, hands down. Its also
down the road from Waterlooplein.

32 **Muziektheater/Stadhuis** (*Music Theater/Town Hall*). Universally known
as the Stopera—not just from the combining of "Stadhuis" (Town
Hall) and "Opera" but from the radical opposition expressed during its
construction—this brick-and-marble complex when viewed from the
south resembles, as a local writer once described it, a "set of dentures."
Another writer grumbled that its "two for one" nature was a tad too
typical of the bargain-loving Dutch. Discontent with this modern complex actually began before the first stone was in place, when locals pro-
tested the razing of the 16th- and 17th-century houses in the old Jewish
Quarter and around Nieuwmarkt to make way for it. Regardless, the
300 million-guilder building was completed, and today has an impressive interior architecture with stunning acoustics. The Muziektheater is
now home base for the Nederlands Opera and the National Ballet and
the ballet orchestra. Tours of the backstage areas are run once a week
(Saturday at noon) or by prior arrangement. From September to May,
the Boekmanzaal is host to a free Tuesday lunch concert.

City Hall is in odd contrast to the grand Music Theater side, with its functional municipal offices and now gay couple–friendly wedding chamber (Dutch marriages all must be performed in the Town Hall, with church weddings optional). Feel free to wander through the interconnecting lobbies, where there is interesting sculpture on display that frighteningly illustrates Amsterdam's position with the sea. ⊠ *Waterlooplein 22 or Amstel 3, Centrum* ☎*020/625–5455* ⊕*www.stopera. nl* ⊠ *Tours €5.00* ⊗ *Mon.–Sat. 10–6; tours Sat. at noon or by arrangement; call 020/551–8103.*

★ ㉖ **Pintohuis.** This Italian Renaissance–style house was grandly renovated in 1680 by Jewish refugee Isaac de Pinto, a grandee who escaped the Inquisition in Portugal to come to Amsterdam and become one of the founders of the East India Company. Six towering Italianate pilasters break up the impressive facade, remodeled by Elias Bouwman in the 1670s. In the early 1970s it was almost demolished so that the street could be widened, but activist squatters saved the building. The Pintohuis is now a public library. Feel free to wander around and admire its lush and historic interior—in particular its cherub-encrusted ceiling painting by Jacob de Wit, a 17th-century master. ⊠*Sint Antoniebreestraat 69, Centrum* ☎*020/624–3184* ⊠*Free* ⊗*Mon. and Wed. 2–8, Fri. 2–5, Sat. 11–2.*

㉞ **Portugees Israelitische Synagoge** *(Portuguese Israelite Synagogue).* With Jerusalem's Temple of Solomon as inspiration, Elias Bouwman and Danield Stalpaert designed this noted synagogue between 1671 and 1675. Its square brick building within a courtyard formed by brick houses was commissioned by the Sephardic Jewish community that had emigrated via Portugal during the preceding two centuries. On its completion it was the largest synagogue in the world, and its spare, elegantly proportioned wood interior has remained virtually unchanged through the centuries. It is still magically illuminated by candles in two immense candelabra during services. The surrounding buildings that form a square around the synagogue house the world-famous Ets Haim ("Tree of Life") library, one of the oldest in the world, and the winter synagogue for use on those draftier days. ⊠*Mr. Visserplein 3, Centrum* ☎*020/624–5351* ⊕*www.esnoga.com* ⊠*€6.50* ⊗*Apr.–Oct., Sun.–Fri. 10–4; Nov.–Mar., Sun.–Thurs. 10–4, Fri. 10–3.*

㉛ **Waterlooplein.** Before its rezoning, this flea market was a swampy neighborhood, bordered by the Leper and Peat canals, that often took the brunt of an overflowing Amstel River and therefore housed only the poorest of Jews. In 1886 it became the daily market for the surrounding Jewish neighborhood—a necessity, since Jews were not allowed to own shops at the time. It became a meeting place whose chaos of wooden carts and general vibrancy disappeared along with the Jewish population during World War II. And yet it still provides a colorful glimpse into Amsterdam's particular brand of pragmatic sales techniques. Its stalls filled with clothes, bongs, discarded electronics, and mountains of Euroknickknacks can sometimes indeed be a battle—although a worthwhile one—to negotiate. ⊠ *Waterlooplein, Centrum* ⊗ *Weekdays 9–4, Sat. 8:30–4:30. Some stalls close earlier, depending on weather.*

★ **㉗ Zuiderkerk** *(South Church)*. Gorgeous enough to have inspired both Sir Christopher Wren and Monet, this famous church was built between 1603 and 1611 by Hendrick de Keyser, one of the most prolific architects of Holland's Golden Age. Legend has it this church hypnotized the great British architect Wren, who went on to build London's St. Paul's Cathedral centuries later; Monet committed the Zuiderkerk to canvas. It was one of the earliest churches built in Amsterdam in the Renaissance style and was the first in the city to be built for the Dutch Reformed Church. The church's hallowed floors—under which three of Rembrandt's children are buried—are now under the reign of the City Planning Office and as such are filled with detailed models of Amsterdam's ambitious future building plans. The church tower—a soaring accumulation of columns, brackets, and balustrades—is one of the most glorious exclamation points in Amsterdam; its bells are played every Thursday between noon and 1. Sadly, until further notice, there are no more tours of the tower because it is unsafe. Hopefully that will change soon. ⊠ *Zuiderkerkhof 72, Centrum* ☎ *020/552-7987* ⊕ *www. zuiderkerk.amsterdam.nl* ✄ *Free* ⊘ *Mon.-Fri. 9–4, Sat. 12–4.*

IF YOU HAVE TIME

㉙ Gassan Diamonds. When diamonds were discovered in South Africa in 1869, there was a near immediate windfall for Amsterdam's Jewish community, a third of whom worked in the diamond trade. Built in 1879, Gassan Diamonds was once home to the Boas diamond-polishing factory, the largest in the world, where 357 diamond-polishing machines were working nonstop. Today, Gassan offers polishing and grading demonstrations and free one-hour tours (for which it's best to book ahead) of the building and its glittering collection of diamonds and jewelry. If you'd like to spend some money on glitter of your own, call ahead to see about arranging a "diamond and champagne" tour, capped off with a champagne reception (and a diamond gift for one lucky prizewinner). ⊠ *Nieuwe Uilenburgerstraat 173, Centrum* ☎ *020/622-5333* ⊕ *www.gassandiamonds.nl* ✄ *Free* ⊘ *Daily 9–5.*

㉕ Montelbaanstoren *(Montelbaans Tower)*. Rembrandt loved to sketch this slightly leaning tower, which dates from 1516; in those more perpendicular days, it formed part of the city's defenses against raiding hordes of attackers. City expansion in 1578 saw it connected by a defensive wall with the Sint Antoniepoort (De Waag in Nieuwmarkt). In 1606, the ubiquitous Hendrick de Keyser oversaw the building of a new tower complete with clockworks. But time soon saw the tower leaning toward Pisa, and in 1611 it had to be reset with lots of manpower and ropes on a stronger foundation. Since 1878, it has housed the City Water Office, which maintains the water levels in the canals and engineers the nightly flushing of the entire city waterway system, closing and opening the sluices to change the direction of the flow and cleanse the waters. Algae and the use of yacht toilets on houseboats make it a thankless job. ⊠ *Oude Schans 2, Centrum.*

Eco Architecture

Dutch architecture is known for its creative approach to practical problems and right now, eco architecture (bringing environmental awareness to building design) is hot. With its focus on sustainability, the current renewal of the Eastern Docklands is a perfect example of this trend. Besides the use of solar panels on the islands east of Centraal Station, the buildings are all connected to a long-term energy storage (LTES) system that will provide collective heating and cooling for the next 15 years. In winter, heat generated is used immediately and cold is stored in the ground at the same time. In summer, the process is efficiently reversed. Another sight worth seeing is the Eco Quarter near Westerpark. More than a decade old, this green and car-free area was built for 600 households and designed as a co-creation project with future inhabitants. Created with an eye towards reducing heating costs, living rooms in the Eco Quarter are south-facing. Green solutions to minimize the use of clean drinking water include grass roofs on top of two building blocks, which catch rainwater before it runs down drainpipes. This allows some of the water to be used to flush toilets. Unfortunately, there was an unforeseen problem: water from the grass roofs unexpectedly brought sand down into the pump systems, causing them to clog and deposit part of the grass roof in people's toilets. Problems aside, the eco architecture in the Netherlands is cutting-edge and incredibly clever.

NEED A BREAK? The best place to view the Montelbaanstoren is from the patio of the **Café Sluyswacht** (⊠ *Jodenbreestraat 1, Centrum* ☎ *020/65–7611*) overlooking Oudeschans. But beware of the slant. You don't want to tumble into the water after a few beers.

30 **Mozes und Aäronkerk** *(Moses and Aaron Church)*. Landmarking the eastern corner of the Waterlooplein flea market, this structure once had a warehouse facade to disguise its function as a clandestine Catholic church. If this rarely used church could speak, it would name-drop the great philosopher Spinoza (it was built on the location of his birth house) and Liszt (it hosted a recital of his that he considered his all-time best). Originally built in 1649, it was rebuilt in 1841 by architect T. Suys the Elder, then refurbished in 1900. The name of the church refers to the figures adorning two gable stones of the original edifice, now to be seen in the rear wall. Today, the nave hosts very occasional exhibitions and concerts. ⊠ *Waterlooplein 205, Centrum* ☎ *020/622–1305* ◷ *Hrs vary.*

180 DEGREES AROUND CENTRAL STATION

Amsterdam was built on water, the source of this city's wealth and cultural history. Although Rotterdam has long surpassed it as the world's busiest port, Amsterdam and its neighboring ports along the North Sea Canal are still bustling. Before Centraal Station was built, the area was the center of the main harbour along the IJ waterway, heading out to open sea. International shipping routes ended here, sluicing bounty into the city via the Amstel river and the man-made canals that radiated outward. Looking at the map and orienting yourself to face the big water passage that is the IJ, you can explore 180 degrees to the east and west around Centraal Station to discover an exciting new fusion of city and water. This massive development has been going on for years and is slated for completion in 2010.

Directly to the west of Centraal Station are the Westerlijke Eilanden (Western Islands). Built on reclaimed land to create dockyards during the Golden Age, this area is living proof of how the city managed to triple in size using engineering that went way beyond the shipbuilding expertise of the day. Today, the old warehouses on the water give this neighborhood a quiet, "village within the city" feel. It borders one of the city's main green areas, the Westerpark, which runs parallel with the train lines coming out of Centraal Station. In the park, the Westergasfabriek ⇨(see Nightlife & the Arts) is the place to go for funky international festivals, art cinema, clubbing and cafés, conferences, music, and experimental exhibits.

Traveling 180 degrees the opposite direction will bring you to the Eastern Docklands, also an area that has been completely redeveloped since the 1990s. Once a squatters' paradise, many buildings have now been replaced by high tech, "microchip"-style architecture, a modern boardwalk, and bicycle bridges linking the islands to the center. Alongside the waterfront, some of the new highlights are the wave-shaped cruiseship Passenger Terminal, the Muziekgebouw Aan 't IJ (Music Building on the IJ) ⇨(see Nightlife & the Arts), and Amsterdam's amazing new library, which is claimed to be the biggest in Europe. The waterfront, once a bleak industrial no-man's-land, is now starting to buzz with internationally oriented sites that can compete with London and Berlin. Modern architecture buffs will enjoy checking out fresh initiatives in this area around Centraal Station and clubbers will appreciate the rollicking nightlife. The residential docklands are off the beaten track, but worth a visit if you want to inhale some cold North Sea wind, find fun little cafés, and experience a slice of up-to-the-minute metropolitan life in Amsterdam.

MAIN ATTRACTIONS

Amsterdamse Openbare Bibliotheek *(Amsterdam Public Library).* Europe's biggest public library opened in July 2007, offering a multifarious collection of information to about 7000 visitors per day. The 80-million-euro building, designed by architect Jo Coenen, replaces the old and sorely cramped Prinsengracht location and is run by 200 employees dressed in imaginative outfits created by fashion guru Aziz Bekkaoui. The "bieb," as locals call it, has a big theater, seminar and conference rooms, art spaces, and an extensive music library. A superb children's section with circular reading corners is set below a terraced central lounge area. Park yourself in the comfy designer furniture and peruse a mind-boggling international magazine collection. With 1,200 desks, half of them connected to internet PCs, you can study and surf in peace, for free. It's so welcoming you might want to hang out all day, or

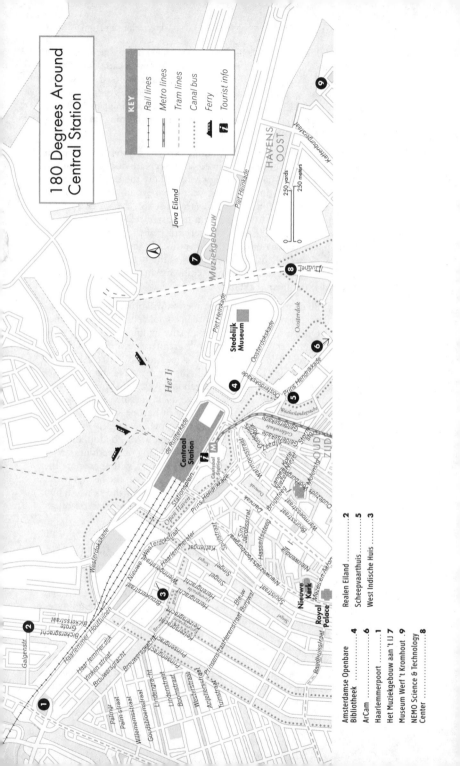

180 Degrees Around Central Station

KEY

⊢⊣⊢⊣	Rail lines
▬▬	Metro lines
-----	Tram lines
....	Canal bus
🚢	Ferry
🛈	Tourist info

Amsterdamse Openbare
Bibliotheek **4**
ArCam **6**
Haarlemmerpoort **1**
Het Muziekgebouw aan 't IJ **7**
Museum Werf 't Kromhout . **9**
NEMO Science & Technology
Center **8**

Realen Eiland **2**
Scheepvaarthuis **5**
West Indische Huis **3**

just drop in to browse the paper, socialize in one of the cafés, or eat a fresh feast in the seventh-floor Marché restaurant, while enjoying a spectacular view over the city. ✉ *Oosterdokskade 143, Centrum* ☎ *020/523–0900* ⊕ *www.oba.nl* ⊙ *Daily 10–10.*

8 NEMO Science & Technology Center. Opened in 1997, this green copper-clad building looks like a ship sinking into the city's boggy harbor. Designed as an international architectural landmark, Renzo Piano—creator of the Pompidou Center in Paris—created a ship's hull rising colossally out of the middle of the water, over the Coen Tunnel entrance to Amsterdam North. A rooftop café and summer 'beach' terrace offer a superb panorama of the area. No time to see the exhibits inside? Take the free entrance via a staircase on the eastern side or via an elevator just inside the entrance to catch the view.

The museum recently shortened its original name, "NewMetropolis," to NEMO, perhaps in nostalgic reference to Jules Verne's notorious sea captain in the evocative tale *The Odyssey,* or to refer to Winsor McCay's 100-year-old fantasy comic strip, *Little Nemo in Slumberland,* depicting the surreal adventures a little boy went on whenever he fell asleep. Kids can enjoy a fantastical, high-tech, hands-on experience at this exploration museum focused on futuristic science. Technical minded smarty pants will love building hydroelectric power stations, constructing a bamboo house, traveling through brains, indulging in dramatic chemistry experiments, playing with a giant domino set, getting charged with static electricity, and working out how to collapse international economies as simulated online bankers. ✉ *Oosterdok 2, Centrum* ☎ *020/531–3233* ⊕ *www.e-nemo.nl* ✒ *€11.50* ⊙ *Oct.–May, Tues.–Sun. 10–5; June–Sept., daily 10–5.*

IF YOU HAVE TIME

6 ArCam. Architecture Centrum Amsterdam is dedicated to modern Dutch architecture. The association organizes exhibits, lectures, and forums on the modern vogue. They also provide references for some excellent tours—including one to the new landmarks arising along the Eastern Docklands and the new residential island Ijburg, built in the middle of the water on the Eastern most outskirts of the city. Its new exhibition space, all swoopy and silver, at the corner of Prins Hendrikkade and Rapenburgerstraat, has already become an architectural icon in and of itself. ✉ *Prins Hendrikkade 600, Centrum* ☎ *020/620–4878* ⊕ *www.arcam.nl* ✒ *Free* ⊙ *Tues.–Fri. 1–5.*

1 **Haarlemmerpoort.** The northern edge of the Jordaan once was marked by city walls and had a historical gateway on the road that led to Haarlem. The current Neoclassical-style gatehouse that was built in 1840 to honor King William II, replaced the Renaissance style gate and bridge, a copy of which still stands in restored glory at the other end of the road in Haarlem. Also known as the Willemspoort, the gatehouse marked the entrance

> **TRULY MOVING MUSIC**
>
> One of the most spectacular features of Amsterdam's Muziekgebouw aan 't IJ is the flexibility of its main auditorium. It has three movable walls, including an acoustic ceiling that can move up and down to allow notes to resonate from 1.5 up to 3.5 seconds at a time (a new musical record).

to Amsterdam until the mid 19th century. Variously used as a military post, train station, fire station and a police station, it was restored in 1986 and converted into private appartments. A bit of a weird white elephant looming in a traffic crossing, it is a handy marker to find your way the Westerpark, one of the city's most hip and upcoming parks. ⊠ *Haarlemmerplein 50, Jordaan.*

7 **Het Muziekgebouw aan 't IJ** *(Music Building on the IJ).* Just 200 meters from Centraal Station and built on a peninsula on the IJ, this spectacular building was also designed on a ship shape theme, by the Danish architects 3xNielsen. Since opening in 2005, it has become a main concert hall for both classical and jazz fans who covet the "building-inside-the building" as the new home of the famous jazz club, Bimhuis. Dubbed Amsterdam's 21st-century Concertgebouw, it is debatable whether the acoustics can compete with the original concert hall on Museumplein. There's no doubt however that the glass building is architecturally stunning, with its ship's ramp entrance and the zen-like simplicity of its three natural colors (concrete, black, and light maple wood). Floor to roof glass walls guarantee angular transparency and spectacular views into the building and out onto the IJ. The changeable weather that the Netherlands normally suffers from is now taken advantage of, as the openness of the building allows clouds, rain, and light to change the atmosphere inside constantly, in a natural way. Its multifunctional main auditorium seats 735 (standing room for 1500); a smaller auditorium seats 100 people, and foyers and extensive conference and catering facilities lure in business visitors who are not strictly here for the music. Pay a lunchtime visit to chill out in café-restaurant Star Ferry and enjoy the waterfront terrace. ⊠ *Piet Heinkade 1, Centrum* ☎ *020/788–2010* ⊕ *www.muziekgebouw.nl.*

9 **Museum Werf 't Kromhout** *(Museum on Kromhout Wharf).* Started in 1757 by Kromhout, a ship's carpenter whose name literally means bent wood, this is one of Amsterdam's oldest functioning shipyards. Almost 300 ships were built here during its heyday in the late 19th century. By the early 20th century, 't Kromhout produced diesel engines used by Dutch canal boats, and to this day, old boats are restored here, so expect to shuffle your way through wood shavings and inhale the smells of tar, diesel, and varnish. The mechanics tend to get particularly

excited by the historical collection of 22 antique engines a
you all about it if you give them a chance. ☒*Hoogte Kadijk 1*
trum 🕾*020/627–6777* ⊕*www.machinekamer.nl* 🖃*€4.50* ☉
10–3, or by prior arrangements for groups larger than 15.

❷ **Realen Eiland.** About a dozen blocks to the west of Centraal Station,
there are three off-the-beaten-track islands that were built on landfill
back in the 17th century. These Western Islands—known in Dutch as
Westelijke Eilanden—were constructed as a safe warehouse zone. The
nautical ambience is particularly beloved by Amsterdammers, who all
seem to have recreational boats, and other seafaring folk. Most visitors
bypass the largest island, Bickers Eiland, jammed as it is with boatyards
and modern apartment buildings. Easier access is via the Nieuwe Teru-
inen and over the bridge to the smallest island, Prinsen Eiland. Follow
the Galgenstraat (Gallows Street)—which once offered a vista of the
town gallows across the water—then head north across the wooden
drawbridge, to Realen Eiland. The island's eastern shore is a peaceful
photogenic waterside getaway. Zandhoek, a street named after a sand
market that used to take place here, reminds you that the city is sinking
and the only way to keep the water at bay was by stacking sandbags
and raising the dikes. A charming row of 17th-century houses were
built here by Laurens Reael, a renegade Catholic famous for smug-
gling religious treasures out of city monasteries before they were confiscated by Protestants during the rather violent Dutch Reformation.
"De Gouden Reael" is the name Reael gave his own house, wittily
referring to his namesake, a valuable gold coin that is also displayed on
the decorative gable stone. Now a waterside café and restaurant, it is a
perfect spot to raise a toast to the old days and watch boats sail along
the Westerdok. ☒*Zandhoek 14 Centrum* ⊕ *follow Haarlemmerstraat/
Haarlemmerdijk from Centraal Station and go under the railway tracks
at Buiten Oranjestraat or at Haarlemmerplein.*

❺ **Scheepvaarthuis** *(Shipping Office).* With its extravagantly phantasma-
goric zinc-roof detailing spilling over various sculpted sea horses, boat
anchors, sea gods (Neptune and his four wives), dolphins, and even
shoals of fish, this is one of Amsterdam's most delightful turn-of-the-
20th-century structures. Built in 1912 to sport a suitably prow-shaped
front, it was used as the headquarters for the major shipping firms
that brought back all that booty from Java and the Spice Islands during the final Dutch colonial years. Later used as a public shipping and
city transport systems office, it has now been renovated into a five-star
hotel, the Grand Amarâth, which opened in June 2007. The 20th-cen-
tury master architects Piet Kramer, Johan van der May, and Michel
de Klerk all contributed to the design of the building; their structure
was one of the opening salvos by the fantastic Amsterdam School. The
design was so expensive to create, it is not surprising that the Amsterdam School's appeal to fantasy suffered an early demise in the 1930s
Depression. After admiring all the ornamentation on the facade, amble
around the sides to take in the busts of noted explorers, such as Barentz
and Mercator, along with patterned brickwork, and strutting iron tracery. Wander inside to check out the Seven Seas restaurant design, enjoy

t the classically restored bar, or book a private tour of the
ors of the building, with its equally lavish interior. ⊠*Prins*
kade 108, Centrum.

sche Huis *(West Indies House).* These former headquarters of
India Trading Company (WIC) have major historical signifi-
nce the WIC was set up as a means to colonize America and
Spaniards abroad. Although not as sovereign as the VOC, it
ntially given free rein to trade on Africa's west coast, the Americas, and all the islands of the West Pacific and New Guinea, and to
oversee the infamous export of 70,000 slaves from West Africa to the
Caribbean between 1626 and 1680. In these rooms, the decision was
made to buy Manhattan for 60 guilders. Silver bullion, piled up by
Piet Pieterszoon Hein (or Pieter Pietersen Heyn) a Dutch naval officer
and folk hero who fought in the Eighty Years' War between the United
Provinces and Spain, was collected here in 1628 after Piet won another
of his infamous sea battles. Now used by local television production
companies and a catering firm, you can come into the courtyard of the
building via its side entrance on Herenmarkt, to see the statue of Peter
Stuyvesant. ⊠*Herenmarkt 93–7, Jordaan.*

THE CANAL RINGS

The *Grachtengordel* (Canal Ring) is one of Amsterdam's prettiest areas
to wander through. As you explore, keep in mind that when these
impressive canal houses were built for the movers and shakers of the
17th-century Golden Age, home owners were taxed on their houses'
width, not height. Wealth and prestige was measured by the width of
the house, the number of windows facing the canal, and the ornate
gable work.

Numbers in the margin correspond to numbers on the Canal Rings map.

WESTERN CANAL RING

The grand, crescent-shape waterways of the Grachtengordel, which
surround the old center, are made up of Prinsengracht, Keizersgracht,
and Herengracht (Prince, Emperor, and Gentlemen canals). The intersecting canals and streets were originally built to house and provide
work space for artisans and workers, but are now magnets to discerning shoppers, diners, and drinkers. The construction of the Canal
Rings, which began at the beginning of the 17th century, proceeded
from west to east.

MAIN ATTRACTIONS

❸ Anne Frankhuis *(Anne Frank House).* Anne Frank is by far one of the
Fodor'sChoice most famous authors of the 20th century, testimony to the inspiring
★ story of a girl who died at age 15 in a tragic end of the two-year saga.
In the pages of *The Diary of Anne Frank* (published in 1947 as *The
Annex* by her father after her death) the young Anne kept her sad
record of two increasingly fraught years living in secret confinement

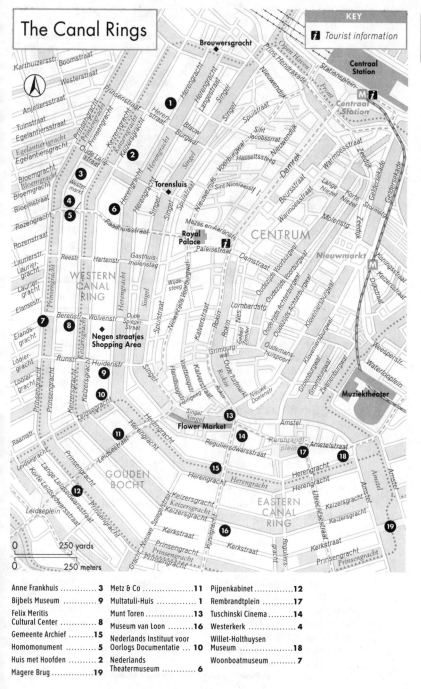

The Canal Rings

WESTERN CANAL RING

CENTRUM

Nieuwmarkt

Negen straatjes Shopping Area

Royal Palace ℹ

Torensluis

GOUDEN BOCHT

EASTERN CANAL RING

Flower Market

Muziektheater

Centraal Station

Brouwersgracht

0   250 yards
0   250 meters

Gables & Hooks

Amsterdam's famous neck gables. Keep an eye peeled for bell and step gables.

The gabled houses on the Canal Ring are Amsterdam's most picture-perfect historic feature. Starting in the 16th century, the tops of these narrow houses were richly ornamented with gables in various styles. This architecture garnish was the result of a tariff system that taxed width along the waterfront. To get the most bang for their gulden, houses were built on long, narrow lots, angled for optimum floor space, and with the slimmest side facing the canal. However, roof points had to be built facing the street full on; to hide the angle of the house, artists were asked to camouflage with decorative gables in the form of steps, vase necks, extended bottle necks, bells, and elegantly framed decorative pictures. Gable styles came and went, so the type of gable reflects how old a house is. The Brouwersgracht (brewers' canal) has colorful house fronts harking back to Amsterdam's first economic impulse, which was the right to tax and brew beer from grains traded with medieval Hanses-

tad cities in Northern Europe. Some gables show what different merchant companies had stored—grain, wood, gold, and coffee. Others have symbolic pictorial decorations and many carry the merchant family's shield. The gabled houses on the Keizersgracht (Emperor's canal) are altogether different, as fabulously wealthy 18th-century noblemen decorated their double houses in a grander, sober style reminiscent of palaces of the Holy Roman Empire. One thing all canal houses have in common is the hook in the gable, oftentimes with a pulley wheel and rope hanging from it. This handy manual elevator system was developed from medieval shipping tactics and helps to avoid moving bulky goods up the precariously steep staircases. Boxes, pianos, couches or whatever are winched up using the rope and pulley, and hauled in through exceptionally wide windows. Keep your eyes peeled as you walk through the city and you may see a few Dutch movers in action.

from the Nazis. Along with the van Daan family, the Frank family felt the noose tighten, and so decided to move into a hidden warren of rooms at the back of this 1635-built canal house.

Anne Frank was born in Germany in 1929; when she was four her family moved to the Netherlands to escape growing anti-Jewish sentiment. Otto Frank operated a pectin business and decided to stay in his adopted country when the war finally reached the Netherlands in 1940. In July 1942, the five adults and three children sought refuge in the attic of the annex "backhouse," or *achterhuis*, of Otto's business in the center of Amsterdam, in a hidden warren of rooms screened behind a hinged bookcase. Here, as one of many *onderduikers* ("people in hiding") throughout all of Amsterdam, Anne dreamed her dreams, wrote her diary, and pinned up movie-star pictures to her wall (still on view). The van Pelsen family, including their son, Peter (van Daan in Anne's journal), along with the dentist Fritz Pfeffer (Dussel) joined them in their cramped quarters. Four trusted employees provided them with food and supplies. In her diary, Anne chronicles the day-to-day life in the house: her longing for a best friend, her crush on Peter, her frustration with her mother, her love for her father, and her annoyance with the petty dentist, Dussel. In August 1944, the Franks were betrayed and the Gestapo invaded their hideaway. All the members of the annex were transported to camps, where Anne and her sister, Margot, died of typhoid fever in Bergen Belsen a few months before the liberation. Otto Frank was the only survivor of the annex. Miep Gies, one of the friends who helped with the hiding, found Anne's diary after the raid and kept it through the war. Now, millions of children read it and its tale of humanity's struggle with fascism. ✉*Prinsengracht 267, Centrum* ☎*020/556–7105* ⊕*www.annefrank.nl* ✍*€7.50* ◷*Sept.–Mar., daily 9–7; Apr.–Aug., daily 9–9.*

INTERNATIONAL CELEBRITY

Anne's diary has been translated into more than 65 languages and sold more than 30 million copies, making her the international celebrity she always dreamed of being.

BE AWARE

The line to get into the Anne Frank House is extremely long, especially in the summer. It moves (sort of) quickly, but it's best to arrive early and avoid the worst crowds.

★ ❷ **Huis met Hoofden** (*House with Heads*). The Greek deities of Apollo, Ceres, Mars, Minerva, Bacchus, and Diana welcome you—or rather, busts of them do—to this famous example of Dutch Neoclassic architecture, one of the grandest double houses of 17th-century Amsterdam. Delightfully graced with pilasters, pillars, and a step gable, the 1622 mansion is attributed to architect Pieter de Keyser, son of the more famed Hendrick. The house is now headquarters to the Monumentenzorg—custodian to many of the city's public monuments—and is not open to the public. A stroll past it and a few pictures are still highly recommended. ✉*Keizersgracht 123, Centrum* ☎*020/522–4888* ⊕*www. bmz.amsterdam.nl.*

6 **Nederlands Theatermuseum** *(Nether-*
★ *lands Theater Museum).* Amsterdam has dozens of Golden Age
house museums, but few are as
gilded as this one. Currently home
to part of the Theater Instituut
Nederland (Netherlands The-
ater Institute), the **Bartolotti Huis**
(Nos. 170–172) is made up of two
spectacular examples of Hendrick
de Keyser's work. The rest of the
museum takes up the equally delectable White House (No. 168), built
in 1638. Its original owner, Michiel
Pauw—as one of the initiators of
the West India Company—could

TOWERS BRIDGE
A bust of Dutch writer Multatuli holds a place of honor on the **Torensluis** *(Towers Bridge)*, the oldest (and the widest) bridge in Amsterdam. It was originally built over a 17th-century sluice gate and bookended with towers. The rooms with barred windows that you see at the base of the bridge were used as a lockup for drunks. ⊠ *Singel between Torensteeg and Oude Leliestraat, Centrum.*

easily afford its interior of marble-lined corridors, sweeping monu-
mental staircases, densely rendered plasterwork, and ceiling paintings
by Jacob de Wit. All of these attributes have been restored and provide a lush backdrop for exhibitions about the history of theater in
all its forms: circus, opera, musical, puppetry, and drama. There are
costumes, models of stage sets, and an extensive library with archives
focused on the theatrical scene in the Netherlands. Its stellar back garden—alone worth the price—is the perfect place to sip a coffee from
the café while imagining it as the setting for Baroque-era barbecues.
⊠ *Herengracht 168–170, Centrum* ☎ *020/551-3300* ⊕ *www.tin.nl*
⊠ *€4.50* ⊗ *Mon.–Fri. 11–5, weekends 1–5.*

1 **Multatuli-Huis.** This museum honors the beliefs and work (and continues
the legacy) of Eduard Douwes Dekker (1820–87), aka Multatuli (from
the Latin, meaning "I have suffered greatly"), who famously wrote
Max Havelaar, or the Coffee Auctions of the Dutch Trading Company,
a muckraking book that uncovered the evils of Dutch colonialism. The
son of an Amsterdam sea captain, Dekker accompanied his father to the
Dutch Indies (Indonesia) and joined the Dutch Civil Service. After years
of poverty and wandering, in 1860 he wrote and published his mag-
num opus, denouncing and exposing the colonial landowners' narrow
minds and inhumane practices. Today, Dutch intellectuals and progressive thinkers respect him mightily. ⊠ *Korsjespoortsteeg 20, Centrum*
☎ *020/638-1938* ⊕ *www.multatuli-museum.nl* ⊗ *Weekends noon–5
and Tues. 10–5. Closed Sat. in July.*

★ **4** **Westerkerk** *(Western Church).* Built between 1602 and 1631 by Hendrick de Keyser, the Dutch Renaissance Westerkerk was the largest
Protestant church in the world until the St. Paul's Cathedral in London
was built. Its tower is topped by a gaudy copy of the crown of the
Habsburg emperor Maximilian I (or, rather, to avoid a potential bar
brawl, a later model of the crown used by Rudolph II). Maximilian
gave Amsterdam the right to use his royal insignia in 1489 in gratitude
for help from the city in his struggle for control of the Low Countries,
and the crown's "XXX" marking was quickly exploited by the city's
merchants as a visiting card of quality.

The tower rates as the city's highest. Its gigantic bell rings every half hour but with a different tone to mark the half before the hour—in other words, the 12 rings of 11:30 are different from the rings of 12. The playing of the church's organ, which still occurs every Tuesday between noon and 1, is often mentioned in the diary of Anne Frank. Another immortal, Rembrandt, lived nearby on Rozengracht 188 during his poverty-stricken last years. He (as well as his son, Titus) was buried in the church in an unmarked grave on October 4, 1669. Rembrandt's posthumous reputation inspired some very surreal television three centuries later, when a body was unearthed that was mistakenly thought to be his. While exposed to the glare of the news cameras, the skull turned to dust. ⊠*Prinsengracht 281 (corner of Westermarkt), Centrum* ☎*020/624–7766* ⊕*www.westerkerk.nl* ◷ *Tower Jun.–Sept., Tues., Wed., Fri., and Sat. 2–5; interior Apr.–Sept., Mon.–Fri. 11–3; tower by appointment* ☎*020/689–2565* ⊡*Free.*

IF YOU HAVE TIME

❾ **Bijbels Museum** *(Bible Museum)*. Although this museum does indeed have a massive collection of Bibles—as well as exhibits with archaeological finds from the Middle East and models of ancient temples that evoke biblical times—what probably draws more people is the building itself. The two enjoined canal houses (dating from 1662) have had their interiors restored, including incredible 18th-century ceiling paintings by Jacob de Wit. ⊠*Herengracht 366–368, Centrum* ☎*020/624–2436* ⊕*www.bijbelsmuseum.nl* ⊡*€7.50* ◷ *Mon.–Sat. 10–5, Sun. 11–5.*

❽ **Felix Meritis Cultural Center.** If we are to believe its name, HAPPINESS THROUGH ACHIEVEMENT, which is chiseled over its entrance, then this is a very happy building indeed—not to mention an enlightened one, since its Neoclassical architecture arose in the year of the French Revolution, 1789. Felix Meritis was a society whose building housed committees dedicated to the study and promotion of economics, science, painting, music, and literature. It held an observatory, and its concert hall had the likes of Schumann and Brahms dropping by to tickle the ivories. Between 1949 and 1968, the Communist Party took over the building. Then various experimental theater companies began calling it home before it settled into its current role as European Center for Art and Science. Readings, panels, and discussions are hosted here regularly with the aim of "connecting cultures." Drop by to pick up a program or to check the hours of its Philosophy Café. ⊠*Keizersgracht 324, Centrum* ☎*020/623–1311* ⊕*www.felix.meritis.nl* ◷ *Café has changeable hrs, call ahead.*

❺ **Homomonument** *(Homosexual Monument)*. This, the world's first memorial to persecuted gays and lesbians, was designed by Karin Daan, who employed three huge triangles of pinkish granite—representing past, present, and future—to form a larger triangle. On May 4 (Remem-

---

ENGRAVED IN STONE

A line from a poem is engraved on one of the marble triangles of the Homomonument reads, "Naar vriendschap zulk een mateloos verlangen" (Such an endless desire for friendship). This text is an extract from the poem, "To a Young Fisherman" by Jacob Israël De Haan (1881-1924).

brance Day), there are services here commemorating the homosexual victims of World War II, when thousands were killed (the 50,000 sentenced were all forced to wear pink triangles stitched to their clothing). Flowers are laid daily for lost friends, especially on the descending triangle that forms a dock of sorts into Keizersgracht. Signs will lead you to the **Pink Point of Presence** (☎020/428–1070 ⊕*www.pinkpoint. org*), one of the stalls along the east side of Westermarkt, which acts as an information point to visiting gays and lesbians. It is open daily noon–6 March through December; and Friday–Sunday noon–6 January through February and is the best source of gay info in Amsterdam. ✉*Westermarkt, Centrum.*

⓫ Metz & Co. When the New York Life Insurance Company opened this building in 1891, its soaring six floors brought a touch of Manhattan to Amsterdam's canals—literally, as architect J. van Looy had also designed the company's lofty skyscraper in Manhattan. By 1908, the Metz department store had converted the offices into showcases for Liberty fabrics and De Stijl teapots. Shop if you must, but don't fail to take the circular staircase up from the sixth-floor café to discover the penthouse created by master designer Gerrit Rietveld in 1933 as a showroom to highlight functionalist furniture (his own included). Its glass roof offers dazzling views of this particularly alluring section of Amsterdam, and the café itself is a favorite time-out spot. ✉*Leidsestraat 34, Centrum* ☎*020/520–7020* ⊗*Mon. 11–6, Tues.–Thurs. and Sat. 9:30–6, Sun. noon–5, café open same hrs.*

⓾ Nederlands Instituut voor Oorlogs Documentatie *(Netherlands Institute for War Documentation).* Established in 1945, this institute has collected vast archives of documents, newspapers, 100,000 photos, and 50,000 books relating to the occupation of World War II. This is where Otto Frank donated his daughter's diary. More recently, the institute has expanded its sights to take in the period between World War I to present day, with particular emphasis on the former colony of Indonesia. Although the institute is essentially not open to the merely curious, it is very welcoming to people doing academic or family-related research. Walk past just to see the Loire-style château exterior and its rich and obsessive sculptures of frolicking mythical figures. ✉*Herengracht 380, Centrum* ☎*020/523–3800* ⊕*www.niod.nl* ⊗*Mon. 1–6, Tue.–Fri. 9– 6, closed weekends.*

⓬ Pijpenkabinet *(Pipe Cabinet).* Considering Amsterdam's rich history of tobacco trading and its population's long tradition of rolling its own "shag," there should actually be a much larger museum dedicated to this subject. Perhaps this theoretical museum could relate such local facts as how urine-soaked tobacco was hailed as an able aphrodisiac in the 16th century, how "tobacco-smoke enema applicators" were used until the mid-19th-century in attempts to revive those found unconscious in the canals, and how Golden Age painters employed tobacco and its smoke as a metaphor for the fleeting nature of life. But as things stand, there is only this focused collection of more than 2,000 pipes. You might also want to check out the library or buy a pipe in the

Smokiana shop. ⊠*Prinsengracht 488, Centrum* ☎*020/421–1779* ⊕*www.pijpenkabinet.nl* 💶*€5* ⏲ *Wed.–Sat. noon–6.*

NEED A BREAK?

Along Westermarkt's southerly side is an excellent fish stall where you can sample raw herring or smoked eel (if you're so inclined). An equally traditional Dutch way of keeping eating costs down is to pack one's belly with pancakes. The Pancake Bakery (⊠*Prinsengracht 191, Centrum*

> ### POLITICAL PUNCH
>
> The release of the Netherlands Institute for War Documentation's government-commissioned report on the role of a Dutch battalion (Dutchbat) in the 1995 fall of Srebrenica in the former Yugoslavia and the ensuing mass murder of 8,000 Muslim men resulted in Prime Minister Wim Kok stepping down and dissolving his Cabinet.

☎*020/625–1333*) is one of the best places in Amsterdam to try them, with a menu that offers a near infinite range of topping possibilities—from the sweet to the fruity to the truly belly-gelling powers of cheese, pinapple, and bacon.Foodism (⊠*Oude Leliegracht 8, Centrum* ☎*020/427–5103* ⊕*www. foodism.nl* ⏲*Mon.–Fri. 11:30 AM–10 PM, weekends until 6 PM*) is one of the city's best and hippest cafés. It is also cheap and the food is plentiful. Sandwiches and smoothies are the best bet.

☝ ❼ **Woonboatmuseum** *(Houseboat Museum).* In Amsterdam nearly 8,000 people (and a whole gaggle of cats at the cat asylum that floats opposite Singel 38) live on more than 2,400 houseboats. This converted 1914-built sailing vessel, the *Hendricka Maria,* provides a glimpse into this unique lifestyle. It almost feels as if you are visiting Grandma—there's even a special child-play zone. ⊠*Prinsengracht opposite No. 296, Centrum* ☎*020/427–0750* ⊕*www.houseboatmuseum.nl* 💶*€3.25* ⏲*Mar.–Oct., Tues.–Sun. 11–5; Nov.–Feb., Fri.–Sun. 11–5.*

EASTERN CANAL RING & REMBRANDTPLEIN

The Eastern end of the Canal Ring is known as the Gouden Bocht (Golden Bend), where elaborate gables, richly decorated facades, colored marbles, and heavy doors create an imposing architecture that suits the bank headquarters of today as well as it did the grandness of yore. Because the properties were so narrow, though, many well-heeled home owners decided to buy two adjoining allotments and build double-wide houses. This area is currently much less residential and largely devoted to banks, businesses, and hotels.

MAIN ATTRACTIONS

🔟 **Magere Brug** *(Skinny Bridge).* Of Amsterdam's 60-plus drawbridges, the Magere Brug is the most famous. It is one of Amsterdam's prettiest bridges, and offers a gorgeous view of the Amstel and surrounding area. The Magere Brug was purportedly built in 1672 by two sisters living on opposite sides of the Amstel, who wanted an efficient way of sharing that grandest of Dutch traditions: the *gezellig* (socially cozy) midmorning coffee break. Walk by at night when it's spectacularly lighted, and

Fodor'sChoice
★

Amsterdam's Hofjes—the Historic Almshouses

If you're lucky, you can catch a glimpse inside of the Van Brienenhof.

Hidden behind innocent-looking gateways throughout the city center, most notably along the main ring of canals and in the Jordaan neighborhood, are some of Amsterdam's most charming houses. There are about 30 *hofjes* (little courtyards surrounded by almshouses), mainly dating back to the 18th century when the city's flourishing merchants established hospices for the old and needy. Their philanthropy was supposed to be rewarded by a place in heaven. But be warned (and be prepared for disappointment): today's residents of these hofjes like their peace and quiet, and often lock their entrances to keep out visitors.

Begijnhof (*Beguine Court*). Here, serenity reigns just feet away from the bustle of the city. The Begijnhof is the tree-filled courtyard of a residential hideaway, built in the 14th century for the Begijntes, a lay Catholic sisterhood. Created as conventlike living quarters for unmarried or widowed laywomen—of which there were

many since most able-bodied men were shipped off and killed in the Crusades—this almshouse required them to follow three simple rules: no hens, no dogs, no men. Rent was paid in the form of caring for the sick and educating the destitute. One resident loved living in the Begijnhof so much that she asked to be buried in the gutter here in 1654—so out of respect, don't tap-dance on the slab of red granite on the walkway on the left side of De Engelse Kerk.

No. 34 is the oldest house in Amsterdam and one of only two remaining wooden houses in the city center (horrific fires forced the city to outlaw the construction of wooden buildings in the 15th century). The small **Engelse Kerk** (English Church) across from No. 48 dates from 1400. Its pulpit panels were designed by a young and broke Piet Mondriaan. After the Calvinst coup (the Altercation of 1578) the church was confiscated from the Beguines, who later built the supposedly clandestine **Mirakel-** or **Begijn-hof-Kapel** (Miracle- or Begijn-Chapel), across the lane at No. 29. ✉ *Entrances on the north side of Spui and on Gedempte Begijnensloot opposite Begijnensteeg, Centrum ⏱ Mirakel- or Begijnhof-Kapel Mon. 1–6:30, Tues.–Fri. 9–6:30, weekends 9–6.*

The Begijnhof is by far the most famous hofje, but there are a few other little gems that you could explore in a day. The **Sint Andrieshofje** (✉ *Egelantiersgracht 105–141, Jordaan*), founded in 1614, is the second-oldest almshouse in Amsterdam. Take notice of the fine gables, including a step gable in the style of Hendrick de Keyser.

The **Claes Claeszhofje** (✉ *Junction of Egelantiersstraat 28–54, Eerste Egelantiersdwarsstraat 1–5, and Tuinstraat 35–49, Jordaan*) was founded in 1616 by the textile dealer Claes Claesz Anslo (note his coat of arms atop one entry). The houses here were renovated and are now rented out to artists, the happiest of whom must occupy the **Huis met de Schrijvende Hand** ("House with the Writing Hand"), the oldest and most picturesque of the lot, topped by a six-stepped gable.

The **Zevenkeurvorstenhofje** (✉ *Tuinstraat 197–223*) was founded around 1645, though the houses standing today are from the 18th century, and the **Karthuizerhof** (✉ *Karthuizerstraat 21–131, Jordaan*) was founded in 1650 and has a courtyard with two 17th-century pumps.

On the Prinsengracht, between the Prinsenstraat and the Brouwersgracht, are two hofjes right close to one another. The **Van Brienen** (Prinsengracht 85–133, closed to the public)

The Karthuizerhof and a happy occupant.

and **De Zon** (Prinsengracht 159–171, open weekdays 10–5) both have plaques telling their stories.

For a moment of peace, visit the **Suykerhoff-hofje** and take in its abundantly green courtyard. These houses opened their doors in 1670 to Protestant "daughters and widows" (as long as they behaved and exhibited "a peace-loving humor") and provided each of them with free rent, 20 tons of turf, 10 pounds of rice, a vat of butter, and some spending money each year. If only the same was done today. ✉ *Lindengracht 149–163, Centrum.*

often drawn up to let boats pass by. Many replacements to the original bridge have come and gone, and this, dating from 1969, is just the latest. ⊠*Between Kerkstraat and Nieuwe Kerkstraat, Centrum.*

★ ⑯ **Museum van Loon.** Once home to one of Rembrandt's most successful students, Ferdinand Bol, this twin house, built in 1672 by Adriaan Dortsman, was occupied by the Van Loon family from 1886 to 1960. After extensive restoration of the house and facade, the museum opened to depict opulent canal-side living. Along with wonderful period rooms, the house is filled with 80 portraits of the Van Loon family, which follow their history back to the 17th century when one of them helped found the East India Company. Up the copper staircase are salons containing paintings known as *witjes,* illusionistic depictions of landscapes and other scenes. Don't miss the real landscape out back: an exquisitely elegant garden of trimmed hedgerows. ⊠*Keizersgracht 672, Centrum* ☎*020/624–5255* ⊕*www.museumvanloon.nl* ☒*€6* ⊗ *Wed.–Mon. 11–5. Closed Tues.*

⑭ **Tuschinski Cinema.** Although officially the architect of this "Prune Cake"—as it was described when it first opened in 1921—was H. L. De Jong, the financial and spiritual force was undoubtedly Abram Icek Tuschinski (1886–1942), a Polish Jew who after World War I decided to build a theater that was "unique." And because interior designers Pieter de Besten, Jaap Gidding, and Chris Bartels came up with a dizzying and dense mixture of Baroque, Art Nouveau, Amsterdam School, Jugendstil, and Asian influences, it is safe to say that he achieved his goal. It began as a variety theater welcoming such stars as Marlene Dietrich, but it soon became a cinema, and to this day watching movies from one of the extravagant private balconies remains an unforgettable experience—especially if you order champagne. Sobering note: Tuschinski died in Auschwitz. ⊠*Reguliersbreestraat 26–28, Centrum* ☎*0900–1458* ⊕*www.tuchinski.nl.*

⑱ **Willet-Holthuysen Museum.** Few houses are open to the public along the
FodorśChoice   Herengracht, so make a beeline to this mansion to see Grachtengordel
★   (Canal Ring) luxury at its best. In 1895, the widow Sandrina Louisa Willet-Holthuysen donated the house and contents—which included her husband's extensive art collection—to the city of Amsterdam. You can wander through this 17th-century canal house, now under the management of Amsterdam's Historisch Museum, and discover all its original 18th-century interiors, complete with that era's mod cons from ballroom to *cabinet des merveilles* (rarities cabinet). You can air out the aura of Dutch luxury by lounging in the French-style garden in the back. ⊠*Herengracht 605, Centrum* ☎*020/523–1822* ⊕*www. willetholthuysen.nl* ☒*€5* ⊗ *Weekdays 10–5, weekends 11–5.*

IF YOU HAVE TIME

⑮ **Gemeente Archief** *(Municipal Archives).* Established in 1914, this noble institution, which is open to the public, is filled with all the archives and collections relevant to Amsterdam. Although you won't be able to actually hold the piece of paper from 1275 by which Floris V extended toll privileges to the then tiny town and thereby initiated its growth

toward global dominance, you can eyeball this par[t]
of their brand-new and permanent "Treasures" exh[i]
lent on-site bookstore sells every available Amster-rele
⊠ *Vijzelstraat 32 (from Aug. 7), Centrum* ☎*020/57*[2]
gemeentearchief.amsterdam.nl 🎫*Free* 🕐*Tue.–Sat. 10*
Closed Mon.

⓭ **Munt Toren** (*Mint or Coin Tower*). This tower received its na[me in 163]2,
when French troops occupied much of the surrounding Re[p]ublic and
Amsterdam was given the right to mint its own coins here for a brief
two-year period. Although the spire was added by Hendrick de Keyser in 1620, the medieval tower and the adjoining guardhouse were
part of a gate in the city's fortifying wall from 1490. The guardhouse,
which now houses a touristy Dutch porcelain shop, has a gable stone
above its entrance, which portrays two men and a dog in a boat. This
is a symbolic representation of the city, where warrior and merchant
bonded together by loyalty—that would be the dog—are sailing toward
the future. ⊠*Muntplein, Centrum.*

⓱ **Rembrandtplein.** Smaller than the Leidseplein, this square is the focus for
hotels, restaurants, cafés, and nightlife venues and it is lively enough
to justify picking it out from its surroundings. Rembrandtplein is
renowned for hosting travelers, so finding menus in English, a pint of
Old Speckled Hen, or overpriced clubs is easy. If you find yourself on
the main square, dart off to the side streets as quickly as possible. For
arts lovers interested in getting up close and personal with Rembrandt,
check out the 3-D, life-like sculpture of The Nightwatch, donated as
part of Rembrandt's 400th birthday celebrations in 2005. In addition,
a gigantic silkscreen billboard of the painting adorns one side of the
square. ⊠*One block south of the Amstel River Centrum.*

THE JORDAAN

This area—pronounced Yoarh-*dahn* and bound by Brouwersgracht,
Lijnbaansgracht, Looiersgracht, and Prinsengracht—is by far the city's
most singular neighborhood. It was built to house workers, many of
whom constructed the canal belt or worked the city's smellier industries such as tanning and brewing. Living conditions were miserable,
and with so many proletarians packed into such a small space, it soon
became a hotbed for rising socialist and unionist ideas. Even today,
the inhabitants of the Jordaan have a reputation for rebelliousness and
community spirit. Longtime residents speak "Jordaans," a dialect com-
parable to London's Cockney slang. It's rumored that they have as
many words for "drunk" as the Eskimos reputedly have for "snow."
Jordaaners even have their own kind of music called *smartlap*. Don't
miss a chance to experience live "Jordaans" music in local cafés such
as the Twee Zwaantjes or Café No 1. In the 1950s, the Jordaan identity
reached mythical proportions—aided by nationally popular local sing-
ers depicting an idealized vision of a poor but tight-knit and socially
aware community—its residents successfully fought city plans to fill in
the remaining canals.

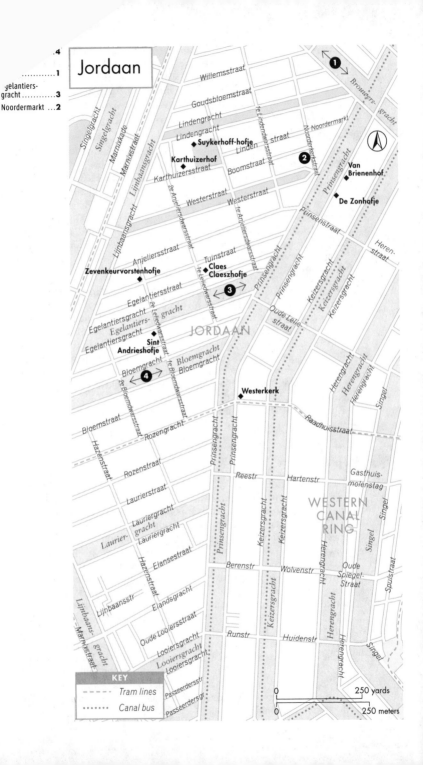

Jordaan

Willemsstraat

Brouwers-gracht

1

Goudsbloemstraat

Lindengracht

Lindengracht

♦ **Suykerhoff-hofje**

Karthuizerstraat

♦ **Karthuizerhof**

1e Lindendwarsstraat

Linden straat

Boomstraat

Noordermarkt

2

Prinsengracht

♦ **Van Brienenhof**

♦ **De Zonhofje**

Singelgracht

Singelgracht

Marnixkade

Marnixstraat

Lijnbaansgracht

2e Anjeliersdwarsstraat

Westerstraat

Westerstraat

Prinsenstraat

Prinsengracht

Prinsenstraat

Heren-straat

Anjeliersstraat

Tuinstraat

♦ **Claes Claeszhofje**

Zevenkeurvorstenhofje ♦

1e Leliedwarsstraat

3

Prinsengracht

Keizersgracht

Keizersgracht

Keizersgracht

Egelantiersstraat

Egelantiersgracht

Egelantiers-gracht

Egelantiers-gracht

Egelantiersgracht

1e Leliedwarsstraat

gracht

Oude Lelie-straat

JORDAAN

♦ **Sint Andrieshofje**

Bloemgracht

Bloemgracht

Bloemgracht

2e Bloemdwarsstraat

1e Bloemdwarsstraat

4

Herengracht

Herengracht

Herengracht

Singel

♦ **Westerkerk**

Raadhuisstraat

Bloemstraat

2e Bloemdwarsstraat

Rozengracht

Prinsengracht

Prinsengracht

Hazenstraat

Rozenstraat

Reestr

Hartenstr

Gasthuis-molenstag

Laurierstraat

Keizersgracht

Keizersgracht

WESTERN CANAL RING

Herengracht

Singel

Lauriergracht

Laurier-gracht

Laurier-

Lauriergracht

Hazenstraat

Elansestraat

Berenstr

Wolvenstr

Oude Spiegel-Straat

Spuistraat

Lijnbaansstr

Elandsgracht

Herengracht

Lijnbaans-gracht

Marnixstraat

Oude Looiersstraat

Looiersgracht

Looiersgracht

Looiersgracht

Runstr

Huidenstr

Herengracht

Singel

Passeerdersstr

Passeerdersgr

0   250 yards

0   250 meters

1

Since the 1980s, the Jordaan has moved steadily upmarket, and now it is one of the trendiest parts of town. Its 1895 population of 80,000, which made it one of the densest in Europe, has declined to a mere 14,000. But in many ways, the Jordaan will always remain the Jordaan, even though its narrow alleys and leafy canals are now a wanderer's paradise lined with quirky boutiques, excellent restaurants, and galleries.

Numbers in the text correspond to numbers in the margin and on the Jordaan map.

MAIN ATTRACTIONS

★ ❹ **Bloemgracht** *(Flower Canal)*. Lined with suave "burgher" houses of the 17th century, this canal was once so stately it was called the "Herengracht of the Jordaan" (Gentlemen's Canal of the Jordaan). In due course, it became a center for paint manufactories, which made sense, because Egelantiersgracht, an address favored by Golden Age artists, is just one canal to the north. Although modern intrusions have been made, Bloemgracht is still proudly presided over by "De Drie Hendricken," three houses set at Nos. 87 to 91. These 1642 mansions, built by Hendrick de Keyser (hence their nickname) and restored by the De Keyser Foundation, allure with their stepped gables, paned windows, and gable stones, carved with a farmer, a city settler, and a sailor. Plainly said, this is a nice street. ✉ *Between Lijnbaansgracht and Prinsengracht, Centrum.*

❶ **Brouwersgracht** *(Brewers' Canal)*. One of the most photographed spots in town, this pretty, tree-lined canal at the northern border of the Jordaan district is bordered by residences and former warehouses of the brewers who traded here in the 17th century when Amsterdam was the "warehouse of the world." Without sacrificing the ancient vibe, most of the buildings have been converted into luxury apartments. Of particular note are the houses at Nos. 188 to 194. The canal is blessed with long views down the main canals and plenty of sunlight, perfect for photo-ops. Also, The Brouwersgracht runs westward from the end of the Singel (a short walk along Prins Hendrikkade from Centraal Station) and forms a cap to the western end of the Grachtengordel. On top of the old canal mansions dotting the Brouwersgracht are symbols referring to the old breweries that used this waterway to transport their goods to thirsty drinks hundreds of years ago. ✉ *Centrum.*

Fodor's Choice
★

❸ **Egelantiersgracht** *(Eglantine Canal)*. Named for the flowering "eglantine" or sweetbriar, this is one of the loveliest canals in the area. Its tree-lined streets form a leafy canopy over the water and flower boxes adorn its bridges in summer. Many of the houses along this canal were first occupied by Golden Age painters and artisans. Hidden here is the **St. Andrieshofje,** famous for its Delftware entryway. Certainly not hidden (it is usually jammed with people) is the famed **Café 't Smalle,** (on the corner of the Prinsengracht). This ivy-covered *proeflokaal* (tasting house), complete with waterside terrace, was where Pieter Hoppe began his *jenever* distillery in 1780, an event of such global significance that 't Smalle is re-created in Japan's Holland Village in Nagasaki. ✉ *Between Lijnbaansgracht and Prinsengracht, Centrum.*

The city's best apple pie can be had at **Winkel** (✉ *Noordermarkt 43, Centrum* ☎ *020/623-0223*). For a funky setting and perhaps an inspired designer sandwich, head to **Finch** (✉ *Noordermarkt 5, Centrum* ☎ *020/626-2461*). If you're more thirsty than hungry, head to the brown café **Café Chris** (✉ *Bloemstraat 42, Centrum* ☎ *020/624-5942*), up on the next corner, which has been pouring beverages since 1624. Its coziness is taken to absurd lengths in its tiny men's bathroom, whose urinal position outside the door means that pranksters can easily shock you out of your reveries with a quick pull of the flusher. Be warned.

❷ **Noordermarkt** *(Northern Market)*. In 1620, city planners decided to build a church for those too lazy to walk to Westerkerk. **Noorderkerk** (Northern Church), designed by Hendrick de Keyser and completed after his death by his son Pieter, was the first Protestant church that featured a new—more democratic—ground plan, which was formed by the Greek cross (four equal arms) with the pulpit in the middle. Until 1688, the surrounding square, Noordermarkt, was a graveyard whose residents were moved to make room for its present—albeit now sporadic—function as a market. The **Maandag Morgen Noordermarkt** (Monday Morning Northern Market), popularly known as the Monday Morning Flea Market, with an enjoining textile market on Westerstraat, is one of the city's most scenic and best-kept secrets. It's also a prime place to see the typically pragmatic sales techniques of the locals in action. Most restaurants on this street, including **De Buurman** (✉ *Westerstraat 30, Centrum* ☎ *020/425-0788*)are top-notch. ✉ *Bounded by Prinsengracht, Noorderkerkstraat, and Noordermarkt, Centrum.*

THE LEIDSEPLEIN

This is Amsterdam's vortex for the performing arts, with street performers, music venues, theaters, and jazz bars. There are plenty of cheap eateries and the area is served by most trams and buses. The Leidseplein *(Leidse Square)* was once a medieval parking lot for horse-drawn carts that used to be banned from the city center—an enlightened policy that modern city planners might learn from. Today, crowds park their behinds on Leidseplein's many terraces in order to people watch. Frequented by kids out on the town, coffee-shop tourists, and late-night clubbers, the square used to be a hot spot for artists and intellectuals; communists and fascists clashed here between the wars. Cafés like Reijnders (Leidseplein 6), Eijlders (Korte Leidsedwarsstraat 47), and the authentic Art Deco American Hotel still retain something of that old atmosphere. Much of the rest has fallen prey to prefab pubs and fast-food outlets. The adjoining Leidsestraat is a busy pedestrian artery lined with funky shops and designer-brand outlets. ✉ *Main entrances: Leidsestraat, Weteringschans, and Marnixstraat, Museum District.*

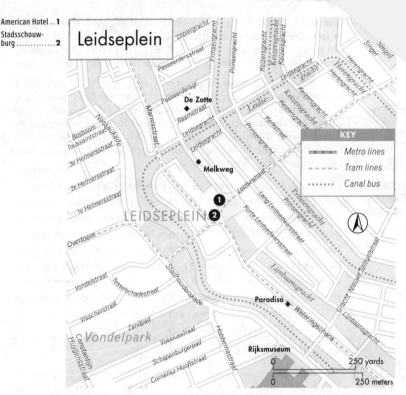

Leidseplein

KEY

≡≡ Metro lines
--- Tram lines
⋯⋯ Canal bus

LEIDSEPLEIN

Numbers in the text correspond to numbers in the margin and on the Leidseplein map.

❶ American Hotel. This landmark was designed by Willem Kromhout in 1902. He grafted Neo-Gothic turrets, Jugendstil gables, Art Deco windows, and a charmingly freestyle clock tower onto a proto–Amsterdam School structure. Its famed Art Deco-style Café Americain, where Mata Hari held her wedding reception, went from bohemian to being boycotted when it banned hippies in the '60s. It's the perfect place for a spot of tea. ✉*Leidekade 97, Museum District* ☎*020/556–3000* ⊕*www. amsterdamamerican.com/.*

❷ Stadsschouwburg *(Municipal Theater).* Built in 1784, the Stadsschouwburg's classical facade still dominates Leidseplein, despite all the neon advertising. In the 18th century, the original building on the Keizersgracht burned down mid-performance and killed many in the audience—a tragedy regarded as poetic justice by Calvinists who thought theater was decadent. After burning down and being rebuilt several more times, the current Neo-Renaissance facade and lushly Baroque horseshoe interior was created in 1890. The nation's theater scene descended into staidness until 1968, when, during a performance of the *Tempest,* the actors were showered with tomatoes. The reaction was a nationwide protest, the "tomato campaign," to show people's discon-

established theater's lack of social engagement. It resulted dies for newer theater groups—many of which now form the rd who regularly play here. Today, Dutch theater is dynamic, y physical and visual, with an often hilariously absurdist sense.

ugh the majority of the programming is in Dutch, there's also a ant stream of visiting international theater and dance companies. international Theater & Film Books store downstairs next to the entrance of the Stadsschouwburg also comes highly recommended by theater lovers. ✉*Leidseplein 26, Museum District* ☎*020/624–2311, 020/622–6489 for the bookstore* ⊕*www.stadsschouwburgamsterdam. nl; www.theaterandfilmbooks.com.*

NEED A BREAK?

Intellectuals and media types hang out at café **De Balie** (✉ *Kleine Gartmanplantsoen 10, Museum District* ☎ *020/553–5151* ⊕ *www.debalie.nl*). Actors and artists relax in the warm ambience of **Café Cox** (✉ *Marnixstraat 429, Museum District* ☎ *020/523–7850* ⊕ *www.stadsschouwburgamsterdam.nl*). Americans will feel right at home at the hilarious improv café and **Boom Chicago Lounge** (✉ *Leidseplein 12, Museum District* ☎ *Tickets 020/423–0101* ⊕ *www.boomchicago.nl/en*). This recently renovated upstairs space allows people to enjoy a decent dinner before seeing Boom's later evening show. In summer there is a terrace option.

THE MUSEUM DISTRICT

The Museumplein offers a solid square mile of Western art. From the Golden Age in the Rijksmuseum, to 19th-century artists at the Van Gogh Museum, through the 20th century at the Stedelijk Museum, this cultural valhalla caters to all tastes.

If museums aren't your thing, the vast expanses of green on the modern Museumplein and charming old Vondelpark are perfect places for people-watching, and the city's best upmarket fashion emporia on the PC Hooftstraat and antiques shops along Nieuwe Spiegelstraat are everything a shopaholic could wish for.

Numbers in the text correspond to numbers in the margin and on the Museum District map.

MAIN ATTRACTIONS

★ ❻ **Concertgebouw** (*Concert Building*). This globally acclaimed concert hall has been home to the Royal Concertgebouw Orchestra since 1892 and welcomed an endless stream of top international artists. With a Viennese classicist facade and golden lyre at its peak, this sumptuous example of Neo-Renaissance style, designed by Al van Gendt, is music mecca to more than 800,000

KRAMER'S BRIDGE

Architectural buffs shouldn't miss the 1925 bridge crossing Singelgracht on the Leidsestraat. Its swoopy Amsterdam School style was designed by Piet Kramer (1881–1961), along with 220 other Amsterdam bridges. For more information on Amsterdam's historic bridges, visit ⊕ *www.bmz. amsterdam.nl.*

1

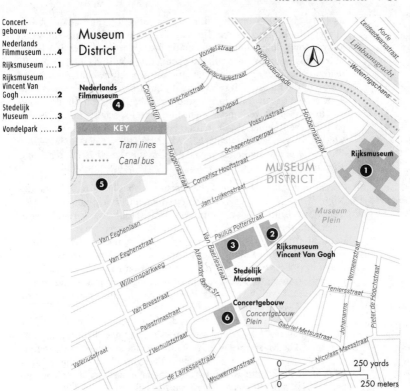

visitors per year. The *Grote* (Large) Hall, while acoustically perfect for classical music, warps amplified sound horribly. There are no tours of the building, but on Wednesdays, from September to June, you can attend a free lunchtime concert and take in your surroundings at the same time. ⊠ *Concertgebouwplein 2–6, Museum District* ☎ *020/671-8345 box office* ⊕ *www.concertgebouw.nl* (Note: tickets can be ordered directly online).

NEED A BREAK?

For Concertgebouw-goers, a handy post-concert dining option is **Bodega Keyzer** (⊠ *Van Baerlestraat 96, Museum District Closed on Sundays* ☎ *020/671-1866*). Although the chic interior exudes top cuisine, the food is unfortunately overpriced for what is really bistro quality. Nevertheless, it's one of the few places in the neighborhood you can order late (until 11:30). To dine before an 8 PM concert, it's worth making a small detour south to Spring (⊠ *Willemsparkweg 177, Museum District* ☎ *020/675-4421* ⊕ *www. restaurantspring.nl*).

★ ❹ **Nederlands Filmmuseum.** Gracing the Vondelpark is the Netherlands Film Museum, an elegant 19th-century pavilion with a museum, film halls, and a permanently packed café Vertigo. Amsterdam's first movie theater, the **Cinema Parisien** is a sumptuous place to see a classic, with its 1910 Art Deco interior, film poster collection, and adjacent film library (the library is open Tuesday–Friday 1–5). The museum's collection covers the whole of cinematic history, from the earliest hand-tinted movies up to recent digital productions. With its internationally renowned collection, major thematic retrospectives, conferences, and research, the museum draws international crowds. There are free outdoor screenings at dusk in the summertime. The theatrical family shows and live music played under silent films are a specialty. Enter Vondelpark via the Roemer Visscherstraat entrance to find this magical place waiting for you. ⊠ *Vondelpark 3, Museum District* ☎ *020/589–1400* ⊕ *www.filmmuseum.nl* ☞ *Free* ☉ *Weekdays 9* AM *–10:30* PM, *weekends 1 hr before screenings.*

❶ **Rijksmuseum** *(State Museum).* The Rijksmuseum is home to Rembrandt's *Night Watch,* Vermeer's *The Kitchen Maid,* and world-famous masterpieces by Steen, Ruisdael, Brouwers, Hals, Hobbema, Cuyp, Van der Helst, and their Golden Age ilk. Sadly, this national treasure is closed until 2010 for extensive renovations. Happily, the South Wing (now renamed the Philips Wing after its sponsors) is open to showcase the museum's "Best of" works. When the museum reopens, you can look forward to more than 150 rooms of paintings, sculpture, and objects with Western and Asian roots, dating from the 9th through the 19th century. The bulk of the collection is of 15th- to 17th-century paintings, mostly by Dutch masters, as well as drawings and prints from the 15th to 20th century. Until 2010, you can view the finest 17th-century collection in The Masterpieces exhibit, and get an overview of more than 400 Golden Age masterpieces in the redesigned Philips Wing. ■TIP→ **Don't leave the country without visiting the mini-museum at Schiphol Airport** ⊠ *Holland Boulevard between piers E and F* ☎ *020/653–5036* ☉ *Weekdays 7* AM *–8* PM ☞ *Free).* To check out the renovations drop in at the Information Center (10 AM–4 PM daily) located in the garden of the Rijksmuseum (take the Jan Luijkenstraat entrance). View a 3-D film on the project or go on the popular "Hard Hat Tour" through the construction site.

Fodor's Choice ★

Designed by P. J. H. Cuypers in the late 1880s, the Rijksmuseum is a magnificent, turreted building that glitters with gold leaf and is textured with sculpture—a fitting palace for a national art collection. ⊠ *Stadhouderskade 42; entrance during renovations: Jan Luijkenstraat 1, Museum District* ☎ *020/674–7000* ⊕ *www.rijksmuseum.nl* ☞ *€10* ☉ *Sat.–Thurs. 9–6, Fri. 9* AM *–10* PM. *Museum ticket counter closes at 5:30* PM *(Fri. at 9:30* PM). *Infocenter (The New Rijksmuseum): Tues.– Sun. 11–4. Library, Print Room, and Reading Room: Tues.–Sat. 10–5. ID required. Rijksmuseum Amsterdam Schiphol (behind the passport control): Daily 7* AM *–8* PM.

NEED A BREAK?

After walking the square mile of art around Museumplein, feed your snack attack at the fish stall on the Rijksmuseum's front east side. **Altena** (⊠ *Jan Luijkenstraat/Stadhouderskade, Museum District*). Here you will learn the finer points of raw herring consumption, Dutch-style, chewing right up to the tail. Not into fish but still looking for kicks? Have a drink at the **Cobra Café**

(✉ *Hobbemastraat 18, Museum District* ☎ *020/470–0111* ⊕ *www.cobraca-fe.nl*) and check out the bizarre bathrooms in the basement.

❷ **Rijksmuseum Vincent Van Gogh** *(Vincent Van Gogh Museum)*. Opened

Fodor'sChoice in 1973, this remarkable, light-infused building, based on a design by
★ famed De Stijl architect Gerrit Rietveld, venerates the short, certainly not sweet, but highly productive career of everyone's favorite tortured 19th-century artist. First things first: Vincent was a Dutch boy, so his name is not pronounced like the "Go" in Go-Go Lounge but rather like the "Go" uttered when one is choking on a whole raw herring. Although some of the Van Gogh paintings scattered throughout the world's high-art temples are of dubious provenance, this collection's authenticity is indisputable: its roots trace directly back to brother Theo van Gogh, Vincent's artistic and financial supporter. The 200 paintings and 500 drawings on display here begin in 1880, when Van Gogh was 27 and end in 1890, when he took his own life. The *Potato Eaters*, the series of *Sunflowers* and landscapes such as *Irises* and *Wheatfield with a Reaper*, are some of Van Gogh's most famous pieces. A bonus of the Van Gogh Museum is that it holds temporary exhibits of other important 19th-century artists and collections of art, graphic design, photography, and sculpture related to Van Gogh's development as a painter. A modern oval extension, opened in 1999, connects the main galleries by an underground walkway. The museum's café and shop are worth taking the time to enjoy. ✉ *Paulus Potterstraat 7, Museum District* ☎ *020/570–5200* ⊕ *www.vangoghmuseum.nl* ▤ *€10* ◷ *Sat.–Thurs. 10–6, Fri. 10–10.*

★ ❸ **Stedelijk Museum** *(Municipal Museum)*. Hot and happening modern art has one of the world's most respected homes at the Stedelijk, normally situated in a wedding-cake Neo-Renaissance structure built in 1895. Until the end of 2009, the museum is undergoing a massive refurbishment and the addition of a new wing by globally acclaimed local architects Benthem/Crouwel. Call ahead or check the Web site to be directed to the Stedelijk's many exhibitions in temporary spaces (more on this below). After World War II the Stedelijk rapidly collected more than 100,000 paintings, sculptures, drawings, and prints, as well as photography, graphic design, applied arts, and new media. Works by 20th-century modernists such as Chagall, Cézanne, Picasso, Monet, and Malevich live alongside the vast post–War melange of CoBrA—including Appel and Corneille; American Pop artists like Warhol, Johns, Oldenburg, and Liechtenstein; abstract Expressionists such as de Kooning and Pollock; and contemporary German Expressionists including Polke, Richter, and Baselitz. Displays of Dutch essentials like de Stijl school (including the amazing *Red Blue Chair* that Gerrit Rietveld designed in 1918, and Mondriaan's 1920 *Composition in Red, Black, Yellow, Blue, and Grey*) are complemented by large retrospectives or themed programs, featuring current hotshots on the art scene.

Until the summer of 2008, the Stedelijk is in a surprising temporary location near Centraal Station: the TPG Post CS building (Oosterdokskade 5). Thanks to the hip café-bar-restaurant **11** (✉ *11th fl.* ☎ *020/625–5999* ⊕ *www.ilove11.nl*) and many experimental groups next door, the Stedelijk has "fallen with its nose in the butter," as the Dutch saying goes. The TPG site has breathtaking views of the city and a hopping club scene that attracts Europe's artistic vanguard. At the end of 2009, you'll again be able to admire the Stedelijk's new home at its original location on Paulus Potterstraat 13 in Museum District. ⌧*Post CS-building, Oosterdokskade 5, 2nd and 3rd fl., Old City Center* ☎*020/573–2911* ⊕*www.stedelijk.nl* ⌧*€12.50* ⊙*Daily 10–6.*

☙ ❺ **Vondelpark.** On sunny days, Amsterdam's "Green Lung" is the most densely populated section of the city. Vondelpark is *the* place where sun is worshipped, joints are smoked, beer is quaffed, picnics are luxuriated over, bands are grooved to, dogs are walked, balls are kicked, lanes are biked, jogged, and rollerbladed on, and bongos are bonged. By evening, the park has invariably evolved into one large outdoor café. The great thing about this park is that, as long as you stay relaxed and go with the flow, you can dress however, hang however, and do whatever. It's all totally cool to Amsterdammers, as they relish the eclectic and unpretentious way of life. For example, a mysterious man has danced around the park for years, on 1970s silver roller skates, wearing silver body paint and a silver G-string (even in winter), shaved legs and chest, headphones, and a silver cap with propeller. Locals watching him don't even blink.

In 1865, Vondelpark was laid out as a 25-acre "walking and riding park" for residents of the affluent neighborhood rising up around it. It soon expanded to 120 acres and was renamed after Joost van den Vondel, the "Dutch Shakespeare." Landscaped in the informal English style, the park is an irregular patchwork of copses, ponds, children's playgrounds, and fields linked by winding pathways. The park's focal point is the open-air theater, which offers free summer entertainment from Wednesday through Saturday. Kids and adults always get a kick out of the llamas and donkeys in the llama field, and the flocks of parrots—apparently the progeny of two escaped pets—that live here year-round. You can also rent Rollerblades at the **Vondeltuin Rent a Skate** (⌧*Vondelpark 7, Museum District* ☎*020/664–5091* ⊕*www. vondeltuin.nl*). If your kids are teeners, join the Friday Night Skate crowd that takes over the city's streets in summer, meeting at the Filmmuseum at 8 PM. Other forms of specialized exercise to be found in the park include spontaneous tai chi, group meditation (usually dotted around the park), and the Oriental laughing sessions, where people come together to laugh (as therapy) every weekday from 8 AM and weekends from 9 AM at the van Eeghenstraat entrance.

Over the years a range of sculptural and architectural gems have made their appearance in the park. Picasso even donated a sculpture, *The Fish,* on the park's centenary in 1965, which stands in the middle of a field to deter football players from using it as a goalpost. The **Round Blue Teahouse,** a rare beauty of functionalist Nieuw Bouw architecture, built beside the lake in 1937, attracts families to its patio during the day and a clubby crowd by evening. ⌧*Stadhouderskade, Museum District.*

OFF THE BEATEN PATH

Amsterdamse Bos. The Amsterdam Woods, the largest of Amsterdam's many parks, covers 2,210 acres and is a few miles south of the city. One hundred thirty seven kilometers (85 mi) of footpaths and 51 km (32 mi) of bicycle paths traverse 50 bridges—many designed in the early-20th-century Amsterdam School style with characteristic redbrick and sculpted stone detailing. The area was planted and constructed from 1934 onward, as a make-work project for 20,000 unemployed people during the Depression. A remarkable feat of engineering, the park was dug out so that it lies about 4 meters (13 feet) below sea level. There are wide recreational fields, a boating lake, the Olympic Bosbaan rowing course plus stadium, and numerous playgrounds and water play areas for toddlers. A popular family attraction is an eco-aware goat farm with a playground and lunchroom, a sunny terrace, and lots of chickens hopping about between the goats. Your kids can feed other kids—the four-legged kind—goat's milk from a bottle, and cuddle bleating babies in the barn. The soft ice cream is made entirely of goat's milk (which does not contain lactose) and homemade goat cheese is on sale. It takes about thirty minutes by bike from the Vondelpark.

Coming out of the southern exit of Vondelpark, take a left onto the Amstelveenseweg and follow this busy road under the highway on the bicycle path until you reach the Van Nijenrodeweg. Turn right into the woods, following signs for the Bosbaan, over old train tracks, past the information posts to the beginning of the Bosbaan rowing course. Buses 170 and 172 are a rapid transfer from the Leidseplein to the Van Nijenrodeweg. You can rent bikes at the entrance of the Amsterdamse Bos from June through August ☎020/644–5473. Maps and signposting are plentiful throughout the park. For example, follow the signs to the **Grote Vijver** (Big Pond) to hire kayaks and pedal boats from April through September ☎020/645–7831. Navigate to the **Bosmuseum** (✉*Koenenkade 56, Amstelveen* ☎*020/676–2152*) to learn about natural history and the management of the woods, open daily 10–5. If you didn't pack your own lunch, the **Boerderij Meerzicht** (✉*Koenenkade 56, Amstelveen* ☎*020/679–2744* ⊕*www.boerderij-meerzicht.nl*) is a traditional Dutch pancake house with a petting zoo and playground for the kids. For the goat farm, follow the blue signs past Boerderij Meerzicht to **Geitenboerderij "De Ridammerhoeve"** (✉*Nieuwe Meerlaan 4, Amstelveen* ☎*020/645–5034* ⊕*www.geitenboerderij.nl*) ✉*Amstelveen*.

THE PIJP

Named for its dirty narrow streets and even narrower gabled houses, De Pijp, (The Pipe) began as a low-income nieghborhood for workers. Today it is *the* up-and-coming bohemian part of town. From his De Pijp grotto, the writer Bordewijk depicted Amsterdam during World War I as a "ramshackle bordello, a wooden shoe made of rock"; Piet Mondriaan began formulating the revolutionary art of De Stijl in an attic studio on Ruysdaelkade (No. 75). From the 1890s through the early 1990s, cheap rents attracted poor families, market hawkers,

students, artists, and wacky radicals, causing a common comparison with Paris' Latin Quarter. De Pijp was also dense with brothels, two of which still occupy seedy strips of the Hobbemakade and Ruysdaelkade. Eduard Jacobs sang absurd, sharply polemical sketches of the neighborhood's pimps, prostitutes, and disenfranchised heroes that figure in the typical Dutch form of musical cabaret called "kleinkunst" (small art), made ragingly popular by national icons like Freek de Jonge and Hans Teeuwen.

The Heineken Brewery attracted the first Spanish guest workers to the neighborhood during the early 1960s. Later, waves of guest workers from Turkey and Morocco and immigrants from the former colonies of Suriname and Indonesia began arriving and were fundamental in revitalizing the area around Albert Cuyp Market with shops, restaurants, and cultural diversity. By the 1980s, De Pijp was a truly global village, with more than 126 nationalities. Construction for a new underground Metro line has literally ripped through this area. Due to be completed by 2013, up-market investors and yuppies have already begun taking over parts of the neighborhood. But for now, De Pijp remains a prime spot for cheap international eats and pub-crawling at local bars and cafés. Plus, you won't find many tourists in this central and lively part of Amsterdam.

Numbers in the text correspond to numbers in the margin and on the Pijp map.

MAIN ATTRACTIONS

② Albert Cuypmarkt *(Albert Cuyp Market)*. Over 100 years old, the Albert Cuypmarkt is one of the biggest and busiest street markets in Europe. Like the majority of street names in De Pijp, it is named after a Golden Age painter; it welcomes 20,000 shoppers daily during the week and double that number on Saturday. Although you can come here for all your fresh food, textiles, and sundries, the atmosphere alone makes a visit worthwhile. With a decades-long waiting list for a permanent booth, things can get dramatic—if not occasionally violent—at 9 every morning on the corner of Sweelinckstraat 1, where the lottery for that day's available temporary spaces takes place. ⊠*Albert Cuypmarkt between Ferdinand Bolstraat and Van Woustraat, De Pijp* ☉ *Mon.–Sat. 9–5.*

> **ORGANIZED CHAOS**
>
> Although it's still a hectic life, an ordinary day for a market vendor on the Albert Cuypmarkt in the early 20th century resembled a Darwinian struggle for survival. After buying their goods early in the morning in the central marketplaces, all vendors lined up at the start of the Albert Cuyp, waiting for a police officer to blow his whistle. This set off a collective sprint to get the best places, occasionally sabotaging the competition along the way.

NEED A BREAK?

The best multicultural snacks can be found around the Albert Cuypmarket. If you want to keep things cheap and speedy, then try Surinamese cuisine—whose history and geography saw the mixing of Indonesian, Chinese, and Caribbean cookeries—at **Albina** (⊠ *Albert Cuypstraat 69, De Pijp* ☎ *020/675–5135*). Fill up on the roti, rice, or noodle dishes. If you've got a sweet tooth, go directly to the kitschy and kid-friendly **De Taart van m'n Tante** (⊠ *Ferdinand Bolstraat 10, De Pijp* ☎ *020/776–4600*), where there's a staggering array of different colorful cakes you can indulge in.

❶ Heineken Brouwerij *(Heineken Brewery)*. Founded by Gerard Heineken in 1863, the Heineken label quickly became one of the world's most famous (and popular) beers. So popular, in fact, that this factory couldn't keep up with the enormous demand—today, most production rolls out of vast plants in The Hague and Den Bosch. The original brewery has now been transformed into the "Heineken Experience," an interactive center that offers tours of the more than 100-year-old facilities. Everything from vast copper vats to beer-wagon dray horses is on view, and if you've ever wanted to know what it feels like to be a beer bottle, the virtual reality ride will clue you in. Others may want to exercise their privilege of drinking multiple beers in a very short time. (Note: this tour is open only to visitors over the age of 18.) Be aware that the brewery is closed until June 2008 because of renovations. ⊠*Stadhouderskade 78, De Pijp* ☎*020/523–9666* ⊕*www.heinekenexperience.com* ⊠*€10* ☉ *Tues.–Sun. 10–6.*

Multicultural Holland

The face of Holland has changed dramatically since World War II. New arrivals have created a melting pot society, and today the Netherlands is one of Europe's most ethnically diverse lands. But many don't realize the country is merely continuing a long tradition.

The first immigrants started arriving in the 17th century, during the Netherlands' Golden Age. While the gulden was pouring into Holland, the rest of Europe struggled with poverty and high unemployment. At the time, around half the people in the city were first generation migrants. Regardless of the what they thought of all these foreigners, the pragmatic Dutch tolerated them because they realized they were vital for keeping the economy moving. The country also gained a reputation as a haven for refugees, and at various times offered shelter to Portuguese and German Jews, French Huguenots, and the Pilgrim Fathers.

In the 20th century, things stepped up a gear. Funded by Marshall Aid, the Dutch economy experienced unprecedented growth in the 1950s and 1960s. Labor was needed, and migrant workers were invited. Initially they came from Italy, Greece and Spain; then in large numbers from Morocco and Turkey. Today there almost one million Muslims in Holland—around 6% of the population. At the same time, the dismantling of the Dutch empire meant new arrivals from ex-colonies such as Surinamand Indonesia.

More recently, refugees arrived from war-torn Somalia. Then, since they joined the EU in 2004, a new wave has flooded in from Poland, Romania and other points east. However, despite the nation's outwardly tolerant face, there are discontented rumblings. Many view the influx of different cultures as a threat to the traditional "Dutch" way of life. This came into sharp focus in 2004, when film director Theo van Gogh was killed by a Dutch-Moroccan youth for "blasphemy". His death shocked the nation and brought about a great deal of soul-searching. For a while relations between the Islamic and Christian communities became severely strained, and the result was a short spate of tit-for-tat violence. Thankfully the situation has since stabilized. While several prominent politicians have tried to appeal to voters by calling for anti-immigration legislation, there are no openly racist political parties with widespread support in Holland.

❸ **Sarphatipark.** This miniature Bois de Boulogne was built by and named after the noted city benefactor Samuel Sarphati (1813–66), whose statue deservedly graces the central fountain. This park, with paths undulating along trees, ponds, and expanses of grass, can be considered a kinder, gentler, and definitely much smaller Vondelpark. It's the perfect place to picnic on everything you picked up at the Albert Cuypmarkt. ✉ *Bounded by Ceintuurbaan and Sarfatipark, De Pijp.*

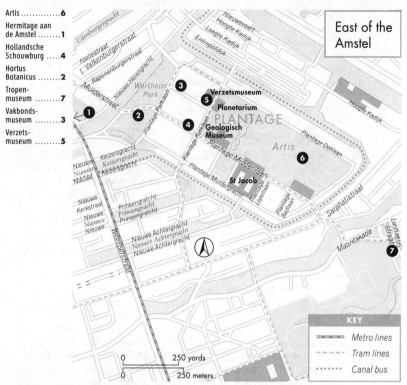

EAST OF THE AMSTEL

A quieter neighborhood, established by wealthier Jewish families from the late 19th century up to the Second World War, this area has wide boulevards, parks, and elegant architecture similar to the neighborhood around the Museum District. This decidedly posh, charming, non-touristy residential area is a great place to wander through. It has a few diverse family attractions and excellent museums.

MAIN ATTACTIONS

6 Artis *(Amsterdam Zoo).* Short for Natura Artis Magistra (Nature Is the Teacher of the Arts), Artis was continental Europe's first zoo and is the world's third oldest. Built in the mid-19th century, the 37-acre park is home to a natural-history museum, a zoo with an aviary, a superb planetarium, and an aquarium with 500 species of freshwater and saltwater fish; the best is a cross section of an Amsterdam canal complete with eels and sunken bicycles. Although many animal cages in the zoo are cramped, others are delightful, including the monkey island and a toy ruin with owls peering out at you from the towers. A modern expansion, including a glassed-in gorilla area and a mini desert for camels and the like, as well as a family-style restaurant, makes this a great stop for kids. The zoo and all its museums are accessible on a single ticket.

The Artis Express canal boat from Centraal Station is an easy way to get there, and Artis has ample parking if you come by car. ⊠ *Plantage Kerklaan 38-40, East of the Amstel* ☎ *020/523–3400* ⊕ *www.artis.nl* ☒€*14.00–17.50* ⊙ *Zoo Oct.–May, daily 9–5; June–Sept., daily 9–6; planetarium times vary depending on program.*

❶ Hermitage aan de Amstel. Taking advantage of 300 years of historical links between Amsterdam and St. Petersburg, Professor Mikhail Piotrovsky, director of The State Hermitage Museum in St. Petersburg, and Ernst Veen, director of the Nieuwe Kerk museum in Amsterdam, chose this spot on the Amstel as the new outpost for the famed Hermitage Russian art museum. With exhibitions culled from one of the most famous art collections in the world, ranging from Venetian painters and ancient Greek jewelry to the treasures of Czar Nicholas and his wife, Alexandra, the Hermitage is the place to go for (currently rather small) rare and specialist exhibits. Be sure to wander into the 17th-century Amstelhof courtyard that surrounds this 19th-century building. Built in 1681–1683 as a nursing home for the elderly, it is one of the finest examples of monumental classicist architecture in the city. The final phase of museum development is due to be completed in 2009. ⊠ *Gebouw Neerlandia, Nieuwe Herengracht 14* ☎ *020/530–8755* ⊕ *www.hermitage.nl* ☒€*7, children under 16 free* ⊙ *Daily 10–5.*

❹ Hollandsche Schouwburg *(Dutch Theater).* From 1892 to 1941, this was *the* theater for Dutch language performances written by luminaries like Herman Heyermans and Esther de Boer-van Rijk and played by artists like Louis "Little Big Man" Davids. In 1941, the Nazis relegated it to a Jewish-only theater, before turning it into a central gathering point for deportation of the city's Jews in 1942. In 1993, the Jewish Historical Museum renovated the theater, turning it into a memorial, where the 6,700 family names of 104,000 Dutch Jews who were murdered are displayed. There is also an upstairs exhibition on the Nazi occupation and an educational program showing documents, photographs, and videos. It is the large and silent courtyard that is perhaps the most effective remembrance of the 80,000 souls that left through this theater's doors to meet their dramatic end in Germany. ⊠ *Plantage Middenlaan 24, East of the Amstel* ☎ *020/531–0340* ⊕ *www.hollandscheschouwburg.nl* ☒ *Free* ⊙ *Daily 11–4.*

★ ❷ Hortus Botanicus. This wonderful botanical garden was originally laid out as an herb garden for doctors and pharmacists in 1682 before

1

the collection expanded to include exotic plants from the East India Company's forays into foreign lands. A labyrinth of ornamental gardens and greenhouses for plant species from a variety of climates (desert, swamp, tropical, and subtropical), a total of 8,000 species are represented here. One of the oldest potted plants in the world, a 300-year-old Cycas palm can be admired near the wonderful café terrace—one of the most peaceful places in the city to enjoy a cup of coffee. In fact, Hortus harbors the leafy descendants of the first coffee plants ever introduced into Europe. A Dutch merchant stole one of the plants from Ethiopia and presented it to Hortus in 1706; they in turn sent a clipping to a botanist in France, who saw to it that further clippings reached Brazil. ✉ *Plantage Middenlaan 2a, East of the Amstel* ☎ *020/625–9021* ⊕ *www.hortus-botanicus.nl* ✉ *€6* ◔ *Sept.–June, weekdays 9–5, weekends 10–5; July and Aug., weekdays 9–9, weekends 10–9.*

> **EXOTIC SUSHI**
>
> Mysterious fish thefts have plagued the Artis Aquarium for years. Illegal exotic fish dealers were prime suspects, but no evidence could be found. Mastermind of the "inside jobs" turned out to be Okkie the octopus, living in a solo tank next door. Crawling out of his aquarium at night, Okkie dropped in on his fishy friends, devouring a few before sneaking back to digest his sushi feast in the peace and quiet of his own home. Okkie's tank has a new glass ceiling that should stop his late-night snacking.

NEED A BREAK?

While in a refreshingly tourist-free zone, why not check out a local brown café (traditional Dutch watering hole) and head to **Eik & Linde** (✉ *Plantage Middenlaan 22, East of the Amstel* ☎ *020/622–5716*)? The history of the Eik & Linde (Oak & Lime) can be tracked back to 1858, and its walls are plastered with historical drawings and photographs to prove it. Located next to the American-style second rate Best Western Lancaster hotel, this old-fashioned, family-run bar has not lost its pre-War charm to the pre-fab fittings or hyper-trendy design. In fact, the clock behind the bar runs backwards, so you can happily lose all sense of time. The owners pride themselves on reasonable pricing and a friendly atmosphere.

⟳ ❼ **Tropenmuseum** *(Museum of the Tropics)*. The country's largest anthropological museum was first built to educate the Dutch about their colonial history in Indonesia and the West Indies, but now excels in hands-on exhibits covering all non-Western cultures. Its gorgeous, skylighted, and tiered interior, rich with wood, marble, and gilt, not only displays endless pieces of antiquity, art, and musical instruments, but also makes these accessible through workshops and in playful, simulated villages and bazaars that you walk through, touching, smelling, hearing music, and feeling the physical experience of life in Java, the Middle East, India, Africa, and Latin America (where you'll also find the city's smallest Internet café, El Cybernetico). There's also a great patio where you can enjoy food from the globe-embracing café. At the **Tropenmuseum Junior** (⊕ *www.tropenmuseumjunior.nl*), children can participate directly in the life of another culture through fun programs involving art, dance, song, and sometimes even cooking. Adults may visit the Junior section but only under the supervision of a child age 6–12. Every weekend the smallest children (under six) and their parents can visit the Kartini Wing, where they can enjoy drawing, building, and folding. For children aged four and over there are special children's routes through the museum. All children's activities are in Dutch only. ⊠ *Linnaeusstraat 2, Plantage* ☎ *020/568–8200* ⊕ *www. tropenmuseum.nl* ✆ *€7.50, Tropenmuseum Junior €2 extra* ⊙ *Daily 10–5. Kindermuseum activities Wed. at 11, 1:30, and 3:15, weekends at 11:30, 1:30, and 3:15.*

❸ **Vakbondsmuseum** *(Trade Union Museum)*. The history of Dutch trade unions may not seem especially scintillating, but its famed architect, H. P. Berlage, considered the building his most successful work. Built in 1900 for the country's first modern labor collective, the Diamond Workers Union, Berlage could incorporate his strong socialist principles into the essential structure. Climb the tower for a view of the neighborhood and enjoy a small display of Berlage's fine architectural blueprints while you're up there. In the various meeting rooms, note the fantastic murals by Richard Roland Holst, stained glass depicting the workers' battle, and the decorative details that fuse Jugendstil with Arts and Crafts stylings on ceilings, doors, and walls. The excellent collection of posters shows the graphic influence of the Soviet avant-garde on designs of the time. ⊠ *Henri Polaklaan 9, East of the Amstel* ☎ *020/624–1166* ⊕ *www.deburcht.org (Web site is in Dutch only)* ✆ *€2.50* ⊙ *Tues.–Fri. 11–5, Sun. 1–5.*

❺ **Verzetsmuseum** *(Dutch Resistance Museum)*. This museum was set up by Dutch Resistance to share stories about how people coped with Nazi occupation during World War II. The Plancius building in which the museum is housed is highly symbolic, as it was home to Jewish choir and stage companies from 1875 to 1940. Recently voted best historical museum in the country, its educational programs cater to school kids aged 10 and up, who increasingly come from multicultural backgrounds. The concept of "Resistance" is given a positive twist, using examples from World War II to make kids aware of the importance of mutual respect, freedom, the fragility of democracy, and their own responsibility in dealing with discrimination and persecution in their own lives. Displays also show how some of today's main Dutch publishers, like *De Parool* ("Password") and *Vrij Nederland* ("Free Netherlands"), began as illegal underground newsletters. If lines at the Anne Frank House are too long and you're short on time, this is a must-see alternative. ⊠ *Plantage Kerklaan 61, East of the Amstel* ☎ *020/620–2535* ⊕ *www.verzetsmuseum.org* ✆ *€5* ⊙ *Tues.–Fri. 10–5, Sat.–Mon. noon–5.*

Where to Eat

WORD OF MOUTH

"We ate at the Pancake Bakery (twice) and really loved it. The big savory pancakes are good, but the proffertjes (half-dollar sized with confectionary sugar) are just wonderful."

—amyb

"The first thing I have after touching down at Schiphol is a Heineken, no matter time of day. The second thing, once in Amsterdam, is to head over to a FEBO and get a frites met mayonnaise!"

—PlalenQ

Updated by
Nicole Chabot

UNTIL A DECADE OR TWO ago, it seemed that eating in Amsterdam was tinged more with the flavor of Calvinism than with any culinary influence. All too often the filling yet unenlightened fare of charred fish or meat, overboiled potatoes, and limp vegetables remained the standard.

Today, happily, things have changed. Many of the city's former industrial- and harbor-related buildings are being transformed into distinctive dining establishments. The term "New Dutch Cuisine," thanks to the emergence of young chefs who are finding their inspiration from around the globe, means exotic foamy-textured pea soup with chanterelles and pancetta, cod smothered in a sauce based on chorizo and fennel, or turbot and truffle wrapped in potato spaghetti, stewed chard, and veal sauce. And international urban eating trends make it highly probable that you'll encounter sushi shacks, soup shops, noodle joints, and organic bakeries selling hearty Mediterranean breads.

Although traditionally hearty Dutch food really shines only in the winter months, there are two imported-but-typically-Dutch culinary trips that cannot be missed: the Indonesian *rijsttafel* ("rice table"), where dozens of differently spiced vegetables, meats, and fish dishes are served with rice; and cheese fondue, which the Dutch appropriated from the Swiss probably because it appealed to their "one pot, many forks" sense of the democratic. The many cheap Suri/Indo/Chin (or some such combination) snack bars serve a combination of Suriname, Indonesian, and Chinese dishes, and although they are remarkably consistent, it is perhaps advisable to choose a dish that matches the cook's apparent roots.

If you're the type who likes to make your own discoveries, here are a few tips to keep in mind. In general, avoid the tourist traps around Leidseplein, Rembrandtplein, the Damrak, and the Red Light District. Cheap global eats are concentrated in the De Pijp district. A broad selection of middle-range eateries can be found around Nieuwmarkt, the Jordaan, and Utrechtsestraat. To find posher purveyors for a true blowout, head to Reguliersdwarsstraat or the Nine Streets (the interconnecting streets of the canal girdle between Raadhuisstraat and Leidsestraat) areas. Befitting a casual town, children are pretty much universally welcomed in Amsterdam.

Note: For a rundown of the best of Amsterdam's famous atmosphere-soaked "brown cafés"—where there is traditionally more imbibing than dining—see Chapter 4, Nightlife & the Arts.

WHAT IT COSTS IN EUROS				
	¢	$	$$	$$	$$$$
AT DINNER	under €10	€10–€15	€15–€22	€22–€30	over €30

Prices are per person for a main course, excluding tax (6% for food and 19% for alcoholic beverages).

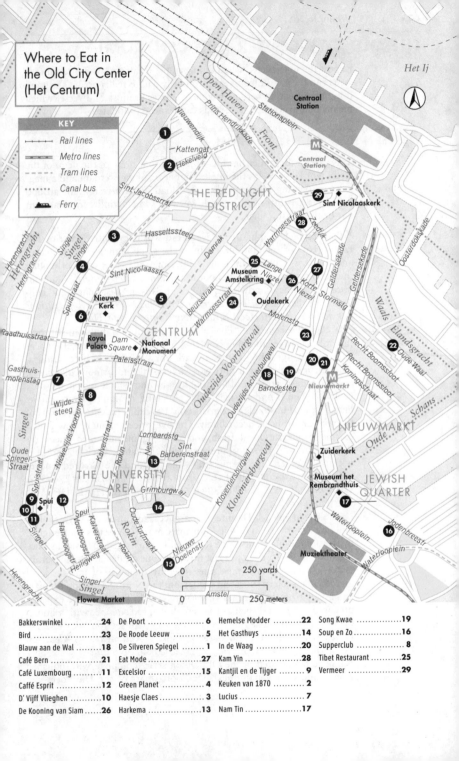

Where to Eat in the Old City Center (Het Centrum)

KEY

┼┼┼┼┼	Rail lines
───	Metro lines
─ ─ ─	Tram lines
· · · · ·	Canal bus
⏏	Ferry

THE OLD CITY CENTER (HET CENTRUM)

Expect the unexpected when dining in the Centrum, where restaurant visits run the gamut from extraordinarily bad to really great. The good thing about eating here is that menu prices are just as diverse, which means that everyone's taste buds can be accommodated.

WESTERN HALF OF THE CENTRUM

This side of the center has lots of history, but none of the neon of the Red Light District. It's the intellectual heart of Amsterdam and a magnet for roaming hipsters, who often load up at a restaurant around Spui square before washing it down with some nightlife in an ancient bar or the latest lounge.

AMERICAN CASUAL

¢–$

✕ **Caffé Esprit** The Spui offers several old-world–evocative eateries, but Esprit (part of the clothing chain of the same name)—with its clean and modern "aluminum design" interior, and windows overlooking the bustling square—reaches out to the homesick by offering contemporary American sandwiches, burgers, pastas, pizzas, salads, and children's menus. ⊠*Spui 10, Centrum* ☎*020/622–1967* ♨*Reservations not accepted* ▭*No credit cards* ✷*No dinner except Thurs.*

$$$–$$$$
Fodor's Choice
★

✕ **D' Vijff Vlieghen.** The "Five Flies" is a rambling dining institution that takes up five adjoining Golden Age houses. Yet the densely evocative Golden Age vibe—complete with bona fide Rembrandt etchings, wooden *jenever* (Dutch gin) barrels, crystal and armor collections, and an endless array of old-school bric-a-brac—came into being only in 1939. You'll find business folk clinching deals in private nooks here, but also busloads of tourists who have dibs on entire sections of the restaurant: book accordingly. The overpriced menu of new Dutch cuisine emphasizes local, fresh, and often organic ingredients in everything from wild boar to purely vegetarian dishes. Lack of choice is not an issue here: the menus, the wine list, and the flavored jenever are—like the decor—all of epic proportions. ⊠*Spuistraat 294–302, Centrum 1012 VX* ☎*020/530–4060 Jacket and tie* ▭*AE, DC, MC, V* ✷*No lunch.*

$$$

✕ **De Silveren Spiegel.** Despite appearances, this precariously crooked building near the solid Round Lutheran Church is here to stay. Designed by the ubiquitous Hendrik de Keyser, it has managed to remain standing since 1614, so it should last through your dinner of contemporary Dutch cuisine. In fact, take time to enjoy their use of famous local ingredients, such as succulent lamb from the North Sea island of Texel and honey from Amsterdam's own Vondelpark. There are also expertly prepared fish plates, such as roasted fillet of red snapper with a homemade vinaigrette. The full five-course menu will set you back €52.50. Lunch is available only for large groups. ⊠*Kattengat 4–6, Centrum* ☎*020/624–6589* ▭*AE, MC, V* ✷*Closed Sun. No lunch.*

$$–$$$

✕ **De Poort.** Restored in the Old Dutch style (complete with polished woods and ceiling paintings), De Poort—part of the Die Poert van

CLOSE UP

Dining Like the Dutch

DINING HOURS

One thing you should be aware of is the Dutch custom of early dining; in fact, the vast majority of the city's kitchens turn in for the night at 10 PM—though many of the newer establishments are moving away from this long-held tradition. It should also be noted that many restaurants choose Monday as their day of rest. Lunches are usually served between noon and 2 PM, but many restaurants in Amsterdam are open for dinner only.

DRESS

Because Amsterdam is a casual sort of town, "jacket and tie" means more "if you feel like it" than "required." The truly elitist dining spots have long learned to have a supply of jackets on hand for the underdressed. So,

"jacket" yes, possibly, though "jacket and tie" is a true rarity.

SMOKING

Although there are strict anti-public smoking laws on the horizon (not set to take effect until at least 2008), the cafés and restaurants of Amsterdam remain puffing paradises. Most restaurants provide no-smoking sections, but the fervently pink-lunged antismoker should really call ahead to get the full scoop.

TIPPING

A 15% service charge is automatically included on the menu prices. However, the trend is for most diners to throw in an extra euro or two on smaller bills and €5 or €10 on larger bills.

Cleve hotel complex—is, in fact, officially Old Dutch. Its roots as a steak brasserie stretch back to 1870, when it awed the city as the first place with electric light. By the time you read this, De Poort will have served well over 6 million of its acclaimed juicy slabs, served with a choice of eight accompaniments. The menu is supplemented with other options such as smoked salmon, a traditional pea soup thick enough to eat with a fork, and a variety of seafood dishes. ☒ *Nieuwezijds Voorburgwal 176–180, Centrum* ☎ *020/622–6429* ☰ *AE, DC, MC, V.*

$$-$$$ ✕**De Roode Leeuw.** Evoking a sense of timeless classicism along a strip that is decidedly middle-of-the-road, De Roode Leeuw has red banquettes, dark paneling, and romantic lighting. It has the city's oldest heated terrace—a good place to enjoy a selection from the impressive champagne list. You'll find poshed-up native fare served here, be it eel (caught fresh from the nearby IJsselmeer before being stewed) in a creamy herb sauce, or Zeeland mussels steamed and served with french fries and salad. Besides attracting passing tourists, the restaurant has also built up a sizable local following ever since it received the coveted *Neerlands Dis* (Netherlands' Dish) award. ☒ *Damrak 93, Centrum* ☎ *020/555–0666* ☰ *AE, DC, MC, V.*

★ **$-$$** ✕**Haesje Claes.** Groaning with pewter tankards, stained glass, leadedglass windows, rich historic paneling, Indonesian paisley *fabriks,* and betasseled Victorian lamps, this restaurant's "Old Holland" ambience and matching menu attract lots of tourists. And why change a winning formula? The Pieter de Hooch–worthy interiors eclipse the food, although the (somewhat overpriced) dishes include an excellent pea soup and a selection of *stampotten* (mashed dishes that combine potato with a variety of vegetables and/or meats). On cold winter nights, opt for the *hutspot*, a stampot of mashed potato and carrot supplemented with steamed beef, sausage, and bacon. ⊠*Spuistraat 273, Centrum* ☎*020/624–9998* ▤*AE, MC, V.*

¢–$ ✕**Keuken van 1870.** This former soup kitchen, where sharing tables is still the norm, offers the best and most economic foray into the world of traditional Dutch cooking. The kitchen serves such warming singularities as hutspot, its more free-ranging variant stampot (a stew made with potatoes, greens, and chunks of cured sausage), *erwtensoep* (a sausage-fortified, extremely thick pea soup), and, naturally, a full range of meat, fish, vegetable, and potato plates. The restaurant continues to serve a daily three-course meal for a measly €7.50. Bless 'em. ⊠*Spuistraat 4, Centrum* ☎*020/620–4018* ▤*No credit cards* ☾*Closed Sun. No lunch.*

ECLECTIC ✕**Supperclub.** The concept is simple but artful. Over the course of an evening, diners casually lounge on mattresses while receiving endless courses of food (and drink …) marked by irreverent flavor combinations. DJs, VJs, and live performances enhance the clublike, relentlessly hip vibe. Supperclub's popularity suggests that one should really go only in large groups; otherwise you may run the risk of being overwhelmed by one of the same. ⊠*Jonge Roelensteeg 21, Centrum 1012 PL* ☎*020/344–6400* ⌲*Reservations essential* ▤*AE, DC, MC, V* ☾*No lunch.*

$$$$
FodorśChoice
★

$–$$ ✕**Café Luxembourg.** One of the city's top grand cafés, Luxembourg has a stately interior and a view of a bustling square, both of which are maximized for people-watching. Famous for its brunch, its classic café menu includes a terrific goat cheese salad, dim sum, and excellent Holtkamp *krokets* (croquettes, these with a shrimp or meat and potato filling). The "reading table" is democratically packed with both Dutch and international newspapers and mags. ⊠*Spuistraat 24, Centrum 1012 XA* ☎*020/620–6264* ▤*AE, DC, MC, V.*

FodorśChoice
★

★ $$–$$$ ✕**Kantjil en de Tijger.** The interior of this large and spacious Indonesian restaurant is a serene take on Jugendstil (a sort of Austrian Art Nouveau). Although you can order à la carte, the menu is based on three different *rijsttafel* (rice tables), with an abundance of meat, fish, and vegetable dishes varying in flavor from coconut-milk sweet to distressingly spicy (tip: the sweet and light local *witbier* beer is an excellent antidote). Groups often come here to line their bellies before a night of drinking in the bars around the nearby Spui and Nieuwezijds Voorburgwal. You can also opt to hit the counter at the adjacent Kantjil To Go (Nieuwezijds Voorburgwal 352, open noon–9 daily) for cheap boxes of noodley goodness. ⊠*Spuistraat 291/293, Centrum* ☎*020/620–0994* ▤*AE, DC, MC, V* ☾*No lunch weekdays.*

$$–$$$ ✕**Lucius.** The plain and informal setting may say "bistro," but this is actually one of the best fish restaurants in town. You can happily linger here over choices like grilled lobster, a deliciously authentic *plateau de fruits de mer* (fruits-of-the-sea platter), or a positively adventurous sea bass served with buckwheat noodles and mushrooms. The intelligent wine list spotlights California, but—attention, oenophiles!—

also sports a Dutch wine from the nation's only vineyard, in Limburg. A three-course meal will set you back €37.50. ⊠ *Spuistraat 247, Centrum* ☎ *020/624–1831* ⌂ *Reservations essential* ⊟ *AE, DC, MC, V* ☉ *No lunch.*

★ ¢–$ ✕ **Green Planet.** You know this is a serious mecca for vegetarians when 90% of the kitchen's ingredients are organic, the resident cat is a dedicated veg (in both diet and manner), and the kitchen employs biodegradable packaging for takeout. The equally noble menu covers everything from wraps to stir-fries but enters true profundity when it comes to the lasagna, the carrot-orange soup with fresh thyme, and the tofu cake. ⊠ *Spuistraat 122, Centrum* ☎ *020/625–8280* ⊟ *No credit cards* ☉ *Closed Sun.*

> **FEASTS TO REMEMBER**
>
> As you hunker down for a good Dutch meal, remember this: holiday celebrations of yesteryear were marked by the drunken gobbling of whole pheasants, just like the boisterous 17th-century depictions of feasts painted by Franz Hals, Jan Steen, and Jacob Jordaens. Dig in!

THE RED LIGHT DISTRICT

The city's Red Light District peddles more than just flesh and porn. It's also host to many bargain Asian restaurants and the fine delicacies of some of Amsterdam's most esteemed eateries.

¢–$$ ✕ **Tibet Restaurant.** This place is famous for its budget prices and late-night hours (daily 1:30 PM–1:30 AM). Although you can get some authentic dishes here, like *momo* (dumplings) and various pork offerings that come either in spicy "folk-style" chunks or milder "family-style" shreds, the majority of the menu is ironically dedicated to standard Chinese Szechuan fare. ⊠ *Lange Niezel 24, Red Light District* ☎ *020/624–1137* ⊟ *MC, V.*

¢–$ ✕ **Kam Yin.** Representative of the many Suriname snack bars found throughout the city, Kam Yin offers this South American country's unique fusion of Caribbean, Chinese, and Indonesian cuisines that arose from its history as a Dutch colony. Perhaps the most popular meal is the *roti*, a flat-bread pancake, which comes with lightly curried potatoes and vegetable or meat additions. If you come for lunch, try a *broodje pom*, a sandwich filled with a remarkably addictive mélange of chicken and cassava root (mmmmm, root vegetable). Basic, clean, convivial, and noisy, Kam Yin shows extra sensitivity with its speedy service, long hours (daily noon–midnight), and a doggy-bag option. ⊠ *Warmoesstraat 6–8, Red Light District* ☎ *020/625–3115* ⊟ *No credit cards.*

¢–$ ✕ **Bakkerswinkel.** This genteel yet unpretentious bakery/tearoom evokes
Fodor's Choice
★ an English country kitchen, one that lovingly prepares and serves breakfasts, high tea, hearty-breaded sandwiches, soups, and divine (almost manly) slabs of quiche. The closely clustered wooden tables don't make for much privacy, but this place is a true oasis if you want to indulge in a healthful breakfast or lunch. It opens at 8 AM daily. There's a second location, complete with garden patio, in the Museum District.

✉ *Warmoestraat 69, Red Light District 1012 HX* ☎ *020/489–8000* ☐ *No credit cards* ☯ *Closed Mon. No dinner.* ✉ *Roelof Hartstraat 68, Museum District & Environs 1071 VM* ☎ *020/662–3594* ☐ *No credit cards* ☯ *Closed Mon. No dinner.*

$$$$
Fodor'sChoice
★

✕ **Vermeer.** With its milk-white walls, dramatic black-and-white patterned floors, Delft plates, fireplace hearths, and old chandeliers, this stately place does conjure up the amber canvases of the great Johannes. Its super-posh vibe, however, suggests that no milkmaid on earth will be able to afford the prices of this restaurant set within the 17th-century wing of the NH Barbizon Palace Hotel. Current chef Chris Naylor aspires to equal heights as his predecessors with such dishes as poached skate with wakame seaweed and fine nicoise ravioli in squid bouillon. An army of waiters are on hand to ensure that the service is always impeccable. ✉ *Prins Hendrikkade 59–72, Red Light District 1012 AD* ☎ *020/556–4885* ☐ *AE, DC, MC, V* ☯ *Closed Sun. No lunch Sat.*

★ **$–$$**
✕ **Harkema.** This brasserie along the city's premier theater strip has infused a former tobacco factory with light, color, and general design savvy. The kitchen, which is open between 11 AM and midnight daily, pumps out reasonably priced lunches and French classics, and a wall of wine is on hand to appeal to all tastes. ✉ *Nes 67, Red Light District* ☎ *020/428–2222* ☐ *MC, V.*

¢–$
✕ **Eat Mode.** One can easily imagine this sleek steel- and Formica-rich snack bar, dedicated to the more popular dishes of Asia, set on a Tokyo subway platform. So it just adds to the charm that it is, in fact, on Amsterdam's oldest street. Order some cheap but tasty yakitori, sushi, noodles, or whatever is on the specials menu that day, and then wait for your number to be called out. ✉ *Zeedijk 105–7, Red Light District* ☎ *020/330–0806* ☐ *No credit cards.*

$$$–$$$$
✕ **Blauw aan de Wal.** In the heart of the Red Light District is a small alley that leads to this charming oasis, complete with the innocent chirping of birds. "Blue on the Quay" is set in a courtyard that once belonged to the Bethanienklooster monastery; it now offers a restful ambience with multiple dining areas (one is no-smoking), each with a unique and serene view. Original wood floors and exposed-brick walls hint at the building's 1625 origins, but the extensive and inspired wine list, and the open kitchen employing fresh local ingredients in its Mediterranean-influenced cuisine, both have a contemporary chic. After starting with a frothy pea soup with chanterelle mushrooms and pancetta, you may want to indulge in a melt-in-the-mouth, herb-crusted lamb fillet. ✉ *Oude Zijde Achterburgwal 99, Red Light District* ☎ *020/330–2257* ☐ *AE, MC, V* ☯ *Closed Sun. No lunch.*

★ **$–$$**
✕ **Bird.** After many years of success operating the chaotic and tiny Thai snack bar across the street, Bird's proprietors opened this expansive 100-seat restaurant. Now they have the extra kitchen space to flash-fry their options from an expanded menu, and enough room to place the chunky teak furnishings they had imported from Thailand. The best tables—where you can enjoy coconut-chicken soup with lemongrass followed by fruity curry with mixed seafood—are at the rear overlooking the canal. ✉ *Zeedijk 72–74, Red Light District* ☎ *020/620–1442* ☐ *AE, DC, MC, V.*

$-$$ ✕ **De Kooning van Siam.** Sitting smack in the middle of the Red Light District, this Thai establishment takes delight in the fact that Brad Pitt (who went local by buying a home in the Jordaan long before coming here to film *Ocean's 12*) once came to dine. It should take more from the fact that it is favored by local Thai residents. Although the ancient beams and wall panels are still visible in this old canal house, the furniture and wall decorations refreshingly dilute the sense of Olde Dutchness. Sensitive to wimpier palates, the menu balances such scorchers as stir-fried beef with onion and chili peppers with milder options. ✉ *Oude Zijde Voorburgwal 42, Red Light District* ☎ *020/623–7293* ▭ *AE, DC, MC, V* ⊘ *Closed Sun. No lunch.*

¢–$ ✕ **Song Kwae.** Perhaps influenced by their Chinese competitors, this buzzing joint offers speedy service and high-quality food for a budget price. Alongside the traditional red and green Thai curries and the stir-fry options, there are specialties such as green papaya salad with crab and *potek*, a searingly spicy mix of meats and fish. In the summer, the seating spills over onto the street with its views of Nieuwmarkt. The owners have also just opened a nearby sister restaurant, Song Kwae Sukiyaki, that specializes in the always socially convivial fondue. ✉ *Kloveniersburgwal 14, Red Light District* ☎ *020/624–2568* ▭ *AE, DC, MC, V* ✉ *Binnenbantammerstraat 11, Red Light District* ☎ *020/422–2444* ▭ *AE, DC, MC, V.*

NIEUWMARKT & ENVIRONS

The Nieuwmarkt & square is an eclectic mix of of upscale eateries like De Waag, at the beating heart of Nieuwmarkt, and student-friendly (read reasonably priced) hangouts that surround it. The adjoining streets are dotted with the type of venues that live up to the reputation of Amsterdam as the laid-back, chilled out European capital. Perfect places to linger over a glass of wine or a pilsje (a little glass of beer), or indulge in local snacks or full-blown meals.

¢–$$ ✕ **Nam Tin.** In the world of culinary imperialism, the Chinese have their formula bolted down. And indeed this massive and massively over-lighted restaurant is like thousands of others the world over in ignoring the setting in favor of an encyclopedic Cantonese menu. As a hangover-curing bonus, they serve dim sum from noon until 5 daily and until 10 on Sunday. The restaurant is known to be kid-friendly. ✉ *Jodenbreestraat 11, Centrum* ☎ *020/428–8508* ▭ *No credit cards.*

$$ ✕**Hemelse Modder.** This bright, stylish, informal, and vegetarian-friendly restaurant is on one of the city's broadest canals and has a long-standing reputation for high quality at a great price. You select from fixed-price menus costing €29.50. The inspired choices show a global sweep but invariably come to rest within the borders of France, Great Britain, and The Netherlands. For a supplement of €6 you can tuck into one of the mountainous grand desserts, including the "heavenly mud" mousse of dark and white chocolate that gives the restaurant its name. ⊠*Oude Waal 11, Centrum* ☎*020/624–3203* ▤*AE, DC, MC, V* ⊘ *Closed Mon. No lunch.*

> ### WORD OF MOUTH
>
> Cafe Bern is a dark paneled wooden bar not far from the Red Light District, metro stop right near by. Great cheese fondue! The bartender and waitstaff were very helpful and there was great service.
>
> —universitylad

★ ¢–$ ✕**Café Bern.** This dark and woody café, as evocative as a Jan Steen 17th-century interior, has been serving the same cheese fondue for decades, and for good reason: it's just about perfect, especially if you enhance digestion—and the frolic factor—with plenty of orders from the fully stocked bar. Just start shredding the accompanying French stick and start dunking those bread bits into that wonderfully gooey mess. Like the Dutch, you, too, may be inspired to establish cheese fondue as your own celebratory meal of choice. ⊠*Nieuwmarkt 9, Centrum* ☎*020/622–0034* ⚘*Reservations essential* ▤*No credit cards* ⊘*No lunch.*

¢–$ ✕**Het Gasthuys.** Bustling and student-filled, this place near the university serves handsome portions of traditional Dutch home cooking, choice cuts of meat with simple sauces, fine fries, and piles of mixed salad. You can sit at the wood bar or take a table high up in the rafters at the back, surrounded by ancient wallpapers. In summer you can watch the passing boats from the enchanting canal-side terrace or watch the junkies selling bikes off the nearby bridge. ⊠*Grimburgwal 7, Centrum* ☎*020/624–8230* ▤*No credit cards.*

$$–$$$$ ✕**Excelsior.** When only the poshest and most elegant will do, take your primped-up selves here. The tinkling of a grand piano, solicitous waiters, knowledgeable sommeliers, laden dessert trolleys, and preparation carts all waltz together here in a setting of towering palms, tall candelabras, shimmering chandeliers, and stunning views over the Amstel River. The menu here is traditional French, but the inspired chef, Jean-Jacques Menanteau, also knows some twists, such as a sublime lobster bisque and a grilled turbot with shrimp and Parmesan risotto. If you're feeling adventurous, opt for his fixed-price five-course *menu excelsior,* for €80 (add €42.50 for wine), which features not only seasonal specialties (think truffles) but occasionally also the acclaimed dishes he creates from such unprepossessing meats as liver and kidneys. ⊠*Hotel de l'Europe, Nieuwe Doelenstraat 2–8, Centrum* ☎*020/531–1705 Jacket and tie* ▤*AE, DC, MC, V* ⊘*No lunch Sat. and Sun.*

2

$$-$$$ ✕ **In de Waag.** The lofty, beamed interior of the historic Waag (weigh house) has been converted into a grand café and restaurant. Although the reading table houses computer terminals with free Internet access, a strict dinner lighting policy of "candles only"—from a huge wooden candelabra, no less—helps maintain the building's medieval majesty. The menu is heartily Burgundian, with such entrées as baked fillet of salmon with braised endive and Noilly Prat sauce or tournedos of entrecôte with roasted beets. The long wooden tables make this an ideal location for larger groups, and if you happen to belong to a party of eight, you should definitely book the spookily evocative tower room. Daytime hunger pangs are also catered to from 10 AM, when you can enjoy a sandwich, a salad, or a snack on the spacious terrace. ⊠ *Nieuwmarkt 4, Centrum* ☎ *020/422-7772* ▭ *AE, DC, MC, V.*

¢ ✕ **Soup en Zo.** Only in the last few years, perhaps because *Seinfeld* is still showing here, has the concept of speedy soup purveyors hit Amsterdam. "Soup Etc." leads the pack by being particularly speedy (at least between 10 and 7:30 daily), as well as health conscious. Four soups are available daily, served with chunky slices of whole-grain breads, and the menu also offers salads and exotic fruit juices imported from Brazil. Once you're fortified, you can rush back to searching for bargains at the Waterlooplein flea market or window-shopping for arts and antiques around its second, Museum District location. ⊠ *Jodenbreestraat 94a, Centrum* ☎ *020/422-2243* ▭ *No credit cards* ⊠ *Nieuwe Spiegelstraat 54, Museum District* ☎ *020/330-7781* ▭ *No credit cards.*

180 DEGREES AROUND CENTRAL STATION

Amsterdam's historical harbor is getting the finishing touches on what is hoped to be an image-polishing boardwalk that will perhaps evolve into the city's premier entertainment zone. And naturally, many once purely industrial buildings have been transformed into dining hot spots.

★ **$-$$** ✕ **Kilimanjaro.** This relaxed and friendly pan-African place serves dishes from all over the continent—including one that may well inspire the outburst from the hammier among us: "this is darn crocodilicious!"—but focuses on the often vegetarian *enjera* pancake-based meals of Ethiopia (which you famously eat with your hands). Have a seat on the summer patio, order either a *mongooza* beer (served in a calabash) or a fruity cocktail (species: exotic), and then later round off your meal with a freshly hand-ground Ethiopian coffee served with popcorn before taking a digestive stroll around the harbor. ⊠ *Rapenburgerplein 6, Centrum* ☎ *020/622-3485* ▭ *No credit cards* ⊙ *Closed Mon. No lunch.*

$$$$ ✕ **Fifteen.** This franchise of superstar chef Jamie Oliver does exactly the same as the London original: it trains young adults as kitchen team players while filming them for a reality television show. Shockingly, it's proven to be a remarkably consistent success, thanks in part to its waterfront location in the up-and-coming Eastern Docklands neighborhood. While the kids learn under the tutelage of well-established chefs, diners indulge in one set menu per day featuring such dishes as

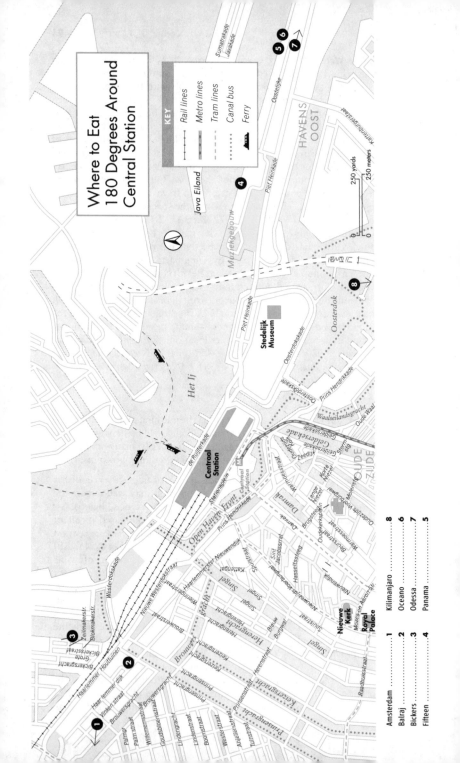

Where to Eat
180 Degrees Around
Central Station

KEY

┼─┼	Rail lines
━━━	Metro lines
─ ─ ─	Tram lines
⋯⋯	Canal bus
⛴	Ferry

Sicilian-style fish soup and veal in a tuna sauce. ✉*Jollemanhof 9, Centrum* 📞*0900/343–8336* 🌐*www.fifteen.nl* 🍴*No credit cards* 🕐*No lunch.*

$$ ✕**Odessa.** This floating restaurant—it's a Ukrainian trawler, hence the name—attracts hipsters and boaties alike. Although you'll pay a pretty price for its international fusion meals, you can get a three-course dinner for €27.50, as well as water views of some acclaimed local architecture. In the summer, the deck is open to diners, and on sporadic Sundays there are all-you-can-eat barbecues. Dancing begins after dark. ✉*Veemkade 259, Centrum* 📞*020/419–3011* 🍴*AE, DC, MC, V* 🕐*No lunch.*

> **EVERYDAY SPECIALS**
>
> Embracing a sense of the democratic is the best advice for lunchtime: just follow the locals into a brown café or bar (also often called an *eetcafe,* eating café) to enjoy a *broodje* (sandwich) or *uitsmijter* (fried eggs with cheese and/or ham served on sliced bread). If you like the vibe, ask what they're serving for dinner. It's probably reasonably priced and based on what was cheapest and freshest at the market that morning.

FRENCH ✕**Amsterdam.** Getting here requires going west of the Jordaan, and
🕐 ★ **$–$$** beyond the Westergasfabriek cultural complex. Like that neighbor (which began its days as a gas factory), this spot is an industrial monument—for a century, this plant pumped water from coastal dunes. Now, under a sky-high ceiling, one can dine on honestly rendered French and Dutch dishes—from rib-eye béarnaise and steak tartare to wonderful fish dishes like grilled tuna with ratatouille—in a bustling atmosphere favored by families and larger groups. If it's too noisy for you, seek refuge on the peaceful terrace. ✉*Watertorenplein 6, Jordaan* 📞*020/682–2666* 🍴*AE, DC, MC, V.*

$–$$ ✕**Bickers.** A true hideaway on Bickers Island, this is a place for which the possibility of getting lost is worth it. With an all-wood terrace, it resembles a harbor with a watery nautical view. The interior is stark, industrial, and modern. The food is tasty—think shrimp croquettes and chips served in a paper cone and accompanied by an excellent mayonnaise. The portions are considerable. ✉*Bickerswerf 2, Bickers Island, Centrum* 📞*020/320–2951* 🍴*MC, V* 🕐*Closed Mon. and Tues.*

$ ✕**Balraj.** For a quarter of a century, Balraj has been a favorite of curry connoisseurs. The ambience is unremarkable—though the restaurant is impeccably clean and the plastic flowers are always fresh. The friendly fellows who serve delicious snacks, soups, and meals from their homeland, however, are a pleasure. You'll break out in the happiest of sweats when indulging in the chicken Madras, which you can wash down with sweet cardamom tea. ✉*Haarlemmerdijk 28, Jordaan* 📞*020/625–1428* 🍴*No credit cards* 🕐*No lunch.*

$$–$$$ ✕**Oceano.** No matter that those plucky Dutch long ago transformed this bay of seawater into a freshwater lake—you can still get plenty of seafood here. The specialities from all over Italy include spaghetti coscolio, a medly of clams, mussels, shrimp, and calamari in a tomato sauce. (It's a favorite of the chef.) You may choose to aid digestion by taking a walk along the very odd Schipstimmermanstraat (a street filled with wacky buildings), as this restaurant is in the heart of a modern architecture mecca. ⊠ *RJH Fortuynplein 29, Borneo Island, Centrum* ☎ *020/419–0020* ⊟ *MC, V* ⊗ *No lunch weekdays.*

$$–$$$ ✗ **Panama.** A posh pioneer in the Eastern Docklands in the harbor's former power station, Panama serves authentic dishes from around the world, with a special emphasis on fish. But you can stop in for a soup, a sandwich, or a salad pretty much any time of the day. Although the original 19th-century industrial architecture is still in view, the furnishings bring everything up to date. Plan to continue your evening in the attached nightspot, where the warm use of red, blue, and gold evokes a vision of an old-fashioned jazz club. ⊠ *Oostelijke Handelskade 4, Centrum* ☎ *020/311–8686* ⚑ *Reservations essential* ⊟ *AE, DC, MC, V.*

THE CANAL RING

If you're in Amsterdam for just one meal, head for the canals. In the midst of a storybook setting you'll find all manner of restaurants from glass-walled bistros to dining rooms that play on the city's rich merchant past. In the summer, outdoor terraces put you at the water's edge.

WESTERN CANAL RING

The intrinsically posh sector of the Grachtengordel ring and its intersecting streets is a foodie paradise. Meals here come equipped with the potential for an after-dinner romantic walk to aid the digestion: the arches of the bridges are prettily lit and their watery reflections pull at the heartstrings of even the most wayworn of travelers.

$$ ✗ **De Belhamel.** Set on the edge of the Jordaan, this restaurant is blessed with Art Nouveau detailing and wallpaper that is so darkly evocative of fin-de-siècle living it may inspire a thirst for absinthe and Symbolist poetry. But the views of the Herengracht canal and the attentive and friendly service help create a more purely romantic setting in which to settle down and enjoy the French-inspired menu. In the winter, hearty game dishes (such as venison with a red-wine and shallot sauce) are featured; in summer, lighter fare is offered, and the seating spills out into the street. ⊠ *Brouwersgracht 60, Canal Ring* ☎ *020/622–1095* ⊟ *AE, MC, V* ⊗ *No lunch.*

★ **$$** ✗ **Van Puffelen.** The ancient Van Puffelen, on a particularly mellow stretch of canal, offers both a startling array of herbed and spiced *jenevers* (Dutch gin) in its role as a *proeverij* (tasting house) and, in addition, a huge restaurant section in which to settle the belly. The menu is of the modern café variety, but it's the frequently changing specials (a three-course dinner costs €19.50, and is served Sunday–Wednesday) that draws so many regulars. Red meat tends to be done rare here. If the main dining room gets too boisterous, you can always escape to the more secluded and intimate mezzanine or, in the summer, the terrace. Reservations are essential for the restaurant. (Also essential is a visit

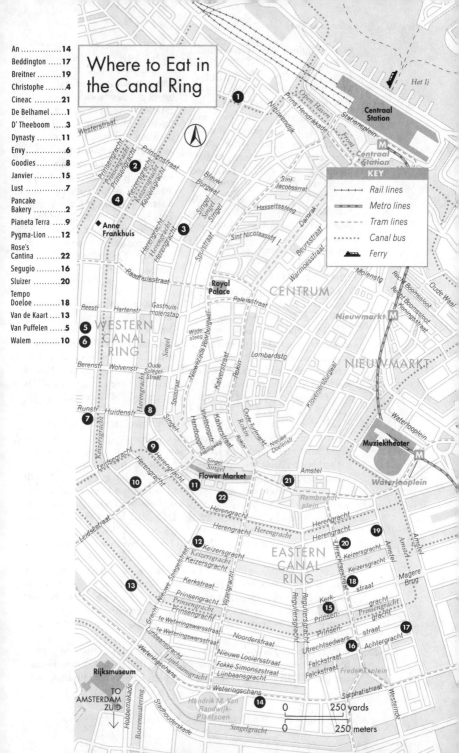

Where to Eat in the Canal Ring

KEY

┣━━━┫	Rail lines
▅▅▅	Metro lines
-----	Tram lines
·····	Canal bus
⛴	Ferry

Centraal Station

Anne Frankhuis

Royal Palace

CENTRUM

Nieuwmarkt

NIEUWMARKT

WESTERN CANAL RING

Muziektheater

Waterlooplein

Flower Market

EASTERN CANAL RING

Magere Brug

Rembrandtplein

Rijksmuseum

TO AMSTERDAM ZUID

Fredriksplein

0		250 yards
0		250 meters

to the "liquor vat" washrooms.)
⊠*Prinsengracht 375–377, Canal Ring* ☎*020/624–6270* ▤*AE, DC, MC, V* ⊘*No lunch Mon.–Wed.*

¢–$ ✕**Pancake Bakery.** It's hard to go wrong when going out for Dutch pancakes in Amsterdam. But the quaint Pancake Bakery rises above the pack of similar eateries with its medieval vibe, canal-side patio, and a mammoth menu with more than 70 choices of sweet and savory toppings. There are also omelets, and a convincing take on the folk dish of *erwtensoep* (a superthick, smoked sausage-imbued pea soup). ⊠*Prinsengracht 191, Canal Ring* ☎*020/625–1333* ▤*AE, MC, V.*

PANCAKE CRAVINGS

With both sweet and savory toppings, *pannenkoeken* (pancakes) are also a mainstay on the menu of many cafés. They are a specialty at such places as the **Pancake Bakery** (see listing), the **Upstairs Pannenkoekenhuis** (Grimburgwal 2, Old Side, 020/626–5603), and the **Boerderij Meerzicht** (Koenenkade 56, Buitenveldert, 0290/679–2744), which is an out-of-the way petting zoo and playground in the heart of Amsterdamse Bos (Amsterdam Forest).

★ $–$$ ✕**Walem.** As if ripped from the pages of *Wallpaper* magazine, this sleekly hip and trendy all-day grand café serves elegant breakfast and brunch options—as well as plenty of both cappuccino and champagne. Dinnertime is fusion time, as the chefs create salads of marinated duck and chicken, crispy greens, and buckwheat noodles, or slather a roast duck with bilberry sauce and serve it with a hodgepodge of arugula. In the summer, you can relax in the formal garden or on the canal-side terrace. Late at night, guest DJs spin hip lounge tunes for an appreciative crowd. ⊠*Keizersgracht 449, Canal Ring* ☎*020/625–3544* ▤*AE, MC, V.*

$$$$ ✕**Christophe.** The William Katz–designed interior, which evokes this artist's acclaimed ballet scenery, remains one of the best reasons to visit Christophe. Chef Jean-Joel Bonsens's ever-evolving menu—always loaded with vegetarian options—may include entrées such as roasted lobster with soft garlic and small "la ratte" potatoes, or sweetbreads of veal with rosemary, asparagus, and compote of preserved lemon. ⊠*Leliegracht 46, Canal Ring* ☎*020/625–0807* ⚲*Reservations essential; Jacket and tie required* ▤*AE, DC, MC, V* ⊘*Closed Sun. and Mon. No lunch.*

$$$–$$$$ ✕**D' Theeboom.** A favorite of the local French business community, this formal, Art Deco–stylish, and fairly priced purveyor of haute cuisine occupies a historic canal-side former cheese warehouse behind the Dam. The flavor of the dishes is only enhanced by the choices on the sophisticated wine list. Take a seat on the terrace on a sunny day, and you'll likely settle in for a long and happy linger. A three-course dinner costs €32.50. ⊠*Singel 210, Canal Ring* ☎*020/623–8420* ▤*AE, DC, MC, V* ⊘*No lunch.*

$$$–$$$$ ✕**Van de Kaart.** This sub-canal-level eatery with its peaceful dining room offers a savvy and stylish balancing of Mediterranean tastes. Though the menu is in continual flux, it may include shrimp sausages, octo-

2

pus with a salad of couscous, basil, and black olives, or a galantine of organic chicken with shiitake mushrooms. You can also opt for one of three surprise menus with matching wines (€37.50 for three courses, €44.50 for four courses, and €52.50 for five courses). Wine arrangements cost €5.50 per glass. ⊠*Prinsengracht 512, Canal Ring* ☎*020/625–9232* ▤*AE, DC, MC, V* ☺*Closed Sun. No lunch Sat.–Tues.*

★ **$$–$$$$** ✕**Envy.** This eatery offers a new take on dining in Amsterdam. The sleek, sexy furnishings are lit by low hanging spotlights. The menu is comprised of appetizer-sized dishes that can be shared by the whole table. Each of these dishes—including prawns and avocados with lemongrass and ravioli filled with baby spinach—are as gorgeously turned out as the waitstaff. The restaurant is perfect for foodies, as they can watch the chefs at work. ⊠*Prinsengracht 381, Canal Ring* ☎*020/344–6407* ⌾*Reservations essential* ▤*AE, DC, MC, V.*

$$–$$$ ✕**Pianeta Terra.** Marble-clad, intimate, and softly lighted, this restaurant has a menu that embraces the whole Mediterranean region (and that pays respect to vegetarians and organic farmers). The daily set menus are a sure bet, and may include carpaccio of swordfish with Pecorino cheese or octopus and mussels prepared in a traditionally Moroccan *tagine* (clay pot). The pasta, like the bread, is made on the premises from organic ingredients. ⊠*Beulingstraat 7, Canal Ring* ☎*020/626– 1912* ⌾*Reservations essential* ▤*AE, DC, MC, V* ☺*No lunch.*

★ **¢–$** ✕**Goodies.** Free from all pretension, this spaghetteria is merely out to serve homemade pastas, healthful salads, and tasty meat and fish dishes of the highest quality for the friendliest of prices. You will, however, be packed like a sardine at the wooden tables and benches (moved onto the street during warm weather). By day, Goodies switches modes and becomes a popular café serving filling sandwiches on wedges of hearty bread, plus salads and deliciously thick fruit shakes. Reservations are essential for dinner. ⊠*Huidenstraat 9, Canal Ring* ☎*020/625–6122* ▤*No credit cards.*

¢ ✕**Lust.** Before you get the wrong idea: "lust" is a much softer word in Dutch and suggests a calmer desire best translated as "appetite." And if you've worked up a lunchy one while wandering the Nine Streets specialty shopping area, this is a truly satiating place for healthful club sandwiches, pastas, and salads. There's a limited dinner menu, too, with entrées costing about €16. Be sure to visit the wacky washroom before you leave. ⊠*Runstraat 13, Canal Ring* ☎*020/626–5791* ▤*AE, DC, MC, V.*

WALL-O-FOOD

The ubiquitous **FEBO** snack bar chain serves patat (french fries) with a stunning variety of toppings (we like the satay sauce and mayo combo), along with mysterious-looking choices of deep-fried meats and cheeses. If you don't want to wait in line, buy your food right out of the wall. It's surprisingly fresh and like all things greasy, it tastes good.

EASTERN CANAL RING & REMBRANDTPLEIN

The Eastern Canal Ring and the Rembrandtplein are packed with some of the city's poshest restaurants. Main streets of culinary interest include upscale Utrechtsestraat, which takes you on an around-the-world culinary trip, and the lively Reguliersdwarsstraat, jammed with sidewalk cafés to satisfy your people-watching urge. Informally dubbed the city's "Gay Street," Reguliersdwarsstraat is as much known for its eateries as for its hip gay patrons.

¢–$$ ✕**Pygma-Lion.** The rather expensive dinner menu here reflects the exotic side of South African cuisine, by offering such exotic meats as crocodile, zebra (served as a minced sausage), and antelope along with a vast array of vegetarian options. The minimalist interior is actually quite small, so expect your conversations to be overheard by your proximate dining neighbors. ⊠*Nieuwe Spiegelstraat 5a, Canal Ring* ☎*020/420– 7022* ⌂*Reservations essential* ☱*MC, V* ☉*Closed Mon.*

$–$$$ ✕**Sluizer.** Sluizer is actually a twin restaurant with a bistrolike atmosphere that once upon a time served meat on one side and fish on the other. Now it's all united, and both areas remain simply decorated and completely unpretentious. Sluizer is known for simple food prepared without an excess of either fanfare or creativity. Because the prices are right and the service swift, it is crowded every night with a predominantly business and pre-theater crowd. ⊠*Utrechtsestraat 41–45, Canal Ring* ☎*020/622–6376* ☱*AE, DC, MC, V* ☉*No lunch.*

★ $–$$ ✕**Cineac.** In a former movie theater, Cineac is now a Chinese restaurant. The massive interior includes a first-floor cocktail bar and a round balcony called the Dragon Ring. The specialty here is small dishes. Even after 11 PM, when the kitchen officially closes, you can still order dim sum. Late at night, the place is transformed into a nightclub. Thursday the DJ plays sexy house, Friday is house with an electric twist, and Saturday is electro pop. ⊠*Reguliersbreestraat 31–33, Canal Ring* ☎*020/616–6664* ☱*AE, DC, MC, V.*

$$$$ ✕**Beddington's.** Although both the flavor and presentation of dishes here are decidedly French, many of chef Jean Beddington's creations hint at other influences: her youth spent in English country kitchens, the three years she spent mastering macrobiotic cooking in Japan, or any number of other influences she has gleaned from her culinary travels across the globe. The frequently changing menu is prepared with a feather-light touch. If you want to find out what the fuss is all about, reserve your table at least a week ahead. ⊠*Utrechtsedwarsstraat 141, Canal Ring* ☎*020/620–7393* ☱*AE, MC, V* ☉*Closed Sun. and Mon. No lunch.*

★ $$$–$$$$ ✕**Breitner.** Whether for romance or the pure enjoyment of fine contemporary dining, Breitner gets high marks. With a formal interior

2

of rich red carpeting and muted pastel colors, and a view across the Amstel River that takes in both the Muziektheater-Stadhuis (Music Theater–City Hall complex) and the grand Carre Theater, this spot serves French-inspired dishes, many of which pack a flavorful punch. The seasonal menu may include such starters as baked quail with goose liver and bacon, and entrées such as skate with Indonesian-style vegetables or smoked rib of beef with a sauce of whole-grain mustard and marinated vegetables. Foie gras, fabulous desserts, and an innovative wine list allow you to step into the realm of pure decadence. As to be expected, the service is flawless and the patrons do their part to reflect Breitner's high standards by dressing smartly. ⊠ *Amstel 212, Canal Ring* ☎ *020/627–7879* ⟁ *Reservations essential* ⊟ *AE, MC, V* ⊘ *Closed Sun., last wk of July, first wk of Aug. No lunch.*

$$$ ✕ **Janvier.** Located in a wooden church that once served as a stable for Napóleon's horses, Janvier has a patio overlooking a scenic square that's a perfect place to linger over wine. (There are 15 varieties offered by the glass.) The lunch menu includes salads, soups, and sandwiches, and dinner brings choices like saltimbocca, chicken cordon bleu, and various fondues. ⊠ *Amstelveld 12, Canal Ring* ☎ *020/626–1199* ⊟ *AE, DC, MC, V* ⊘ *Closed Mon.*

$$–$$$ ✕ **Tempo Doeloe.** For decades, this has been a safe and elegant—albeit somewhat cramped—place to indulge in that spicy smorgasbord of the gods, the Indonesian rice table. Stay alert when the waitstaff points out the hotness of the dishes; otherwise you might wind up having to down several gallons of antidotal *witbier* (a sweet local wheat beer). ⊠ *Utrechtsestraat 75, Canal Ring* ☎ *020/625–6718* ⟁ *Reservations essential* ⊟ *AE, DC, MC, V* ⊘ *No lunch.*

$–$$$ ✕ **Segugio.** Two local and long-respected Italian chefs came together a few years ago to open this temple to the taste buds—and they brought some of their ancient family recipes with them. The Venetian-style stucco walls give the dining room a rustic and genuine feel. In the summer you can have aperitifs on the patio, while in the winter you can request a table by the open fire. Foodies can try the chefs' five-course menu for €52.50. But making a choice from the main menu—perhaps sublime risotto of the day, or a roasted rabbit hopped up with capers and olives—is usually a sure bet, too. ⊠ *Utrechtsestraat 96, Canal Ring* ☎ *020/330–1503* ⟁ *Reservations essential* ⊟ *AE, DC, MC, V* ⊘ *Closed Sun. No lunch.*

$–$$ ✕ **An.** This long-popular Japanese eatery once offered only takeout; now you can linger over an evening meal along with some excellent plum wine (*umeshuu*). Although the menu focuses on sushi, the kitchen also offers fantastic baked tofu (*atsuage*) and some super-delicious *gyoza*—steamed or fried dumplings filled with veggies or seafood. You may still choose to forgo dining in the oddly Mediterranean–style dining room and take your meal to a nearby bench on the Amstel or to the green expanses of Saraphatipark. ⊠ *Weteringschans 76, Canal Ring* ☎ *020/624–4672* ⊟ *No credit cards* ⊘ *Closed Sun. and Mon. No lunch.*

$$ ✕ **Rose's Cantina.** Rose's does what it can to fill the Tex-Mex void in the Amsterdam dining market, serving heaping portions of tacos and burritos alongside daredevil margaritas. If you've got sensitive ears, consider bringing earplugs with you; the noise levels careen up the decibel scale. In summer you can sit in the gardens facing the backs of the stately mansions on the Herengracht. ✉ *Reguliersdwarsstraat 40, Canal Ring* ☎ *020/625–9797* 🖃 *AE, DC, MC, V* ⊘ *No lunch.*

$$–$$$$ ✗**Dynasty.** Although its name has nothing to do with the 1980s television show of the same name, this restaurant's regular clientele (showbiz types, football heroes dangling arm candy) does sometimes resemble a casting call for a soap opera. Although it's not required, you may want to dress up a bit when you come here. The interior is certainly fanciful: the Art Deco starting point blurs into an Asian frenzy of rice-paper umbrellas and golden Buddhas. In the summer, you should try for a table on the "dream terrace" set in a majestic Golden Age courtyard. Chef K. Y. Lee's menu, which is full of Cantonese, Thai, Malaysian, and Vietnamese culinary classics, is as ambitious as the décor; his drunken prawns (jumbo shrimp marinated in an intoxicating broth of Chinese herbs and Xiaoxing wine) are reliably excellent. ✉ *Reguliersdwarsstraat 30, Canal Ring* ☎ *020/626–8400* ⚔ *Reservations essential* 🖃 *AE, DC, MC, V* ⊘ *Closed Tues. No lunch.*

JORDAAN

Its maze of narrow streets lined with leaning gabled houses make the Jordaan a unique backdrop for lunch or dinner. Head for the so-called Nine Streets, where the roads are named after the animals whose pelts were once used in the city's tanning industry. The streets most heavily laden with eateries include Westerstraat and Lindengracht. (Don't look for a canal in the case of the latter one, as it has long been paved over.) Haarlemmerdijk is also a good bet.

★ $$ ✗**Café de Reiger.** This excellent neighborhood brown café ("brown" because of its nicotine-stained nature) has a long history of being packed with boisterous drinkers and diners. Its past is reflected in its tile tableaux and century-old fittings. The Dutch fare is of the bold meat-potato-vegetable variety, always wonderfully prepared and sometimes even with an occasional adventurous diversion, such as the sea bass tastily swimming in a sauce of fennel and spinach. At lunchtime there is a menu of sandwiches and warm snacks. ✉ *Nieuwe Leliestraat 34, Jordaan* ☎ *020/624–7426* ⚔ *Reservations not accepted* 🖃 *No credit cards* ⊘ *No lunch.*

$$ ✗**Cinema Paradiso.** This former art-house cinema has been reinvented as a designer eatery serving excellent starters—both the *bresaola* (an antipasto of air-dried salted beef that has been aged for two months, sliced thin, and moistened with olive oil and lemon) and *gambas* (prawns)

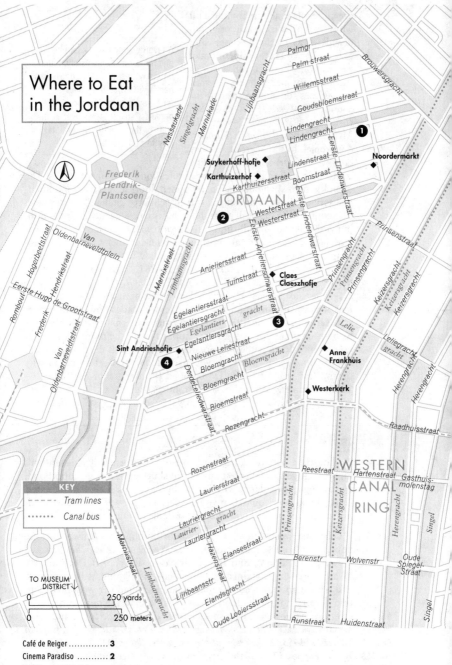

Where to Eat in the Jordaan

KEY

--- *Tram lines*

····· *Canal bus*

TO MUSEUM DISTRICT ↓

| 0 | 250 yards |
| 0 | 250 meters |

Café de Reiger **3**
Cinema Paradiso **2**
De Vliegende Schotel **4**
Toscanini **1**

are pure manna. But for the Full Montini, you can also choose from a wide array of simple pastas and pizzas. The restaurant doesn't take reservations, but you can linger at the pleasant bar while you wait (sometimes for quite a stretch) for a table. ⊠ *Westerstraat 184–186, Jordaan* ☏ *020/623–7344* ▤ *AE, MC, V* ⊘ *Closed Mon. No lunch.*

★ $$ ✕ **Toscanini.** In the heart of Amsterdam is this true-blue Florentine trattoria, a perennial favorite with professionals and media types. The open kitchen, skylighted ceiling, wooden floors and tables, and attentive service all work to create a sort of "country kitchen" atmosphere. The cooks pride themselves on their ability to create any regional dish, but you will undoubtedly find your favorite already listed on the extensive menu. The risottos are profound, the fish dishes sublime, the desserts decadent, and the wine list inspired. What more can one ask? ⊠ *Lindengracht 75, Jordaan* ☏ *020/623–2813* ⌖ *Reservations essential* ▤ *AE, DC, MC, V* ⊘ *Closed Sun. No lunch.*

¢ ✕ **De Vliegende Schotel.** The Flying Saucer has been providing tasty and inexpensive vegetarian fare for a couple of decades now. With buffet-style serving and a squatter's aesthetic, this is alternative Amsterdam at its best, one that you will grow to appreciate all the more if you wash your dinner down with some organic beer or wine. If the dining room's full or your need for spelt hits you around lunchtime, the more kitschy but no less vegan-friendly De Bolhoed (Prinsengracht 60, 020/626–1803), complete with patio, is but a short stroll away. ⊠ *Nieuwe Leliestraat 162, Jordaan* ☏ *020/625–2041* ▤ *AE, MC, V* ⊘ *No lunch.*

LEIDSEPLEIN

The bustling square called Leidseplein is the heart of Amsterdam's nightlife. It gets the shortest amount of shut-eye of any neighborhood, explaining its popularity with late-night munchers. Although the eateries on the square require that you dig deep in your wallet, the surrounding streets are packed with more affordable restaurants.

¢–$$ ✕ **Café Americain.** Though thousands of buildings in Amsterdam are designated historic monuments, few have their *interiors* landmarked as well. This one is, and for good reason: it's an Art Deco display of arched ceilings, stained glass, leaded-glass lamps, wall paintings, and a huge antique reading table. (Mata Hari had her wedding reception here.) Though the food is less notable than the decor (the menu offers everything from light snacks to full dinners), the coffee and cakes are always excellent. ⊠ *American Hotel, Leidsekade 97, Leidseplein* ☏ *020/624–5322* ⌖ *Reservations not accepted* ▤ *AE, DC, MC, V.*

$$–$$$ ✕ **Blue Pepper.** One of the city's most widely acclaimed restaurants,
Fodor'sChoice Blue Pepper features the inspired cooking of chef Sonja Pereira, whose
★ previous restaurant won her a Michelin star. You can order just about

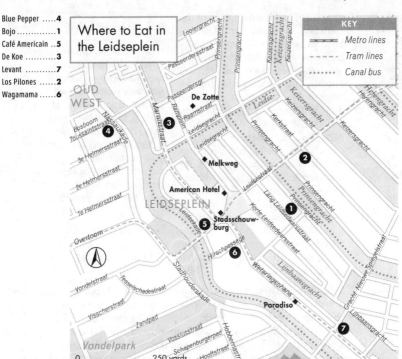

Where to Eat in the Leidseplein

KEY

━━ *Metro lines*
- - - *Tram lines*
······ *Canal bus*

anything and rest assured that it will be excellent. If you're lucky, the ever-changing menu might include *Kambing kecap*, where panfried tender pieces of lamb are cooked with lime leaves, lemongrass, garlic, soy sauce, and chili peppers. Unlike many other Indonesian restaurants, you won't have a thousand different dishes piled on your plate here—just a few obsessively prepared ones. There are full prix-fixe dinners (€40–€55) and a savvy selection of wines. Be warned: the price of a main course is deceiving, since you'll always be inspired to spend more than you planned. ⊠*Nassaukade 366, Leidseplein 1054 AB* ☎*020/489–7039* ⚭*Reservations essential* ▤*AE, DC, MC, V* ⊗*No lunch.*

★ ¢–$ ✕**Bojo.** There are plenty of mediocre late-night eateries around the Leidseplein, but the bambooed Bojo stands out for serving huge portions of enjoyable food. You'll find everything here, from *saté* (skewered and barbecued meats) to vegetarian *gado-gado* (vegetables drowned in a spicy peanut sauce) to the monumental rice table where dozens of different small dishes are served. Bojo is open until 2 AM during the week and 4 AM on the weekend. ⊠*Lange Leidsedwarsstraat 49–51, Leidseplein* ☎*020/622–7434* ▤*AE, DC, MC* ⊗*No lunch.*

$ ✕**Wagamama.** Though it may sound like an Italian restaurant run by a large-bottomed matriarch, this is actually a slick, minimalist eatery recalling a Japanese noodle shop. It's fresh, fast, and fairly cheap; just fill out a menu card and hand it to one of the waitstaff. Moments later, a hearty bowl of noodles and broth supplemented with your choice of meats, fish, and vegetables will arrive. Further sustenance comes in the form of fruit and vegetable shakes. ⊠*Max Euweplein 10, Leidseplein* ☎*020/528–7778* ⊟*AE, MC, V.*

¢–$ ✕**De Koe.** Downstairs at "The Cow," the cooks crowded into the tiny kitchen manage to pump out wonderfully prepared dishes. Despite the restaurant's name, the ever-changing menu tends to favor less beef and more fish and ostrich

> **BELLY UP TO THE BAR**
>
> Most local brown bars and cafés serve a range of snacks meant to be washed down with beer. *Bitterballen* (bitter balls—really just more dainty versions of croquettes), *kaas blokjes* (cheese blocks that are always served with mustard), and *vlammetjes* (pastry puffs filled with spicy beef and served with Thai sweet chili sauce) all work to keep your belly happy through to dinnertime.

(made with truffle sauce). The crowd here is largely local, casual, and friendly: you won't see any yuppies here. Upstairs from the café is an equally earthy and popular bar. ⊠*Marnixstraat 381, Leidseplein* ☎*020/625–4482* ⊟*AE, DC, MC, V* ⊙*No lunch.*

MEXICAN **$** ✕**Los Pilones.** Given how far Amsterdam is from Mexico, it may take a little courage for you to try this eatery's cactus salad (even though the main ingredient is happily de-spiked), or the popular Day of the Dead dish, enchiladas with mole (pronounced *moh*-lay and featuring a spicy chocolate-chili sauce). But even if these aren't the most authentic Mexican dishes you'll ever eat, the charming young staff and casual environment here are winners. Even better, the selection of tequilas is deliciously ample, and the margaritas have all the requisite bite and zest. ⊠*Kerkstraat 63, Leidseplein* ☎*020/320–4651* ⊟*AE, DC, MC, V* ⊙*Closed Mon. No lunch.*

☺ **$$** ✕**Levant.** Welcome to Istanbul Junior, where in a simple and modern setting you can indulge in grilled meats (and the appropriate firewaters with which to wash it all down). All the while, your children will invariably be entertained by the extraordinarily warm staff. This hidden treasure comes with a canal-side terrace (from which, on your way out, you can pay your respects to the bustling kitchen staff). Reservations are especially recommended. ⊠*Weteringschans 93, Leidseplein* ☎*020/662–5184* ⊟*MC, V* ⊙*Closed Sun. No lunch.*

MUSEUM DISTRICT

With such monuments to culture as the Rijksmuseum, the Van Gogh Museum, and the Concertgebouw, it's no surprise that this ultra-posh area attracts the suited and booted. In keeping with the upper-crust tone, you'll find some of the city's most critically acclaimed, and excruciatingly expensive, restaurants.

$$$–$$$$ ✕**Bodega Keyzer.** In the shadow of the golden lyre that tops the Concertgebouw (Concert Building), this institution has been serving musicians and concertgoers alike for almost a century. You can come here at

Where to Eat in the Museum District

KEY
----- Tram lines
······· Canal bus

almost any hour for anything from a drink or a full meal. The appropriately classical, dimly lighted Old Dutch interior—comfortable as an old shoe—is paneled with dark wood and spread with Oriental rugs. Aside from such relative oddities as *ris de veau* (veal sweetbreads) with orange and green-pepper sauce, the tournedos- and schnitzel-rich menu leans toward tradition, with a sole meunière being the house specialty. ✉ *Van Baerlestraat 96, Museum District* ☎ *020/675–1866* 🖃 *AE, DC, MC, V.*

$$–$$$ ✕ **Brasserie van Baerle.** If it's Sunday and you want to brunch on the holiest of trinities—blini, caviar, and champagne—look no further than this brasserie. The elegant modern decor and the professional yet personal service attracts a business crowd at lunch, as well as late-night diners still on an aesthetic roll after attending an event at the nearby Concert Building. The imaginative chef knows how to put on an inspired show with a fusion menu that includes both light and spicy Asian salads and heavier fare such as veal tartlet with sweetbreads, tongue, and winter truffles. There's outdoor dining when the weather cooperates. ✉ *Van Baerlestraat 158, Museum District* ☎ *020/679–1532* ✍ *Reservations essential* 🖃 *AE, DC, MC, V* ⊗ *No lunch Sat.*

☕ **¢–$** ✕ **KinderKookKafé.** Certainly the most child-friendly place in town, the "Children's Cooking Café" gives Dutch-language cooking lessons during the week, then has the kids running the place on weekends. It serves a simple, cheap, and healthful fixed menu. The decor is cheery, using the brightest colors in the paint box. ⊠ *Vondelpark 6, Museum District* ☎020/625–3257 ▤*No credit cards.*

$–$$$ ✕**Vakzuid.** Slightly off the beaten track, this sprawling bar-café-lounge-restaurant is in Section South of the still-new-looking 1928 Olympic Stadium, an architectural monument designed by one of the founders of De Stijl, Jan Wils. With its contemporary take on the functionally modern, Vakzuid fits right in. There's a huge, sunny patio (accessible by water taxi) with comfortable seating under umbrellas; a solo-friendly bar specializing in coffee and designer sandwiches by day and cocktails and sushi by night; a comfortable lounge area with a view over the track field; and a raised restaurant with an open kitchen serving a mix of Mediterranean and Asian cooking. Thursday through Saturday evenings see this spot transform into something resembling a nightclub, complete with noise, smoke, bouncers, and DJs. Reservations are essential for the restaurant. ⊠*Olympisch Stadion 35, Museum District* ☎020/570–8400 ⌂*Reservations essential* ▤*AE, DC, MC, V* ⊘*Closed Sun.*

¢   ✕**Bagels and Beans.** This low-key, bustling hot spot is just what the good doctor ordered: a wealth of fresh-made bagel choices, along with fresh juices and piping-hot coffee. There are two other locations (at Ferdinand Bolstraat 70 in the Pijp, and Keizersgracht 504 near Leidseplein), but the Museum District location wins out with its remarkably pleasant and peaceful back patio. ⊠*Van Baerlestraat 40, Museum District* ☎020/675–7050 ▤*AE, DC, MC, V* ⊘*No dinner.*

$–$$$ ✕**Sama Sebo.** This busy but relaxed neighborhood restaurant acts as a good, albeit not too adventurous, "Intro to Indo" course. Since 1969, Sama Sebo has been dishing out *rijsttafel,* a feast with myriad exotically spiced small dishes, in an atmosphere characteristically enhanced by rush mats and shadow puppets. There are also simpler dishes such as *bami goreng* (spicy fried noodles with vegetables or meat) and *nasi goreng* (the same, but with the noodles). At the bar, you can wait for your table while having a beer and getting to know the regulars. ⊠*P. C. Hooftstraat 27, Museum District* ☎020/662–8146 ⌂*Reservations essential* ▤*AE, DC, MC, V* ⊘*Closed Sun.*

$$$–$$$$ ✕**Le Garage.** This former garage is now a brasserie awash with red-plush seating and kaleidoscopically mirrored walls—handy for local glitterati who like to see and be seen. This is the home of the celebrity "Crazy Chef" Joop Braakhekke, whose busy schedule of TV appearances necessitates his leaving his kitchen in other—very capable—hands. The food is invariably excellent and uses French haute cuisine as its starting point. Particularly sublime is the Flemish *hennepotje,* a starter pâté of chicken, snails, and rabbit, and the Moroccan *pastilla d'anguille,* which seals a mélange of duck liver and eel in a thin pastry dough. Although champagnes, fine wines, and caviar accent the essential poshness of it all, the daily set lunch menu is quite reasonably priced. ⊠*Ruysdaelstraat 54, Museum District* ☎020/679–7176 ⌂*Reservations essential* ▤*AE, DC, MC, V* ⊘*No lunch weekends.*

★ $$ ✕**Bond.** Bond. Jan Bond. With its golden ceiling above and lush lamps, sofas, and sounds below, Bond is as double-oh-so-'70s as it is comfort-

2

A Dizzying Array

CLOSE UP

Holland's famed *rijsttafel*, or rice table, was the ceremonial feast of the Dutch colonists in Indonesia centuries ago. Partake of a serious one and you confront dozens of separate platters—platters, not just dishes—so you may act like its Thanksgiving and starve yourself for a day. When you sit down to face the dizzying array, put two spoonfuls of rice in the center of your plate and limit yourself to one small taste of everything. Otherwise, you're licked from the start.

If you're really ravenous, go for an appetizer of *soto ajam,* a clear chicken broth with rice noodles, or *loempia,* deep-fried rolls of bean sprouts, vegetables, and meat. After this, the staff will bring a number of hot plates, warmed by candles, to the table. The ritual of describing the dishes is a ceremony in itself. The dishes are often arranged according to their level of spiciness. Standard delights include *saté,* a skewer of bite-size morsels of *babi* (pork) or *ajam* (chicken), drenched in a rich peanut sauce.

What else will be served? *Gado-gado* is a mix of cold, cooked vegetables, also in peanut sauce. *Seroendeng,* a mix of fried coconut and peanuts, or *sayur lodeh,* vegetables cooked in coconut milk, can help take the bite out of peppery spiciness. *Daging* is meat, often beef, stewed lovingly in no fewer than 11 spices. *Bali* is the name for dishes made with *sambal,* a red chili–based sauce with a bite, which may be used for meats and fish such as mackerel.

ably experimental. Ditto for the dinner menu, which darts from braised rabbit to steak grilled with heirloom mushrooms to fish roasted with corn, wild parsnips, and oranges. Being close to the similarly gilded Concert Building, Bond can also be a great location for, say, a post-Rossini martini. Lunchtime sees things a tad more restrained, with choices running more along the lines of club sandwiches and decidedly non-McDonald's-like caesar salads. ⊠ *Valeriusstraat 128b, Museum District* ☎ *020/676–4647* ☐ *MC, V.*

$–$$ ✕ **Pulpo.** This trendy hot spot suggests a simple Italian trattoria at first glance—until, that is, you notice the '70s shag carpeting covering the walls. The surprises continue, thanks to Pulpo's remarkable friendliness and reasonable prices. So, settle back, groove to jazzy tunes, and splash some Mediterranean sunshine down with a glass of fine Italian wine. The main courses are simple but always top-notch—few can resist the signature marinated squid with *rucola* (arugula) and lime, or the ever-popular candied duck. And if you arrive before 6:45 PM, a three-course, preconcert menu will set you back only €26. ⊠ *Willemsparkweg 87, Museum District* ☎ *020/676–0700* ☐ *AE, DC, MC, V* ☉ *No lunch Sun.*

THE PIJP

Loud, proud, and bohemian, the Pijp is all things to all people. The original occupants of this staunchly working class area are still around, though they are dwindling in numbers as the area becomes increasingly pricey. Today you'll see more upwardly mobile types, as well as mem-

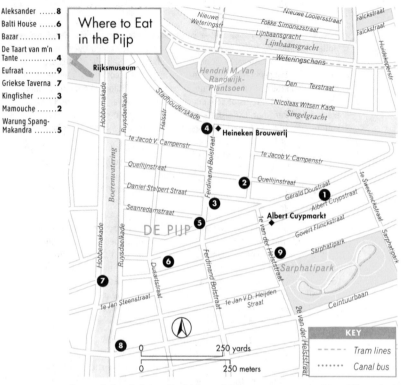

bers of the thriving Turkish and Moroccan communities. The mix is mirrored in the choice of dining options, so you can grab a roti, a bowl of soto ayam, or a plate of seafood linguine.

$$ ✕ **De Taart van m'n Tante.** Looking like the set of a children's television program, "My Aunt's Cake" has funky tables covered with wacky and colorful pies and cakes. Quiche is the menu's only savory option. ⊠ *Ferdinand Bolstraat 10, The Pijp* ☎ *020/776–4600* ⊟ *No credit cards* ☉ *No dinner.*

$$–$$$ ✕ **Aleksander.** With walls dense with knickknacks and paintings evoking the Balkans, this Dalmatian grill sums up the often forgotten spirit of this region, where hospitality and food—particularly grilled meats and fish—reign supreme. Walking in, you may be offered a complimentary shot of the house *slivovitz,* a plum-based hard liquor. Unless you want to rent the whole restaurant for a celebration, things remain fairly quiet here: the clientele is mostly mature locals out for a quiet evening and to take advantage of the three-course daily special for €15. ⊠ *Ceintuurbaan 196, The Pijp* ☎ *020/676–6384* ⊟ *AE, MC* ☉ *No lunch.*

$ ✕ **Griekse Taverna.** You won't find souvlaki or gyros here; nor will you find the activity of plate throwing as a *digestif* (as you will at the neighboring I Kriti [⊠ *Balthasar Floriszstraat 3,* ☎ *020/664–1445*]). But this woody and comfortable taverna does win points for its late hours (it's open until midnight) and its excellent, affordable, and fresh herbed starters (€4.80/plate), which are brought to your table en masse for you to choose from. Since these easily make a full meal, you won't have to worry about choosing one of their grilled main dishes until your inevitable next visit. ⊠*Hobbemakade 64/65, The Pijp* ☎*020/671–7923* ⊟*No credit cards* ⊘*No lunch.*

2

$–$$ ✕ **Balti House.** If you find yourself craving curry, the dishes at this excellent purveyor of Indian cuisine have an actual subtle variance in flavors as opposed to unsubtle variance in tongue-blistering potential. Some of their more addictive choices are any one of their soups or tandooris, the butter chicken, the garlic naan bread, and the homemade *kulfi* ice cream. The patio's a lovely place to sit when the sun is out. ⊠*Albert Cuypstraat 41, The Pijp* ☎*020/470–8917* ⊟*AE, MC, V* ⊘*No lunch.*

¢–$ ✕ **Warung Spang-Makandra.** The Indonesian-inspired food at this local favorite includes *loempias* (egg rolls of sorts). You can also try Javanese *rames*—a mini–rice table–style smorgasbord on a plate. The dressed-down decor might remind you of a snack bar, but the staff is friendly and the food is tasty. No wonder the place is always busy. ⊠*Gerard Doustraat 39, The Pijp* ☎*020/670–5081* ⊟*No credit cards.*

$ ✕ **Kingfisher.** For a taste of the area's reinvented café culture, check out Kingfisher, a long, narrow eatery frequented by a hip young crowd. The stellar kitchen pumps out sandwiches by day and an inventive and inexpensive daily special for dinner at night. Situated on a corner, it's a great spot for people-watching. ⊠*Ferdinand Bolstraat 23, The Pijp* ☎*020/671–2395* ⊟*No credit cards.*

$–$$ ✕ **Eufraat.** A mecca to fans of Eastern food, Eufraat serves lamb-based soups and homemade breads that are a meal in themselves. Dishes like minced veal in a yogurt sauce bear such poetic names as the Garden of Babel. The tasty entrées, which include many vegetarian options—make up for the sparse interior. ⊠*1e Van der Helststraat 72, The Pijp* ☎*020/672–0579* ⊟*AE, DC, MC, V.*

$ ✕ **Bazar.** A golden-angel-capped church provides the singular setting for this kitsch-addled restaurant. Cheap and flavorful North African cooking covering the range from falafel to mixed grilled meats is served here in an atmosphere of convivial chaos. Since it's located alongside the country's largest outdoor market, Bazar is also the perfect place to break for coffee in between rounds of market wandering. ⊠*Albert Cuypstraat 182, The Pijp* ☎*020/675–0544* ⊟*AE, DC, MC, V.*

$$ ✕ **Mamouche.** All signs of this location's past as a Hell's Angels bar have been erased; it's now a North African teahouse that takes delight in the smallest details. Romantic and posh, this spot has been a hit with locals for dishes such as couscous with saffron-baked pumpkin. Chocoholics will say a heartfelt amen when rounding off their meal with the Ahram, a dark, mysterious pyramid embellished with a nut caramel sauce. ⊠*Quelijnstraat 104, The Pijp* ☎*020/673–6361* ⊟*MC, V* ⊘*No lunch.*

FodorsChoice ★

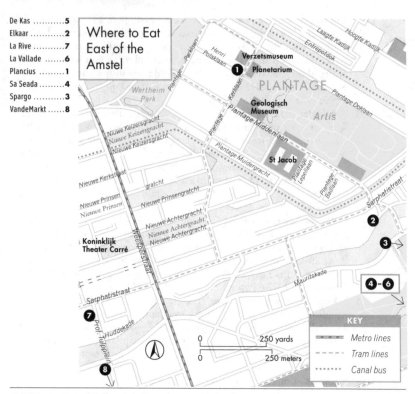

Where to Eat
East of the
Amstel

EAST OF AMSTEL

Head away from the historical center, east of the Amstel River, and toward the tranquil neighborhood known as the Plantage for a truly leisurely meal. The areas around the Hortus Botanicus and the Tropenmuseum are home to some of the nicest places for a leisurely meal.

★ $$ ✕ **Plancius.** With its arty but calming leather-walled interior, Plancius offers a refreshing sense of space after the chaos of the Artis zoo or the cramped exhibits at the Resistance Museum. After breakfast and lunch service, things get kicked up a notch in the evenings, when a fashionable and convivial crowd comes to hobnob. The superb menu is adventurous, mixing and matching everything from Italian *panzarotti* (a folded-over pizza of sorts) to Indian lentil soup to fish steaks with teriyaki and tahini sauce. Everything is made from scratch, right down to the tapenade. ⊠ *Plantage Kerklaan 61a, East of Amstel* ☎ *020/330–9469* ☐ *AE, DC, MC, V.*

$–$$ ✕ **Spargo.** This funky neighborhood eatery always draws a crowd
FodorśChoice   despite its slightly off-the-beaten-path location. A nicely executed menu
★   features such dishes as lamb *tajine* (stew), roasted trout, and entrecote from the neighborhood butcher. The waitstaff, ever ready with a toothy grin, is among the most attractive and friendly in the city. In the sum-

CLOSE UP

Say "Cheese"

To say that the Dutch like cheese is like saying the Italians are partial to pasta. The Dutch have long been known as *kaas-koppen*, or "cheese heads," and not only is it true that they love the stuff, they positively live for it as a glimpse into a local supermarket will attest. Shelves are piled floor to ceiling with cheeses of all colors, shapes, and forms: sliced, diced, grated, or in giant wheels.

The best-known Dutch cheeses are Gouda and Edam. Gouda is traditionally produced in wheels, but today you can also find it in squares and blocks. A young Gouda has a creamy flavor and soft consistency, but as it matures its acquires a more robust flavor and firmer texture. Gouda made with herbs is now popular in Holland, with the cumin seed variety especially pleasing to the palate.

The round shape and bright red color of Edam makes it instantly recognizable even to those with just a passing interesting in cheese. Yet fewer people know that Edam can also wear a yellow or even a black coat. Whatever the color, its appearance is obtained by spraying the cheese with wax to form a protective layer. Edam is very mild, with slightly salty or nutty flavors. Calorie counters rejoice at the thought of Edam, since it is made with low-fat milk. Those in the know recommend the pairing of Edam and dark beer. Naturally, this negates any savings of calories.

Other popular Dutch cheeses include Leyden, which, like Edam, is made with skimmed milk; Frisian Clove, a firm-textured cheese spiced with cumin; the hole-ridden Maasdam; and the orange-rimmed Kernbem.

---

mer you can wine and dine on the sunny terrace. ⊠ *Linnaeusstraat 37a, East of Amstel 1093 EG* ☎ *020/694–1140* 🖃 *AE, DC, MC, V.*

★ **$$$–$$$$** ✕**La Rive.** Located within the Amstel Inter-Continental Hotel—the lodging of choice for royalty, dignitaries, and rock stars—La Rive is the city's unparalleled purveyor of refined French and Mediterranean cuisines. The setting is chic, with views over the river and formal service that is solicitous but not stuffy. If you don't mind emptying your wallet, settle in for one of the two equally succulent five-course choices on offer, priced at €85 and €97.50. Terrine of Jabugo ham with goose liver is a typical starter, and main courses reflect a marked truffle fetish (the turbot and truffle wrapped in potato spaghetti is a much-lauded dish). A meatier choice is the roasted rack of lamb enriched with pulverized rillettes of lamb shoulder, curry, and ginger. You'll need to book two weeks ahead to guarantee a table. ⊠ *Amstel Inter-Continental Hotel, Professor Tulpplein 1, East of Amstel* ☎ *020/520–3264* ⟁ *Reservations essential. Jacket and tie* 🖃 *AE, DC, MC, V* ⊙ *Closed Sun. No lunch Sat.*

★ **$$$** ✕**Elkaar.** In a white-and-red corner building, this new addition to the dining scene is easy to spot. The dark-wood paneling, pressed linen tablecloths, and knowledgeable waitstaff conspire to make a visit feel like a special occasion. And the French-influenced specialties—prawns with celery, sea bass in a mussel broth, and entrecote in red wine sauce—don't disappoint. In summer you can dine alfresco. ⊠ *Alexanderplein 6, East of Amstel* ☎ *020/330–7559* 🖃 *AE, DC, MC, V.*

$–$$$ ✕**Sa Seada.** Named after a Sardinian dish, this slightly out-of-the-way eatery near Ooster Park has some of the best pizza and calzones in town (including one particularly *delizioso* number with ricotta cheese). It also sports a great patio if things inside get a little too cozy. It's just a shame that European Union regulations no longer allow the importing of the famed Sardinian worm cheese. It's not only a crime against cheese plates everywhere, but also prevents this place from being the ultimate in authenticity. But here we can blame the EU, and not this wonderful little treasure. ✉*1e Oosterparkstraat 3–5, East of Amstel* ☎*020/663–3276* ⌕*Reservations essential* ☰*AE* ⊘*Closed Tues. No lunch.*

★ **$$$$** ✕**De Kas.** This 1926-built municipal "greenhouse" must be the ultimate workplace for chefs: they can begin the day picking the best and freshest of homegrown produce before building an inspired Mediterranean menu around them. For diners it's equally sumptuous, especially since the setting includes two very un-Dutch commodities—lots of light and a giddy sense of vertical space, thanks to the glass roof. The frequently changing set menu always consists of a selection of small starters, followed by a main course and a dessert; you can also opt for the whole hog on the chef's table, which will set you back €125, including wine. Don't miss out on the house cocktail: champagne with lemon basil. ✉*Kamerlingh Onnelaan 3, East of Amstel* ☎*020/462–4562* ⌕*Reservations essential* ☰*AE, DC, MC, V* ⊘*Closed Sun. No lunch Sat.*

$$$ ✕**La Vallade.** A candlelit, cozy atmosphere and revered country cooking inspire many to take Tram 9 to this outlying restaurant on the Ringdijk, the city's perimeter dike. Every night a new four-course menu is posted, for just €30, the only constant being a diverse cheese board. A lovely terrace in the summer slightly increases the chances of being able to book a table. ✉*Ringdijk 23, East of Amstel* ☎*020/665–2025* ☰*No credit cards* ⊘*No lunch.*

★ **$$** ✕**VandeMarkt.** "From the Market" truly defines the food here: each course of the day's three- (€36) or four- (€43) course feast is made from the freshest ingredients found at the market that morning. As such, the menu might include anything from a lobster bisque with prawn wontons to wild duck with sage sauce. (Often, dishes exhibit an Asian touch.) The setting is sleek and up-to-the-minute trendy, with simple pine floors contrasting with brightly colored walls. ✉*Schollenbrugstraat 8–9, East of Amstel* ☎*020/468–6958* ⌕*Reservations essential* ☰*AE, DC, MC, V* ⊘*Closed Sun., 3 wks in July and Aug. No lunch.*

Where to Stay

WORD OF MOUTH

"I prefer the Leidseplein area in the southwestern part of the city. It is near many of the museums and the Vondelpark, and is a major public transportation hub. It is not as seedy as the area near the train station. Lots of hotels and restaurants. Also a good location from which to wander the canals."
—smueller

"We stayed in the Western Canal Ring, near the Jordaan, and really liked that area. It is more residential with plenty of bars, restaurants, and boutiques, and easy walking distance to many other parts of the city."

—ms_go

Updated by
Nicole Chabot

A 17TH-CENTURY CANAL-HOUSE GUEST ROOM: Late-morning sunshine streams through a drift of tulle curtains; outside the window floats a Vermeer-worthy view of the Keizersgracht, the most elegant of Amsterdam's canals. After lolling under crisp sheets, the down-stuffed duvet, and a bed canopy, you get ready to face the day by heading for breakfast, stepping down the steep and narrow canal-house stairway. You enter a breakfast nook that is the epitome of *gezellig,* a term that embodies the notions of coziness, comfort, and pleasure. The table is set with ham, rolls, jams, and cheeses, and the lady serving you is as courteous as the *ontbijtkoek* (gingerbread cake) is velvety and rich.

If you consider your hotel an integral part of your travel experience—not simply somewhere to spend the night—then staying in one of Amsterdam's registered historic monuments-turned-guesthouses is a true thrill. These lovely gabled buildings, which often overlook canals and have carefully tended gardens, allow you to intimately experience this city's rich sense of history—from the inside.

Of course, not everyone likes the idea of beaming themselves back to the 17th century, so it's good that Amsterdam is equally famous for its sleekly modern, ultra-designed hotels catering to savvy business types. And for those who'd rather combine some historic charm with present-day amenities, there are also a few top places (like the Dylan Amsterdam and the Pulitzer) that combine the best of the old and the new. These properties offer a kind of *trompe l'oeil* experience: the exteriors are historic, but their interiors are all high-gloss and luxury. No matter where you stay, though, chances are your room will have been scrubbed only hours, or minutes, before your arrival. In the world of Amsterdam accommodations, cleanliness is truly next to godliness.

WHAT IT COSTS IN EUROS				
	¢	$	$$	$$$	$$$$
HOTELS	under €75	€75–€120	€120–€165	€165–€230	over €230

Prices are for two people in a standard double room in high season, including the 6% VAT (value-added tax).

THE OLD CITY CENTER (HET CENTRUM)

If you want to stay in the heart of Amsterdam, head for the area surrounding Dam Square. Its bustling crowds mean you'll always have company. The adjacent Red Light District may cast a less-than-rosy glow, but this part of Amsterdam is a must-see area that remains one of the city's most historic neighborhoods.

$$$$
Fodor's Choice
★

Grand Amsterdam Sofitel Demeure. For captivating elegance, nothing tops the facade of the Grand, with its Neoclassical courtyard, white sash windows, carved marble pediments, and roof abristle with chimneys and gilded weather vanes. If it seems lifted from a Rembrandt painting, that's because this hotel's celebrated city-center site has a long and varied history: it was built in the 14th century as a convent, then went on to house the offices of the Amsterdam Admiralty. After being rezoned by Napoléon, it became Amsterdam's city hall from 1808 to 1988, and then finally reopened in 1992 as one of the city's most deluxe hotels, where guests like Mick Jagger and President Jacques Chirac of France have made their home-away-from-home. The guest rooms here feature traditional-luxe furniture, fine fabrics, and quiet hues, plus every manner of business mod con. The Café Roux, an oak-and-black-trim Art Deco–ish brasserie, sports a Karel Appel mural and some of the most stylish French dishes in town. The Admiralty, a more casual nook that opens out onto a glorious garden, is a great place to enjoy afternoon tea. **Pros:** beautiful courtyard, variety of dining options, a good chance of spotting a celebrity. **Cons:** run-down neighborhood, rather noisy location. ⊠ *Oudezijds Voorburgwal 197, 1012 EX, Centrum* ☏ *020/555–3111* ⊕ *www.thegrand.nl* ✆ *129 rooms, 37 suites, 16 apartments* ⟁ *In-room: safe, kitchen (some), refrigerator (some), DVD (some), VCR (some), dial-up, Wi-Fi (some). In-hotel: restaurant, room service, bar, pool, gym, spa, bicycles, laundry service, concierge, public Internet, public Wi-Fi, parking (fee), no-smoking rooms* ▭ *AE, DC, MC, V.*

$$$$ ✕⊞**Grand Hotel Amrâth Amsterdam.** Perfect for anyone into Amsterdam School–style architecture and design (basically art nouveau, but more sober), or looking for quiet luxury without unnecessary extravagance. Originally the office for the major Dutch shipping companies, the appropriately called "Shipping House" (Scheepvaarthuis) was reopened as the Amrâth Hotel in June 2007, after a massive renovation. Fortunately, almost all the original owners' symbols, sculptures, wood paneling and stained glass art remain even the furniture, wallpaper patterns and signage. While the rooms themselves are everything you would expect, the public areas lack the grandeur often found in five-star hotels. The atmosphere may be studiously restrained but the service is friendly, professional, and prompt. Across from the Centraal Station and around the corner from the Red Light District, the Amrâth offers well-heeled customers a genuine Amsterdam experience. **Pros:** architecturally unique, intimate, impressive wellness center. **Cons:** modest public areas, small bar, diminutive entrance. ⊠ *Prins Hendrik-kade 108, 1011 AK, Centrum* ☏ *020/552–0000* ⊕ *www.amratham-sterdam.com* ✆ *142 rooms, 22 suites* ⟁ *In-room: safe, refrigerator (some), DVD (some), VCR (some), dial-up, Wi-Fi. In-hotel: restaurant, room service, bar, spa, laundry service, concierge, public Internet, public Wi-Fi, no-smoking rooms* ▭ *AE, DC, MC, V.*

$$$$ ✕⊞**Hotel Amsterdam–De Roode Leeuw.** On the corner of Dam Square and across from the city's leading department store, De Bijenkorf, the Hotel is a cut above the rest of the competition on the Damrak. The front guest rooms, showcasing the elegant 18th-century facade, have soundproof window that serve as a buffer to the outside

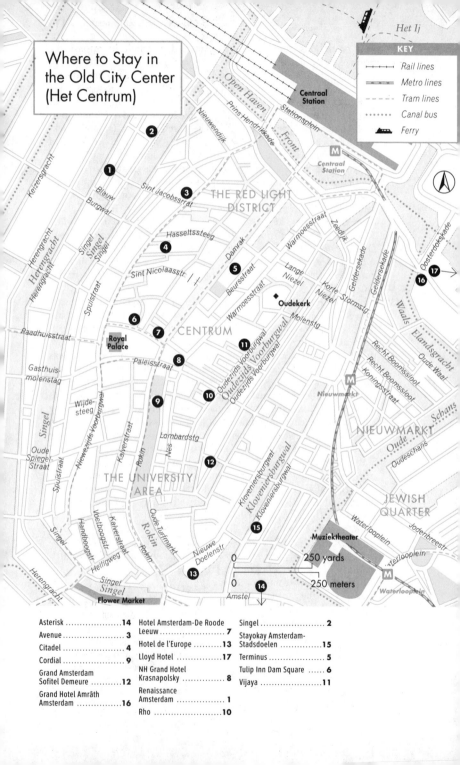

Where to Stay in the Old City Center (Het Centrum)

KEY

Rail lines
Metro lines
Tram lines
Canal bus
Ferry

Het Ij

Open Haven Front

Centraal Station

Stationsplein

Centraal Station

THE RED LIGHT DISTRICT

Nieuwendijk

Prins Hendrikkade

Sint Jacobsstraat

Hasseltssteeg

Sint Nicolaasstr

Damrak

Beursstraat

Warmoesstraat

Lange Niezel

Korte Niezel

Oudekerk

Molenstg

Zeedijk

Gelderskade

Geldersekade

Oosterdokskade

Waals

Elandsgracht

Oude Waal

CENTRUM

Oudezijds Voorburgwal

Oudezijds Voorburgwal

Oudezijds Voorburgwal

Recht Boomssloot

Recht Boomssloot

Koningsstraat

Nieuwmarkt

NIEUWMARKT

Oude Schans

Oudeschans

Schans

Royal Palace

Paleisstraat

Raadhuisstraat

Gasthuis-molensteg

Wijde-steeg

Spuistraat

Keizersgracht

Herengracht

Herengracht

Herengracht

Singel

Singel

Singel

Blauw Burgwal

Nieuwezijds Voorburgwal

Kalverstraat

Rokin

Nes

Lombardstg

THE UNIVERSITY AREA

Oude Turfmarkt

Rokin

Kalverstraat

Voetboogstr

Handboogstr

Heiligweg

Nieuwe Doelenstr

Oude Spiegel-Straat

Spuistraat

Singel

Singel

Herengracht

Singel

Flower Market

Amstel

Kloveniersburgwal

Kloveniersburgwal

Kloveniersburgwal

Muziektheater

Waterlooplein

Waterlooplein

Waterlooplein

Jodenbreestr

JEWISH QUARTER

0   250 yards

0   250 meters

Asterisk **14**	Hotel Amsterdam-De Roode Leeuw **7**
Avenue **3**	Hotel de l'Europe **13**
Citadel **4**	Lloyd Hotel **17**
Cordial **9**	NH Grand Hotel Krasnapolsky **8**
Grand Amsterdam Sofitel Demeure **12**	Renaissance Amsterdam **1**
Grand Hotel Amrâth Amsterdam **16**	Rho **10**

Singel **2**	
Stayokay Amsterdam-Stadsdoelen **15**	
Terminus **5**	
Tulip Inn Dam Square **6**	
Vijaya **11**	

world. The rooms at the back or on the "executive floor" are also safe bets. The hotel's restaurant, De Roode Leeuw, has built up a sizable following thanks to its heated terrace, Dutch haute cuisine, and encyclopedic champagne list. It was the recipient of the coveted *Neerlands Dis* (Netherlands' Dish) award, and serves a succulent roast Gelderland chicken in tarragon sauce, as well as an array of *stampots* (hotchpotches) made with smoked sausage, beef steak, and bacon. **Pros:** easy access to transportation, central location, excellent restaurant. **Cons:** small lobby, lackluster room decor. ⊠*Damrak 93–94, 1012 LP, Centrum* ☎*020/555–0666* ⊕*www.hotelamsterdam.nl* ⬩*79 rooms, 2 suites* ⬩*In-room: safe, refrigerator, Ethernet, dial-up. In-hotel: restaurant, laundry service, concierge, public Internet, public Wi-Fi, some pets allowed, no-smoking rooms* ☰*AE, DC, MC, V.*

★ $$$$ ☷ **Hotel de l'Europe.** Owned by Freddy Heineken's daughter, Charlene de Carvalho, this quiet, gracious, and plush hotel has a history extending back to 1638 (although its delightful, storybook facade dates only to the 19th century). Overlooking the Amstel River, the Muntplein, and the Flower Market, it may be familiar to those who remember the setting of Hitchcock's *Foreign Correspondent*. The chandeliered lobby leads off to the lounge, aglow with gold-trimmed ceiling coves and blackamoor lamps—the perfect setting for high tea (served in full glory here). Guest rooms are furnished with reserved, classical elegance: the city-side rooms are full of warm, rich colors; riverside rooms are in brilliant whites and have French windows. All have Victorian-style draperies as canopies over the beds. The restaurant's fine French food is ooh-la-la. **Pros:** Statuesque building, cozy bar serving free snacks, balconies perfect for people-watching. **Cons:** Cavernous yet largely unused lobby area, outdated room furnishings. ⊠*Nieuwe Doelenstraat 2–8, 1012 CP, Centrum* ☎*020/531–1777* ⊕*www.leurope.nl* ⬩*77 rooms, 23 suites* ⬩*In-room: safe, kitchen (some), refrigerator, Wi-Fi. In-hotel: 2 restaurants, room service, bar, pool, gym, spa, bicycles, laundry service, concierge, public Internet, public Wi-Fi, parking (fee), some pets allowed, no-smoking rooms* ☰*AE, DC, MC, V.*

$$$$ ☷ **NH Grand Hotel Krasnapolsky.** Until the Hilton came along, this hotel was Holland's biggest. As you'll see when you take a table in the Kras's soaringly beautiful Wintertuin (Winter Garden), Amsterdam's loveliest place for luncheon, it was also one of the best. Sitting in this masterpiece of 19th-century allure, replete with potted palms, greenhouse roof, Victorian chandeliers, and buffet tables stocked with cakes and roses, will make you feel like a countess or duke. Sadly, the rest of this 1866 landmark isn't as impressive. Unfortunately, a mishmash of revamping over the years was done with a progressively penurious attitude toward living space. Last renovated in 2003, the guest rooms—now numbering more than 468—vary greatly in size and tend toward disappointingly serviceable functionality. There are some memorable dining spots here, however; you can linger over a *jenever* gin cocktail at the Proeflokaal Wynand Fockink (Tasting House Wynand Fockink), dine in France, or feast on Japanese delights at the Edo teppanyaki restaurant. **Pros:** well situated on the Dam Square, great view of Royal Palace, near transportation. **Cons:** garagantuan size, impersonal feel. ⊠*Dam 9, 101*

JS, Centrum ☎*020/554–9111* ⊕*www.nh-hotels.com* ⤶*426 rooms, 7 suites, 35 apartments* ⟳*In-room: safe, kitchen (some), refrigerator, Wi-Fi. In-hotel: 3 restaurants, room service, bar, gym, spa, bicycles, laundry service, concierge, public Internet, public Wi-Fi, parking (fee), some pets allowed, no-smoking rooms* ▤*AE, DC, MC, V.*

☾ **$–$$$$**

Fodor's Choice

★

Lloyd Hotel. From the outside, the Art Deco–style Lloyd Hotel looks slightly severe, but its appearance fits with its history. Built in 1921 as a hotel for Eastern European immigrants, it then became a prison, then a detention center, before finally emerging as accommodations for artists. The vast café-cum-lobby is effortlessly stylish, with colossal white walls and plenty of natural light streaming in through windows. Its rooms are quirkily and almost all uniquely designed, with unusual furniture that has been featured in many fashion magazine spreads. One of the funkiest lodging choices is the "rough music room," with its log cabin–style walls, bed big enough for eight, and lime-green bathroom. Most rooms have extra-large tables, grand pianos, and kitchens. The hotel includes a cultural embassy, which, according to hotel literature, "offers a total service package, giving personal advice, obtaining tickets for theatrical performances, or arranging an informal encounter with a kindred spirit." Clearly, the Lloyd is unconventional. **Pros:** Historic building, quirky interior, rooms priced for all budgets. **Cons:** Out-of-the-way location, some of the more popular rooms are difficult to reserve. ⊠*Oostelijke Handelskade 34, 1019 BN, Eastern Docklands* ☎*020/561–3636* ⊕*www.lloydhotel. com* ⤶*117 rooms, 16 with shared bath, 14 suites* ⟳*In-room: no a/c, kitchen (some), no TV. In-hotel: restaurant, room service, bar, laundry service, concierge, public Internet, public Wi-Fi, parking (fee), no-smoking rooms* ▤*AE, MC, V.*

$$$

Renaissance Amsterdam. It's not every day that a 17th-century church is part of a hotel, but an underground passage connects the Renaissance with the domed Koepelkerk, an erstwhile Lutheran church that now serves as this hotel's conference center. Smack-dab in the middle of the Centrum (city center), between Dam Square and Centraal Station, this ultramodern hotel's top floors provide panoramic views of the city. Another high point is the hotel's highly popular fitness center, Splash, where you can have a complete workout or relax with a massage, steam bath, whirlpool, or sauna. The soaring lobby is basically modern, trimmed out with wood and equipped with wireless Internet access. **Pros:** a stone's throw from Centraal Station, on a charming thoroughfare. **Cons:** basic rooms, corridors resemble university residence halls. ⊠*Kattengat 1, 1012 SZ, Centrum* ☎*020/621–2223* ⊕*www.renaissancehotels.com* ⤶*375 rooms, 6 suites, 24 apartments* ⟳*In-room: safe (some), refrigerator, Ethernet, dial-up, Wi-Fi. In-hotel: 2 restaurants, room service, bar, gym, laundry service, concierge, executive floor, public Internet, parking (fee), no-smoking rooms* ▤*AE, DC, MC, V.*

★ **$$$**

Tulip Inn Dam Square. Just around the corner from the Royal Palace, this hotel is a surprisingly quiet oasis, because of its location on a narrow, pedestrians-only street. The Amsterdam School–style building is adorned with storybook-ornate brick and stone trim and a gabled roof; inside, rooms are modern and comfortable with terra-cotta and dark green furnishings. The building once housed a liquor distillery, and you can still enjoy a visit to the tasting house next door. A nice plus here is the hotel's level of service—at times, the staff coddles you. It's no surprise that visitors return again and again. **Pros:** gorgeous building, on a meandering lane just off Dam Square. **Cons:** rooms fill up fast, can be hard to find. ⊠ *Gravenstraat 12–16, 1012 NM, Centrum* ☎ *020/623-3716* ⊕ *www.tulipinndamsquare.com* ➽ *38 rooms, 1 suite* ⟨△⟩ *In-room: Wi-Fi. In-hotel: bar, laundry service, public Internet, no-smoking rooms* ☰ *AE, DC, MC, V* ⟨⦿⟩ *CP.*

$$–$$$ ⊞ **Singel.** The three renovated 17th-century canal houses that make up this property are charmingly lopsided and quirky-looking, with cheerful, striped window canopies. The historic exterior belies the modern furnishings and comforts you'll discover within, which include an elevator and express ironing and shoeshine service. If you want a view of the Singel canal, book a front or side room. From the hotel, it's just a short stroll to the Kalvertoren and Magna Plaza shopping malls, as well as the Dam Square. **Pros:** near Amsterdam's best restaurants and bars, lovely facade, doting service. **Cons:** often noisy on weekends, not all rooms have views. ⊠ *Singel 13–17, 1012 VC, Centrum* ☎ *020/626–3108* ⊕ *www.singelhotel.nl* ➽ *32 rooms* ⟨△⟩ *In-room: no a/c, safe, dial-up, Wi-Fi. In-hotel: room service, bar, laundry service, public Wi-Fi, some pets allowed, no-smoking rooms* ☰ *AE, DC, MC, V* ⟨⦿⟩ *CP.*

$–$$$ ⊞ **Citadel.** Set in a spiffy brick seven-story building, and topped with a jaunty two-story mansard roof, the Citadel is on a busy main street near the Royal Palace, Dam Square, and the Magna Plaza shopping mall. Rooms at the back of the building are quieter, but top-floor rooms at the front provide a sweeping view of gabled rooftops. All are furnished no-frills style, with modern wood furniture and patterned upholstery. **Pros:** lovely building, a stone's throw from sights like the Anne Frank House. **Cons:** rooms devoid of charm, no particular Dutch flavor. ⊠ *Nieuwezijds Voorburgwal 98–100, 1012 SG, Centrum* ☎ *020/627–3882* ⊕ *www.hotelcitadel.nl* ➽ *38 rooms* ⟨△⟩ *In-room: Wi-Fi. In-hotel: room service, bar, laundry service, no-smoking rooms* ☰ *AE, DC, MC, V* ⟨⦿⟩ *CP.*

$–$$$ ⊞ **Rho.** Few hotels have as marvelous a lobby as this one, thanks to the building's origins as a 1910s theater. Jugendstil ornament, tile trim, and etched glass all conjure up the soigné style of the turn of the 20th century. A rich maroon color is carried out in furnishings throughout the hotel, conveying a bit of the music-hall tinkle; guest room furnishings for the most part, however, are modern and standard issue. Happily located on a quiet side street off the Dam Square, the Rho is within walking distance of theaters, nightlife, and shopping. **Pros:** gorgeous high-ceilinged lobby, near some fabulous restaurants. **Cons:** alley entrance, basic rooms. ⊠ *Nes 5–23, 1012 KC, Centrum* ☎ *020/620–7371* ⊕ *www.rhohotel.com* ➽ *167 rooms* ⟨△⟩ *In-room: safe, refrigerator, Wi-Fi. In-hotel: bar, bicycles, laundry service, public Wi-Fi, parking (fee), no-smoking rooms, some pets allowed* ☰ *AE, MC, V* ⟨⦿⟩ *CP.*

$$ ⚄**Cordial.** Young international travelers are drawn to this hotel because it is easy on the budget, informal, and centrally located. Front rooms face the busy Rokin shopping street, and there's a terrace in front of the hotel for people-watching while enjoying a drink. All units are sparely outfitted with utilitarian furnishings, but are bright and clean. There's a cold breakfast buffet included in the price. **Pros:** easy on the budget, good location. **Cons:** basic rooms, noise from nearby construction. ⊠ *Rokin 62–64, 1012 KW, Centrum* ☎ *020/626–4411* ⊕ *www.cordialhotel.nl* ⇆ *52 rooms* ⌂ *In-room: no a/c, safe. In-hotel: bar, laundry service* ⊟ *AE, DC, MC, V* ⌽⦶CP.

> **HIDDEN ROOMS**
>
> The Anne Frank House is not the only place where smart carpentry hid Jewish refugees from the Nazi Gestapo in World War II. If you stay in an apartment built between 1910 and 1939 there may still be a hidden bedroom behind the walls or in the stairwell. Recent renovations in a penthouse apartment in Amsterdam South revealed a children's alcove under the narrow floorboards, complete with storybooks, pillows, and a forlorn little teddy bear waiting for its long lost owner to come back for a hug.

$–$$ ⚄**Avenue.** This hotel occupies several historic buildings, including one that used to be a warehouse for the United East India Company. Its rooms, though small, are comfortable, and are furnished in a bright, cheerful contemporary style. Double window glazing and extra-thick walls ensure that you won't be disturbed by street noise or rambunctious neighbors. The large and varied breakfast buffet gets consistent raves. **Pros:** historic building, quiet interior despite bustling neighborhood. **Cons:** smallish rooms. ⊠ *Nieuwezijds Voorburgwal 33, 1012 RD, Centrum* ☎ *020/530–9530* ⊕ *www.embhotels.nl* ⇆ *80 rooms* ⌂ *In-room: no a/c, dial-up, Wi-Fi. In-hotel: bar, laundry service, public Wi-Fi, no-smoking rooms* ⊟ *AE, DC, MC, V* ⌽⦶CP.

$–$$ ⚄**Terminus.** Eleven 18th-century town houses make up the Terminus, between the Berlage Exchange and the Oudekerk (Old Church), two famed historic sites. The views of the Old Church—Amsterdam's oldest—are wonderful, but unfortunately, its bell chimes every half hour around the clock, which means it can be heard in some rooms even through double-glazed windows. The modern glass-paneled entrance manages not to detract from the traditional beauty of the buildings, and there's a solarium for sunny days. The guest room decor is elegantly modern, comfortable, and boring. The location is the greatest draw here: you're in the heart of the city, surrounded by landmarks and in the major shopping district. **Pros:** close to historic monuments, pleasant and helpful staff. **Cons:** no-frills accommodations, nearby streets attract late-night revelers. ⊠ *Beursstraat 11–19, 1012 JT, Centrum* ☎ *020/622–0535* ⊕ *www.terminus.nl* ⇆ *85 rooms, 9 suites* ⌂ *In-room: no a/c (some), safe (some), refrigerator. In-hotel: bar, laundry service, public Internet, public Wi-Fi, some pets allowed, no-smoking rooms* ⊟ *AE, DC, MC, V* ⌽⦶CP.

$–$$ ⊞**Vijaya.** As with many 18th-century canal-house hotels, the exterior here is eye-catching—this one has a particularly ornate gable—and the inside is modernized. Comfortably furnished rooms in front have a canal view, but the rooms at the back are quieter. The family rooms sleep five. Near Dam Square, the main shopping streets and Centraal Station, you are also just a short tram ride away from

3

the major museums. **Pros:** authentic Amsterdam vibe, near plenty of restaurants, rooms for families. **Cons:** near Red Light District, some unsavory characters milling around. ⊠*Oudezijds Voorburgwal 44, 1012 GE, Centrum* ☎*020/638–0102* ⊕*www.hotelvijaya.com* ⇨*30 rooms* ⚒*In-room: no a/c, Ethernet. In-hotel: 2 restaurants, no elevator, public Internet, some pets allowed (no fee), no-smoking rooms* ⊟*AE, MC, V* ⓦ*CP.*

☾ **¢–$** ⊞**Asterisk.** A touch of the 19th century still hovers about this very friendly hotel. Some guest rooms feature decorative ceiling moldings and chandeliers. Major art museums, the Leidseplein, the Flower Market, and the Rembrandtsplein are all within walking distance of the hotel, which is on a quiet street. For children, cots and high chairs are available if you request them in advance. Only the main building has an elevator. Breakfast is included in the price only if you pay cash in advance. **Pros:** kid-friendly environment, good value for money, good deal on breakfast. **Cons:** not all rooms have private baths, Web site often outdated. ⊠*Den Texstraat 16, 1017 ZA, Centrum* ☎*020/626–2396* ⊕*www.asteriskhotel.nl* ⇨*40 rooms, 7 with shared bath* ⚒*In-room: no a/c, safe. In-hotel: bar, Internet, some pets allowed* ⊟*MC, V.*

★ **¢** ⊞**Stayokay Amsterdam-Stadsdoelen.** Located in a canal house at the edge of the Red Light District, this hostel is a backpacker's Ritz. Usually filled with young, friendly international travelers, it has a reputation as the most *gezellig,* or cozy, place to stay in Amsterdam. Some say if you're looking for simple accommodation at a bargain-basement price, you can't do better. The dormitories are immaculate, with breakfast and bedsheets included in the price. You can get meals and drinks at the café. Everyone congregates in the lobby to make new friends, watch TV, or use the Internet. **Pros:** cheap and cheerful, friendly vibe, near the city's best second-hand bookstores. **Cons:** dorm-style accommodations, books up fast. ⊠*Kloveniersburgwal 97, 1011 KM, Centrum* ☎*020/624–6832* ⊕*www.stayokay.com* ⇨*10 dormitories, 172 beds* ⚒*In-room: no a/c, no phone, no TV. In-hotel: restaurant, bar, bicycles, laundry facilities, public Internet, public Wi-Fi, no-smoking rooms* ⊟*AE, MC, V* ⓦ*CP.*

THE CANAL RINGS

Most Grachtengordel (Canal Ring) lodgings are in older buildings with all the Golden Age trimmings. As for neighborhoods, these canal-side hotels are listed as either in the Western Canal Ring, northwest of the Golden Bend area, or the Eastern Canal Ring, to its southeast.

WESTERN CANAL RING

The Western Canal Ring is separated from its eastern counterpart by the Leidsestraat, a narrow street running from the Leidseplein in the south to the Koningsplein in the north. West of the Leidsestraat lies the Nine Streets shopping area, with roads named for the animals whose hides were used in the district's tanning industry.

$$$$ ✕🖼 **Dylan Amsterdam.** Known for her chic London properties, Anouska
Fodor'sChoice Hempel opened this Amsterdam outpost as the city's first "designer"
★ hotel. It's located at (and incorporates a stone-arch entranceway from) the site of the historic Municipal Theater, which burned down in the 17th century. Today, the elegant rooms here are decorated with lacquered trunks, mahogany screens, modernist hardwood tables, and luxurious upholstery. One suite commands a view of the canal; many other rooms overlook a serene central courtyard. The hotel's restaurant ($$$–$$$$) offers an acclaimed French menu in a vogueish setting that functioned as a bakery between 1787 and 1811. **Pros:** a taste of old Amsterdam, good for celebrity spotting, updated business facilities. **Cons:** some parts of the hotel feel overdesigned, not all rooms have water views. ✉*Keizersgracht 384, 1016 GB, Western Canal Ring* ☎*020/530–2010* ⊕*www.dylanamsterdam.com* ➪*33 rooms, 8 suites* ⚖*In-room: safe, refrigerator, DVD (some), Wi-Fi. In-hotel: restaurant, room service, bar, gym, spa, bicycles, concierge, laundry service, public Internet, public Wi-Fi, parking (fee), no-smoking rooms* ▤*AE, DC, MC, V.*

★ $$$$ 🖼 **Seven One Seven.** Designer Kees van der Valk savvily applied his discerning eye to the decor of this hotel. Men's suiting fabrics have been used to upholster the overstuffed armchairs and sofas, and guest rooms—each of which is named for a different composer, artist, or writer—are filled with classical antiquities, framed art, flowers, and candles. Breakfast can be served in the suites or downstairs in the Stravinsky Room, where coffee, tea, cakes, wine, and beer are available for the asking throughout the day and evening. There's also a plush library and a pretty back patio. **Pros:** wonderful atmosphere, free refreshments throughout the day. **Cons:** no restaurant, staff is not big on smiles. ✉*Prinsengracht 717, 1017 JW, Western Canal Ring* ☎*020/427–0717* ⊕*www.717hotel.nl* ➪*8 suites* ⚖*In-room: no a/ c (some), refrigerator, DVD, Wi-Fi. In-hotel: bicycles, no elevator, laundry service, concierge, public Internet, public Wi-Fi, no-smoking* ▤*AE, DC, MC, V* ⍵*CP.*

★ $$$–$$$$ 🖼 **Pulitzer.** A clutch of 17th- and 18th-century houses—25 in all—were combined to create this rambling hotel sprinkled with landscaped garden courtyards that are featured in the blockbuster movie *Ocean's*

Twelve. It faces the Prinsengracht and the Keizersgracht canals and is just a short walk from both the Dam Square and the Jordaan. The place retains a historic ambience: most guest rooms—which are surprisingly spacious compared with its labyrinth of narrow halls and steep stairs—have beam ceilings and antique stylings. An appropriately historical soundtrack is provided every half hour when the

nearby Westerkerk chimes. Modern touches include heated bathroom floors and wireless Internet. **Pros:** friendly vibe, efficient staff, beautiful high-beam ceilings in some rooms. **Cons:** clanging of church bells, rooms vary in quality. ⊠*Prinsengracht 315–331, 1016 GZ, Western Canal Ring* ☎*020/523–5235* ⊕*www.luxurycollection.nl* ⬗*230 rooms, 3 suites* ⟁*In-room: safe (some), kitchen (some), refrigerator, dial-up, Wi-Fi. In-hotel: restaurant, room service, bar, gym, bicycles, laundry service, concierge, public Internet, public Wi-Fi, parking (fee), some pets allowed (fee), no-smoking rooms* ⊟*AE, DC, MC, V.*

\$–\$\$\$\$ 🔲 **Estheréa.** This hotel, which incorporates six 17th-century houses, has been run by the same family for three generations. The property has been modernized but still retains its historic charm; the lobby is filled with antiques and brass chandeliers, and the smallish, pastel-hued rooms have Adamesque ceilings and doors, along with plush headboards made from cushions and brass rods. The owners and staff are young, enthusiastic, and highly professional. Free coffee and tea are available 24 hours a day in the lounge. **Pros:** efficient and friendly staff, harmoniously decorated public areas, lovely breakfast room. **Cons:** no restaurant. ⊠*Singel 303–309, 1012 WJ, Western Canal Ring* ☎*020/624–5146* ⊕*www.estherea.nl* ⬗*71 rooms* ⟁*In-room: safe, refrigerator, DVD (some),VCR (some), Wi-Fi. In-hotel: room service, bar, laundry service, public Internet, public Wi-Fi, some pets allowed, no-smoking rooms* ⊟*AE, MC, V.*

\$\$\$
Fodor'sChoice
★
🔲 **Ambassade.** Ten 17th- and 18th-century houses have been folded into this hotel on the Herengracht near the Spui square. Friday's book market on the square might explain the Ambassade's popularity with book-world people: Doris Lessing, John Le Carré, Umberto Eco, and Salman Rushdie are regulars, and novelist Howard Norman set part of his book *The Museum Guard* here. Two lounges—one of which functions as breakfast room—and a library are elegantly decorated with Oriental rugs, chandeliers, clocks, paintings, and antiques. The canal-side rooms are spacious, with large floor-to-ceiling windows and solid, functional furniture. The rooms at the rear are quieter but smaller and darker; attic rooms have beamed ceilings. Service is attentive and friendly, and if by the smallest of chances you do end up getting out of sorts, you can always seek refuge in the flotation tanks. **Pros:** on a picturesque canal, hub for literati. **Cons:** slightly way-worn interiors, rooms at rear can be small and dark. ⊠*Herengracht*

341, 1016 AZ, Western Canal Ring ☎*020/555–0222* ⊕*www. ambassade-hotel.nl* ⤶*52 rooms, 7 suites, 1 apartment* ⚄*In-room: kitchen (some), DVD (some), VCR (some), dial-up. In-hotel: restaurant, room service, bicycles, no elevator, laundry service, public Internet, public Wi-Fi, some pets allowed, no-smoking rooms* ▭*AE, MC, V.*

$$–$$$

Fodor'sChoice

★

▣**Canal House.** A lot of love has gone into the refurbishment of this 1640 canal-house hotel. It's a beautiful old home with high plaster ceilings, antique furniture, old paintings, and a backyard garden bursting with plants and flowers. Every room is unique in size and furnishings, but you can probably count on a grandmotherly quilt on the bed. The elegant chandeliered breakfast room with burled-wood grand piano overlooks the garden, and there is a small bar in the front parlor. Wandering the halls is a treat. **Pros:** beautiful breakfast room with grand piano, abundance of curios. **Cons:** worn rooms, narrow corridors are easy to get lost in. ✉*Keizersgracht 148, 1015 CX, Western Canal Ring* ☎*020/622–5182* ⊕*www.canalhouse.nl* ⤶*26 rooms* ⚄*In-room: no a/c, Wi-Fi. In-hotel: bar, public Internet* ▭*AE, DC, MC, V* ⧆*CP.*

$$–$$$

▣**Hampshire Inn Prinsengracht.** With vast town-house windows overlooking the houseboat-graced Prinsengracht Canal, these two 18th-century canal houses are a popular choice. When the weather is fine, it's delightful to breakfast in the hotel's garden, which also has its own small guesthouse, a simple affair that sleeps up to four. Front rooms have a view of the Prinsengracht; back rooms overlook the garden. A short walk takes you to the Rembrandtplein, the Flower Market, and the main shopping area by the Kalverstraat. **Pros:** great location, some rooms have garden views. **Cons:** rooms are on the poky side, rooms tend to book up fast. ✉*Prinsengracht 1015, 1017 KN, Western Canal Ring* ☎*020/623–7779* ⊕*www.prinsengrachthotel.nl* ⤶*34 rooms* ⚄*In-room: no a/c, safe, Wi-Fi. In-hotel: room service, bar, bicycles, laundry service, public Internet, public Wi-Fi, no-smoking rooms* ▭*AE, DC, MC, V.*

★ **$$–$$$**

▣**Toren.** The historic setting for the founding of the Free University, this canal-side hotel's two buildings date from 1638 and are overlooked by the Westerkerk *toren* (Western Church tower). The guest rooms cultivate an aura of romance with marble fireplaces and chandeliers (although some also offer such modern conveniences as double whirlpool bathtubs). There's a beautifully carved mirrored bar in the bar/breakfast room area, and a charming garden cottage that serves as a bridal suite and enjoys its own sun lounge and terrace. The service at this family-run place often exceeds even its four-star status. **Pros:** wonderful salon, helpful staff. **Cons:** rooms are a bit of a letdown after the public areas, bathrooms need to be modernized. ✉*Keizersgracht 164, 1015 CZ, Western Canal Ring* ☎*020/622–6352* ⊕*www.hoteltoren.nl* ➽*38 rooms, 2 suites* ⌂*In-room: safe, refrigerator, VCR (some), dial-up. In-hotel: room service, bar, bicycles, concierge, laundry service, public Internet, some pets allowed, no-smoking rooms* ▤*AE, DC, MC, V.*

CAR TROUBLE

Amsterdam is a pedestrian's paradise, but it is a driver's nightmare. Few hotels have parking lots (those that do charge accordingly). Cars are perhaps best abandoned in one of the city's multistory lots for the duration of your stay.

3

$$ **⊡'t Hotel.** Guests return year after year to this romantic canal-side hotel. It occupies an 18th-century house and is a national monument (which is why there is no elevator). Rooms here are larger than those in similar historic lodgings; those in the rear are especially quiet. Room 8 on the top floor has a garden view. Antiques and hats are for sale in a small shop within the hotel. **Pros:** on a quiet stretch of canal, close to dining options. **Cons:** no real communal area, no restaurant. ✉*Leliegracht 18, 1015 DE, Western Canal Ring* ☎*020/422–2741* ⊕*www.thotel.nl* ➽*8 rooms* ⌂*In-room: no a/c, safe, Wi-Fi. In-hotel: no elevator, public Internet, public Wi-Fi, no-smoking rooms* ▤*AE, MC, V* ❑*CP.*

$ **⊡Keizersgracht.** Appealing to youthful and budget-minded travelers, this hotel sits along its namesake canal, and is a five-minute walk from Centraal Station. The lodgings here are basic, but all rooms have private bathrooms. There's a downstairs bar where you can socialize, watch TV, and play pool, pinball, or video games. Light meals and snacks can be ordered throughout the day. **Pros:** inexpensive rate, convivial atmosphere, near Centraal Station. **Cons:** downstairs bar can get rowdy, utilitarian room furnishings. ✉*Keizersgracht 15–17, 1015 CC, Western Canal Ring* ☎*020/625–1364* ➽*26 rooms* ⌂*In-room: no a/c, no phone, no TV. In-hotel: bar, no-smoking rooms* ▤*AE, DC, MC, V.*

¢–$ **⊡Hegra.** In a 17th-century building on the Herengracht canal, this hotel embodies what the Dutch call *klein maar fijn* (small but good). Rooms are unpretentious but comfortable, and the ones in front have a canal view. Some have shared baths. The absence of amenities is offset by the cordiality of the family that runs the property, the great location (near the Anne Frank House, shopping streets, and the major art museums), and the relatively gentle price tag. **Pros:** pleasant staff, good value. **Cons:** basic furnishings, not all rooms have private bathrooms. ✉*Herengracht 269, 1016 BJ, Western Canal Ring* ☎*020/623–7877* ➽*11 rooms, 2 with shared bath* ⌂*In-room: no a/c, no phone, no TV, Wi-Fi. In-hotel: no elevator, public Internet, public Wi-Fi, parking (fee), some pets allowed, no-smoking rooms* ▤*MC, V* ❑*CP.*

EASTERN CANAL RING & REMBRANDTPLEIN

Rembrandtplein may be a glaring tribute to neon and nightclubs, but the area to east of the square offers a peaceful respite. Here you'll find kid-friendly attractions like Artis Zoo, the Hortus Botanicus, and the Tropenmuseum.

$–$$$$

Fodor'sChoice ★

Seven Bridges. One of the famous canal sights in Amsterdam is the lineup of seven consecutive bridges that can be seen gracing Reguliersgracht. This atmospheric little retreat, which looks over these bridges, also takes its name from them. Occupying an 18th-century house in the heart of "Golden Bend" country (yet just a few blocks from Rembrandtplein), this hotel offers uniquely stylish guest rooms, all meticulously decorated with dark woods, Oriental rugs, handcrafted and inlaid bed frames, and Art Deco tables. The proud owner scouts the antiques stores and auction houses for furnishings, and all have thorough documentation. The top-floor, beam-ceilinged rooms are the smallest and are priced accordingly; the first-floor room No. 5 is practically palatial, with its own private terrace. Nail down your reservation well in advance. **Pros:** friendly owners, breakfast delivered to your room, wonderful view. **Cons:** no public areas, next door to a coffee shop. ⊠ *Reguliersgracht 31, 1017 LK, Eastern Canal Ring & Rembrandtplein* ☎ *020/623–1329* ⊕ *www. sevenbridgeshotel.nl* 🛏 *8 rooms* ⚫ *In-room: no a/c (some), Wi-Fi. In-hotel: no elevator, public Internet, public Wi-Fi, no-smoking rooms* ⊟ *AE, MC, V* ❙❁❙ *CP.*

¢–$$$$

Armada. A superb canal-side location at the corner of the Utrechtsestraat—where there's excellent shopping and dining—is the main draw here. The rooms are simple, and some have shared bathrooms. The breakfast room has an aquarium, and—in 17th-century style—small Oriental carpets covering the tables. **Pros:** friendly staff, excellent location near Rembrandtplein. **Cons:** basic furnishings, some rooms don't have their own bathrooms, some carpets are worn. ⊠ *Keizersgracht 713, 1017 DX, Eastern Canal Ring & Rembrandtplein* ☎ *020/623–2980* 🛏 *26 rooms, 8 with shared bath* ⚫ *In-hotel: bar, no-smoking rooms* ⊟ *AE, DC, MC, V* ❙❁❙ *CP.*

★ **$$–$$$**

NH Schiller. Frits Schiller built this hotel in 1912 in the Art Nouveau variant known as Jugendstil. He may have been an artist of modest ability, but a huge number of his paintings, whose colors inspired the inventive furnishings of the modernized rooms, are proudly displayed throughout the hotel. His friends, bohemian painters and sculptors, came to the Schiller Café, which became a famous meeting place and is still an informal and popular bar with Amsterdammers. In the lobby lounge you can check your e-mail to the hum of the espresso machine from the Brasserie Schiller. A winter film series is held on Sunday afternoons in the restaurant, with cocktails and dinner included. **Pros:** friendly staff, popular bar. **Cons:** noise from nearby nightclubs, lacks the charm of a smaller property. ✉ *Rembrandtplein 26–36, 1017 CV, Eastern Canal Ring & Rembrandtplein* ☎ *020/554–0700* ⊕ *www.nh-hotels.com* ⬲ *91 rooms, 1 suite* △ *In-room: no a/c, refrigerator, Wi-Fi. In-hotel: restaurant, room service, bar, laundry service, public Internet, public Wi-Fi* ⊟ *AE, DC, MC, V.*

$–$$$ ⬚**Albus Grand.** The Albus Grand's exterior has been graciously designed to conjure up the look of yesteryear. Inside, seven floors offer rooms of a comfortable size. Even the street-side rooms, which overlook the Munt tower and Flower Market, are remarkably quiet because of their double-paned windows. The hotel lobby and guest rooms are tastefully decorated with wicker chairs and contemporary paintings from the owners' collection. The buffet in the light and cheerful breakfast room serves Dutch specialties as well as more run-of-the-mill fare. **Pros:** Dutch specialities at breakfast, close to Kalverstraat shopping. **Cons:** restaurant has disappointing view, noise from ongoing construction near hotel. ✉ *Vijzelstraat 49, 1017 HE, Eastern Canal Ring & Rembrandtplein* ☎ *020/530–6200* ⊕ *www.albusgrandhotel.com* ⬲ *74 rooms, 3 apartments* △ *In-room: no a/c, kitchen (some), dial-up (some). In-hotel: restaurant, bar, laundry service, concierge, public Internet, public Wi-Fi, no-smoking rooms* ⊟ *AE, DC, MC, V.*

$–$$$ ⬚**Best Western Eden.** Although it can get very noisy when the discos empty in the wee hours, this gigantic hotel is perfectly situated for those who like the club scene and surrounding nightlife. Rooms in front have views of the Amstel River, whereas rooms elsewhere have few views but are quieter. The street appears to be down at the heels, but the inside of the hotel is clean, comfortable, and modern. There is wireless Internet access in the lobby and on the second floor. **Pros:** views of the Amstel, close to Rembrandtplein, cheerful lobby. **Cons:** on a run-down street, lots of traffic noise. ✉ *Amstel 144, 1017 AE, Eastern Canal Ring & Rembrandtplein* ☎ *020/530–7878* ⊕ *www.edenhotelgroup. com* ⬲ *218 rooms, 8 apartments* △ *In-room: no a/c (some), safe, kitchen (some), refrigerator, dial-up, Wi-Fi (some). In-hotel: restaurant, bar, concierge, laundry service, public Wi-Fi, no-smoking rooms* ⊟ *AE, DC, MC, V.*

$–$$ ⬚**Imperial.** This Parisian-looking hotel is on a pedestrian-only street with cobblestones and a terraced square. Rooms are individually decorated, in styles ranging from sedate to cheerful to bold, to appeal to every kind of taste. This is a no-smoking hotel. There is no elevator, and although the stairs are modern (as opposed to steep traditional Dutch staircases), you must walk up at least two flights of them. **Pros:** efficient staff, close to Rembrandtplein. **Cons:** some of the rooms are lackluster, slightly run-down location. ✉ *Thorbeckeplein 9, 1017 CS, Eastern Canal Ring & Rembrandtplein* ☎ *020/622–0051* ⊕ *www. imperial-hotel.com* ⬲ *14 rooms* △ *In-room: no a/c, safe, dial-up, Wi-Fi. In-hotel: room service, no elevator, public Internet, public Wi-Fi, no-smoking rooms* ⊟ *MC, V* ⦿*CP.*

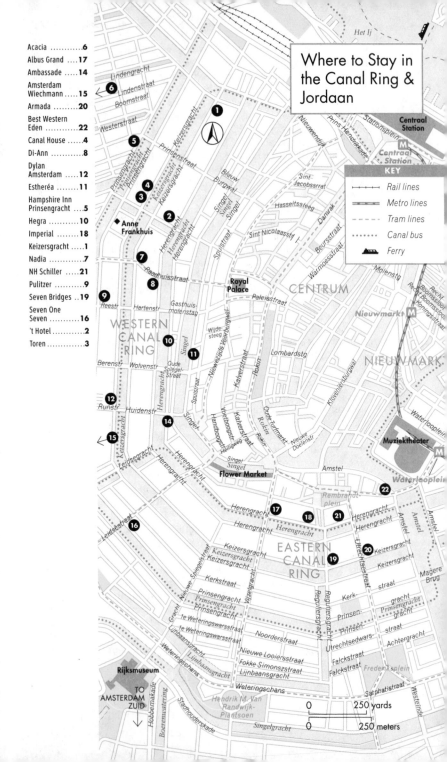

Where to Stay in the Canal Ring & Jordaan

KEY

Rail lines

Metro lines

Tram lines

Canal bus

Ferry

Het IJ

Centraal Station

CENTRUM

NIEUWMARKT

WESTERN CANAL RING

Anne Frankhuis

Royal Palace

Nieuwmarkt

Muziektheater

Waterlooplein

Flower Market

EASTERN CANAL RING

Rembrandtplein

Rijksmuseum

TO AMSTERDAM ZUID

Hendrik M. Van Randwijk-Plantsoen

Magere Brug

0   250 yards

0   250 meters

JORDAAN

While wandering this most singular of neighborhoods, you may decide it's your favorite in the city. So why not stay here? The bells from the Westertoren take you back in time; sleepy little canals and narrow cobblestone streets with lopsided 17th-century houses give the area a special charm. On the surface, the neighborhood still looks very much as it did when Anne Frank lived here, although behind the weather-worn exteriors it now sports numerous fascinating boutiques and antiques shops.

> **TAXING SITUATION**
>
> Most of the pricing includes a VAT (Value Added Tax) of 6%, and in some cases the city tax of 5% may be included. Many hotels operate on the European Plan (with no meals), although some are on the Continental Plan and serve anything from rolls and coffee to a generous buffet.

★ $$ ⬚**Amsterdam Wiechmann.** A favorite with rock musicians—of both the punk (Sex Pistols) and country (Emmy Lou Harris) persuasions—the Wiechmann's main claim to fame is announced by a gold record displayed in the lobby, the pride and joy of the owner, John Boddy. There are delightful personal touches, like a teapot collection and framed Delft blue tiles, throughout the lobby and adjoining breakfast room, and fresh flowers are everywhere. The maze of hallways through the hotel's three buildings lead to guest rooms of wildly varying sizes; these are plainly decorated but enlivened by quilted bedspreads and floral drapes. Some have bedside tables covered by rugs (an old Dutch tradition). It's worth the extra money to get a room with views over the canal. **Pros:** smiling staff, spic-and-span rooms, quiet location. **Cons:** rooms are a little corny, no restaurant. ⊠*Prinsengracht 328–332, 1016 HX, Jordaan* ☎*020/626–3321* ⊕*www.hotelwiechmann.nl* ⬚*37 rooms, 1 suite* ⬚*In-room: no a/c, no TV (some), Wi-Fi. In-hotel: bar, no elevator, public Internet, public Wi-Fi, some pets allowed, no-smoking rooms* ⊟*MC, V* ⦿*CP.*

★ ¢–$$ ⬚**Nadia.** The exterior of this 19th-century building is an architectural extravaganza, complete with kiosk corner turret, Art Nouveau–y portals, and redbrick trim. Inside, rooms are white, modern, and casual, and some have adorable views overlooking the canals. (Sleepers bothered by noise should opt for rooms in the rear.) The breakfast room is idyllic, bathed in a rosy orange glow and topped by a chandelier, with leafy views out the windows. The friendly staff will encourage you to help yourself to a welcome drink at the check-in minibar when you arrive. **Pros:** multilingual staff, lovely views. **Cons:** steep staircase, no-frills rooms. ⊠*Raadhuisstraat 51, 1016 DD, Jordaan* ☎*020/620–1550* ⊕*www.nadia.nl* ⬚*52 rooms* ⬚*In-room: no a/c, refrigerator, Wi-Fi. In-hotel: room service, no elevator, laundry service, public Internet, public Wi-Fi, parking (fee), no-smoking rooms* ⊟*AE, MC, V* ⦿*CP.*

★ $ ⬚**Acacia.** This small family-run hotel makes a good ambassador for the Jordaan, thanks to its quiet, clean, and welcoming vibe. The dining room here is cozy—even grandmotherly—and the rooms are clean and colorful, but you might opt to "go native" and book one of the two self-catering houseboats moored out front (each is equipped with shower, toilet, cable TV, and telephone). The Acacia is within walking distance of the Anne Frankhuis and the Westertoren, and is right next door to a typical Jordaan café, Café de Gijs, noted for its charming *gezelligheid*. The whole district is full of interesting, quirky shops offering collectibles, handmade jewelry, and antiques. **Pros:** good location, canal views, chance to stay on a houseboat. **Cons:** spartan rooms, dining room is a bit fussy. ✉*Lindengracht 251, 1015 KH, Jordaan* ☎*020/622–1460* ⊕*www.hotelacacia.nl* ⬚*14 rooms, 2 studios* ♿*In-room: no a/c, no phone. In-hotel: no elevator* ▤*MC, V* ❘◎❘*CP.*

¢–$ ▦**Di-Ann.** Just a few minutes' walk from the Westertoren, Anne Frankhuis, and the Royal Palace, this friendly hotel occupies a gorgeously historic building with gable roofs, Romanesque balconies, and half-moon windows. Perched above a ground floor filled with shops, overlooking the regal Herengracht, and several blocks from the hectic Dam Square, the Di-Ann is right in the middle of all the action (perhaps too so: delicate sleepers should opt for a room in the rear). When you enter, you need to climb a traditional narrow, steep staircase, so if you have any mobility problems, this isn't the hotel for you. Some of the attractively modern guest rooms have balconies, and those in the rear overlook a garden. Other rooms have views of the Westertoren, Royal Palace, or canal. The breakfast room allures with crown moldings, chandelier, and flowered wallpaper. **Pros:** good views, close to Dam Square. **Cons:** steep staircase, noisy location. ✉*Raadhuisstraat 27, 1016 DC, Jordaan* ☎*020/623–1137* ⊕*www.diann.nl* ⬚*33 rooms* ♿*In-room: no a/c, safe. In-hotel: no elevator, public Internet, public Wi-Fi, no-smoking rooms* ▤*AE, DC, MC, V* ❘◎❘*CP.*

LEIDSEPLEIN

It can be noisy in the city's busiest square, but then again sometimes it pays to be centrally located.

$$$–$$$$ ▦**Park.** At first glance, the Park looks like everyone's dream of a grand Netherlandish hotel: it's topped by a picturesque pepper-pot tower, and its 18th-century building set with regal windows is mirrored charmingly in the Singel River. But though this stately Amsterdam fixture has one foot in history, the other is firmly entrenched in today, thanks to its modern-luxe decor and amenities. The neon lights of Leidseplein's shops, casino, and clubs are around the corner, and the sylvan glades of Amsterdam's gorgeous Vondelpark are just across the road, beckoning you to take an early morning jog. The major art museums are also within walking distance. **Pros:** stylishly appointed rooms, convenient location between Leidseplein and the Vondelpark. **Cons:** no particular Dutch flavor, bureaucratic staff

> **WORD OF MOUTH**
>
> I stayed at Park hotel, right at Vondelpark and across the street from Hard Rock and Holland Casino. Great location and easy walk to Dam Square and Red Light. Rijksmuseum and Van Gogh Museum is right next door.
>
> — Englcedave

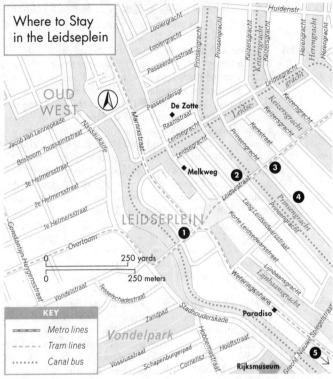

Where to Stay in the Leidseplein

is slow to answer requests. ⊠*Stadhouderskade 25, 1071 ZD, Leidseplein* ☎*020/671–1222* ⊕*www.parkhotel.nl* ⟿*187 rooms, 6 suites* ♿*In-room: no a/c (some), safe (some), refrigerator (some), Ethernet. In-hotel: restaurant, room service, bar, laundry service, public Internet, public Wi-Fi, parking (fee), no-smoking rooms* ☰*AE, DC, MC, V.*

★ **\$\$–\$\$\$\$** 🏨 **Amsterdam-American.** Housed in one of the city's most fancifully designed buildings—one that is said to form the missing link between Art Nouveau and the Amsterdam School—the American (the name everyone knows it by) is a beloved Amsterdam landmark. Directly on Leidseplein, this 1902 castle-like structure is an agglomeration of Neo-Gothic turrets, Jugenstil gables, Art Deco stained glass, and an Arts and Crafts clock tower. Gloriously overlooking the Stadhouderskade (the reason the hotel has its own boat landing), this place is near everything—nightlife, dining, sightseeing, and shopping. Guest rooms are sizable, bright, and furnished in a modern Art Deco style, and you have a choice between canal and bustling-square views—the latter option having the bonus of small balconies. Newlyweds might want to indulge in the Mata Hari Honeymoon Suite, which is named after the spy fatale who celebrated her own wedding here. **Pros:** alluring history, great for celebrity spotting, near canal boat dock. **Cons:** busy lobby, late check-in time. ⊠*Leidsekade 97, 1017 PN, Leidseplein* ☎*020/556–3000* ⊕*www.amsterdamamerican.com* ⟿*161 rooms, 14 suites* ♿*In-room:*

safe, refrigerator, Ethernet, dial-up. In-hotel: restaurant, room service, bar, gym, concierge, laundry service, public Internet, public Wi-Fi, no-smoking rooms ☰AE, DC, MC, V.

★ $$–$$$$ 🏨**Dikker and Thijs Fenice.** "Lavish," "classical," and "cozy" are some of the adjectives typically used to describe this hotel, which has a regal address on the Prinsengracht canal. The hotel, first opened as a shop in 1895, has been renowned for fine dining since its founder, A. W. Dikker, entered into a partnership in 1915 with H. Thijs, who had apprenticed with the famous French chef Escoffier. The busy location—happily, all the majestic sash windows are double-glazed—is convenient to the major shopping areas and one block from the Leidseplein, nightlife center of the city. The Art Deco–style rooms are fully modernized, although they retain a regal ambience with dark-wood furniture, scarlet upholstery, and gilt-edged mirrors. Room 408 has a wonderful beamed ceiling. Of the upper-price hotels, this is one of the few that includes breakfast in the basic room rate. **Pros:** water views, good location, lots of dining options nearby. **Cons:** small lobby gets crowded, rooms book up fast. ✉*Prinsengracht 444, 1017 KE, Leidseplein* ☎*020/620–1212* ⊕*www.dtfh.nl* ➦*42 rooms* ⌂*In-room: no a/c (some), refrigerator, dial-up, Wi-Fi. In-hotel: room service, bar, laundry service, public Internet, public Wi-Fi, some pets allowed (no fee), no-smoking rooms* ☰*AE, DC, MC, V* ⦿*CP.*

$$ 🏨**Marcel's Creative Exchange Bed & Breakfast.** How would you like to stay in a renovated 17th-century home decorated with fine antiques and original works of art, located in the heart of the city and all for a sweetly gentle price? Internationally renowned artist/designer Marcel van Woerkom has been renting rooms in his house since 1970 and has since hosted royalty, travelers, and artists from a variety of disciplines. All guests surely drool over the modern interiors with furniture from Charles and Ray Eames, Alvar Alto, Philippe Starck, and Marcel Breuer. Because of the location on the Leidsestraat next to De Uitkijk, Amsterdam's oldest existing art cinema, you're right in the thick of things. **Pros:** modern furnishings, personal concierge, convenient location. **Cons:** some rooms share bathrooms, books up fast. ✉*87 Leidsestraat, 1017 NX, Leidseplein* ☎*020/622–9834* ⊕*www. marcelamsterdam.com* ➦*3 rooms; 1 suite, 2 with shared bath* ⌂*In-room: no a/c, no phone, safe (some), refrigerator (some). In-hotel: no elevator, public Internet, some pets allowed (no fee), no kids under 4 yrs, no-smoking rooms* ☰*V, MC.*

$–$$ 🏨**Nicolaas Witsen.** If you're just looking for a place to hang your hat and get a quiet night's sleep, the Nicolaas Witsen is a good choice. Run by the same affable family for two generations, the redbrick-and-white-trim hotel is on a peaceful street within walking distance of the Rijksmuseum and the Heineken Brewery. The standard-issue guest rooms have white walls punctuated by lots of windows, Swedish-wood furniture, and modern bathrooms. The breakfast room is cheery, and there is a family room that sleeps up to four people. **Pros:** quiet location, close to numerous dining options. **Cons:** no-frills decor, rooms on the small side. ✉*Nicolaas Witsenstraat 4–8, 1017 ZH, Leidseplein* ☎*020/623–6143* ⊕*www.hotelnicolaaswitsen.nl* ➦*28 rooms* ⌂*In-room: no a/c,* *kitchen (some), Wi-Fi. In-hotel: bar, laundry service, public Wi-Fi, no-smoking rooms* ▤*AE, MC, V* ▯*CP.*

¢ 🖭**Hans Brinker.** Housed in a brick building that was a monastery about half a century ago, this hostel has rooms that are no-frills but sparkling clean, with white walls and blue floors. The dorms have bunk beds, and the private rooms have bathroom facilities. As basic as it all is, it's never boring. You can boogie in the disco, drink at the bar, enjoy incredibly cheap meals (guests only) in the dining room. From 5 PM to 6 PM, you'll find your fellow backpackers guzzling beer in the bar during happy hour. And it's all "happening" at Leidseplein, just around the corner. What more could you want? **Pros:** offers lots of facilities under one roof, you'll meet people from all over the globe. **Cons:** staff can be brusque, checking in seems to take forever. ⊠*Kerkstraat 136, 1017 GR, Leidseplein* ☎*020/622–0687* ⊕*www.hans-brinker.com* 🛏*120 rooms, all with shared bath, 500 beds* ⚐*In-room: no a/c, no phone, safe (some), no TV. In-hotel: restaurant, bar, public Internet* ▤*MC, V* ▯*CP.*

MUSEUM DISTRICT

If you've come to Amsterdam for its reputation as the city of the arts, then you should book a room in this quarter. All the city's top museums are here, the priciest shopping strip is just around the corner, and the lovely green Vondelpark is just to the west. Little wonder that this entire area has been colonized by fine hotels.

★ $$$–$$$$ ✕🖭**The College Hotel.** This hotel occupies an 1895 school building, giving it a unique atmosphere. It's owned by an educational institute, the ROC of Amsterdam, and operated as a training ground for students of the hotel management program (which accounts for the fresh-faced staff). The building has wide, grand corridors and stairwells, and the rooms have high ceilings, carpets you can sink into, and gleaming bathrooms. The in-house restaurant is one of only a few that serves New Dutch cuisine; you can try warm smoked eel here, with radish, apple syrup, and grated lemon. **Pros:** historic building, trendy bar, in-room massages. **Cons:** staff can be easily distracted, location not very convenient. ⊠*Roelof Hartstraat 1, 1071 VE, Museum District & Environs* ☎*020/571–1511* ⊕*www.steinhotel.com/college* 🛏*40 rooms* ⚐*In-room: safe, Ethernet, DVD (some), VCR (some). In-hotel: restaurant, room service, bar, bicycles, laundry service, concierge, public Wi-Fi, no-smoking rooms* ▤*AE, DC, MC, V.*

★ $$–$$$$ 🖭**Bilderberg Jan Luyken.** This small, formal, and stylish town-house hotel offers a peaceful sanctuary, complete with serene garden and restrained Art Nouveau stylings. Located in a trio of quaint 19th-century five-story town houses, its exterior is fitted out with wrought-iron balconies, cute gables, and the usual ugly roof extension. The interior decor is largely *Wallpaper*-modern—tripod lamps, steel ashtrays, Knoll-ish chairs. Guest rooms can be on the snug side, and service and housekeeping leave a bit to be desired. The hotel is just one block away from the Museumplein and fashionable shopping streets; perhaps this explains its popularity with musicians in town who play the nearby Concertgebouw. There's a lovely little "relaxation" room with a tanning lounge, Turkish bath, and hot tub, and the hotel's trendy bar, Wines and Bites, serves high-quality wine along with snacks and lunches. **Pros:** leafy environs, modern rooms, proximity to museums. **Cons:** slightly unwelcoming entrance, can be hard to find. ⊠*Jan Luykenstraat 58, 1071 CS, Museum District & Environs* ☎*020/573–0730* ⊕*www.bilderberg.nl* ⊃*62 rooms* ⟐*In-room: safe, Wi-Fi. In-hotel: room service, bar, laundry service, public Internet, some pets allowed (fee), no-smoking rooms* ⊟*AE, DC, MC, V.*

★ **$$–$$$$**   ⊡ **Gresham Memphis.** Classically proportioned, mansard-roofed, and ivy-covered—what more do you want from an Amsterdam hotel facade? This elegant, exceptionally spacious hotel was once the private residence of Freddy Heineken, of brewery fame. Formerly decorated in a classical style, the entire hotel is now fresh, modern, and airy, so if you want Vermeer-style interiors, this isn't the place for you. But the new design is energizing, not to say empowering (lots of businesspeople stay here): the breakfast room is bright and welcoming, the bar-lounge is sleek contempo, the guest rooms are modern and tranquil. As formal but not as expensive as the deluxe hotels, and embraced by a serene residential neighborhood, the Memphis is near the Concertgebouw. Extra beds are available, and children under 12 are welcome at no additional charge. The large bar has comfortable armchairs and tables and serves light meals. **Pros:** pleasant modern lobby and bar area, lovely rooms, equally suited to business and leisure travelers. **Cons:** rooms on the small size, location is a bit far from the sites. ⊠*De Lairessestraat 87, 1071 NX, Museum District & Environs* ☎*020/673-3141* ⊕*www. memphishotel.nl* ⊃*74 rooms* ⟐*In-room: safe (some), Ethernet, Wi-Fi. In-hotel: room service, bar, laundry service, public Internet, public Wi-Fi, parking (fee), no-smoking rooms* ⊟*AE, DC, MC, V.*

$$–$$$$ ⊡ **Vondel Amsterdam Centre.** On a quiet street next to the Vondelpark and very close to the Leidseplein, this hotel is refined and contemporary. The lobby and bar are filled with comfortable suede sofas, light-wood furnishings, sunlight, and flowers. The similarly colored rooms and apartments, generous in size, are enhanced with flashes of crimson, and a small garden terrace makes for a verdant oasis. Suites are on the top floor and have large windows that follow the shape of the roof and give you a scenic view of the neighborhood. Throughout the hotel are paintings by Amsterdam artist Peter Keizer. The hotel, like the park, gets its name from the 17th-century poet Joost van den Vondel, and the rooms are named after his poems. A lavish breakfast buffet is available, but is not included in the rate. **Pros:** artsy vibe, pleasant staff, lovely garden terrace. **Cons:** staff could be friendlier, rooms book up fast. ⊠*Vondelstraat 20, 1054 GD, Museum District & Environs* ☎*020/612–0120* ⊕*www.vondelhotels.nl* ⊃*75 rooms, 3 suites* ⟐*In-room: no a/c, safe, Ethernet, Wi-Fi. In-hotel: restaurant, room service, bar, bicycles, laundry service, concierge, public Wi-Fi, no-smoking rooms* ⊟*AE, DC, MC, V.*

$$–$$$ ⊡ **Atlas.** Just a block from the Vondelpark, this hotel, housed in an Art Nouveau mansion, is renowned for its personal, friendly, and generally relaxing atmosphere. Although the Atlas discreetly blends into its well-to-do residential area and is within easy walking distance of the museums, the convivial nature of its lounge-bar-restaurant seems to exert a holding suction effect on many of the guests. Rooms are decorated with contemporary artwork on the walls. **Pros:** friendly staff, well-used public areas, close to the Vondelpark. **Cons:** mostly residential area, room furnishings feel randomly assembled. ⊠ *Van Eeghenstraat 64, 1071 GK, Museum District & Environs* ☎*020/676–6336* ⏚*www. hotelatlas.nl* ⤳*23 rooms* ⚹*In-room: no a/c, safe, VCR (some), dial-up. In-hotel: room service, bar, bicycles, concierge, laundry service, some pets allowed, no-smoking rooms* ⊟*AE, DC, MC, V.*

★ **$$–$$$** ▦**Piet Hein.** Salons don't come any sleeker than the ones inside this ornate brick Vondelpark mansion, with their cube-shape chairs, gleaming Swedish woods, sisal-like carpeting, and white-on-white hues. The bright bursts of navy blue are perhaps in homage to Piet Hein, the legendary 17th-century Dutch privateer and vice admiral. Other maritime touches include paintings of sailing ships, navy blue carpets with patterns of seaman's knots, and cozy rooms that make you feel like you're in a ship's cabin. Some bedrooms here are so sprightly done up you will feel 10 years younger. Real color lies outside the windows, as front rooms have fine views of the park (always in demand—even booking far in advance doesn't guarantee you one of these rooms). Those in the back look over a garden. The P. C. Hooftstraat, the Concertgebouw, and the city's major art museums are nearby. **Pros:** attracts a young crowd, close to the Vondelpark. **Cons:** staff could be friendlier, lobby has a slightly worn look. ⊠ *Vossiusstraat 51–53, 1071 AK, Museum District & Environ* ☎*020/662–7205* ⏚*www.hotelpiethein.nl* ⤳*60 rooms* ⚹*In-room: no a/c (some), safe, Wi-Fi. In-hotel: room service, bar, laundry service, no-smoking rooms* ⊟*AE, DC, MC, V.*

$$–$$$ ▦**Toro.** In a prim and proper 19th-century-style villa on the southern border of the Vondelpark, this hotel offers a relaxing atmosphere. The views of the park and a small lake, and an interior tastefully furnished with antiques, oil paintings, and chandeliers provide a special home-like environment that is rare in Amsterdam. Rooms are bright and spacious, and some have balconies. Set near the area of the park far from the museum quarter and its shops, slightly outside the city center in a chic residential area, the hotel is, nevertheless, convenient to tram lines and lends itself to a lovely stroll through the park from the heart of Amsterdam. **Pros:** peaceful atmosphere, cozy interior, views of the Vondelpark. **Cons:** out-of-the-way location, staff can be hard to find. ⊠ *Koningslaan 64, 1075 AG, Museum District & Environs* ☎*020/673–7223* ⏚*www.hoteltoro.nl* ⤳*22 rooms* ⚹*In-room: safe, refrigerator, VCR (some), dial-up. In-hotel: room service, bar, bicycles, concierge, laundry facilities, laundry service, some pets allowed, no-smoking rooms* ⊟*AE, DC, MC, V.*

� **$$** ▦**Fita.** The couple that runs this property, Hans and Loes de Rapper, places an emphasis on the spic-and-span. Therefore, this peaceful hotel, a turn-of-the-20th-century town house, is not only dustless but is off-limits to smokers. In the morning, you can enjoy fresh-baked bread and homemade jam, along with freshly squeezed orange juice, at the buffet breakfast. Another plus: you won't be charged for telephone calls within Europe and to the United States. The Rijksmuseum, Van Gogh Museum, Stedelijk Museum, and Concertgebouw are literally around the corner. You can buy your tickets here and get a 20% discount. **Pros:** staff with a sense of humor, free telephone calls, free laundry service. **Cons:** no real public areas, decor is on the twee side. ⊠ *Jan Luyken-straat 37, 1071 CL, Museum District & Environs* ☎ *020/679–0976* ⊕ *www.fita.nl* ☞ *15 rooms* △ *In-room: no a/c, Wi-Fi. In-hotel: laundry service, public Internet, no-smoking rooms* ⊟ *AE, DC, MC, V* ☉ *Closed Dec. 15–Jan. 15* ⏀ *CP.*

$$ **Prinsen.** P. H. H. Cuijpers, the architect of the Rijksmuseum and Centraal Station, also created this adorable hotel. A chalet roof, dormers, bay window, jigsaw trim, Neoclassical columns, and sculpted reliefs of cats (one showing a cat chasing mice) all decorate the exterior, which was built around 1870. The storybook feeling, however, ends as soon as you step in the door: the interiors have all been gutted and renovated. Many of the bedrooms are still cheery and gracious, though, and on the ground floor, there's a bright yellow breakfast room overlooking a lovely garden. On a quiet street next to the Vondelpark, the hotel makes all its guests very welcome. **Pros:** fanciful facade, gay-friendly vibe, close to the Vondelpark. **Cons:** bland interior, staff can be brusque. ⊠ *Vondelstraat 36–38, 1054 GE, Museum District & Environs* ☎ *020/616–2323* ⊕ *www.prinsenhotel.nl* ☞ *45 rooms, 1 suite* △ *In-room: no a/c, safe, Wi-Fi. In-hotel: bar, laundry service, public Internet, some pets allowed (no fee), no-smoking rooms* ⊟ *AE, DC, MC, V* ⏀ *CP.*

$$ **Sander.** The Sander offers rooms best described as traditionally Dutch: clean and comfortable. Seating areas in window bays give some rooms additional charm. The bar and breakfast room open out onto a garden. The hotel is welcoming to everyone. **Pros:** gay-friendly vibe, close to museums, inexpensive rates. **Cons:** simple furnishings, rooms book up fast. ⊠ *Jacob Obrechtstraat 69, 1071 KJ, Museum District & Environs* ☎ *020/662–7574* ⊕ *www.hotel-sander.nl* ☞ *20 rooms* △ *In-room: no a/c, safe. In-hotel: room service, bar, laundry service, public Internet* ⊟ *AE, MC, V* ⏀ *CP.*

$–$$ **Aalders.** Occupying a cozy, charming town house, this busy (and completely smoke-free) hotel has reasonably-sized rooms with large windows overlooking a quiet street. All rooms have shower or bath; double rooms have twin beds. Breakfast is served in a large and beautiful second-floor room. **Pros:** friendly staff, close to museums. **Cons:** doubles have twin beds, rooms vary in size. ⊠ *Jan Luykenstraat 13–15, 1071 CJ, Museum District & Environs* ☎ *020/662–0116* ⊕ *www.hotelaalders.nl* ☞ *28 rooms* △ *In-room: no a/c, Wi-Fi. In-hotel: bar, laundry service, public Internet, public Wi-Fi, no-smoking rooms* ⊟ *AE, DC, MC, V* ☉ *Closed 2 wks, in mid-Dec.* ⏀ *CP.*

$–$$ **Europa 92.** You can't miss the Europa: it has a neon sign nearly larger than its four-story facade. Within easy walking distance of the Vondelpark and the elegant shopping street P. C. Hooftstraat, this family-run hotel has a lovely garden, which you may wish to escape to after realizing that the No. 1 tram passes the front—be sure to opt for the quieter rooms at the back, two of which contain small kitchenettes and provide a garden view. **Pros:** friendly staff, close to the Vondelpark. **Cons:** slightly run-down location, rooms can be noisy. ✉*1e Constantijn Huygenstraat 103–107, 1054 BV, Museum District & Environs* ☎*020/618–8808* ⊕*www.europa92.nl* 🛏*47 rooms, 2 suites* ⚓*In-room: no a/c, no phone, safe, Ethernet, dial-up, Wi-Fi. In-hotel: bar, laundry service, public Wi-Fi, parking (fee), some pets allowed (fee), no-smoking rooms* ▤*AE, DC, MC, V* ▢*CP.*

$–$$ 🏨 **Hestia.** On a street of extraordinary 19th-century houses, the Hestia is parallel to the Vondelpark and close to the Leidseplein. Fitted out with red brick, white trim, and a cute mansard roof, it's certainly easy on the eyes. The Hestia is family operated, with a helpful and courteous staff, and is the kind of place that reinforces the image of the Dutch as a clean and orderly people. The hotel's breakfast room has a view of the garden, and a large family room has a charming sitting area in a bay window with stained glass that also overlooks the garden. The rooms are basic, light, and simply modern. Four of the rooms are very small, but so is their cost. **Pros:** friendly staff, close to museums. **Cons:** some rooms are on the small side, rooms book up fast. ✉*Roemer Visscherstraat 7, 1054 EV, Museum District & Environs* ☎*020/618–0801* ⊕*www.hotel-hestia.nl* 🛏*18 rooms* ⚓*In-room: no a/c, safe, Wi-Fi. In-hotel: room service, laundry service, public Wi-Fi, some pets allowed (no fee), no-smoking rooms* ▤*AE, DC, MC, V* ▢*CP.*

★ $–$$ 🏨 **Hotel de Filosoof.** Bona fide Amsterdam philosophers are regularly to be found ensconced in this hotel's comfy armchairs. Monthly lectures and discussion evenings are hosted here for locals, many of whom are, naturally, artists, writers, and thinkers. Even the decorator of this hotel has picked up on the philosophical motif: each of the guest rooms is decorated with a different theme. (There is an Aristotle room furnished in Greek style, with passages from the works of Greek philosophers hung on the walls, and a Goethe room adorned with Faustian texts.) Some of the rooms are a little silly—the Walden, for instance, sports some landscape daubs on the wall—but the Spinoza is a total knockout: an homage to Golden Age style, complete with black-and-white floors, 19th-century library lamp, and framed paintings, it is a jewel that fancier hotels in town could well take as a model. Enjoy breakfast, or merely relax, in the large garden. **Pros:** off-the-wall interior, interesting guests. **Cons:** can be hard to find, furnishings are a tad wayworn. ✉*Anna van den Vondelstraat 6, 1054 GZ, Museum District & Environs* ☎*020/683–3013* ⊕*www.hotelfilosoof.nl* 🛏*34 rooms, 4 suites* ⚓*In-room: no a/c. In-hotel: bar, laundry service, no-smoking rooms, public Internet* ▤*AE, MC, V* ▢*CP.*

$–$$ 🏨 **Museum Square.** Small and refined, with a cherry and white facade, this hotel is within walking distance of the Concertgebouw and the major art museums, as well as a large selection of good restaurants and trendy brasseries. The Vondelpark is nearby, but you can enjoy your own little piece of private heaven in the hotel's tranquil Japanese garden. Rooms are attractively furnished. **Pros:** light and airy rooms, efficient staff. **Cons:** no particular Dutch flavor, no real public area. ✉*De Lairessestraat 7, 1071 NR, Museum District & Environs* ☎*020/671–9596* ⊕*www.amsterdamcityhotels.nl* 🛏*34 rooms* ⚓*In-*

room: no a/c (some), safe, Wi-Fi. In-hotel: bar, laundry service, public Internet, no-smoking rooms ☰AE, DC, MC, V ⦿CP.

$-$$

Fodor'sChoice

★

☷ Washington. Just a stone's throw from the Museumplein, this hotel often attracts international musicians in town to perform at the nearby Concertgebouw—except perhaps those who play the cello (the steep staircase is hard to navigate with bulky baggage). Owner Johan Boel-houwer is helpful and will lend from his collection of guidebooks. The breakfast room and lounge are filled with antiques and marvelous brass chandeliers, and the hotel is meticulously polished and sparkling clean. The rooms are simply and charmingly decorated in white and pastel shades. Large windows let in a flood of light. There are also four comfortable and cozy apartments with their own kitchens; some also have living rooms, bathtubs, and pianos. **Pros:** laid-back atmosphere, friendly staff, popular with musicians. **Cons:** no elevator, books up fast. ⊠*Frans van Mierisstraat 10, 1071 RS, Museum District & Environs* ☎*020/679–7453* ⊕*www.hotelwashington.nl* ⟿*22 rooms, 4 with shared bath, 1 suite, 4 apartments* ⟁*In-room: no a/c, safe, Wi-Fi. In-hotel: no elevator* ☰AE, V ⦿CP.

$

Fodor'sChoice

★

☷ Museumzicht. The name "Museum View" is accurate: this hotel is directly across the street from the Rijksmuseum. The owner once ran an antiques shop, so the house is filled with wonderful objects such as Art Deco wardrobes, streamlined lamps, and Lloyd Loom chairs. The breakfast room–lounge has a Murano glass chandelier and Art Deco pottery on the chimney walls. Elsewhere hang 19th- and 20th-century landscapes and portraits. The rooms are simple but delightful, with pastel-striped wallpaper and little etchings. The hotel is on the top floors of the building, and guests must climb a narrow and steep stairway with their luggage to the reception desk and to the rooms—the owners highly recommend traveling light. **Pros:** quiet location, clean rooms, view of the Rijksmuseum. **Cons:** steep staircase, no particularly Dutch flavor. ⊠*Jan Luykenstraat 22, 1071 CN, Museum District & Environs* ☎*020/671–2954* ⟿*14 rooms* ⟁*In-room: no a/c, safe (some), no phone. In-hotel: no elevator* ☰AE, DC, MC, V ⦿CP.

$

Fodor'sChoice

★

☷ Smit. Despite its location, at the foot of the exclusive P. C. Hooftstraat and south entrance to the Rijksmuseum, this hotel is anything but pretentious. It's a lively and friendly place and a good choice for those who want to enjoy the Leidseplein nightlife. The neighboring restaurant is open for lunch and afternoon snacks but closes at 6 PM. The rooms are very plain and the bathrooms are spacious. **Pros:** friendly staff, close to museums. **Cons:** rooms facing the tram lines are a bit noisy, rooms can be cramped. ⊠*P. C. Hooftstraat 24, 1071 BX, Museum District & Environs* ☎*020/671–4785* ⊕*www.hotelsmit.com* ⟿*51 rooms* ⟁*In-room: no a/c, safe, Wi-Fi. In-hotel: restaurant, laundry service, public Internet, public Wi-Fi, no-smoking rooms* ☰AE, MC, V ⦿CP.

¢-$

☷ Jupiter. On a quiet residential street not far from the Vondelpark, the Jupiter hotel, though its arched doorway and windows are rimmed with neon lighting, has a plain, homey interior and an elevator. You're a short walk away from the Rijksmuseum and the Concertgebouw, as well as the shops in the chic P. C. Hooftstraat. **Pros:** quiet location, close to museums, nice bathrooms. **Cons:** no particular Dutch flavor, staff could be friendlier. ✉ *2e Helmersstraat 14, 1054 CJ, Museum District & Environs* ☎ *020/618–7132* ⊕ *www.jupiterhotel.nl* 🛏 *20 rooms* ♿ *In-room: no a/c, safe, dial-up. In-hotel: concierge, some pets allowed, no-smoking rooms* ▤ *No credit cards* ⑩ *CP.*

★ ¢–$ 🏨 **Quentin England.** The intimate Quentin England is one of a series of adjoining buildings dating from 1884, each of which is built in an architectural style of the country whose name it bears. A connoisseur's delight—adorned with a Tudor gable and five-step gable—the Quentin occupies the England and Netherlands buildings. Rooms are simple and vary greatly in size, but are all cozy and clean. The tiny breakfast room is particularly enchanting, with flower boxes on the windowsills, dark-wood tables, and fin-de-siècle decorations. Behind the reception desk is a small bar and espresso machine (perhaps on loan from the neighboring Italian building?). The hotel offers tremendous character and attention in place of space and facilities. **Pros:** friendly staff, close to museums. **Cons:** no-frills rooms, guests must pay in advance. ✉ *Roemer Visscherstraat 30, 1054 EZ, Museum District & Environs* ☎ *020/616–6032* ⊕ *www.quentinhotels. com* 🛏 *40 rooms, 3 with shared bath* ♿ *In-room: no a/c, no phone. In-hotel: no elevator* ▤ *AE, DC, MC, V.*

★ ¢ 🏨 **Flying Pig Palace Hostel.** For those backpackers who like to chill out and save a load of money, the Flying Pig Palace is the favored choice of "piggies" everywhere. The admittance policy is strict: if you're not a backpacker aged 16 to 35, you'll have to look elsewhere. The price includes not only breakfast and sheets, but also free Internet, and the use of in-line skates (so lace up and explore the park, or join the once-weekly night skate throughout the city). There's a bar claiming to serve the cheapest beer in town, and you can cook with other guests in the kitchen. If you're traveling with an amour or don't mind sharing with a friend, the best deal is to book a queen-size bunk bed in one of the dorms. **Pros:** fun atmosphere, tons of activities. **Cons:** no particular Dutch flavor, can be noisy. ✉ *Vossiusstraat 46, 1071 AJ, Museum District & Environs* ☎ *020/400–4187* ⊕ *www.flyingpig.nl* 🛏 *4 rooms, 20 dormitories* ♿ *In-room: no a/c, no phone, no TV (some), Wi-Fi (some). In-hotel: bar, no elevator, no-smoking rooms* ▤ *AE, MC, V* ⑩ *CP.*

★ ¢ 🏨 **Stayokay Amsterdam-Vondelpark.** Word of mouth has made this hostel so popular that more than 75,000 backpackers stay here every year. Hidden on a small side path within the Vondelpark, the location is almost like being in a secret forest, despite being only minutes away from the hustle and bustle of the city. Put your bike in the hostel's covered shed, breakfast on the terrace, ogle the parrots in the trees, then do a few rounds of the park (a great place to connect with new people). Accommodations range from rooms that sleep two to dormitories for 20, and sheets are included in the price. In the spacious lounge, you can use the Internet, watch TV, play pool, or get acquainted with backpackers from around the world. Some rooms are available for those with disabilities. This is probably the cleanest hostel anywhere—your mother would definitely approve. **Pros:** quiet location in the Vondelpark, clean rooms. **Cons:** no particular Dutch flavor, harried staff. ⊠*Zandpad 5, 1054 GA, Museum District & Environs* ☎*020/589–8996* ⊕*www. stayokay.com* ↩*100 rooms, 536 beds* ⚿*In-room: no a/c, no phone, no TV. In-hotel: restaurant, bar, bicycles, no elevator, laundry facilities, public Internet, no-smoking rooms* ▤*AE, MC, V* ❍|*CP.*

DE PIJP

Both budget and posh, homey and businesslike, accommodations come together in the more quiet residential neighborhoods of De Pijp and the high-toned Oud Zuid (Old South). They are set a mere 15-minute canal ride away from Centraal Station, but far enough removed from center-city crowds.

★ ☾ $$$$ ✕⊞**Okura Amsterdam.** This local landmark sports the largest barometer in the Netherlands; every day after the sun goes down, the building forecasts the next day's weather by changing color. Inside, there's a cavernous, dramatic lobby with inch-thick carpeting, guest rooms with dark-wood furniture and flat-screen TVs, and two marvelous, Michelin-starred restaurants to choose from: Yamazato ($$$$), serving Japanese food that's touted as the best in the city, and the classic French Le Ciel Bleu ($$$$). One interesting extra that's sure to help you get back on your feet if you've arrived after a long flight is the hotel's jet-lag program, which uses light therapy to help you adjust to your new surroundings. **Pros:** wonderful rooms, cozy top-floor bar, close to many dining options. **Cons:** lacks a personal touch, staff can have difficulties with simple requests. ⊠*Ferdinand Bolstraat 333, 1072 LH, De Pijp & Environs* ☎*020/678–7111* ⊕*www.okura.nl* ↩*301 rooms, 34 suites* ⚿*In-room: safe, kitchen (some), refrigerator (some), dial-up. In-hotel: 4 restaurants, room service, bars, pool, gym, bicycles, concierge, laundry facilities, laundry service, public Internet, public Wi-Fi, parking (fee), no-smoking rooms* ▤*AE, DC, MC, V.*

$$–$$$$ ⊟**Golden Tulip Apollo Amsterdam.** Amsterdam is often called the "Venice of the North," and five of its canals converge near the Apollo. A modernist palace framed by lovely trees, it's in the swank and suave Apollolaan district, known for its elegant shops and within easy walking distance of the Museum Quarter. Guest rooms are luxurious and modern, with nice touches like plasma televisions. Downstairs, the tangerine and terra-cotta–hued La Sirene offers a French-Mediterranean menu. Few can resist feasting on fish on the restaurant's beautiful canal-side terraces (higher-priced rooms also offer great views of the canals). As *un touche finale,* the hotel even has its own private marina. **Pros:** quiet location, refurbished rooms. **Cons:** slightly out-of-the-way location, overburdened staff. ⊠*Apollolaan 2, 1077 BA, De Pijp & Environs* ☎*020/673–5922* ⊕*www.goldentulipapolloamsterdam.com* ↩*219 rooms, 18 suites* ⚿*In-room: refrigerator, Wi-Fi. In-hotel: restaurant, room service, bar, gym, bicycles, laundry service, concierge,*

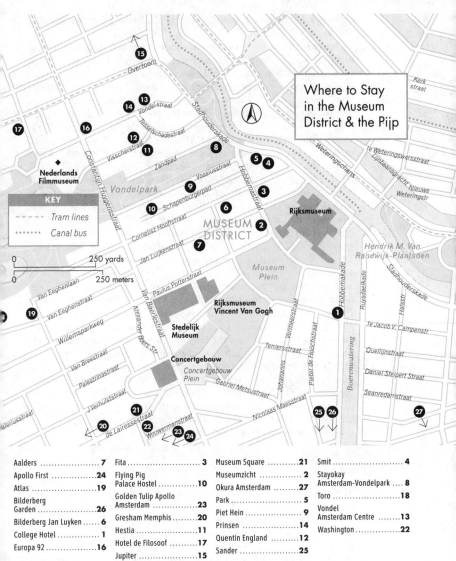

Where to Stay in the Museum District & the Pijp

KEY

- - - - - Tram lines
········· Canal bus

0 _____ 250 yards
0 _____ 250 meters

executive floor, public Internet, public Wi-Fi, parking (fee), no-smoking rooms ⊟*AE, DC, MC, V.*

$$–$$$ ⊡**Apollo First.** The big neon sign here seems more suitable for a cinema, but once you're inside this family-run hotel you'll be surrounded by quiet elegance. Black walls, gold trim, overstuffed chairs, and glittering chandeliers and sconces make the lobby a modern jewel box. Upstairs, you'll want to opt for a quieter room at the back: these chambers allow you to fully savor the tranquillity of the hotel's sylvan garden terrace. A few steps out the door the chic shops of the Apollolaan start; you're also within walking distance of Museum Square. **Pros:** atmospheric interior, gorgeous garden terrace, upper-crust neighborhood. **Cons:** out-of-the-way location, expensive breakfast. ⊠*Apollolaan 123, 1077 AP, De Pijp & Environs* ☎*020/577–3800* ⊕*www.apollofirst.nl* ↩*40 rooms, 3 suites* ⌂*In-room: no a/c, safe, kitchen (some), dial-up, Wi-Fi. In-hotel: room service, bar, concierge, laundry service, public Internet, some pets allowed, no-smoking rooms* ⊟*AE, DC, MC, V.*

$$–$$$ ⊡**Bilderberg Garden.** This bulky modern hotel looms over a tree-lined street in Oud Zuid (Old South), Amsterdam's poshest neighborhood. The hotel underwent a dramatic top-to-toe face-lift in 2006, giving the whole place a bright and cheery atmosphere. Bathrooms have robes and slippers, and a trouser press in every room. The hotel is most often noted for its top restaurant, the Mangerie De Kersentuin (The Cherry Orchard). Although the property lacks any sort of historic allure, you can find plenty of that within walking distance: the Vondelpark, Concertgebouw, and the elegant shops in the Apollolaan are just short strolls away. **Pros:** refurbished rooms, excellent restaurant. **Cons:** mostly business clientele, rooms near lobby can be noisy. ⊠*Dijsselhof-plantsoen 7, 1077 BJ, De Pijp & Environs* ☎*020/570–5600* ⊕*www.gardenhotel.nl* ↩*124 rooms, 2 suites* ⌂*In-room: safe, DVD (some), dial-up, Wi-Fi. In-hotel: restaurant, room service, bar, bicycles, laundry service, public Internet, public Wi-Fi, parking (fee), some pets allowed, no-smoking rooms* ⊟*AE, DC, MC, V.*

EAST OF THE AMSTEL

The small tranquil neighborhood known as the Plantage is a great choice if you want a more relaxed stay. The Hortus Botanicus, Artis Zoo, and the Tropenmuseum dominate this *Oost* (East) Amsterdam area. The Tropenmuseum backs on to the Oosterpark neighborhood, which is bordered by the Linneausstraat, Populierenweg, Amstel River, and Mauritskade. It's a mainly residential area with the exception of the busy Wibautstraat.

$$$$ ⊡**InterContinental Amstel Amsterdam.** Elegant enough to please a queen,
Fodor's Choice   extroverted enough to welcome Madonna, Michael Jackson, and the
★   Rolling Stones, this grand dowager has wowed all onlookers since it opened its doors in 1867. With its palatial facade, sash windows, and historic roof dormers this is a fairy-tale setting guaranteed to bring out your inner prince or princess. You'll feel like a visiting dignitary when entering the magnificent lobby, with its grand double staircase

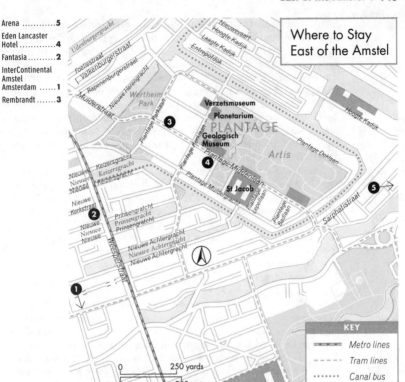

Where to Stay
East of the Amstel

that demands you glide, not walk, down it. The guest rooms are the most spacious in the city (though they shrink considerably on the top floor), and the decor features Oriental rugs, brocade upholstery, Delft lamps, and a color palette of warm tones inspired by Makkum pottery. Fresh tulips are placed in all of the rooms, and the bathrooms spoil guests with showerheads the size of dinner plates. The generous staff-to-guest ratio, the top-notch food—in particular, at the lovely La Rive restaurant—the riverside terrace, the Amstel Lounge (perfect for drinks), and the endless stream of extra "little touches" (such as yacht service) will make for a truly baronial experience. **Pros:** historic building, suites large enough to do cartwheels in, the most attentive hotel staff in Amsterdam. **Cons:** the door between the pool and the changing rooms is noisy, hard to find elevator. ⊠*Professor Tulpplein 1, 1018 GX, East of the Amstel* ☎*020/622–6060* ⊕*www.intercontinental.com/ams-amstel* ⊅*55 rooms, 24 suites* ☐*In-room: safe (some), kitchen (some), DVD, VCR (some), Wi-Fi. In-hotel: 2 restaurants, room service, 2 bars, pool, gym, laundry service, public Internet, public Wi-Fi, parking (fee), no-smoking rooms* ☐*AE, DC, MC, V.*

★ $$–$$$ **Arena.** This grand complex in a former 19th-century orphanage consists of the hotel, a restaurant, and a dance club (complete with frescoed walls that reflect its former function as a clandestine church). For those who like spare minimal style the hotel is strikingly austere. The lobby is minimalist black with an impressive cast-iron staircase leading up to the rooms. The hotel uses the hottest young Dutch architects and designers in the hotel's continual evolution. Rooms—some of which are split-level to form a lounge area—are furnished with modernist furniture by Gispen, Eames, and Martin Visser. **Pros:** fun atmosphere, stylish decor, good range of bar. **Cons:** no-frills room, out-of-the-way location. ⊠*'s-Gravesandestraat 51, 1092 AA, East of the Amstel* ☏*020/850–2400* ⊕*www.hotelarena.nl* ⤿*127 rooms, 6 suites* ♿*In-room: no a/c, safe (some), Wi-Fi (some). In-hotel: 2 restaurants, 3 bars, laundry service, public Internet, public Wi-Fi, parking (fee), no-smoking rooms* ⊟*AE, DC, MC, V* ⦿❘*CP.*

♻ **$–$$$**   🏨 **Eden Lancaster Hotel.** The higher-priced rooms in this hotel have a view of a verdant lawn—a reminder of the hotel's location in the district known as the Plantage. The Artis zoo is opposite the hotel, and the Tropenmuseum is within walking distance, which makes the hotel a great choice for kids. Rooms are light and cheerful, if a bit unremarkable. **Pros:** rooms designed for families, leafy neighborhood, close to zoo. **Cons:** no particular Dutch flavor, out-of-the-way location. ⊠*Plantage Middenlaan 48, 1018 DH, East of the Amstel* ☏*020/535–6888* ⊕*www.edenlancasterhotel.com* ⤿*92 rooms* ♿*In-room: no a/c, safe, Ethernet, dial-up. In-hotel: restaurant, laundry service, public Internet, public Wi-Fi, parking (fee), no-smoking rooms* ⊟*AE, DC, MC, V.*

$ 🏨 **Fantasia.** Peace and quiet await you at this friendly hotel occupying an 18th-century canal house. Ornamental cows are found everywhere in the hotel (there's a history of farming in the owner's family). There's a room to suit everyone, from a small attic room (complete with bath) to a family-sized room that sleeps four. There's also a pleasant hotel garden where you can relax and pet the resident dog. **Pros:** staff members are real characters, leafy location, relaxed vibe. **Cons:** out-of-the-way location, books up fast due to regular guests. ⊠*Nieuwe Keizersgracht 16, 1018 DR, East of the Amstel* ☏*020/623–8259* ⊕*www.fantasia-hotel.com* ⤿*19 rooms, 2 with shared bath* ♿*In-room: no a/c, no phone, no TV, Wi-Fi (some). In-hotel: no elevator, public Internet, public Wi-Fi, no-smoking rooms* ⊟*AE, MC, V* ⦿❘*CP.*

★ **$**   🏨 **Rembrandt.** Because it is close to the University of Amsterdam, Hortus Botanicus, and Tropenmuseum, the Hotel Rembrandt is often populated with academics and museum people—which explains the library of 1,800 books. The rarified air is particularly thick in the remarkable breakfast room: the 18th-century paintings and exquisitely painted woodwork on the ceiling, and the wood paneling and beams dating from 1558, were brought here in the 19th century. Most of the rooms at the back of the hotel facing the garden are quiet, though there are now double-glazed windows in front. **Pros:** great atmosphere, near museums. **Cons:** no real public areas, rooms at the front can be noisy. ⊠*Plantage Middenlaan 17, 1018 DA, East of the Amstel* ☏*020/627–2714* ⊕*www.hotelrembrandt.nl* ⤿*17 rooms* ♿*In-room: no a/c, Wi-Fi. In-hotel: room service, no elevator, laundry service, public Wi-Fi* ⊟*AE, MC, V* ⦿❘*CP.*

Nightlife & the Arts

WORD OF MOUTH

"For the really traditional Amsterdam 'brown café' experience, look for some combination of that special Dutch sort of swirly 18th-century-style script on the windows, lace café-curtains, lots of dark wood, and carpet-patterned chenille table-coverings."
—PatrickLondon

"Amsterdam has a popular comedy show called Boom Chicago that might be fun."
—Travelnut

Updated by
Karina Hof

AMSTERDAM'S NIGHTLIFE CAN HAVE YOU careening between smoky coffee shops, chic wine bars, mellow jazz joints, laid-back lounges, and clubs either intimate or raucous. The bona fide local flavor can perhaps best be tasted in one of the city's ubiquitous brown café-bars—called "brown" because of their woody walls and nicotine-stained ceilings. Here, both young and old, the mohawked and the merely balding, come to relax, rave, and revel in every variety of coffee and alcohol. The Dutch are very sociable people who enjoy going out. Don't hesitate to join the revelry. It will definitely make for a memorable trip.

BROWN CAFÉS

Along with French's *ennui* and Portuguese's *saudade*, a Dutch word often makes linguists' list of culturally untranslatable terms. *Gezelligheid,* however, is a positive one, referring to a state of total coziness created by warm social circumstances. People, places, and things are all contributing factors, though if you want to experience *gezelligheid* like a true Lowlander, learn this equation: drink + conversation ÷ friends = *gezellig*! The best place for these pleasures is a traditional brown café, or *bruine kroeg*. Wood paneling, wooden floors, comfortably worn furniture, and walls and ceilings stained with eons' worth of tobacco smoke are responsible for their name—though today a little artfully stippled paint achieves the same effect. Customarily, there is no background music, just the hum of *kletsen* (chitchat) and the house-cat meowing. There will also be a beer or two, and perhaps a *jenever* (Dutch gin) as the evening wears on.

Café Chris. This venue has been pouring beverages since 1624, when it served as the local bar for builders of the Westerkerk. The cozy factor is enhanced by the smallest washrooms in town. ⊠*Bloemstraat 42, Jordaan* ☎*020/624–5942* ⊕*www.cafechris.nl.*

Café Sluyswacht. Beware: the slant of this oldie-but-goodie can lead to nausea after one too many beers on the patio. A quintessential Amsterdam view of the Oudeschans, however, has been bringing relief since 1695. ⊠*Jodenbreestraat 1, Jewish Quarter and Plantage* ☎*020/625–7611* ⊕*www.sluyswacht.nl.*

De Admiraal. Once the tasting house of an old family distillery, two hundred years later, this Jordaan spot still serves potent liqueurs, including Dutch *jenever*. ⊠*Herengracht 319, The Canal Ring* ☎*020/625–4334* ⊕*www.de-ooievaar.nl.*

De Doktertje. Beer and liquor are just what "the little doctor," the tiniest brown bar in the country, have been ordering for centuries. ⊠*Rozenboomsteeg 4, The Old City Center (Het Centrum)* ☎*020/626–4427.*

De Engelse Reet. Also referred to as "The Pilsner Club," this decidedly ancient and unmistakably brown venue is like stepping back into some lost age when beer was the safest alternative to drinking water. ⊠*Begijnensteeg 4, The Old City Center (Het Centrum)* ☎*020/623–1777.*

A Jenever Primer

The indigenous liquor of the Netherlands is *jenever*, a potent spirit that was invented in the mid-1600s, when an alchemist in Leiden discovered a way to distill juniper berries. It was first sold as medicine but by the late 17th century, people liked it so much that they soon started drinking it for fun. Soon the English got in on the *jenever* game. They bumped up the alcohol content, smoothed over the rough-edged flavor, and called it gin.

There are two basic kinds of *jenever—oude* (old) and *jonge* (young). The names aren't a matter of aging, but of distilling techniques. Young *jenever* uses a newer (post WWII) distilling techique that produces a lighter, less outspoken spirit. Old *jenever* has a much more pronounced flavor. If you want to drink *jenever* like a true Lowlander, find yourself a *proeflokaal*, an old-fashioned "tasting house." We recommend the legendary **Wynand Fockink,** which has been hydrating Amsterdammers since 1679. Once you have made your choice from the milder *jonge* saps or the more sophisticated *oude* spirits, let the fun begin. The bartender fills a sherry-like glass until it is so precariously full that you must lean over the bar, hands behind you back, and take your first sip without touching the glass. Only then are you free to lift the glass by its dainty stem. When *jenever* is served with a beer it is called a *kopstoot*, literally meaning "headbang." This should be taken as a warning to the uninitiated.

De Prins. Like a number of cafés in the Jordaan, this mainstay is blessed with a canal-side patio. ✉*Prinsengracht 124, Jordaan* ☎*020/624–9382.*

De Reiger. With a distinctive Jugendstil bar and highly touted food, this joint is a favorite of beautiful people and seasoned locals alike. ✉*Nieuwe Leliestraat 34, Jordaan* ☎*020/624–7426.*

De Twee Zwaantjes. If you want to hear the locals sing folk music on a Saturday evening or a Sunday afternoon, stop by this classic canal-side café. ✉*Prinsengracht 114, Jordaan* ☎*020/625–2729* ⊕*www.detweezwaantjes.nl.*

Nol. Only getting started at 9 each night (except Tuesday), Nol resonates with lusty-lunged native Jordaaners having the time of their lives. ✉*Westerstraat 109, Jordaan* ☎*020/624–5380* ⊕*www.cafenol-amsterdam.nl.*

Rooie Nelis. Despite the area's tendency toward trendiness, this café has kept its traditional Jordaan atmosphere. ✉*Laurierstraat 101, Jordaan* ☎*020/624–4167* ⊕*www.caferooienelis.nl.*

FodorśChoice ★ **'t Smalle.** Set with Golden Age chandeliers, leaded-glass windows, and the patina of centuries, this charmer is one of Amsterdam's most glorious spots. The after-work crowd always jams the waterside terrace here, though you are just as well to opt for the historic interior, once home to one of the city's first *jenever* distilleries. It's not surprising to learn that a literal copy of this place was created for Nagasaki's Holland Village in Japan. ✉*Egelantiersgracht 12, Jordaan* ☎*020/623–9617.*

Cheers to Dutch Beers

If you think Dutch beer begins and ends with Heineken, think again! The Netherlands has a thriving little industry of microbrews and produces some top-notch stuff. While most of the beer can be roughly broken down into three mouthwatering categories (*pils, witte bier,* and *bokbier*), *pils* (pilsner) is by far the most popular and commonly consumed. A refreshing light golden lager, it is served in smaller glasses and with more foam (two fingers worth) than you're probably used to. In summer, Amsterdammers find refreshment in *witte bier,* a white zesty brew served with a twist of lemon. *Bokbier,* a stronger variety of *pils,* is made with warming spices. The Dutch also love Belgium brews, so you'll have no problem finding Trappist beers, Lambics, fruit beers, wheat beers, and dark brown ales.

OUR FAVORITE WATERING HOLES

Brouwerij 't IJ. Perched under a windmill on the eastern outskirts of the city is an evocative, if out of the way, microbrewery. Choose from any one of their coveted home brews (Plzen, Natte, Zatte, Struis, Columbus). ✉ *Funenkade 7, East of the Amstel* ☎ *020/622–8325* ⊕ *www.brouwerijhetij.nl* ☾ *Daily from 3–8.*

Café Belgique. As the name suggests, this welcoming little café, located right behind Nieuwe Kerk, has an excellent selection of Belgian ales. ✉ *Gravenstraat 2, The Old City Center (Het Centrum)* ☎ *020/625–1974.*

Café Gollem. Very popular with students and locals, the well-known brown café near Dam Square has far too many beers to try in one go. Ditto for its same-named sister in The Pijp. ✉ *Raamsteeg 4, The Old City Center (Het Centrum)* ☏ *No phone* ⊕ *www.cafegollem.nl* ✉ *Daniel Stalpertstraat 74, The Pijp* ☎ *020/676–7117.*

Het Elfde Gebod. Right in the heart of the Red Light District, this cozy bar has five Belgian beers on tap and over 50 bottled. ✉ *Zeedijk 5, The Old City Center (Het Centrum)* ☏ *No phone* ⊕ *www.hetelfdegebod.com.*

In de Wildeman. This busy, jolly brown café attracts a wide range of types and ages. There are two hundred bottled brews to chose from, 17 beers on tap, and a featured beer of the month. ✉ *Kolksteeg 3, The Old City Center (Het Centrum)* ☎ *020/638–2348* ⊕ *www.indewildeman.nl.*

De Zotte. The name of this little pub off of the Leidseplein translates to "really really drunk," and with around 100 Belgian beers available, it's aptly named. ✉ *Raamstraat 29, Jordaan* ☎ *020/626–8694* ⊕ *www.dezotte.nl.*

Fodor'sChoice ★ **Wynand Fockink.** This is Amsterdam's most famous—and miraculously least hyped—*proeflokaal* (tasting room). Opened in 1679, this dimlit, blithely cramped little bar just behind the Hotel Krasnapolsky has a menu of over 60 Dutch spirits that reads like poetry: *Bruidstranen* (bride's tears) and *Boswandeling* (a walk in the woods) are just two favorite flavors. Call ahead for a guided tour of the distillery. ✉ *Pijlsteeg 31, The Old City Center (Het Centrum)* ☎ *020/639–2695* ⊕ *www.wynand-fockink.nl* ☾ *Daily 3* PM*–9* PM.

BARS, CAFÉS & LOUNGES

Perhaps like the diners of New Jersey, brown cafés will remain an institution as much for the sake of wood-paneled nostalgia as for practical reasons: affordability and coziness. In recent years though, brown has given way to black, as Amsterdam's watering holes take on a sleeker intercontinental vibe. If a Berlin DJ hasn't popped in for the evening, a digital jukebox pulsates loungey deep house beats. Diners go gaga over Asian-fusion menus. Frosted walls shed mood lighting onto the latest Droog furniture. And even the Jack Russell faces threat as favorite purse pooch from hip rivals like the French bulldog.

Absinthe. If pot or prostitutes aren't your thing, Amsterdam permits another oft-forbidden substance. Absinthe is where seekers of the same-named sap can get safely starry-nighted—this in spite of the fact that the green fairy may be what fueled Van Gogh's little ear episode. Traditional tonics are also on tap for those who seek a more generically gothic vibe in the grotto-like bar. ⊠*Nieuwezijds Voorburgwal 171, The Old City Center (Het Centrum)* ☎*06/4607–6476* ⊕*www. absinthe.nl.*

Bar With No Name. Too popular to be incognito, this Nine Streets mainstay is now referred to by its address, the coordinates of which fall right where hiply understated intersects with charmingly pretentious. The '70s-style decor and dim-sum-y menu attract advertising types, but a housecat named Jippie keeps all the anonymity in check. ⊠*Wolvenstraat 23, The Canal Ring* ☎*020/320–0843.*

Bep. Since opening, Bep has attracted a smart artistic crowd for mellow afternoons and lively evenings. ⊠*Nieuwezijds Voorburgwal 260, The Old City Center (Het Centrum)* ☎*020/626–5649.*

Boom Bar. If you're a lounging American, you'll find a familiar home at this part and parcel of the same-named comedy club. The music will be comfortingly retro for most Generation Xers, and there's a terrace and an array of fruity cocktails for those on the summer backpack circuit. ⊠*Leidseplein 12, Museum District* ☎*020/423–0101* ⊕*www. boomchicago.nl.*

Brasserie De Brakke Grond. As would be expected from a theater-happy neighborhood, the Nes offers some prime drinking holes. Fans of Belgian beer should stop by this café next door to the Flemish Cultural Center to select from dozens of options, consumable out on the spacious patio or within the classy restaurant. ⊠*Nes 43, The Old City Center (Het Centrum)* ☎*020/626–0044* ⊕*www.brasseriedebrakkegrond.nl.*

Café Cox. The Stadsschouwburg's restaurant provides a pleasant retreat from the tourist and tram clamor outside on the city's second-busiest square. It's also a good bet for speedy service if ever there was one: courtesy may not be a top priority to the Dutch, but promptness is, especially among theatergoers. ⊠*Marnixstraat 429, Leidseplein* ☎*020/523–7851* ⊕*www.cafecox.nl.*

Café Cuba. The always lively Nieu-wmarkt mainstay serves relatively cheap cocktails and offers a jazzy electronic sound track that inspires many of the hipster and student regulars to light up a joint in the back. ⊠ *Nieuwmarkt 3, The Old City Center (Het Centrum)* ☎ *020/627–4919.*

> ### KOEKJE BIJ?
>
> As frugal as the Dutch are, one act of their generosity is found in the *koekje bij* phenomenon: a small "cookie on the side" (or sometimes, piece of chocolate) is always served perched on the saucer of a hot beverage.

Café de Jaren. This light and airy multilevel café has a lovely terrace overlooking the Amstel. It's exceedingly popular with a big cross-section of the population, from students and hipster knitting circles to artists and businessmen. ⊠ *Nieuwe Doelenstraat 20, The Old City Center (Het Centrum)* ☎ *020/625–5771* ⊕ *www.cafedejaren.nl.*

Café de Koe. Hardly bovine, the "Cow's Café" is a fine place to chew the cud or graze a little, and is especially favored by local musicians and students. ⊠ *Marnixstraat 381, Leidseplein* ☎ *020/625–4482* ⊕ *www.cafedekoe.nl.*

★ **Café Luxembourg.** This favorite haunt of the famous food critic Johannes van Dam is known for its dark Art Deco interior and a glassed-in terrace that's perfect for watching people on the Spui. Those with less interest in urban sociology can entertain themselves at the communal table with an assortment of international newspapers and magazines. ⊠ *Spui 24, The Old City Center (Het Centrum)* ☎ *020/620–6264* ⊕ *www.luxembourg.nl.*

Café Schiller. Part of the same-named hotel, this place has a real sense of history thanks to a wooden fin-de-siècle interior that other grand cafés would sell their souls for. Still, the glory is fast fading as Rembrandtplein gets seedier and a long-patronizing media crowd finds other places to slake their thirst. ⊠ *Rembrandtplein 26, Rembrandtplein* ☎ *020/624–9846.*

★ **Café Vertigo.** Not only does the Nederlands Filmmuseum have an atmospheric cellar restaurant, great for a pre-movie meal or post-flick refreshments, but the stunningly scenic terrace provides open-air seating for watching the chaos that is the Vondelpark. ⊠ *Vondelpark 3, Museum District* ☎ *020/612–3021* ⊕ *www.vertigo.nl.*

Fodor'sChoice **College Hotel.** Seeking a little New Amsterdam in Old Amsterdam? Stop
★ by the lounge-bar of this relatively new hotel, where dark oak floors, sleek black tables, low lights, and sequestered seating arrangements evoke an old boys' club in midtown Manhattan—minus the elitism. In fact, almost all the staff are service-industry students in training. Seek the fireplace out on a chilly night, and on Sundays from September through June there's live samba. ⊠ *The College Hotel, Roelof Hartstraat 1, Museum District* ☎ *020/571–1511* ⊕ *www.steinhotels. com/college.*

De Balie. Like Wi-Fi antennae, dark-rimmed eyeglasses peek over PowerBooks as a well-read and socially conscious crowd fills the café/bar of this center for culture and politics. It's the ideal spot to pick up local event flyers or, for that matter, a date. ⊠*Kleine Gartmanplantsoen 10, Leidseplein* ☎*020/553–5131* ⊕*www.balie.nl.*

De Buurvrouw. In this small sawdusted and kitsch-strewn haven, students and alternative types don't mind yelling over the latest in loud guitars and funky beats. They also enjoy a pool tournament every now and then. ⊠*St. Pieterspoortsteeg 29, The Old City Center (Het Centrum)* ☎*020/625–9654* ⊕*www.debuurvrouw.nl.*

De Kroon. This grand café dating back to 1898 is popular for both its intimate seating arrangements and a U-shape bar surrounding old-style wooden museum cases filled with zoological specimens. In the evenings, a yuppie clientele sits pretty, high above the noisy, street-level clubs on Rembrandtplein, including the Club Escape conglomerate next door. ⊠*Rembrandtplein 17, Rembrandtplein* ☎*020/625–2011* ⊕*www.dekroon.nl.*

Dantzig. With a view of the Amstel River, this grand café jutting out from the Stopera complex is the perfect point for a pre- or post-performance bevvy. The staff is as allegro as you'll get in this city. ⊠*Zwanenburgwal 15, The Old City Center (Het Centrum)* ☎*020/620–9039* ⊕*www.dantzig.info.*

Dulac. The mazelike den attracts all types by offering sensory overload in the form of strong drinks, good food, DJs, and a decor that suggests it was built by a Gaudi reborn as an inspired junkyard artist. ⊠*Haarlemmerstraat 118, Jordaan* ☎*020/624–4265.*

Finch. With a funky interior and epic views of a canal and a church square, the café attracts thirsty, artsy types. ⊠*Noordermarkt 5, Jordaan* ☎*020/626–2461.*

The Getaway. True to its name, this bar-restaurant provides a cool and convenient retreat to the students and local shop proprietors whose life may be getting a little stagnant on Spui. Regular DJs assist in the common goal of escapism. ⊠*Nieuwezijds Voorburgwal 250, The Old City Center (Het Centrum)* ☎*020/627–1427.*

Het Blauwe Theehuis. The Vondelpark's quietly pulsating epicenter is a blue space-ship–shaped "teahouse" with a massive, multi-tiered terrace attracting all manner of folks by day and a hip clubby crowd by night. On Sunday nights and summertime Fridays, DJs are on hand to provide a gentle but beat-driven sound track. ⊠*Vondelpark 5, Museum District* ☎*020/662–0254* ⊕*www.blauwetheehuis.nl.*

Kadinsky Café. By establishing its own café-bar, right across the street from its central-most coffee shop, the Kadinsky chain has found a way to avoid getting tangled up in the circus of legislation that prohibits venues from selling both alcohol and soft drugs. So, if you'd like smokes in one hand and sips in the other, buy your buds at Zoutsteeg 14, cross the road, and order a drink. ⊠*Zout-steeg 9–11, The Old City Center (Het Centrum)* ☎*020/627–3258.*

Kapitein Zeppos. Nestled on an easy-to-miss alley, this former cigar factory is still redolent of jazzy times past. On weekdays neighboring University of Amsterdam scholars talk books and drink espressos. Evenings are perfect for a memorable glass of wine or a simple meal, especially with live music on some Sundays. ⊠*Gebed Zonder End 5, The Old City Center (Het Centrum)* ☎*020/624–2057* ⊕*www.zeppos.nl.*

KING OF BEER

Located behind Dam Square, Bierkoning is the best beer store in Amsterdam, and possibly even the Netherlands. They have more than 950 beers in stock and tons of glassware and other accessories. The friendly, knowledgeable staff can tell you everything you ever wanted or needed to know about Belgian and Dutch beers. ⊠*Paleisstraat 125, The Old City Center (Het Centrum)* ☎*020/625–2336* ⊕*www.bierkoning.nl.*

Kingfisher. For a flavor of the neighborhood's regentrified café culture, check out this favorite corner bar that fills up most nights with parched Pijpers. ⊠*Ferdinand Bolstraat 24, The Pijp* ☎*020/671–2395.*

Lime. This slick, minimalistic lounge sandwiched between the Red Light District and Chinatown offers a nicely unpretentious atmosphere. ⊠*Zeedijk 104, The Old City Center (Het Centrum)* ☎*020/639–3020.*

Lokaal 't Loosje. An old tram warehouse where the arty and the student unite. The place dates back over two centuries, with tile wall hangings from 1912 adding to the authenticity of antiquity. ⊠*Nieuwmarkt 32–34, The Old City Center (Het Centrum)* ☎*020/627–2635.*

Lux. A fantastic 1960s look and an attractive young crowd keeps it lively at this Marnixstraat club. ⊠*Marnixstraat 397, The Old City Center (Het Centrum)* ☎*020/422–1412.*

The Mansion. The loungey bar-club-restaurant opened its doors in 2005 and still exudes that distinctive London-style of classy. It's for folks who have money and like showing it off. ⊠*Hobbemastraat 2, Museum District* ☎*020/616–6664* ⊕*www.the-mansion.nl.*

NL-Lounge. Taking its name from the national car code, NL is one of the hippest local lounges. It's so classy, it makes you feel as if you have been transported back to the Rat Pack days. ⊠*Nieuwezijds Voorburgwal 169, The Old City Center (Het Centrum)* ☎*020/622–7510* ⊕*www.nieuwezijdslounge.nl.*

The Tara. This labyrinth of an Irish bar is large enough to host live music and large-screen football (soccer) matches. Yet, there are still plenty of cozy nooks left over for a quiet meal, Wi-Fi web surfing, or cuddling with ye olde sweetheart. ⊠*Rokin 89, The Old City Center (Het Centrum)* ☎*020/421–2654* ⊕*www.thetara.com.*

FodorsChoice
★

Twenty Third. The newest addition to the Okura, already with two highly acclaimed restaurants and perhaps the country's finest hotel service, is this champagne bar so named after the top floor on which it perches. Besides the eagle-eye view of Amsterdam South, there are 17 different kinds of champagne and snacks (if caviar could be so categorized) from the highly touted Ciel Bleu restaurant next door. ⊠ *Hotel Okura, Ferdinand Bolstraat 333, The Pijp* ☎ *020/678–8344* ⊕ *www.okura.nl.*

Twstd. It may be small and vowelless, but this lounge belongs to the organizers of the mega Dance Valley festival (www.dancevalley.nl) and is famous for its annual DJ contest. Don't be surprised if a top turntablist drops by to spin some latest dance grooves. ⊠ *Weteringschans 157, The Canal Ring* ☎ *020/320–7030* ⊕ *www.twstd.nl.*

4

Star Ferry. Whether or not you have the musical motivation to visit the Muziekgebouw aan 't IJ, the building's café is worth the hike alone. On a clear afternoon or night, stop by for a meal or a drink and take in the panoramic views of the harbor and the ever-booming docklands of Amsterdam. ⊠ *Muziekgebouw aan"t IJ, Piet Heinkade 1, Eastern Docklands* ☎ *020/788–2090* ⊕ *www.starferry.nl.*

Werck. This former coach house to the Westerkerk is now a watering hole for yuppies, Jordaanites, and the loungey house DJs who serve them their smooth late-night beats. During the day, tourists from the nearby Anne Frank House bring brighter-colored clothing to the café-scape, both on the bi-level interior and outside on the spacious patio. ⊠ *Prinsengracht 277, Jordaan* ☎ *020/627–4079* ⊕ *www.werck.nl.*

Wildschut. This 1920s Amsterdam School edifice is a delightful place for coffee, Wi-Fi Web-surfing, or a pre- or post-recital stop, with the Concertgebouw just down the road. At nightfall, it's also the place to meet pin-striped-suited yuppies by the dozen. The large terrace has great views for architecture enthusiasts. ⊠ *Roelof Hartplein 1-3, Museum District* ☎ *020/676–8220* ⊕ *www.goodfoodgroup.nl.*

Winkel. This corner café's eminent *appeltaart* (apple pie) beckons locals and travelers alike. The mastermind behind Saturday's organic market once owned the place, so you can bet there's living memory here of fresh food and conscious consumership. ⊠ *Noordermarkt 43, Jordaan* ☎ *020/623–0223.*

CLOSE UP

Lighting-Up in Amsterdam

Unless you're a regular user, checking out one of those euphemistically named venues where marijuana is sold is hard to justify from a "when in Rome" rationale. The coffee shop industry caters mostly to travelers, and the Dutch are reported to smoke less pot than most other European populations. That said, if you do decide to indulge in Amsterdam's infamous weed scene, there are a few things you should know.

THE SELECTION
Most coffee shops offer a robust selection of both weed and hash, sold anywhere from €5 to €20 per gram Don't hesitate to describe your dream high to the dealer, and he (or, rarely, she) will try to accommodate you.

HANDLING YOUR HIGH
Be wary. Dutch-sold marijuana is potent and blows the socks off the most hard-core potheads. If cannabis is not your usual drug of choice, don't feel you have to play cool: ask questions of the staff and use caution whatever your medium—joint, bong, or brownie. If you do over-indulge, try not to panic. Find a quiet place, take deep breaths, and remember that the discomfort will pass. Sometimes consuming something sweet will help to soften the high.

THE DEAL ON DEALING
Amsterdam is home to an estimated 240 coffee shops, but statistics are looking grim for those who go gaga for ganja. An April 2007 law that prohibits the side-by-side sale of marijuana and alcohol has forced proprietors to dry out their bars to retain coffee shop licenses. What's more, as of July 1, 2008, Amsterdam, like many other cities, will have become

a smoke-free service city and though such a law could potentially turn the whole industry on its head, coffee shops, it seems, will be allowed to keep *blowen*. Currently, it's acceptable to sell small amounts of marijuana via the "front door" of a coffee shop where the customer enters. However, the "back door," through which the product arrives, is linked to the illegal world of the mysterious wholesale supplier. Technically, selling marijuana is a no-no, officially prohibited, but the government has barely bothered to enforce this legislation—the buzzword here is "decriminalized." Thanks to the Dutch Opium Act of 1976, an important distinction is made between hard drugs and soft drugs—weed being soft.

STAYING LEGAL
The Netherlands currently allows up to 5 grams of marijuana and several other cannabis-laden comestibles (pot brownies, space cakes, ganja cookies) to be dispensed at a licensed venue to anyone over 18. It also condones possession of up to 30 grams by individuals, solely for personal use. While marijuana must be purchased on regulated premises, takeaway to a more discreet spot is another option. Most of the city frowns upon smoking joints in restaurants, bars, and cafés, though nightclubs tend to be kosher (if you're in doubt, simply ask an employee). The ins and outs of the trade can get as fuzzy as a stoner's Monday morning. So, what's the Lowlands' logic to all this? Cannabis is recognized as a substance that has the potential for psychological addiction, yes, but it is not believed to create an "unacceptable risk" to the body or, for that matter, to society.

COFFEE SHOPS

Coffee shops (that really sell weed) tend to be dim, noxious places, with an interior decor rivaling that of your local deli. However, below are a few of the cleaner and more sophisticated establishments in the city. Still, the atmosphere is very different (almost the antithesis) to the *gezelligheid* of Amsterdam's precious brown cafés.

Abraxas. Down a small alley, just a stone's throw from the Dam, you'll come upon what would seem to be the multilevel home of a family of hip hobbits. You'll think better once you make out the poor-postured travelers smoking joints or nibbling on ganja cakes. A small satellite branch, Abraxas Too, can be found at Spuistraat 51. ✉ *Jonge Roelensteeg 12–14, The Old City Center (Het Centrum)* ☎ *020/625–5763* ⊕ *www.abraxasparadise.nl.*

> ### READY, SET, TOKE!
>
> During November, a conspicuous number of tourists with glazed-over eyes and smiles that stretch from dreadlock to dreadlock can be spotted around Amsterdam. No, Phish isn't in town—it's **Cannabis Cup**, the weeklong contest sponsored by *High Times* magazine. The premise of this event is to provide a friendly competition among the city's pot purveyors to see who has the best stuff. Winners are selected by public judges who have all-access to the pot at stake, though at the cost of a €200 judges' pass.

Barney's. This regular Cannabis Cup–winning coffee shop brings together two stand-alone concepts: a wide variety of smokeables and all-day breakfasts of the world (served from 9:30–1 in the coffee shop). Barney's Brasserie serves breakfast all day long and is located a few doors up at Haarlemmerstraat 98. ✉ *Haarlemmerstraat 102, Jordaan* ☎ *020/625–9761* ⊕ *www.barneys.biz.*

Dampkring. As much as being stoned and being starstruck seem antithetical, this coffee shop has become even more popular after its use as a set for *Ocean's Twelve* (and the tacky decision to loop movie clips above the bar). The possibility of sitting where Brad may have toked-up notwithstanding, the weed menu is exceptional and the smoothie selection remarkable. ✉ *Handboogstraat 29, The Old City Center (Het Centrum)* ☎ *020/638–0705* ⊕ *www.dedampkring.nl.*

Fodor's Choice ★ **De Rokerij.** For over a decade, this coffee shop has managed to maintain a magical-grotto feel that, ironically enough, requires no extra indulgences to induce a state of giddy transcendence. Dim lights, Indian-inspired murals, and low-to-the-ground seating keep the ambience chill regardless of how busy the Leidseplein headquarters can get. De Rokerij's other branches may inspire smaller-scale out-of-body experiences. ✉ *Lange Leidsedwarsstraat 41, Leidseplein* ☎ *020/622–9442* ⊕ *www.rokerij.net* ✉ *Amstel 8, The Canal Ring* ☎ *020/620–0484* ✉ *Singel 8, The Canal Ring* ☎ *020/422–6643* ✉ *Elandsgracht 53, Jordaan* ☎ *020/623–0938.*

Green House. Another Cannabis Cup darling, and a not uncommon docking station for celebrities staying at the Grand Hotel up the block, this chain is renowned for quality weeds and seeds. Artful mosaics provide a trippy background, and storefront tables let patrons take in a breath of fresh air. ⊠ *Oudezijds Voorburgwal 191, The Old City Center (Het Centrum)* ☎ *020/627–1739* ⊕ *www.greenhouse.org* ⊠ *Waterlooplein 345, The Old City Center (Het Centrum)* ☎ *020/622–5499* ⊠ *Tolstraat 91, Amsterdam East* ☎ *020/673–7430.*

Kadinsky. This chain offers mellow jazz and scrumptious chocolate-chip cookies, providing a refreshingly understated approach to getting high. ⊠ *Rosmarijnsteeg 9, The Old City Center (Het Centrum)* ☎ *020/624–7023* ⊠ *Langebrugsteeg 7A, The Old City Center (Het Centrum)* ☎ *020/620–4715* ⊠ *Zoutsteeg 14, The Old City Center (Het Centrum)* ☎ *020/620–4715.*

> **SOWING WEEDS**
>
> Those with a green thumb (who do not live in a country where growing of pot is punishable with jail time) may want to consider getting to the root of their high. Marijuana seeds can be purchased from seed shops, coffee shops, and smart shops. A 10-pack can cost somewhere between €30 and €100. Amsterdam's legendary seed shops include **Dutch Passion** (Utrechtsestraat 26, 020/625–1100, www.dutch-passion.nl), **The Flying Dutchman** (Oudezijds Achterburgwal 131, 020/428–4110), and **Homegrown Fantasy** (Nieuwe Nieuwestraat 25, 020/423–2859, www.homegrownfantaseeds.com).

Other Side. Apropos of its location on one of the city's three main gay streets, the clientele at this coffee shop are primarily queer men. The atmosphere is no less welcoming, however, to the straight, the female, or the undecided. ⊠ *Reguliersdwarsstraat 6, Rembrandtplein* ☎ *020/421–1014* ⊕ *www.theotherside.nl.*

Paradox. Perhaps the paradox is that this storefront in the charming Jordaan comes across more like a health-food café than a coffee shop. ⊠ *1e Bloemdwarstraat 2, Jordaan* ☎ *020/623–5639* ⊕ *www.paradox-amsterdam.demon.nl.*

Yo-Yo. This is a quintessential friendly neighborhood coffee shop, which—lucky for its bohemian bourgeoisie neighbors—is in the heart of the multicultural Pijp. ⊠ *2e Jan van der Heijdenstraat 79, De Pijp* ☎ *020/664–7173.*

DANCE CLUBS

If you feel the need to get up off the bar stool and shake your groove thing, Amsterdam has a few venues for just that.

Akhnaton. If you're a world-music buff, think about heading to this renowned venue known for its tight and sweaty African and salsa club nights. ⊠ *Nieuwezijds Kolk 25, The Old City Center (Het Centrum)* ☎ *020/624–3396* ⊕ *www.akhnaton.nl.*

Psilocybin—uh, can you spell that?

Only two decades after the Dutch government condoned the sale of marijuana and hash under the Opium Act of 1976, another "soft drug" came onto the scene: psilocybin. More commonly known as magic mushrooms, psilocybin can be purchased at a number of Amsterdam's various "smart shops." Smart shops sell a veritable salad of other "natural" high-producing substances—peyote, aphrodisiacal herbs and oils, and herbal XTC. If you choose to take any of these products, use your own innate smarts: not only are many of them illegal if carried outside the Netherlands, they can produce strong—and not necessarily pleasant—judgment-impairing hallucinations. In 2007, the legalization of *paddos,* as they are locally termed, was once again called into question after a series of fatal incidents involving tripping tourists. There's an ongoing national debate about whether to impose a ban, so do confirm local laws before you go foraging for fresh fungi.

Conscious Dreams. Hans van den Hurk is attributed for having opened this very first smart shop in 1994, as a place to promote mind-body awareness. Besides the usual suspects of "natural" drugs, you'll find a selection of "harm reduction kits" said to speed up the recovery process after a hyperconscious weekend. Lounge beats play overhead and Internet awaits your access. ✉ *Kerkstraat 113, The Canal Ring* ☎ *020/627–1739* ⊕ *www. consciousdreams.nl* ✉ *Warmoesstraat 12, The Old City Center (Het Centrum)* ☎ *020/421–7000.*

Inner Space. "The only legal coke alternative" and liquid drops to produce "that real MDMA feeling" are among the products sold here. So are mushroom grow kits, marijuana seeds, and some good ol' Vitamin C. ✉ *Spuistraat 108, The Old City Center (Het Centrum)* ☎ *020/624–3338* ⊕ *www.innerspace.nl* ✉ *Staalstraat 5, The Old City Center (Het Centrum)* ☎ *020/ 320–0064.*

Bitterzoet. The relatively new kid on the block has a packed program of DJs, bands, and even theater. Thursday through Saturday offers a hearty serving of hip-hop, soul, and funk. ✉ *Spuistraat 2* ☎ *020/521–3001* ⊕ *www.bitterzoet.com.*

Club More Amor. What used to be plain old "Club More" has gotten a whole new load of Latin-flavored love. DJs play salsa, Caribbean, and other Hispanophilic beats. ✉ *Rozengracht 133, Jordaan* ☎ *020/624–2330* ⊕ *www.clubmoreamor.nl.*

Escape. Thursdays through Sundays, this megaclub opens its doors to some 2,500 people. The great Escape is meant for those who take "dress to impress" literally and are keen to dance under laser lights as DJs spin techno and all its new-millennial derivatives. In celebration of its recent 20-year anniversary, the conglomerate, also comprising the more intimate club Escape deLux (with its own entrance on Amstel 70), has expanded with a studio of MTV-esque aspirations, an LED-ceilinged lounge, and a café. ✉ *Rembrandtplein 11–15, Rembrandtplein* ☎ *020/622–1111* ⊕ *www.escape.nl.*

Jimmy Woo's. Thursday through Sunday, this is probably the hottest club in town for the rich and the famous and their wannabes. The urban grooves are funky and the sound system, not-too-shabby. ✉*Korte Leidsedwarsstraat 18, Leidseplein* ☎*020/626–3150* ⊕*www.jimmywoo.nl.*

Korsakoff. This is a dark but friendly magnet for the pierced and tattooed among us who like their music industrially rough and ready. And somehow, as only the complexities of Dutch culture will permit, the club feels cozy. ✉*Lijnbaansgrach 161, Jordaan* ☎*020/625–7854* ⊕*www.korsakoffamsterdam.nl.*

Odeon. If you feel like some weekend dancing in a gracious old canal house, head for this 17th-century beer brewery turned 19th-century concert hall, which reopened in 2005 to provide cocktails, dining, fashion shows, and spinning from superhip DJs. Many of its rooms retain their spectacular painted and stucco ceilings. ✉*Singel 460, The Old City Center (Het Centrum)* ☎*020/521–8555* ⊕*www.odeonamsterdam.nl.*

The Power Zone. Amsterdam's relatively new megaclub can pack in thousands of revelers and often does, thanks to a fairly easygoing door policy (just don't come as a pack!). There is plenty of room for lounging and dancing to the latest happy house tunes. ✉*Daniel Goedkoopstraat 1–3, Museum District* ☎*020/681–8866* ⊕*www.thepowerzone.nl.*

Studio 80. This newcomer to the square is unlikely to share its clientele with the neighboring clubs, who tend to attract those with a penchant for hair product. On any given night, you'll find underground house producers, Israeli DJs, or unapologetic pop programs that cater to a smart young crowd. ✉*Rembrandtplein 17, The Canal Ring* ☎*020/521–8333* ⊕*www.studio-80.nl.*

Panama. A pioneer in the up-and-coming nightlife and culture zone of the Eastern Docklands is this nightclub with a plush and golden interior. Sadly, in 2005 it was forced to trade in its inspired programming—which included everything from tango orchestras to circus acts—for more commercially viable house music. ✉*Oostelijke Handelskade 4, Eastern Docklands* ☎*020/311–8686* ⊕*www.panama.nl.*

GAY, LESBIAN & MIXED BARS

GAY

Whether or not Amsterdam is the "Gay Capital of the World," as proclaimed by some admirers of the Netherlands' long-standing acceptance of gays and their right to marry, the city undoubtedly has a *trés* gay nightlife. While every nook and cranny is fair game to experience the whole gamut of Amsterdam's sexual orientations and gender-based identities, the gay scene divides into something of a three-ring circus throughout the city center.

Reguliersdwarsstraat Predictable and pretty, the venues here attract mostly men in their 20s, 30s, or 40s (with the occasional sugar daddy grandpa who still has pecs of steel). It's trendy but tactful, cruisey but only after a certain hour. This is not to say, however, that things can't get a little bit X-rated. The dark room at Club Exit, a favorite late-night disco for gay men and a dusting of women, is certainly conducive to lascivious liaisons. What's more, just the thought of the Thermos Saunas (*see below*), not too far away on Kerkstraat, has a way of steaming up the scene. Of the three districts, the one that has evolved along **Warmoestraat** is considerably the least egalitarian. One of the main streets that borders the Red Light District, it feels a little too cut off from the rest of the city. There are a few bars that do welcome all walks of life (including straight folks), but the majority of the clubs found here are men-only, leather-heavy, and dungeon-prone. Your surest bet at all-encompassing *homo-gezelligheid* is **Amstel,** located right off of Rembrandtplein. These coordinates make it likely you'll have to dodge some drunken Rembrandtplein tourists or their speeding taxis, but it's well worth it. Kitschy gay pubs, lively lesbian clubs, and drag bars, Amstel is a haven of pansexual hospitality.

FOR LAVENDER LADIES

Lesbians on the lookout for parties should stop by the bookstore **Xantippe Unlimited,** which specializes in women's literature. ✉ *Prinsengracht 290, The Canal Ring* ☎ *020/623–5854* ⊕ *www. xantippe.nl.*

Another fine resource for seeing what's down with dames is the gay and lesbian bookstore **Boekhandel Vrowlijk.** ✉ *Palesisstraat 135, The Old City Center (Het Centrum)* ☎ *020/623–5142* ⊕ *www.vrolijk.nl.*

Women should consider consulting **COC Amsterdam** for their list of highly recommended reverie. ✉ *Rozenstraat 14, Jordaaan* ☎ *020/626–3087* ⊕ *www.cocamsterdam.nl* ⊙ *Office hours 9 AM– 5 PM. Event times vary.*

April. The front side of this later night lounge makes for classic cruising, with a few females always on the loose. When the place becomes particularly crowded during the weekend, management opens up the backside where a fabulous rotating bar gives everyone at least one 15-minute round of fame. ✉ *Reguliersdwarsstraat 37, Rembrandtplein* ☎ *020/625–9572* ⊕ *www.cafeapril.eu.*

ARC. With fusion-inspired finger food and €5 Wednesday cocktail nights, this lounge is suited for a scene from Sex and the City. Passé as the premise may be, it remains a magnet for fashionable gay men and pansexual hipsters. ✉ *Reguliersdwarsstraat 44, Rembrandtplein* ☎ *020/689–7070* ⊕ *www.bararc.com.*

Club Exit. The late-night multilevel disco and bar attracts a smart young crowd of gay men and their female friends unafraid to dance right into the top-floor dark room. ✉ *Reguliersdwarsstraat 42, Rembrandtplein* ☎ *020/625–8788* ⊕ *www.clubexit.eu.*

Club Stereo. Opened in summer 2007, this city-center gay bar is the new kid on the block, but proving itself an old hand at the DJ+dancefloor equation. ⊠*Jonge Roelensteeg 4, The Old City Center (Het Centrum)* ⊕*clubstereo.nl.*

Cockring. This strictly men-only venue is almost an institution in the leather scene. It also stays open 'til the wee hours of the morning. ⊠ *Warmoestraat 96, The Old City Center (Het Centrum)* ☎*020/623–9604* ⊕*www.clubcockring.com.*

Cuckoo's Nest. Back in 1984, this bar was so leather-lined it put San Francisco's Folsom Street to shame. Today it attracts a more diverse crowd, many of whom find their way to, what's rumored to be, one of the biggest dark rooms in Europe. (See the Web site for a concise chart of "common hanky codes.") ⊠*Nieuwezijds Kolk 6, The Old City Center (Het Centrum)* ☎*020/627–1752* ⊕*www.cuckoosnest.nl.*

Dirty Dick's. Let's just say that the name of this leather cruise bar has a bite that doesn't even come close to its bark. ⊠ *Warmoestraat 86, The Old City Center (Het Centrum)* ☎*020/627–8634.*

Downtown. With its sunny terrace, this café is a pleasant daytime pit stop for coffee and sandwiches. ⊠*Reguliersdwarsstraat 31, Rembrandtplein* ☎*No phone* ⊕*www.coffeeshopdowntown.nl.*

Le Montmartre. This kitschy corner attracts a comfortably out, all-ages, all-classes crowd stopping in for a drink and perhaps a sing-along before heading out clubbing. ⊠*Halvemaansteeg 17, Rembrandtplein* ☎*020/620–7622.*

Queen's Head. You won't find Queen Beatrix here, but a mainstream crowd of well-built and fun-loving princes enjoying DJ beats and parties that pour out onto the sidewalk. ⊠*Zeedijk 20, The Old City Center (Het Centrum)* ☎*020/420–2475* ⊕*www.queenshead.nl.*

Soho. Varnished wood, red leather seats, and brass-framed mirrors provide the backdrop for the outrageous flirting that goes down in this English-style pub. The ever-popular happy hour makes Soho a go-to for locals as well as a magnet for visitors. ⊠*Reguliersdwarsstraat 36, Rembrandtplein* ☎*020/ 422–3312* ⊕*www.pubsoho.eu.*

Thermos Night Sauna. Men interested in more than just a little dip into the city's gay scene might consider taking the plunge at Amsterdam's most luxurious saunas for men, which provides ample opportunity for fraternizing in the Finnish sauna, Turkish steam bath, whirlpool, the "rest cabins," or at the bar. ⊠*Kerkstraat 58–60* ☎*020/623–4936* ⊘*11* PM *to 8* AM.

Thermos Day Sauna. Experience all the amenities, including a swimming pool, rooftop terrace, restaurant, and, for the multi-media-minded, a video room and Internet service. ⊠*Raamstraat 33* ☎*020/623–9158* ⊕*www.thermos.nl.* ⊘*Noon–11* PM.

The Web. Leather, piercing, and tattoos predominate, but meeting one's soul mate at this cruise bar is not out of the question. ⊠*Sint Jacobstraat 6, The Old City Center (Het Centrum)* ☎*020/623–6758.*

LESBIAN

Compared to many other coordinates on the globe, Amsterdam has had women's rights and gay rights down pat for several decades. What can still use a little more loving, however, is society's accommodation of gay women, particularly when it comes to nightlife. This sector of sex in the city still has some evolving to do, yet the scene is steadily expanding its repertoire with an increasing number of lesbian bars and nightclubs.

HERE AND QUEER?

For more information about gay life in Amsterdam, visit the gay and lesbian information kiosk Pink Point (www.pinkpoint.org) located at the Homomonument on the corner of Keizersgracht and Westermarkt; it's open daily from 10–6. For details on gay nightlife, consult the listings at ⊕ www.gayamsterdam.nl and ⊕ www.amsterdam4gays.com.

Saarein II. Amsterdam's best lesbian bar, as it's been labeled, has a cozy brown-café atmosphere in the Jordaan and a relatively new "mixed" policy. Hence the "II." ✉ *Elandsstraat 119, Jordaan* ☎ *020/623–4901* ⊕ *www.saarein.nl.*

Sappho. Finally, the classy dyke bar that this city has always been screaming for. Straight-friendly and especially hospitable to musicians, the venue is popular for its open-mike Tuesdays and live performances on Wednesdays. The rarified air on weekdays, however, can turn into chaos during the weekend dance parties, when even the butch women let their hair down. ✉ *Vijzelstraat 103, Rembrandtplein* ☎ *06/1714–0296* ⊕ *www.sappho.nl.*

Sugar Custom Café. This rather new lesbian-owned bar is a sweet choice for ladies who like ladies, though it also attracts a mix of other tastes. ✉ *Hazenstraat 19, Jordaan* ☎ *No phone* ⊕ *les-bi-friends.com.*

Vive-la-Vie. For almost three decades pretty women have been vying for space in these petite quarters on the edge of Rembrandtplein. Today the bar is popular as ever, also being straight-friendly and open to men—so long as they behave. ✉ *Amstelstraat 7, Rembrandtplein* ☎ *020/624–0114* ⊕ *www.vivelavie.nl.*

MIXED

With a population of just 750,000 inhabiting what are essentially a series of canal-determined concentric circles, it's hard for Amsterdam residents not to bump into one another. Some confluences are less felicitous than others, but you can always count on the ones at "mixed" bars to be merry and gay. As with most mixed venues, gay men usually outnumber lesbians and straight folk.

Amstel Taveerne. Tankards and brass pots hanging from the ceiling reflect the friendly crowd of locals around the bar. Go just for the raucous sing-alongs that erupt whenever an old favorite is played. ✉ *Amstel 54, Rembrandtplein* ☎ *020/623–4254* ⊕ *www.amsteltaveerne.nl.*

COC. Founded in 1946, this center of the Dutch Association for the Integration of Homosexuality is the oldest organization of its kind in the world and today has several chapters throughout the country. Stop by to see what's happening while you're in town. ⊠ *Rozenstraat 8, Jordaan* ☎ *020/623–4596* ⊕ *www. cocamsterdam.nl.*

Getto. Every color and chromosome combination is welcome at this self-proclaimed "place for like minded people." The menu of typical Americana fair and fun cocktails—virgin and experienced—reads as though under the influence of a John Waters script. ⊠ *Warmoes-straat 51, The Old City Center (Het Centrum)* ☎ *020/421–5151* ⊕ *www.getto.nl.*

Habibi Ana. Meaning "my sweetheart" in Arabic, Habibi Ana is a one-of-a-kind experience in Amsterdam and, quite possibly the world over. Founded by the same-titled foundation, this bar caters to gay, bisexual, and transsexual men and women of Arab descent. ⊠ *Lange Leidsedwarsstraat 4–6, Leidseplein* ☎ *No phone* ⊕ *www.habibiana.nl.*

> ### CHEERS TO YOUR (SEXUAL) HEALTH
>
> Less than a year after opening, **PRIK** has already solidly established itself, and not just as a fun café in the pink pages of nightlife listings. In March 2007, PRIK hosted the first ever speed-dating session for HIV+ men, according to the HIV association Poz and Proud. The event sold out and left the city waiting for a follow-up. Promoting sexual health awareness throughout the year, the Spuistraat venue has also invited patrons to get free PRIK pricks, namely hepatitis-B vaccinations administered by city health officials.

Lellebel. This decade-old drag-show bar is renowned for its extravagant weekend performances. Recent additions to the weekday program include karaoke, salsa, and a Wednesday night Transgender Café. ⊠ *Utrechtse-straat 4, The Canal Ring* ☎ *020/427–5139* ⊕ *www.lellebel.nl.*

Fodor'sChoice ★ **PRIK.** Not only is this highly popular bar-café a new kid on the block, but its block is rather off the beaten queer path, which was intended by its founding gay couple as a means to be as all-inclusive as possible. The staff and clientele are as effervescent as the venue's name—*prik* means bubbles in Dutch and (among other things) refers to the Prosecco on tap. Tuesdays are movie nights and weekend brunch is served until 8 PM. ⊠ *Spuistraat 109, The Old City Center (Het Centrum)* ☎ *020/320–0002* ⊕ *www.prikamsterdam.nl.*

De Trut. Every Sunday night since the mid-'80s, the basement of an old squat in an unmarked building has opened its doors to a rainbow of folk—particularly *potten en flickers* (dykes and fags). The nice thing about partying here (besides the fact that it's a blast) is that all of the workers are volunteers, and all proceeds from the evening go to various gay-rights nonprofit organizations. The beer and the entrance fee are cheap, but be sure to arrive 15 minutes before the doors open at 11; the line gets long and you'll be turned away once capacity is reached. ⊠ *Bilderdijkstraat 165, Amsterdam West* ☎ *020/612–3524* ⊕ *www. trutfonds.nl.*

JAZZ CLUBS

Amsterdam has provided a happy home-away-from-home for jazz musicians since the early '50s, when such legends as Chet Baker and Gerry Mulligan would wind down after their official show at the Concertgebouw by jamming at one or another of the many bohemian bars around the Zeedijk. For the last quarter century, the world-statured but intimate Bimhuis has taken over duties as the city's major jazz venue with an excellent programming policy that welcomes both the legendary jazz performer and the latest avant-garde up-and-comer.

Alto. Every night hear the top picks of local ensembles and some well-respected locals in the smoky, jam-packed atmosphere of one of Amsterdam's oldest jazz joints. A little blues can be enjoyed here as well. ⊠*Korte Leidsedwarsstraat 115, Leidseplein* ☎*020/626–3249* ⊕*www.jazz-cafe-alto.nl.*

Bamboo Bar. Cool Latin sounds and a warm crew bring Leidseplein south of the equator for the night. ⊠*Lange Leidsedwarsstraat 64, Leidseplein* ☎*020/776–9614* ⊕*www.bamboobar.nl.*

Fodor'sChoice ★ **Bimhuis.** The best-known jazz place in town left its classic digs in 2005 in favor of the brand-spanking-new—and utterly awesome—Muziekgebouw aan 't IJ. Everyone, from old legends to the latest avant-gardist, agrees: it's close to perfect. Views of the city are breathtaking and the music you'll hear inside has been known to leave listeners panting for more. ⊠*Piet Heinkade 3, Eastern Docklands* ☎*020/788–2150 office, 020/788–2188 box office* ⊕*www.bimhuis.nl.*

Bourbon Street Jazz & Blues Club. Mainstream blues and jazz are served up to a largely out-of-town clientele, but it does the job—and a late one at that, open until 5 in the morning Fridays and Saturdays and 4 all other days. ⊠*Leidsekruisstraat 6–8, Leidseplein* ☎*020/623–3440* ⊕*www.bourbonstreet.nl.*

Café Meander. This student-friendly dance club go-to offers a mixed selection of live music, from soul to swing. ⊠*Voetboogstraat 3, The Old City Center (Het Centrum)* ☎*020/625–8430* ⊕*www.cafemeander.nl.*

Casablanca. On the edge of the Red Light District sits this neighborhood's classic club, dating back to the 1940s. For better or for worse, cracks are appearing in its jazzy foundation as the programming gets diluted with cabaret, DJ sets, and karaoke. ⊠*Zeedijk 24–26, The Old City Center (Het Centrum)* ☎*020/625–5685* ⊕*www.casablanca-amsterdam.nl.*

Cotton Club. Fans of more traditional jazz should check out the legendary venue named after its original owner, the Surinamer trumpet player Teddy Cotton. Although the club's music is not usually live, its gregarious crowd is certainly lively. ⊠*Nieuwmarkt 5, The Old City Center (Het Centrum)* ☎*020/626–6192.*

ROCK MUSIC VENUES

Quaint yet cosmopolitan, Amsterdam has been the place where many of the world's musicians dream of one day playing. The Melkweg and Paradiso have savvily kept their fingers on the pulse of every major musical trend since the late '60s. Today both legendary venues and a whole new-millennial phalanx of other clubs manage to keep the music real. The long-clichéd unholy trinity of sex, drugs, and rock and roll may not define Amsterdam as well as it used to, but the city remains one of the defining places for musicians worldwide to indulge in dreams of excess. And this makes for a rocking dance floor.

Heineken Music Hall. The relatively new and rather-out-of-the-way concert hall with a capacity for 5,500 offers a sterile but acoustic-rich environment. It's usually for touring bands that have outgrown (and most likely sold out) the Melkweg and Paradiso. ⊠*Arena Boulevard 590, Amsterdam Southeast* ☎*0900/300–1250* ⊕*www.heineken-music-hall.nl.*

Hotel Arena Tonight. From tabernacles to turntables: yet another of Amsterdam's churches has been refurbished to accommodate the city's nightlife. Part of Hotel Arena complex, this club is popular for its hip roster of DJs and weekend programs. ⊠*'s-Gravensandestraat 51, East of the Amstel* ☎*020/850–2420* ⊕*www.hotelarena.nl.*

The Last Waterhole. A favorite with tourists, this Leidseplein landing strip usually features a blues and rock cover band of dubious distinction—but it remains a smoke-friendly place to trade tales of the road. ⊠*Korte Leidsedwarsstraat 49, Museum District* ☎*020/620–8904* ⊕*www.lastwaterhole.nl.*

★ **Maloe Melo.** What could be nicer than a friendly hangout dive and venue for rock, blues, and roots musicians? Sometimes said characters are joined on stage by bigger musical celebrities, fresh from their gigs at more reputable venues. ⊠*Lijnbaansgracht 163, Jordaan* ☎*020/420–4592* ⊕*www.maloemelo.com.*

Melkweg. The legendary "Milk Way" has a broad programming policy that takes in everything from punk to house to world music. Named in homage to the building's previous function as a milk factory, this space began as a hippie squat in the '60s before evolving into a music venue for the major trends that followed. Today it's a slickly operated multimedia center equipped with two concert halls, a theater, cinema, gallery, and café-restaurant. On any day of the week you may walk into an evening of rock, reggae, drum'n'bass, hip-hop, soul, hard core, or any other imaginable genre. ⊠*Lijnbaansgracht 234–A, Leidseplein* ☎*020/531–8181* ⊕*www.melkweg.nl.*

OCCII. The former squat and slightly out of the way hole-in-the-wall is just beyond the gates of the Vondelpark's western exit. Nevertheless, OCCII (pronounced "oh-chee") has stayed true to its punky vibe over the years, and also softened enough to let a little world music programming in. ⊠*Amstelveenseweg 134, Museum District* ☎*020/671–7778* ⊕*www.occii.org.*

IN THE NEWS

For the latest on what's happening, you'd do well to browse through the many fliers, pamphlets, booklets, and magazines that can be picked up at cafés such as De Balie, Café De Jaren, and Dantzig. The Dutch-language *Uitkrant* can be found at its headquarters at the **Amsterdams Uitboro (AUB)** ⊠ *Leidseplein 26, Leidseplein* ☏ *0900/0191 (Daily 9–6)* ⊕ *www.aub.nl* ⊙ *Monday–Saturday 10–7:30, Sunday noon–7:30.* An English-language *Village Voice-*esque newspaper emerged to provide both natives and expats a cool-o-meter of the city's arts and culture scene, *Amsterdam Weekly* (⊕ *www.amsterdamweekly.nl*) is an invaluable resource for listings as well as articles that document the zanier sides of cosmopolitan Amsterdam living. *What's On in Amsterdam* is a comprehensive, albeit a tad dull, English-language publication distributed by the tourist office that lists art and performing-arts events around the city.

★ **Paradiso.** This former church of a pop temple is the country's most famous concert space, intact with vaulted ceilings and stained glass. It began its days as a hippie squat allowed by the local government in hopes that it might encourage the emptying of the Vondelpark (then serving as the crash pad for a generation). To this day, Paradiso remains an epic venue for both music's legends and up-and-comers, regardless of their genre. Most concerts are followed by a club night extending into the early hours that showcases the latest dance sounds. Flexible staging arrangements also make this a favorite venue for performance artists and multimedia events. ⊠ *Weteringschans 6–8, Leidseplein* ☏ *020/626–4521* ⊕ *www.paradiso.nl.*

Sugar Factory. Self-stylized as a "night theater," the Factory opened its doors across from the Melkweg in 2005 with big ambitions: taking clubbing into the 21st century and beyond. An average evening may involve DJs, as well as bands, theater, dance, spoken word, and slam poetry. ⊠ *Lijnbaansgracht 238, Leidseplein* ☏ *020/626–5006* ⊕ *www. sugarfactory.nl.*

Westergasfabriek. A potential pleasure-palace extraordinaire is found in a gas factory founded in 1883 and reopened in 2003 as an arts and cultural center. The site comprises 13 monumental buildings of various sizes and shapes that play host to film and theater companies, fashion shows, corporate functions, movie shoots, art exhibitions, operas, techno parties, and assorted festivals. There are also bars, nightclubs, and restaurants. ⊠ *Haarlemmerweg 8–10, Amsterdam West* ☏ *020/586–0710* ⊕ *www.westergasfabriek.nl.*

Winston. If a small-scale club is what you're after, take a hike up the Warmoesstraat. But when it comes to quality programming, size doesn't matter. Winston offers a bit of everything—from punk to DJs, from neo-Christian to the easiest of easy tunes. ⊠ *Warmoesstraat 129–131, The Old City Center (Het Centrum)* ☏ *020/623–1380* ⊕ *www.winston.nl.*

THE ARTS

Although a relatively small city, Amsterdam packs a giant cultural wallop with its numerous venues—from former churches and industrial monuments to the acoustical supremacy of the Concertgebouw—and festivals that invariably feature both homegrown and international talent. So book that ticket fast! Amsterdam's theater and music season begins in September and runs through June, when the Holland Festival of Performing Arts is held.

Tickets can be purchased at either the **AUB Ticketshop** ⊠ *Leidseplein 26 Leidseplein* ☎ *0900/0191 (Daily 9–6)* ⊕ *www.aub.nl* ⊗ *Monday–Saturday 10–7:30, Sunday noon–7:30.* or at **VVV Ticketmaster** ⊠ *Stationsplein 10, Centraal Station* ⊗ *Daily 10–4, Sunday noon–4.* or at theater box offices. Reserve tickets to performances at the major theaters before your arrival through the AUB Web site or by calling +31 020/621–1288 from abroad.

CABARETS

September marks the official start of the cultural season, as the greater majority of Amsterdam's performing arts do not give shows during the summer. But don't fret: June, July, and August are jam-packed with festivals (both in the city and its environs), outdoor concerts and movie screenings, and appearances by many foreign artists stopping through Amsterdam on their summer tours.

Boom Chicago. This is what happens when a bunch of zany expat Americans open their own restaurant-theater to present improvised comedy inspired by life in Amsterdam and the rest of the world. Dinner and seating begin at 6, with show time at 8:15; on weekends there are also late shows. ⊠ *Leidseplein 12, Leidseplein* ☎ *020/423–0101* ⊕ *www.boomchicago.nl* ⊗ *Daily 6:00* PM.

Comedy Café Amsterdam. For some straight—and often English—stand-up, check the schedule of this club next door to the Hard Rock Café. ⊠ *Max Euweplein 43–45, Leidseplein* ☎ *020/638–3971* ⊕ *www.comedycafe.nl.*

De Kleine Komedie. For many years, this riverside theater has been the most vibrant venue for cabaret and comedy mainly in Dutch. ⊠ *Amstel 56–58, East of the Amstel* ☎ *020/624–0534* ⊕ *www.dekleinekomedie.nl.*

Toomler. Borrowing its name from the Yiddish word for "noisemaker," this is the podium for the Dutch standup group Comedytrain. The programming is often English-friendly, with regular appearances by international guests. ⊠ *Breitnerstraat 2, Amsterdam South* ☎ *020/670–7400* ⊕ *www.toomler.nl.*

FILM

Have you ever wondered how the Dutch came to speak such impeccable English? History's answer to this is that a small nation with few resources had no choice but to speak the language of the people with whom they traded. Pop culture's answer to this is much simpler: Hollywood! All films and TV are subtitled, not dubbed, so viewers are constantly exposed to English. What's more, in a nation whose last half-century would generally be characterized by political peace and social harmony, it's no wonder local folks yearn for a bit of good old-fashioned American cussing and carnage. The Dutch have a big soft spot for master of unease David Lynch, and they can never get enough of Tarantino and the Coen Brothers. Conversely, a number of Dutch directors—alienated by the long lackluster local scene—have manifested their blockbuster destinies in Hollywood. Creator of *Basic Instinct* and *RoboCop,* the notorious Paul Verhoeven is the nation's most famous export.

> ## FILM FESTIVALS
>
> If you're a film lover with a flexible schedule, plan your trip around Holland's big film events. The International Film Festival Rotterdam (⊕ *www.filmfestivalrotterdam.com*), is in late January/early February; the International Documentary Film Festival Amsterdam (⊕ *www.idfa.nl*) and the smaller budget documentary sideshow The Shadow Festival (⊕ *www.shadowfestival.nl*) are in November; the Amsterdam Fantastic Film Festival (⊕ *www.afff.nl*) is in June.

Cinecenter. Sleek, modern decor fills the lounge of this theater opposite the Melkweg, while four screens downstairs play artier and more internationally acclaimed films. ⊠ *Lijnbaansgracht 236, Leidseplein* ☏ *020/623–6615* ⊕ *www.cinecenter.nl.*

Filmhuis Cavia. One of several repertory cinemas that show a savvy blend of classics and modern world cinema, with programming that is decidedly edgy and politically alternative. ⊠ *Van Hallstraat 52-I, Amsterdam West* ☏ *020/681–1419* ⊕ *www.filmhuiscavia.nl.*

Kriterion. This film house is run by students and reflects their world-embracing tastes (especially during its late shows that encourage the more cultish of movies). The adjoining café is always buzzing with chatty humanities types, but that's not to say that the long-graduated among us are unwelcome. ⊠ *Roetersstraat 170, East of the Amstel* ☏ *020/623–1708* ⊕ *www.kriterion.nl.*

The Movies. A full-swing 1920s ambience sets the stage for artsy and indie flicks at this filmhouse. The cozy restaurant, lively bar, and smiling staff could leave you wanting little more. ⊠ *Haarlemmerdijk 157–165, Jordaan* ☏ *020/624–5790* ⊕ *www.themovies.nl.*

Nederlands Filmmuseum *(Netherlands Film Museum).* True film buffs should definitely pay a visit to this treasure trove of more than 35,000 films and a library open to the public. Not only are revival screenings culled from this collection, but there are also special programs that comprise outdoor screenings and silent films accompanied by live piano music. ✉ *Vondelpark 3, Museum District* ☎ *020/589–1400* ⊕ *www.filmmuseum.nl.*

Rialto. Away from the maddening crowd, this little theater is noted for showing world cinema and more highbrow film classics. ✉ *Ceintuurbaan 338, The Pijp* ☎ *020/662–3488* ⊕ *www.rialtofilm.nl.*

Studio K. The Amsterdam foundation Kriterion, which has been promoting student-run business ventures since World War II, has added yet another venue to its resume. Opened in autumn 2007, this two-screen movie house shows not only art and foreign films, but with a theater, an open stage, and a restaurant-bar, it's is a multidisciplinarian's dream come true. ✉ *Timorplein 62, East of the Amstel* ☎ *020/692–0422* ⊕ *www.studio-k.ntenlen wat we zijn gramma.*

★ **Tuschinski.** Since 1921, this eclectic Art Deco reverie has been the most dazzling—not to mention central—place for moviegoers to escape from reality. Owned by the country's main movie distributor, the theater has six screens showing the latest Hollywood blockbusters and the occasional Dutch film or art-house number. ✉ *Reguliersbreestraat 26, Rembrandtplein* ☎ *0900/1458.*

De Uitkijk. Opened in 1913, this small canal-side "lookout," as its name means in Dutch, ranks as the city's oldest cinema. No longer just a one-hit wonder, the theater was spruced up in 2007 and now offers a more diverse program consisting of documentaries, kid flicks, and movies screened in cooperation with the Filmmuseum. ✉ *Prinsengracht 452, Leidseplein* ☎ *020/623–7460* ⊕ *www.uitkijk.nl.*

MUSIC

Some of Amsterdam's most esteemed music venues also happen to be in the city's most beautiful structures. Enjoy a night of music in a breathtaking, and accoustically stellar, setting.

Fodor'sChoice **Concertgebouw.** There are two auditoriums, large and small, under one
★ roof at the Netherlands' premier concert hall, famous for having one of the finest sound systems the world over. With its Viennese Classicist facade surmounted by a golden lyre, this building opposite the Rijksmuseum draws 800,000 visitors to 800 concerts per year. In the larger of the two theaters, the **Grote Zaal**, Amsterdam's critically acclaimed **Koninklijk Concertgebouworkest** (Royal Concert Orchestra), whose recordings are in the collections of most self-respecting lovers of classi-

cal music, is often joined by international soloists. Their reputation has only grown in the last decade under the baton twirling of conductor Riccardo Chailly, who has just passed the honor to the highly regarded Latvian Mariss Jansons. Guest conductors read like a list from the musical heavens: Mstislav Rostropovich, Nikolaus Harnoncourt, and Bernard Haitink. Visiting maestros like these naturally push the prices up, but the range remains wide: expect to pay anything between €5 and €100. But throughout July and August, tickets for the Robeco Summer Concerts, which involve high-profile artists and orchestras, are an excel-

> **OPEN-AIR ENTERTAINMENT**
>
> Theatrical events in the Vondelpark have a long and glorious history. Nowadays, during the **Openluchttheater** season, there's a lunchtime concert and a midafternoon children's show on Wednesdays, Thursday night shows are in the bandstand, and there's theater every Friday night. Various activities take place on Saturdays, and theater events and pop concerts are held on Sunday afternoons. It's a full agenda!

4

lent bargain. The **Koorzaal,** (the "Choir Hall"), is a smaller venue for chamber music and up-and-coming musicians, and is the usual setting for the free lunchtime concerts on Wednesdays at 12:30, that take place from September through June. ✉ *Concertgebouwplein 2–6, Museum District* ☎ *020/671–8345* ⊕ *www.concertgebouw.nl.*

Beurs van Berlage. The architectural landmark and progenitor of the Amsterdam School has two concert halls—including the unique glass-box "diamond-in-space" Amvest Zaal—with the Netherlands Philharmonic and the Netherlands Chamber Orchestra as the in-house talent. ✉ *Damrak 213, The Old City Center (Het Centrum)* ☎ *020/521–7575* ⊕ *www.beursvanberlage.nl.*

Muziekgebouw aan 't IJ. It only opened in 2005, yet this self-monickered "Concerthall for the 21st Century" is already a huge asset to the city's arts and culture scene. What's more, it's home to legendary jazz club Bimhuis *(see above),* and the Star Ferry café has a splendid panoramic view of the IJ's harbor. ✉ *Piet Heinkade 1,* ☎ *020/788–2010* ⊕ *www. muziekgebouw.nl.*

Fodor'sChoice
★

Muziektheater. Seating 1,600 people to witness its international performances throughout the year, this urban coliseum is home to **De Nederlandse Opera, Het Nationale Ballet,** and the newly established **Holland Symphonia,** all of whose repertoires embrace both the classical and the 20th century. On Tuesdays from September through May, you can catch free lunchtime concerts in the Boekmanzaal from the Nederlands Kamerorkest, Opera Studio Nederland, and Holland Symfonia. Doors open at 12:15, and are first-come, first-served. ✉ *Amstel 3/Waterlooplein 22, The Old City Center (Het Centrum)* ☎ *020/625–5455* ⊕ *www.muziektheater.nl.*

Bethanienklooster. Many of the city's churches are being used these days by music lovers and players *(see also Nieuwe Kerk, Noorder Kerk, Nicolaas Kerk, and Oude Kerk in Exploring Amsterdam).* This former monastery still provides a calm and holy setting for regular chamber music concerts. ✉ *Barndesteeg 6B, The Old City Center (Het Centrum)* ☎ *020/625–0078* ⊕ *www.bethanienklooster.nl.*

★ **Engelse Kerk.** The former Pilgrims' hangout has weekly concerts of baroque and classical music that always seeks to employ period instruments. English-language church service is on Sunday mornings at 10:30. ✉ *Begijnhof 48, The Old City Center (Het Centrum)* ☎ *020/624–9665* ⊕ *home.tiscali.nl/~t451501/ercadam.*

NES TIX

Amsterdam's Off Broadway–type theaters are centered along the Nes, an alley leading off the Dam. One-stop ticket shopping for the Brakke Grond, De Engelenbak, and Frascati can be done at the central ticket office (⊕ www.indenes. nl). You can also visit the office located at **Brakke Grond** ✉ Nes 45, The Old City Center (Het Centrum). or reserve tickets by calling 020/626–6866 (Monday–Saturday, from 1 PM up until showtime).

★ **Waalse Kerk.** Founded in 1409, restored in 1647, and rebuilt in 1816, this courtyarded church is as intimate as it is elegant. Musicians from both the Netherlands and abroad give regular concerts. A mass in French is given on Sunday mornings at 11. ✉ *Walenpleintje 159, The Old City Center (Het Centrum)* ☎ *020/623–2074* ⊕ *www.waalsekerk-amsterdam.nl.*

Orgel Park. In this newest church-turned-cultural venue, just off of the Vondelpark, an international roster of professional organists and students perform thematically inspired concerts and genre-bending improvisational pieces. The organ was never so hip. ✉ *Gerard Brandtstraat 26, Museum District* ☎ *020/515–8111* ⊕ *www.orgelpark.nl.*

★ **Vondelpark Openluchttheater.** Skaters, joggers, cyclists, and sun worshippers gather in the Vondelpark each summer to enjoy the great outdoors. Between late May and September, they're joined by the culture vultures all heading to the park's open-air program of music, dance, cabaret, and children's events. ✉ *Vondelpark Museum District* ☎ *020/428–3360* ⊕ *www.openluchttheater.nl.*

OPERA & BALLET

Fodor'sChoice **Muziektheater.** This theater's huge and flexible stage acts as a magnet
★ for directors with a penchant for grand-scale décor, such as Robert Wilson, Willy Decker, and Peter Sellars. ✉ *Amstel 3/Waterlooplein 22, The Old City Center (Het Centrum)* ☎ *020/625–5455* ⊕ *www.muziektheater.nl.*

Dutch-Style Theater

Such internationally statured companies as **Dogtroep** (⊕ *www.dogtroep.nl*), **PIPS:lab** ⊕ *www.pipslab.nl*), and **Vis-à-Vis** (⊕ *www.visavis.nl*) are specialists in the typically Dutch school of spectacle theater, which is hardly bound by language and goes in search of unique locations—and other dimensions—to strut its stuff. Groups like this usually participate, along with many others of like mind from around the world, in the amazing annual **Over het IJ Festival** ☎*020/492–2229* ⊕ *www.ijfestival.nl*. This festival is held every July at the abandoned shipyard-turned-post-modern-culture-center NDSM in Amsterdam North *(see above)*, gathering together dozens of dance and theater troupes dedicated to the more wild and physical

aspects of the arts. If you happen to be in town for the first two weeks of August, don't miss **Parade** ✉*Martin Luther Kingpark, Amsterdam South* ☎*033/465–4555* ⊕*www.deparade.nl*, a traveling tent city that specializes in quirky performances and a social and carnival-esque ambience. And, finally, get ready to return to NDSM in September, for the **Robodock Festival** (www.robodock.org), a three-day theater extravaganza that puts a totally punk-rock twist on recycling. For more than 10 years, the international squatter-friendly collective have been creating out-of-this-world performances around massive structures made of found industrial objects and other modern-day disposables—like cars.

FodorsChoice
★ **Stadsschouwburg.** The red-and-gold plushness of the city theater is home to the underrated **Nationale Reisopera** (National Travelling Opera). It also regularly hosts visiting companies from all over the world. ✉*Leidseplein 26, Leidseplein* ☎*020/624–2311* ⊕*www.ssba.nl*.

Koninklijk Theater Carre. Although more focused on commercial and large-scale musicals, this former circus theater also schedules many acclaimed Eastern European companies performing ballet and opera classics. Tom Waits liked the ambience so much that he did a two-night stand here in 2005. ✉*Amstel 115–25, East of the Amstel* ☎*0900/252–5255* ⊕*www.theatercarre.nl*.

DANCE & THEATER

Although many associate the Dutch dance scene with two names—Het Nationale Ballet and Nederlands Dans Theater—there are many more innovative local companies. Certainly the Hungarian ex-pat Krisztina de Châtel (⊕ *www.dechatel.nl*) has turned Amsterdam into a jumping-off point for international acclaim, thanks to her physical approach that also often employs the latest technologies in the visual arts. A certain multimedia savvy is also seen in the works of other acclaimed Amsterdam-based troupes such as Dance Company Leine & Roebana, the Shusaku & Dormu Dance Theater & Bodytorium, and the absurdity-seeking and mime-loving Hans Hof Ensemble. One annual not-to-be-missed event—that mixes both local and international names of a cutting-edge nature—is the month-long Julidans (⊕ *www.julidans.nl*), which is centered around the Stadsschouwburg.

Brakke Grond. Part of the Flemish cultural center, the Brakke Grond is infamous for welcoming experimental theater and dance performances from the Netherlands' neighbor to the south. ⊠*Nes 45, The Old City Center (Het Centrum)* ☎*020/622–9014* ⊕*www.brakkegrond.nl.*

De Engelenbak. This venue is best known for its "Open Bak," an open-stage event each Tuesday where virtually anything goes. It's the longest-running theater program in the Netherlands, where everybody gets their 15 minutes of potential fame; arrive at least half an hour before the show starts to get a ticket. Otherwise, the best amateur groups in the country perform between Thursday and Saturday. ⊠*Nes 71, The Old City Center (Het Centrum)* ☎*020/626–3644* ⊕*www.engelenbak.nl.*

> **MIDNIGHT MUSEUM CRAWL**
>
> For one night in early November, all the city's major museums stay open until the wee hours to host a variety of themed parties. If you only have a very short period of time to visit Amsterdam, elasticize those euros by arriving for **Museum Nacht**. At this fantastic party, you'll find activities such as tangos under Rembrandt's *Night Watch*, house beats at the Jewish Historical Museum, bossa nova in the Stedelijk, how to paint like Bob Ross masterclasses, and ghost stories for kids in the Bible Museum. For annual details see ⊕*www.n8.nl.*

Frascati. The three stages here all create a sense of intimacy for both performers and spectators. The close-knit feel is reinforced on Frascati's regular open-stage nights, when audience members are invited to take the stage. ⊠*Nes 63, The Old City Center (Het Centrum)* ☎*020/751–6400* ⊕*www.theaterfrascati.nl.*

International Theaterschool. Handily located near the Waterlooplein, this institution unites students and teachers from all over the world to share their experiences, learning and creating in the fields of dance and theater. Dance performances—some of which are announced in *Uitkrant*—vary from studio shots to evening-long events in the Philip Morris Dans Zaal theater. Also worth checking out is the international theater school festival hosted every June. ⊠*Jodenbreestraat 3, The Old City Center (Het Centrum)* ☎*020/527–7700* ⊕*www.theatreschool.nl.*

Koninklijk Theater Carre. For lavish, large-scale productions, this former circus home built in the 19th century is the place to go. ⊠*Amstel 115–125, East of the Amstel* ☎*0900/252–5255* ⊕*www.theatercarre.nl.*

Melkweg. The relatively small stage of this multimedia center brings together both local and international dance names to strut their stuff in a more intimate setting. ⊠*Lijnbaansgracht 234a, Leidseplein* ☎*020/531–8181.*

Muiderpoorttheater. Although not within the Nes zone, this theater also follows an Off Broadway path by presenting new faces of the international drama and dance scene in an intimate setting. ⊠*2e Van Swindenstraat 26, East of the Amstel* ☎*020/668–1313* ⊕*www. muiderpoorttheater.nl.*

Muziektheater. This gracious and spacious hall also hosts the **Nederlands Dans Theater** (⊕ *www.ndt. nl*), which has evolved into one of the most celebrated modern dance companies in the world under choreographers Jiri Kylian and Hans van Manen. ⊠ *Waterlooplein 22/ Amstel 3, The Old City Center (Het Centrum)* ☎*020/625–5455* ⊕*www.muziektheater.nl.*

NDSM. What were once industrial shipyards have been reinvented as, quite possibly, the city's largest *broedsplaats*, or government-sponsored "breeding ground" for the arts, where regular theater performances and festivals take place. And with a ferry departing from behind Centraal Station, getting there has never been easier. ⊠*TT Neveritaweg 15, Eastern Docklands* ☎*020/330–5480* ⊕*www.ndsm.nl.*

Stadsschouwburg. Host of the Julidans festival, this theater often has a variety of modern dance offerings. The red-velvet is primarily paved for those attending Dutch theater, though there are occasional English programs. ⊠*Leidseplein 26, Leidseplein* ☎*020/624–2311* ⊕*www. ssba.nl.*

Sugar Factory. The club and "night theater" opened its doors in 2005 with the agenda to infuse the witching hours with theater, dance, art, and poetry—often all in one go. ⊠*Lijnbaansgracht 238, Leidseplein* ☎*020/626–5006* ⊕*www.sugarfactory.nl.*

Tropeninstituut Theater. Part of the Tropics Institute, this theater hosts international companies dedicated to non-Western dance—from classical Indian to reinvented tango. ⊠*Linnaeusstraat 2, East of the Amstel* ☎*020/568–8500.*

Warner en Consorten. Formed in 1993, this group embraces an interdisciplinary concept of street theater: sculpture, dance, physical acting (such as mime), and music collide and challenge the concepts of theater, urban life—and reality. The results are often Dada-istically hilarious. Public space is the starting point: streets are analyzed, crowd behavior studied, passersby observed. During the winter months, the company

---

SPECTACLE SPECIALISTS

Alternative forms of theater are *very* Amsterdam. Not unlike the *stamppot*—a traditional Dutch peasant's stew made of mashed potatoes and pretty much any other vegetable and scrap of meat you can find in your pantry—anything goes. Multimedia, multidimensional, and multicultural are the three basic components to such pieces. Be warned: some performers are not shy about trying to convert the uninitiated. If you decide to attend a show, therefore, keep in mind that your position as a spectator can quickly transmogrify into participant.

4

finds abandoned warehouses and factories for venues; in the summer, city streets are the theaters. ✉*Hemkade 18, Zaandam (just a 20-minute train ride from Amsterdam's Centraal Station)* ☎*075/631–1980* ⊕*www.warnerenconsorten.nl.*

Westergasfabriek. The former gas-factory complex *(see Dance & Rock Clubs)* employs its singular performance spaces for a variety of shows and festivals that often embrace the more visual and more avant-garde of the entertainment spectrum. ✉*Haarlemmerweg 8–10, Amsterdam West* ☎*020/586–0710* ⊕*www.westergasfabriek.nl.*

Shopping

WORD OF MOUTH

"The quintessential department store of Amsterdam is de Bijenkorf. It is on the left side of the Damrak. On the south side it faces the Dam and Hotel Kraznapolsky."

—hopscotch

"Check out the daily flea market on the Waterlooplein, the book sale at the Oudemanshuispoort, the Albert Cuypstraat market and, of course, the Bloemenmarkt on the Singel where you can buy some tulips for your hotel room."

—artstuff

Updated by
Karina Hof

THE DUTCH, FAMOUS FOR THEIR savvy business skills and wily ways with trade, are considered either frugal or cheap (hence the phrase "going Dutch"). And while it's true that Lowlanders monitor their wallets they do have a *very* healthy consumer culture. What does this mean for you? First, there is ample shopping to be had—a bit of something for everyone; and second, you won't have to take out a second home mortgage for that dandy trinket you like so much.

Most of the city's major shopping districts are hard to miss. Just down the road from Centrale Station is **Nieuwendijk.** Besides the national chains, this street has a busy pedestrian mall catering to bargain hunters and a younger crowd of urbanites. To the south of the Dam is the city's principal shopping strip, **Kalverstraat** (one of the only areas open on Sundays). Here you'll find the international chains and favorite Dutch franchises. (Avoid this area on the weekend if you don't like crowds.) **Leidsestraat** offers a scaled-down version of Kalverstraat with an escape-route of canal-side cafés. Here you'll find some one-of-a-kinds, including the grand Madam of high-end department store shopping, Metz & Co *(see Department Stores).* Just east is the **Spiegelkwartier,** one of Europe's most fabled agglomerations of antiques shops.

If these main drags excite you about as much as the mall back home—minus the food court—go where the locals go. Explore the unique clothing and jewelry boutiques, crafts ateliers, and funky consignment stores dotted along the **Nine Streets,** which radiate from behind the Royal Palace to the periphery of the **Jordaan.** Take time to browse this neighborhood's art galleries, jewelry shops, and purchasable homages to interior design. If you head all the way north on Prinsengracht, you're sure to pass the Noordermarkt *(see Markets)* and eventually reach the trendy trappings of **Haarlemerstraat,** with its gamut of high-end specialty stores.

Not far from the Museum District is **Van Baerlestraat.** This street is lined with bookstores specializing in art, music, and language and clothing shops that are smart—but not quite smart enough to have made it to the adjoining **P.C. Hooftstraat.** This is the Madison Avenue of Amsterdam: all the main fashion houses are here, from Armani to Vuitton. Continue farther south, through to the other side of the Vondelpark, and you'll come upon **Amsterdam South,** and a burgeoning cluster of small clothing and shoe boutiques, sleek home furnishers, and pricey delicatessens.

To get back to Amsterdam's democratic roots, stop in the neighborhood of **The Pijp.** Skip the clothing and shoe chains more and more branded with "Made-in-China" tags to peruse the working-class shops hidden behind the stands of the Albert Cuypmarkt *(see Markets).* Finally, if you need a decent yet still slightly decadent foray into Amsterdam shopping, have yourself a stroll along **Utrechtsestraat,** perhaps one of the city's most underrated avenues. You may well find just what you were always looking for, from that high-quality Japanese pressing of a Blue Note record to baby-blue ballerina flats made of antique goat's leather.

DEPARTMENT STORES

C & A. Perched on the ever-busy Damrak, across the road from the Beurs van Berlage, this representative European chain department store is a longtime fixture on Amsterdam's shopping landscape. The budget-minded come here for clothing and accessories, and the basement caters to Generation Y. On the ground floor, there are always sales racks; if you have the patience to paw through them, you may be rewarded with some amply discounted finds. ⊠*Beurspassage 2 or Damrak 79, The Old City Center (Het Centrum)* ☎*20/510–6000* ⊕*www.c-en-a.nl.*

De Bijenkorf. Akin to Macy's, if not as stylish as Paris's Galleries Lafayette, is "The Beehive," the nation's best-known department store and the swarming ground of its monied middle classes. Top international designer lines of housewares and clothing are available, along with gourmet goodies, and the usual repertoire of suitcases, shoes, appliances, and hipster bric-a-brac. The store eateries are way upscale, and makeup makeovers on the ground floor offer surprise "theater" to tourists. ⊠*Dam 1, The Old City Center (Het Centrum)* ☎*0900–0919* ⊕*www.bijenkorf.nl.*

★ **HEMA.** The *Hollandsche Eenheidsprijzen Maatschappij Amsterdam* or "De Hema" as it's called by locals, stocks not only your basic needs, but also some surprisingly hip designer items—and for the friendliest of prices. Cosmetics, vitamins, undergarments, and power tools are some of the best bargains, and the chain is cherished for its store-brand sausage and coveted cakes. ⊠*Nieuwendijk 174–176, The Old City Center (Het Centrum)* ☎*020/623–4176* ⊕*www.hema.nl* ⊠*Kalvertoren, Kalverstraat 212, The Old City Center (Het Centrum)* ☎*020/422–8988* ⊠*Ferdinand Bolstraat 93–93A, The Pijp* ☎*020/676–3222.*

★ **Maison de Bonneterie.** With its Paris-style skylights, chandeliers, silently gliding assistants, and coat of arms, this is Amsterdam's most gracious department store. It has basics such as linens and appliances, but is most loved for its array of women's fashions, ranging from cutting-edge supermodel frocks to the most proper basics for ladies who dutifully match their handbags with their shoes. Browse on the ground floor: you're likely to come upon a great buy among the limited supplies of designer lamps, bedding, and other homewares on special offer. ⊠*Rokin 140–142, The Old City Center (Het Centrum)* ☎*020/531–3400* ⊕*www.maisondebonneterie.nl.*

Metz & Co. Landmarked by its cupola, the historic and stately department store has presided over the Grachtengordel since 1908 (it first set up shop elsewhere in 1740). Now an outpost of London's famous Liberty store, it carries a decent range of breathtakingly expensive designer articles from around the world. Stop in at the top-floor café where you can enjoy a lovely bird's-eye view of the city. ⊠*Leidsestraat 34–36, The Canal Ring* ☎*020/520–7020* ⊕*www.metzenco.nl.*

Peek & Cloppenburg. This Dam mainstay specializes in durable, middle-of-the-road clothing. The shop has recently been adding more European lines, including attractive Italian and French knitwear and casuals.

✉*Dam 20, The Old City Center (Het Centrum)* ☎*020/ 623–2837* ⊕*www.peekundcloppenburg.com.*

Vroom & Dreesmann. V & D, as its called by the locals, is an upmarket version of Sears, selling clothing, shoes, office supplies, and household items. You'll also find a large stationery section and a fine array of computer software. The adjacent eatery, La Place, makes for convenient refueling, and its bakery spills back into the department store to offer vitrines of exceptionally tasty chocolates, marzipan, and souvenir candies. ✉*Kalverstraat 203, The Old City Center (Het Centrum)* ☎*0900/235–8363* ⊕*www. vroomendreesmann.nl.*

> **THANK GOD IT'S THURSDAY**
>
> Most shops close between 5 and 6 except on Thursday evenings, which are famously known as *koopavonden* (buying nights). But in a country where many people work part-time (and "overtime" is a dirty word), something's gotta give. Many shops therefore have delayed openings on Mondays. An H&M storefront at noon on a Monday makes you question the country's policy on school truancy.

MARKETS

Whether hunting for treasures or trash, you can unearth terrific finds, often at rock-bottom prices, at any of Amsterdam's open-air markets. It's also a good excuse to enjoy freshly squeezed orange juice, pickled herring on a bun, or a *stroopwaffel* (syrup-filled waffle) hot off the griddle.

Albert Cuypmarkt. This century-old market, found on Albert Cuypstraat between Ferdinand Bolstraat and Van Woustraat, is the heart of The Pijp, and is arguably the best open-air market in Amsterdam. It's open Monday through Saturday from 9–5, rain or shine, and you're likely to hear the vendors barking out their bargain deals over the pleasant sound track of a street musician. Interspersed among the colorful crowd, stalls sell food, clothing, fabrics, plants, and household goods from all over the world. Just about every ethnic culture is represented here by purveyors, their goods, and their buyers. Be sure to try some of the exotic nibbles, or just order the Dutchman's favorite fast food—*frites met mayonnaise* (french fries with mayonnaise) served piping hot in a paper cone. Look for Belgian *frites,* as these are the tastiest. ⊕*www.albertcuypmarkt.com.*

★ **Bloemenmarkt.** Hands down, this is one of Amsterdam's must-sees. Along the Singel canal, between Koningsplein and Muntplein, the renowned Flower Market is where blooming wonders are purveyed from permanently moored barges. Besides bouquets of freshly cut flowers, you'll find plants, small trees, bulbs, seeds, and a colorful array of souvenir trinkets. The market is open Monday–Saturday 9:30–5:30, Sunday 11-5:30.

Boekenmarkt. It's not for nothing that Amsterdam has been named the 2008 World Book Capital by UNESCO. The city has a number of book markets, though its most famous takes place every Friday on Spui Square, from 10–6. Under the little white tents, it's an antiquarian and used book–browsing paradise.

Lapjesmarkt. Fabric lovers will think they've taken a magic carpet to heaven when they visit the so-called "rag market", which takes place on Mondays from 8–noon, adjacent to Noordermarkt. Down along Westerstraat, you'll find stalls with every possible kind of fabric—beautiful rainbow-colored Asian silks embedded with mirrors and embroidery, batiks from Indonesia, Suriname, and Africa, fabulous faux furs, lace curtains, velvet drapery materials, calicos, and vinyl coverings, all being admired and stroked by eager shoppers. Couturiers rub elbows with housewives, vendors measure out meters, and the crowds keep getting denser.

Lindenmarkt. On Saturday from 9–5 check out the less yuppie-fied sister to the Noordermarkt, which winds around Noorderkerk and runs down the length of Lindengracht. Fresh produce, discounted toiletries, clothes, linens, and small electronics are this market's humble offerings.

Modern Art Market. Fair weather on Sundays from March through December brings good opportunity for a rotating series of some 25 artists to sell their paintings, lithographs, textiles, and other objets d'art in the Rembrandtplein area. Organized by the Kunstkring Thorbecke Foundation (*052/720–1559;* ⊕ *www.modern-art-market.nl*), the market takes place on Thorbeckeplein (just off the Rembrantplein) from 10:30–6.

Nieuwmarkt. At the northern end of Kloverniersburgwal, the square known as Nieuwmarkt hosts its own smaller-scale market offering the basics in Amsterdam open-air trade. Every Saturday from 9–5, a *boerenmarkt,* or organic farmers' market, hosts specialist stalls selling essential oils and other New Age fare alongside the oats, legumes, and vegetables. From May through October, you can find curiosa, art, and books when the *antiekmarkt* (antique market) sets up its weekly shop.

★ **Noordermarkt.** The Noordermarkt is probably most cherished by Amsterdammers for its weekly *boerenmarkt,* the organic farmers' market held every Saturday from 9–6 around the perimeter of the Noorderkerk. With comestibles such as free-range meats, cruelty-free honey, homemade pestos, and vegan cakes on offer, it's an orgasm for the organic-loving. Just be prepared to open your wallet. On Mondays, from 9–1, the Noordermarkt shapeshifts into what is locally known as the *maandagmarkt* (Monday Market). Evocative of the Old World, it's a sprawling affair, mostly of used clothing, books, and toys, but careful collectors can find a range of good stuff, from antique silverware and pottery to wartime and advertising memorabilia.

Postzegelmarkt. Philatelists, take heart. During good weather, you'll find the city's stamp market set up near the Spui along Nieuwezijds Voorburgwal, held on Wednesdays and Saturdays from 1–4. And there are some coins for you numismatists, too.

Waterlooplein. Few markets compare with Amsterdam's famous flea market that hugs the backside of the Stopera (the complex whose descriptive name derives from an ever-pragmatic blending of *stadhuis* for "city hall" and "opera," in reference to the Muziektheater *(see Nightlife & the Arts chapter)*. Waterlooplein is a descendant of the haphazard pushcart trade that gave this part of the city its distinct, lively character in the early part of the 20th century. It's amusing to see the old telephones, typewriters, and other arcana all haphazardly displayed—as well as the shoppers scrambling and vying with each other to reacquire such items. Professional dealers sell secondhand and vintage clothing, hats, and purses. New fashions are mostly for generic alterna-types who will enjoy a wide selection of slogan T-shirts, hippie bags, and jewelry for every type of piercing. The flea market is open Monday–Saturday 9–6.

SPECIALTY STORES

ANTIQUES & GOLDEN AGE ART

Fodor's Choice
★
Anouk Beerents. The Hall of Mirrors at the Palace of Versailles may be evoked should you have the opportunity to visit the dazzling, skylighted quarters of this Jordaan atelier-cum-store. For 20 years, the ever-gracious Anouk Beerents has been buying 18th- and 19th-century antique mirrors from France and Italy, and then restoring them for local and international clients (including, for example, Ralph Lauren shops in the U.S.). Replete with ornate gold or silver gilded frames, some four hundred museum-quality mirrors (some actually from the Palace of Versailles) hang upon the walls of this space, which is so large that customers are invited to park their cars inside. Visits are by appointment only and shipping can be arranged to other countries. ✉ *Prinsengracht 467, Jordaan* ☎ *020/622–8598* ⊕ *www.anoukbeerents.nl.*

Bruno de Vries. An unusual collection of antique money banks is displayed at this gallery, along with Art Deco and Jugendstil lamps, as well as items from the Amsterdam School of Architecture. ✉ *Elandsgracht 67, Jordaan* ☎ *020/620–2437* ⊕ *www.brunodevries.com.*

Christie's Amsterdam. The internationally known auction house hosts sales of art, furniture, wines, jewelry, and porcelain. Even if you leave empty-handed, the surrounding neighborhood is well worth the journey. ✉ *Cornelis Schuytstraat 57, Amsterdam South* ☎ *020/575–5255* ⊕ *www.christies.com.*

D. I. Haaksman. Among a glittering array of 18th- and 19th-century crystal chandeliers here, you'll find just the illumination you're looking for from leading names such as Bagues and Baccarat. ✉ *Elandsgracht 55, Jordaan* ☎ *020/625–4116* ⊕ *www.dihaaksman.nl.*

Antiquing on a Budget

For more gently priced collections, you might rather opt to tiptoe past the 18th-century tulipwood armoires and explore an increasingly popular neighborhood for adventurous collectors—the Jordaan. In stark contrast to the elegant stores in the Spiegelkwartier with their beautiful displays, the tiny, unprepossessing shops dotted along the Elandsgracht and connecting streets, such as the 1e Looiersdwarsstraat, offer equally wonderful treasures. Those who take the time to carefully examine the backroom shelves, nooks, and crannies of a small shop may be rewarded with a big find. Prices here are also more in keeping with a downtown〈 for interior decor. Indeed, th〈 of the best-kept secrets of N ... fork's antiques shop dealers, who often scour the Jordaan for their imported wares. You can also enjoy happy hunting in the shops on Rozengracht and Prinsengracht, near the Westerkerk, which offer country Dutch furniture and household items; take a look at the antiques and curio shops along the side streets in that part of the city. Many of the antiques shops in the Spiegelkwartier and the Jordaan keep irregular hours and some are open by appointment, so it's wise to call first.

Jan Beekhuizen Kunst en Antiekhandel. For antique European pewter from the 15th through the 19th centuries, Jan Beekhuizen is the authority. His store also carries antique furniture, Delftware, metalware, and other collectible objects. ⊠*Nieuwe Spiegelstraat 49, The Canal Ring* ☎*020/626–3912* ⊕*www.janbeekhuizen.nl.*

Kunst & Antiekcentrum De Looier. For a broad range of vintage and antique furniture, curios, jewelry, clothing, and household items, try this cooperative housing more than 80 dealers, making it the largest covered art and antiques market in the Netherlands. You wouldn't be the first to get a great buy on an antique doll, a first-edition book, military memorabilia, or even a jeweled trinket here. The best days to go are Wednesday, Saturday, or Sunday, when all the vendors, including the *tafeltjesmarkt* (one-day table rentals), are present. Right after a book on *Delftsblauw* (Delft Blue porcelain) collectibles was published some years ago, a virtual army of dealers from the United States descended on De Looier market and snapped up just about every piece of Delft (if foolishly ignoring the large assortment of equally interesting and collectible Makkumware). ⊠*Elandsgracht 109, Jordaan* ☎*020/624–9038* ⊕*www.looier.com.*

★ **Prinsheerlijk Antiek.** Spanning 1,800 square feet, this emporium sells a princely assortment of furniture, bric-a-brac, and chandeliers dating from the early 18th century, as well as unique clock cases, Swedish-style birchwood furniture, and Dutch hand-painted folk pieces. Many items come from royal families and palaces, such as the spectacular sofa with griffin's arms that originally graced a Swedish castle. The shop also includes a renowned work studio, where antique furniture is upholstered and refurbished. ⊠*Prinsengracht 579, The Canal Ring* ☎*020/638–6623* ⊕*www.prinsheerlijkantiek.nl.*

Shopping

Salomon Stodel. Museum curators and collectors do their shopping at this nearly 150-year-old rare antiques store. ⊠ *Rokin 70, The Old City Center (Het Centrum)* ☎ *020/623–1692* ⊕ *www.salomonstodel.com.*

Sotheby's. Many antiques dealers buy from the fabled auctions held at the Amsterdam branch of this auction house. The Dutch are some of the savviest businesspeople in the world, but you can try to beat them to the bid. ⊠ *De Boelelaan 30, Buitenveldert* ☎ *020/550–2200* ⊕ *www.sothebys.com.*

Fodor's Choice ★ **Spiegelkwartier.** A William and Mary–era harpsichord? One of the printed maps that figured prominently in Vermeer's *Lutenist*? An 18th-century bed-curtain tie-up? Or a pewter nautilus cup redolent of a Golden Age still life? All these and more may be available in Amsterdam's famous array of antiques stores in the city's "Mirror Quarter," centered around Nieuwe Spiegelstraat and its continuation, Spiegelgracht. But—with shops on both sides of the street and canal for five blocks, from the Golden Bend of the Herengracht nearly to the Rijksmuseum—this section of town often requires a royal House of Orange budget.

Wildschut Antiquiteiten. Once you squeeze past the marvelous wooden wardrobes that fill this store, chances are you'll encounter owner Michael Wildschut at the back, restoring his latest acquisition. A tribute to European craftsmanship, the chests and armoires come mainly from northern France and are made of fine woods such as mahogany. These pieces have been restored with loving care, and can be fit with shelves or drawers as you so desire, and then shipped to your home address. ⊠ *1e Looiersdwarsstraat 8B, Jordaan* ☎ *020/320–8119* ⊕ *www.wildschut-antiek.nl.*

Willem Vredevoogd. Specializing in top names such as Lalique, Cartier, and Boucheron, Willem's is where to go for antique jewelry. ⊠ *P. C. Hooftstraat 82, Museum District* ☎ *020/673–6804.*

ART: MODERN TO CONTEMPORARY

Many of the galleries that deal in modern and contemporary art are centered on the Keizersgracht and Spiegelkwartier, and others are found around the Western Canal Ring and the Jordaan. Artists have traditionally gravitated to low-rent areas. De Baarsjes, a neighborhood in Amsterdam West, is increasingly attracting small galleries that showcase exciting works of art. With a shabbiness reminiscent of the early days of New York's Soho, it's worth a detour for adventurous art lovers. *Day by Day in Amsterdam*, published by the tourist office, is a reasonable source of information on current exhibitions and can be purchased for a small fee at one of the city's four VVV tourist information points. Other helpful sources are the Dutch-language publication *Alert* and the Web site ⊕ *www.galeries.nl.* Opening times vary greatly, so it's a good idea to check out the listings or first call the gallery for information.

De Beeldenwinkel. Whether you're looking for a serious art piece, a funny ornament, or an item that blends with your home home interior, the pieces on view here are always interesting. The shop is filled with sculpture made from metal, ceramic, and glass, with something to please every taste and budget. ⊠ *Berenstraat 29, The Canal Ring* ☎ *020/676–4903* ⊕ *www.beeldenwinkel.nl.*

Elisabeth Den Bieman de Haas. This gallery is a top contender in the Spiegelkwartier, showcasing art from the international CoBrA collection, with a specialization in Corneille's early works. ⊠ *Nieuwe Spiegelstraat 44, The Canal Ring* ☎ *020/626–1012* ⊕ *www.biemandehaas.nl.*

Galerie De Stoker. Though mainly featuring sculptures in papier-mâché and stone, this Amsterdam West venue is also noted for its innovative ceramic fountains. The atelier behind the gallery is open to visitors. ⊠ *Witte de Withstraat 124, Amsterdam West* ☎ *020/612–3293* ⊕ *www.destoker.nl.*

Galerie Ei. Artist Judith Zwaan displays her whimsical, colorful paintings and papier-mâché sculptures, influenced by Niki de Saint-Phalle and the CoBrA group, as well as the art and culture of West Africa. Other exciting new artists regularly exhibit at the small gallery. ⊠ *Admiraal de Ruijterweg 154, De Baarsjes* ☎ *020/616–3961.*

Kunsthandel M.L. De Boer. Founded in 1945, this gallery is renowned for showing contemporary figurative and abstract works by Dutch, French, and Belgian artists, as well as by Dutch and French masters from the 19th century and early 20th century. Since M.L. De Boer's death in 1991, the gallery has been kept open by his son expressly for exhibitions of modern works from the gallery's own collection. ⊠ *Keizersgracht 542, The Canal Ring* ☎ *020/623–4060* ⊕ *www.kunsthandeldeboer.com.*

Peter Donkersloot Galerie. Formerly known as Galerie Hoopman, this is a top stop for contemporary art along the Spiegelkwartier. It was rechristened in 2006, when Mr. Hoopman joined forces with Peter Donkersloot. ⊠ *Spiegelgracht 14–16, The Canal Ring* ☎ *020/623–6538* ⊕ *www.peterdonkerslootgalerie.nl.*

BOOKS

ABC Treehouse. For the past decade, the American Book Center has been hosting bookshop-related events and exhibitions in their former warehouse space, just across from their new headquarters on the Spui. The Treehouse has also built a solid reputation for all kinds of Anglophonic activities, such as English language readings, open-mike nights, and its annual Thanksgiving potluck dinner. ⊠ *Voetboogstraat 11, The Old City Center (Het Centrum)* ☎ *020/423–0967* ⊕ *www. treehouse.abc.nl.*

★ **American Book Center.** What began in the early '70s as an erotic magazine outlet has grown into reputedly the largest English-language book emporium on the continent. True to its name, the stock is strongly oriented toward American tastes and expectations, with its vast selection spread over seven stories. Since opening in its new location in 2006, now with a 20-foot-high poplar tree trunk in its entry reminding readers of the source of all literature, the store is bustling more than ever. (Students, senior citizens, and teachers receive a 10% discount.) ✉*Spui 12, The Old City Center (Het Centrum)* ☎*020/625–5537* ⊕*www.abc.nl.*

★ **Antiquariaat Kok.** This antiquarian's heaven has, for the last 60 years, offered readers oodles of treasures on Amsterdam history. It also takes pride in housing the city's largest secondhand Dutch-language book collection and a fair share of other literature nicely shelved according to subject. ✉*Oude Hoogstraat 14–18, The Old City Center (Het Centrum)* ☎*020/623–1191* ⊕*www.nvva.nl/kok.*

Architectura en Natura. Rarely does anyone leave the shop empty-handed—not with its stock of beautiful oversized art and photography books spanning architecture, nature, landscape design, and gardening. ✉*Leliegracht 22, Jordaan* ☎*020/623–6186* ⊕*www.architectura.nl.*

Athenaeum Boekhandel. Since the late '60s, this mainstay on the Spui has been one of the Netherlands's largest independent bookshops. Celebrity authors sometimes pop in, and scholars and university students often rely on the stock for academic literature. ✉*Spui 14–16, The Old City Center (Het Centrum)* ☎*020/514–1460* ⊕*www.athenaeum.nl.*

Athenaeum Nieuwscentrum. For the city's best selection of international periodicals and newspapers, as well as a smattering of cool local zines, follow your way to the unmissable red-and-white awning on the Spui. ✉*Spui 14–16, The Old City Center (Het Centrum)* ☎*020/514–1470* ⊕*www.athenaeum.nl.*

Book Exchange. Redolent of a bygone era in a rural New England town, this browse-worthy shop sells used English-language books on all subjects and many a secondhand paperback. ✉*Kloveniersburgwal 58, The Old City Center (Het Centrum)* ☎*020/626–6266* ⊕*www.book exchange.nl.*

Cortina Papier. Poet or paper-pusher, you'll find a luscious array of notebooks, albums, stationery, gift wrap, and 26 colors of writing ink here. And if even for five minutes, you'll forget all about the invention of the computer. ✉*Reestraat 22, The Canal Ring* ☎*020/623–6676* ⊕*www. cortinapapier.nl.*

De Slegte. Possibly the largest bookstore in Amsterdam, this is a true haven for book hunters. Every floor stocks tomes in various languages, across all genres, and covering many subjects. The shop is known for its large nonfiction collection of popular titles at bargain prices, and upstairs floors have a humongous antiquarian book section. ✉*Kalverstraat 48–52, The Old City Center (Het Centrum)* ☎*020/622–5933* ⊕*www.deslegte.com.*

The English Bookshop. Get served tea in a cozy little shop while the staff recommend reading according to your personal tastes. Secondhand books, Dutch authors translated into English, children's books, and lots of fine literature are at your fingertips. ✉*Lauriergracht 71, Jordaan* ☎*020/626–4230* ⊕*www.englishbookshop.nl.*

Evenaar Literaire Reisboekhandel. Armchair travelers and ground-stomping wayfarers visit this store for publications on travel, anthropology, and literary essays. What you need to know about foreign cultures you'll discover here. ⊠ *Singel 348, The Old City Center (Het Centrum)* ☎ *020/624–6289* ⊕ *www.evenaar.net.*

Oudemanhuis Book Market. This tiny, venerable covered book market is snuggled in the heart of the University of Amsterdam's meandering edifices. Booksellers in this alleyway have been hawking used and antiquarian books, prints, and sheet music for more than a century. ⊠ *Oudemanhuispoort, The Old City Center (Het Centrum).*

Premsela. Tempting window displays allure browsers into this specialty shop for art books. ⊠ *Van Baerlestraat 78, Museum District* ☎ *020/662–4266.*

Selexyz Scheltema. With five floors of books on every imaginable subject, plus an international spread of newspapers and magazines, and a Bagels & Beans café on the first floor, this is one of Amsterdam's busiest and best-stocked international bookstores. It'll come close to satisfying Americans jonesing for a Barnes & Noble fix. ⊠ *Koningsplein 20, The Canal Ring* ☎ *020/523–1402* ⊕ *www.selexyz.nl.*

Waterstone's. Take refuge from Amsterdam's hectic shopping street in this four-floor edifice of English-language books, ranging from children's stories to computer manuals. There's also a huge selection of magazines from the U.K. ⊠ *Kalverstraat 152, The Old City Center (Het Centrum)* ☎ *020/638–3821* ⊕ *www.waterstones.com.*

CERAMICS & CRYSTAL

Breekbaar. Here you'll find a top-brand selection of zany glassware and unique china, including a splendid menagerie of Ritzenhoff stems and saucers. The owner is a jovial, cigar-smoking gent who seems he could have been created by Lewis Carroll. ⊠ *Weteringschans 209, The Canal Ring* ☎ *020/626–1260.*

Frides Lamëris. For superb porcelain, glass, and tiles, all minted before 1800, visit this Spiegelkwartier venue. ⊠ *Nieuwe Spiegelstraat 55, The Canal Ring* ☎ *020/626–4066* ⊕ *www.frideslameris.nl.*

De Glaswerkplaats. If you're seeking a personalized souvenir, consider stopping by this studio on the Nine Streets, where you can order custom-made designs in fused or stained glass. Classes and workshops are also held at the shop. ⊠ *Berenstraat 41, The Canal Ring* ☎ *020/420–2120* ⊕ *www.glassierkunst.nl.*

Hogendoorn & Kaufman. Fancy a gift fit for a king? Well-oiled shoppers and devout collectors know there is only one address in Amsterdam that can please. This shop sells the crème de la crème, with the best designs from Baccarat, Lalique, Daum, and Swarovski in crystal, Royal Delft, Makkum, Lladró, Herend, and special designs from Fabergé, Meissen, Mats Jonasson, and others (with free worldwide shipping, too). Some items are moderately affordable, such as a Royal Delft dish with Dick Bruna's Miffy bunny, personalized with your child's name for less than €100. ⊠*Rokin 124, The Old City Center (Het Centrum)* ☎*020/638–2736* ⊕*www.hogendoorn-kaufman.com.*

't Winkeltje. This rummager's delight is a charming spot to search for small souvenirs. It's easy to pass the time pawing through the jumble of hotel porcelain, glass, and vintage postcards. ⊠*Prinsengracht 228, Jordaan* ☎*020/625–1352.*

CHILDREN

Azzurro Kids. Designer togs, shoes, and accessories for babies, boys, and girls can be found here. Armani Jr., Braez, Dolce & Gabbana, and other notable labels are ready to turn your little one into a walking advertisement. ⊠*P. C. Hooftstraat 122, Museum District* ☎*020/673–0457.*

FodorśChoice ★

Couzijn Simon. You may be hypnotized by the magenta-dyed mustache that the eponymous shop owner sports, but it's Simon's toy treasures that will make your child as pop-eyed as some of the vintage dolls here. The 35-year-old shop is crammed with wonders: an 18th-century rocking horse as finely carved as an 18th-century sculpture; a 4-foot-long wooden ice skate (a former store sign); a 1-inch doll with tiny hinged limbs; vintage trains and collector teddy bears; and porcelain dolls dressed for a costume ball. Some of the toys here even date back to the mid-18th century, which was when this shop first opened as a pharmacy. In the back is a small garden and a cottage, now the atelier of Dutch painter Anton Hoeboeur, whose works are for sale. ⊠*Prinsengracht 578, The Canal Ring* ☎*020/624–7691.*

De Beestenwinkel. The delightful corner store has nothing but animal toys of every breed and in all price ranges, as well as some fine souvenir choices for the young at heart. ⊠*Staalstraat 11, The Old City Center (Het Centrum)* ☎*020/623–1805* ⊕*www.beestenwinkel.nl.*

De Speelmuis. If your toddler back home simply must have a dollhouse version of a four-story gabled canal house, head to this Jordaanian gem. Also available here are kiddie carts in the shape of jumbo jets and fire engines, collectible medieval-style castles, figures from Schleigh, Papo, and Plastoy, and unusual wooden rocking "horses" in the shapes of bears, ducks, and motorcycles. ⊠*Elandsgracht 58, Jordaan* ☎*020/638–5342* ⊕*www.speelmuis.nl.*

De Winkel van Nijntje. Most department stores and toy shops in the Netherlands carry the classic children's brand, but here, at one of only three shops in the country, you'll find every imaginable Nijntje product—clothes, books, night-lights, tooth-fairy boxes, car seats, and more. ⊠*Beethovenstraat 71, Amsterdam South* ☎*020/671–9707* ⊕*www.dewinkelvannijntje.nl.*

★ **Exclusive Oilily Store.** Children's clothing has never been the same since Willem "Olli" Olsthoorn and wife Marieke Olsthoorn launched the first Oilily branch in the Netherlands' famous cheese market city of Alkmaar. In 1963, the couple wowed the fashion scene with colorful, funky, and wildly chic clothing and accessories. Today Oilily is most famous for dazzling colors and nearly psychedelic patterns that evoke kaleidoscope visions and glass millefleurs. Now a global name, Oilily caters to women and children, with offerings like mukluk booties for babies, fleece coats with penguin-shape buttons for older kids, and vibrant separates for moms who want to color-coordinate wardrobes with their Mini Mes. ✉ *P. C. Hooftstraat 131–133, Museum District* ☎ *020/672–3361* ✉ *Kalvertoren, Kalverstraat 212–220* ☎ *020/422–8713* ⊕ *www.oil-ily-world.com.*

Gone with the Wind. Specializing in mobiles from around the world, this mecca of mirth also sells unusual handcrafted wooden flowers and toys and spring-operated jumping toys. ✉ *Vijzelstraat 22, The Old City Center (Het Centrum)* ☎ *020/423–0230* ⊕ *www. gonewind-mobiles.com.*

★ **Pinokkio.** Your child may feel like an heir to the House of Orange if lucky enough to receive some of the beautifully carved old-fashioned wooden toys on offer at this shop vaulted away in the city center's veritable mall. Don't miss the array of old-fashioned greeting cards, apt for any age. ✉ *Magna Plaza, Nieuwezijds Voorburgwal 182, The Old City Center (Het Centrum)* ☎ *020/622–8914* ⊕ *www.pinokkio.net.*

't Schooltje. Your toddler in Armani, Versace, and Da-Da? If that's a yes, pay a visit to the Little School boutique where high-end clothing and shoes for infants to 16-year-olds are the curriculum. ✉ *Overtoom 87, Museum District* ☎ *020/683–0444* ⊕ *www.schooltje.nl.*

CLOTHING

Fodor'sChoice **English Hatter.** This beacon to times past offers pullovers, tweed jack-
★ ets, deerstalkers, and many other trappings of the English country gentleman. The cozy shop barely has room in which to turn around, but the inventory is large and the business bustling. Women can also buy hats here. ✉ *Heiligeweg 40, The Old City Center (Het Centrum)* ☎ *020/623–4781* ⊕ *www.english-hatter.nl* ✉ *Heiligeweg 53, The Old City Center (Het Centrum)* ☎ *020/626–2605.*

H&M. Like IKEA, this sensational Swedish chain has gone global, while offering remarkably cheap, classic, and trendy threads. H&M is the perfect sartorial answer to the Dutch's sense of democracy, and Amsterdammers swarm its various franchises in droves. ✉ *Kalverstraat 125, The Old City Center (Het Centrum)* ☎ *0900–1988* ⊕ *www. hm.com* ✉ *Nieuwendijk 141, The Old City Center (Het Centrum)* ☎ *0900–1988.*

THE GLOBE-HOPPING BUNNY

Created by Utrecht native Dick Bruna in 1955, Nijntje is to the Netherlands what Mickey Mouse is to the U.S. Rarely does a Dutch child today go without at least one Bruna book or toy. The beloved storybook bunny is named after the Dutch word for "little rabbit," *konijntje,* though you may know her by her less dipthongy international handle, Miffy. Experts in cuteness, the Japanese are especially fond of Miffy as well as her diverse animal friends, whose simple lines and expressionless features are no doubt a pre-pastel-colored harbinger to Hello Kitty.

5

McGregor. Chunky knitwear and the odd flash of tartan are characteristic of this international chain with a distinctly Scottish air. ✉*P. C. Hooftstraat 113, Museum District* ☎*020/675–3125* ⊕*www.mcgregor-fashion.com.*

Mulberry Company. Stylish fashions and luxury goods come from across the English Channel to please those with an affinity for the fox hunting look. ✉*P. C. Hooftstraat 46, Museum District* ☎*020/673–8086* ⊕*www.mulberry.com.*

Oger. Wives accompany their corporate husbands to this Dutch purveyor of Italian custom-tailored suits, so they can ogle the shop clerks who look like moonlighting male runway models. This store takes "dressed to the nines" to a ten in their self-proclaimed goal to "Latinize" their clients' sense of style. ✉*P. C. Hooftstraat 75–81, Museum District* ☎*020/676–8695* ⊕*www.oger.nl.*

Sissy-Boy. Casual yet colorful threads are found at this Dutch chain, which will prove edgy to Esprit types, but somewhat dull to H&M regulars. ✉*Van Baerlestraat 15, Museum District* ☎*020/671–5174* ✉*Kalverstraat 199, The Old City Center (Het Centrum)* ☎*020/638–9305* ⊕*www.sissy-boy.nl* ✉*Leidsestraat 15, Leidseplein* ☎*020/623–8949* ✉*Leidsestraat 15, Leidseplein* ☎*020/623–8949.*

Society Shop. This mainstay among the museums sells all the classics that Dutch politicians and businessmen dig. ✉*Van Baerlestraat 20–22, Museum District* ☎*020/664–9281.*

WOMEN'S WEAR **American Apparel.** The international franchise famous for cruelty-free cotton knits and infamous for its pornographic-like marketing campaign may just as well have been called "Amsterdam Apparel." ✉*Westerstraat 59–61, Jordaan* ☎*020/330–2391* ⊕*www.americanapparel.net.*

Bodysox. A modern-day hosiery haven that sells socks, tights, nighties, and lingerie. ✉*Leidsestraat 35, The Canal Ring* ☎*020/422–3544.*

Concrete. The Cyberdog's synthetic fabrics aspiring towards "futuristic" have been kicked to the curb by this new streetwear boutique, selling esoteric urban labels and vintage Levi's and Nike. You can bet on the obligatory stock of high-tops, hoodies, and plastic Japanese toys that are requisite to stores of this milieu. ✉*Spuistraat 250, The Old City Center (Het Centrum)* ☎*0900–CONCRETE* ⊕*www.concrete.nl.*

Cora Kemperman. This Dutch minichain offers architecturally designed clothes that are ageless and elegant. ✉*Leidsestraat 72, The Canal Ring* ☎*020/625–1284* ⊕*www.corakemperman.nl.*

Edgar Vos. The creations of this Dutch designer cater to women who seek garments that are classic and feminine, but never frilly. Hand-beaded and hand-embroidered details on fine silk, wool, and linen make his clothes especially attractive and spotlight the influence of his apprenticeship to Dior and Balmain. ✉*P. C. Hooftstraat 136, Museum District* ☎*020/671–2748* ⊕*www.edgarvos.nl* ✉*Beethovenstraat 57Amsterdam South* ☎*020/662–7460.*

★ **Individuals Statement Store.** The Amsterdam Fashion Institute proudly sells the creations of its third-year students just next door to the Maagdenhuuis, a university building notorious as the site of history-making student sit-ins. Print-wary and asymmetrically inclined as these aspiring new designers may be, the clothes are surprisingly wearable and small gift items affordable. ✉ *Spui 23, The Old City Center (Het Centrum)* ☎ *020/525–8133* ⊕ *www.individualsatamfi.nl.*

Marlijn. Those who really want to make an individual fashion statement should make an appointment with couturiere Marlijn Franken. This Dutch designer has created looks for numerous celebrities, and if you're keen on having a transparent plastic suit, an iridescent, slashed-silk dress, or anything else outrageously luscious, she can do it. ✉ *Govert Flinckstraat 394 hs, The Pijp* ☎ *020/671–4742* ⊕ *www.marlijnamsterdam.nl.*

Pauw. It's a wonder that the shops in this chain always appear in clusters, with two or three sharing the same block, when you consider how pricey their collection is. For those who can afford it, however, Madeleine Pauw's pieces are just plain beautiful, particularly for the sophisticated and perhaps equestrian-inspired type of woman, be she a professional or society dame. ✉ *Van Baerlestraat 48, 66, 72, Museum District* ☎ *020/662–6253* ⊕ *www.pauw.nl* ✉ *Leidsestraat 16, Leidseplein* ☎ *020/626–5698.*

★ **Van Ravenstein.** The chic boutique is one of a handful of retail outlets in Holland for Viktor & Rolf ready-to-wear. But instead of A-bomb fashion—seldom seen outside museums and off the runway—you'll find the duo's smart, beautifully cut ready-to-wear clothing. The shop also carries top Belgian designers such as Martin Margiela, Dirk van Saenne, and Dries van Noten. On Saturdays, they open the bargain basement and the deals are outrageously well-priced. ✉ *Keizersgracht 359, The Canal Ring* ☎ *020/639–0067* ⊕ *www.van-ravenstein.nl.*

DIAMONDS & JEWELRY

Diamonds are hardly ever a bargain. But compared with other cities, and thanks to Amsterdam's centuries-old ties to South Africa, they brilliantly border on that category here. The city's famous factories even allow one-stop shopping.

Amsterdam Diamond Center. Several diamond sellers are housed in this large tourist's to-do opposite the Dam. Besides diamonds, one can shop for other jewelry, watches, and silver gifts. ✉ *Rokin 1–5, The Old City Center (Het Centrum)* ☎ *020/624–5787* ⊕ *www.amsterdamdiamondcenter.nl.*

BLGK. This Nine Streets stop specializes in handmade Byzantine-inspired silver and gold jewelry. ✉ *Hartenstraat 28, The Canal Ring* ☎ *020/624–8154.*

★ **Bonebakker.** In business since 1792, this is one of the city's oldest and finest jewelers. Founder Adrian Bonebakker was commissioned by King Willem II to design and make the royal crown for the House of Orange. Today you'll find watches by Piaget, Corum, Chaumet,

Cartier, and Jaeger-LeCoultre, and beautiful silver and gold tableware. Some of the silver designs produced here in the 1920s have been exhibited in Dutch museums, such as the Willet-Holthuysen. ⊠ *Rokin 88–90, The Old City Center (Het Centrum)* ☎ *020/623–2294.*

Coster Diamonds. Kitty-corner to the Rijksmuseum, this store-disguised-as-a-museum hasn't really maintained its luster. The shabby interior decor notwithstanding, you can purchase some nice ice or other jewelry. ⊠ *Paulus Potterstraat 2–8, Museum District* ☎ *020/ 305-5555* ⊕ *www.costerdiamonds.com.*

> **DIAMOND DRILL**
>
> Even if you're not in the market for new rocks, a visit to Coster is worth one of its free guided tours. You'll learn all about the diamond industry's "four Cs"—carat, color, clarity, and cut—and get to watch workers plying their trade. There's also a replica of the factory's most famous cut—the Koh-I-Noor diamond, one of the prize gems of the British crown jewels.

Galerie RA. This gallery tucked into the armpit of an ABN-AMRO bank shows wearable art by Dutch and international jewelry designers. ⊠ *Vijzelstraat 80, The Old City Center (Het Centrum)* ☎ *020/626–5100* ⊕ *www.galerie-ra.nl.*

Grimm Sieraden. Small but savvy, this boutique is known for unearthing the latest in jewelry by trendy young designers. ⊠ *Grimburgwal 9, The Old City Center (Het Centrum)* ☎ *020/622–0501* ⊕ *www.grimmsieraden.nl.*

Hans Appenzeller. Situated on a tiny street near the university is one of the international leaders in contemporary jewelry design. ⊠ *Grimburgwal 1, The Old City Center (Het Centrum)* ☎ *020/626–8218* ⊕ *www.appenzeller.nl.*

Premsela & Hamburger. Fine antique silver and jewelry have been purveyed here since 1823. And—how progressive!—it's open most Sundays. ⊠ *Rokin 98, The Old City Center (Het Centrum)* ☎ *020/624–9688* ⊕ *www.premsela.com.*

Schaap and Citroen. The century-old company carries top brands like Rolex, but also more moderately priced wristwatches and jewelry. ⊠ *P. C. Hooftstraat 40, The Old City Center (Het Centrum)* ☎ *020/671–4714* ⊕ *www.schaapcitroen.nl.*

FOOD & BEVERAGES

CHEESE   **De Kaaskamer.** This store stinks—of a smell testifying to its terrific selection of cheese. In addition to the usual Dutch suspects (Edam, Gouda, Old Amsterdam, and the smoked curds), this family business also sells choices from France, Greece, Italy, and Switzerland. There's also a rich assortment of accompanying cold cuts, olives, freshly made sauces, and dried fruits. ⊠ *Runstraat 7, The Canal Ring* ☎ *020/623-3483.*

CHOCOLATE   **Arti Choc.** Chocoholics, take note, this Amsterdam South secret not only sells handmade bonbons, but will also custom-design just about anything you can imagine made from chocolate. The staff is lovely, and serves a very generous scoop of gelato, ideal to take along on a walk through the nearby Vondelpark. ⊠*Koninginneweg 141, Amsterdam South* ☎*020/470–9805* ⊕*www.artichoc.nl.*

Australian Homemade. This Nijmegen-founded, now global chain's chocolate is consumed en masse by Amsterdammers—its silver, space-age vacuum-sealed packaging finds a way onto the racks of many third-party vendors (including the local Albert Heijn grocery chain). But, no doubt, Australian's all-natural ingredients do make delectable chocolate and ice cream, as well as the best milk shake in town. ⊠*Singel 437, The Old City Center (Het Centrum)* ☎*020/428–7533* ⊕*www.australianhomemade.com* ⊠*Spui 5, The Old City Center (Het Centrum)* ☎*020/627–4430* ⊠*Leidsestraat 101, Leidseplein* ☎*020/622–0897.*

Chocolaterie Pompadour. After 40 years, the civilized still sit here for afternoon tea and tart. The front of the store attends to a steady stream of chocoholics—no less cultivated, just on the go. The Florentines are an éclat in their own right. ⊠*Huidenstraat 12, The Canal Ring* ☎*020/623–9554* ⊠*Kerkstraat 148, The Canal Ring* ☎*020/330–0981.*

★ **Puccini Bomboni.** Amsterdam's best handmade chocolates come from this shop seemingly dreamed up by Roald Dahl for the modern-day metropolitan. Each bonbon is a knockout: one is usually enough to satiate the most gluttonous among us. The unusual ingredients include cognac, prune, pepper, and tamarind. ⊠*Singel 184, The Old City Center (Het Centrum)* ☎*020/427–8341* ⊕*www.puccinibomboni.com* ⊠*Staalstraat 17, The Canal Ring* ☎*020/626–5474.*

COFFEE, TEA & SPIRITS

Cave Rokin. As its name suggests, this liquor store can be found in a cellar finely stocked with a range of European and New World wines, *jenevers* (Dutch gins), and *advocaats* (eggnogs made with brandy). The staff is knowledgeable and helpful. Tastings can be arranged for larger parties. ⊠*Rokin 60, The Old City Center (Het Centrum)* ☎*020/625–0628* ⊕*www.caverokin.nl.*

De Bierkoning. Nearly one thousand different types of beer can be purchased at this veritable museum of a specialty shop. The 300 beer-brand glasses on offer also make for a unique gift (and assuage long guilt-ridden pub pilferers). ⊠*Paleisstraat 125, The Old City Center (Het Centrum)* ☎*020/625–2336* ⊕*www.bierkoning.nl.*

Geels & Co. Since 1880, this Warmoesstraat store has sold tea, coffee, and brewing utensils. It's a great place to find gifts like replica antique spice necklaces and traditional Dutch candy (not easy to find elsewhere). Don't miss the tiny museum upstairs with its display of antique coffee paraphernalia from around the world. ⊠*Warmoesstraat 67, The Old City Center (Het Centrum)* ☎*020/624–0683* ⊕*www.geels.nl.*

Jacob Hooy & Co. Filled with teak-wood canisters and jars bearing Latin inscriptions, fragrant with the perfume of seeds, flowers, and medicinal potions, this health and wellness store has been in operation on Nieuwmarkt since 1743. Gold-lettered wooden drawers, barrels, and bins contain not just spices and herbs, but also a daunting array of *dropjes* (hard candies and medicinal drops) and teas. ✉*Kloveniersburgwal 12, The Old City Center (Het Centrum)* ☎*020/624–3041* ⊕*www.jacobhooy.nl.*

Kaldi. Most of the city's few (though steadily growing) number of takeaway coffee corners are found on the busiest of cross-sections, so this shop's emergence on the quiet Nine Streets is most welcome. One of a few franchises throughout the country, Kaldi also sells specialty coffees and teas from around the world, as well as everything related to their preparation, from brewing apparatus to accompanying biscotti. ✉*Herengracht 300, The Canal Ring* ☎*020/428–6854* ⊕*www.kaldi.nl.*

> **CO-OPTING THE CLOG**
>
> You can't visit Holland and not buy a pair of *klompen* (clogs), can you? Clogs may not be the best choice for backpacking throughout Europe, but these wooden shoes are still used by farmers, fishermen, and factory workers. Traditionally worn over a thick pair of *geitenwollen sokken* (socks made from goat's wool), *klompen* help keep toes warm while providing durable soles to stomp through wet and muddy surfaces. While you're in town, you may notice how some of the bohemian city folk have co-opted the clog, using it as a wall-mounted flowerpot on their terraces.

GIFTS & SOUVENIRS

Baobab. This shop's interior is like something out of Ali Baba's cave of treasures or 1001 Nights. You'll find a rich trove of jewelry, statuary, and all kinds of objects from such locales as India and the Middle East. ✉*Elandsgracht 105, Jordaan* ☎*020/626–8398* ⊕*www.baobab-aziatica.nl.*

★ **Brilmuseum.** A must-visit when you're strolling the Nine Streets, this boutique displays a collection of eyeglasses from antique to contemporary in a setting that evokes the atmosphere of the 17th century (the upstairs galleries actually have museum status). It's open only Wednesday through Saturday. ✉*Gasthuismolensteeg 7, The Canal Ring* ☎*020/421–2414* ⊕*www.brilmuseumamsterdam.nl.*

Cats & Things. Cat lovers return again and again to Ine van Bercum's headquarters for feline-related gifts and useful items for the kitty. Ms. Van Bercum is also a very knowledgeable cat breeder, and of course, a real cat named Annabel is on hand to welcome customers with a purrfect greeting. ✉*Hazenstraat 26, Jordaan* ☎*020/428–3028* ⊕*www.catsandthings.nl.*

De Condomerie. A discreet, well-informed staff promote healthful sexual practices at this condom emporium (with an equally handy online store). It's also strategically located on one of the city's boulevards for gay nightlife. ✉*Warmoesstraat 141, The Old City Center (Het Centrum)* ☎*020/627–4174* ⊕*www.condomerie.com.*

De Witte Tanden Winkel. Anyone for champagne-flavored toothpaste? Whether concerned about dental hygiene or looking for some kind of oral novelty, consider visiting this small shop stocked with everything teeth-related. The toothbrush Ferris wheel in the window is also worth a gander. ✉ *Runstraat 5, The Canal Ring* ☏020/623–3443 ⊕*www. dewittetandenwinkel.nl.*

★ **The Fair Trade Shop.** In the market for Colombian coffee, silver jewelry, a set of salad tongs, new salsa beats, or a handcrafted photo album from India? You'll find a rainbow of such items from this shop of the same-named global organization promoting the fair compensation of products imported from developing communities. ✉ *Heiligewg 45, The Old City Center (Het Centrum)* ☏020/625–2245 ⊕*www.fairtrade.nl.*

Kerkhof. Holland's leading fashion and theatrical costume designers frequent this funky archive of unusual ribbons, tassels, lace edgings, and other fashion trim available for retail customers. (The store is closed Friday through Sunday.) ✉ *Wolvenstraat 9, Jordaan* ☏020/623–4084.

Knuffels/De Klompenboer. Located in a former metro station, Knuffels is the upstairs venue that sells toys, including a fun-loving selection of *knuffels* (the word for hugs and, by extension, cuddle toys). Downstairs is the *klompen* (clog) shop, where you can order wooden shoes in all sizes and colors, as well as request hand-painted or wood-burned designs. ✉ *Sint Anthoniesbreestraat 39–51, The Old City Center (Het Centrum)* ☏020/427–3862.

Nieuws. Small, quirky presents can be found at this crossroads for gag gifts, kitsch, and novelty items. ✉ *Prinsengracht 297, The Canal Ring* ☏020/627–9540 ⊕*www.peoplesgiftstore.com.*

RoB Flagship Store. Serving a largely gay men's community for nearly 30 years, this self-touted "epicenter of Amsterdam leather life" sells hides, rubber, and other pliable gear to those of a dungeon-y demeanor. ✉ *Warmoesstraat 71, The Old City Center (Het Centrum)* ☏020/428–3000 ⊕*www.rob.nl.*

★ **Skatezone.** The dike-plugging Dutch boy Hans Brinker would have loved this modern skating outlet, which stocks well over 150 models of ice skates in all styles: from those made for wintertime canal gliding (becoming an increasingly unlikely possibility thanks to global warming) to hockey skates. The shop carries top brands such as Viking, Raps, Bauer, CCM, Zandstra, Graf, with a large variety of *noren,* the most popular style of speed skates for adults, as well as traditional Dutch wooden training skates for children (the double blades make for easier balance). Skatezone is also the place to rent in-line skates manufactured by all the bigwigs in extreme sports, including Rollerblade, K2, and Powerslide. ✉ *Ceintuurbaan 57–59, The Pijp* ☏020/662–2822 ⊕*www.skatezone.nl.*

Souvenir Shop Holland. Although souvenir shops can be found on every other street corner in Amsterdam, this one is distinguished by its better class of products, such as Delft cuckoo clocks and automated miniature windmills. Sure, you may find a number of these items elsewhere, but they're often displayed just across the aisle from total kitsch, risqué mementos, or drug paraphernalia. In other words, feel free to bring your grandmother to this shop. ⊠*Nieuwendijk 226, Dam* ☎*020/624–7252* ⊕*www.souvenirshopholland.com.*

A Space Oddity. This little shop combs a big world for robots, toys, and memorabilia from TV and film classics. ⊠*Prinsengracht 204, Jordaan* ☎*020/427–4036* ⊕*www.spaceoddity.nl.*

HAIR & BEAUTY

Ariane Inden. This salon has a full line of Dutch cosmetics and does makeovers. The upstairs parlor also offers a range of skin treatments. ⊠*Utrechtsestraat 127, The Canal Ring* ☎*020/420–2332* ⊕*www.arianeinden.com.*

Barrio. What happens when a young Dutch couple spend a year camping out of their Winnebago, on adventures from Berlin to Barcelona? They go back to their hometown to open a hair salon-cum-streetwear boutique, bringing the latest threads of an understated urban variety to down-to-earth hipsters. They also give it a Spanish name, in remembrance of their community-spirited inspiration for new cuts in hair and clothes. ⊠*Voetboogstraat 20, The Old City Center (Het Centrum)* ☎*020/663–2918* ⊕*www.barrio.nl.*

Hairpolice. The daring and dreadlocked frequent this salon, right off the Bloemenmarkt, for wild dos, colorful extensions, and the rigmarole of dread maintenance. ⊠*Geelvincksteeg 10, The Canal Ring* ☎*020/420–5841* ⊕*www.hairpolice.nl.*

Ici Paris XL. Only the top brands in makeup and perfumes are sold at this chain of cosmetics. The staff is as polished and professional as the shop—the salesladies and occasional salesgents look airbrushed, which isn't necessarily a bad thing. ⊠*P. C. Hooftstraat 132–134, Museum District* ☎*020/675–8032* ⊕*www.iciparisxl.nl* ⊠*Leidsestraat 67, Leidseplein* ☎*020/320–9751.*

Kiehl's. This global chain of herbal-friendly cosmetics, which first began as a New York City apothecary in 1851, is a perfect addition to the swanky little shops along the P. C. Hooftstraat periphery. ⊠*Hobbemastraat 4, Museum District* ☎*020/675–0891* ⊕*www.kiehls.com.*

Kinki Kappers. This city chain attracts mainstream hipsters exploring the realm of asymmetrical bangs and whatnot. ⊠*De Bijkenkorf, Dam 1, The Old City Center (Het Centrum)* ☎*020/330–7471* ⊕*www.kinki.nl* ⊠*Utrechtsestraat 34, The Canal Ring* ☎*020/625–7793*

A TWOFER THAT TURNS HEADS

Pontifex Essential Oils and Incense/Doll Hospital E. Kramer. If on the off chance you're looking for a potion that will promote inner peace and harmony, and you also happen to have an antique porcelain doll that needs a tune-up, you have only one place to go. On one side of this Nine Streets shop, you'll find candles, incense, and nearly 200 types of ethereal and spiritual oils. On the other side, shopkeeper Kramer carries on a 40-year-old tradition of doll repair and re-capitation (there are shelves of body-less heads to chose from). ⊠*Reestraat 18–20, The Canal Ring* ☎*020/626–5274.*

⊠ *Overtoom 245, Amsterdam West* ☎ *020/689–4553.*

★ **La Savonnerie.** For 10 years, this sweet little shop has been hand-making its own brand of palm oil soap. There are over 70 different scents, colorfully ranging from Aqua to Winterberry, and, best of all, bars can be custom-engraved. ⊠ *Prinsengracht 294, Jordaan* ☎ *020/428–1139* ⊕ *www.savonnerie.nl.*

CUT AND GO

Returning home with that cool Euro coif you always wanted just got cheaper and chiller. On Fridays from 7–9 PM, **Barrio** welcomes walk-ins who, for just €20, can get "cut and go"—that is, full salon service minus the blow-dry.

Lush. Enticing scents and spunky staff lure you into this modern-day beauty shop, where the handmade soaps, "bath bombs," and massage stones appear good enough to eat (if you don't mind getting a little glitter on your tongue). ⊠ *Leidsestraat 14, Leidseplein* ☎ *020/423–4315* ⊕ *www.lush.nl* ⊠ *Kalverstraat 98, The Old City Center (Het Centrum)* ☎ *020/330–6376.*

Rob Peetoom. The ultramodern surroundings at this hair and makeup salon are full of beautiful people trying to get more beautiful. ⊠ *Elandsgracht 68, Jordaan* ☎ *020/528–5722* ⊕ *www.robpeetoom.nl* ⊠ *De Bijenkorf, Dam 1, The Old City Center (Het Centrum)* ☎ *020/422–3902.*

★ **Skins Cosmetics.** A Sephora gone small-town, this Nine Streets boutique carries an extensive selection of exclusive brands of cosmetics and hair-care products. On-site hairdressers for men and women and makeup artists will tend to your looks. ⊠ *Runstraat 9, The Canal Ring* ☎ *020/528–6922* ⊕ *www.skins.nl.*

HOUSEWARES

Bebob Design Interior. Collectors and galleries stock up here on hard-to-find historic designs of chairs, sofas, tables, office chairs, and lighting fixtures from top lines. ⊠ *Prinsengracht 764, The Canal Ring* ☎ *020/624–5763* ⊕ *www.bebob.nl.*

Blond Amsterdam. In some places, goofy-captioned caricature portraiture went out of fashion along with street fairs and mall kiosks, but Holland can't seem to get enough of it—in the form of hand-painted cups and plates created by two (blond) Amsterdam art school grads. In fall 2007, Blond went platinum with a new "lifestyle" megastore. ⊠ *Gerard Doustraat 69, The Pijp* ☎ *020/428–4929* ⊕ *www.blond-amsterdam.nl.*

Capsicum. Not your run-of-the-mill fabric store, this place makes fabricholics drool with all its gorgeous weaves, prints, and colors. ⊠ *Oude Hoogstraat 1, The Old City Center (Het Centrum)* ☎ *020/623–1016* ⊕ *www.capsicum.nl.*

★ **Coco-Mat.** Since opening this Dutch flagship shop in May 2003, the Greek chain has been crowded with customers seven days a week. Troll

CLOSE UP

Cutting Edge Dutch Design

Ever since Gerrit Rietveld produced his "Red and Blue Chair," the Dutch have been in the international limelight, famous for graphic design, fashion (clothing, jewelry, accessories), industrial design, interior design, furniture design, advertising, and architecture. Rietveld has been followed by the likes of Bruno Ninaber van Eyben (inventor of the pendant watch and the Dutch Euro), Trude Hooykaas (architect), Frans Molenaar (fashion), Jan Jansen (shoes), Ted Noten (jewelry), KesselsKramer (advertising), and Marcel Wanders (industrial designer best known for his Knitted Chair). These, and other equally acclaimed designers have works displayed in commercial galleries and modern art museums alike. Since 45,000 Dutch designers produce more than 2.5 billion euros worth of new stuff per year, you'd think somebody could tell you exactly what "Dutch Design" is. But it's too diverse to pin down, and ranges from modern, conceptual, kitsch, functional, sober, conceptual, innovative, ironic, experimental, intelligent, and alternative to everything in between. Each year, a steady stream of new talent, graduating from one of the numerous national institutes

A Droog table and chair, produced and designed by Richard Hutten.

dedicated to design, make Dutch Design a perennially hot topic that takes center stage no matter what time of year you visit. The Utrecht School for the Arts (HKU), Design Academy Eindhoven (dubbed the "School of Cool" by Time magazine), the Industrial Design department at TU Delft, and the Rietveld Academy in Amsterdam are talent pools feeding into the trend mecca that the Netherlands has become. To dive deep into Dutch Design, visit Droog design (dry design) (✉ *Staalstraat 7A & B, The Old City Center* ☎ *020/626-9809* ⊕ *www.droogdesign.nl*), an enterprise for witty young designers. Its shop features numerous articles and a "new talent" gallery that changes every two months. The Frozen Fountain (✉ *Prinsengracht 629–645, The Canal Ring* ☎ *020/622-9375* ⊕ *frozenfountain.nl*) is filled with the most fabulous furniture and lighting. ⇨ (See Shopping for more design stores)

Marcel Wanders' famous egg vase.

for decadently comfortable ortho-
pedic beds, ergonomic sofas, pretty
tables, curtains, and bed and bath
linens. Glass floor panels reveal the
downstairs area, which is devoted
to children's furnishings and adorable soft toys. The staff welcomes
you with Mediterranean hospitality: gifts of olive oil, wine, nut-filled
figs, or a fresh-pressed fruit juice,
which you can enjoy in the peaceful
garden. ⊠ *Overtoom 89, Museum
District* ☎ *020/489–2927* ⊕ *www.
coco-mat.nl.*

Dreamz. Everything here is handmade by European designers exclusive to the store. Browse and you'll
discover art glass objects from
Prague, elaborate Parisian chairs
resembling thrones, and stunning
chrome wine racks. The owner will customize lamps according to
your desires. ⊠ *Willemsparkweg 8, Museum District* ☎ *020/470–4718*
⊕ *www.dream-z.nl.*

> ## THE TUMBLE MAN
>
> **Duikelman** is named in honor of
> the original "Tumble Man." In the
> 1940s, Joop van Hal, grandfather
> to David Appelboom, the busi-
> ness's current owner, had invented
> a flashlight that automatically
> shut off when flipped over
> in a downward tumbling—
> "*duikelen*"—motion. This timely
> device was a crucial invention,
> helping to keep the Dutch army
> strategically obscured from enemy
> sight. It also began the Appel-
> boom family's tradition of selling
> simple yet well-designed tools,
> now in more tranquil times.

Fodor'sChoice
★ **Droog Design.** Besides exhibiting highlights of its collection, this design
collective also sells a number of its edgy, often industrial, furniture and
home accessories. What began as a decidedly Dutch group now comprises designers from all over the globe, who have together cultivated
an international reputation for groundbreaking interior design. ⊠ *Staalstraat 7A & B, The Old City Center (Het Centrum)* ☎ *020/626–9809*
⊕ *www.droogdesign.nl.*

Fodor'sChoice
★ **Duikelman.** Kitchen supplies never had it so good, and neither did the
professional or amateur cooks who shop here. At the flagship store,
just off Ferdinand Bolstraat, you'll find 10,000 top-quality cooking
utensils and kitchenware items. Cross the street (⊠ *Gerard Doustraat
54* ☎ *020/673–1385.*), and you'll come upon the company's two latest
additions: a shop selling cookbooks, porcelain dishes, and art school-
designed tea towels, and a shop offering ovens that take baking to a
whole new level. ⊠ *Ferdinand Bolstraat 68–68a, The Pijp* ☎ *020/671–
2230, 020/671–7569* ⊕ *www.duikelman.nl.*

★ **The Frozen Fountain.** This gallery-cum-store carries contemporary furniture and innovative home accessories from such top Dutch designers as
Hutten, Arad, Newson, Starck, Wanders, and Jongerius. You can find
custom-made scrapwood cabinets by Piet Hein Eek, as well as artistic
perfume dispensers, jewelry, and carpets. The store juxtaposes minimalism with paper-cut chandeliers and rococo seats. Part of the space
serves as a museum shop for the Netherlands Textile Museum, where
original European fabrics are on offer. ⊠ *Prinsengracht 629–645, The
Canal Ring* ☎ *020/622–9375* ⊕ *www.frozenfountain.nl.*

HEMA. Even the Dutch equivalent of Sears has high-style household items at reasonable prices, and a cool, minimalist design. ✉ *Nieuwendijk 174–176, The Old City Center (Het Centrum)* ☎ *020/623–4176* ⊕ *www.hema.nl.*

De Kasstoor. This three-floor home store began in 1892 on the very same city block where it purveys sleek, contemporary furniture and household goods. Across the street are two other equally reputable Kasstoor businesses. **Wonen2000 Bed & Bad** (✉ *Rozengracht 215–217* ☎ *020/521–8712*) sells plush linens and bathroom accessories. **Wonen IDC** (✉ *Rozengracht 219–221* ☎ *020/521–8710*) sells innovative European furniture, while also offering forth its in-house group of architects and interior designers. ✉ *Rosengracht 202–210, Jordaan* ☎ *020/521–8112* ⊕ *www.dekasstoor.nl.*

> **EAT IN (AND ON) STYLE**
>
> Nothing works up an appetite like shopping for Scandinavian sofas or Italian countertops. But whether you've come to the De Kasstoor/Wonen2000 complex with hopes of totally overhauling your home or for just a browse, take a seat at the on-site eatery. Brasserie 2000 (✉ *Rozengracht 219* ☎ *020/521–8710*) is the perfect place for a Mediterranean-inspired lunch or an afternoon espresso and, from saucer to seat, customers are treated to the very same kind of well-designed European houseware that the store sells. The back patio is idyllic in the summer.

Kitsch Kitchen. This is a supermarket of wacky, tacky, plasticy housewares that greatly appeals to the Dutch's postmodern approach to interior design. Here's where Amsterdammers pick up that Virgin of Guadalupe votive candle to accompany the Alessi pepper grinder on an IKEA coffee table. ✉ *Rozengracht 8–12, Jordaan* ☎ *020/622–8261* ⊕ *www.kitschkitchen.nl.*

& Klevering Zuid. You'll find yourself in a rainbow world at this quiet corner thanks to its wide range of tints in porcelain and glass tableware, colorful household accessories, and bright table linens. Top European design brands are all here, including stainless steel cookware from Iittala, Peugeot pepper mills, lush towels and bathrobes from Van Dijck Sanger, and artistic storage boxes from Galerie Sentou. ✉ *Jacob Obrechtstraat 19a, Amsterdam South* ☎ *020/670–3623* ⊕ *www.klevering.nl.*

Nico van Ooorschot. World-renowned for his hand-patinated goat's leather chairs, Nico Van Oorchot has even sold chairs to Barbra Streisand. The coloring process is a family secret. ✉ *Bosboom Toussaintstraat 20, Old West* ☎ *020/612–5961* ⊕ *www.oorschotbv.nl.*

MUSIC

Fodor'sChoice
★ **Broekmans & Van Poppel.** Apropos of the neighboring Concertgebouw, this store specializes in recordings, sheet music, and accessories for classical and antiquarian music. ✉ *Van Baerlestraat 92–94, Museum District* ☎ *020/675–1653* ⊕ *www.broekmans.com.*

Concerto. This bi-level, multi-doored music mecca is filled with new and used records and CDs covering all imaginable genres. If you're looking for a particular recording, this should be your first stop. The staff members give off *High Fidelity*-esque vibes. ⊠*Utrechtsestraat 54–60, The Canal Ring* ☎*020/626–6577* ⊕*www.concerto.nu.*

★ **Rush Hour.** In the Netherlands, this is *the* premiere record shop for quality house, techno, left field vinyl releases, and international imports from Detroit to Tokyo. It's also a world-renowned mail-order outlet, an exclusive record label, and a bunch of boys who know how to throw a good party. ⊠*Spuistraat 98, The Old City Center (Het Centrum)* ☎*020/427–4505* ⊕*www.rushhour.nl.*

South Miami Plaza. The vast SMP has just about every music category, including the Dutch answer to country music, *smartlap*. Listening booths are available, too. ⊠*Albert Cuypstraat 116, The Pijp* ☎*020/662–2817.*

SHOES

Antonia By Yvette. Two generations of women, each with their own doorway, under one roof and one motto: "Crazy about shoes." Yvette carries hip footwear from top European designers for men and women. Her mother next door carries slippers, clogs, Birkenstocks, and boots for every kind of precipitation. ⊠*Gasthuismolensteeg 18–20, The Canal Ring* ☎*020/320–9433* ⊠*Gasthuismolensteeg 16, The Canal Ring* ☎*020/627–2433* ⊕*www.antoniabyyvette.nl.*

Dr. Adams. The good doctor sells chunkier, more adventurous styles of shoes for men and women. ⊠*P. C. Hooftstraat 90, Museum District* ☎*020/662–3835* ⊕*www.dradams.nl* ⊠*Leidsestraat 25, The Canal Ring* ☎*020/626–4460* ⊠*Oude Doelenstraat 5–7, The Old City Center (Het Centrum)* ☎*020/622–3734* ⊠*Kalvertoren, Kalverstraat 212–220, The Old City Center (Het Centrum)* ☎*020/427–2565* ⊠*Magna Plaza, Nieuwezijds Voorburgwal 182, The Old City Center (Het Centrum)* ☎*020/489–0576.*

★ **Fred de La Bretoniere.** This is *the* shop to find a classic style that still lets you walk with your own unique verve. Fred de la Bretoniere has been selling men's and women's leather footwear since 1970, and it's no surprise that his shoes have been entered into the permanent collections of several Dutch design museums. ⊠*Sint Luciënsteeg 20, The Old City Center (Het Centrum)* ☎*020/623–4152* ⊕*www.bretoniere. nl* ⊠*Utrechtsestraat 77, The Canal Ring* ☎*020/626–9627.*

Hester van Eeghen. Since 2000, cool, contemporary Dutch design has been available for ladies' feet—that is, after being manufactured from fine leather in Italy. And if you like Ms. Van Eeghen's shoes, walk west to her eponymous handbag boutique (⊠*Hartenstraat 37* ☎*020/626–9212*). Geometry never before seemed so colorful or portable. ⊠*Hartenstraat 1, The Canal Ring* ☎*020/626–9211* ⊕*www. hestervaneeghen.com.*

Jan Jansen. Forget fairy godmothers: this is where today's urban Cinderella finds her glass slippers. Since age 18, Jansen, the Nijmegen-born artist and craftsman has been creating footwear beloved for its conceptual design, outrageous color, and uncompromised wearability. After numerous design awards and contributions to museum collections, the 40-something-year-old offers a manufactured line of shoes perfect for any ball or business affair. ⊠ *Rokin 42, The Old City Center (Het Centrum)* ☎ *020/625–1350* ⊕ *www.janjansenshoes.com* ⊠ *Vijzelstraat 111, The Canal Ring* ☎ *020/428–8260.*

Onitsuka Tiger. With just a few flagships stores scattered throughout the world, Amsterdam provides some uppity canal-side real estate for this hip Japanese line of Asics sneakers. There seems to be a style for every breed of tulip. ⊠ *Herengracht 365, The Canal Ring* ☎ *020/528–6183* ⊕ *www.onitsukatiger.nl.*

Patta. Named for the Surinamese slang for "shoes," this boutique for the urban-hip sells an exclusive selection of sneakers from all over the globe. It's where to find those limited-edition retro suede New Balances you've always wanted. Preview the current stock on the store's Web site. ⊠ *Nieuwezijds Voorburgwal 142, The Old City Center (Het Centrum)* ☎ *020/528–5994* ⊕ *www.teampatta.nl.*

Shoebaloo. One might mistake the interior of this store for that of a disco, if not a spaceship. Some of the shoe styles are just as wild (the Day-Glo tiger-striped stilettos, for example), though many are simply the high-end leather kickers of fashionistas. ⊠ *P. C. Hooftstraat 80, Museum District* ☎ *020/671–2210* ⊕ *www.shoebaloo.nl* ⊠ *Leidsestraat 10, Leidseplein* ☎ *020/330–9147* ⊠ *Koningsplein 7, The Canal Ring* ☎ *020/626–7993* ⊠ *Cornelis Schuytstraat 9, Amsterdam South* ☎ *020/662–5779.*

Day Trips from Amsterdam

WORD OF MOUTH

"Try to arrive at the Keukenhof gardens not later than 10 AM. The earlier you arrive the more time you will have to enjoy the landscapes in tranquillity. However, the most spectacular views are not of the gardens, in my opinion, but of the miles and miles of adjacent bulb fields that are best viewed after climbing the ladder stairs up to the second story of the windmill. Take your time, even if the small porch is crowded, to get good photos. They will probably be the best of your whole trip."

—chasi

Updated by
Ann Maher

THE NETHERLANDS IS SUCH A manageably small country that there's practically no excuse not to explore a little further afield. Castles, seaside resorts, historic towns, and tulip fields are just outside the city, and with Amsterdam's great transport connections, very accessible. Most historic towns and attractions are under an hour away—even the Wadden Islands can be reached in a couple of hours.

> **EXCLUSIVE BLOOM**
>
> In the 17th century floral futures market, fortunes were made and lost in a day with reckless gambling on the price of tulip bulbs. One Semper August bloom clocked in at 3,000 guilders—at that time, the cost of a decent house in Amsterdam.

Whether you are driving or cycling, the routes are well maintained and clearly signposted. Trains and regional buses are frequent and punctual with a range of passes for discount travel. The tourist board can print out a travel schedule for a specific destination which is particularly useful if you are having to switch between metro, bus, and train all on one journey.

THE BULB FIELDS

In the spring (late March until mid-May) the bulb fields of South Holland are transformed into a vivid series of Mondriaan paintings through the colors of millions of tulips and other flowers. The bulb fields extend from just north of Leiden to the southern limits of Haarlem with the greatest concentration beginning at Sassenheim and ending between Hillegom and Bennebroek. Floral HQ is the town of Lisse and the fields and glasshouses of the Keukenhof Gardens. It is an unmissable and unforgettable sight. The bulb, rather than the bloom, is the prize and to promote growth and subdivision, tulips are decapitated in the field by specialized machines designed by fanatical breeders. Timing can be volatile but there's a general progression from crocus in the middle of March, daffodils and narcissi from the end of March to the middle of April, early tulips and hyacinths from the second week of April to the end of the month, and late tulips immediately afterward. An early or late spring can move these approximate dates forward or backward by as much as two weeks.

Fodor'sChoice **Bollenstreek Route** *(Bulb District Route)*, more popularly known as ★ the Bloemen Route (Flower Route), is a series of roads that meander through the bulb-growing region. It was originally designed by Dutch motoring organization ANWB, which began life as a a cycling association. Look out for the small blue-and-white signs marked Bollenstreek. Driving from Amsterdam, take the A4 towards Leiden then the N207 signposted Lisse. By train, head for Haarlem and take bus 50 or bus 51, which allows you to embark and disembark along the route. Tour companies and the local VVVs (Tourist Information Offices) also organize walking and bicycle tours that usually include a visit to Keukenhof.

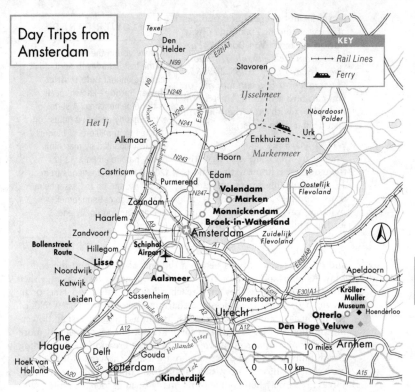

Day Trips from Amsterdam

KEY
⊦––––⊣ *Rail Lines*
⚓ *Ferry*

Texel
Den Helder
Stavoren
IJsselmeer
Noordoost Polder
Urk
Het Ij
Alkmaar
Enkhuizen
Hoorn *Markermeer*
Oostelijk Flevoland
Castricum
Purmerend
Edam
Volendam
Marken
Zaandam
Monnickendam
Haarlem
Broek-in-Waterland
Zandvoort
Amsterdam
Zuidelijk Flevoland
Bollenstreek Route
Hillegom
Schiphol Airport
Noordwijk
Lisse
Katwijk
Aalsmeer
Apeldoorn
Leiden
Sassenheim
Amersfoort
Kröller-Muller Museum
Hoenderloo
Otterlo
Utrecht
Den Hoge Veluwe
The Hague
Delft
Gouda
0   10 miles   Arnhem
Hoek van Holland
Rotterdam
0   10 km
Kinderdijk

6

Some of the towns along the Bollenstreek are worth a little detour. The dunes of **Noordwijk** make it a popular seaside resort with a vast, sandy nature reserve almost as big as the bulb district itself. It is also the home of **Space Expo,** Europe's first permanent space exhibition for those with budding astronauts in the party. Part of the historic white church in **Noordwijkerhout** is made from the remains of a ship that dates from the year 1000. In **Sassenheim,** there is an imposing 13th-century ruined castle.

LISSE

27 km (17 mi) southwest of Amsterdam.

GETTING HERE

By car from Amsterdam take the A4 in the direction of Schiphol and Den Hague then take exit 4. Continue on the N207 to Lisse and follow the signs for the Keukenhof. Parking costs €6. You can buy a ticket in advance from the Web site ⊕*www.keukenhof.nl.* You can also take the train to Leiden Centraal and then bus 54 (aka "Keukenhof Express"). For bus departure times, call ☏0900/9292. There are also bus connections from Haarlem (bus 50 or bus 51) or Lisse (bus 57).

Bicycles can be rented at a number of places including Haarlem railway station or from **Van Dam** (✉ *Parkeerterrein De Keukenhof, Stationsweg 166a, Lisse* ☎ *06/12089858* ⊕ *www.rent-a-bikevandam.nl*) or you can hire a bike in Amsterdam and take it with you (the bike will also need a train ticket).

WHAT TO SEE

The heart of Tulip country, the town of Lisse is home to the famous 17-acre Keukenhof park and greenhouse complex. Founded in 1950 by Tom van Waveren and other leading bulb growers, the Keukenhof is one of the largest open-air flower exhibitions in the world, and draws steady crowds between the end of March and the end of May. As many as 7 million tulip bulbs bloom here every spring, either in hothouses (where they may reach a height of nearly 3 feet) or in flower beds along the sides of a charming lake. In the last weeks of April you can catch tulips, daffodils, hyacinths, and narcissi all flowering simultaneously. In addition there are 50,000 square feet of more exotic blooms under glass. Keukenhof is the creation of the leading Dutch bulb-growing exporters, who use it as a showcase for their latest hybrids. Unfortunately, this means that commercial, not creative, forces are at play here. Some of the many open gardens are filled with rather gaudy tulip varieties, and the layout of the property is charming but not particularly interesting (there are lots of meandering streams, placid pools, and paved paths traversed by hordes of people). Any sense of history—Keukenhof's roots extend way back to the 15th century, when it was the herb farm (Keukenhof means "kitchen courtyard") of one of Holland's richest ladies—has been obliterated. This is the Netherlands' most popular springtime attraction, which is easy to reach from all points of the country. Traveling independently rather than in an organized group should present no problem: just follow the crowds. ✉ *N207, Lisse* ☎ *0252/465–555* ⊕ *www.keukenhof.nl* 💶 *€13.50* ⊗ *Late Mar.–May, daily 8–7:30.*

> ### THE FLOWER PARADE
>
> If you're visting the Netherlands on the last Saturday in April, don't miss the annual **Bulb District Flower Parade**—known locally as the *Bloemencorso*. A series of extravagantly designed floats constructed from millions of blooms, and accompanied by marching bands, parade along a 32-km (20-mi) route that extends from Noordwijk and on to Sassenheim, Lisse, Hillegom, Bennebroek, Heemstede, and finally ends in Haarlem.

AALSMEER

20 km (12 mi) east of Keukenhof.

GETTING HERE

By car from Amsterdam from the A10 (ring) take the A4 in the direction of Den Haag then exit 3 signposted Aalsmeer (N201). Follow signs for Bloemenveiling and, once inside the complex, follow the route to the visitors' car park. Or take bus 172 from Amsterdam and Amstelveen.

WHAT TO SEE

At Aalsmeer, about 19 km (12 mi) southwest of Amsterdam near Schiphol Airport, the **Bloemenveiling Aalsmeer** *(Aalsmeer Flower Auction)* is held five days a week from the predawn hours until midmorning. The largest flower auction in the world, held in the biggest commercial building in the world, it has

> ### BOAT RENTALS
>
> When exploring various villages, go native and rent a canoe or a kayak from **Kano & Electroboot Waterland** (⊠ *Drs. J. van Disweg 4, Broek-in-Waterland* ☎ *020/403–3209).*

three auction halls operating continuously in a building the size of 120 football fields. You can watch the proceedings by walking on a catwalk above the rolling carts that move on tracks past the auctioneers. The buying system is what is called a Dutch auction—the price goes down, not up, on a large "clock" on the wall (though there are also Internet buyers these days). The buyers sit lecture-style with buzzers on their desks; the first to register a bid gets the bunch, and they work their way through 20 million of the things daily. Note that you can reach the auction hall by taking NZH Bus 172 from the stop opposite the American Hotel near Amsterdam's Leidseplein. ⊠ *Legmeerdijk 313, Aalsmeer* ☎ *0297/392–185* ⊕ *www.vba.nl* 🎫 *€5.00* ⊗ *Weekdays 7:00–11* AM.

STORYBOOK HOLLAND

Much of the Netherlands is so picturesque that it's almost postcard perfect. Volendam and Marken are sleepy little fishing ports lost in time, where boys can still be seen wearing Hans Brinker costumes and canal vistas recall ink sketches by Rembrandt. Kinderdike is so darn pretty that it was awarded UNESCO World Heritage status.

BROEK-IN-WATERLAND

14 km (9 mi) northeast of Amsterdam. Follow route N247 and take exit S116 from the ring road.

GETTING HERE

By car from Amsterdam and the S116, take the N247 (Nieuwe Leeuwarderweb) and follow signs to Broek-in-Waterland. There is no train station in Broek-in-Waterland, so from Amsterdam public transportation is by bus. The 110, 112, 114, 116, and 118 all leave from Amsterdam Centraal with the directions Volendam/Edam, Monnickendam/Marken, and Hoorn. You can buy a Waterland all-day family bus ticket (Arriva) for €10 (two adults, two children) and combine visits to several villages in this region in one day.

This is a popular cycling trip suitable for enthusiastic eight-year-olds upwards. Take one of the free ferries behind central station that cross the IJ, and follow the signs.

No 18th-century visitor on the Dutch leg of a grand tour would miss this picturesque, wealthy Waterland village where even the local grocer is called *Posch*. Broek-in-Waterland has a centuries-old reputation of being the cleanest town in all the Netherlands and everything is still immaculate. The village is full of pretty 17th- and 18th-century wooden houses built for merchants and farmers (83 of the houses have national historic status). Back in the day, the residents here amassed legendary fortunes. The 16th-century church is the burial place for VOC businesswoman Neeltje Pater who left the enormous sum of 7 million guilders when she died in 1789. Today's inhabitants include media moguls and finance types. (Check out the super-chic houseboats,with matching speedboats, on the dike leading into the village.) It's a charming step-back-in-time stroll around the village where you can admire the fine houses with their garden mosaics and clipped hedges. Don't miss the

★ **De Kralentuinen,** or Bead Gardens, where hedges are clipped Baroque patterns and mosaics studded with antique blue glass beads. Hundreds of years ago, Dutch sea merchants used these beads to trade with primitive cultures for spices and other goods; the beads that were left over and brought back to Holland were used to decorate such gardens. There's an old-fashioned pancake house and a slightly funkier café for a spot of lunch or, if you prefer, bring a picnic. It's a lovely area to explore by boat, canoe, or kayak and you can rent all of them here. Potter round the **Havenrak,** the large lake which is popular with ice skaters in the winter, or go for a more extensive Waterland tour.

MONNICKENDAM

4.7 km (3 mi) north from Broek-in-Waterland, 16 km (10 mi) northeast of Amsterdam. Take Route N247.

If you're driving from Amsterdam and the S116, take the N247 (Nieuwe Leeuwarderweg) and follow signs to Monnickendam. It's a trip of 10-15 minutes. By bus it's a few minutes further from Broek-in-Waterland on the 110, 111, 114, or 116 from Amsterdam Centraal.

The historic town of Monnickendam owes its name to the monks who created a dam here in the 12th century. Granted city rights in 1355 and a prominent port by the 1660s, Monnickendam still has a large yacht harbor where swanky, spanking new 125-foot trophy vessels (some of which are constructed here) bob alongside old Dutch sailing barges. The center of town is well preserved with narrow canals and bridges, cobbled streets, and pretty gabled houses. If you need a pit stop, take a table under the portico of the 17th century weigh house, which is now an elegant café and restaurant. Even if you get lost as you stroll about, you won't lose track of time. Every quarter of an hour, the mellifluous bells of the Speeltoren ring out, and on the hour are accompanied by knights-on-horseback galloping round the clockwork under the watchful gaze of a female angel. The bells are part of the oldest

(1597) carillon in the world and on Saturdays at 11am, a carillonneur climbs the ladders inside the narrow tower to give a recital. The 16th-century tower is attached to the former town hall (dating from 1764) which is now home to the **Museum De Speeltoren,** where you can view a collection of decorative blue-and-white tiles and majolica, historical artifacts, exhibits, and films on local history. You can also inquire here about walking tours—almost every building has an interesting history: one house was a hiding place for Jews during World War II. ✉ *Noordeinde 4* ☎ *0299/652–203* ⊕ *www.despeeltoren.nl/* 🎫 *€1.50* 🕐 *April 14–May 29, Sat. 11–4:30, Sun. 1–4:30; May 26–Sept. 16 daily (except Mon.) 11:00–4:30; Sept. 22–Oct. 14 Sat. and Sun.*

> **WORD OF MOUTH**
>
> Biking in Amsterdam was AWESOME. We rented great bikes from the Marriott for 12 euros a day. The first day we went to a market then got a bike map from MacBike and took the ferry behind the train station and headed through the countryside for a 20 mile ride to Marken.
>
> —Jeff

MARKEN

8.9 km (6 mi) east of Monnickendam, 16 km (10 mi) northeast of Amsterdam. Take Route N518.

GETTING HERE

From Amsterdam by car and on the S116, go through the IJ tunnel and take the N247 (Nieuwe Leeuwarderweg) and follow signs to Marken. Marken has no railway station so from Amsterdam take the 111 bus from Amsterdam Centraal. The Marken Express ferry travels between Marken and Volendam. You can board it at either harbor. It is also possible to arrange a boat tour or charter from Volendam. Visit the local VVV for further details.

WHAT TO SEE

The tidal wave that hit the Netherlands in 1916 was a defining factor in the decision to drain the Zuiderzee, but with the construction of the enclosing dam (Afsluitdijk), traditional Dutch fishing villages like Marken lost their livelihood. Heritage tourism has now taken over on this former island (a causeway to the mainland was built in 1957) that, despite the busloads of visitors, retains its charm. Many of the green-and-white gabled homes are built on timber piles, dating from when the Zuiderzee used to flood, and a maritime past is revealed in the sober Calvinist church (1904) with its hanging herring boats and lugger. There is a klompen (clog) maker and kleding (dress) shop that includes designs dating from the 1300s, some of which are worn today. The floral chintzes are inspired by the Dutch East Indies and the caps, in particular, are incredibly intricate. The full folkloric effect can be viewed in the films showing at the local museum.

The intimate **Marker Museum** consists of six former smokehouses (where the smoke left in a hole in the ceiling rather than a chimney) with exhibits showing the past and present life of Marken. You can see how a fisherman's family lived until about 1932 ⊠ *Kerkbuurt 44–47* ☎ *0299/601–904* ⊕ *www.marker-museum.nl* ⊠ *€2.50* ⊘ *Apr.–Nov. Mon.–Sat. 10–4:30; Sun. noon–4.*

VOLENDAM

6.7 km (4 mi) northwest of Marken, 18 km (11.5 mi) northeast of Amsterdam. Take Routes N247–N517.

GETTING HERE

Drive through the IJ tunnel on S116 and take N247 to Marken and Monnickendam. Buses 110, 112, 116, or 118 leave from Amsterdam Centraal.

WHAT TO SEE

Volendam once had the largest fleet of ships in the Zuiderzee. It was a star destination on the tours of American Express and Thomas Cook and a colony of artists holed up at the Hotel Spaander—now a rather charming three-star Best Western with a legacy of a thousand 18th-century artworks from those same painters. Tourism is of course more important than fishing these days, although a number of places sell smoked eels and other fishy delicacies. If you arrive at Volendam by boat (the best way to go) you will alight at the main drag full of restaurants and shops and places to have your photo taken in traditional costume. On high days and holidays, you may see the real thing as residents stroll around in traditional dress immortalized by Dutch dolls the world over. The men wear dark baggy pantaloons fastened with silver guilders instead of buttons, striped vests, and dark jackets with caps. Women wear long dark skirts covered with striped aprons and blouses with elaborately hand-embroidered floral panels. Their coral necklaces and famous winged lace caps complete the picture. Of course, everyone wears *klompen* (clogs).

You can learn about Volendam's history at the **Volendams Museum**, next to the VVV, which has reconstructed rooms, such as a school filled with mannequins adorned with folkloric costumes; there's even a photograph of Josephine Baker clad in traditional garb! ⊠ *Zeestraat 41, Volendam* ☎ *0299/369–258* ⊕ *www.volendams-museum.com* ⊠ *€1.75* ⊘ *Mar.–Dec., daily 10–5.*

★ **Kaasboerderij Alida Hoeve** is a working cheese farm where you can learn how cheese is made, and purchase various cheeses. ⊠ *Zeddeweg 1 41, Volendam* ☎ *0299/365–830* ⊠ *Free* ⊘ *Daily 8:30–6.*

CLOSE UP

Holding the Waters at Bay

Amsterdam's scenic windmills were instrumental in keeping the land drained and dry.

6

There's a good reason the Dutch countryside looks as it does, crisscrossed by canals and dikes, and dotted with more than 1,000 windmills. Those picturesque mills used to serve a vital role in keeping everyone's feet dry. About a quarter of the land, including most of the Randstad, lies below sea level, and without major human intervention, large swathes of the Netherlands would either be underwater, or uninhabitable swamp. Just think, when you land at Schiphol—the name, "ship's hole," is a clue—you should be about 20 feet below the surf.

The west coast has always been protected by high dunes, but the rest of the land had to take its chances for centuries. The first to begin the fight against the sea were early settlers who built mounds in the north of the country around 500 BC, and the battle has continued ever since. Real progress was made around 1200 AD when dikes began appearing. In the 14th century canals were dug, and the first windmills were built to pump the water off the land (a job now done by electric pumps). This transformed the fertile alluvial landscape, turning it into a farmer's paradise.

War on nature has waged ever since, as Holland gradually clawed back territory, by closing off the Zuiderzee inland sea in 1932 to form the Ijssel Lake, and by a century-long land reclamation program of polder building. The sea bit back with a vengeance one wintry night in 1953. On January 31 that year, a combination of exceptionally high tides and strong winds sent a storm surge pouring up the Rhine delta, killing around 2,000 and inundating a thousand square miles of land.

Dutch engineers vowed this disaster would never be repeated. They responded by closing off the river mouth by building the Delta Works (F*see* Rotterdam, *chapter 7*), one of the great engineering feats of the 20th century. If you're driving over the barrier (southwest of Rotterdam), stop off to visit the exhibition at the midpoint that shows you how this man-made marvel came about.

KINDERDIJK

55 km (34 mi) southwest of Amsterdam.

GETTING HERE

It is a bit of a trek (2½hours) from Amsterdam and there are a number of ways to go. The most straightforward route is to head for Rotterdam Zuid on the train. From there, take the metro to Rotterdam Zuidplein, then Bus 154 to Albasserdam. By car, Kinderdijk is 20 km (12½mi) from Rotterdam. Follow directions to Rotterdam, then take A15 to exit 22. There are (small) car parks by the mills. Waterbus (⊕*www.water-bus.nl)* runs a fast ferry service from the Erasmusbrug in Rotterdam to Ridderkerk (line 1) and then you change onto another ferry (line 3) to pop across to Kinderdijk. Ferries are every half hour and it takes about half an hour. Other tour boats are available from Rotterdam and there is also (a pricey) water taxi.

WHAT TO SEE

★ The sight of the 19 windmills at **Kinderdijk** under sail is magnificently, romantically impressive. Not surprisingly, this is one of the most visited places in the Netherlands and on the UNESCO World Heritage list. These are water pumping mills whose job was to drain water from the Alblasserwaard polder enclosed by the rivers Noord and Lek—a function now performed by the 1950 pumping station with its humongously-sized water screws, which you pass on the way to the site. The somewhat chocolate-boxy name (which means "child's dike") comes from a legend involving a baby which washed up here in a cradle after the great floods of 1421, with a cat sitting on its tummy to keep them both from tumbling out.

These windmills date back to 1740. Just 150 years ago 10,000 windmills were in operation across the country but today only 1,000 remain. These have been saved from the wrecking ball thanks to the help of heritage organizations. The windmills are open in rotation, so there is always one interior to visit. A walk through a working windmill gives fascinating insight into how the millers and their families lived. The mills are under sail from 2 PM to 5 PM on the first Saturday in May and June, then every Saturday in July and August. Throughout the second week in September the mills are illuminated at night, really pulling out the tourist stops. You can walk around the mills area whenever you like, so it's a great way to spend an leisurely afternoon. There are a couple of cafés for snacks but if the weather is good, bring a picnic. ⊠*Molenkade, Kinderdijk* ☏*078/691–5179* ⊡*Interior of mill €3.00* ⊙*Interior Apr.–Sept., daily 9:30–5:30.*

OTTERLO/DE HOGE VELUWE

78 km (49 mi) southeast of Amsterdam, 20 km (13 mi) south of Apel-doorn, 35 km (22 mi) southeast of Amersfoort.

When German heiress Hélène Müller married Dutch industrialist Anton Kröller at the turn of the 20th century, their combined wealth and complementary tastes were destined to give pleasure to genera-tions to come. She loved art and could afford to collect it; he bought up land in Gelderland and eventually created a foundation to maintain it as a national park, building a museum to house the fruits of their expensive and discriminating taste. Today you can wander through the vast forests, heath, dunes, and moors of the Hoge Veluwe National Park, Kröller's land, and see the descendants of the wild boar and deer with which he stocked the estate. Or you can visit the world-famous museum in the middle of the park, established by Hélène and contain-ing one of the best collections of Van Goghs in the world, as well as an excellent selection of late-19th-century and modern art. Additionally, you can visit the philanthropists' own house and hunting lodge. Chil-dren can caper about the largest sculpture garden in Europe, and the whole family can pick up one of the free bikes that are available in the park and trundle off down wooded lanes. (Note that Otterlo is only one entrance of several to the Hoge Veluwe, but it is widely considered the main gateway to the park.)

WHAT TO SEE

Hoge Veluwe, once the private property of the Kröller-Müller family, is the largest national park in Holland, covering 13,300 acres of forest and rolling grassland, moors, and sand dunes, where it is possible to stroll without limit, apart from a few areas reserved for wildlife. The traditional hunting grounds of the Dutch royal family, it is populated with red deer, boar, roes, mouflons (wild sheep), and many birds; it is also filled with towering pines and hardwood trees (oak, beech, and birch), dotted with small villages (**Hoge Soeren,** near Apeldoorn, is par-ticularly charming), and laced with paths for cars, bicycles, and walk-ers, more than 42 km (27 mi) of which are specifically designated for bicycling. Indeed, there are more than 1,000 white bicycles at your disposal here, free to use with the price of entrance (available at the entrances to the park, at the visitor center, De Koperen Kop restaurant, and at the Kröller-Müller museum; return them to any bike rack when you are finished).

There is a landlocked, always shifting sand dune to marvel at; the world's first museum of all things that live (or have lived) underground; plus an old hunting lodge beside a pond that provides a nice stop-ping place. At the heart of the park is the visitor center (**Bezoekers Cen-trum**), which contains exhibits on the park and an observation point for game-watching. **Jachthuis Sint Hubertus** (St. Hubert Hunting Lodge) was the private home and hunting lodge of the Kröller-Müllers, a monu-mental house planned in the shape of antlers, built between 1914 and

1920 by Dutch architect H. P. Berlage around the legend of St. Hubert, the patron saint of hunters. Rooms with Art Deco furniture follow in sequence from dark to light, representing Hubert's spiritual development and path of enlightenment from agnostic to saint. Free guided tours of the lodge, which is still used as a residence for visiting dignitaries, may be arranged at the park entrance only.

Museonder is the first underground museum in the world, offering visitors a fascinating look at life below the surface, including a simulated earthquake. A campsite at the Hoenderloo entrance is open from April to the end of October (☎ 055/378–2232), and there are four restaurants in the park: the stylish Rijzenburg, at the Schaarsbergen entrance (☎ 026/443–6733; closed Monday and February); De Koperen Kop, a self-service restaurant in the center of the park opposite the visitor center (☎ 031/859–1289); another self-service one at the Kröller-Müller Museum; and a kiosk near the Jachthuis (open only in summer). The best opportunity for game-watching is at the end of the afternoon and toward evening, and park officials advise that you stay in your car when you spot any wildlife. Special observation sites are signified by antlers on the maps that are provided at the entrances. To enter the park from the A1, A50, or A12 motorways, follow the signs to "Park Hoge Veluwe." ⊞Entrances at Hoenderloo, Otterlo, and Schaarsbergen ℙ 0318/591627, 0900/464–3835 at €0.45 per min ⊕ www.hogeveluwe. nl €5, cars €5; half-price entrance after 5 PM, May–Sept.; weekly tickets available ⊙Nov.–Mar., daily 9–5:30; Apr., daily 8–8; May and Aug., daily 8–9; June and July, daily 8–10; Sept., daily 9–8; Oct., daily 9–7.

The **Kröller-Müller Museum** ranks as the third-most-important museum of art in the Netherlands, after the Rijksmuseum and the Vincent van Gogh Museum in Amsterdam. Opened in 1938, it is the repository of a remarkable private collection of late-19th-century and early-20th-century paintings, the nucleus of which are 278 works by Van Gogh (about 50 of which rotate on display at any given time) that, when combined with the collection in the Amsterdam museum, constitutes nearly four-fifths of his entire oeuvre. Hélène Kröller, née Müller, had a remarkable eye as well as a sixth sense about which painters created art for the ages. Her first purchase was most likely Van Gogh's *Faded Sunflowers*. Among his other well-known paintings in her collection are the *Potato Eaters, Bridge at Arles,* and *L'Arlesienne*, copied from a drawing by Gauguin.

But Hélène Kröller-Müller was not myopic in her appreciation and perception. She augmented her collection of Van Goghs with works by Georges Seurat, Pable Picasso, Odile Redon, Georges Braque, and Piet Mondriaan. The museum also contains 16th- and 17th-century Dutch paintings, ceramics, Chinese and Japanese porcelains, and contemporary sculpture. The building itself, designed by Henry van de Velde, artfully brings nature into the galleries through its broad windows, glass walkways, and patios. The gardens and woods around the museum form a stunning open-air gallery, the largest in Europe with a collection of 20th-century sculptures that include works by Auguste Rodin, Richard Serra, Barbara Hepworth, and Alberto Giacometti. There is a gift shop and self-service restaurant on-site. E *Houtkampweg 6, in Hoge Veluwe National Park, 6730 AA Otterlo P 0318/591241* ⊕*www.kmm.nl A Park and museum €10 C Park and museum Tues.– Sun. 10–5; sculpture garden closes at 4:30*

See and buy is the game plan at the **Nederlands Tegelmuseum** (Netherlands Tile Museum), where all manner of Dutch tiles, from as far back as the 13th century, including those old Dutch standbys, Makkum and Delft, are displayed in a former summerhouse in the village of Otterlo, not far from the Hoge Veluwe. For those with a decorative eye, the tiles for purchase in the gift shop will be irresistible. E *Eikenzoom 12, 6731 BH Otterlo P 0318/591519 A €2.75 C Tues.–Fri. 10–5, weekends 1–5.*

DAY TRIP ESSENTIALS

CONTACTS & RESOURCES

GUIDED TOURS

Entrepreneurs in the Netherlands offer a smorgasbord of excursions for individuals and groups.

Contacts **VVV** (⊠ *Just in front of Centraal Station, Amsterdam* ☎*0900/4004040*). A special bicycle **Tulip Tour** of the bulb fields in April can be booked through the Amsterdam VVV tourist office. **Wetlands Safari** (☎*020/686-3445* ⊕*www. wetlandssafari.nl*). Travel through a 17th-century landscape in a canoe. Guided tours last five hours and the €33 fee covers transport, coffee, and lunch. They can also organize customized tours. Be sure to wear rain boots or old footwear.

Rederij JC Vos en Zn. Lines (☎*0180/512174*). From May to October you can join a guided tour and take a half-hour boat trip out to see the Kinderdijke windmills. Based off Molenkade in Kinderdijk, tours are offered daily from 10 to 5 for €3.

Rebus Varende Evenementen (☎*010/218-3131* ✉*€12.50 and various group rates*). A boat tour of Rotterdam and a cruise to Kinderdijk along the river Lek. A three-hour trip is available from mid-April to the end of September. Boats leave from Boompjeskade where there is a ticket office, or you can buy tickets from the Rotterdam VVV. 10:45 AM and 2:15 PM departures.

Orangebike. Provides a wide range of guided bike tours to the beaches, historical cities, and Waterland, with some architectural and culinary tours within Amsterdam itself. Average time of tours is four hours. (☎*020/528-9990* ⊕*www.orangebike.nl*). From €22.50.

VISITOR INFORMATION

Most towns and cities in the Netherlands have a Visitor Information booth. It's usually in the vicinity of the train station.

Tourist Information **VVV Aalsmeer** (✉ *Drie Kolommenplein 1, 1431 LA, Aalsmeer* ☎ *0297/325–374* ⊕ *www.vvvaalsmeer.nl*).

VVV Lisse (✉ *Grachtweg 53, 2161 HM* ☎ *0900/222–2333* ⊕ *www.vvvlisse.nl*).

VVV Haarlem/Regio Zuid Kennemerland (✉ *Stationsplein 1, 2011 LR, Haarlem* ☎ *023/531–9413* ⊕ *www.vvvzk.nl*).

VVV Noordwijk (✉ *De Grent 8, 2202 EK, Noordwijk* ☎ *0900/222–3333* ⊕ *www. vvvnoordwijk.nl*).

VVV Volendam (✉ *Zeestraat 37, 1131 ZD, Volendam* ☎ *0299–363747* ⊕ *www. vvv-volendam.nl*).

The Randstad

HAARLEM, DELFT, ROTTERDAM & UTRECHT

WORD OF MOUTH

"Delft is a beautiful and tranquil town. I fell in love with it the moment I arrived. Time flew by very quickly, and I was very sad when I had to leave."
—yk

"Rotterdam is a vibrant and very interesting city. Especially if you like modern architecture. The city was bombed in WW II and instead of rebuilding the 'old' city, Rotterdam became sort of a showcase for modern architecture. So don't except canals and other typical Dutch-city features! It is also one of the largest harbors in the world. There are a lot of interesting museums, restaurants, some shopping. So yeah, if you can go for free, it really is a fun city to visit."

—TommieG

www.fodors.com/forums

By Tim Skelton

THE TOWNS AND CITIES OF Zuid-Holland (South Holland) cluster around Amsterdam like filings round the end of a magnet. Each has prospered and grown independently, and today their borders virtually overlap one another to such an extent that the region is now dubbed the *Randstad* (Border City), because locals consider it one mammoth megalopolis. A quarter of Holland's 16 million residents live within 80 km (50 mi) of the capital.

TOP REASONS TO GO

■ See the Old Masters in Haarlem's Frans Hals Museum

■ Wander Delft's canal-lined medieval streets—Amsterdam in miniature

■ Climb Utrecht's Domtoren—the Netherlands' tallest church tower

■ Check out the country's busiest harbor in Rotterdam

Among the cities of the Randstad, Rotterdam is the industrial center of Holland and the world's largest port. Contrasting with the quaintness of many other Dutch towns, it is brash, forward-looking, and home to some of Europe's most dazzling modern architecture. The imposing, futuristic skyline has led to it being dubbed by some as Manhattan-on-the-Maas.

Elsewhere, the past is more in evidence. You can pursue the ghost of Frans Hals through the Golden Age streets of Haarlem; explore the time-stained center of Utrecht; and wander through the ancient cobbled streets of Delft, which once colored the world blue. In fact, although the area is small enough to drive through in an afternoon, it would take you weeks to explore fully.

Whereas Amsterdam tends to pander to the demands of tourists, this is the beating heart of the Netherlands where the "real" people live. And it's all the more fascinating for that.

ORIENTATION

The towns and cities of the Randstad are all within easy reach of Amsterdam, and can be visited on day trips, for overnight stays, or incorporated into a circular tour. Rotterdam lies farthest from the capital, yet is still only 73 km (45 mi) to the south, and little more than an hour away by train or car.

Indeed, unless you want to make a detailed exploration of the Dutch countryside, you may find it more convenient and less stressful to leave your car behind when touring the Randstad. The region is crossed by a dense network of freeways, but these are frequently clogged with commuter traffic, and often grind to a halt at peak times. Avoid the jams by hopping on a train, which is the cheap, convenient, and usually reliable way to get around. Every city in this chapter is connected to Amsterdam (and most to each other) by direct services that run at least twice each hour throughout the day. Rotterdam, Utrecht, and Delft have hourly train service to Amsterdam all night.

PLANNING

TIMING

This part of Holland is at its best in late spring or early autumn. High summer means too many visitors, and touring in winter often puts you at the mercy of the weather (bring your umbrella year-round). For flora lovers, mid- to late April is ideal for a trip around Haarlem, as the fields are bright with spring bulbs. Many restaurants are closed Sunday (also Monday); museums tend to close Monday.

If you're into the arts, you might prefer to schedule your trip to catch one of the area's two world-renowned festivals: the International Film Festival Rotterdam, where 300 noncommercial films are screened in late January and early February, and the Festival Oude Muziek (Festival of Early Music), where 150 concerts are held in venues across Utrecht in late August. Jazz lovers will want to time their arrival in Rotterdam to coincide with the North Sea Jazz Festival, which takes place over three days in mid-July.

ABOUT THE RESTAURANTS & HOTELS

Although this area of Holland is home to some of the country's most worldly restaurants, keep in mind that most bars also offer house specials whose prices are usually cheap enough to keep students and young people sated (keep an eye out for the *kleine kaart,* or lighter meal menu, usually offered in the bar area and available throughout the day). Perennially popular dishes such as satay and pepper steak never come off the menu.

Hotels in the Randstad range from elegant canal houses to cross-country chains with anonymous decor. Most large towns have one or more deluxe hotels that exceed all expectations. Accommodation in Rotterdam—a big convention city—is at a premium, so book well in advance, although the situation is usually not as tight as it is in Amsterdam. The VVVs (tourist offices) in the region have extensive accommodation listings, and can book your reservations. Assume all rooms have air-conditioning, TV, telephones, and private bath, unless otherwise noted. Assume hotels operate on the EP meal plan (with no meals) unless stated otherwise.

WHAT IT COSTS IN EUROS				
	¢	$	$$	$$$	$$$$
RESTAURANTS	under €10	€10–€15	€15–€22	€22–€30	over €30
HOTELS	under €75	€75–€120	€120–€165	€165–€230	over €230

Restaurant prices are per person for a main course only. Hotel prices are for a standard double room in high season.

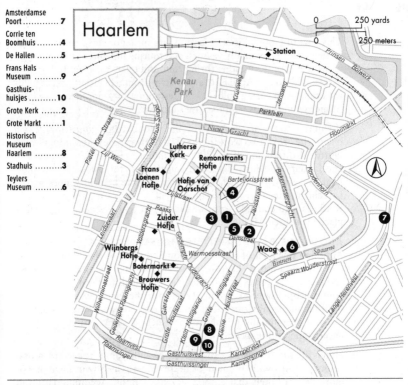

HAARLEM

Walking past the charming *hofjes* (historic almshouse courtyards), and between the red brick gabled facades lining Haarlem's historic streets, it is easy to feel transported back to the Netherlands' Golden Age, especially around the central market square where the hulking form of Sint Bavo's church dominates the city skyline and evokes a bygone age. In fact, the intrusive motorized transport apart, much of Frans Hals' hometown appears unchanged for centuries. Yet despite its many picturesque monuments and rich supply of fascinating museums, Haarlem isn't a city rooted in the past. It is home to a lively population of students—often the overspill who can't find lodgings in Amsterdam or Leiden—who bring with them a youthful vibrancy, especially at night. With its close proximity to the dunes and the seaside resort of Zandvoort, Haarlem also attracts hordes of beach-going Amsterdammers and Germans every summer. The result is an intoxicating mix of old and new that makes the town well worth checking out.

TO & FROM
20 km (12 mi) west of Amsterdam, 41 km (26 mi) north of The Hague.

Getting to Haarlem by rail is a simple matter. Around six trains make the 15 minute trip from Amsterdam's Centraal Station every hour during the day. Driving will take around 20–25 minutes—you'll need to head west out of Amsterdam on the N200/A200. If you have the energy, you can bike.

EXPLORING

Haarlem is a compact city and easy to cover on foot. From the main railway station it is about five minutes' walk south to the Grote Markt. The Frans Hals Museum is another five minutes beyond that. You may want to keep a street map handy when you explore—most Dutch cities have locater maps posted at regular intervals, but they don't seem to have made it here yet.

MAIN ATTRACTIONS

⑨ Frans Hals Museum. Named after the celebrated man himself, this not-to-be-missed museum holds a collection of amazingly virile and lively group portraits by the Golden Age painter, depicting the merrymaking civic guards and congregating regents for which he became world famous. The building itself is one of the town's smarter hofjes: an entire block of almshouses grouped around an attractive courtyard. In the 17th century this was a home for elderly men, an *oudemannenhuis*. The cottages now form a sequence of galleries for paintings, period furniture, antique silver, and ceramics. But the focal point is the collection of 17th-century paintings that includes the works of Frans Hals and other masters of the Haarlem School.

Many of the works on display represent Hals at his jovial best—for instance, the *Banquet of the Officers of the Civic Guard of St. Adrian* (1624–27) or the *Banquet of the Officers of the St. George Militia* (1616), where the artist cunningly allows for the niceties of rank (captains are more prominent than sergeants, and so on down the line) as well as emotional interaction: he was also the first painter to have people gaze and laugh at each other in these grand portraits.

As respite from nearly 250 canvases, step into the museum's courtyard—lovely, and planted with formal-garden baby hedges, of which you get only fleeting glimpses as you work your way through the galleries (most of the blinds are shut against the sunlight to protect the paintings). In one room, with curtains drawn for extra protection, is **Sara Rothè's Dolls' House**; nearby is an exquisitely crafted miniature version of a merchant's canal house. On leaving, *View of Haarlem* (1655) by Nicolaes Hals, Frans's son, bids you good-bye. ✉ *Groot Heiligland 62* ☎ *023/511-5775* ⊕ *www.franshalsmuseum.com* ☞ *€7* ☉ *Tues.–Sat. 11–5, Sun. noon–5.*

⑩ Gasthuis-huisjes *(Guesthouse–little houses).* Don't miss this series of houses with their identical step

> ### WHICH WAY TO GO?
>
> If you arrive by train, take a good look around before you leave the railway station—it's a fabulous Art Nouveau building dating from 1908. Next, head down Jansweg (to the left of the station as you exit) for several blocks, over the Nieuwe Gracht canal and into the city center. It will take you right to the Grote Markt.

Dutch Art—Then & Now

Few countries can boast of so many great artists. During the Golden Age of the 17th century, an estimated 20 million paintings were executed and every home seemed to have an oil painting tacked on the wall. Even before the arrival of Rembrandt and Vermeer, the country had a rich artistic history.

In the late 16th century, the Netherlands were divided into a Flemish south under Catholic Spanish rule, and an independent northern alliance of Dutch Protestant provinces. Before then, most painters hailed from the southern cities of Gent, Antwerp, and Brugge, and their subject matter was mostly biblical and allegorical—Jan van Eyck (1385–1441) founded the Flemish School, Hieronymus Bosch (1450–1516) crafted meticulous, macabre allegories, and Pieter Bruegel the Elder (1525–69) depicted scenes of Flemish peasant life.

In the north, a different style began surfacing. Around Haarlem, Jan Mostaert (1475–1555) and Lucas van der Leyden (1489–1553) brought a new realism into previously static paintings. In Utrecht, Gerrit van Honthorst (1590–1656) used light and shadow to create realism never seen before on canvas.

From these disparate schools flowed the Golden Age of Dutch painting, and Hals, Rembrandt, and Vermeer all borrowed from each diverse technique. Frans Hals (1581–1666) has been called the first modern painter. A fantastically adept and naturally gifted man, he could turn out a portrait an hour. He delighted in capturing the emotions—a smile or grimace—in an early manifestation of impressionism.

Rembrandt van Rijn (1606–69) is regarded as the most versatile artist of the 17th century. Born in Leiden, he grew rich from painting and tuition. His early works were overly ornamental, but as the years went by he dug deeper into the metaphysical essence of his subjects. When his material world collapsed around him—he was blackmailed and ruined—he somehow turned out even greater art, showing off a marvelously skilled use of light and shadow.

Jan Vermeer (1632–72), the third in this triumvirate, was a different case altogether. He produced only 35 known paintings, but their exquisite nature make him the most precious painter of his time. He brought genre art to its peak; in small canvases with overwhelming realism he painted the soft calm and everyday sameness of middle-class life.

Around the middle of the century, Baroque influences began permeating Dutch art, heralding a trend for landscapes. Artists such as Albert Cuyp and Meindert Hobbema's scenes of polder lanes, grazing cows, and windswept canals were coveted by 17th- and 18th-century collectors. Other masters were more playful in tone. Jan Steen's (1625–79) lively, satirical, and sometimes lewd scenes are imbued with humor.

The greatest Dutch painter of the 19th century is undoubtedly Vincent van Gogh (1853–90). During his short but troubled life, he produced an array of masterworks, although he famously sold only one. He only began painting in 1881, and his first paintings often depicted dark peasant scenes. But in his last four years,

Johannes Vermeer's (1632–75) most haunting work, *Girl with a Pearl Earring*, inspired Tracy Chevalier's 1999 best-selling novel as well as the 2003 film starring Scarlett Johansson.

spent in France, he produced endlessly colorful and arresting works. In 1890, he committed suicide after struggling with depression. To this day, his legacy continues to move art lovers everywhere.

The 20th century brought confusion to the art scene. Unsure what style to adopt, many artists reinvented themselves. Piet Mondriaan (1872–1944) is someone who evolved with his century. Early in his career he painted bucolic landscapes. Then, in 1909, at the age of 41, he began dabbling, first with expressionism and then cubism. He eventually developed his own style, called neo-plasticism. Using only the primary colors of yellow, red, and blue set against neutral white, gray, and black, he created stylized studies in form and color. In 1917, together with his friend Theo van Doesberg (1883–1931), he published an arts magazine called *De Stijl* (*The Style*) as a forum for a design movement attempting to harmonize the arts through purified abstraction. Though it lasted only 15 years, the movement's effect was felt around the world.

The most vibrant movement to emerge after World War II was the experimental CoBrA (artists from Copenhagen, Brussels, and Amsterdam), cofounded by Karel Appel (1921–2006) and Constant (née Constant Nieuwenhuis, 1920–2005). With bright colors and abstract shapes, their paintings have a childlike quality. The artists involved continue to have influence in their respective countries.

gables at the southern end of Groot Heiligland, across the street from the entrance to the Frans Hals Museum. They originally formed part of the St. Elizabeth hospital and were built in 1610.

BIKING IN HAARLEM

Like the Netherlands in general, Haarlem is small, flat, and easy to navigate by bike. If you feel like peddling around the city, **De Wolkenfietser** (✉ *Koningstraat 36z* ☎ *023/532–5577*) has bicycles for rent. You can also rent bicycles from **Pieters** (✉ *Stationsplein 7* ☎ *023/531–7066*).

⑤ De Hallen *(The Halls).* A branch of the Frans Hals Museum, De Hallen has an extensive collection, with the works of Dutch impressionists and expressionists, including sculpture, textiles, and ceramics, as well as paintings and graphics. The complex consists of two buildings—the Vleeshal and the Verweyhal House.

The **Vleeshal** (Meat Market) building is one of the most interesting cultural legacies of the Dutch Renaissance, with a fine sweep of stepped gables that seems to pierce the scudding clouds. It was built in 1602–03 by Lieven de Key, Haarlem's master builder. The ox heads that look down from the facade are reminders of the building's original function: it was the only place in Haarlem where meat could be sold, and the building was used for that sole purpose until 1840. Today it is used for exhibitions—generally works of modern and contemporary art, usually by local artists. Note the early landscape work by Piet Mondriaan, *Farms in Duivendrecht,* so different from his later De Stijl shapes.

The **Verweyhal Gallery of Modern Art** was built in 1879 as a gentlemen's club, originally named *Trou moet Blijcken* (Loyalty Must Be Proven). The building now bears the name of native Haarlem artist Kees Verwey, who died in 1995. It is used as an exhibition space for selections from the Frans Hals Museum's enormous collection of modern and contemporary art. In addition to the works of Kees Verwey, the exhibition covers such artists as Jacobus van Looy, Jan Sluijters, Leo Gestel, Herman Kruyder, and Karel Appel. Note, too, a fine collection of contemporary ceramics. ✉ *Grote Markt 16* ☎ *023/511–5775* ⊕ *www.dehallen.com* ✉ *€5* ☉ *Tues.–Sat. 11–5, Sun. noon–5.*

② Grote Kerk *(Great Church).* Late Gothic Sint Bavo's, more commonly called the Great Church, dominates the main market square. It was built in the 14th century, but severe fire damage in 1370 led to a further 150 years of rebuilding and expansion. This is the burial place of Frans Hals—a lamp marks his tombstone behind the brass choir screen. Laurens Coster is buried here too. It is rumored that he was the first European to use movable type in 1423 (sorry, Gutenberg), which he discovered while carving letters for his children; he was inspired when one of the bark letters fell into the sand and made an imprint. The church is the home of the Müller organ, on which both Handel and Mozart played. Installed in 1738, and for centuries considered the finest in the world, it has been meticulously restored to protect the sound planned by its creator, Christian Müller. Between May and October organists perform free concerts every Tuesday at 8:15 PM, and occasionally on

Thursday at 3 PM. Bach fugues have never sounded so magisterial. ⊠*Grote Markt* ☎*023/533–2040* 🏷*€2* 🕙*Mon.–Sat. 10–4.*

❶ Grote Markt. Around this great market square the whole of Dutch architecture can be traced in a chain of majestic buildings ranging from the 14th to the 19th century (with a smile and a little bravado, you can enter most of them for a quick look), but it is the imposing mass of Sint Bavo's church that catches the eye and towers over everything.

NEED A BREAK?

The spacious **Grand Café Brinkmann** (⊠*Brinkmannpassage41* ☎*023/532–3111*), adorned with cherubic ceiling paintings, offers baguettes, pancakes, and other light snacks. Windows edged with Art Deco stained glass overlook the Grote Markt and Sint Bavo's church across the square.

HAARLEM'S HIDDEN COURTYARDS

Throughout the old city center are the many historic *hofjes* (almshouse courtyards)—hidden little courtyards that make Haarlem an incredibly pleasant place to explore. Look for the Zuider Hofje, the Hofje van Loo, the Wijnbergs Hofje, and the Brouwershofje (they are all signposted). Closer to the Grote Markt are the Remonstrants Hofje, the Luthershofje, and the Frans Loenen Hofje. These secluded gardens are filled with flowers and birdsong, and offer peace and respite away from the city streets.

★ **❻ Teylers Museum.** Just north of the **Waag** (Weigh House)—built entirely of stone in 1598 and now a café—Teylers is the best sort of small museum: it is based on the eclectic whims of an eccentric private collector, in this case the 18th-century merchant Pieter Teyler van der Hulst. Founded in 1784, it's the country's oldest museum and has a mixture of exhibits—fossils and minerals sit alongside antique scientific instruments, such as a battery of 25 Leiden jars, dating from 1789 and used to store an electric charge. The museum itself is a grand old building with mosaic floors; its major artistic attraction is the legendary collection of drawings and prints by Old Masters, such as Michelangelo, Rembrandt, and Raphael, based on a collection that once belonged to Queen Christina of Sweden. Much of the collection is housed in the original 18th-century museum building. ⊠*Spaarne 16* ☎*023/516–0960* ⊕*www.teylersmuseum.nl* 🏷*€7* 🕙*Tues.–Sat. 10–5, Sun. noon–5.*

IF YOU HAVE TIME

❼ Amsterdamse Poort (*Amsterdam Gate*). Built around 1400, this is Haarlem's only remaining city gate; remains of the city wall can be seen at its base.

❹ Corrie ten Boomhuis (*Corrie ten Boom House*). Just off the Grote Markt, and tucked into a small gabled building above a shop, this house honors a family of World War II resistance fighters who successfully hid a number of Jewish families before being captured themselves by the Germans in 1944. Most of the Ten Boom family died in the concentration camps, but Corrie survived and returned to Haarlem to tell the story in her book *The Hiding Place.* The family clock shop is preserved on the street floor, and their living quarters now contain displays, documents, photographs, and memorabilia. Visitors can also see the hiding closet, which the Gestapo never found, even though they lived six days in the house hoping to starve out anyone who might be concealed here. The upstairs living quarters are not accessible through the shop, but via the side door of No. 19, down a narrow alley beside the shop. Meeting instructions giving the time of the next guided tour are posted on the door. ⊠*Barteljorisstraat 19* ☎*023/526–8481* ⊕*www.corrietenboom. com* ⊡*Donations accepted* ⊙*Apr.–Oct., Tues.–Sat. 10–4; Nov.–Mar., Tues.–Sat. 11–3.*

OFF THE BEATEN PATH

Zandvoort is only 9 km (5½ mi) from Haarlem and has the area's biggest and best beach around—it's a favorite of sun-starved Amsterdammers. It can get crowded but if you wander south for 10 minutes or so, you can find isolated spots among the dunes; after about 20 minutes, you come to the nude, in places gay, sunbathing beach.

❽ Historisch Museum Haarlem. Located near the Frans Hals Museum, with two or three small temporary exhibitions a year, the town's history museum makes the most of its limited resources, offering insight into the history of the city and the surrounding area. Video screenings (in English), models of the city, and touch-screen computers relate stories that take you back in history. There are fascinating old prints and maps, and some apparently random exhibits, including one of the earliest printing presses, dating from the 17th century. Also on view here is an incisive exhibition on modern Dutch architecture, **ABC Architectuur Centrum Haarlem,** with plans and photographs from city projects already finished and still in the planning stages (De Bruijn's Woonhuis is particularly ingenious). ⊠*Groot Heiligland 47* ☎*023/542–2427 Historisch Museum* ⊕*www.historischmuseumhaarlem.nl* ⊡*€2* ⊙*Tues.–Sat. noon–5, Sun. 1–5.*

❸ Stadhuis *(Town Hall).* On the market square, this 14th-century former hunting lodge belonged to the Count of Holland, who permitted it to be transformed into Haarlem's Town Hall in the 14th century. The large main **Gravenzaal** (Count's Hall) is worth a visit—if you can sneak in between bouts of confetti throwing, as there are a good number of bridal parties ascending its steps on a regular basis—to study its collection of 16th-century paintings amassed by the Count of Holland. If you wish to tour the premises, call in advance to get permission. ⊠*Grote Markt 2* ☎*023/511–3000* ⊡*Free* ⊙*Weekdays 10–4 (when not closed for civic functions).*

WHERE TO STAY & EAT

$$$ ✕**Peter Cuyper.** In a 17th-century mansion that was once a bank, this small, gracious restaurant has a traditional beamed dining room that is brightened with flowers, crisp linens, and light filtering through the mullioned windows. Ask for a table with a view of the enclosed garden (open in summer) if you've missed out on a table outside. Try the wild sea bass with parmesan risotto and lobster jus, or one of the delicious soups. The restaurant is convenient to both the Frans Hals

SHOP 'TIL YOU DROP

The pedestrianized Barteljorisstraat has lots of top fashion chains, such as Vanilia, Esprit, and MEXX, as well as a number of street-wear shops for men. The top end of Kruisstraat has furniture shops, from antiques to designer, and a lot in between. Flowers can be found on Krocht, on the corner junction of Kruisstraat and Barteljorisstraat—the sumptuous displays echo the nearby tulip fields between Haarlem and the Keukenhof.

If it's art you're after, check out **Theo Swagemakers** (⊠ *Stoofsteeg 6* ☎ *023/532–7761* ✉ *€3.50*), a gallery that sells artwork by Swagemakers (1898–1994) himself, as well as others. It's open Thursday–Sunday 1–5. Other more commercial art galleries can be found along Koningstraat. For Art Nouveau and Art Deco, visit **Kunsthandel Hermine Guldemond** (⊠ *Frankestraat 39* ☎ *023/531–8725*).

and the Teylers museums. ⊠ *Kleine Houtstraat 70* ☎ *023/532–0885* ⌖ *Reservations essential* ☰ *AE, DC, MC, V* ☾ *Closed Sun. and Mon. No lunch Sat.*

$–$$ ✕ **De Lachende Javaan.** Stepping into "The Laughing Javanese" off an old Haarlem street that hasn't changed in centuries, you are hit with a flash of color and pungent smells. You can sit upstairs at one of the window tables and look out over the sober gabled houses while eating *kambing saté* (skewers of lamb in soy sauce) and *kipkarbonaade met sambal djeroek* (grilled chicken with a fiery Indonesian sauce), but the menu options are enormous, so you can mix and match, choosing a meal of 12 small dishes if you want. ⊠ *Frankestraat 27* ☎ *023/532–8792* ☰ *AE, DC, MC, V* ☾ *Closed Mon. No lunch.*

★ ¢–$$ ✕ **XO.** A very funky restaurant-bar, XO has chunky silver graphics, purple-and-gray walls, and oversize but softly lighted lamps. Throw in some fun touches—"king" chairs, complete with claw feet and red cushions; nifty recesses at the bar for extra intimacy; big stone candlesticks—and you've got an alluring setting for lunch and evening edibles. The dinner menu changes regularly but always contains mouth-watering and exquisitely presented dishes, such as cod filet baked in a sun-dried tomato-and-truffle crust, with black pasta, spinach, and a white-wine cream sauce. For a lunchtime snack try the imaginative bread rolls stuffed with marinated salmon and horseradish cream, or a cucumber salad; a fine range of tapas are served all day. ⊠ *Grote Markt 8* ☎ *023/551–1350* ☰ *AE, MC, V.*

¢–$$ ✕ **Jacobus Pieck.** One of Haarlem's best *eetlokaals* (dining spots), this attracts locals with its long bar, cozy tables, and lovely sun trap of a garden. The menu offers standards but with a twist: try the Popeye Blues Salad—a wild spinach, blue cheese, and bacon number, with creamy mustard dressing for a lighter option—or, for dinner, lamb with ratatouille and rosemary jus. As you'll see, the food makes this restaurant-café very popular, so get here early or book ahead to snag a table.

7

✉ *Warmoestraat 18* ☎ *023/532–6144* ⊟ *No credit cards* ⊙ *Closed Sun. No dinner Mon.*

$$–$$$ ⊡ **Golden Tulip Lion d'Or.** This modern hotel is in a pretty 18th-century building just 50 yards from the railway station and within walking distance of major downtown sights. Rooms are spacious with good lighting and upscale chain-hotel-style furnishings. The bathrooms all have tubs as well as showers. Downstairs are meeting rooms, and a reasonably priced restaurant and bar. A jogging path runs behind the hotel. ✉ *Kruisweg 34–36, 2011 LC* ☎ *023/532–1750* ⊟ *023/532–9543* ⊕ *www.goldentulip.com* ⊅ *32 rooms, 2 suites* ⚲ *In-room: dial-up. In-hotel: restaurant, bar, parking (fee), some pets allowed* ⊟ *AE, DC, MC, V* ⍟ *BP.*

¢–$ ⊡ **Carillon.** This is an old-fashioned hotel with a friendly staff, set in the shadow of Sint Bavo's across the Grote Markt. Small rooms are spartan but fresh and comfortable, with impeccable bathrooms that include showers but not tubs. The central location and reasonable rates make it a top spot to accommodate a day of exploring and then a night out. The café-bar has a nice terrace on the square. ✉ *Grote Markt 27, 2011 RC* ☎ *023/531–0591* ⊟ *023/531–4909* ⊕ *www.hotelcarillon.com* ⊅ *21 rooms, 15 with bath* ⚲ *In-room: no a/c, dial-up. In-hotel: restaurant, bar, no elevator* ⊟ *AE, DC, MC, V* ⍟ *CP.*

¢ ⊡ **Faber.** Within walking distance of the beaches of Zandvoort, this is a small family-style hotel with bright, tidy rooms and a summer terrace. It's run by two brothers, Hans and Martin, who make a point of making sure your stay is comfortable. Rooms book up very quickly in summer, so make reservations early. ✉ *Kostverlorenstraat 15, 2042 PAZandvoort* ☎ *023/571–2825* ⊟ *023/571–6886* ⊕ *www.hotel-faber.nl* ⊅ *32 rooms* ⚲ *In-room: no a/c. In-hotel: restaurant, bar* ⊟ *AE, MC, V* ⍟ *CP.*

NIGHTLIFE & THE ARTS

Haarlem is more than a city of nostalgia. The **Patronaat** (✉ *Zijlsingel 2* ☎ *023/517–5858*) is an excellent rock music venue: it's Haarlem's answer to the Melkweg in Amsterdam only without the really big bands.

Daytime cafés often metamorphose into busy nightspots. For example, **Mickie's** (✉ *Kruisstraat 22* ☎ *023/551–8661*), is a mellow café by day, but turns into a rowdy nightclub with a DJ, serious lighting, and enormous speakers to ensure the ambience is just right.

If you feel like bar hopping but don't want to wear a hole in your shoe, head to Lange Veerstraat or the Botermarkt square, where you'll find a lot of bars and cafés. The **Café de Linde** (✉ *Botermarkt 21* ☎ *023/531–9688*) is a mellow place for a drink or a light meal. Located in a converted Art Deco cinema on the Grote Markt, **CaféStudio** (✉ *Grote Markt 25* ☎ *023/531–0033*) has an exceptional range of Belgian beers. **Gay Cafe Wilsons** (✉ *Gedempte Raamgracht 78* ☎ *023/532–5854* ⊙ *Weekends only*) is the in gathering place for gays in Haarlem.

DELFT

For many travelers, few spots in Holland are as intimate and attractive as this town. With time-burnished canals and cobblestone streets, Delft possesses a peaceful calm that recalls the quieter pace of the 17th-century Golden Age, back when Johannes Vermeer was counted among its citizens. Imagine a tiny Amsterdam, with smaller canals and narrower bridges, and you have the essence of Old Delft. But even though the city has one foot rooted in the past, another is planted firmly in the present: Delft teems with hip cafés, and being a college town, revelers pile in and out of bars almost every day of the week.

> ### ORGAN IMPROV
>
> Haarlem hosts an **International Organ Improvisation Competition** in even-numbered years for a week in early July, giving people ample opportunity to hear the renowned Müller organ in Sint Bavo's church at full throttle. Entry costs €5 for the early rounds, and €10 for the final. For more information, call ☎020/488–0479, or visit ⊕ www.organfestival.nl.

TO & FROM

14 km (9 mi) southeast of The Hague, 71 km (44 mi) southwest of Amsterdam.

Direct trains leave Amsterdam Central Station for Delft every half hour throughout the day——the journey time is a little under one hour. If driving, take the A10 then the A4 south from Amsterdam. The drive will take between 45 minutes and one hour, depending on traffic.

7

EXPLORING

Compact and easy to traverse despite its web of canals, Delft is best explored on foot, although water taxis are available in summer to give you an armchair ride through the heart of town. Everything you might want to see is in the old center. If arriving by train, look for the computer information terminals outside by the bus station, which will print out a handy map with directions to any sight you care to request.

MAIN ATTRACTIONS

❷ Bagijnhof. On the Oude Delft, just north of the Lambert van Meerten Museum, is a weather-beaten 13th-century Gothic gate, with ancient-looking stone relief, that leads through to a small courtyard. The city sided with the (Protestant) Dutch rebels during the Eighty Years' War, and when the (Catholic) Spanish were driven out in 1572, the city reverted to Protestantism, leaving many Catholic communities in dire straits. One group of women was permitted to stay and practice their religion, but according to a new law, their place of worship had to be very modest: a drab exterior in the Bagijnhof hides their sumptuous Baroque church.

❽ Gemeenlandshuis. The pretty, tree-lined Oude Delft canal has numerous historic gabled houses along its banks, and takes the honors for being the first canal in the city, and possibly the first city canal anywhere in the Netherlands. One of the finest buildings along its length, the

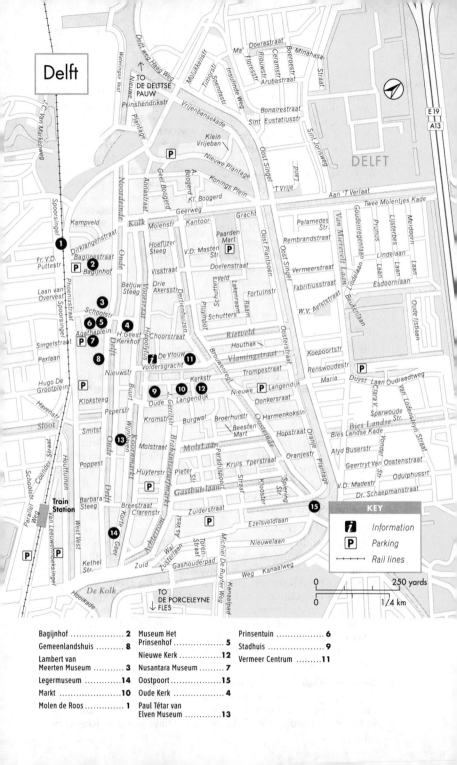

Delft

KEY

🛈   Information

Ⓟ   Parking

⊢⊢⊢   Rail lines

0   250 yards

0   1/4 km

A Brief History of Delft

Delft has more than painterly charm—many great men lived and died here. Toward the end of the 16th century Prince William of Orange (known as William the Silent) settled in Delft to wage his war against Spanish rule. He never left: the nation's founder was assassinated in his mansion in 1584 by a spy of the Spanish Duke of Alva, and buried in the Nieuwe Kerk (New Church). Also buried here is Grotius, the humanist and father of international law. And Delft was home to Anthonie van Leeuwenhoek, who mastered the fledging invention of the microscope and was born the same year as Vermeer, 1632. Vermeer was just one of many artists who set up shop in the city—which had grown rich with the trade in butter, cloth, beer, and pottery.

Delft's history was often turbulent. In the 17th century, the canal water became tainted, forcing 180 of the 200 resident breweries to close. In 1654, the "Thunderclap," an accidental gunpowder explosion, leveled half the town and killed hundreds. But Delft rebounded thanks to riches it had amassed as the headquarters of the Dutch East India Company. The porcelains their traders brought back from the Far East proved irresistible, and in 1645 De Porceleyne Fles started making and exporting the famous blue-and-white earthenware that soon became known the world over as Delft Blue.

Gemeenlandshuis, is a spectacular example of 16th-century Gothic architecture and is adorned with brightly painted shields and a coat of arms. A few yards east of here, across the canal on the corner of Hippolytusbuurt and Cameretten, are a row of *visbanken* (fish stalls), built along the canal in 1650. Fish has been sold over the counter here pretty much ever since. (⊠ *Oude Delft 167*)

NEED A BREAK?

Kleyweg's Stads-Koffiehuis (⊠ *Oude Delft 133* ☎ *015/212–4625)* **looks out over the oldest and one of the most beautiful canals in Delft. Inside, you'll find a** *stamtafel,* **a large table laid out with newspapers and magazines, where anyone may sit and chat. There are also smaller individual tables where you can enjoy good coffee, delicious pancakes, and terrific apple pie. In fine weather, the tables on the barge moored on the canal are very popular. The café is closed Sunday.**

★ ❸ **Lambert van Meerten Museum.** Within the shadow of the Oude Kerk, this Renaissance-era, canal-side mansion has gloriously paneled rooms which provide a noble setting for antique tiles, tin-glazed earthenware, paintings, and an extensive collection of ebony-veneer furniture. Although much of the works on display are not the original patrician owner's (who lost a fortune when his distillery burned down and he had to auction off everything), the house and some of his collection was bought back by Van Meerten's friends. Note especially the great collection of tiles, whose subjects range from foodstuffs to warships. The gardens here are alluring, with a spherical sundial, two busts, and a stone gateway leading the eye through to the tangled woods beyond. ⊠ *Oude Delft*

199   ☎*015/260–2358*   ⊕*www. gemeentemusea-delft.nl*   ✆*€3.50; combined ticket to Het Prinsenhof, Nusantara, and Lambert van Meerten museums €6* ⊙*Tues.–Sat. 10–5, Sun. 1–5.*

RENT A BIKE?

If you want to rent a bike, pick one up from the **railway station** (☎*015/214-3033*), open weekdays 5:45 AM–midnight, weekends 6:30 AM–midnight. Fees run €6.50–€7.50 per day, with ID and a security deposit of €50. For biking routes through Delft, Delfshaven, and Schiedam, get maps from the Delft Tourist Information Point.

❿ **Markt.** Delft's main square is bracketed by two town landmarks, the Stadhuis (Town Hall) and the Nieuwe Kerk. Here, too, are cafés, restaurants, and souvenir shops (most selling imitation Delftware) and, on Thursday, a busy general market. Markt 52 is the site of Johannes Vermeer's house, where the 17th-century painter spent much of his youth. Not far away is a statue of Grotius, or Hugo de Groot, born in Delft in 1583 and one of Holland's most famous humanists and lawyers.

❶ **Molen de Roos** *(Rose Windmill).* Just to the west of Oude Delft is Phoenixstraat, where you'll find this former flour mill that originally stood on the town ramparts. The hexagonal base dates back to 1728. The platform encircling the mill about halfway up was restored in 1990. The mill sails get going every Saturday, when you can climb up the vertiginous stairs to get a view from the platform as the sails swoosh by. ⊠*Phoenixstraat 112* ☎*015/212–1589* ⊕*www.molenderoos.nl* ✆*Free* ⊙*Sat.–Sun. 10–4, but only when a blue flag is flying from the sails.*

★ ❺ **Museum Het Prinsenhof.** A former dignitary-hosting convent of St. Agatha, the Prinsenhof museum is celebrated as the residence of Prince William the Silent, beloved as *Vader des Vaderlands* (Father of the Nation) for his role in the Spanish Revolt and a hero whose tragic end here gave this structure the sobriquet "cradle of Dutch liberty." The complex of buildings was taken over by the government of the new Dutch Republic in 1572 and given to William of Orange for his use as a residence. On July 10, 1584, fevered by monies offered by Philip II of Spain, Bathasar Gerard, a Catholic fanatic, gained admittance to the mansion and succeeded in shooting the prince on the staircase hall, since known as Moordhal (Murder Hall). The fatal bullet holes—the *teykenen der koogelen*—are still visible in the stairwell. Today, the imposing structure is a museum, with a 15th-century chapel, a quaint courtyard, and a bevy of elegantly furnished 17th-century rooms filled with antique pottery, silver, tapestries, and House of Orange portraits, along with exhibits on Dutch history. ⊠*Sint Agathaplein 1* ☎*015/260–2358* ⊕*www.gemeentemusea-delft.nl* ✆*€5; combined ticket to Het Prinsenhof, Nusantara, and Lambert van Meerten museums €6* ⊙*Tues.–Sat. 10–5, Sun. 1–5.*

⓬ **Nieuwe Kerk** *(New Church.)* Presiding over the Markt, this Late Gothic edifice was built between 1483 and 1510. It represents more than a

CLOSE UP

Buying Delftware

It's corny, even sometimes a little tacky (miniature clogs, anyone?), but no visit to Delft would be complete without stopping at a Delft Porcelain Factory, to see plates and tulip vases being painted by hand and perhaps picking up a souvenir or two. **De Porceleyne Fles** (⊠ *Royal Delftware Factory, Rotterdamseweg 196* ☎ *015/251–2030*) is the original and most famous home to the popular blue-and-white pottery. Regular demonstrations of molding and painting pottery are given by the artisans. These wares bear the worthy name of De Porceleyne Fles. On the bottom of each object is a triple signature: a plump vase topped by a straight line, the stylized letter "F" below it, and the word "Delft." Blue is no longer the only official color. In 1948, a rich red cracked glaze was premiered

depicting profuse flowers, graceful birds, and leaping gazelles. There is New Delft, a range of green, gold, and black hues, whose exquisite minuscule figures are drawn to resemble an old Persian tapestry; the Pynacker Delft, borrowing Japanese motifs in rich oranges and golds; and the brighter Polychrome Delft, which can strike a brilliant sunflower-yellow effect.

Another favorite place for picking up Delftware is at the pottery factories of **De Delftse Pauw** (⊠ *Delftweg 133* ☎ *015/212–4920*), which, although not as famous as De Porceleyne Fles, produce work of equally high quality. **Atelier de Candelaer** (⊠ *Kerkstraat 14* ☎ *015/213–1848*) is a smaller pottery, and its city center location makes it a convenient stop-off for comparisons of Delftware with other pottery.

century's worth of Dutch craftsmanship—it's as though its founders knew it would one day be the last resting place of the man who built the nation, William the Silent, and his descendants of the House of Orange. In 1872 the noted architect P. J. H. Cuypers raised the tower to its current height. There are 22 columns surrounding the ornate black marble and alabaster tomb of William of Orange, which was designed by Hendrick de Keyser and his son. The small dog you see at the prince's feet is rumored to have starved to death after refusing to eat following his owner's death. Throughout the church are paintings, stained-glass windows, and memorabilia associated with the Dutch royal family. There are other mausoleums, most notably that of lawyer-philosopher Hugo de Groot, or Grotius. In summer it is possible to climb the 380-odd steps of the church tower for an unparalleled view that stretches as far as Scheveningen to the north and Rotterdam to the south. ⊠ *Markt 2* ☎ *015/212–3025* ▭ *Combined ticket for Oude Kerk and Nieuwe Kerk €3, tower €2.50* ☉ *Apr.–Oct., Mon.–Sat. 9–6; Nov.–Mar., Mon.–Sat. 11–4.*

❹ **Oude Kerk.** *(Old Church)* At the very heart of historic Delft, the Gothic Oude Kerk, with its tower 6 feet off-kilter, is the last resting place of Vermeer. The tower seems to lean in all directions at once, but then, this is the oldest church in Delft, having been founded in 1200. Building went on until the 15th century, which accounts for the combination of architectural styles, and much of its austere interior dates from the latter part of the work. The tower, dating to 1350, started leaning in the Middle Ages, and today the tilt to the east is somewhat stabilized by the 3-foot tilt to the north. The tower, whose tilt prevents ascension by visitors, holds the largest carillon bell in the Netherlands; weighing nearly 20,000 pounds, it now is used only on state occasions. ☒ *Heilige Geestkerkhof* ☎ *015/212–3015* ☒ *Combined ticket to Oude Kerk and Nieuwe Kerk €3* ☉ *Apr.–Oct., Mon.–Sat. 9–6; Nov.–Mar., Mon.–Fri. 11–4, Sat. 10–5.*

⑪ Vermeer Centrum. Opened in 2007, and housed in the former St. Lucas Guild, where Delft's favorite son was dean for many years, the Vermeer Center takes visitors on a multimedia journey through the life and work of Johannes Vermeer. Touch screens, projections, and other interactive features are interspersed with giant reproductions of the master's work, weaving a tale of 17th-century Delft and drawing you into the mind of the painter. The centerpiece is a huge model of the city as it would have looked in Vermeer's day. ☒ *Voldersgracht 21* ☎ *015/213–8588* ⊕ *www.vermeerdelft.nl* ☒ *€8* ☉ *Apr.–Oct., Mon.–Sat. 10—6, Sun. 10–5; Nov.–Mar., daily 10–5.*

IF YOU HAVE TIME

⑭ Legermuseum *(Netherlands Army Museum).* Delft's former armory makes an appropriate setting for an impressive military museum. Despite the gentle images of Dutch life, the origins of the Dutch Republic were violent. It took nothing less than the Eighty Years' War (1568–1648) to finally achieve independence from the Spanish crown. In addition to the guns, swords, and other implements of warfare, all periods of Dutch military history are explored in detail, from Roman times to the German occupation during World War II. ☒ *Korte Geer 1* ☎ *015/215–0500* ⊕ *www.armymuseum.nl* ☒ *€6* ☉ *Tues.–Fri. 10–5, weekends noon–5.*

❼ Nusantara Museum. In the same courtyard as the Prinsenhof Museum, the Nusantara has a colorful collection of ethnographic costumes and artifacts from the Dutch East Indies—most of it is ill-gotten gains from the 17th century by members of the Dutch East India Company. A large Javanese *gamelan* (percussion orchestra) takes center stage inside, and is surrounded by Indo-European batik, Hindu statuettes, shields and intricately carved spears, diamond-encrusted daggers, *wayang kulit* (shadow puppets), and a beautifully carved tomb. Other displays chart the history of the spice trade. ☒ *Sint Agathaplein 4* ☎ *015/260–2358* ⊕ *www. gemeentemusea-delft.nl* ☒ *€3.50; combined ticket to Het Prinsen-*

RETAIL THERAPY

In Delft, Friday is *koopavond* (evening shopping), the only day that stores are open until 9 PM (the rest of the week everything closes at 5 PM). A large weekly market is held every Thursday from 9 to 5 on the Markt, with a flower market along the Hippolytusbuurt also on Thursday from 9 to 5. Every Saturday, there is a general market at the Brabantse Turfmarkt/Burgwal. Saturday in summer, there is a flea market on the canals in the town center and an art market at Heilige Geestkerkhof.

Vermeer: Sphinx of Delft

As one of the world's most adored artists, Johannes Vermeer (1632–75) has been the subject of blockbuster exhibitions, theater pieces, and best-selling novels (Tracy Chevalier's *Girl with a Pearl Earring*, also a sumptuous movie). He enjoys cult status, yet his reputation rests on just 35 paintings. Of course, those canvases—ordinary domestic scenes depicting figures caught in an amber light—are among the most extraordinary ever created. But Vermeer's fame is relatively recent. He died aged 42, worn out by economic woes. Only since the mid-19th century have critics rightfully revered his work. And when Proust proclaimed his *View of Delft* "the most beautiful painting in the world," audiences worldwide became enraptured.

How Vermeer painted scenes of such incomparable quietude, while living in a house filled with his 11 children is a difficult question to answer, and little is known about his early life. We do know that his father ran an inn, and was also an art dealer, as was Johannes himself. But that doesn't seem important—the "reality" that matters is the one Vermeer captured on his canvases. The way his light traps the most transient of effects is so perfect, you almost find yourself looking around to see where the sunlight has fallen, expecting it to be dappling your own face.

hof, Nusantara, and Lambert van Meerten museums €6 ⊙ Tues.–Sat. 10–5, Sun. 1–5.

⑮ Oostpoort *(East Gate.)* At the southern end of the Oosteinde canal, the fairy-tale twin turrets of the Oostpoort form Delft's only remaining city gate. Dating back to 1400, with the spires added in 1514, parts of it are now a private residence, but you can still walk over the drawbridge. It is a short walk out of the center, but the effort of getting there is more than rewarded by the view.

⑬ Paul Tétar van Elven Museum. This 18th-century canal-side mansion was the former home of 19th-century painter Paul Tétar van Elven. The interior he created is charmingly redolent of Ye Olde Delft, complete with painted ceilings, antiques, and even a reproduction of an artist's atelier done up in the Old Dutch style. ⊠ *Koornmarkt 67* ☎ *015/212–4206* ⊠ *€2.50* ⊙ *Apr.–Oct., Tues.–Sun. 1–5.*

⑥ Prinsentuin *(Prince's Garden.)* Between the Prinsenhof and the Nusantara Museum is Agathaplein, a late Gothic leafy courtyard built around 1400, which has huge chestnut trees shading an adjacent green. At the center is the Prinsentuin, a somewhat cultivated square that offers a calming respite from the city streets.

⑨ Stadhuis *(Town Hall).* At the west end of the Markt, only the solid 13th-century tower remains from the original medieval town hall building. The gray-stone edifice that looms over has picturesque red shutters and lavish detailing. It was designed in 1618 by Hendrick de Keyser, one of the most prolific architects of the Golden Age. Inside is a grand staircase and Council Chamber with a famous old map of Delft. You can view the Town Hall interior only by making arrangements through the Delft tourist office, which can also issue you a ticket to visit the torture chamber in Het Steen, the 13th-century tower. ⊠ *Markt 87* ⊙ *Weekdays 10–4.*

WHERE TO STAY & EAT

★ $$$–$$$$ ✕**De Zwethheul.** Delft's classiest restaurant is also its best hidden: set a little outside town, it can easily be reached by cab. In a restored 18th-century building, this award-winner actually began as a humble pancake house. In fine weather, you can eat on a beautiful terrace overlooking the Schie River. Specialties of the house include Bresse chicken ravioli with baked crayfish, and lamb in basil sauce. The sommelier and his wine list are among the best in Holland. ⊠ *Rotterdamseweg 480* ☎ *010/470–4166* ᐃ *Reservations essential* ⊟ *AE, DC, MC, V* ⊙ *Closed Mon. No lunch weekends.*

$$–$$$$ ✕**Le Vieux Jean.** The tiny, family-run restaurant serves tasty meat-and-potatoes fare as well as good fish dishes such as *kabeljauw* (cod) with asparagus sauce. In the adjoining *proeflokaal* (tasting room) you can buy wine and spirits. ⊠ *Heilige Geestkerkhof 3* ☎ *015/213–0433* ᐃ *Reservations essential* ⊟ *AE, DC, MC, V* ⊙ *Closed Sun. and Mon.*

★ $$$ ✕**L'Orage.** In cool shades of blue, with pristine white linen, Restaurant L'Orage has a sublime aura; as soon as you walk through the door, you anticipate the sensational dining options on offer. It is owned and run by Denmark-born Jannie Munk—Delft's very own prizewinning lady chef—who is now reaching out to a wider public thanks to the professional classes she offers in her kitchen. Her architect-husband, Pim Hienkans, was the mastermind behind the look of the place, which is accented by a huge, hinged glass roof to create an indoors-outdoors feeling. Munk creates delicious fish dishes, many based on recipes from her native country. Sometimes if the kitchen is in the mood, you'll be treated with *amuse-bouches*—three or four of the tastiest dishes on the menu in miniature—to accompany your drinks. Best bet for your main course is the roasted Scottish steak with truffle sauce. ⊠ *Oude Delft 111b* ☎ *015/212–3629* ᐃ *Reservations essential* ⊟ *AE, DC, MC, V* ⊙ *Closed Mon. No lunch.*

★ $–$$ ✕**Stadscafé de Waag.** The ancient brick-and-stone walls of this cavernous former weigh house are adorned with hulking 17th-century balance scales. Tables on the mezzanine in the rear overlook the Wijnhaven canal, while those on the terrace in front nestle under the magnificent, looming, town clock tower. All the while, tastefully unobtrusive music creates a cool vibe for a mixed clientele. Happily, dishes such as Flemish asparagus with ham and egg, or *parelhoen* (guinea fowl) in a rich dark broth, are equal to the fabulous setting. ⊠ *Markt 11* ☎ *015/213–0393* ⊟ *AE, MC, V.*

¢–$$ ✕**Café Vlaanderen.** Board games keep you entertained on a rainy day inside the extensive café, but sunny skies will make you head for the tables set under leafy lime trees out front on the Beestenmarkt. Out back is an equally shady garden. The deluxe fish wrap makes a delicious light lunch, while evening options include a delicious tuna and swordfish brochette. ⊠*Beestenmarkt 16* ☎*015/213–3311* ➡*MC, V.*

¢–$$ ✕**Willem van Oranje.** You might normally be wary of any large establishment on a main tourist crossroads that offers its menu in six languages, but what redeems this place, with its view to die for between the town hall and the New Church, is the wide selection of good value Dutch pancakes. Fill up from a choice of around 50 sweet or savory (and sometimes both) flavor concoctions to suit every taste. Or if you still can't make up your mind, there are also all the usual Dutch café standards on the menu, including omelets, rolls, and salads. A more sophisticated dinner menu with heartier fish and meat favorites appears on weekend evenings. ⊠*Markt 48a* ☎*015/212–3059* ➡*MC, V.*

¢–$ ✕**De Wijnhaven.** This Delft staple has loyal regulars, drawn by the many terrace tables on a small square overlooking a narrow canal, and a mean Indonesian satay. There's a smart restaurant on the first floor, but the bar and mezzanine have plenty to offer, with lunch snacks, a reasonable menu for dinner with the latest tracks on the speakers, and great fries and salads. ⊠*Wijnhaven 22* ☎*015/214–1460* ➡*MC, V.*

¢ ✕**De Nonnerie.** In the vaulted cellar of the famous Prinsenhof Museum, this luncheon-only tearoom has a sedate, elegant atmosphere. If you can, get a table in the grassy courtyard under an umbrella, and—since you're within the House of Orange—order an Oranjeboom beer to wash down the fine *Delftsche Meesters palet* (three small sandwiches of pâté, salmon, and Dutch cheese) served here. Entry is via the archway from Oude Delft into the Prinsenhof Museum, down a signposted path beside the gardens. ⊠*Sint Agathaplein* ☎*015/212–1860* ➡*No credit cards* ✪*Closed Mon. No dinner.*

$$–$$$ ▥ **Best Western Delft Museumhotel & Residence.** Spread through a complex of 11 buildings and a warren of corridors, this sprawling hotel is opposite the Oude Kerk and adjacent to the Prinsenhof Museum. Unfortunately, the historic charm of the rooms was lost in an anonymous chain-hotel makeover—only the canal views compensate. As if to make amends, the management has cut loose with an over-the-top display of antiques in the public areas. ⊠*Phoenixstraat 50a, 2611 AM* ☎*015/215–3070* 🖷*015/215–3079* ⊕*www.museumhotel.nl* ⤶*49 rooms, 2 suites* ♿*In-room: no a/c (some), safe, refrigerator, Wi-Fi* ➡*AE, DC, MC, V.*

$–$$$ ▥ **Bridges House.** The history of this hotel goes back to Jan Steen—one of the great painters of The Hague School—who lived and painted here. His contemporaries didn't recognize his talent, so he opened an inn and operated a brewery to supplement his income. The current owner has re-created a patrician's house in a tasteful refurbishment. Antiques grace each spacious room, all adorned with extra-long beds with bespoke Pullman mattresses. The bathrooms are fitted with enormous showerheads for a wake-up blast, and all have tubs. The breakfast room overlooks the canal. For longer stays, consider one of the apartments. ⊠*Oude Delft 74, 2611 CD* ☎*015/212–4036* 🖷*015/213–3600* ⊕*www.bridges-house.com* ⤶*10 rooms, 2 studio apartments* ♿*In-room: no a/c, dial-up. In-hotel: no elevator* ➡*MC, V* ❙⊘*BP.*

7

★ $$ ☷**Johannes Vermeer.** It's surprising that no one else thought of it before, but this is the first Delft hotel to pay homage to the town's most famous local son. The buildings of this former cigar factory were completely modernized and turned into a sumptuous hotel in 2000. You'll be spoiled for choice of Old-Master views: rooms at the front overlook a canal, while rooms at the back have a sweeping city view that takes in three churches. In tasteful greens and yellows, the decor is unobtrusive, and the staff are pleasantly friendly. The garden behind the hotel is a mellow place to have a drink. The restaurant is open only for groups (advance arrangements essential). It's too bad, because the walls of the restaurant are adorned with painted copies of the entire works of Vermeer, with his *Girl with a Pearl Earring* inevitably taking center stage. ✉*Molslaan 18–22, 2611 RM* ☎*015/212–6466* 🖷*015/213–4835* ⊕*www.hotelvermeer.nl* 🛏*24 rooms, 1 suite* ♿*In-room: dial-up. In-hotel: no elevator* 🖃*AE, DC, MC, V* ⦿*BP.*

★ $–$$ ☷**Leeuwenbrug.** Facing one of Delft's quieter waterways, this traditional and well-maintained hotel has an Old Dutch–style canal-side lounge, an ideal spot to sip a drink and rest up aching feet after a hard day's touring and shopping. The rooms are large, airy, and tastefully contemporary in decor; those in the annex are particularly appealing. Rooms at the front have canal views. The staff are very friendly and helpful, and often go out of their way to make guests feel welcome. ✉*Koornmarkt 16, 2611 EE* ☎*015/214–7741* 🖷*015/215–9759* ⊕*www.leeuwenbrug.nl* 🛏*36 rooms* ♿*In-room: no a/c, dial-up. In-hotel: bar* 🖃*AE, MC, V* ⦿*BP.*

¢–$ ☷**Soul Inn.** In a quiet residential neighborhood ten minutes' walk from the train station and the old center, the large '70s logo above the door of this 19th-century town house barely hints at the eclectic nature of this soul-inspired B&B. Each of the rooms is individually bedecked with a chaotic mixture of chintz and glitz that harks back to a time when big Afro hair was the only way to go, and color coordination had yet to be invented. It's bright, it's unique, and it's fun. The three apartments are also equipped with kitchen facilities. ✉*Willemstraat 55, 2613 DS* ☎*015/215–7246* ⊕*www.soulinn.nl* 🛏*10 rooms, 3 apartments* ♿*In-room: no a/c. In hotel: no elevator* 🖃*MC, V* ⦿*BP.*

¢   ☷**B&B Oosteinde.** This small yet friendly bed-and-breakfast is the only one of its kind in the city. Located behind the Beestenmarkt, near the fairy-tale twin towers of the city gate at Oostpoort, this welcoming house makes you feel like one of the family. Larger rooms can sleep three or four. A minimum stay of two nights is required. There are sinks in the rooms, but bathroom facilities are shared. ✉*Oosteinde 156, 2611 SR* ☎🖷*015/213–4238* ⊕*www.bb-oosteinde.nl* 🛏*3 rooms without bath* ♿*In-room: no a/c. In-hotel: some pets allowed, no elevator* 🖃*No credit cards* ⦿*BP.*

NIGHTLIFE

Delft is home to one of the country's most important technical universities, and the large student population ensures the bars are always lively at night. Two good places to find a profusion of watering holes are the Markt and the Beesten-markt. The latter is a peaceful little square where the discerning drinkers go on summery evenings to sit out under the leafy lime trees. The most humming nightspot—in fact, the only club (nearly all others are students-only)—in Delft is **Speakers** (⊠ *Burgwal 45–49* ☎ *015/212-4446* ⊕ *www.speakers.nl*). Each night there is something different going on. Stand-up comedy, in English as well as Dutch, is usually on Wednesday, with concerts on Thursday; Friday night sees theme night (1970s, for instance); Saturday hosts the techno-beat crowd; and Sunday offers salsa parties. Open regular hours are a restaurant, bar, and sidewalk café.

With its idyllic location on Delft's nicest square, **Café Vlaanderen** (⊠ *Beestenmarkt 16* ☎ *015/213-3311*) is not only a good place to eat, it's also a fine place to chill out with a cold one. For beer lovers looking to be pleasantly bewildered by a choice of around 200 different Belgian beers, **Locus Publicus** (⊠ *Brabantse Turfmarkt 67* ☎ *015/213-4632*) is the place to go.

> ## PARTY TOWN
>
> From February until December, there are annual festivals throughout Delft. Highlights include the De Koninck Blues Festival in mid-February; canal-side concerts from the end of June through July and August; a week of chamber music during late August; the African Festival in early August; the Delft Jazz and Blues Festival at the end of August; a waiters' race in the Beestenmarkt in early September; and the City of Lights in mid-December. For more details, log on to (⊕ *www.delft.com*) or contact the **Delft Tourist Information Point** (⊠ *Hippolytusbuurt 4* ☎ *0900/515-1555*).

ROTTERDAM

Rotterdam looks to the future like almost nowhere else. The decision to leave the past behind wasn't made entirely through choice however—the old town disappeared overnight on May 14, 1940, when Nazi bombs swept away 30,000 buildings in a few torrid hours. Since then, a new landscape of concrete, steel, and glass has risen from the ashes, and today this world port is home to some of the 21st century's most architecturally important creations.

Thanks to its location on the deltas of the Rhine and Maas rivers, Rotterdam has become the world's largest seaport. Through its harbors and the enormous Europoort pass more tons of shipping than through all of France combined. The rapid expansion of the port in the post-war years created a huge demand for labor, bringing waves of migrants from Italy, Spain, Greece, Turkey, Morocco, Cape Verde, and the Netherlands Antilles, turning Rotterdam into one of the most ethnically diverse cities in Europe.

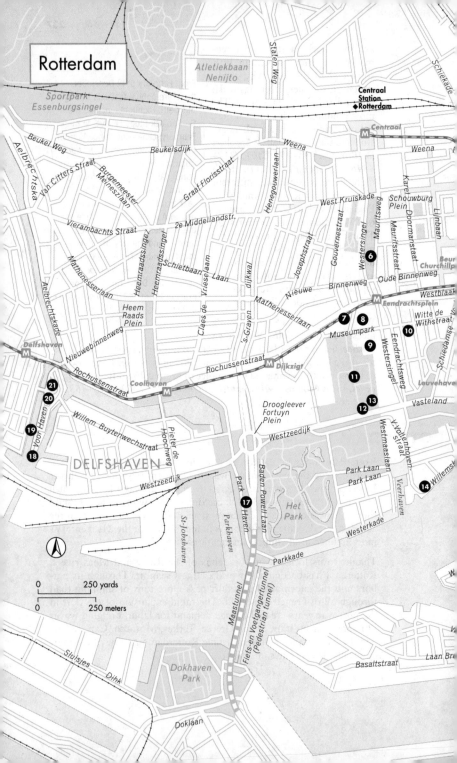

7

KEY

├─┼─┤ Rail lines

═══ Metro lines

ORIENTATION

The city divides itself naturally into a number of main sectors. The **Central** area, south and east of the main railway station, is focused on the pedestrianized zone around the Lijnbaan and Van Oldenbarnevelt-straat. This is where the city goes out to shop—all the major department stores and many exclusive boutiques are located here. Along the river are three old harbors, **Delf-shaven, Oude Haven,** and **Leuvehaven,** although there is little similarity

between them. Charming Delfshaven is so narrow it looks like a canal, and is lined with gabled houses dating back centuries, creating a classic Dutch scene. The Oude Haven, by contrast, is surrounded by modern buildings, some of which, like the Blaak Rail Station and Kijk-Kubus, are among Rotterdam's most-iconic buildings. To the south of the river, across the Erasmus Bridge, the **Kop van Zuid** and **Entrepot** districts are where famous architects such as Sir Norman Foster and Renzo Piano have been given free rein to design housing projects, theaters, and pub-lic buildings to complete the area's transformation into a modern and luxurious commercial and residential district. **Museumpark** is the cul-tural heart of the city, and home to four museums and bordered by a Sculpture Terrace. Because these different areas are fairly spread out, to get between them you may want to make use of the efficient public transport network (taxis are expensive). Buses and trams fan out across the city above ground, while two underground metro lines—one north-south, one east-west—offer an even faster way of getting about. To use the network you'll need an **OV-chipkaart** (public transport chip card)—a new electronic payment system that's being tested in Rotterdam before being rolled out nationally in 2009 *(see Transport Essentials at the end of this chapter)*.

TO & FROM

Direct trains leave Amsterdam Centraal Station for Rotterdam as often as six times an hour throughout the day, and hourly through the night—the journey time is around one hour. If driving, take the A10, A4, and A13 freeways south from Amsterdam. The drive will take about one hour, depending on traffic.

EXPLORING

MAIN ATTRACTIONS

The Nieuwe Maas River has flowed through Rotterdam for 700 years, dividing the city in two, and acting as the city's lifeline. A continual procession of some 30,000 oceangoing ships and some 130,000 river barges passes annually through Rotterdam to and from the North Sea. A top option for visitors to the city is boat tours around the harbor, ranging from a hydrofoil called the *Flying Dutchman* to the very popular **Spido boat tours** (✉ *Willemsplein 85* ☎*010/275–9988*); a variety of water taxis and water buses also operate in the Waterstad (the docks and harbors along the banks of the river). There is also a water-bus link between Rotterdam and Dordrecht, which stops at several places along the way, including Alblasserdam, home of the famous Kinderdijk windmills.

★ ⑲ **Delfshaven.** The last remaining nook of old Rotterdam is both an open-air museum with rows of gabled houses lining the historic waterfront, and an area full of trendy galleries, cafés, and restaurants. Walk along the Voorhaven, Achterhaven, and neighboring Piet Heynplein and marvel at the many historic buildings; most of the port area has been reconstructed to appear just as it was when originally built. For historic sights in the environs, check out the working mill of **Korenmolen de Distilleerketel** (open Wednesday and Saturday only), the fascinating **Museum de Dubbelde Palmboom** on Rotterdam city history, and the **Oudekerk/Pilgrimvaders Kerk.** Tram No. 4 connects Delfshaven with the rest of the city, as does the nearby Delfshaven metro station. ✉*Achterhaven and Voorhaven, Delfshaven.*

⑰ **Euromast.** For a bird's-eye view of the contrast between Delfshaven and the majority of the city, as well as a spectacular panorama of city and harbor, visit the 600-foot-high Euromast. Designed by Maaskant in 1960, it was the Netherland's tallest building for many years; when a new medical facility was built for the Erasmus University, an additional 25 feet were added to the tower in six days, restoring it to its premier position. On a clear day, you can just about see the coast. The tower not only offers great vistas, but also packs in a number of other attractions. The **Euroscoop** is a rotating panoramic elevator that carries you another 300 feet from the observation deck up to the top of the mast. For the thrill-seekers among us, skip the elevator and rappel down from the roof (make reservations via the Web at ⊕ *www.abseilen.nl*). The park at the base of the Euromast is where many Rotterdammers spend their time when the weather is good. ✉*Parkhaven 20, Delfshaven* ☎*010/436–4811* ⊕*www.euromast.com* 🎫*€8.30, rappel €42.50* ⏲*Apr.–Sept., daily 9:30* AM*–11* PM*; Oct.–Mar., daily 10* AM*–11* PM.

⑬ **Kunsthal.** This "art house" sits at one end of the visitor-friendly museum quarter and hosts major temporary exhibitions. There is no permanent collection, other than the massive, multistory boxlike center itself, designed by architect-prophet Rem Koolhaas. Opinions about the building are sharply divided: some say the design bridging the gap between the Museumpark and the dike is a clever spatial creation; others consider it an ugly mix of facades (part glass, part brick, and part corrugated iron) that has led to rusted iron, stained concrete, and cracks in the central walkway. The biggest complaint is the lack of elevator, compounded by the hazards of the central ramp, whose steep angle makes this a potential ski slope for wheelchair users. Fortunately, the eclectic exhibitions, usually three or four at any one time, are always fascinating, regardless of the setting. ✉ *Westzeedijk 341, Museumpark* ☎*010/440–0301* ⊕*www.kunsthal.nl* 🎫*€8.50* ⏲*Tues.– Sat. 10–5, Sun. 11–5.*

🐤 ★ ❺ **Maritiem Museum Rotterdam.** A sea lover's delight, the Maritime Museum is Rotterdam's noted nautical collection. Appropriately perched at the head of the Leuvehaven harbor, it was founded by Prince Hendrik in 1874. Set against the background of modern and historical maritime objects, the seafaring ways of old Rotterdammers make more sense. Star attraction of the ground floor is a large model of the Europoort, which shows how the Rotterdam area has developed over the centuries into the major seaport of today. The upper floors are mainly given over to rotating exhibitions on seafaring themes. Children have half a floor dedicated to them, called "Professor Plons" (Professor Plunge), where museum staff are on hand to help with looking through a real periscope, donning a hard hat and taking to the driving seat of a scaled-down crane, and engaging in many other activities dealing with the themes of water and ships. Kids will also love the museum's prize exhibit, the warship *De Buffel,* moored in the harbor outside, dating back to 1868. The ship has been perfectly restored and is fitted out sumptuously, as can be seen in the mahogany-deck captain's cabin. ✉*Leuvehaven 1, Witte de With* ☎*010/413–2680* ⊕*www.maritiemmuseum.nl* 🎫*€5* ⏱*July and Aug., Mon.–Sat. 10–5, Sun. 11–5; Sept.– June, Tues.–Sat. 10–5, Sun. 11–5.*

❾ **Museum Boijmans van Beuningen.** Rotterdam's finest shrine to art, with
Fodor'sChoice treasures ranging from Pieter Bruegel the Elder's 16th-century *Tower*
★ *of Babel* to Mondriaan's extraordinary *Composition in Yellow and Blue,* this museum ranks among the greatest art galleries in Europe. The top attraction here is the collection of Old Masters, which covers West European art from the 14th to the 19th century. In particular 15th to 17th century Dutch and Flemish art are well represented, including painters such as Van Eyck, Rubens, Hieronymous Bosch, and Rembrandt. The modern art section runs the gamut from Monet to Warhol and beyond, picking up Kandinsky, Magritte, and Dalí in between. In the Decorative Art and Design collection, both precious ornamental objects and everyday utensils dating from medieval times are displayed. In the museum café, note the fantastic collection of chairs, each by a different designer. Nearby, more artworks embellish the museum gardens. ✉*Museumpark 18–20, Museumpark* ☎*010/441–9400* ⊕*www. boijmans.nl* 🎫*€9* ⏱*Tues.–Sat. 10–5, Sun. 11–5.*

⓴ **Museum de Dubbelde Palmboom** *(Double Palm Tree Museum).* Devoted to the history of Rotterdam and its role as an international nexus, this museum traces the city's history from prehistoric times to the current day. The focus is on how exotic wares imported by the East India Company affected the city. The building itself is redolent of history: not only do its heavy beams and brick floors waft you back to yesteryear, but there even seems to be a faint smell of grains, recalling its many years spent as a warehouse. Ask for the informative guide in English, as all labeling is in Dutch. The first floor has some fascinating archaeological finds: one of the spouted ancient jugs has been traced to a town near Cologne, providing proof of trading contacts with the region, as traveling merchants were apparently very active in trading ceramics. ✉*Voorhaven 12, Delfshaven* ☎*010/476–1533* ⊕*www.dedubbelde-*

palmboom.nl ✉️€3, *ticket also valid for a same-day visit to the Schie-landshuis* ⊙*Tues.–Sun. 11–5.*

🔔 ⑫ **Natuurmuseum** *(Natural History Museum).* Located in a historic villa-like structure together with an enormous glass wing (echoing the hip Kunsthal next door), the Natural History Museum lures its visitors with glimpses of the exhibits within, including skeletons of creatures you'll be hard put to identify. As soon as you enter the foyer, you are face-to-face with a mounted scary-hairy gorilla. It doesn't stop there: in one room the skeleton of a giraffe stretches as far up as you can crane your own neck. Continue on to be met by a tiger and arching elephant tusks. There is an "ironic" re-creation of a trophy hunter's display, with turtles mounted on a wall, arranged according to size. In another area, a dinner table is set, with the skulls of a human, a cow, an anteater, a lion, a zebra, and a pig as guests. Before each of them is a plate laden with their respective dining preferences. Children, meanwhile, are drawn to the 40-foot-long skeleton of a sperm whale. ✉️*Westzeedijk 345, Museumpark* ☎010/436–4222 ⊕*www.nmr.nl* ✉️€4 ⊙*Tues.–Sat. 10–5, Sun. 11–5.*

❼ **Nederlands Architectuurinstituut.** Fittingly, for a city of exciting modern architecture, Rotterdam is the home of the **NAi**, or the Netherlands Architecture Institute. The striking glass-and-metal building—designed by Rotterdam local Joe Conen in 1993—hosts temporary displays on architecture and interior design in seven exhibition spaces, giving a holistic interpretation of the history and development of architecture, especially the urban design and spatial planning of Rotterdam. Outside, the gallery under the archive section is illuminated at night. ✉️*Museumpark 25, Museumpark* ☎010/440–1200 ⊕*www.nai.nl* ✉️€8 ⊙*Tues.–Sat. 10–5, Sun. 11–5.*

㉑ **Oudekerk/Pilgrimvaders Kerk** *(Pilgrim Fathers' Church).* On July 22, 1620, 16 men, 11 women, and 19 children sailed from Delfshaven on the *Speedwell.* Their final destination was America, where they helped found the Plymouth Colony in Massachusetts, New England. Puritan Protestants fleeing England for religious freedom usually went to Amsterdam, but this group, which arrived in 1608, decided to live in Leiden, then 10 years later opted to travel on to the New World by leaving from Rotterdam. On July 20, 1620, they left Leiden by boat, and via Delft they reached Delfshaven, where they spent their last night in Holland. After a sermon from their vicar, John Robinson, in what has since become this church, they boarded the *Speedwell,* sailing to Southampton, England, then left on the *Mayflower* on September 5, reaching Cape Cod 60 days later.

The church was built in 1417 as the Chapel of Sint Anthonius, then extended and restyled in the Late Gothic period. However, in 1761 the ceilings were raised, and the current style dates back to this Regency revamp, when an ornate wooden clock tower was also added. Next to the choir is a vestry from 1819, where you can find a memorial plaque to the Pilgrim Fathers on the wall. The bell tower has a tiny balcony.

The church is now owned by the Trust for Old Dutch Churches. ⊠ *Aelbrechtskolk 16, Delfshaven* ☎ *010/482–3041* ⊙ *Sat. 1–4.*

★ ❹ **Schielandshuis.** Staunchly defending its position against the high-rise Robeco Tower and the giant Hollandse Banke Unie surrounding it, this palatial 17th-century mansion is almost engulfed by the modern city. Happily, it holds its own as a part of Rotterdam's historical museum (the other half is the Dubbelde Palmboom in Delfshaven). Built between 1662 and 1665 in Dutch Neoclassical style by the Schieland family, it burned down in 1864, but the facade survived, and the interior was carefully restored. Inside are Baroque- and Rococo-style rooms reconstructed from houses in the area, clothing from the 18th century to the present day, and the famous collection of maps, the Atlas von Stolk. Because of the frailty of the paper, only a tiny selection of vintage maps is on display at any one time, usually under a specific theme. The museum's café is in a lovely garden. ⊠ *Korte Hoogstraat 31, Centrum* ☎ *010/217–6767* ⊕ *www.historischmuseumrotterdam.nl* ⊠ *€3, ticket also valid for a same-day visit to the Dubbelde Palmboom Museum* ⊙ *Tues.–Fri. 10–5, weekends 11–5.*

⟳ ⓮ **Wereld Museum.** On a corner of rustic Veerhaven, surrounded by old sailing boats moored alongside modern yachts, this museum is devoted to non-Western cultures, many of which have had a sizable influence on Rotterdam. One of the permanent exhibitions is "Rotterdammers," which explores how the city developed in the 20th century with the arrival of immigrants from around the world. Another attraction is wonderful for children: the **Hotel "Het Reispaleis"** ("The Travel Palace" Hotel), a collection of "hotel" rooms of travelers from different countries that kids can explore either with museum staff or with parents, learning about other cultures as they visit the room of a "guest" in the "hotel" (who is supposedly out in town): knickknacks spell out the occupant's culture, job, and religion (one, for instance, is for a Moroccan photographer), and children are encouraged to try on clothes, shoes, and hats, and look in bedside tables to see what journals the guest has been reading. Video displays allow the guest to talk about his or her job, home, and friends (in pictures around the room). Result: children explore someone else's culture, seeing what is important to that person, in a "real" context. ⊠ *Willemskade 25, Scheepvaartkwartier* ☎ *010/270–7172* ⊕ *www.wereldmuseum.nl* ⊠ *€6* ⊙ *Tues.–Sun. 10–5.*

OFF THE BEATEN PATH
FodorsChoice
★
⟳

If you want to see the dike to end all dikes, drive South along the coast to see the Delta works and visit **Waterland Neeltje Jans.** This impressive museum offers a firsthand tour of the most important achievement of Dutch hydraulic engineering—the Delta Works, a massive dam and flood barrier that closed up the sea arms in response to the flood disaster of 1953. There are also exhibits documenting the 2,000-year history of the Dutch people's struggle with the sea. Films and slide shows, working scale models, and displays of materials give a comprehensive overview of dikes, dams, and underwater supports. The visit includes a boat trip in good weather. There is also a water playground with all kinds of interesting aquatic-based contraptions, a storm surge barrier one can stand on, a new futuristic-style whale pavilion, and even a hurricane simulator. Some attractions are closed in winter. ⊠ *Eiland Neeltje Jans, Burgh-Haamstede* ☎ *0111/652–702* ⊕ *www.neeltjejans.nl* ⬚ *€9.50 Apr.–Oct., €15 Nov.–Mar.* ☉ *Apr.–Oct., daily 10–5:30; Nov. –Mar., Wed. –Sun. 10–5*

IF YOU HAVE TIME

8 Chabot Museum. This museum displays the private art collection of leading Dutch expressionist painter and sculptor Henk Chabot, who was active between the two world wars, depicting peasants, market gardeners, and, later, refugees and prisoners. ⊠ *Museumpark 11, Museumpark* ☎ *010/436–3713* ⊕ *www.chabotmuseum.nl* ⬚ *€5* ☉ *Tues.–Fri. 11–4:30, Sat. 11–5, Sun. noon–5.*

18 Korenmolen de Distilleerketel. Set in the historic district of Delfshaven, this mill is the only working flour mill in the city. Formerly employed to grind malt to make jenever, the dusty-hair miller now mills grain for specific bakeries in the city, which means it is closed most of the week. ⊠ *Voorhaven 210, Delfshaven* ☎ *010/477–9181* ⬚ *€2* ☉ *Wed. 11–5 and Sat. 10–4.*

16 Nederlands Fotomuseum. Although Holland's Photography Museum doesn't have any permanent exhibits, the changing exhibitions are well worth looking at, and there is an extensive library open during the week for reference. The museum is now housed in the **Las Palmas** building in the Kop van Zuid neighborhood. ⊠ *Wilhelminakade 332, Kop van Zuid* ☎ *010/203–0405* ⊕ *www.nederlandsfotomuseum.nl* ⬚ *€6* ☉ *Tues.–Fri. 10–5, weekends 11–5.*

11 Museumpark. A project masterminded by Rem Koolhaas's Office for Metropolitan Architecture (OMA) in collaboration with French architect Yves Brunier, this modern urban garden is made up of different zones, extending from the Museum Boijmans van Beuningen to the Kunsthal. The idea is that each section is screened off from the last and creates a different impression—but each block of the garden isn't as radically different as this theory builds it up to be. The one part you should linger over is just before the bridge, where there is a memorial to city engineer G. J. de Jongh. Various artists had a hand in this, with Henk Chabot responsible for the inscription on the wall and Jaap Gidding designing the beautiful mosaic at the base of the monument, which represents Rotterdam and its surroundings at the end of the 1920s. Sculptor R. Bolle designed the bronze railings, with harbor and street scenes from the period when De Jongh was working in Rotterdam. ⊠ *Museumpark to the north, Westersingel to the east, Westzeedijk to the south, and bounded by a canal on the west side, Museumpark.*

1 Nationaal Oonderwijsmuseum *(National Education Museum).* In a 1920s classroom you can take a seat at an old desk and try your hand at writing with an ink-dip pen or using chalk on a slate, making for a charming journey back to the good old days. ⊠ *Nieuwemarkt 1a, Meent* ☎ *010/404–5425* ⊕ *www.onderwijsmuseum.nl* ⬚ *€4* ☉ *Tues.–Sat. 10–5, Sun. 1–5.*

6 Sculpture Terrace. Set along the Westersingel, this outdoor venue exhibits sculptures of the past 100 years, dotting the grassy bank of the canal and creating a sculpture garden. Highlights here include Rodin's headless *L'homme qui marche* (Walking Man), Henri Laurens's *La Grande Musicienne* (The Great Musician), and Umberto Mastroianni's *Gli Amanti* (The Lovers), a fascinating jumble of triangular-shape points. ⊠ *Museumpark.*

2 Sint Laurenskerk. Built between 1449 and 1525, this church is juxtaposed against its modern surroundings. Of the three organs contained inside, the main organ ranks as one of Europe's largest. Hendrick de Keyser's statue of Erasmus in the square was buried in the gardens of the Museum Boijmans van Beuningen during the war and miraculously survived. ⊠ *Grotekerkplein 27, Sint Laurenskwartier* ☎ *010/413–1494* ⊙ *Tues.–Sat. 10–4.*

3 Stadhuis *(City Hall).* At the top of the Coolsingel, this elegant 1920s building is the hallowed seat of the mayor of Rotterdam and is open for guided tours on weekdays. A bronze bust of the architect, Henri Evans, is in the central hall. With the neighboring post-office building, the two early-1920s buildings are the sole survivors of their era. ⊠ *Coolsingel 40, Centrum* ☎ *0800/1545 (toll-free).*

10 TENT Centrum Beeldende Kunst. The Rotterdam Center for Visual Arts is usually simply called TENT, an apt acronym for showcasing modern art by local artists of the last decade. Shows range from edgy, current event type of stuff to tranquil designs for city gardens. The ground floor is devoted to up-and-coming artists, and the upper floor exhibits established artists' work. Artists also have a workplace to experiment with new projects. All exhibitions are temporary, lasting a maximum of three months, so call ahead to find out about the current show. Every first and third Thursday of the month there is an exciting free evening program. ⊠ *Witte de Withstraat 50, Witte de With* ☎ *010/413–5498* ⊕ *www.tentplaza.nl* ☞ *€3* ⊙ *Tues.–Sun. 11–6.*

15 Toren op Zuid. An office complex by celebrated modern architect Renzo Piano, this structure houses the head offices of KPN Telecom. Its eye-catching billboard facade glitters with 1,000-odd green lamps flashing on and off, creating images provided by the city of Rotterdam, in addition to images provided by KPN and an art academy. The facade fronting the Erasmus Bridge leans forward by 6 degrees, which is the same as the angle of the bridge's pylon. It is also said that Piano could have been making a humorous reference to his homeland, as the Tower of Pisa leans at the same angle. ⊠ *Wilhelminakade 123, Kop van Zuid.*

WHERE TO EAT

★ $$$$ ✕ **Parkheuvel.** Overlooking the Maas, this posh restaurant, run by chef-owner Cees Helder, is said to be popular among the harbor barons, who can oversee their dockside territory from the bay windows of this tastefully modern, semicircular building. Tables are covered with cream-color linens and wood-frame chairs are elegantly upholstered.

The service here is as effortlessly attentive as you would expect from one of Holland's top three restaurants. Luxuries such as truffles are added to the freshest ingredients, with the day's menu dictated by the availability of the best produce at that morning's markets. Kudos and salaams are offered up by diners to many of the chef's specialties, including the grilled turbot with an anchovy mousse and crispy potatoes. ✉*Heuvellaan 21, Centrum* ☎*010/436–0530* ⌦*Reservations essential* ▤*AE, DC, MC, V* ⊘*Closed Sun. No lunch Sat.*

$$$–$$$$ ✗**Brancatelli.** Around the windblown environs of the Erasmus Bridge you can find several eateries specializing in Mediterranean cuisine, Brancatelli being the best. "Kitsch" is the word that springs to mind when you spot the large glass animals on every table; add a preprogrammed player piano, and you are going to either laugh or cringe. If you feel a smile tickling, then the (very) pink table settings won't be too much, either. The friendly staff really play on being Italian, making, as they say, "a nice evening" of it, especially for groups. A typical four- or five-course menu is usually fish-based. Even if the price pushes up your expectations, the presentation and sheer quality of the dishes justify the cost. ✉*Boompjes 264, Centrum* ☎*010/411–4151* ⌦*Reservations essential* ▤*AE, DC, MC, V* ⊘*No lunch weekends. Closed mid-Jul.–mid-Aug.*

$$$–$$$$ ✗**De Engel.** The international kitchen of this former town house has created a loyal following, who flock here for excellent food, a sash-window view over the Westersingel, and an intimate setting (tables are very close together). The very friendly staff are more than helpful with their recommendations, as are your next-table neighbors. For a special taste treat, try the truffle soup, or the skate wing with garlic sauce. Note that this is not the same establishment as Grand Café Engels, on the Stationsplein, which is much more mainstream. ✉*Eendrachtsweg 19, Centrum* ☎*010/413–8256* ⌦*Reservations essential* ▤*AE, MC, V* ⊘*Closed Sun. No lunch Sat.*

★ $$$ ✗**Kip.** Dark wooden floors, unobtrusive lighting, and a big fireplace make Kip's traditional interior warm and cozy. As befits the restaurant's name (which means chicken), the chicken breast (from a special Dutch breed called *Hollandse blauwhoender*) with truffles is the most popular dish, but the kitchen offers a whole lot more. There's always a daily-changing fish option, such as cod with saffron and fennel sauce, and plenty of meatier fare, such as veal in wild mushroom sauce. The menu must work, because this spot is always packed. In summer, a leafy garden at the back provides welcome respite from the bustle of the big city. ✉*Van Vollenhovenstraat 25, Scheepvaartkwartier* ☎*010/436–9923* ⌦*Reservations essential* ▤*AE, DC, MC, V* ⊘*No lunch.*

$$–$$$ ✗**Zeezout.** On the corner of an elegant, riverfront terrace, around the corner from the venerable Veerhaven moored with old sailing ships, the charming "Sea Salt" restaurant mirrors the freshness of its sea-based menu in crisp linen tablecloths and its spotlessly clean open kitchen, where watching the staff work whets your appetite. A large fish mosaic on the wall looks out across the river to the floodlighted Erasmus Bridge; a window awning adds to the romance of the view. Try the turbot accompanied by thyme-and-rosemary-flavored polenta and

snow peas. ⊠ *Westerkade 11b, Scheepvaartkwartier* ☎010/436–5049 ⌂*Reservations essential* ⊟*AE, DC, MC, V* ⊘*Closed Sun. and Mon. No lunch Sat.*

$–$$$ ✕**Asian Glories.** Reputed to be the city's best Cantonese restaurant, Asian Glories serves lunches, dinners, and Sunday brunches in a tasteful modern Asian interior or outdoors on its terrace. It's hard to choose what is most delicious; their dim sum, fresh oysters, mussels in black bean sauce, and Peking Duck consistently get raves from fussy eaters. Leave room for an exotic dessert such as ice cream with rice and red bean sauce. ⊠*Leeuwenstraat 15, Centrum* ☎010/411–7107 ⊟*AE, DC, MC, V* ⊘*Closed Wed.*

$–$$$ ✕**Loos.** In the grand style of Rotterdam's cafés, Loos has a range of international magazines and newspapers on its reading racks, and in a fun gesture, six clocks with different time zones decorate one wall. You enter and see what looks like a forest of tables, but this trompe l'oeil effect is largely caused by a wall-size mirror. As for the food, some dishes are excellent, including such delights as roasted-pepper-and-smoked-apple soup with aniseed cream; monkfish with truffle-butter sauce; and steak with Armagnac-soaked raisins and a duck-liver-and-truffle sauce. If you want to eat less luxuriously, try the bar menu. ⊠*Westplein 1, Scheepvaartkwartier* ☎010/411–7723 ⊟*AE, MC, V* ⊘*No lunch weekends.*

$$ ✕**Bla Bla.** Just around the corner from the historic heart of Delfshaven, this restaurant is always lively and frequently crowded. There is always a choice of four main vegetarian dishes, inspired by cuisines from around the world, and the menu changes often. Make sure you're having dinner on the early side to get the freshest ingredients—and a seat. ⊠*Piet Heynsplein 35, Delfshaven* ☎010/477–4448 ⊟*V* ⊘*Closed Mon. and Tues. No lunch.*

$–$$ ✕**Café Floor.** Adjacent to the Stadsschouwburg (Municipal Theater), Café Floor doesn't look too inviting from the outside, but the interior is modern, light, and airy; the staff are friendly; and the kitchen produces excellent food. Try the lamb brochette so tender the meat practically dissolves on your tongue. The delicious passion-fruit cheesecake comes from Café Dudok's kitchen. The beautiful garden at the back, and accompanying birdsong from the local fauna, make this a restful stop. This place is very popular with local and international regulars, so be prepared to be patient if you go late-ish on a Saturday. ⊠*Schouwburgplein 28, Centrum* ☎010/404–5288 ⊟*AE, MC, V.*

★ ¢–$$ ✕**Café Dudok.** Lofty ceilings, a cavernous former warehouse, long reading tables stacked with international magazines and papers—little wonder this place attracts an artsy crowd. At its most mellow, this spot is perfect for a lazy afternoon treat of delicious homemade pastries, but you can come here for breakfast, lunch, high tea, dinner, or even a snack after midnight. They also offer a small selection for vegetarians. The brasserie, on a mezzanine above the open kitchen at the back, looks out over the Rotte River. Since it's terribly crowded at times, you should get here unfashionably early to avoid disappointment—there's nowhere else like it in Rotterdam. ⊠*Meent 88, Centrum* ☎010/433–3102 ⊟*AE, DC, MC, V.*

¢–$$ ✕**Dewi Sri.** This restaurant has rijsttafel (rice table) to dream about, with creative takes on traditional Indonesian dishes. Rice table is like Indonesian smorgasbord with samplings from the menu. Choose from a multitude of tantalizing options from Indonesian, Javanese, and Sumatran menus. Some diners may find the mock wood carvings a little heavy, given the subtle flavors of the food being served. The large restaurant upstairs could feel quite empty midweek, but the staff are incredibly polite, appearing discreetly at your table just as soon as you feel the need to ask for something. All in all, this probably has the best Indonesian food in Rotterdam, so don't let the decor faze you. If you can't find space in the Dewi Sri, it shares its premises with the adjacent Warisan restaurant, which serves similarly priced and equally mouthwatering Thai food. ⊠ *Westerkade 20–21, Scheepvaartkwartier* ☎*010/436–0263* ⊟*AE, DC, MC, V* ⊘*No lunch weekends Sept.–June.*

$ ✕**Rotown.** This arts center venue is more celebrated for its funky bar than for its restaurant proper. A buzz fills the dining area, a spillover from the crowd up front. The menu is quite extensive, but the staff doesn't write down your order, so expect an informal, slapdash approach (if you're very unlucky, courses could even come in the wrong order, and a main course, brought out too early, will be reheated and returned later). But if you like a stylish, party-hearty atmosphere (bands often play at the bar), this could be worth it. ⊠*Nieuwe Binnenweg 17–19, Centrum* ☎*010/436–2669* ⊟*AE, DC, MC, V for dinner only.*

¢ ✕**Le Marché.** A market stall in the V&D department store, Le Marché has a nice luncheon option: a tempting variety of reasonably priced sandwiches. On the top floor the self-serve café La Place transforms the roof into a sunny terrace in summer. ⊠*Hoogstraat 185, Centrum* ☎*0900/235–8363* ⊟*No credit cards* ⊘*Closed Sun.*

WHERE TO STAY

★ $$$$ ☷ **The Westin.** The only five-star hotel in the city is on the first 14 floors of the Millennium tower, smack opposite Centraal Station. Although this is primarily a business hotel, the slick-yet-friendly service of this landmark draws celebrity guests, such as pop and rock stars Robbie Williams and Kylie Minogue. With regal purple corridors, lined with copies of masterpieces from Vermeer to Van Gogh, and bright spacious rooms—each fitted out with a luxuriously huge bed, topped with a 10-layer mattress and sumptuous snowy-white linen—it's hard not to feel like a member of the glitterati yourself. All the lavish bathrooms have tubs. The panorama across town makes the extra rates for rooms from the fourth floor up more than worthwhile, with many looking out over the Erasmus Bridge and the skyline (both dramatically floodlighted after dark). In the Lighthouse restaurant, chef Fred Smits serves superb nouvelle cuisine. Try the Irish Black Angus beefsteak served with tiger prawns or the fried brill fish fillet with anchovy risotto and smoked emperor salmon, accompanied by crispy ham and salsify. In keeping with the spirit of Rotterdam, the decor has a maritime theme; even the bar is in the form of a ship's prow. Fans adore the four-course after-

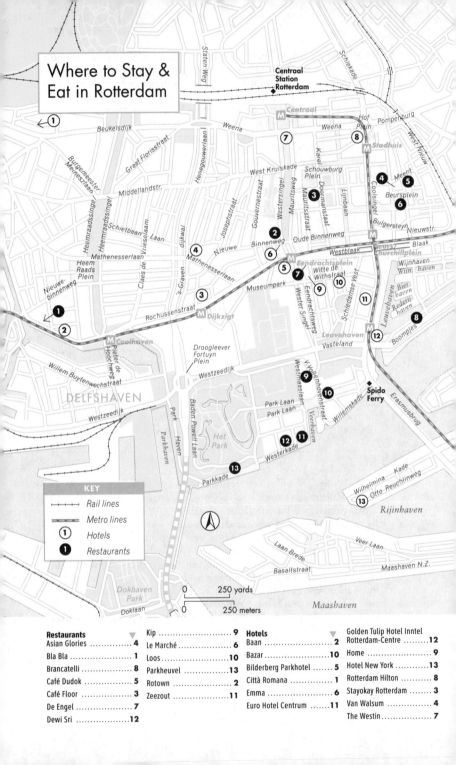

Where to Stay & Eat in Rotterdam

KEY

- ┼─┼─┼ Rail lines
- ━━━━ Metro lines
- ① Hotels
- ● Restaurants

0 —— 250 yards
0 —— 250 meters

noon high tea. There's a glass-covered skywalk to De Doelen concert and business center on the Stadsschouwburgplein, so on concert nights make the most of the Lighthouse's special dining offers to see just how good the chef really is. ⊠ *Weena 686, 3012 CN, Centrum* ☎*010/430–2000, 00800/325–95959 (toll-free within Holland)* 🖷*010/430–2001* ⊕*www.westin.nl* ⊃*224 rooms, 7 suites* ⚿*In-room: safe, refrigerator, dial-up. In-hotel: restaurant, bar, gym, laundry service, some pets allowed, Wi-Fi* ⊟*AE, DC, MC, V.*

$$$–$$$$ ⊞**Rotterdam Hilton.** During the International Film Festival at the end of January, this hotel often hosts some of the notable participants, thanks in part to its top facilities, a number of suites, meeting rooms, and luxury appointments and amenities. A major plus is its location, right in the middle of downtown. Since it tends to appeal to visitors who want a name they can rely on, it can get filled with tour groups. ⊠ *Weena 10, 3012 CM, Centrum* ☎*010/710–8000* 🖷*010/710–8080* ⊕*www.rotterdam.hilton.com* ⊃*246 rooms, 8 suites* ⚿*In-room: refrigerator, Wi-Fi. In-hotel: bar, gym, laundry service, some pets allowed* ⊟*AE, DC, MC, V.*

$$–$$$ ⊞**Bilderberg Parkhotel.** Although this hotel welcomes you with a town-house facade dramatically yoked to a metallic skyscraper, the interior bears few reminders of its 80-year history. Rooms have been renovated in uncluttered, modern styles, while those at the back overlook a quiet garden. The Bilderberg also offers a wide spectrum of top-brass services. The Restaurant 70 serves an interesting fusion of nouveau global and traditional cuisine in the classical surroundings of the old wing of the hotel. Just a few minutes' walk from the Museum Boijmans van Beuningen, this spot is centrally located. Another plus is the staff, which offers the sort of apparently effortless, unobtrusive attention to your every need that makes a stay here very pleasant. ⊠ *Westersingel 70, 3015 LB, Centrum* ☎*010/436–3611, 0800/024–5245 (within Holland), 800/641–0300 (from the U.S.)* 🖷*010/436–4212* ⊕*www.parkhotelrotterdam.nl* ⊃*186 rooms* ⚿*In-room: no a/c (some), refrigerator, Wi-Fi. In-hotel: restaurant, bar, gym, laundry service, some pets allowed* ⊟*AE, DC, MC, V.*

★ **$–$$$** ⊞**Hotel New York.** Rotterdam is very much a commercial harbor city, with hotels aimed primarily at the business trade; the Hotel New York, a converted shipping office from the first part of the 20th century, is a particularly atmospheric exception. The twin towers rising over the water of the Nieuwe Maas, across from the city center, were known to Rotterdammers for decades as the headquarters of the Holland-America Line, before being renovated and opened as a hotel. Rooms are individually decorated, with high ceilings contrasting with the modern decor, so it's not just the view that boosts the price. The enormous restaurant (which seats 400) somehow maintains an intimate café atmosphere, although those in the know delight in the afternoon tea served here but don't stay for dinner. Other amenities include an oyster bar, tea salon, and water taxi connecting the Kop van Zuid with the city center (€2.70 per person, one way). ⊠*Koninginnenhoofd 1, 3072 AD, Kop van Zuid* ☎*010/439–0500* 🖷*010/484–2701* ⊕*www.hotelnewyork.*

nl ↩*71 rooms, 1 penthouse apartment* ⚹*In-room: no a/c, Wi-Fi. In-hotel: restaurant, room service* ☰*AE, DC, MC, V.*

$–$$ ▧ **Emma.** At this hotel on social, busy Nieuwe Binnenweg, plenty of shops and nightspots are conveniently close; the nearest sidewalk café is right opposite the hotel. This is the third generation of the Orsini family seeing to the comfort of the hotel's guests. Furnishings are modern, and there is an elevator. Staffed by a friendly and approachable team, this place offers special rates for groups and those staying longer. ✉*Nieuwe Binnenweg 6, 3015 BA, Centrum* ☎*010/436–5533* 📠*010/436–7658* ⊕*www.hotelemma.nl* ↩*24 rooms* ⚹*In-room: no a/c, refrigerator, dial-up. In-hotel: bar, some pets allowed, parking (fee)* ☰*AE, DC, MC, V* ⦿|*CP.*

$–$$ ▧ **Golden Tulip Hotel Inntel Rotterdam-Centre.** The majority of the rooms in this modern high-rise, built at the opening to the Leuvehaven inner harbor, have water views. All guest rooms are simply but tastefully decorated, wearing a designer-look edge. The conservatory-style breakfast room overlooks a terrace for true relaxation. Hotel guests can use two neighboring restaurants, then add dinner to the hotel bill. The staff are incredibly friendly and make all efforts to make your stay pleasant. The top-floor restaurant, Le Papillon, has long-reaching views across the Maas, as do the rooftop health club and swimming pool. ✉*Leuvehaven 80, 3011 EA, Centrum* ☎*010/413–4139* 📠*010/413–3222* ⊕*www.goldentuliprotterdamcentre.com* ↩*263 rooms* ⚹*In-room: no a/c, refrigerator, Wi-Fi. In-hotel: restaurant, pool, gym* ☰*AE, DC, MC, V.*

$ ▧ **Baan.** This is a comfortable family-run hotel overlooking the Coolhaven harbor, and only five minutes from the waterside at Delfshaven. After a renovation in 2004, the bright rooms have tasteful furnishings and accessories in blue and yellow pastel shades. ✉*Rochussenstraat 345, 3023 DH, Centrum* ☎*010/477–0555* 📠*010/476–9450* ⊕*www.hotelbaan.nl* ↩*14 rooms* ⚹*In-room: no a/c* ☰*AE, MC, V* ⦿|*CP.*

★ $ ▧ **Bazar.** The well-traveled owner has created havens from his wanderings, with hot, deep colors evoking Turkey and Morocco throughout the individually styled rooms on the second floor, and motifs conjuring up Africa and South America on the third and fourth floors respectively. Although there is an elevator, it goes only to the third floor. The restaurant of the same name on the ground floor has, needless to say, a very international menu. The location on the young, busy Witte de Withstraat draws a nicely "in" crowd to both hotel and restaurant. ✉*Witte de Withstraat 16, 3012 BP, Witte de With* ☎*010/206–5151* 📠*010/206–5159* ⊕*www.bazarrotterdam.nl* ↩*27 rooms* ⚹*In-room: no a/c, dial-up, minibar. In-hotel: restaurant, some pets allowed* ☰*AE, DC, MC, V* ⦿|*CP.*

$ ▧ **Euro Hotel Centrum.** Despite the business-like, anonymous name, this is a welcoming and comfortable modern hotel with lots of flowers and plants, so the overall feeling is spruce and well cared for. They have family rooms, in case you're traveling with children. This place is particularly handy for Museumpark and strolls along the Westersingel. Enjoy the buffet breakfast before setting out. ✉*Baan 14–20, 3011 CB, Centrum* ☎*010/214–1922* 📠*010/214–0187* ⊕*www.eurohotel-*

centrum.nl ⤵*53 rooms, 2 suites* ⚅*In-room: no a/c, dial-up. In-hotel: bar* ⊟*AE, MC, V* ⦿|*CP.*

$ 🖼 **Van Walsum.** On a residential boulevard within walking distance of the Museum Boijmans van Beuningen and major attractions, the Van Walsum is near the Euromast. The friendly and gregarious owner proudly restores and reequips his rooms, floor by floor, on a continuously rotating basis, with the always-modern decor of each floor determined by that year's best buys in furniture, carpeting, and bathroom tiles. There is a bar-lounge and a small restaurant that has a summer garden extension. ✉*Mathenesserlaan 199–201, 3014 HC, Centrum* ☎*010/436-3275* 🖷*010/436-4410* ⊕*www.hotelvanwalsum.nl* ⤵*29 rooms* ⚅*In-room: no a/c, Wi-Fi. In-hotel: restaurant, bar, public Internet, parking (fee)* ⊟*AE, DC, MC, V* ⦿|*CP.*

¢–$ 🖼 **Città Romana.** You generally don't think of resorts when you think of Rotterdam, but this vast place is considered a pleasant retreat set a half hour from the city center. More than 200 charming thatch-roof, gable-window cottages are stylishly furnished (although we could do without those mock-orange columns in the public areas). Located 10 minutes' drive from the North Sea and five minutes' walk from a local lake, Haringvliet, its two- and three-bedroom villas sleep four to six people, come fully furnished, and even have chairs and sun beds for the gardens. The living room is complete with open kitchen, and most villas have two bathrooms. ✉*Parkweg 1, 3220 AB, Hellevoetsluis* ☎*0181/334455* 🖷*0181/334433* ⊕*www.cittaromana.com* ⤵*263 villas* ⚅*In-room: no a/c. In-hotel: restaurant, pool, gym, parking (fee), no elevator* ⊟*MC, V.*

¢ 🖼 **Home.** On the liveliest street in town, five minutes from the Museumpark, this hotel is right in the middle of Rotterdam's best dining, shopping, and nightlife. When you're back at the hotel, incredibly helpful staff are on hand for recommendations and assistance, making this a pad you'll really want to come back to. The rate drops the longer you stay, by as much as 50% if you stay more than 30 days—and plenty of people do, as en-suite kitchenettes and sitting areas in each room make this a popular choice for longer stays. ✉*Witte de Withstraat 81a, 3012 BN, Witte de With* ☎*010/411–2121* 🖷*010/414–1690* ⊕*www.home-hotel.nl* ⤵*80 rooms* ⚅*In-room: no a/c, no phone, kitchen. In-hotel: no elevator* ⊟*AE, MC, V.*

¢ 🖼 **Stayokay Rotterdam.** If you're running on a budget, this modern hostel right in the middle of the city, between Delfshaven and the Museumpark, is just the ticket. Dorms are shared with three, five, or seven others, and you can use a fully-equipped kitchen. If you book way in advance, you might be lucky and get one of the double rooms, best for extra privacy, where you have your own en-suite facilities. ✉*Rochussenstraat 107–109, 3015 EH, Centrum* ☎*010/436–5763* 🖷*010/436–5569* ⊕*www.stayokay.com* ⤵*2 rooms for 2 people, 20 dorm rooms with shared baths* ⚅*In-room: no a/c, kitchen, no TV. In-hotel: bar, laundry facilities* ⊟*MC, V* ⦿|*CP.*

7

NIGHTLIFE & THE ARTS

THE ARTS

Rotterdam's arts calendar extends throughout the year. You can book tickets and find out what's on around town through the local tourist information office, the VVV. **VVV Rotterdam** (⊠*Coolsingel 5, 3011 AA, Centrum* ☎*010/271–0120* ⊕*www.rotterdam.nl*).

DANCE Rotterdam's resident modern dance company, **Scapino Ballet,** has the reputation of being one of the most formidably talented troupes in the country. It performs at **Rotterdamse Schouwburg** (⊠*Schouwburgplein 25, Centrum* ☎*010/411–8110* ⊕*www.scapinoballet.nl*).

FILM Partly because of the annual avant-garde **International Film Festival Rotterdam,** held in late January–early February, there is a lot of general interest in film in this city—as a result, you have many screens to choose from. The **Pathé** (⊠*Schouwburgplein 101, Centrum* ☎*0900/1458*) is the place to head for blockbusters. The **Theater Lantaren/Venster** (⊠*Gouvernestraat 133, Centrum* ☎*010/277–2266*) has an interesting program that shows art films in addition to hosting small-scale dance and theater performances. There's an open-air cinema at the Museumpark in September.

MUSIC Rotterdam's renowned concert orchestra is the excellent **Rotterdam Philharmonic Orchestra,** which performs at the large concert hall **De Doelen** (⊠*Schouwburgplein 50, Centrum* ☎*010/217–1717* ⊕*www.dedoelen.nl*). Attracting 400,000 visitors a year, the orchestra is known for its adventurous range of music—this troupe plays not just Beethoven but has also tackled the score from the film *Jurassic Park.*

THEATER The leading theater company of Rotterdam is **RO Theatergroup,** which performs at its own theater, **RO Theater** (⊠*William Boothlaan 8, Meent* ☎*010/404–6888*); the RO Theatergroup's subsidiary venue is the **Rotterdamse Schouwburg** (⊠*Schouwburgplein 25, Centrum* ☎*010/411–8110*). The majority of RO Theater's productions are in Dutch, as are, unfortunately, Onafhankelijk Toneel's, the city's other leader in the field. The **Luxor Theater** (⊠*Posthumalaan 1, Kop van Zuid* ☎*010/484–3333* ⊕*www.luxortheater.nl*) has 1,500 seats, and was specifically designed to cater to major stage musicals and other popular events. The theater, one of the Netherlands' largest, was designed by Australian architect Peter Wilson and has a marvelous view of Rotterdam's harbor and skyline. Performances are often in English.

Rotterdam's cultural climate facilitates the staging of productions from many semiprofessional groups, such as Turkish folk dance, classical Indian dance, and Capoeira Brazilian martial art troupes. The **Theater Zuidplein** (⊠*Zuidplein 60–64, Charlois* ☎*010/203–0203* ⊕*www.theaterzuidplein.nl*) is particularly known for its multicultural program.

NIGHTLIFE

To get your bearings and find your way around the party scene, look out for glossy party fliers in cafés, record stores, and clothes shops selling clubbing gear. The best nights tend to be Thursday to Saturday, 11 PM to 5 AM. Most venues have a clubbing floor, with DJs working the crowd and more ambient rooms for smoking or just plain relaxing. From hard-core techno—which has been popular here since the early '90s—to early-hour chill-out cafés, there is a wide gamut of night-time entertainment. West Kruiskade (also known as China Town) is the place to go if you want lively bars and music from around the world. Nieuwe Binnenweg and Witte de Withstraat have many busy late-night cafés and clubs. Oude Haven is particularly popular with students, and the Schouwburgplein is favored by visitors to the nearby theaters and cinemas. Stadshuisplein has a number of tacky discos and bars.

CAFÉS **Breakaway** (✉ *Karel Doormanstraat 1, near Centraal Station, Centrum* ☎ *010/233–0922*) is busy, with a young international crowd, and the nearest you'll get to a Dutch take on an American bar. **Café Rotterdam** (✉ *Wilhelminakade 699, Kop van Zuid* ☎ *010/290–8442*) is on the Wilhelminakade in the up-and-coming Kop van Zuid district, between the architectural designs of Sir Norman Foster and Renzo Piano. This former shipping terminal is now a massive meeting center, with a large café and fantastic view of the white Erasmus Bridge. **Cambrinus** (✉ *Blaak 4, Blaak* ☎ *010/414–6702*) is a cozy café opposite Blaak station, with a terrace on the Oude Haven. This is a popular mecca for beer lovers, with a dizzying 150 to choose from. **Locus Publicus** (✉ *Oostzeedijk 364, Blaak* ☎ *010/433–1761*) is another favorite with Belgian beer enthusiasts, with a menu that tops 200 varieties. Best of all, this one room brown café a few minutes' walk east from Blaak station has an open log fire in winter.

De Consul (✉ *Westersingel 28, Museumpark* ☎ *010/241–7534*) offers movies, as well as new age and pop music. With two floors, music drifts through the place from the bar upstairs. **De Schouw** (✉ *Witte de Withstraat 80, Witte de With* ☎ *010/412–4253*), an erstwhile brown café and former journalists' haunt, is now a trendy brown bar with a mix of artists and students. **Temptation Swingcafé** (✉ *Stadhuisplein 43, Meent* ☎ *010/414–6400*) attracts a late-night crowd with an intimate dance floor and music, including salsa, merengue, and rhumba, that gets everyone's feet moving. Temptation is closed Monday and Tuesday.

CLUBS In a former pedestrian tunnel, the **Blauwe Vis** (✉ *Weena-Zuid 33, Centrum* ☎ *010/213–4243*), or Blue Fish, is a seafood restaurant until the late hours, when the mood changes and the music really kicks in with soul, jazz, and funk. The long, narrow **Club Vibes** (✉ *Westersingel 50a, Museumpark* ☎ *010/436–6389*) has a friendly staff who chat at the bar with early punters—this is another place you shouldn't arrive at before 1:30 AM. Music is mostly 1970s and 1980s, with some more mainstream 1990s nights. Three floors and one of the best live music lineups make **Nighttown** (✉ *West Kruiskade 26–28, Centrum* ☎ *010/436–5283* ⊕ *www.nighttown.nl* 🎫 *€12–€20, €1.80 membership fee required*)the place to be in Rotterdam. If you can't get tickets for the big-band nights, make sure you catch the after-event party, definitely not to be missed. Music ranges from hip-hop to drum and bass, funk, techno, and pop. The adjoining café Fresh Up has very mellow music Thursday night, with R&B 'til late. **Now & Wow** (✉ *Graansilo, Maashaven ZZ 1, Rotterdam Zuid/Maashaven* ☎ *010/477–1074* 🎫 *€15*) is the wildest addition to the clubbing scene in Rotterdam. It's in a warehouse by metro station Maashaven. On Saturday night, a weekly MTC Party (Music Takes Control) pushes the envelope for excess. **Rotown** (⊠ *Nieuwe Binnenweg 19, Museumpark* ☎ *010/436–2669*), a high-style restaurant, has new-talent bands playing on Saturday night.

GAY & LESBIAN BARS

Club Vibes (⊠ *Westersingel 50a, Museumpark* ☎ *010/436–6389*) hosts gay-only nights on Sunday."Very much part of the late-night scene, **Gay Palace** (⊠ *Schiedamsesingel 139, Centrum* ☎ *010/414–1486*) attracts crowds of young gay and lesbian Rotterdammers to its large dance floor.

JAZZ

For three days in mid-July, jazz lovers from around the world descend on Rotterdam for the **North Sea Jazz Festival** (☎ *015/214–8393* ⊕ *www.northseajazz.nl*), which fills the Ahoy' arts complex with music. Around 180 artists perfom on 15 different stages in what is one of Europe's largest and most popular celebrations of jazz.

Dizzy (⊠ *'s-Gravendijkwal 127, 's-Gravendijkwal* ☎ *010/477–3014* ⊕ *www.dizzy.nl*) is *the* jazz café if you appreciate live performances. A big terrace out back hosts both Dutch and international musicians every Tuesday and Sunday. The café also serves good, reasonably priced food. Come early if you want a seat. Concerts and jamming sessions are free.

POP & ROCK

For mega-events, choose between the **Ahoy'**, which holds pop concerts and large-scale operas, and **De Kuip**, Rotterdam's major football stadium, which boasts of its Bob Dylan, Rolling Stones, and U2 concerts. Tickets for both venues often sell out quickly, but De Kuip has a better sound system. **Ahoy'** (⊠ *Ahoyweg 10, Zuidplein* ☎ *010/293–3300* ⊕ *www.ahoy.nl*) hosts major pop concerts for big names such as Kylie Minogue, Green Day, and Jamiroquai, but also hosts classical philharmonic orchestras, top jazz musicians, and top performance companies like Cirque du Soleil. Despite being able to seat more than 51,000 people, concerts at **De Kuip/Feyenoord Stadion** (⊠ *Van Zandvlietplein 1, Kop van Zuid* ☎ *010/492–9455*) usually sell out.

SHOPPING

Rotterdam is the number one shopping city in South Holland. Its famous Lijnbaan and Beurstraverse shopping centers, as well as the surrounding areas, offer a dazzling variety of shops and department stores. Here you'll find all the biggest chains in Holland, such as Mango, MEXX, Morgan, Invito, and Sacha. The archways and fountains of the Beurstraverse—at the bottom of the Coolsingel—make this newer, pedestrianized area more pleasing to walk around. It is now one of the most expensive places to rent shop space, and has a nickname: *Koopgoot,* which can mean "shopping channel" (if you like it) or "shopping gutter" (if you don't). The Bijenkorf department store has an entrance here on the lower-street level. Van Oldenbarneveldtstraat and Nieuwe Binnenweg are the places to be if you want something different. There is a huge variety of alternative fashion to be found here.

DEPARTMENT STORES

De Bijenkorf (✉ *Coolsingel 105, Centrum* ☎*0900/0919*) is a favorite department store, designed by Marcel Breuer (the great Bauhaus architect) with an exterior that looks like its name, a beehive. The best department store in Rotterdam, it covers four floors. There's a good range of clothing and shoes from both designers and the store's own label, plus a selection of cosmetics and perfume on the ground floor, with a Chill Out department on the same floor geared toward street- and club-wear; here, on some Saturdays a DJ keeps it mellow, and you can even get a haircut at in-store Kinki Kappers. De Bijenkorf is well known for its excellent household-goods line, ranging from lights and furniture to sumptuous fabrics and rugs. Check out the second-floor restaurant with its view out over the Coolsingel and Naum Gabo's sculpture *Constructie.* **V&D** (✉ *Hoogstraat 185, Centrum* ☎*0900/235–8363*) is great for household goods, stationery, and other everyday necessities. Rest your tired tootsies and admire the city view from the rooftop café, La Place, where you can indulge in a wide selection of snacks and full meals.

SHOPPING DISTRICTS & STREETS

Exclusive shops and boutiques can be found in the Entrepotgebied, Delfshaven, Witte de Withstraat, Nieuwe and Oude Binnenweg, and Van Oldenbarneveldtstraat. West Kruiskade and its vicinity offer a wide assortment of multicultural products in the many Chinese, Surinamese, Mediterranean, and Arabic shops. The shops in the city center are open every Sunday afternoon, and there is late-night shopping—until 9—every Friday.

SPECIALTY STORES

There are numerous specialty stores all across town, and depending on what you are looking for, you should be able to find it somewhere. If in doubt, ask a fellow shopper or the tourist office.

ANTIQUES Look along the **Voorhaven** and its continuation **Aelbrechtskolk,** in Delfshaven, for the best antiques. On Sunday head to the **Schiedamsdijk,** where you can expect to find a market that specializes in antiques and old books, open noon–5.

ART GALLERIES Many galleries provide the opportunity both to look at art and buy it. These can be found along the Westersingel and in the Museumpark area, but the top galleries are on Witte de Withstraat, also lined with numerous cafés, making it an ideal street to spend some time window-shopping.

Mama Showroom for Media and Moving Art (✉ *Witte de Withstraat 29–3* ☎*010/433–0695* ⊕*www.showroommama.nl*) encourages the collaboration of emerging, experimental artists. If you're looking for new, exciting, and innovative art with high standards, you'll find it here. Some of the work may shock; some might make you laugh out loud in delight; but all of it is art-critic-worthy. Consider film- and video-based art by the Dutch Galleon of Mayhem or the inflatable sculptures by a group of "artoonists," including a giant rabbit by Florentijn Hofman. The gallery is open Wednesday–Sunday 1–6.

BOOKS **Selexyz Donner** (✉ *Lijnbaan 150, Centrum* ☎*010/413–2070*) is the biggest bookstore in Rotterdam. Its 10 floors include an excellent range of English-language books, which are distributed throughout the shop under specific headings.

DESIGN **Dille & Kamille** (✉ *Korte Hoogstraat 22, Centrum* ☎*010/411–3338*) is a fantastic store for anyone interested in cooking. From herbs to sturdy wooden spoons to recipe books, this is a browser's heaven. It is one of the few shops in the Netherlands that still carries traditional Dutch household items, such as a huge water kettle to make tea for 25, a nutmeg mill, or a *zeepklopper,* a device that holds a bar of soap and can whip up bubbles—a forerunner to liquid dish-washing detergent. In the **Entrepot Harbor design district,** alongside the city marina at Kop van Zuid, are several interior-design stores. More like a museum of modern art and home furnishings than a mere gallery, the **Galerie ECCE** (✉ *Witte de Withstraat 17a–19a, Witte de With* ☎*010/413–9770* ⊕*www.galerie-ecce.nl*) has an exclusive collection of ultramodern furniture, lamps, and glassware from Dutch and European designers and offers a custom-design service. You'll find a variety of smaller unique design items, suitable for gifts, such as coasters and wall sconces. The gallery has a new exhibition of paintings and sculpture every two months, and also specializes in the production of trompe l'oeil wall paintings.

FASHION For fashion suggestions, start with **Sister Moon** (✉ *Nieuwe Binnenweg 89b, Centrum* ☎*010/436–1508*), which has a small collection of exclusive hip clothing for men and women in the party scene; part of the boutique is devoted to trendy secondhand togs. Graffiti artists favor **Urban Unit** (✉ *Nieuwe Binnenweg 53, Centrum* ☎*010/436–3825*), loving the look of the men's sneakers and street wear on sale (while stocking up on spray cans and other graffiti supplies). On Van Oldenbarneveldtstraat the prices rise as the stores get more label based. **Van Dijk** (✉ *Van Oldenbarneveldtstraat 105, Centrum* ☎*010/411–2644*) stocks Costume National and Helmut Lang, and the owner, Wendela, has two of her own design labels. You can find trendy shoes, bags, and accessories here and have plenty of room to try on clothes in the *paskamers* (fitting rooms).

Where there's fashion, there's music: keep in mind that Holland's largest concentration of international music stores can be found on the Nieuwe Binnenweg, ranging from techno to ambient, rock to Latin and African.

STREET MARKETS

The expansive **Binnenrotteplein,** between Sint Laurenskerk and Blaak railway station, is home to one of the largest street markets in the country, every Tuesday and Saturday from 9 to 5 and Friday from noon to 5. Among the 520 stalls you can find a flea market, book market, household items, used goods, food, fish, clothes, and flowers. From April to December, a fun shopping market with 200 stands is held on Sunday from noon to 5. There are often special attractions for children, and you can chill out on the terrace.

UTRECHT

58 km (36 mi) northeast of Rotterdam, 40 km (25 mi) southeast of Amsterdam.

Birthplace of the 16th-century pope Adrian VI (the only Dutch one), Utrecht has been a powerful bishopric since the seventh century and is still a major religious center. First settled by Romans, Utrecht achieved its first glory in the 16th century, when the religious power of the town was made manifest in the building of four churches at points of an enormous imaginary cross, with the **Dom** (cathedral) in the center. It was in Utrecht that the Dutch Republic was established in 1579 with the signing of the Union of Utrecht. In addition to being home to Holland's largest university, the city has so many curiosities, high-gabled houses, fascinating water gates, hip shops, artsy cafés, and winding canals that the traveler can almost forgive the city for being one of the busiest and most modern in Holland. Happily, the central core remains redolent with history, particularly along the Oudegracht (Old Canal), which winds through the central shopping district (to the east of the train station shopping complex).

TO & FROM

Utrecht forms the central hub of the national rail network, and tracks fan out from here in all directions. Around five trains an hour make the 25 minute trip between Amsterdam and Utrecht throughout the day. If driving, the A2 southeast from Amsterdam will get you to Utrecht in around 30 minutes, but the trip can take much longer at peak times.

EXPLORING

If you arrive by train, you might be forgiven for thinking Utrecht is one enormous covered shopping mall, since the station is incorporated into the warren of 200-plus shops that is the Hoog Catharijne. You could get lost here for a day, but if you follow signs for *Centrum* (town center) and keep walking with determination, you will eventually come out in the historic center. The soaring tower of Domtoren, or "the cathedral that is missing," on the skyline will direct you to the center of the action. Most of the main sights are in a fairly compact area and reachable on foot within a few minutes of the Domtoren.

MAIN ATTRACTIONS

7 **Centraal Museum.** This vast and eclectic collection ranges from a 10th-century boat to a Viktor and Rolf A-Bomb coat, and from Golden Age paintings to minimalist home furnishings. What you see depends on the theme of the current temporary exhibitions, but of the permanent displays, don't miss the **Utrecht Boat,** the complete 1,000-year-old wooden hull of a ship, excavated from a nearby riverbed in 1930, which has survived remarkably intact. The museum also has a collection of Golden Age art and artists from the Utrecht school. Across the square, modern-art lovers will make a beeline for the **Gerrit Rietveld Wing,** focused on the most famous of all De Stijl architects and designers. There is a reconstruction of his studio and lots of original Rietveld

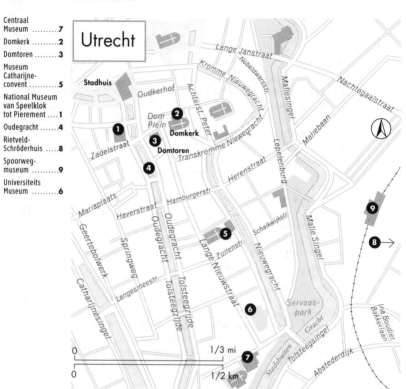

furniture. ✉*Nicolaaskerkhof 10* ☎*030/236–2362* ⊕*www.centraal-museum.nl* ✉*€8* ⊙*Tues.–Sun. 12–5, Fri. until 9.*

❷ **Domkerk.** Holding its own against the imposing Domtoren across the square, this grand Gothic Cathedral was built during the 13th and 14th centuries and designed in the style of Tournai Cathedral in Belgium. It has five chapels radiating around the ambulatory of the chancel, as well as a number of funerary monuments, including that of a 14th-century bishop. The entire space between the tower and the Domkerk was originally occupied by the nave of the huge cathedral, which was destroyed in a freak tornado in 1674 and not rebuilt. Many other buildings were damaged, and the exhibition inside Domkerk shows interesting before-and-after sketches. Today only the chancel and tower remain, separated by an open space, now a sunny square edged by a road. Behind the chancel is the **Pandhof,** a 15th-century cloister with a formal herb garden with medicinal herbs, replanted in the 1960s. If you're lucky you'll come upon classical musicians, making the most of the wondrous acoustics. A free concert is held every Saturday at 3:30. ✉*Achter de Dom 1* ☎*030/231–0403* ✉*Free, donations appreciated* ⊙*May–Sept., weekdays 10–5, Sat. 10–3:30, Sun. 2–4; Oct.–Apr., weekdays 11–4, Sat. 10–3:30, Sun. 2–4.*

❸ **Domtoren** *(Cathedral tower).* Soaring lancet windows add to the impression of majestic height of the famous tower of "the cathedral that is missing," the 14th-century Domtoren. The sole remnant of an enormous house of worship that was destroyed by a storm late in the 17th century (the outline of its nave can still be seen in the paving squares of the Domplein), it is more than 367 feet high. Not only is it the highest tower in the country, but its more than 50 bells make it the largest musical instrument in Holland. The tower is so big that city buses drive through an arch in its base. You can climb the tower, but make sure you feel up to the 465 steps. The panoramic view is worth the pain, though, for it stretches 40 km (25 mi) to Amsterdam on a clear day. ⊠ *Domplein* ☎ *030/236–0010* ☎€*7.50* ⊙ *Apr.–Sept., Tues.–Sat. 10–5, Sun.–Mon. noon–5; Oct.–Mar., Sun.–Fri. noon–5, Sat. 11–5; view by tour only; last tour at 4.*

> **INFORMATION**
>
> Make your way to the central Domplein, where you'll find the one-stop cultural and historical information center for the historic quarter. Inexplicably named **RonDom,** this is where you can buy tickets for almost everything as well as book a guided tour or barge trip. There is an excellent range and display of free leaflets, to which you should help yourself. ⊠ *Domplein 9* ☎ *030/236–0010* 🖷 *030/236–0037* ⊕ *www.domtoren.nl* ⊙ *Sun.–Mon. 12–5, Tue.–Fri. 10–6, Sat. 10–5.*

☝ ❶ **Nationaal Museum van Speelklok tot Pierement** *(National Musical Box and Street Organ Museum).* This super-charming and tuneful museum is housed in an old church, and has a large collection of automated musical instruments from the 15th to the 19th century. You can wander around by yourself, but it's far more rewarding to wait for a tour (also in English), for only on these are the dazzling automata put into play. The highlight for everyone, young and old, is the tiny music box in the form of an ancient furry rabbit, which pops up out of a fading cabbage and beats time to the music with its ears. Fittingly for Holland, the development of the barrel organ—still the bane of shoppers on many busy streets—is charted from the Renaissance onward. Away from the main collection, the children's Music Factory has displays of historical instruments hardy enough for three-year-olds to try—they can go at it on percussion instruments, bicycle bells, and harps. There are also interactive stands where children can shout into voice distorters, or watch themselves on a TV screen as they sing. ⊠ *Steenweg 6* ☎ *030/231–2789* ⊕ *www.museumspeelklok.nl* ☎€*7* ⊙ *Tues.–Sun. 10–5; guided tours every hr.*

❹ **Oudegracht.** Utrecht's long central sunken canal—which suffers a confusing name change at several points en route through the city—is unique in Holland, for its esplanade has upper and lower levels, with shops and galleries opening onto street level, and restaurants and cafés on the walkway just above the water (sinking water levels centuries ago led to the excavation of a lower story).

★ **8** **Rietveld-Schröderhuis.** This house exemplifies several key principles of the De Stijl movement that affected not only art but also modern architecture, furniture design, and even typography in the early part of the 20th century. The house was designed for the Schröder family by Gerrit Rietveld, one of the leading architects of De Stijl, who has many objects on view in Utrecht's Centraal Museum. The open plan, the direct communion with nature from every room, and the use of neutral white or gray on large surfaces, with primary colors to iden-

> **PEDAL POWER**
>
> Whether you're into exploring by road or canal, pedal power can be a great way to see Utrecht. Rent bikes from the **Rijwiel Shop** (⊠ *Centraal Station Utrecht* ☎ *030/231–1159*). Costs are €6.50–€7.50 with ID and a €50 deposit. The shop is by the north end of track 19. Water ski–bikes can be found at **Canal Bike** (⊠ *Oudegracht, opposite City Hall* ☎ *020/626–5574* .

tify linear details, are typical De Stijl characteristics. Rietveld is best known outside Holland for his "Red-Blue-Yellow" chair design. Tours must be reserved in advance. Meet at the Centraal Museum 30 minutes before the scheduled tour time, and a shuttle bus takes you to the house, which is about a mile east of the city center. ⊠ *Prins Hendriklaan 50* ☎ *030/236–2310* ⊕ *www.centraalmuseum.nl* ☑ *€16 (includes guided tour and entry to Centraal Museum)* ⊗ *By appointment only Tues.–Sat. 11–5.*

☺ ★ **9** **Spoorwegmuseum** *(Railway Museum).* Beyond the converted 19th-century station that serves as the entrance to this excellent museum is a vast exhibition space in the style of a rail yard. In addition to dozens of locomotives, three large sheds, called *werelden* (worlds), take you on a tour of rail history. In World 1, dealing with the birth of the railways, you follow an audio tour (available in English) through an early-19th-century English coalmine. World 2 stages a theater production based on the Orient Express. In World 3, you sit in carriages and ride the rails, while all around you the bright lights, sounds, and billowing steam evoke the Golden Age of train travel. Outside, kids can ride the *Jumbo Express* on an adventure trip past lakes, and through tunnels and water jets. The museum is an easy walk from the city center. Alternatively, trains run between here and Utrecht Centraal Station eight times daily for €2 round trip. ⊠ *Maliebaanstation* ☎ *030/230–6206* ⊕ *www.spoorwegmuseum.nl* ☑ *€13.50* ⊗ *Tues.–Sun. 10–5; daily 10– 5 during school vacations.*

IF YOU HAVE TIME

5 **Museum Catharijneconvent** *(Convent of St. Catherine Museum).* Just a few blocks south of the Dom, this former convent houses a vast collection of religious history and sacred art. There are magnificent altarpieces, ecclesiastical vestments, beautifully illustrated manuscripts, sculptures, and paintings—including works by Rembrandt and Frans Hals. Note the painting of a silvery-bearded God, by Pieter de Grebber (1640), holding what appears to be a crystal ball, inviting Jesus to sit at his right hand, in a cherub-bedecked chair. Temporary exhibitions here are first-rate. Cross the first-story walkway to get a great view of the cloister gardens. ⊠ *Lange Nieuwestraat 38* ☎*030/231–3835* ⊕*www.catharijneconvent.nl* ☞*€8.50* ☉*Tues.–Fri. 10–5, weekends 11–5.*

☝ ❻ **Universiteits Museum.** The University Museum deals with both the history of Utrecht University and the fields of science. The first thing to grab your attention is the building itself: architects visit specially to look at Koen van Velsen's square building and his garden "boxes." A glassed-in corridor runs the length of the building, giving an immense

> ### ART YOU CAN WEAR
>
> Utrecht is fiercely proud of Holland's own *enfants terribles* of the catwalk Viktor and Rolf, whose clothes hover between visual art and couture, taking a subtle yet witty stand against traditional design. Their provocative yet innovative work has elevated them to such prominence that they are seen as the visionaries of haute couture's future, not just by the city of Utrecht, but by the whole fashion world.

feeling of space. One collection, bought by William I and donated to the museum, verges on the ghoulish: skulls, anatomical models, and preserved "things" in jars; medical ethics would prevent these exhibits from being preserved now, most notably the embryos, which only increases their fascination for youngsters. On the third floor kids can have a field day. In the Youth Lab children put on mini–lab coats to do experiments and play with optical illusions (with assistants patrolling the floor to provide guidance and assistance on Wednesday, Saturday, and Sunday afternoons). A former orangery is now a garden-fronted café. ⊠*Lange Nieuwestraat 106* ☎*030/253–8008* ⊕*www.museum. uu.nl* ☞*€7* ☉*Tues.–Sun. 11–5.*

WHERE TO STAY & EAT

Utrecht hotel rooms are much in demand, since the city is a business and college center. Always book as far in advance as you can. The **Utrecht VVV** (☎*0900/128–8732*) can help with bookings.

$$–$$$ ✕**Polman's Huis.** This grand café of the old school is a Utrecht institution. Its spacious Jugendstil–Art Deco interior is authentic. Other reasons to find your way here are the relaxing atmosphere and range of meal choices, from a simple quiche to a steamed fish dinner, from a kitchen that uses Mediterranean influences. ⊠*Keistraat 2* ☎*030/231–3368* ▤*MC, V* ☉*Closed Sun.*

$$ ✕**De Artisjok.** This gracious old canal-house restaurant overlooking the fashionable New Canal has been spruced up and given a bright new lick of paint in colors that reflect the Mediterranean cuisine. The changing menu offers such tempting selections as tuna steak with basil and tomato, or lamb with asparagus and caramelized onions. ⊠*Nieuwegracht 33* ☎*030/231–7494* ⌂*Reservations essential* ▤*AE, DC, MC, V* ☉*No lunch.*

$–$$ ✕**Café le Journal.** This spot has the widest terrace and so catches the most sun (when there is sun to be had) of the cafés along Winkenburgstraat and Neude. Large trees soften the view across the square, so this is a prime place for lazy weekend afternoons. Inside, floor-to-ceiling framed magazine covers reflect the general news theme. The long communal table inside is stocked with newspapers, including a few English-language titles. The menu is excellent and wide-ranging. Although the café is relatively big, there is no feeling of being processed when you come here, thanks to the charming staff. Even when it is busy, you can linger over a *koffie verkerd* (café au lait) as long as you want. ✉*Neude 32* ☎*030/236–4839* ▤*No credit cards.*

★ **$–$$** ✕**De Zakkendrager.** As you walk down the narrow alleyway to this gem, it's easy to be misled by its unassuming exterior. Students, concertgoers from the nearby Vredenburg Music Center, and fashionable young locals come here for generous portions of grilled meats, excellent salads, and an unusually large vegetarian range. The atmosphere is even better—the restaurant is cozy, friendly, and informal. The rear half opens out into a breezy conservatory with panoramic views through glass walls and ceiling panels. In the walled garden at the back, a 180-year-old beech tree towers over everything. The green decor inside echoes the foliage, creating an oasis of calm away from the bustle of the city. ✉*Zakkendragerssteeg 26* ☎*030/231–7578* ▤*AE, DC, MC, V.*

★ **$–$$** ✕**Winkel van Sinkel.** This Neoclassical *paleis* (palace) started out in the 18th century as Holland's first department store, before becoming Utrecht's foremost social hot spot. Fronted with columns and cast-iron statues of women, it conjures up images of Grecian luxe and abundance. The enormous statues were produced in England in the mid–19th century and shipped over, but they were too heavy for the crane that unloaded them, which collapsed, thereby earning the ladies the nickname "the fallen women." You can dine either on the terrace overlooking the canal or in the high-ceilinged Grote Zaal. The menu is designed to satisfy all tastes, with tempting selections such paella, rib-eye steaks, or, for vegetarians, a delicious spring vegetable ravioli. If you fancy eating after-hours, the Nachtrestaurant serves tapas until late, and a nightclub kicks in late every weekend. Monthly events include salsa and Latino nights. Check out the Web site for more details. ✉*Oudegracht 158; Nachtrestaurant entry via Aan de Werf* ☎*030/230–3030* ⊕*www.dewinkelvansinkel.nl* ▤*No credit cards.*

$ ✕**Eetcafé de Poort.** This place is on Ledig Erf, one of Utrecht's small squares, which becomes a hive of energy and is filled with huge shade umbrellas when the sun comes out. This café's tables spill over the bridge, so you can sit overlooking canal-side gardens. On the far side of the plaza, black-and-white squares are painted onto the pavement, carrying out a popular chess theme from the surrounding cafés. The spareribs here are a perennial favorite. ✉*Tolsteegbarriere 2* ☎*030/231–4572* ▤*No credit cards.*

$$$$ ✕▨**Grand Hotel Karel V.** This former military hospital and restored 11th-century convent has been transformed into Utrecht's most luxurious hotel. The Garden Wing is a separate building surrounded by extensive gardens but lacks the historic aura of the main building, where Napoléon's brother Louis once resided. Canopied guest bedrooms are comfortably large, if the terra-cotta and gold furnishings are a bit overdone. Accent pieces are very new and yet not modern, and enormously heavy curtains are roped back to reveal almost floor-to-ceiling sash windows. The sumptuous dining room glitters with opulent metallic murals, and designer-oversize vases—a regal setting for the excellent fare. A lighter-eating alternative is the Brasserie Goeie Louisa, where you can be served in the gardens or courtyard, if the weather is fine; note the afternoon tea and garden barbecue menus. ⊠*Geertebolwerk 1, 3511 XA* ☎*030/233–7461* ⊜*030/233–7580* ⊕*www.karelv. nl* ⇙*70 rooms, 21 suites* ⇘*In-room: refrigerator, dial-up. In-hotel: restaurant, bar, gym, some pets allowed* ⊟*AE, DC, MC, V.*

★ **$–$$$** ⊞ **NH Centre Utrecht Hotel.** In the shadow of Sint Janskerk and opposite a leafy square, this friendly, modern hotel in a 19th-century jacket offers pretty and well-kept rooms at excellent prices. The attractive exterior of the 1870 building has Art Nouveau leanings, while the interior is very 21st century. Rooms are airy and stylishly understated, with floral-theme paintings on the walls. Some bathrooms have tubs. In the center of town, the hotel is within walking distance of the canals, as well as plenty of shopping and dining. ⊠*Janskerkhof 10, 3512 BL* ☎*030/231–3169* ⊜*030/231–0148* ⊕*www.nh-hotels.com* ⇙*47 rooms* ⇘*In-room: no a/c, Wi-Fi, refrigerator. In-hotel: restaurant, bar, public Wi-Fi* ⊟*AE, MC, V.*

$–$$ ⊞ **Malie Hotel.** Located on a tree-lined avenue behind a stylish 19th-century facade, this classically designed hotel is both modern and attractive. Guest rooms are brightly decorated, though simply furnished. The breakfast room overlooks a pretty garden, which guests have access to, and the bar-lounge doubles as a small art gallery. ⊠*Maliestraat 2, 3581 SL* ☎*030/231–6424* ⊜*030/234–0661* ⊕*www.maliehotel.nl* ⇙*45 rooms* ⇘*In-room: Wi-Fi. In-hotel: bar, public Internet* ⊟*AE, MC, V* ⦿*CP.*

$ ⊞ **Hotel Ouwi.** A convivial family hotel, this is just off one of the main transit routes to the city center. The rooms are tight and simple in furnishings and decor, but they're very clean and tidy. ⊠*F. C. Dondersstraat 12, 3572 JH* ☎*030/271–6303* ⊜*030/271–4619* ⊕*www.hotelouwi.nl* ⇙*34 rooms, 4 studios* ⇘*In-room: no a/c, no phone, Wi-Fi. In-hotel: some pets allowed* ⊟*AE, DC, MC, V* ⦿*CP.*

¢ ⊞ **Stayokay Hostel Bunnik.** Backpackers and travelers on a budget can find a bargain bunk in shared dorms just outside Utrecht, only 10 minutes from town by bus. The hostel enjoys a peaceful wooded location on the banks of the Kromme Rijn river. ⊠*Rhijnauwenselaan 14, 3981 HH, Bunnik* ☎*030/656–1277* ⊜*030/657–1065* ⊕*www.stayokay. com* ⇙*23 dorm rooms of 2, 3, 4, 5, 6, 7, 8, or 12 beds* ⇘*In-room: no a/c, no phone, no TV. In-hotel: restaurant, bar, public Internet* ⊟*AE, V* ⦿*CP.*

NIGHTLIFE & THE ARTS

THE ARTS In Utrecht you can find dance on the programs of **Stadsschouwburg** (⊠*Lucas Bolwerk 24* ☎*030/230–2023* ⊕*www.stadsschouwburg-utrecht.nl*), which has a major performance hall as well as the Blauwe Zaal (Blue Room) for small productions. The annual **Spring Dance** festival brings international performers to town in June, with the biggest events usually on the big squares in the center of town, the Neude.

The **Vredenburg Muziek Centrum** (⊠ *Vredenburgpassage 77* ☎ *030/231–4544 box office, 030/286–2286 information* ⊕ *www.vredenburg.nl*) is the biggest venue in Utrecht for classical and pop concerts.

Utrecht's **Festival Oude Muziek** (☎ *030/232–9010* ⊕ *www.oudemuziek.nl*), or Festival of Early Music, in late summer each year is immensely popular, selling out rapidly. Check the Web site for locations and events.

A full program of concerts is performed in many of Utrecht's fine churches. The best are usually heard in the **Dom** (☎ *030/231–0403*).

The 10-day annual late-September **Nederlands Film Festival** (☎ *030/232–2684* ⊕ *www.filmfestival.nl*) is a seriously taken review of the past year of Dutch productions held in Winkel van Sinkel café and most of the town's cinemas. Many international movies, often in English, are given their Dutch premieres here, and at the gala event the "Golden Calves"—the Dutch Oscars—are dished out to the year's best. More than 100,000 visitors attend the many screenings. Tickets can be bought online, by phone, or in person from the temporary pavilion that appears on the Neude square at festival time. Most tickets cost €8.

NIGHTLIFE Utrecht's students strike a lively note at cafés around the center, more during the week than over weekends. Larger cafés such as the **Winkel van Sinkel** and **Oudaen** are gathering spots for all ages.

Nachtwinkel (⊠ *Oudegracht 158 a/d werf* ☎ *030/230–3030*) hosts Winkel van Sinkel's weekend serious fun nights, packing both floors with frenetic clubbers.**Polman's Huis** attracts a lively crowd of students and thirtysomethings.

Trianon (⊠ *Oudegracht 252* ☎ *030/231–6939*) is a fast-growing salsa club that organizes great dance events—on some nights there are salsa classes earlier in the evening before the party starts. There are also demonstrations, dance lessons, and workshops on offer at the center, as well as Spanish- and Portuguese-language lessons.

SIDE TRIP TO KASTEEL DE HAAR

10 km (6 mi) northwest of Utrecht.

78 The spectacular **Kasteel de Haar** is not only the largest castle in the Neth-
Fodor'sChoice erlands, but also the most sumptuously furnished. Thanks to the for-
★ tuitous way the Barons van Zuylen had of marrying Rothschilds, their family home grew into a Neo-Gothic extravaganza replete with moat, fairy-tale spires, and machicolated towers. The castle was founded back in 1165, but several renovations and many millions later, the family expanded the house under the eye of P. J. H. Cuypers, designer of Amsterdam's Centraal Station and Rijksmuseum in 1892. Inside the castle are acres of tapestries, medieval iron chandeliers, and the requisite ancestral portraits snootily studying you as you wander through chivalric halls so opulent and vast they could be opera sets.

At de Haar, be sure to explore the magnificent gardens and park, dotted with romantic paths, fanciful statues, and little bridges. As was the wont of aristo owners in the 19th century, entire villages were relocated to expand their estate parks, and in this case, Haarzuilens was reconstructed a mile from the castle. Designed in 1898 around a village square, all its cottages have red-and-white doors and shutters, reflecting the armorial colors of the Van Zuylen family. Every year in September, the village funfair is kicked off by the current baron to the accompaniment of a fireworks display. As for the castle itself, you can view its grand interiors only via one of the guided tours (no kids under five), which leave on the hour and are led only in Dutch. No matter, the objects of beauty on display can be understood in any language. Once you explore this enchanted domain, you'll easily understand why Marie-Hélène van Zuylen, who grew up here, went on to become Baroness Guy de Rothschild, the late-20th-century's "Queen of Paris," famous for her grand houses and costume balls. Directions for car travelers are given on the castle Web site. For public transport, take Bus No. 127 from Utrecht Centraal Station, direction Breukelen/Kockengen, until the Brink stop in Haarzuilens, a 15-minute walk from the castle. You can also train it to Vleuten and then take a taxi. ✉ *Kasteellaan 1, near Haarzuilens* ☎ *030/677–8515* ⊕ *www.kasteeldehaar.nl* 🎟 *€8, grounds only €3, parking €3* ⊙ *Grounds daily 10–5; castle Tues.–Fri. 11–4, weekends noon–4. Hrs vary slightly through the year; call to confirm.*

7

RANDSTAD ESSENTIALS

TRANSPORTATION

In combination with trains, the efficient system of buses and trams in the metropolitan area will easily take care of most of your transportation needs. Bus service is available in all cities in this region, and trams operate within The Hague, Rotterdam, and Utrecht. Trams also run between Delft and The Hague; buses offer services across the Randstad to certain smaller towns served only by secondary rail connections. Bus lanes are shared only with taxis, meaning they remain uncongested, ensuring that you travel more swiftly than the rest of the traffic in rush hour.

Rotterdam also has a subway, referred to as the metro, with only two lines (east to west and north to south) that extend into the suburbs and cross in the city center for easy transfers. All three options are excellent for transport within the city. To get around by bus, tram, or metro in Rotterdam you'll need an **OV-chipkaart** (public transport chip card)—a new electronic payment system that's being tested in the city before being rolled out nationally in 2009. These credit card–sized tickets can be loaded up with credit from machines in the railway and metro stations, and are debited as you board and leave trains and buses. There are information and sales points in the Beurs and Centraal Station metro stations, as well as in the main bus station. Or call the help desk ☎0900/500–6010 for more information.

Contact **Public Transportation Information** (☎0900/9292).

BY AIR

Amsterdam Schiphol Airport is 50 km (30 mi) north of Rotterdam and has efficient road and rail links. Its comprehensive Web site provides real-time information about flight arrivals and departures, as well as all transport and parking facilities. **Rotterdam Airport,** 17 km (11 mi) northwest of Rotterdam, is the biggest of the regional airports, providing daily service to a number of European cities. However, to reach the airport from Rotterdam you need to take Bus No. 33 from Centraal Station, or a taxi, as there are no rail links. If you take a taxi, expect to pay around €25.

Airport Information **Amsterdam Schiphol Airport** (☎0900/0141 ⊕www. schiphol.nl). **Rotterdam Airport** (☎010/446–3444 ⊕www.rotterdam-airport.nl).

BY BIKE

In this flat land, a bicycle is an ideal means of getting around, and cities have safe cycle lanes on busy roads. Bikes are best rented at outlets near most railway stations, called **Rijwiel** shops. These shops are generally open long hours every day, and the bikes are invariably new and well maintained. Rates are €6.50–€8.40, and you must show ID and pay a deposit of €50. Cheaper bikes have back-pedal brakes and no gears. Other local rental centers can be found in the regional *Gouden Gids* (Yellow Pages), under *Fietsen en Bromfietsen.*

BY BOAT

TOURS   The best way to see Rotterdam's waterfront is by boat; **Spido Harbor Tours** offers excursions lasting from just over an hour to a full day. In Delft, Dordrecht, Kinderdijk, Leiden, Rotterdam, and Utrecht guided sightseeing boat tours allow you to explore the cities. Ask at the local VVV office in the towns you would like to tour for the latest departure information and routes. In Utrecht, opt for one of the many guided tours operated by the **RonDom,** a one-stop cultural and historical information center for the museum quarter, where you can buy tickets for almost everything as well as book a guided tour or a barge trip.

Contacts **RonDom** (✉Domplein 9, Utrecht ☎030/236–0010 ⊕www.rondom.nl). **Rondvaart Delft** (✉Koornmarkt 113 ☎015/212–6385 ⊕www.rondvaartdelft.nl). **Spido Harbor Tours** (✉Willemsplein 85 ☎010/275–9988 ⊕www.spido.nl).

Contacts **PO North Sea Ferries** (✉Beneluxhaven, Havennummer 5805, Rotterdam/Europoort ☎020/200–8333 ⊕www.poferries.nl).**Stena** (✉Hoek van Holland Terminal, Stationsweg 10, Hoek van Holland ☎0174/389333, 0900/8123 reservations [10¢ per min.] ⊕www.stenaline.nl).

BY CAR

Using a car in the Randstad, with the complexity of one-way streets in city centers, makes driving a real headache, let alone the added burdens of parking and expense. In addition, there is also the consideration of traffic, especially around rush hour, when driving between Haarlem and Delft can take up to three times longer than traveling by train. If you decide to travel by car, you can reach Rotterdam directly from Amsterdam by taking A4 via Amsterdam Schiphol Airport. The city is bounded by the A20 on the northern outskirts, the A16 on the east, the A15 on the south, and the A4 on the west. N200 or A9 goes to Haarlem from Amsterdam; to reach Delft directly from Amsterdam, take A4 via Amsterdam Schiphol Airport; to reach Utrecht take A2.

Car-Rental Agencies **Avis** (⊠ *Bredestraat 17–19, Rotterdam* ☎ *010/433–2233* ⊕ *www.avis.nl).* **Budget** (⊠ *Koperstraat 15, Rotterdam* ☎ *010/415–1833* ⊕ *www. budget.nl).* **Europcar** (⊠ *Walenburghof 17, Rotterdam* ☎ *010/465–6400* ⊠ *Rotterdam Airport* ☎ *010/437–1826* ⊕ *www.europcar.nl).*

BY TAXI

Taxis are available at railway stations, at major hotels, and, in larger cities, at taxi stands in key locations. You can also order a taxi by using the telephone numbers below. Expect to pay at least €35 for a 30-minute journey between Rotterdam and Delft.

When you buy your train ticket from a station office, you can buy a *treintaxi* (a taxi that operates out of train stations) ticket from some smaller stations for a standard €4.30 per person, per ride. It doesn't matter where you're going, so long as it's within the city limits. The fare is so cheap because it's shared—but with waiting time at a guaranteed maximum of 10 minutes following your call, you won't be hanging around long. Treintaxis are ideal for getting to sights on the outskirts of smaller towns. Call one of the numbers below to order a taxi in metropolitan Holland, but for treintaxis, simply go to the ticket window at the smaller train station; note that not all small towns have this service.

Taxi Companies **Delft** (☎ *015/361–3030).* **Haarlem** (☎ *023/540–0600).* **Rotterdam** (☎ *010/462–6060 or 010/425–7000).* **Utrecht** (☎ *030/230–0400).*

BY TRAIN

Getting about by rail is the ideal means of intercity transport in the metropolitan area. Trains are fast, frequent, clean, and reliable, and stations in all towns are centrally located, usually within walking distance of major sights. All international and intercity trains from Brussels and Paris stop in Rotterdam Centraal. From here connections can be taken to travel directly to Delft (15 minutes northwest), and Haarlem (55 minutes northwest), on a twice-hourly *sneltrain* (express train) in the direction of Amsterdam. Intercity trains to Amsterdam traveling via Schiphol also stop in Delft and Haarlem. There are regular direct intercities to Utrecht from Rotterdam. Seat reservations aren't permitted. When traveling around the metropolitan area, direct trains leave Amsterdam for Haarlem, Delft, Rotterdam, and Utrecht several times an hour.

Information **Intercity** (☎ *0900/9292).* **Rotterdam Centraal** (☎ *0900/9292).* **Treintaxi** (☎ *0900/873–4682).*

CONTACTS & RESOURCES

EMERGENCIES

Pharmacies stay open late on a rotating basis. Call one of the hospital numbers listed below for addresses on a given night.

Emergency Services **National Emergency Alarm Number** (☎*112 for police, fire, and ambulance*).

Hospitals **Delft** (✉*Reinier de Graaf Gasthuis, Reinier De Graafweg 3–11* ☎*015/260–3060*). **Haarlem** (✉*Spaarne Ziekenhuis, Spaarnepoort 1, Hoofddorp* ☎*023/890–8900*). **Rotterdam** (✉*Erasmus MC, 's-Gravendijkwal 230* ☎*010/463–9222*). **Utrecht** (✉*Universitair Medisch Centrum Utrecht, Heidelberglaan 100* ☎*030/250–9111*).

VISITOR INFORMATION

Each VVV (tourist board) across the country has information principally on its own town and region. Contact the VVV of the area you plan to travel to, and ask directly for information, as there is no one central office; information lines cost €.70 per minute.

Tourist Information **Toeristen Informatie Punt Delft (Delft Tourist Information Point)** (✉*Hippolytusbuurt 4, 2611 HN* ☎*0900/515–1555*). **VVV Haarlem** (✉*Stationsplein 1, 2011 LR* ☎*0900/616–1600*). **VVV Rotterdam** (✉*Coolsingel 5, 3012 AC* ☎*0900/403–4065*). **VVV Utrecht** (✉*Domplein 9* ☎*0900/128–8732*).

The Hague

WORD OF MOUTH

"While in The Hague, don't forget to visit the new Escher Museum. The collection is very extensive and includes family photo albums. On the top floor there is a virtual reality exhibit that fits right in with his work."

—wen47

"The Mauritshuis and the beautiful old parliament buildings right next door to it are a must."

—Rockknocker

By Tim Skelton   **IT'S EASY TO SEE THE** Hague as nothing more than Amsterdam's prissy maiden aunt—it's Holland's seat of government, and also home to the Dutch royal family and the International Court of Justice. Yet those who experience the city up close will find a lively metropolis that is both elegant and quirky. Explore the 25-plus public parks and the narrow winding streets where contemporary architecture sits comfortably beside grand 17th-century mansions. Relax at sidewalk cafés and watch as they fill with civil servants spilling from the offices around the 13th-century Ridderzaal. Or visit the galleries and museums to find masterpieces by Johannes Vermeer, or the dazzling optical conundrums of Dutch graphic artist M. C. Escher. If you find yourself tiring of The Hague's grace, escape to the neighboring fishing port of Scheveningen; a tacky beach resort par excellence. Here you can lose your shirt in the city's casino or lose your dignity by taking a dip in the stupendously icy North Sea.

> **TOP REASONS TO GO**
>
> ■ Marvel at Vermeer's *Girl with a Pearl Earring* in the Mauritshuis
>
> ■ Make yourself bug-eyed deciphering the graphic puzzles in the Escher in Het Paleis Museum.
>
> ■ Step into history inside the 13th-century Knights' Hall.
>
> ■ Teach the kids all about Holland in 30 minutes at the miniature world of the Madurodam

The Hague's official name is 's-Gravenhage (literally "the Count's Hedge"), harking back to the 13th century when the Count of Holland's hunting lodge was based in a village called Die Haghe. But to the Dutch the city is known simply as Den Haag, and that's the name you'll hear used on the street.

ORIENTATION

For a city that sees so much political, legal, and diplomatic action, The Hague can seem surprisingly quiet, and a pleasure to those who want to escape the crowds. It's a flat, compact city and most of the sights in the town center are within a 15-minute walk from either of the city's train stations. Tram lines 3 and 17 cover many of the sights in town, and Tram No. 10 will get you to the outlying Statenkwartier museums. Tram No. 9 goes to Madurodam. For information on specific lines, ask at the HTM offices in The Hague's stations, or at offices listed below. For information on public transport (trains, buses, trams, and ferries), call the national information line.

Contacts **HTM** (✉ *Wagenstraat 35* ☎ *070/390–7722* ✉ *Venestraat 9* ☎ *070/390–7722*). **Public Transportation Information** (☎ *0900/9292* ∰ *www.9292ov.nl*).

PLANNING

TIMING

Done at a pace that will allow you to soak up The Hague's historical atmosphere, a minimal tour around the city center should take about three or four hours. If you stop to visit the main sights en route, you're looking at a very full day. At the very least, allow 30 minutes for each site you visit.

Before you start out, bear a couple of things in mind. First, as in all other Dutch cities, both walking surfaces and the weather can change at short notice; if you're going to be on your feet all day, make sure you're equipped with an umbrella and sturdy walking shoes. Second, most museums and galleries close at 5 PM, and many sites are also closed Monday, so plan accordingly.

ABOUT THE RESTAURANTS & HOTELS

For a good selection of a restaurant's fare, opt for a set menu. This will give you three or more courses, sometimes including appropriate wines, for a bargain price. As elsewhere in Holland, you don't have to dress up to chow down. Local diners usually start their evening meal around 7 PM, fashionably late compared to the 5:30–6 dinner hour elsewhere in the country. It's generally wise to reserve ahead on weekends, although if you arrive early without a prior booking, you may be lucky.

As a hub of international business, and with more than 20 million visitors a year, The Hague needs plenty of beds. Hotels here can quickly fill up, so rooms at the better places should be booked well in advance. With the exception of the super swanky Des Indes hotel, accommodations can be a little on the bland side; The Hague's smaller, family-run bed-and-breakfast facilities offer homey, more individual surroundings. Assume all rooms have air-conditioning, TV, telephones, and private bath, unless otherwise noted.

If you arrive in The Hague without a room, the reservations department of **Den Haag Marketing & Events** (☎ *070/338–5800* ⊕ *www.den-haag.com*) should be able to help you. It's open weekdays 8:30–5.

WHAT IT COSTS IN EUROS				
¢	$	$$	$$$	$$$$
HOTELS under €10	€10–€15	€15–€22	€22–€30	over €30
RESTAURANTS under €75	€75–€120	€120–€165	€165–€230	over €230

Restaurant prices are per person for a main course; Hotel prices are for a standard double room in high season

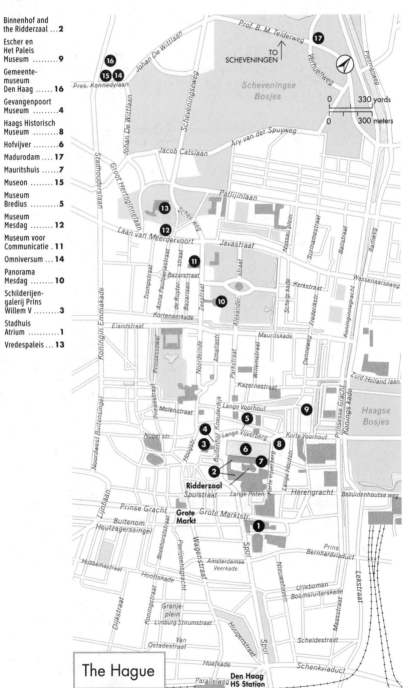

The Hague

EXPLORING

The Hague's center is crammed with the best the city has to offer in terms of art, history, and archi-tecture. An exploration of a rela-tively small area will take you into the famed Mauritshuis Museum, through the Binnenhof, home to the famous Ridderzaal (Knights' Hall), or along the leafy Lange Voorhout, for a stroll through what in the 19th century was the place to see and be seen.

MAIN ATTRACTIONS

❷ **Binnenhof and the Ridderzaal** *(Inner Court and the Knights' Hall)*. The
Fodor'sChoice governmental heart of the Netherlands, the Binnenhof (or Inner Court)
★ complex is in the very center of town yet tranquilly set apart from it, thanks to the charming Hofvijver (court lake). The setting creates a poetic contrast to the endlessly dull debates that go on within its walls—the basis of everyday Dutch politics. Pomp and decorum are in full fig every third Tuesday of September, when Queen Beatrix arrives at the 13th-century Ridderzaal, or Knights' Hall, in a golden coach to open the new session of Parliament.

For many centuries the Binnenhof was the court for the Counts of Hol-land; it is now a complex of buildings from several eras. As you enter, the twin-turreted former castle of the Earls of Holland dominates the scene. It was originally built by Count Floris V and became a meeting hall for the Knights of the Order of the Golden Fleece (one of the most regal societies of the Middle Ages). The interior of the Great Hall sim-ply drips with history: there are vast wooden beams, flags of the Dutch provinces, and a massive rose window bearing coats of arms. In 1900 the hall was restored to its original 13th-century glory; it is still called Knights' Hall and you can almost feel the feasts and revelries that took place there. The room still plays a key role in Dutch legislative life.

The Binnenhof also incorporates the halls used by the First and Second Chambers of Parliament (equivalent to the U.S. Senate and House of Representatives). You can wander freely around the open outer court-yard, but entrance to the Knights' Hall and other interior rooms is by guided tour only. The vaulted reception area below the Knights' Hall contains a free exhibition detailing the political history of the Low Countries. ✉*Binnenhof 8a* ☎*070/364–6144* 💶*€7* 🕐*Mon.–Sat. 10–4 (some areas may be closed when government meetings are tak-ing place).*

🧒 ❾ **Escher in Het Paleis Museum** *(Escher Museum)*. First known as the Lange
Fodor'sChoice Voorhout Palace, this lovely building was originally the residence of
★ Caroline of Nassau, daughter of Prince Willem IV—in 1765 Mozart performed for her here. In 2001 the palace was transformed into a museum devoted to Dutch graphic artist M. C. Escher (1892–1972),

8

whose prints and engravings of unforgettable images—roofs becoming floors, water flowing upward, fish transforming into birds—became world famous in the 1960s and '70s. Replete with ever-repeating Baroque pillars, Palladian portals, and parallel horizons, Maurits Cornelis Escher's visual trickery presages the "virtual reality" worlds of today. Fittingly, the museum now features an Escher Experience where you don a helmet and take a 360-degree digital trip through his unique world. Concave and convex, radical metamorphoses, and dazzling optical illusions are on view in the impressive selection of his prints (including the famed *Day and Night* and *Ascending and Descending*); distorted rooms and video cameras make children big and adults small; and there are rooms that are Escher prints blown up to the nth power. Don't forget to look up as you walk around—the latest addition to the museum is a series of custom-designed chandeliers by Dutch sculptor Hans van Bentem that are inspired by Escher's work. These delightfully playful creations include umbrellas, sea horses, birds, and even a giant skull and crossbones. A family ticket for €20 makes this an even more attractive museum for kids. ⊠ *Lange Voorhout 74* ☎ *070/427–7730* ⊕ *www.escherinhetpaleis.nl* 🎫 *€7.50* ⊗ *Tues.–Sun. 11–5.*

NEED A BREAK? Down a quiet side street, off Vos in Tuinstraat and very near the Escher in Het Paleis Museum, the friendly Le Café Hathor (⊠ *Maliestraat 22* ☎ *070/346–4081*) is a great spot for a snack, a full lunch, or just a quiet drink. Wood-paneled walls and flickering candles on each table create an intimately cozy atmosphere inside, while in good weather, tables on a raft outside overlook a gently flowing canal.

16 Gemeentemuseum Den Haag *(Hague Municipal Museum).* Designed by H. P. Berlage (the grand old master of modern Dutch architecture) and completed in 1935, this is considered one of the finest examples of 20th-century museum architecture. Although its collection ranges from A to Z—Golden Age silver, Greek and Chinese pottery, historic musical instruments, and paintings by Claude Monet and Vincent van Gogh—it is best known for the world's largest collection of works by Piet Mondriaan (1872–1944), the greatest artist of the Dutch De Stijl movement. The crowning masterpiece, and widely considered one of the landmarks of modern art, is Mondriaan's *Victory Boogie Woogie*—an iconic work, begun in 1942 but left unfinished at the artist's death. The painting's signature black-and-white grid interspersed with blocks of primary color arrived only in 1998, when the Netherlands Institute for Cultural Heritage controversially paid 80 million guilders for the (then American-owned) work. Also be sure to see the dollhouse with real doll-size Delft Blue chinaware. Elsewhere, the museum's Costume Gallery contains no fewer than 55,000 items (not all are on display at one time!), providing endless inspiration for dedicated students of fashion. ⊠ *Stadhouderslaan 41* ☎ *070/338–1111* ⊕ *www.gemeentemuseum.nl* 🎫 *€8.50* ⊗ *Tues.–Sun. 11–5.*

Fodor'sChoice ★

6 Hofvijver *(Court Lake).* Beside the Binnenhof, this long, rectangular reflecting pool—the venerable remains of a medieval moat—comes complete with tall fountains and a row of pink-blossomed horse-chestnut trees. Today, the lake is spectacularly surrounded by some of The Hague's most elegant historic buildings and museums.

Fodor's Choice ★ ➐ **Mauritshuis.** One of Europe's greatest museums, it's an incomparable feast of art in only a dozen rooms and includes 14 Rembrandts, 10 Jan Steens, and 3 Vermeers. The latter's remarkable *View of Delft* takes pride of place; its rediscovery in the late 19th century assured the artist's eternal fame. In the same room is Vermeer's (1632–75) most haunting work, *Girl with a Pearl Earring,* which inspired Tracy Chevalier's 1999 best-selling novel as well as the 2003 filmed version. For something completely different, look to Jan Steen (1626–79), who portrayed the daily life of ordinary

> ## WHO'S THAT GIRL?
>
> Johannes Vermeer's immortal *Girl with a Pearl Earring* is one of the few paintings ever to have its own spin-off novel and movie. The enigma surrounding the work remains to this day—despite extensive investigations, historians have never been able to determine who this sphinxlike lady actually is. Some think she is Maria, the eldest of Vermeer's 11 children. The novel claims she is Vermeer's maid. Considering the complete lack of ostentatious dress and iconographic symbols, the latter could be a real possibility.

people in the Netherlands of the 17th century. His painting *The Way You Hear It Is the Way You Sing It* is particularly telling. Don't miss local boy Paulus Potter's vast canvas *The Bull,* complete with steaming cow dung; the 7-foot-by-11-foot painting leaves nothing to be said on the subject of beef on the hoof.

As an added treat, the building itself is worthy of a 17th-century master's brush: a cream-color mansion tucked into a corner behind the Parliament complex and overlooking the Hofvijver. It was built around 1640 for one Johan Maurits, Count of Nassau-Siegen and governor-general of Dutch Brazil. The pair behind its creation, Jacob van Campen and Pieter Post, were the two most important Dutch architects of their era. ✉ *Korte Vijverberg 8* ☎ *070/302–3456* ⊕ *www.mauritshuis.nl* 🎟 *€9.50* 🕐 *Tues.–Sat. 10–5, Sun. 11–5.*

★ ➓ **Panorama Mesdag.** Long before TV was capable of reproducing reality, painted panoramas gave viewers the chance to immerse themselves in another world. The *Panorama Mesdag,* painted in 1880 by the renowned marine artist Hendrik Willem Mesdag and a team including his wife, Sientje Mesdag-van Houtenback, is one of the largest and finest surviving examples of the genre. The cinematic vision is a sweeping view of the sea, the dunes, and the picturesque fishing village of Scheveningen. To enhance the effect of the painting, you are first led through a narrow, dark passage, then up a spiral staircase, and out onto a "sand dune" viewing platform. To the southeast is The Hague, detailed so perfectly that old-time residents can identify particular houses. So lifelike is the 45-foot-high panorama with a 400-foot circumference that it's hard to resist the temptation to step across the guardrail onto the dune and stride down to the water's edge. ✉ *Zeestraat 65* ☎ *070/364–4544* ⊕ *www.panorama-mesdag.nl* 🎟 *€5* 🕐 *Mon.–Sat. 10–5, Sun. noon–5.*

8

★ ⑬   **Vredespaleis** *(Peace Palace).* Facing the world across a broad lawn, this building houses the International Court of Justice plus a 500,000-volume law library. The court was initiated in 1899 by Czar Nicolas II of Russia, who invited 26 nations to meet in The Hague to set up a permanent world court of arbitration. The current building was constructed in 1903 with a $1.5 million gift from Scottish-American industrialist Andrew Carnegie. Built in Flemish style, its red-and-gray granite-and-brick pile has become a local landmark. Gifts from the participating nations embellish the interior and include statuary, stained-glass windows,

> **STREET MARKETS**
>
> The main traditional street market (an organic farmers' market at that) in The Hague is generally held outside the **Grote Kerk** on Wednesday from 11 to 6. From the beginning of May until the end of October on Thursday and Sunday, there's an antiques market on **Lange Voorhout**. Wandering through the stalls on a fine day, perhaps to the accompaniment of a street musician, makes for a lovely experience. Plus there's an alfresco café for that all-important coffee and apple cake.

doors and clocks. Comparatively few litigations are heard here these days, although some still make headlines, such as the famous trial of Slobodan Milosevic. ⊠ *Carnegieplein 2* ☎ *070/302–4242* ⊕ *www.vredespaleis.nl* 🎫 *€5* ⊙ *Weekdays, guided tours only, at 10, 11, 2, 3, and 4 when court is not in session.*

OFF THE BEATEN PATH

Ⓒ

Fodor'sChoice
★

Madurodam. Statistically, the Dutch are the tallest people in Europe, and never must they be more aware of their size than when they visit this miniature version of their own land. Set in a sprawling "village" with pathways, tram tracks, and a railway station, every important building of the Netherlands is reproduced here, on a scale of 1:25. Many aspects of Dutch life ancient and modern are also on view: medieval knights joust in the courtyard of Gouda's magnificent Town Hall; windmills turn; the famous cheese-weighing ritual is carried out in Alkmaar; a harbor fire is extinguished; the awe-inspiring Delta Works storm surge barrier (constructed after the disastrous flooding of 1953) holds the ocean at bay; and planes land at Schiphol Airport. The world's longest miniature railway is here, too. Madurodam has two restaurants, a picnic area, a playground, and the entire exhibit is surrounded by gardens. The sunset hour is a fairy-tale experience as some 50,000 lights are turned on in the little houses. In July and August there is also an after-dark sound-and-light presentation, free to park visitors. Madurodam is in the woods that separate The Hague from the port of Scheveningen to the north. To get there take Tram No. 9 from either railway station in the city center. ⊠ *George Maduroplein 1* ☎ *070/416–2400* ⊕ *www.madurodam.nl* 🎫 *€13* ⊙ *Sept.–mid-Mar., daily 9–6; mid-Mar.–June, daily 9–8; July and Aug., daily 9 AM–11 PM.*

ALSO WORTH SEEING

④ Gevangenpoort Museum *(Prison's Gate Museum)*. This site is now a museum showcasing enough instruments of inhumanity to satisfy any criminologist. Originally a gatehouse to the local duke's castle, Gevangenpoort was converted to a prison around 1420. In 1882, it opened in its current incarnation as both a monument to its own past and a museum to apparatuses of punishment. After a slide presentation, the guided tour will take you through the torture chamber, the women's section, and the area where the rich were once imprisoned. If you're drawn to the macabre, the Gevangenpoort Museum offers a fascinating, if chilling, experience. ✉*Buitenhof 33* ☎*070/346–0861* ⊕*www. gevangenpoort.nl* 🎫*€4* ⊗*Tues.–Fri. 10–5, weekends noon–5. Guided tours only, every hr on the hr (last tour at 4).*

★ **⑧ Haags Historisch Museum** *(Hague Historical Museum)*. One of the series of museums that encircle the Hofvijver lake, the Historical Museum is in the Sebastiaansdoelen, a magnificent Classical-Baroque mansion dating from 1636. Worthy of a visit in itself, the mansion houses collections that offer an in-depth look at The Hague's past. Treasures include Jan van Goyen's enormous 17th-century panoramic painting of the city, a collection of medieval church silver, and a dollhouse from 1910. The idyllic views out the windows over the Hofvijver lake and the greensward of the Lange Voorhout are good for the soul. ✉*Korte Vijverberg 7* ☎*070/364–6940* ⊕*www.haagshistorischmuseum.nl* 🎫*€4* ⊗*Tues.–Fri. 10–5, weekends noon–5.*

☝ **⑮ Museon.** With hands-on, interactive displays, frequent special exhibitions, and archaeological and intercultural subjects with common themes, plus children's workshops on Wednesday and Sunday afternoons (book in advance), Museon claims to be "the most fun-packed popular science museum in the Netherlands," and perhaps they're right. Permanent exhibitions center on the origins of the universe and evolution. The Museon is right next door to the Gemeentemuseum, so you can easily combine a visit to both. ✉*Stadhouderslaan 37* ☎*070/338–1338* ⊕*www.museon.nl* 🎫*€7.50* ⊗*Tues.–Sun. 11–5.*

★ **⑤ Museum Bredius.** Housed in an 18th-century patrician mansion, the collection of traveler and art connoisseur Abraham Bredius (1855–1946) supports the argument that the private collections are often the best. It includes works by Jan Steen, as well as nearly 200 paintings by Dutch "little masters"—whose art Bredius trumpeted. Once curator of the Mauritshuis, Bredius was the first art historian to question the authenticity of Rembrandt canvases (there were zillions of them in the 19th century), setting into motion a seismic quake that reduced the master's oeuvre to fewer than 1,000 works. The house itself, overlooking the Hofvijver, makes a fittingly elegant setting for the art. ✉*Lange Vijverberg 14* ☎*070/362–0729* ⊕*www.museumbredius.nl* 🎫*€4.50* ⊗*Tues.–Sun. 11–5.*

8

★ ⑫ **Museum Mesdag.** Literally wall-papered with grand paintings and exquisite fabrics and tapestries, this oft-overlooked treasure-house is former residence of noted 19th-century Dutch painter H. W. Mesdag. Famed for his vast *Panorama Mesdag*, he left this house as a repository for his collection of works from The Hague School, which often featured seascapes and the life of fisherfolk in nearby Scheveningen. ⊠ *Laan van Meerdervoort 7f* ☎ *070/364–6940* ⊕ *www.museummesdag.nl* ⊠ *€5* ⊗ *Tues.–Sun. noon–5.*

☾ ⑪ **Museum voor Communicatie** *(Communication Museum).* Ultramodern and with lots of space, light, and activities, the Communication Museum looks at the ways in which people have gotten in touch with one another over the years, from carrier pigeon to e-mail. Some exhibits are specifically designed for young children, allowing them to play with old telex machines or design their own cell phone ringtones. Much of the signage is in Dutch, although English-speaking audio guides are available. ⊠ *Zeestraat 82* ☎ *070/330–7500* ⊕ *www.muscom.nl* ⊠ *€6* ⊗ *Weekdays 10–5, Sat. and Sun. noon–5.*

⑭ **Omniversum.** The IMAX theater shows a rotating program of film spectaculars, including several with nature-based and futuristic themes, on a screen six stories high. It's also one of the few Hague sights open in the evenings. ⊠ *Pres. Kennedylaan 5* ☎ *0900/666–4837* ⊕ *www.omniversum.nl* ⊠ *€9* ⊗ *Showing times vary–check the Web site or phone to confirm.*

★ ③ **Schilderijengalerij Prins Willem V** *(Prince William V Painting Gallery).* One of the last remaining Dutch art *kabinets*, this princely gallery is packed with old-masters hung in 18th-century *touche-touche* fashion (with barely an inch between paintings). Opened in 1773 it became the Netherlands' first public museum (until then, most collections were seen only by special appointment). The cream of the collection was later moved to the Mauritshuis, but many fine works remain. The long, narrow room has grand Louis XVI stucco ceilings, but it nevertheless exudes an intimate, homey atmosphere, as if a friend who just happened to own a collection that included works by Jan Steen and Rembrandt had asked you over to see them. The museum is scheduled to re-open in 2008 following major renovation work—check the Web site for the latest information. ⊠ *Buitenhof 35* ☎ *070/362–4444* ⊕ *www.mauritshuis.nl* ⊠ *€1.50 (free with entry to Mauritshuis)* ⊗ *Tues.–Sun. 11–4.*

① **Stadhuis Atrium** *(Town Hall).* Richard Meier's Neo-Modernist 1995 complex, comprising the Town Hall, Central Library, and Municipal Record Office, is an awe-inspiring creation in aluminum, glass, and white epoxy resin. Inside, take the elevator to the 11th floor (weekdays only) to get the full effect of the building's light and space. The architect's attention to mathematical relationships–every aspect of the design is based on measurements that are multiples of 17.73 inches—makes for mesmerizing effect. Meier has endeavored to show the building, both literally and metaphorically, in its best light—the quality of light in the vast central lobby belies the fact you are actually indoors. ✉*Spui 70* ☎*070/353–3629* ⊕*www.atriumdenhaag.nl* 🎟*Free* ⊙*Mon.–Wed. and Fri. 7* AM*–7* PM, *Thurs. 7* AM*–9:30* PM, *Sat. 9:30–5.*

WHERE TO STAY & EAT

$$$–$$$$ ✕**Restaurant Julien.** A glamorous belle epoque interior, lush with Tiffany-style chandeliers and ornate mirrors, echoes an equally decadent menu. Try the mouth-watering lamb with truffle purée or the open ravioli with turbot. Finish off with a Dutch cheese plate or one of the delicious house desserts, such as the banana crème brûlée. Julien prides itself on an extensive wine list. ✉*Vos in Tuinstraat 2a* ☎*070/365–8602* ⊕*www.julien.nl* ⊟*AE, DC, MC, V* ⊙*Closed Sun.*

★ $$–$$$$ ✕**It Rains Fishes.** Crown Prince Willem Alexander has been known to pop in here, so you know it must be good. A gleaming eggshell, ivory, and mirrored jewel box, It Rains Fishes is run by a team of five international chefs, whose predominantly aquatic specialties combine Thai, Malaysian, Indonesian, and French flavors. Its name, taken from a Thai folktale of fishes jumping from the river after a heavy rainfall, finds a few echoes in the restaurant's decor, with the occasional painted fish leaping around on the ceiling and walls. Specialties include sea bass with lemon and tarragon oil and king crab in the shell with Malay black pepper sauce. For an unorthodox but totally winning dessert, choose the Thai basil and chocolate sorbet. Outdoor dining is available in good weather. ✉*Noordeinde 123* ☎*070/365–2598* ⊕*www. itrainsfishes.nl* ⊟*AE, DC, MC, V* ⊙*No lunch Sat. and Sun.*

★ $$–$$$ ✕**Garoeda.** Named after a golden eagle in Indonesian mythology, a symbol of happiness and friendship, Garoeda is something of an institution among Hagenaars, many of whom consider it the best Indonesian spot in town. Established in 1949 and spread over five floors, the restaurant is decorated with Eastern art, and filled with wicker chairs and lush plants to give it a unique "colonial" atmosphere. Waiters are dressed in traditional costume and are more than happy to advise patrons new to the Indonesian dining experience. In addition to a choice of no less than seven different rijsttafels (an exotic smorgasbord of Indonesian dishes), there is also an extensive à la carte menu, featuring some unusual finds, such as spicy mussels and crispy roasted chicken in soy sauce. ✉*Kneuterdijk 18a* ☎*070/346–5319* ⊕*www. garoeda.com* ⊟*AE, DC, MC, V.*

8

★ $–$$$ ✕ **Le Haricot Vert.** In a 17th-century building that once housed the staff of the nearby Noordeinde palace, Le Haricot Vert is a popular haunt for locals who come to enjoy good food in an intimate, candlelit atmosphere. Every possible wall surface is hung with china, sections of stained glass, pictures, and mirrors, and the overall effect is one of beguiling, romantic clutter. Dishes such as grilled sardines with ratatouille, and lamb fillet served with rosemary and sweet peppers, combine Dutch classics with French flair. The menu changes seasonally, so you can expect irresistible asparagus in spring and game in winter. ✉ *Molenstraat 9a–11* ☎ *070/365–2278* 🖃 *AE, MC, V* ☉ *No lunch Mon.–Wed.*

> ## BAR FOOD
>
> When sitting down to a glass of beer, there's little the Dutch like more than a portion of hot *bitterballen:* half a dozen or so deep-fried, breadcrumb-coated "balls," with a side of mustard for dipping. When you bite into one you'll encounter finely-ground meat-based goo with negligible nutritional value. What this is exactly, no one seems to know for sure. The meat part may have once belonged to a cow, but you can bet your life it wasn't finest rump. We love them!

$–$$$ ✕ **'T Goude Hooft.** Magnificently dating from 1423 but rebuilt in 1660, the oldest restaurant in The Hague has a well-preserved interior, with plenty of wooden beams, brass chandeliers, and "antique" furniture all richly redolent of the Dutch Golden Age. In warm weather, the large terrace overlooking the market square makes a pleasant spot in which to enjoy a drink and a platter of *bitterballen.* For something more substantial, try the wine-enriched beef stew. ✉ *Dagelijkse Groenmarkt 13* ☎ *070/346–9713* 🖃 *MC, V.*

★ $–$$ ✕ **Dudok Brasserie.** These days, Dudok is *the* in place in The Hague. It's ideal for people-of-every-stripe-watching, from politicians debating over a beer, to the fashionistas toying with their salads, to pensioners tucking into an afternoon tea of cream cakes and salmon sandwiches. The vast granite-and-metal interior looks like a cross between a 1930s railway station and an ultracontemporary factory, and besides the countless small tables and roomy bar area, there's a communal central table and a packed magazine rack to keep solo diners busy. The menu combines international dishes—carpaccio of beef, steaks, and grilled chicken—with traditional Dutch fare such as mustard soup (surprisingly mild and flavorsome) and sausage with cabbage. Additional pluses include a terrace for outdoor dining and a 1:30 AM closing on Saturday. ✉ *Hofweg 1a* ☎ *070/890–0100* ⊕ *www.dudok.nl* 🖃 *AE, DC, MC, V.*

★ ¢–$ ✕ **Eetlokaal Lokanta.** A well-priced menu and funky, colorful decorations, like floral oilcloths on the tables and gilded tissue holders, make this eatery popular with trendy young locals, who flock in to enjoy a delicious combination of Greek, Turkish, and Moroccan dishes. Try the *imam beyildi* (Turkish for "the imam fainted"), the name for a dish of eggplant stuffed with a spicy meat mixture. Because Lokanta is less expensive than some other places on this central street, it fills up fast, so get there early or reserve ahead. ✉*Buitenhof 4* ☎*070/392–0870* ▤*MC, V* ⊘*No lunch Sun.*

¢–$ ✕**Greve.** Take your place at one of many wooden tables spread out between the giant cacti and huge earthenware pots in this airy and trendy café. Opt for the mouthwatering delight of grilled swordfish with guacamole or the hearty chicken soup thick with fresh vegetables. You'll need to make your mind up fairly quickly, as service in this chatty, communal, and informal eatery is surprisingly speedy. Greve also has a formal dining room, which offers the same menu in slightly more formal surroundings. ✉*Torenstraat 138* ☎*070/360–3919* ▤*AE, DC, MC, V (restaurant only)* ⊘*Restaurant closed Sun. and Mon.*

★ $$$$ ✕▦**Le Méridien Hotel Des Indes.** A stately grande dame of the hotel world and once a 19th-century mansion built principally for grand balls and entertainment, Des Indes has a graciousness that makes it one of the world's premier hotels. Stay here and you'll be following in the footsteps of Empress Josephine of France, Theodore Roosevelt, and the legendary ballerina Anna Pavlova (who, sorry to note, died here after contracting pneumonia on her travels). Des Indes sits on one of the city's most prestigious squares, in the heart of The Hague, surrounded by all the important buildings: the Parliament, embassies, ministries, and the best shops. The interior is a harmonious blend of belle epoque elements: marble fluted columns, brocaded walls, a good deal of gilding. Luxurious and ample bedrooms have all the best facilities—there are even Jacuzzis in some of them (although not the belle epoque ones). The former inner courtyard is now a towering domed lounge leading to the superb formal dining room—all crystal and linen—called Le Restaurant. On offer here is ambitious French-Mediterranean cuisine. Chef Van-Beusekom changes the Menu Royal every week, so the ingredients are always in season; and there is always a dish that brings Holland's East Indies past to mind. After all, this hotel isn't called Des Indes for nothing. ✉*Lange Voorhout 54–56, 2514 EG* ☎*070/361–2345* 📠*070/361–2350* ⊕*www.hoteldesindes.nl* ⇆*79 rooms, 13 suites* ⊜*In-room: refrigerator, dial-up. In-hotel: public Wi-Fi, restaurant, pool, gym, parking (fee), no-smoking rooms* ▤*AE, DC, MC, V.*

★ $$–$$$$ ▦**Parkhotel Den Haag.** Situated in lovely Molenstraat, a boutique- and café-busy street with a bohemian feel, the Parkhotel has been sheltering visitors since 1912. The building still exults in plenty of Art Nouveau detailing; architecture buffs won't want to miss its fabulous five-story brick-and-stone stairway, for example. Today, friendly staff plus light, airy rooms complete with all the modern conveniences (including snazzy bathrooms) add to its charms. ✉*Molenstraat 53, 2513 BJ* ☎*070/362–4371* 📠*070/362–4525* ⊕*www.parkhoteldenhaag.nl* ⇆*120 rooms* ⊜*In-room: no a/c, dial-up. In-hotel: restaurant, bar, parking (fee)* ▤*AE, DC, MC, V* ⧉*BP.*

$$–$$$ ▦**Novotel.** It's a case of "Lights, camera, action!" in this Novotel, housed as it is in what was once a cinema. Its interior designers have cleverly capitalized on this former life, with the entrance foyer and lounge atmospherically decorated with movie posters, cameras, and directors' chairs. It all helps to create a sense of individuality in what

8

might otherwise be just another bland chain hotel. The guest rooms, safely decorated in shades of peach and blue, aren't quite as interesting, but what they lack in imagination they more than make up for in cleanliness and modern conveniences. And the Novotel's location is ideal for shopping and sightseeing. ⌧*Hofweg 5–7, 2511 AA* ☎*070/364–8846* 🖷*070/356–2889* ⊕*www.accorhotels.nl* 💬*104 rooms, 2 suites* ⚡*Inroom: refrigerator, Wi-Fi. In-hotel: restaurant, bar, parking (fee)* ▤*AE, DC, MC, V.*

$ 🏨**Petit.** This quiet, family-style hotel, operated by a young couple and fronted by a pretty garden, is on a residential boulevard between the Peace Palace and The Hague Municipal Museum. Occupying two large houses that date from 1895, Petit is tastefully furnished in warm shades of red and gold, with the occasional period stained-glass accent. The wood-paneled bar-lounge is a nice place to relax. ⌧*Groothertoginnelaan 42, 2517 EH* ☎*070/346–5500* 🖷*070/346–3257* ⊕*www.hotelpetit.nl* 💬*20 rooms* ⚡*In-room: no a/c, refrigerator, Wi-Fi. In-hotel: bar, parking (fee)* ▤*AE, DC, MC, V* ⭘*BP.*

$ 🏨**Sebel.** The friendly owners of this hotel have expanded it into two buildings between the city center and the Peace Palace. Tidy and comfortable, the rooms are large but sparsely furnished, and have high ceilings and tall windows for lots of light and air. ⌧*Prins Hendrikplein 20, 2518 JC* ☎*070/345–9200* 🖷*070/345–5855* ⊕*www.hotelsebel.nl* 💬*27 rooms* ⚡*In-room: no a/c, dial-up. In-hotel: bar, parking (fee)* ▤*AE, DC, MC, V* ⭘*BP.*

¢ 🏨**Stayokay.** Stayokay is one of the leading hostel chains in Holland, and this one enjoys a location close to Hollands Spoor train station. Besides the 12 double rooms, there are rooms for three to nine. Clean, modern, and light, the hostel is in a renovated former warehouse and has a deck on the water plus a library, Internet stations, and a pool table for when you just can't sightsee any more. ⌧*Scheepmakersstraat 27, 2515 VA* ☎*070/315–7888* 🖷*070/315–7877* ⊕*www.stayokay. com* 💬*49 rooms each with 2–9 beds and shared baths* ⚡*In-room: no a/c, no phone, no TV. In-hotel: restaurant, bar, parking (fee), public Internet* ▤*No credit cards* ⭘*BP.*

NIGHTLIFE & THE ARTS

NIGHTLIFE

Though The Hague seems fairly quiet at night, don't be fooled. Behind the reserved facade are plenty of clubs and bars tucked away, often discreetly hidden down tiny backstreets. However, if you like your nightlife of the pumpingly loud variety, you'd best hop on a train to Amsterdam.

BARS

Tapperij Le Duc (⌧*Noordeinde 137* ☎*070/364–2394*) has a delightful old-world ambience, with lots of wood, tiles, and a magnificent fireplace.

De Paap (✉ *Papestraat 32* ☏ *070/ 365–2002*) has live music most nights and a cozy, welcoming atmosphere. The beer's cheap, too. **Boterwaag** (✉ *Grote Markt 8a* ☏ *070/365–9686* ⊕ *www.september.nl*) is a favorite—located in a 17th-century weigh house, its high, vaulted brick ceilings make this magnificent bar feel open and airy even when packed. It draws a trendy young crowd.

Paas (✉ *Dunne Bierkade 16a* ☏ *070/ 360–0019*) sits beside a picturesque canal between Hollands Spoor Station and the city center. A haven for beer connoisseurs, it offers 150 brews, by far the best selection in town. Dunne Bierkade is also home

to many other bars and restaurants, and has been dubbed the city's "Avenue Culinaire." **Schlemmer** (✉ *Lange Houtstraat 17* ☏ *070/360–9000*) is a comfortable brown-style bar that is one of Den Haag's top places to see and be seen.

To enjoy an aperitif in an upmarket setting and surrounded by The Hague's bold and beautiful, a trip to **Bodega de Posthoorn** (✉ *Lange Voorhout 39a* ☏ *070/360–4906*) is a must. You can have light meals here and the leafy terrace is particularly appealing. **Frenz** (✉ *Kazernestraat 106* ☏ *070/363–6657*) is a lively gay outpost for both sexes. The friendly and relaxed **Stairs** (✉ *Nieuwe Schoolstraat 11* ☏ *070/364–8191*) is gay-oriented, but women are welcome here too.

MUSIC CLUBS

The latest local and international bands can be heard at **Het Paard** (✉ *Prinsengracht 12* ☏ *070/750–3434*), where you can also dance and watch movies and multimedia shows.

The huge **Marathon** (✉ *Wijndaelerweg 3* ☏ *070/368–0324*) offers a wide variety of music and attracts a young, energetic crowd.

THE ARTS

The Hague has a thriving cultural life—look no further than the gleaming Spui theater complex for proof. The resident orchestra and ballet company are so popular that advance reservations are essential if you want to be sure of a ticket. If you do catch a show, you'll note an unusual phenomenon from the otherwise normally reserved Dutch: the compulsory standing ovation. For some mysterious reason, this response seems to be given with far greater frequency here than in other countries. For information on cultural events, call the **Uit information**

(⊠ *Uitpost Den Haag* ☏*070/363–3833 weekdays 9–5*) in The Hague. In addition, pick up the monthly *Den Haag Agenda,* published by the VVV tourist office, which will keep you up-to-date on every worthwhile event that's happening in town during your stay.

MUSIC, THEATER & DANCE

De Appel company has a lively, experimental approach to theater and performs at its own **Appeltheater** (⊠ *Duinstraat 6* ☏*070/350–2200* ⊕*www.toneelgroepdeappel.nl*). Mainstream Dutch theater is presented by the national theater company **Het Nationale Toneel,** which performs at the **Royal Schouwburg** (⊠ *Korte Voorhout 3* ☏*0900/345–6789* ⊕*www.ks.nl*).

For an outing with children, visit **Kooman's Poppentheater** (⊠ *Frankenstraat 66* ☏*070/355–9305* ⊕*www.kooman-poppentheater.nl*), which performs musical shows with puppets every Wednesday and Saturday. Advance booking is recommended.

The **Nederlands Danstheater** (⊠ *Spuiplein 152* ☏*070/880–0333* ⊕*www.ldt.nl*) is the national modern dance company and makes its home at the Lucent Dance Theatre, the world's only theater built exclusively for dance performances. It has an international reputation for groundbreaking productions, which might cause a run on tickets.

The Hague's **Residentie Orkest** has an excellent worldwide reputation and performs at **Dr. Anton Philipszaal** (⊠ *Spuiplein 150* ☏*070/880–0333* ⊕*www.residentieorkest.nl*).

SHOPPING

There is a plethora of intimate, idiosyncratic specialty boutiques to explore in The Hague, and in the larger department stores you can kid yourself that you're there only to admire the architecture—several are housed in period gems. With its historic and artistic connections, the city's art and antiques trade has naturally developed a strong reputation, and you can certainly find treasure here. Despite the Dutch reputation for thrift, haggling for antiques isn't "done." That said, you can almost always secure some kind of discount if you offer to pay in cash. Late-night shopping in The Hague is on Thursday until 9. Increasingly in the center of town, you'll find larger stores open on Sunday. Many shops take a half day or don't open at all on Monday.

DEPARTMENT STORES

De Bijenkorf (⊠ *Wagenstraat 32 [entrance on Grote Markstraat]* ☏*070/426–2700*) is Holland's premier department-store chain. It has a reputation for combining class with accessibility and is excellent for cutting-edge housewares, fashion accessories, and clothing basics. Do look, too, at the building's period detailing: the stained-glass windows, carvings, and original flooring that adorn the sweeping stairway on the left of the store.

The **Maison de Bonneterie** (⊠ *Gravenstraat 2* ☎*070/330–5300*) is The Hague's most exclusive department store—and it's got the "By Royal Appointment" labels to prove it. Built in 1913 and with an enormous central atrium, it's a glittering mixture of glass and light. On Maison de Bonneterie's four floors you'll find everything from Ralph Lauren shirts to wax candles.

SPECIALTY STORES

ANTIQUES & FINE ART

There are so many reputable antiques and art specialists on Noordeinde and Denneweg that a trip down either street is sure to prove fruitful.

Smelik & Stokking (⊠*Noordeinde 150* ☎*070/364–0768*) specializes in contemporary art, welcomes browsers, and has a pretty sculpture garden full of unusual pieces.

Voorhuis Kunst en Antiek (⊠*Noordeinde 88* ☎*070/392–4138*) has a suit of armor positioned outside its door that seems to demand that shoppers enter. Inside, various rooms are filled with seemingly every style of furniture, dating from the 17th century onward.

BOOKS & PRINTS

M. Heeneman (⊠*Prinsestraat 47* ☎*070/364–4748*) is a respected dealer who specializes in Dutch antiquarian prints, maps, and architectural renderings. Staff in this small shop are happy to advise customers, and purchases are wrapped in beautiful paper that depicts a fantasy old Dutch town. You'll always be able to buy English-language newspapers at the city's train stations, but otherwise the centrally located **Verwijs** (⊠*Passage 39* ☎*070/311–4848*), one of a chain of bookstores, sells a good range of English-language magazines and books. **A. Houtschild** (⊠*Papestraat 13* ☎*070/346–7949*) has a broad selection of books, including great coffee-table art titles.

CLOTHING

Both men and women can find classics with a twist in natural linens, cottons, and wools at **Hoogeweegen Rouwers** (⊠*Noordeinde 23* ☎*070/365–7473*). The service is as timeless as the clothes—it's the sort of place where purchases are carefully wrapped in tissue paper. For handmade men's shirts, visit the diplomats' favorite supplier, **FG Van den Heuvel** (⊠*Hoge Nieuwstraat 36* ☎*070/346–0887*), in business since 1882.

WHERE TO SHOP

Denneweg, Frederikstraat, and Noordeinde are best for antiques shops, galleries, and boutiques. For quirky, one-of-a-kind gift shops, try Molenstraat and Papestraat. You'll find chain stores in the pretty, light-filled Hague Passage (Spuistraat 26), which dates from the 1880s and is the Netherlands' last remaining period mall. In the little streets behind the Passage are more fashion and home-ware boutiques. Between the Venestraat and Nieuwstraat is the charmingly named Haagsche Bluf (the name is akin to the "hot air" coming out of Washington, D.C.) pedestrian mall, featuring mainly clothing chain stores.

8

CRYSTAL, CHINA & HOUSEWARES

Ninaber van Eyben (⊠ *Hoogstraat 5* ☎ *070/365–5321*) sells the classic Dutch lifestyle look—antique-finish globes, silverware, and traditional blue-and-white china. There's plenty of room to look around without fear of breaking anything.

To see the cutting-edge side of contemporary Dutch housewares, visit **Steitner & Bloos** (⊠ *Molenstraat 39* ☎ *070/360–5170*). You'll find steel bathroom accessories, geometrically shaped lights, and sofas, tables, and chairs designed along clean, graphic lines.

GIFTS, SOUVENIRS & JEWELRY

Tucked away from the crowds is **Emma** (⊠ *Molenstraat 22* ☎ *070/345–7027*), a tiny, very feminine store complete with white-washed walls and a wooden floor. The owner specializes in silver plate and costume jewelry, much imported from Paris and Berlin. She also stocks a small range of fabulous chandeliers, sometimes in unusual colors such as purple.

The tiny, family-run store **Loose** (⊠ *Papestraat 3* ☎ *070/346–0404*) is a toy shop for grown-ups. Glass cabinets are filled with rolling pins, pots, and pans no bigger than a fingernail just perfect for dollhouse enthusiasts. Meanwhile there are also larger wooden toys, a wonderful selection of old Dutch books and albums, and, in the rear of the store, a wide range of old prints.

If you want to make your own gifts or kill some time with older kids, a good place to visit is the funky DIY-jewelry store **Bija** (⊠ *Prinsestraat 60* ☎ *070/362–8186*). You can choose delicate beads—candylike glass ones, metallic baubles, or fake pearls—then join the others at the big table and string them into pretty necklaces and earrings.

Customers at **Backers & Zoon** (⊠ *Noordeinde 58* ☎ *070/346–6422*) receive the sort of personal, attentive service one would expect from an old-fashioned family jeweler. There's a sophisticated stock of pieces, including signet rings, diamond rings, and Fabergé-style accessories. Prices are not for the fainthearted.

Papier Damen (⊠ *Noordeinde 186* ☎ *070/360–0166*) sells exquisite handmade papers and gift wrapping, as well as covered notebooks.

THE HAGUE ESSENTIALS

TRANSPORTATION

BY CAR

To reach The Hague directly from Amsterdam, take E19 via Amsterdam Schiphol Airport. To reach the city from Utrecht, take the A12. Once you're approaching the city, follow the signs for the central parking route. This is an extremely helpful ring road that covers the many inexpensive parking lots within the city center.

Car Rentals **Avis** (⊠ *Theresiastraat 216* ☎ *070/385–0698*). **Europcar** (⊠ *De Savornin Lohmanplein 5* ☎ *070/361–9191*).

BY TAXI

Taxis are available at the railway stations. Alternatively, to get one to collect you from your location, try one of the taxi firms recommended by the VVV: HTMC, ATC Taxi, or Baantax. You can't hail cabs in the street.

Contacts **ATC Taxi** (☎ *070/317–8877*). **Baantax** (☎ *070/350–4924*). **HTMC** (☎ *070/390–7722*).

BY TRAIN

There are two railway stations in The Hague: one is in the central business district, the **Station Hollands Spoor** (⊠ *Stationsweg*). The other station, **Centraal Station** (⊠ *Koningin Julianaplein*), is in the residential area. Trains from Amsterdam run directly to both the Centraal and Hollands Spoor stations, but the Centraal stop is an end stop, whereas Hollands Spoor is a through destination and is used as a stop for trains to and from Amsterdam, Delft, and Rotterdam. Travel from Hollands Spoor to these cities is more often by Intercity (express) train and will not involve a transfer.

Contact **Intercity Express Trains** (☎ *0900/9292*).

CONTACTS & RESOURCES

EMERGENCIES

Pharmacies stay open late on a rotating basis; call for addresses on a given night. Tourist Assistance Service is an organization serving foreign tourists who've fallen victim to crime or been involved in an accident; it's open seven days a week.

Emergency Services **National Emergency Alarm Number** (☎ *112 for police, fire, and ambulance*).

Hospital **The Hague** (⊠ *Bronovolaan 5* ☎ *070/312–4141*).

Hotline **Tourist Assistance Service** (☎ *070/424–4000*).

Late-Night Pharmacies **Late-Night Pharmacy Information** (☎*070/345–1000*).

TOURS

A Royal Tour that takes in the palaces and administrative buildings associated with Queen Beatrix operates April–September; the cost is €27.50 per person. The VVV also arranges a variety of tours covering everything from royalty to architecture. Or you can purchase booklets that will allow you to follow a walking tour at your own pace. The VVV does tours and has brochures for them, as well as tickets, at the VVV offices.

De Ooievaart runs boat tours around The Hague's canals. The boats depart from Bierkade and offer a peaceful and relaxing way to see the city. Trips last 1½ hours, cost €9.50, and tickets can be bought from the VVV.

Contacts **Day Trips Department, Den Haag Marketing** (☎*070/338–5800*). **De Ooievaart** (☎*070/445–1869* ⊕ *www.ooievaart.nl*).

VISITOR INFORMATION

Tourist Information **VVV City Mondial** (⊠ *Wagenstraat 193* ⊘ *Tues.–Sat. 10–5* ☎*070/402–3336*).

Side Trips to Belgium

WORD OF MOUTH

"If you only have two days, Brugge would be a perfect stop between the Netherlands and Paris."
—artstuff

"Bruges (Brugge) is the brightest jewel in Belgium and if you pass up the chance of seeing it you will be a poorer person. Belgian railways are easy, reliable and cheap - it's a small country. Brussels is not the most striking capital in Europe but there are nevertheless many beautiful places depending on your interests and requirements. Belgium is a delightful country and offers the finest beer on the continent, and just about the best food as well."

—stfc

Updated by
Susan Carroll

BELGIUM HAS ATTRACTIONS OUT OF proportion to its diminutive size. Brussels' vibrant, cosmopolitan atmosphere and multicultural beat make it much more than simply the administrative hub of Europe. For all its world-class restaurants, architecture, and art, though, the city keeps a relatively low profile, so you'll have the breathing room to relish its landmarks, cobbled streets, and beautiful parks.

The smaller cities of Brugge and Gent are ancient towns whose heritage has been well preserved. Gent and particularly Brugge get crowded during the summer, but in the quiet, colder seasons, the cities offer a peaceful refuge, and you can feel the rhythm of life centuries ago.

ORIENTATION

An expanding network of high-speed trains puts Brussels, Brugge, and Gent within commuting distance of many European cities. An extensive regional rail network makes it easy to hop around Belgium, and the country is also covered by a large network of four-lane highways. It's an easy drive from Amsterdam, Düsseldorf, and Paris.

Belgian Railways sends two trains each hour to Brugge from Brussels (52 minutes) and two trains an hour from Gent (27 minutes). The trains all pass through Brussels' three main stations: Gare du Nord/ Brussel Nord, Gare Centrale/Brussel Centraal, and Gare du Midi/Brussel Zuid. Of these three, the Gare du Midi/Brussel Zuid is the largest and has the clearest signage and directions. It's also the terminus for the Eurostar service connecting London and Paris, as well as the Thalys network that links Amsterdam, Brussels, Cologne, and Paris. You can also travel to Brugge and Gent from Amsterdam through Antwerp station, where there is one train an hour to each city.

PLANNING

TIMING
Travelers can cover the main sights of Brussels in a weekend. To add on the Flemish splendor of Gent and Brugge, it's best to allow at least a day for each city.

ABOUT THE RESTAURANTS & HOTELS
Belgium's better restaurants are on a par with the most renowned in the world. Prices are similar to those in France and Great Britain—and often cheaper. The Belgian emphasis on high-quality food filters down to more casual options as well, from main-square cafés to the street vendors you'll find in towns large and small. The restaurants we list in this book are the cream of the crop in each price category. Properties indicated by ✕⛩are lodging establishments whose restaurant warrants a special trip.

Belgium offers a range of options, from the major international hotel chains and small, modern local hotels to family-run restored inns and historic houses. Prices in metropolitan areas are significantly higher than those in outlying towns and the countryside.

	WHAT IT COSTS IN EUROS				
	¢	$	$$	$$$	$$$$
HOTELS	under €10	€10–€15	€15–€22	€22–€30	over €30
RESTAURANTS	under €75	€75–€120	€120–€165	€165–€230	over €230

Restaurant prices are per person for a main course; Hotel prices are for a standard double room in high season

BRUSSELS

204 km (122 mi) south of Amsterdam.

Brussels started life as a village towards the end of the 10th century and by end of the 19th century was one of the liveliest cities in Europe. In 1958 it became the European Economic Community's headquarters, a precursor to its hosting of the EU's administrative and political arms. As a by-product of Europe's increasing integration, international business has invaded the city. The result: city blocks of steel-and-glass office buildings set only a few steps from cobblestoned streets. Diversity is now the capital's greatest strength; one-third of the city's million-strong population are non-Belgians, and you're as likely to hear Arabic or Swedish spoken on the streets as French or Flemish.

TO & FROM

If you are traveling by car from Amsterdam, take the A1/E19 motorway. Once you reach the E40, follow the signs to the city. The trip takes around 2½ hours.

Brussels is connected to Amsterdam by the high-speed Thalys train network, which requires advance reservations. One train an hour leaves the Dutch capital for Brussels, and the journey takes just over 2½ hours. This is set to drop to 1½ hours in 2008, once high-speed tracks and signaling systems are in place. An InterCity train also leaves from Schiphol Airport and takes just over 2½ hours.

ORIENTATION

Brussels is small enough that you can get a superficial impression of it from a car window in a single day. For a more substantial appreciation, however, you need one day for the historic city heart, another for the uptown squares and museums, and additional days for museums outside the center and excursions to the periphery.

While Brussels technically includes 19 communes, or suburbs, most sights, hotels, and restaurants are clustered in the center. Locals simply call this the *centre,* but the tours here distinguish a Lower Town and Upper Town. The Lower Town is physically lower, including the area around the Grand'Place and the Bourse. A steep slope leads up to the Upper Town, around rue de la Régence, place Royale, and the Sablon squares.

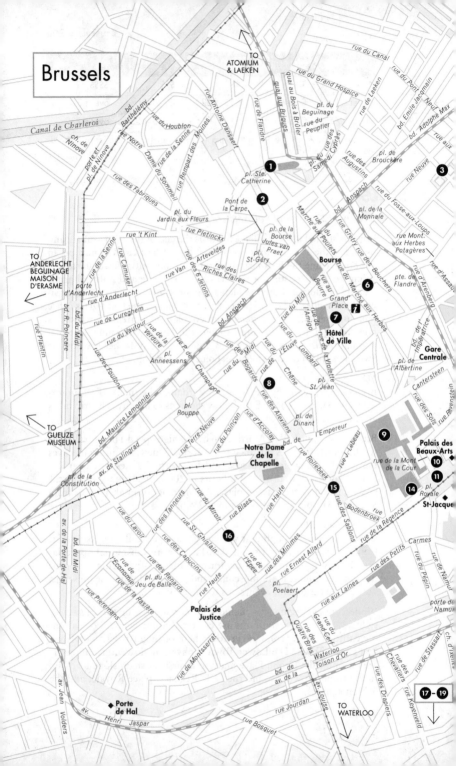

9

KEY

Metro

Rail lines

Tram

Tourist Information

IF YOU ONLY HAVE 1 DAY

Head for the Grand'Place to drink in the gilded splendor of its medieval buildings. Wander the narrow, cobbled lanes surrounding the square and visit the graceful, arcaded Galeries St-Hubert, an elegant 19th-century shopping gallery. Head down rue de l'Etuve to see the Manneken Pis, the statue of the little boy who according to legend saved Brussels by urinating to extinguish a fire. Walk to the place du Grand Sablon to window-shop at its many fine antiques stores and galleries. If it's a weekend, enjoy the outdoor antiques market. Have lunch in one of the cafés lining the perimeter, and don't forget to buy chocolates at one of the top chocolatiers on the square. Then cross over rue de la Régence to see the place du Petit Sablon before walking down the street to the Musée d'Art Moderne and the Musée d'Art Ancien to view collections ranging from the Surrealism of Belgian artist René Magritte to the delicately wrought details of Pieter Bruegel the Elder's *The Fall of Icarus*. Pick out a restaurant on the fashionable rue Antoine Dansaert for dinner. Finally, return to the Grand'Place to cap off the evening with a drink at one of the cafés to see the shimmer of the golden facades under the glow of lights.

EXPLORING THE LOWER TOWN

MAIN ATTRACTIONS

❼ Grand'Place. This jewel box of a square is arguably Europe's most ornate and most theatrical. It's a vital part of the city—everyone passes through at some point. At night the burnished facades of the guild houses and their gilded statuary look especially dramatic: from April to September, the square is floodlit after sundown with waves of changing colors, accompanied by music. Try to be here for the *Ommegang*, a magnificent historical pageant re-creating Emperor Charles V's reception in the city in 1549 (the first Tuesday and Thursday in July). You'll find here a flower market, frequent jazz and classical concerts, and in December, under the majestic Christmas tree, a life-size crèche with sheep grazing around it. The Gothic **Hôtel de Ville,** which dates from the early 15th century, dominates the Grand'Place. It's nearly 300 years older than the surrounding guild houses, as it survived the devastating fires of 1695. The left wing was begun in 1402 but was soon found to be too small. Charles the Bold laid the first stone for the extension in 1444, and it was completed four years later. The extension left the slender belfry off center; it has now been fully restored. The belfry is topped by a bronze statue of St. Michael crushing the devil beneath his feet, and is a beautiful and useful landmark for navigating Brussels' winding streets. Over the gateway are statues of the prophets, female figures representing lofty virtues, and effigies of long-gone dukes and duchesses. Inside the building are a number of excellent Brussels and Mechelen tapestries, some of them in the Gothic Hall, where recitals and chamber-music concerts are frequently held. Locals still get married in the town hall, so keep an eye out for brides stepping gingerly over the cobbles on summer mornings. ✉ *Grand'Place, Lower Town*

Fodor$Choice
★

☎ *02/279–4365* 🎫 *€2.50* 🕐 *Guided tours available in English, call for times or ask at the tourist office in the right wing of the building.* On the same side of the Grand'Place as the Hôtel de Ville, the **Maison de la Brasserie** was once the brewers' guild. The building, also known as l'Arbre d'Or (the Golden Tree), now houses a modest brewery museum, appropriate enough in a country that still brews 400 different beers. There are audio-guides in English. ✉ *Grand'Place 10, Lower Town* ☎ *02/511–4987* 🎫 *€2.50* 🕐 *Daily 10–5.*

8 **Manneken Pis.** This cocky emblem of Brussels has drawn sightseers for centuries—but after all the hype, you may be underwhelmed by the minuscule statue of the peeing boy, an image that launched a thousand tchotchkes. The first mention of the Manneken dates from 1377, and he's said to symbolize what Belgians think of the authorities, especially those of occupying forces. The present version was commissioned from sculptor Jerome Duquesnoy in 1619. It is a copy; the original was seized by French soldiers in 1747. In restitution, King Louis XV of France was the first to present *Manneken Pis* with a gold-embroidered suit. The statue now has 517 other costumes for ceremonial occasions, an ever-increasing collection whose recent benefactors include John Malkovich and Dennis Hopper, and his own personal dresser. On one or two days of the year, he spouts wine or beer, rather than water. A female version set up by an enterprising restaurateur, the *Jeanneke Pis,* can be found off the rue des Bouchers. ✉ *Rue de l'Etuve at rue du Chêne, Lower Town.*

ALSO WORTH SEEING

☕ ★ **4** **Centre Belge de la Bande Dessinée.** It fell to the land of Tintin, a cherished cartoon character, to create the world's first museum dedicated to the ninth art—comic strips. Despite its primary appeal to children, comic strip art has been taken seriously in Belgium for decades, and in the Belgian Comic Strip Center it is wedded to another strongly Belgian art form: Art Nouveau. Based in an elegant 1903 Victor Horta–designed building, the museum is long on the history of the genre but sadly short on kid-friendly interaction and anglophone-friendly information. Tintin, the cowlicked adventurer created in 1929 by the late, great Brussels native Hergé, became a worldwide favorite cartoon character. But many other artists have followed in Hergé's footsteps, some of them even more innovative. The collection includes more than 400 original plates by Hergé and his Belgian successors and 25,000 cartoon works; those not exhibited can be viewed in the archive. There are also good temporary exhibitions from time to time, a large comic strip shop, a library, and a lovely Art Nouveau brasserie. Most information is in French. If you enjoy this, keep an eye out for the comic-strip murals dotted on walls around the city. ✉ *Rue des Sables 20, Lower Town* ☎ *02/219–1980* 🌐 *www.comicscenter.net* 🎫 *€7.50* 🕐 *Tues.–Sun. 10–6.*

NEED A BREAK?

A la Mort Subite (✉ *rue Montagne-aux-Herbes-Potagères 7, Lower Town* ☎ *02/513–1318*) is a Brussels institution named after a card game called Sudden Death. This 1920s café with its high ceilings, wooden tables, and mirrored walls brews its own traditional Brussels beers, Lambik, Gueuze, and Faro, and is a favorite of beer lovers from all over the world. The sour, potent beer may be an acquired taste, but, like singer Jacques Brel, who came here often, you'll find it hard to resist the bar's gruff charm.

❸ Place des Martyrs. This square holds a monument to the 445 patriots who died in the brief but successful 1830 war of independence against the Dutch. The square itself is a neoclassical architectural ensemble built in 1795 in the cool style favored by the Austrian Habsburgs. ✉ *Rue du Persil, Lower Town.*

❶ Place Ste-Catherine. If you find the Grand'Place overrun by tourists, come to this square, a favorite of locals. It's a working market every weekday from 7 to 5, where people come to shop for necessities and banter with fishmongers. There's a stall where you can down a few oysters, accompanied by a glass of ice-cold muscadet. In the evening the action moves to the old **Vismet** (fish market), which branches off from the Eglise de Ste-Catherine. A canal used to run through here; it's now reduced to a couple of elongated ponds, but both sides are lined with seafood restaurants, some excellent, many overpriced. In good weather, there's outdoor waterside dining. ✉ *Intersection of rue Ste-Catherine, rue du Vieux Marché aux Grains, rue de Flandre, quai aux Briques, quai au Bois à Bruler, pl. du Samedi, rue Plateau, and rue Melsens, Lower Town.*

★ ❻ Quartier de l'Îlôt Sacré. Flimflam artists and jewelry vendors mingle with the crowds in the narrow rue des Bouchers and even narrower petite rue des Bouchers. While many streets in central Brussels were widened as part of the preparations for the 1958 World's Fair, these tiny routes escaped being demolished after locals complained. The area was given special protection in 1959 and there are strict rules governing what changes can be made to its historic buildings. As long as you watch out for pickpockets, it's all good-natured fun in the liveliest area in Brussels, where restaurants and cafés stand cheek by jowl, their tables spilling out onto the sidewalks. One local street person makes a specialty of picking up a heaped plate and emptying it into his bag. The waiters laugh and bring another plate. The restaurants make strenuous efforts to pull you in with huge displays of seafood and game. The quality, alas, is a different matter, and there have been arrests in recent years for large-scale credit-card fraud in these restaurants. *(For some outstanding exceptions, see Where to Eat, below.)* ⊕ *www.ilotsacre.be.*

❷ Rue Antoine Dansaert. This is the flagship street of Brussels' fashionable quarter, which extends south past St-Géry and Ste-Catherine. Avant-garde boutiques sell Belgian-designed men's and women's fashions along with more familiar designer labels. There are also inexpensive restaurants, cozy bars and cafés, edgy galleries, and stylish furniture shops.

EXPLORING THE UPPER TOWN

MAIN ATTRACTIONS

★ ⓫ Place Royale. There's a strong dash of Vienna in this white, symmetrical square; it was built in the neoclassical style by Austrian overlords. Elegantly proportioned, it is the centerpiece of the Upper Town, which became the center of power during the 18th century. The equestrian statue in its center, representing Godefroid de Bouillon, Belgian crusader and King of Jerusalem, is a romantic afterthought. The buildings are being restored one by one, leaving the facades intact. Place Royale was built on the ruins of the palace of the Dukes of Brabant, which had burned down. The site has been excavated, and it is possible to see the underground digs and the main hall, Aula Magna, where Charles V was crowned Holy Roman Emperor in 1519 and where, 37 years later, he abdicated to retire to a monastery. The church on the square, **St-Jacques-sur-Coudenberg**, was originally designed to look like a Greek temple. After the French Revolution reached Belgium, it briefly served as a "Temple of Reason." The Art Nouveau building on the northwest corner is the former Old England department store, now home[HAC6] of the Musée des Instruments de Musique.

⓰ **Les Marolles.** If the Grand'Place stands for old money, the Marolles neighborhood stands for old—and current—poverty. This was home to the workers who produced the luxury goods for which Brussels was famous. There may not be many left who still speak the old Brussels dialect, mixing French and Flemish with a bit of Spanish thrown in, but the area still has raffish charm, although gentrification is in progress. The Marolles has welcomed many waves of immigrants, the most recent from Spain, North Africa, and Turkey. Many come to the daily **Vieux Marché** (flea market) at the place du Jeu de Balle (7-1), where old clothes are sold along with every kind of bric-a-brac, plain junk, and the occasional gem. For more browsing, hit the smattering of antiques shops on rue Haute and rue Blaes. This area can be sketchy at night, so you may want to leave by sunset, particularly if you're alone, though groups can enjoy some fun bars and restaurants. ⊠ *Bordered by blvd. du Midi, blvd. de Waterloo heading southwest from Palais de Justice, and imaginary line running west from pl. de la Chapelle to blvd. Maurice Lemonnier, Upper Town.*

★ ⓯ **Place du Grand Sablon.** "Sand Square" is where the people of Brussels come to see and be seen. Once, as the name implies, it was nothing more than a sandy hill. Today, it is an elegant square, surrounded by numerous restaurants, cafés, and antiques shops, some in intriguing alleys and arcades. Every weekend morning a lively antiques market of more than 100 stalls takes over the upper end of the square. It isn't for bargain hunters, however. For a little tranquillity, pop into the beautiful Notre Dame du Sablon church or across the street to the lovely little Place du Petit Sablon garden. ⊠ *Intersection of rue de Rollebeek, rue Lebeau, rue de la Paille, rue Ste-Anne, rue Boedenbroeck, rue des Sablons, petite rue des Minimes, rue des Minimes, and rue Joseph Stevens, Upper Town.*

ALSO WORTH SEEING

⑤ **Cathédrale St-Michel et Ste-Gudule.** The twin Gothic towers and outstanding stained-glass windows of the city's cathedral look down over the city. One namesake, Saint Michael, is recognized as the patron saint of Brussels, but mention Saint Gudule and most people will draw a blank. Very little is known about this daughter of a seventh-century

Carolingian nobleman, but her relics have been preserved here for the past 1,000 years. Construction of the cathedral began in 1226 and continued through the 15th century; chapels were added in the 16th and 17th centuries. The remains of an earlier, 11th-century Romanesque church that was on the site can be glimpsed through glass apertures set into the floor. These, as well as the crypt and treasure rooms, can be visited for a nominal fee. Among the windows in the cathedral, designed by various artists, those by Bernard van Orley, a 16th-century court painter, are the most spectacular. The window of *The Last Judgment,* at the bottom of the nave, is illuminated from within in the evening. All royal weddings and christenings take place here. ⊠ *Parvis Ste-Gudule, Upper Town* ☎ *02/217–8345* ⊕ *www.cathedralestmichel. be* ☉ *May–Sept., weekdays daily 7–7, weekends 8:30–7; Oct.–Apr., weekdays 8:30–7, weekends 8:30–6.*

★ ⓮ **Musée d'Art Ancien.** In the first of the interconnected art museums, the Ancient Art Museum pays special attention to the so-called Flemish Primitives of the 15th century, who revolutionized the art of painting with oil. The Spanish and the Austrians pilfered some of the finest works, but there's plenty left by the likes of Memling, Petrus Christus, Rogier van der Weyden, and Hieronymus Bosch. The collection of works by Pieter Bruegel the Elder is outstanding; it includes *The Fall of Icarus,* in which the figure of the mythological hero disappearing in the sea is but one detail of a scene in which people continue to go about their business. Bruegel the Younger's wonderful *Fight between Carnival and Lent* is also here. There are English-language brochures and guided tours available, as well as an excellent brasserie. ⊠ *Rue de la Régence 3, Upper Town* ☎ *02/508–3211* ⊕ *www.fine-arts-museum. be* ☜ *€5* ☉ *Tues.–Sun. 10–5.*

★ ⓽ **Musée d'Art Moderne.** Rather like New York's Guggenheim Museum in reverse, the Modern Art Museum burrows underground, circling downward eight floors. You can reach it by an underground passage from the Musée d'Art Ancien or you can enter it from the house on place Royale where Alexandre Dumas (*père*) once lived and wrote. The collection is strong on Belgian and French art of the past 100 years, including such Belgian artists as the Expressionist James Ensor and the Surrealists Paul Delvaux and René Magritte, as well as Pierre Alechinsky and sculptor Pol Bury. Highlights include Magritte's *The Empire of Light* and Delvaux's *Pygmalion,* and Ensor's *Skeletons Fighting for a Smoked Herring.* Notable works by non-Belgian artists include Francis Bacon's *The Pope with Owls.* There are English-language explanatory brochures and guided tours available. ⊠ *Pl. Royale 1, Upper Town* ☎ *02/508–3211* ⊕ *www.fine-arts-museum.be* ☜ *€5* ☉ *Tues.–Sun. 10–5.*

☾ ⓾ **Musée des Instruments de Musique (MIM).** If you've ever been curious to
FodorśChoice know what a gamelan or Tibetan temple bell sounds like, here's your
★ chance. In addition to seeing the more than 1,500 instruments on display, you can listen to them via infrared headphones; you can hear musical extracts from almost every instrument as you stand in front of it. The more than 200 extracts range from ancient Greek tunes to

mid–20th century pieces. Paintings and ancient vases depicting the instruments being played throughout history complete the experience. The four-story museum features a complete 17th-century orchestra, a precious 1619 spinet-harpsichord (only two such instruments exist), an armonica, a rare Chedeville bagpipe, and about 100 Indian instruments given to King Leopold II by the rajah Sourindro Mohun Tagore. Head to the rooftop café for fantastic views of the city and call for information about occasional free concerts. ⊠ *Rue Montagne de la Cour 2, Upper Town* ☎ *02/545–0130* ⊕ *www.mim.fgov.be* ☎ *€5* ☉ *Tues.–Fri. 9:30–5, weekends 10–5.*

⓭ **Palais de Charles V.** Under the Place Royale lie the remains of a massive palace first constructed in the 11th century, and upgraded over hundreds of years in line with the power and prestige of Brussels' successive rulers. Destroyed by a great fire in 1731, the palace was never reconstructed. Parts of the palace, and one or two of the streets that surrounded it, have been excavated and the underground site is a fascinating glimpse into Brussels' past. You can see the remains of palace rooms and walk up the steep cobbled rue Isabelle, once the busiest street in the city. Access is through the Musée BELvue, which focuses on Belgium history and its royal family. ⊠ *Pl. Palais 7, Upper Town* ☎ *02/545–0800* ☎ *€5, combined with the Musée BELvue* ☉ *June–Sept., Tues.–Sun. 10–6; Oct.–May, Tues.–Sun. 10–5.*

EXPLORING CINQUANTENAIRE & SCHUMAN

Often known as the European Union quarter, this area combines the behemoth buildings of the government institutions, the lovely Parc du Cinquantenaire, and many of the city's best museums and sights. The area lies to the east of the city center. To get here, take Metro Line 1A or 1B to Schuman or Merode. If you are driving, simply follow the signs pointing toward the "European institutions."

The European Union project brought jobs and investments to the city, but in the process entire neighborhoods were razed to make room for unbendingly modern, steel-and-glass buildings, and as more countries join the EU, more massive complexes are being built. What remains of the old blocks has seen an influx of ethnic restaurants catering to the tastes of lower-level Eurocrats; the grandees eat in splendid isolation in their own dining rooms. The landmark, star-shape **Berlaymont** (⊠ *rue de la Loi 200*) is the home of the European Commission, the executive arm of the EU. The **European Council of Ministers** (⊠ *rue de la Loi 170*) groups representatives of the EU national governments and occupies the pink-marble Justus Lipsius building. The **European Parliament building,** (⊠ *rue Wiertz 43*) known for its rounded glass summit, looms behind the Gare du Quartier Leopold. ⊠*Place Schuman and Place du Luxembourg, Etterbeek.*

⑰ Koninklijk Museum voor Midden Afrika/Musée Royal de l'Afrique Centrale. Stellar holdings, contemporary concerns, and a history of the jaundiced colonial mind-set make for a fascinating mix at the Royal Museum of Central Africa. Part of King Leopold II's legacy to Belgium, it holds an incredible collection of 250,000 objects, including masks, sculpture, paintings, and zoological specimens. There's also a wealth of memorabilia from the central African explorations commissioned by Leopold, most notably by Henry Morton Stanley (of "Doctor Livingston, I presume?" fame), whose archive is kept here. Some sections of the museum, such as the entrance hall, are virtually time capsules from the early 20th century, while others have been updated. The attached research center has a "Living Science" exhibition open to the public, focusing on its studies of African flora and fauna. While many parts of the museum's collection are invaluable from a scholarly point of view, they came at an incalculable cost, rooted in Leopold's brutal colonial rule. The museum has been undergoing a period of soul-searching, and is in the process of updating its exhibitions to more accurately reflect the horrific nature of Belgium's time in the Congo. The renovations are due to be completed in April 2010, the museum's 100th anniversary. There's descriptive information available in English throughout. Save some time for a walk through the museum's beautifully landscaped park. To get here from place Montgomery, take tram 44 to Tervuren. ⊠*Leuvensesteenweg 13, Tervuren* 🕾*02/769–5211* ⊕*www.africamuseum.be* 🎫*€4* ☉*Tues.–Fri. 10–5, weekends 10–6.*

NEED A BREAK? The Maison Antoine (⊠*pl. Jourdan, Etterbeek*) frites stand sells the best fries in the capital, accompanied by a dizzying range of sauces. This is a great place to try Belgium's famous snack (the country's secret is frying the potatoes twice in beef tallow) and most of the bars that line the square will let you sit down and order a beer to go with your paper cone of frites.

☺ ⑱ Musée des Sciences Naturelles. The highlights of the Natural Sciences Museum are the skeletons of 14 iguanodons found in 1878 in the coal mines of Bernissart—these are believed to be about 120 million years old. It has a fine collection of 50,000 stones and 30,000 minerals and there are also displays on mammals, insects, and tropical shells, as well as a whale gallery. Unfortunately, there's little information in English, but an extensive renovation due to be completed in 2008 should remedy this situation. ⊠*Rue Vautier 29, Etterbeek* 🕾*02/627–4238* ⊕*www.sciencesnaturelles.be* 🎫*€4, free 1st Wed. of every month 1– 4:45* ☉*Tues.–Sat. 9:30–4:45, Sun. 10–6.*

★ ⑲ Musées Royaux d'Art et de l'Histoire. For a chronologically and culturally wide-ranging collection of artworks, hit the sprawling Royal Museums of Art and History in the lovely Parc du Cinquantenaire, which is worth a visit in itself. The vast numbers of antiquities and ethnographic treasures come from all over the world; the Egyptian and Byzantine sections are particularly fine. Don't miss the colossal Easter Island statue.

There's also a strong focus on home turf, with significant displays on Belgian archaeology and the immense and intricate tapestries for which Brussels once was famous. There's some information in English and guided tours are available. Take a break from the dizzying collection of exhibits in the pleasant café. ⊠ *Parc du Cinquantenaire 10, Etterbeek* ☎ *02/741–7211* ⊕ *www.kmkg-mrah.be* ⌨ *€4, free 1st Wed. of every month 1–5* ⊙ *Tues.–Fri. 9:30–5, weekends 10–5.*

EXPLORING IXELLES

Lying just south of the city center, Ixelles includes the city's most upmarket shopping district and the vibrant beat of Brussels' African quarter, the Matonge. A favored haunt of artists and writers, it's now home to the bourgeois and bohemian alike. Its Art Nouveau homes give the area a lot of the charm that the city center has lost through overdevelopment. To get here, take Metro Line 2 to Porte de Namur or Louise. If you're driving, take the Louise exit from the Ring Road.

🕙 ⑳ **Musée d'Architecture.** If Ixelles' Art Nouveau houses have made you hungry for information about Brussels' architectural past, present, and future, head to the Architecture Museum. Set in a former Masonic Lodge, the knowledgeable staff and displays of documents, drawings, and photographs provide a wealth of information. The museum mounts particularly good temporary exhibitions from time to time, such as one examining the depiction of animals in architecture. ⊠ *Rue de l'Ermitage 86, Ixelles* ☎ *02/649–8665* ⊕ *www.aam.be* ⌨ *€4* ⊙ *Tues.–Sat. 10–5.*

🕙 ㉑ **Musée des Enfants.** At this museum for two- to 12-year-olds, the purpose may be educational—learning to handle objects and emotions—but the results are fun. Kids get to plunge their arms into sticky goo, dress up in eccentric costumes, walk through a hall of mirrors, crawl through tunnels, and take photographs with an oversize camera. English-language guide booklets are available. To reach the museum by public transit, take tram 93 or 94 to the Buyl stop. ⊠ *Rue du Bourgmestre 15, Ixelles* ☎ *02/640–0107* ⊕ *www.museedesenfants.be* ⌨ *€6.85* ⊙ *Sept.–July, Wed. and weekends 2:30–5.*

9

NEED A BREAK?

Cafe Belga (⊠ *pl. Flagey 18, Ixelles* ☎ *02/640–3508*), in an ocean-liner-like Art Deco building, is a favorite among Brussels' beautiful people. Sip a cocktail or mint tea at the zinc bar or sit outside and gaze at the swans on the Ixelles ponds.

★ ㉒ **Musée Horta.** The house where Victor Horta (1861–1947), the creator of Art Nouveau, lived and worked until 1919 is the best place to see his mesmerizing interiors and furniture. Horta's genius lay in his ability to create a sense of opulence, light, and spaciousness where little light or space existed. Inspired by the direction of the turn-of-the-20th-century British Arts and Crafts movement, he amplified such designs into an entire architectural scheme. He shaped iron and steel into fluid, organic curves; structural elements were revealed. The facade of his home and studio, built between 1898 and 1901 (with extensions a few years later), looks somewhat narrow, but once you reach the interior stairway you'll be struck by the impression of airiness. A glazed skylight filters light down the curling banisters, lamps hang like tendrils from the ceilings, and mirrored skylights evoke giant butterflies with multicolor wings of glass and steel. Like Frank Lloyd Wright after him, Horta had a hand in every aspect of his design, from the door hinges to the wall treatments. You can reach the house by tram 91 or 92, getting off at the Ma Campagne stop. Note that you're not allowed to take photos. There's very little information in English, but you can buy books, postcards, and posters in the well-equipped shop. For more examples of how Horta and his colleagues transformed the face of Brussels in little more than 10 years, ride down avenue Louise to Vleurgat and walk along rue Vilain XIII to the area surrounding the ponds of Ixelles. ⊠ *Rue Américaine 25, Ixelles* ☎ *02/543–0490* ⊕ *www.hortamuseum.be* ⊡ *€7* ☉ *Tues.–Sun. 2–5:30.*

WHERE TO EAT

LOWER TOWN

$$$$
Fodor'sChoice
★ ✕ **Comme Chez Soi.** Pierre Wynants, the perfectionist owner-chef of what many consider the best restaurant in the country, has decorated his bistro-size restaurant in Art Nouveau style. The superb cuisine, excellent wines, and attentive service complement the warm decor. Wynants is ceaselessly inventive, and earlier creations are quickly relegated to the back page of the menu. One all-time favorite, fillet of sole with a white wine mousseline and shrimp, is, however, always available. Book weeks in advance to be sure of a table. ⊠ *Pl. Rouppe 23, Lower Town B1000* ☎ *02/512–2921* ⊸ *Reservations essential Jacket and tie* ⊟ *AE, DC, MC, V* ☉ *Closed Sun., Mon., July, and Dec. 25–Jan. 1.*

★ **$$$–$$$$** ✕ **L'Ogenblik.** This split-level restaurant, on a side alley off the Galeries St-Hubert, has all the trappings of an old-time bistro: green-shaded lamps over marble-top tables, sawdust on the floor, and laid-back waiters. There's nothing casual about the French-style cuisine, however: wild duck with apples and pepper, mille-feuille of lobster and salmon with a coulis of langoustines, saddle of lamb with spring vegetables and potato gratin. The selection of Beaujolais is particularly good. ⊠ *Galerie des Princes 1, Lower Town* ☎ *02/511–6151* ⊟ *AE, DC, MC, V* ☉ *Closed Sun.*

★ **$$$–$$$$** ✕ **Sea Grill.** Dashing superstar chef Yves Mattagne presides over the kitchen of arguably the best seafood place in town. Gastronomes rub shoulders here with tycoons and aristocrats, as they tuck into king crab from the Barents Sea, Dublin Bay prawns, Brittany lobster pressed table-side, and line-caught sea bass crusted with sea salt. Inevitably, because of its hotel location, the restaurant feels rather corporate, but it's spacious and elegant, and service is impeccable. ⊠ *Radisson SAS Hotel, 47 rue du Fossé-aux-Loups, Lower Town* ☎ *02/227–9225* ⊟ *AE, DC, MC, V* ☉ *Closed weekends.*

☾ **$–$$$$** ✕ **Aux Armes de Bruxelles.** A reliable choice among the many tourist traps of the Ilôt Sacré, this kid-friendly restaurant attracts a largely local clientele with its slightly tarnished middle-class elegance and Belgian classics: turbot waterzooi, a variety of steaks, and mussels prepared every conceivable way. The place is cheerful and light, and service is friendly if frequently overstretched. ⊠ *Rue des Bouchers 13, Lower Town* ☎ *02/511–5550* ⊟ *AE, DC, MC, V* ⊘ *Closed Mon.*

★ $$–$$$ ✕ **La Roue d'Or.** Bright orange and yellow murals pay humorous homage to Surrealist René Magritte in this excellent Art Nouveau brasserie. Bowler-hatted gentlemen ascend serenely to the ceiling, a blue sky inhabited by tropical birds. The good cuisine includes traditional Belgian fare—a generous fish waterzooi and homemade frites—as well as such staples of the French brasserie repertory as lamb's tongue vinaigrette with shallots, veal kidneys with tarragon and watercress cream, and foie gras. Menus in English are on hand. ⊠ *Rue des Chapeliers 26, Lower Town* ☎ *02/514–2554* ⊟ *AE, DC, MC, V* ⊘ *Closed mid-July–mid-Aug.*

★ $–$$$ ✕ **Chez Léon.** More than a century old, this cheerful restaurant has expanded over the years into a row of eight old houses, while its franchises can now be found across Belgium and even in France. It's a reliable choice on the restaurant-lined rue des Bouchers—just don't expect to see any locals eating here. Heaped plates of mussels and other Belgian specialties, such as *anguilles en vert* (eels in an herb sauce), and fish soup, are continually served. ⊠ *Rue des Bouchers 18, Lower Town* ☎ *02/511–1415* ⊟ *AE, DC, MC, V.*

★ $–$$ ✕ **In 't Spinnekopke.** True Brussels cooking flourishes in this charming restaurant. The low ceilings and benches around the walls remain from its days as a coach inn during the 18th century. Choose from among 100 artisanal beers, then tuck into dishes made with the tipple, such as *lapin à gueuze* (rabbit stewed in fruit beer). Go with an appetite, as portions are huge. The knowledgeable waiters will recommend the best beers to go with your food. ⊠ *Pl. du Jardin aux Fleurs 1, Lower Town* ☎ *02/511–8695* ⊟ *AE, DC, MC, V* ⊘ *Closed Sun. No lunch Sat.*

$–$$ ✕ **'t Kelderke.** Head down into this 17th-century vaulted cellar restaurant (watch out for the low door frame) for traditional Belgian cuisine served at plain wooden tables. Mussels are the house specialty, but the *stoemp et saucisses* (mashed potatoes and sausages) are equally tasty. It's a popular place with locals, as it's open from noon to 2 AM. There are no reservations, so turn up early to be sure to snag a table. ⊠ *Grand'Place 15, Lower Town* ☎ *02/513–7344* ⊟ *AE, DC, MC, V.*

¢–$$ ✕ **Kika Caffe.** This retro-style eatery is a great place for supper. It's a symphony in brown, with wallpaper copied from a Pedro Almodóvar film, and formica-topped tables. The food is Mediterranean fusion, served in hearty portions. ⊠ *Blvd. Anspach 177, Lower Town* ☎ *02/513–3832* ⊟ *MC, V* ⊘ *Closed Mon. and Tues.*

★ ¢–$$ ✕ **Mirante.** Don't be put off by the kitsch decor; this busy and popular Italian restaurant serves the best pizzas in town, alongside specialties from Puglia. Try the Fiorentina, a spinach pizza with a raw egg yolk in its center. ⊠ *Plattesteen 13, Lower Town* ☎ *02/511–1580* ⊟ *AE, DC, MC, V.*

★ ¢–$$ ✕ **Taverne Falstaff.** Students, pensioners, and everyone in-between flock to this century-old huge tavern with an Art Nouveau terrace and legendarily grumpy waiters. While the menu devotes itself to straightforward Belgian cuisine throughout the day and into the night, Cuban

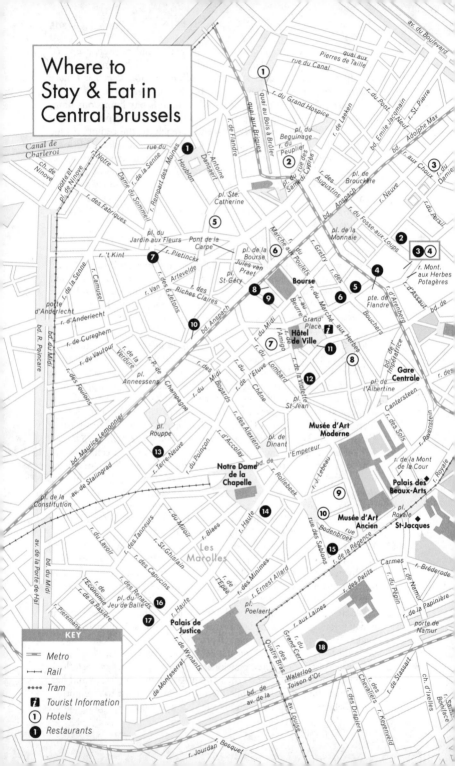

Where to Stay & Eat in Central Brussels

KEY

- Metro
- Rail
- Tram
- Tourist Information
- ① Hotels
- ● Restaurants

Canal de Charleroi

Les Marolles

Bourse

Grand Place

Hôtel de Ville

Musée d'Art Moderne

Musée d'Art Ancien

Notre Dame de la Chapelle

Palais de Justice

Palais des Beaux-Arts

St-Jacques

Gare Centrale

pl. Ste. Catherine

pl. du Jardin aux Fleurs

pl. Rouppe

pl. du Jeu de Balle

pl. Poelaert

pl. de la Constitution

pl. du Beguinage

pl. du Peuplier

pl. de Brouckère

pl. de la Monnaie

Restaurants ▼	
Amadeus	**2**
Au Vieux Saint Martin	**14**
Aux Armes de Bruxelles	**6**
Au Vieux Bruxelles	**19**
Bazaar	**16**
Chez Léon	**5**
Comme Chez Soi	**13**
De la Vigne á l'Assiette	**20**
Eetcafe Het Warm Water	**17**
In 't Spinnekopke	**7**
Kika Caffe	**10**
La Roue d'Or	**12**
La Truffe Noire	**21**
Le Pain Quotidien	**1, 15**
Le Pain et le Vin	**22**
L'Ogenblik	**4**
Maison du Bœuf	**18**
Mamy Louise	**23**
Mirante	**8**
Sea Grill	**3**
Taverne Falstaff	**9**
't Kelderke	**11**

Hotels ▼	
Alfa Sablon	**10**
Amigo	**7**
Atlas	**5**
Brussels Marriott Hotel	**6**
Hotel Silken Berlaymont	**11**
Jolly Grand Sablon	**9**
Le Dixseptième	**8**
Monty Hotel	**12**
Manos Premier	**13**
Noga	**1**
Radisson SAS Hotel	**4**
Sleep Well	**3**
Welcome Hotel	**2**

9

music and cocktails take over after 11 PM. (The kitchen is open until 5 AM on weekends.) The same group owns the next-door Montecristo Café, which is another loud, popular, late-night spot with Latin flavor. ☒ *Rue Henri Maus 19, Lower Town* ☎ *02/511–9877* ⊟ *AE, DC, MC, V.*

¢–$ ✕ **Le Pain Quotidien.** These bakeries are a popular brunch spot on weekend mornings. They have spread like wildfire all over Europe (and even to New York and Los Angeles) with the same satisfying formula: hearty homemade soups, open-face sandwiches on farm-style bread, and bowls of café au lait, served at a communal table from 7:30 AM to 7 PM. ☒ *Rue Antoine Dansaert 16, Lower Town* ☎ *02/502–2361* ☒ *Rue des Sablons 11, Upper Town* ☎ *02/513–5154* ⌂ *Reservations not accepted* ⊟ *No credit cards.*

UPPER TOWN

★ $$$$ ✕ **Maison du Boeuf.** Red-meat lovers are drawn to chef Michel Thueurel's exceptional beef rib steak roasted in salt, the house specialty. There are other tempting traditional French and Belgian choices too, mostly beef but with a couple of other choices (coq au vin for example) as well. Upscale in every way, with gliding waiters, heavy silver cutlery, and linen tablecloths, the eatery is a favorite of politicians and high society. ☒ *Hilton Hotel, blvd. de Waterloo 38, Upper Town* ☎ *02/504–1111* ⌂ *Reservations essential Jacket and tie* ⊟ *AE, DC, MC, V.*

$$$–$$$$ ✕ **Bazaar.** The building along a side street in the Marolles may once have been a convent, but it now exudes a seductive allure. Candles burn in its cavernous dining room, where Moroccan lamps and sofas create intimacy in a bric-a-brac setting. It's young and fashionable; there's a disco on the lower floor on weekends. The eclectic menu includes such choices as chicken *tajine* (slow-cooked with gravy in a deep, glazed earthenware dish) with olives and lemon. Later in the evening, it becomes a lively bar. ☒ *Rue des Capucins 63, Upper Town* ☎ *02/511–2600* ⊟ *AE, DC, MC, V* ☉ *Closed Sun. and Mon. No lunch.*

★ $$–$$$ ✕ **Au Vieux Saint Martin.** Even when neighboring restaurants on Grand Sablon are empty, this one is full. A rack of glossy magazines is a thoughtful touch for lone diners, and you're equally welcome whether you order a cup of coffee or a full meal. The short menu emphasizes Brussels specialties, and portions are substantial. The owner, a wine importer, serves unusually good wine for the price, by the glass or bottle. ☒ *Grand Sablon 38, Upper Town* ☎ *02/512–6476* ⌂ *Reservations not accepted* ⊟ *MC, V.*

$$ ✕ **Amadeus.** It's not so much the food (goat cheese with honey, vegetable tart, spareribs, tagliatelle with salmon) as the decor that makes this converted artist's studio near the place Stéphanie a must. Ultra-romantic, not to say kitschy, the dining rooms have an abundance of mirrors, candles, and intimate alcoves, creating a trysty, almost conspiratorial baroque feel. ☒ *Rue Veydt 13, St-Gilles* ☎ *02/538–3427* ⊟ *AE, DC, MC, V* ☉ *Closed mid-July–mid-Aug. No lunch.*

¢–$ ✕ **Eetcafe Het Warm Water.** Just above the place de Jeu de Balle in the heart of the Marolles, this café is a local institution known for its set brunches. These are rib-sticking meals, with muesli, yogurt, eggs, croissants, and some combination of cheese and ham. It's a staunchly Flemish place; the staff doesn't appreciate orders in French (English is preferable). When the neighborhood had no running water, this is where residents would come to get hot water—hence the name. Before wandering down the street to the *Vieux Marché* (flea market), get a snack of tasty bread and cheese or an omelet here, washed down with a bowl of *lait russe* (milky coffee). ⊠*Rue des Renards 19, Upper Town* ☎*02/213–9159* ⚐*Reservations not accepted* ⊟*No credit cards.*

IN & AROUND IXELLES

★ $$$–$$$$ ✕**La Truffe Noire.** Luigi Ciciriello's "Black Truffle" attracts a sophisticated clientele with its modern design, well-spaced tables, and cuisine that draws on classic Italian and modern French cooking. Carpaccio is prepared at the table and served with long strips of truffle and Parmesan. Entrées may include Vendé pigeon with truffles and steamed John Dory with truffles and leeks. In summer you can eat in the garden. ⊠*Blvd. de la Cambre 12, Ixelles* ☎*02/640–4422* ⚐*Reservations essential. Jacket and tie* ⊟*AE, DC, MC, V* ☉*Closed Sun., Jan. 1–10, last wk July and 1st 2 wks Aug. No lunch Sat.*

★ $$–$$$$ ✕**De la Vigne à l'Assiette.** When you take into account the high quality of the food and the wine list of this no-frills bistro off avenue Louise, the combination proves to be an exceptionally good value. The modern French cuisine of chef Eddy Dandrimont is embellished with such exotic flourishes as star anise sauce, and crisp angel-hair pasta atop grilled salmon. The excellent wine list refrains from the usual hefty markup. ⊠*Rue de la Longue Haie, Ixelles* ☎*02/647–6803* ⊟*AE, DC, MC, V* ☉*Closed Sun. and Mon. No lunch Sat.*

★ $$$ ✕**Le Pain et le Vin.** The plain-spoken name, "Bread and Wine," signals an equally pared-down aesthetic in this excellent restaurant. It's co-owned by acclaimed sommelier Eric Boschman; hence, the cellar is impressively deep, and wines can be ordered by the glass to accompany different courses. The food takes the minimalist route with choices such as risotto with asparagus and tuna steak. The large garden is a plus in fine weather. ⊠*Chaussée d'Alsemberg 812A, Uccle* ☎*02/332–3774* ⊟*AE, MC, V* ☉*Closed Sun. No lunch Sat.*

★ $–$$$ ✕**Au Vieux Bruxelles.** Open since 1882, this Brussels institution is a fun, lively place to have dinner and a firm local favorite. The cuisine is decidedly Belgian, with *anguilles au vert* (eels in a green sauce) and hearty carbonnades on the menu, and best accompanied by a good beer. Naturally, everything is served with frites, and be sure to ask for the tasty homemade mayonnaise. If you're feeling too full to tackle a whole dessert, you can order a half portion. ⊠*Rue St-Boniface 35, Ixelles* ☎*02/503–3111* ⊟*AE, DC, MC, V* ☉*Closed Mon.*

¢–$$ ✕**Mamy Louise.** This is one of several good quality lunch spots on the pedestrianized rue Jean Stas, just off avenue Louise. With Hamptons-style decor and outdoor tables in warm weather, the varied menu includes Belgian staples like *boudin* (blood sausage), as well as quiches and salads. It's also a great place to grab a morning or afternoon coffee and a delicious slice of cake. ⊠*Rue Jean Stas 12, Ixelles* ☎*02/534–2502* ⊟*AE, DC, MC, V.*

WHERE TO STAY

LOWER TOWN

★ $$$$ ⬚ **Amigo.** A block from the Grand'Place, the Amigo pairs contemporary design with antiques and plush wall hangings. Rooms are decorated in green, red, or blue, with silk curtains, leather headboards, and a mix of modern furniture and antiques. Works by Belgian artists hang on the walls, while Tintin pictures and figurines cheer up the mosaic-tiled bathrooms. If you'd like a view over the surrounding rooftops, ask for a room on one of the higher floors (these also have a higher rate). Pros: understated luxury, polished service, central location. Cons: some bathrooms are small, nearby streets can be noisy. ⊠ *Rue d'Amigo 1–3, Lower Town B1000* ☎ *02/547–4747* ⊕ *www.roccofortehotels. com* ⟿ *174 rooms, 19 suites* ⌂ *In-room: safe, refrigerator, Ethernet. In-hotel: restaurant, room service, bar, gym, public Wi-Fi, parking (fee)* ⊟ *AE, DC, MC, V.*

★ $$$$ ⬚ **Brussels Marriott Hotel.** This branch of the Marriott chain opposite the stock exchange has a striking cream-marble lobby, and each floor has a different theme for its guest rooms. Guest rooms are done in universal corporate-travel style: cherrywood furniture, green- or yellow-striped wallpaper, and marble bathrooms. Quieter ones face an internal courtyard; those on upper floors have city views. Nearly half of the rooms are especially geared toward business travelers, with ergonomic desk chairs and no-glare lamps. Pros: easy access to the city center, sound-proofed rooms. Cons: bland decor, slightly chilly staff. ⊠ *Rue A. Orts 1–7, Lower Town B1000* ☎ *02/516–9090* ⊕ *www.marriott.com* ⟿ *202 rooms, 16 suites* ⌂ *In-room: safe, refrigerator, Wi-Fi. In-hotel: restaurant, bar, gym, parking (fee)* ⊟ *AE, DC, MC, V* ⦿ *BP.*

$$$ ⬚ **Le Dixseptième.** Here you can stay in what was once the residence
Fodor's Choice   of the Spanish ambassador. The stylishly restored 17th-century build-
★   ing lies between the Grand'Place and the Gare Centrale. Rooms surround a lovely interior courtyard, and suites are up a splendid Louis XVI staircase. Named after Belgian artists, rooms have whitewashed walls, plain floorboards, exposed beams, and suede sofas. Suites have decorative fireplaces and the honeymoon suite is particularly romantic. Pros: romantic setting, gorgeous rooms. Cons: not so much fun for singles. ⊠ *Rue de la Madeleine 25, Lower Town B1000* ☎ *02/517–1717* ⊕ *www.ledixseptieme.be* ⟿ *22 rooms, 2 suites* ⌂ *In-room: safe, kitchen (some), refrigerator, Ethernet. In-hotel: bar, public Wi-Fi* ⊟ *AE, DC, MC, V.*

$–$$$ ⬚ **Alfa Sablon.** On a quiet street between the Sablon and the Grand'Place, this hotel offers spacious and attractive rooms, some with canopy beds. Some rooms are a bit dark. Suites arranged in duplex style favor comfort over corporate entertainment, with a gingham-covered sofa, a spiral staircase leading up to a tiny landing, and a modern classic-style bedroom in cherrywood and cream. Pros: Near two of the city's prettiest squares, service with a smile. Cons: Some rooms are a bit dark, not the most memorable building. ⊠ *Rue de la Paille, Lower Town B1000* ☎ *02/513–6040* ⟿ *32 rooms, 4 suites* ⌂ *In-room: safe. In-hotel: bar, gym, parking (fee)* ⊟ *AE, DC, MC, V* ⦿ *CP.*

$–$$$ ⊞**Atlas.** This hotel offers unpretentious comfort and a convenient location in a building dating from the 18th century. The small rooms have cream and yellow walls, gray carpets, and blue-and-white furniture. Suites, on two floors, each have a kitchenette in the lounge area. Buffet breakfasts are served in the blue-and-white basement with abstract art and the exposed brick of an ancient city wall. Pros: good value, convenient location. Cons: no-frills rooms, standard decor. ⊠*Rue du Vieux Marché aux Grains 30, Lower Town*B1000 ☎*02/502–6006* ⊕*www. atlas-hotel.be* ⌑*83 rooms, 5 suites* ⌂*In-room: refrigerator, Wi-Fi. In-hotel: parking (fee)* ▤*AE, DC, MC, V* ⍾*BP.*

⊞**Noga.** The hotel's Web site promises a "cosy, cosy, very cosy" spot, and indeed it is. Opened in 1958, the well-maintained Noga is packed with mementos of the Jazz Age, from table lamps to black-and-white photographs of the period. There are rooms on four floors for two, three, or four people—larger rooms have sofas great for socializing. You can rent a bike, borrow a book from the library, or even order a picnic lunch to take sightseeing with you. The hotel is in the popular Béguinage quarter, near the Ste-Catherine fish market. Pros: trendy spot, great service, super-friendly staff. Cons: bathrooms lack tubs, hotel fills up quickly. ⊠*Rue du Béguinage 38, Lower Town B1000* ☎*02/218–6763* ⊕*www.nogahotel.com* ⌑*19 rooms* ⌂*In-room: safe, refrigerator, Wi-Fi. In-hotel: bar, bicycles, parking (fee)* ▤*AE, DC, MC, V* ⍾*BP.*

★ **$** ⊞**Welcome Hotel.** Among the charms of the smallest hotel in Brussels are the young owners, Michel and Sophie Smeesters. The rooms, divided into economy, business, and first class, are as comfortable as those in far more expensive establishments. Each is strikingly decorated to evoke a certain place; the Bali and China rooms are particularly lovely, with their masks and dragon motifs. Around the corner on the Vismet (fish market), Michel doubles as chef of the excellent seafood restaurant La Truite d'Argent ($$$), where hotel guests get a special rate. Pros: fantastic decor, lovely staff. Cons: rooms fill up quickly. ⊠*Rue du Peuplier 5, Lower Town*B1000 ☎*02/219–9546* ⊕*www. brusselswelcomehotel.be* ⌑*14 rooms, 1 suite* ⌂*In-room: safe. In-hotel: restaurant, parking (no fee)* ▤*AE, DC, MC, V.*

¢ ⊞**Sleep Well.** This youth hostel is bright, well-run, and conveniently located for transportation links. The basic rooms sleep from one to eight people with shared bathrooms, and you have to pay extra for sheets. The more upscale rooms in the Star section have private bathrooms, and pretty striped bedspreads (sheets are included in the price). There's a comic-strip mural in the lobby, a TV room, Internet center, and lively bar with karaoke. Pros: clean rooms, great security, a great place to meet fellow travelers. Cons: extra cost for Internet access, can be noisy at night. ⊠*Rue du Damier 23, Lower Town B1000* ☎*02/218–5050* ⊕*www.sleepwell.be* ⌑*82 rooms* ⌂*In-room: no phone, no TV. In-hotel: restaurant, bar, bicycles, public Internet* ▤*MC, V* ⍾*CP.*

UPPER TOWN

$$$–$$$$ ⊞**Jolly Grand Sablon.** Part of the Sablon square's lineup of antiques shops, cafés, and chocolate makers, the Jolly offers discreet luxury behind an elegant white facade. The reception area is set within a hushed arcade of private art galleries, and there's a pretty interior cobbled courtyard. The rooms are unadventurously decorated in shades of pink or peach. Some bathrooms have only showers, but the plush suites have whirlpool baths. Ask for a room at the back, as the square outside is often clogged with traffic and the weekend antiques market gets going at 6 AM. Pros: lovely older building, full of art, shady courtyard. Cons: some baths have only showers, some front rooms are noisy. ⊠ *Rue Bodenbroeck 2–4, Upper Town B1000* ☎ *02/518–1100* ⊕ *www. jollyhotels.be* ☞ *193 rooms, 6 suites* ⌂ *In-room: refrigeratoar, dial-up. In-hotel: restaurant, bar, parking (fee)* ▭ *AE, DC, MC, V* ⦿ *BP.*

★ $$$ 🏠 **Radisson SAS Hotel.** Near the northern end of the Galeries St-Hubert shopping arcade, this hotel has an Art Deco facade and is decorated in a variety of styles, including "Maritime" rooms with blue and yellow walls and wood floors. The greenery-filled atrium incorporates a 10-foot-high section of the 12th-century city wall and serves excellent Scandinavian-style open sandwiches. Pros: great extras like self-filling minibars and trouser presses, near super shopping, eye-popping decor. Cons: location is sketchy at night, staff can be scarce during the day. ⊠ *Rue du Fossé-aux-Loups 47, Upper Town B1000* ☎ *02/219–2828* ⊕ *www.radisson.com/brusselsbe* ☞ *261 rooms, 24 suites* ⌂ *In-room: safe, Ethernet, Wi-Fi. In-hotel: 2 restaurants, bar, gym, parking (fee), minibar* ▭ *AE, DC, MC, V* ⦿ *BP.*

CINQUANTENAIRE & SCHUMAN

$–$$$ 🏠 **Hotel Silken Berlaymont.** Contemporary photography inspires the Berlaymont's signature look. Each room is decorated with works of a different photographer, and the navy, black, and dark-wood furnishings are sober and smart. Attention to perspective and style are evident in the chrome, black marble, and spotlights around the hotel. Eight rooms have showers only. The green mosaic-tiled sauna, hammam, spa, and fitness center are inviting. There's a good café on-site. Pros: smartly turned-out hotel, pleasantly busy atmosphere, great perks for business travelers. Cons: often overrun with groups, not the place for a romantic getaway. ⊠ *Blvd. Charlemagne 11–19, Etterbeek B1000* ☎ *02/231–0909* 📠 *02/230–3371* ⊕ *www.hoteles-silken.com* ☞ *214 rooms, 2 suites* ⌂ *In-room: safe, dial-up. In-hotel: restaurant, bar, gym, spa, parking (fee)* ▭ *AE, DC, MC, V.*

★ $–$$ 🏠 **Monty Hotel.** A stay here is like an overnight in a contemporary design showroom—with breakfast in the morning. Guest rooms have ingenious lighting, like winged lightbulbs by Ingo Maurer, Mario Bellini "Cuboglass" televisions, and gray-tiled bathrooms with Philippe Starck fittings. The comfortable lounge with its tomato-red walls is peppered with equally modern-classic furniture. Unlike some boutique hotels, the Monty doesn't tip over into chilly attitude; its warmth is demonstrated at breakfast, served at a friendly communal table. Pros: great design, delicious breakfasts, lively atmosphere. Cons: a little off the beaten track, few parking spaces. ⊠ *Blvd. Brand Whitlock 101, Laeken B1200* ☎ *02/734–5636* ⊕ *www.monty-hotel.be* ☞ *18 rooms* ⌂ *In-room: dial-up, Wi-Fi. In-hotel: bar, no elevator, parking (fee)* ▭ *AE, DC, MC, V* ⦿ *BP.*

SOUTH OF CENTER

★ **$$$$** ⊞ **Manos Premier.** This upscale hotel has expansive terraces, a rose-filled garden populated by waterfowl and songbirds, and a good restaurant, Kolya. The well-appointed rooms have Louis XV and Louis XVI antiques and inviting bedspreads in green, cream, and pink. The sauna has a decadent Moroccan flavor with tiling and arched doorways. Pros: handsome hotel, lovely garden. Cons: doesn't quite live up to its high price, a few shabby carpets and corners. ⊠*Chaussée de Charleroi 100–104, St-Gilles B1060* ☎*02/537–9682* ⊕*www.mano-shotel.com* ⌨*55 rooms, 15 suites* ⌂*In-room: safe, dial-up. In-hotel: restaurant, bar, gym, spa* ⊟*AE, DC, MC, V* |⊙|*CP.*

NIGHTLIFE & THE ARTS

Although the presence of both French and Flemish drives a wedge or two through the capital's cultural landscape, it also delivers some advantages. Both Flemish- and French-language authorities inject funds into the arts scene; one notable combined effort is the annual Kunsten-FESTIVALdesArts, a contemporary arts festival held in May. A glance at the "What's On" section of weekly English-language newsmagazine the *Bulletin* reveals the breadth of the offerings in all categories of cultural life. Tickets for major events can be purchased by calling **FNAC Ticket Line** (☎*0900/00600* ⊕*www.fnac.be*).

THE ARTS

CLASSICAL MUSIC The principal venue for classical music concerts is the Horta-designed **Palais des Beaux-Arts** (⊠*rue Ravenstein 23, Upper Town* ☎*02/507–8200* ⊕*www.bozar.be*). The complex, which also houses an art gallery and a theater, was the first multipurpose arts complex in Europe when it opened in 1928. Its Henry Le Boeuf concert hall has world-class acoustics.

NIGHTLIFE

There's a café on virtually every street corner, most serving all kinds of alcoholic drinks. Although the Belgian brewing industry is declining as the giant Inbev firm (the brewers of Stella Artois) muscles smaller companies out of the market, Belgians still consume copious quantities of beer, some of it with a 10% alcohol content. Most bars here have artisanal beers along with the major-brand usual suspects. The place St-Géry, rue St-Boniface, and the Grand'Place area draw the most buzz.

HIPSTER BARS The stylish, Art Deco **Archiduc** (⊠*rue Antoine Dansaert 6, Lower Town* ☎*02/512–0652*) attracts a thirtyish, fashionable crowd; it gets smoky up on the balcony. The sidewalk outside **Au Soleil** (⊠*rue du Marché-au-Charbon 86, Lower Town* ☎*02/513–3430*) teems with the hip and would-be hip, enjoying relaxed trip-hop sounds and very competitive prices. Another favorite with the arty crowd is Flemish bar **Monk** (⊠*rue Ste-Catherine 43, Lower Town* ☎*02/503–0880*), which used to be a schoolhouse.

TRADITIONAL BARS Beer is one of Brussels' biggest tourist draws, and the city has a few traditional-style bars where you can sample everything from the sour delights of local Lambic to the six Trappist treasures, brewed by

9

monks in Orval, Chimay, Roche-fort, Westmalle, and Westvleteren and revered the world over. One of the best is **Bier Circus** (✉*rue de l'Enseignement 57, North city center* ☎*02/218–0034*), which has a huge list of brews on its menu, including some excellent organic beers. With its wooden decor and friendly staff, this is a great place to start learning about Belgian beer, and there's good food, too. The grungy **Chez Moeder Lambic** (✉*rue de Savoie 68, St-Gilles* ☎*02/539–1419*) claims to stock 600 Belgian beers and a few hundred more foreign ones, as well as comic books to read while you sip.

WHO'S SPINNING

The club scene is lively, and world-famous DJs as well as homegrown mavericks spin regularly. Many places stay open until dawn. For a rundown on upcoming DJ parties and other late-night events, one resource is the online magazine **Noctis** (⊕*www. noctis.com*).

JAZZ CLUBS   After World War II, Belgium was at the forefront of Europe's modern jazz movement: of the great postwar players, harmonica maestro Toots Thielemans and vibes player Sadi are still very much alive and perform in Brussels. Other top Belgian jazz draws include guitarist Philip Catherine, pianist Jef Neve, and the experimental ethno-jazz trio Aka Moon. Tiny **New York Café Jazz Club** (✉*chaussée de Charleroi 5, Upper Town* ☎*02/534–8509*) models itself on the Blue Note in the Big Apple, down to the table service. **The Music Village** (✉*rue des Pierres 50, Lower Town* ☎*02/513–91345*) hosts a plethora of international jazz musicians. **Sounds** (✉*rue de la Tulipe 28, Ixelles* ☎*02/512–9250*) dishes up contemporary jazz along with good food. An established jazz club with its own record label and festival, **Travers** (✉*rue Traversière 11, Upper Town* ☎*02/218–4086*) pulls in aficionados.

GAY BARS

The city's small but lively gay quarter can be found around rue des Pierres, rue du Marché au Charbon, and rue St Géry in the Lower Town. Keep an eye out for rainbow flags in the windows. **Tels Quels** (✉*rue du Marché-aux-Charbon 81, Lower Town* ☎*02/512–4587*) is not only a bar, but also a resource for up-to-date information about the capital's gay scene and the publisher of a monthly magazine. **Chez Maman** (✉*rue des Grands Carmes 7, Lower Town* ☎*02/502–8696*), a disco with a fun drag show, is presided over by Maman herself. For night owls, **Le Why Not** (✉*rue des Riches Claires 7, Lower Town* ☎*02/512–6343*) is a popular club bar that pulses until dawn.

SHOPPING

For generations, Brussels has been the place to indulge a taste for some of the finer things in life: chocolate, beer, lace, and lead crystal. Brussels is also heaven for comic book collectors, and there are lots of offbeat shops to tempt magpies. While the city may not be bursting with bargains, there are inexpensive items to be found in the markets. Value-added tax (TVA) inflates prices, but visitors from outside the EU can obtain refunds. Sales take place in January and July.

SHOPPING DISTRICTS

The stylish, upper-crust shopping area for clothing and accessories spans the upper end of **avenue Louise; avenue de la Toison d'Or,** which branches off at a right angle; **boulevard de Waterloo,** on the other side of the street; **Galerie Louise,** which links the two avenues; and **Galerie de la Toison d'Or,** another gallery two blocks away. The **City 2** mall on place Rogier and the pedestrian mall, **rue Neuve,** are fun and inexpensive shopping areas (but not recommended for women alone after dark).

There are galleries scattered across Brussels, but low rents have made **boulevard Barthélémy** the "in" place for avant-garde art. The **Windows** (✉ *blvd. Barthélémy 13, Upper Town*) complex houses several galleries. On the **place du Grand Sablon** and adjoining streets and alleys you'll find antiques dealers and smart art galleries.

The **Galeries St-Hubert** is a rather stately shopping arcade lined with posh shops selling men's and women's clothing, books, and objets d'art. In the trendy **rue Antoine Dansaert** and **place du Nouveau Marché aux Grains,** near the Bourse, are a number of boutiques carrying fashions by young designers and interior design and art shops. Avenue Louise and its surrounding streets in Ixelles have a number of chic boutiques offering clothes new and vintage, jewelry, antiques, and housewares.

STREET MARKETS

Bruxellois with an eye for fresh farm produce and low prices do most of their food shopping at the animated open-air markets in almost every commune. Among the best are those in **Boitsfort** in front of the Maison Communal on Sunday morning; on **place du Châtelain,** Wednesday afternoon; and on **place Ste-Catherine,** all day, every day except Sunday. In addition to fruits, vegetables, meat, and fish, most markets include traders with specialized products, such as cheese or wild mushrooms. The most exotic market is the Sunday morning **Marché du Midi,** where the large North African community gathers to buy and sell foods, spices, and plants, transforming the area next to the railway station into a vast bazaar. You can also join the thousands of shoppers in the meat and produce market in **Anderlecht's,** housed in a 19th-century former abattoir every Friday, Saturday, and Sunday 7–2.

9

BRUSSELS ESSENTIALS

BY AIR

AIRPORTS Brussels National Airport (BRU), known locally as Zaventem, is 15 km (9 mi) northeast of the city center. This large international airport is easy to navigate, as signs are in English as well as French and Dutch. It has plenty of facilities, including shops, a bank, a travel agency, a post office, Internet stations for last-minute e-mail, restaurants, and bars, including ones specializing in Belgian beer.

Brussels South Airport (CRL) in Charleroi is 55 km (34 mi) south of the city. This small airport is home to low-cost airlines like Ryanair and WizzAir, but is immensely popular due to rock-bottom prices and good service to central and Eastern Europe. The facilities are limited to a self-service restaurant and a newspaper shop.

AIRPORT
TRANSFERS

By Bus: The number 12 bus runs between the Zaventem airport and the city center every half hour. One-way tickets cost €3. Courtesy buses serve airport hotels and a few downtown hotels; inquire when making reservations. A shuttle bus service runs between Brussels South Airport and the Gare du Midi. It leaves the station 2½ hours before each flight is due to depart and the airport after each flight lands. The hour-long ride costs €10 each way.

By Taxi: From Zaventem, a taxi to the city center takes about half an hour and costs roughly €35. ■ TIP➔ You can save 25% on the fare by buying a voucher for the return trip if you use the Autolux taxi company. Don't accept the offers of freelance taxi drivers who hawk their services in the arrival hall. A taxi from Brussels South Airport can cost up to €100; if you miss the shuttle bus, you might ask other stranded passengers if they'd like to share the cab and split the cost.

By Train: SNCB's Airport City Express trains run between Zaventem airport and all three main railway stations in Brussels: Midi (South), Central (Central), and Nord (North). The trains leave every 20 minutes from about 5:30 AM to midnight, every day; the ride takes 23 minutes. A one-way ticket costs €2.60.

Airport Information **Brussels National Airport** (☎ 0900–70000 ⊕ www. brusselsairport.be).**Brussels South** (Charleroi ☎ 071/251–211 ⊕ www.charleroi-airport.com).

Contact **Airport City Express** (☎ 02/555–2525 ⊕ www.b-rail.be). **Autolux** (☎ 02/411–1221).

BY BUS

Eurolines offers up to three daily express bus services from Amsterdam, Berlin, Frankfurt, Paris, and London. One-way trips cost from €20 to €50. The Eurolines Coach Station is at CCN Gare du Nord.

Depot **CCN Gare du Nord** (✉ rue du Progrès 80, St-Josse ☎ 02/203–0707).

Lines **Eurolines** (✉ rue du Progrès 80, St-Josse ☎ 02/274–1350 ⊕ www. eurolines.be).

BY CAR

GETTING
THERE

Belgium is covered by an extensive network of four-lane highways. Brussels is 204 km (122 mi) from Amsterdam on E19; 222 km (138 mi) from Düsseldorf on E40; 219 km (133 mi) from Luxembourg City on E411; and 308 km (185 mi) from Paris on E19.

If you piggyback on Le Shuttle through the Channel Tunnel, the distance is 213 km (128 mi) from Calais to Brussels; the route from Calais via Oostende is the fastest, even though on the Belgian side the highway stops a few kilometers short of the border. If you take the ferry to Oostende, the distance is 115 km (69 mi) to Brussels on the six-lane E40.

GETTING
AROUND

Brussels is surrounded by an inner and outer beltway, marked RING. Exits to the city are marked CENTER/CENTRUM. Among several large underground parking facilities, the one close to the Grand'Place at rue Duquesnoy is particularly convenient if you're staying in a downtown hotel.

BY PUBLIC TRANSPORTATION

GETTING AROUND The metro, trams, and buses operate as part of the same system and are run by the city's transport authority, STIB/MIVB (Société des Transports Intercommunaux de Bruxelles/Maatschappij voor het Intercommunaal Vervoer te Brussel). You can buy the tickets in metro stations, train, and in some shops. ■TIP→A single "Jump" ticket, which can be used among all three systems in an hour-long time frame, costs €1.50 (or €2 if you buy your ticket onboard a tram or bus). The best buy is a 10-trip ticket, which costs €11.

Detailed maps of the Brussels public transportation network are available in most metro stations and at the Tourist Information Brussels in the Grand'Place. ■TIP→Get a map free with a Tourist Passport (also available at the tourist office), which, for €7.50, allows you a one-day transport card and discount admissions at museums.

Information **STIB/MIVB** (☎02/515–2000 ⊕ www.stib.irisnet.be). **Tourist Information Brussels** (☎02/513–8940 ⊕ www.brusselsinternational.be).

BY TAXI

The easiest way to ensure a cab is to call Taxis Verts or Taxis Oranges. You can also catch a taxi at stands around town, which are indicated with yellow signs. All officially registered taxis have a yellow-and-blue sign on their roofs. A cab ride within the city center costs between €6.20 and €12.40. Tips are included in the fare.

Companies **Taxis Oranges** (☎02/349–4343). **Taxis Verts** (☎02/349–4949).

BY TRAIN

Brussels is one of the hubs for the Belgian National Railways (SNCB/NMBS). Passenger trains are clean and efficient. Domestic trains use the capital's three stations: Gare du Midi, Gare Centrale, and Gare du Nord. National service is extensive and frequent. For example, four to five trains an hour link Antwerp with Brussels; the trip takes about 45 minutes.

Thayls high-speed trains to Paris, Bordeaux, Avignon, Marseille, Liège, Cologne, Aachen, Amsterdam, Rotterdam, and The Hague leave from the Gare du Midi. It takes under an hour and a half to get to Paris, and trains leave every half hour between 6 AM and 7 PM. The trip to Amsterdam takes 2 hours and 38 minutes. In 2008, thanks to new high-speed tracks and upgraded signaling systems will reduce this trip by an hour.

Stations **Gare Centrale** (✉carrefour de l'Europe 2, Upper Town ☎02/528–2828). **Gare du Midi** (✉rue de France, Lower Town ☎02/528–2828). **Gare du Nord** (✉rue du Progrès 76, St-Josse ☎02/528–2828).

BANKS & EXCHANGE SERVICES

Currency exchange offices are clustered around the Grand'Place, while the major banks, Fortis and ING, have branches around the city. Branch hours are usually weekdays 9 AM to 1 PM and 2 PM to 4:30 PM. There are 24-hour ATMs, called Bancontact or Mister Cash and marked with blue-and-yellow signs, all around Brussels, though not as many as in most European cities. This is why long lines often sprout from downtown ATMs on weekend nights. Frustratingly, ATMs are often out of order and can be totally out of cash by Sunday evenings.

EMERGENCIES

The police and fire departments both have immediate-response emergency hotlines. One pharmacy in each district stays open 24 hours; the rotating roster is posted in all pharmacy windows.

Contacts **Ambulance and Fire Brigade** (☎ *100*). **24-Hour English-Speaking Info and Crisis Line** (☎ *02/648–4014*).

VISITOR INFORMATION

The tourist information center in the Hôtel de Ville is open weekdays 9–6. The office has an English-speaking staff.

Tourist Information **Tourist Information Brussels** (*TIB ⊠ Hôtel de Ville, Grand'Place, Lower Town* ☎ *02/513–8940* ⊕ *www.brusselsinternational.be*).

GENT

210 km (130 mi) south of Amsterdam.

Gent's old town has been almost totally restored to its original form, and it now has the largest pedestrian area in Flanders. You'll have to walk along cobblestone streets and pavements, which can be tricky if you wear high-heeled shoes or open sandals. The gray-stone city center looks like a puzzle piece, surrounded as it is by the river Leie, its tributaries, and canals. Although many people live and work in this area, most reside in neighboring quarters.

One of the nicest neighborhoods to explore is the Gravensteen (also known as Patershol) area, once the residential quarter for the textile workers from the Gravensteen. Its layout is medieval but its spirit is modern—the streets are now crammed with chic cafés and restaurants. It's the in place to live for well-off young couples.

TO & FROM

To reach Gent by car, take the A4 motorway to Antwerp, and then follow the E17. The journey takes around two hours. By train, take a Thalys high-speed train to Brussels' Gare de Midi/Brussel Zuid station, then change to a Belgian Railways (SNCB/NMBS) train bound for Gent. There are two an hour, and the trip from Brussels takes 27 minutes. Gent St Pieters station is a little distance from the city center, so hop on a bus or take a taxi when you arrive.

EXPLORING

MAIN ATTRACTIONS

6 **Belfort.** Begun in 1314, the 300-foot belfry tower symbolizes the power of the guilds and used to serve as Gent's watchtower. Since 1377, the structure has been crowned with a gilded copper weather vane shaped into a dragon, the city's symbol of freedom. (The current stone spire was added in 1913.) Inside the Belfort, documents listing the privileges

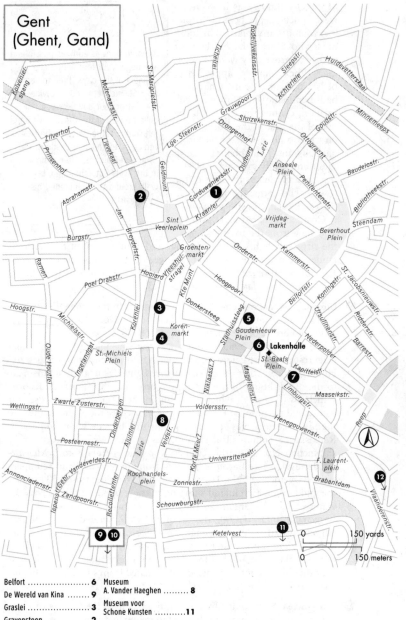

Gent
(Ghent, Gand)

of the city (known as its *secreets*) were once kept behind triple-locked doors and guarded by lookouts who toured the battlements hourly to prove they weren't sleeping. When danger approached, bells were rung—until Charles V had them removed. Now a 53-bell carillon, claimed by experts to be one of the best in the world, is set on the top floor. One of the original bells, the Triumphanta, cast in 1660 and badly cracked in 1914, rests in a garden at the foot of the tower. The largest original bell, Klokke Roeland, is still sung about in Gent's anthem of the same name. The view from the tower is one of the city's highlights. Note that you need a guide to visit the carillon; guides are available afternoons between May and September. ⊠ *St-Baafsplein, Torenrij* ☎ *09/269–3730* 🎫 *€3, guided tour €6* ⊙ *Mid-Mar.–mid-Nov., daily 10–12 and 2—5:30.*

> **IF YOU ONLY HAVE 1 DAY**
>
> Arrive in Gent as early as possible and begin your tour with a classic view of the city's three towers from St. Michael's bridge. Divide the rest of your day between the guild houses of the Graslei district, the Gothic cathedral, and the Gravensteen, the ancient castle of the counts of Flanders. After a dinner in the lively Patershol area, take a walk around the illuminated historic district.

★ ❸ **Graslei.** This magnificent row of guild houses in the original port area is best seen from across the river Leie on the **Korenlei** (Corn Quay). The guild house of the **Metselaars** (Masons) is a copy of a house from 1527; the original, which stands near the Sint-Niklaaskerk, has also been restored. The **Eerste Korenmetershuis** (the first Grain Measurers' House), representing the grain weigher's guild, is next. It stands next to the oldest house of the group, the brooding, Romanesque **Koornstapelhuis** (Granary), which was built in the 12th century and served its original purpose for 600 years; this was where the grain claimed by the tax collectors was stored. It stands side by side with the narrow Renaissance **Tolhuis** (Toll House), where taxes were levied on grain shipments. No. 11 is the **Tweede Korenmetershuis** (Grain Measurers' House), a late Baroque building from 1698. The **Vrije Schippers** (Free Bargemen), at No. 14, is a late Gothic building from 1531, when the guild dominated inland shipping. Almost opposite this, across the water at No. 7 Korenlei, is the **Huis der Onvrije Schippers** (Unfree Bargemen), built in 1740 and decorated with a gilded boat. The free bargemen had right of passage along the canals inside the city; the unfree had to unload their cargoes outside the city, and transfer them to the boats of the guild of free bargemen. Every night the Graslei and the other historic monuments are illuminated from sunset to midnight. ⊠ *Graslei, Gravensteen/Patershol.*

❷ **Gravensteen.** Surrounded by a moat, the Castle of the Counts of Flanders resembles an enormous battleship steaming down the sedate Lieve Canal. From its windswept battlements there's a splendid view over the rooftops of old Gent. There has been a fortress on this site for centuries. The Gravensteen, modeled after a Syrian crusader castle, was built in 1180 by the Count of Flanders on top of an existing fortress, and has been rebuilt several times since then—most recently in the 19th century to reflect what the Victorians thought a medieval castle should look like. Above the entrance is an opening in the shape of a cross, which symbolizes the count's participation in the Crusades, resulting in his death in the Holy Land.

Today's brooding castle has little in common with the original fortress, built by Baldwin of the Iron Arm to discourage marauding Norsemen. Its purpose, too, changed from protection to oppression as the conflict deepened between feudal lords and unruly townspeople. Rulers entertained and feasted here throughout the Middle Ages, and the Council of Flanders, the highest court in the land, met in chambers here for over 500 years. At various times the castle has also been used as a mint, a prison, and a cotton mill. It was here, too, that the country's first spinning mule was installed after being spirited away from England; soon the castle's chambers echoed with the clattering of looms, and Gent became a textile center to rival Manchester. ⊠ *Sint-Veerleplein, Gravensteen/Patershol* ☎ *09/225–9306* 🎟 *€6* ⏲ *Apr.–Sept., daily 9–6; Oct.–Mar., daily 9–5.*

> ## BOATING
>
> Boating is popular along the river and canals and a fantastic way to see the city and surrounding area. Take a boat tour or rent a motorboat from the **Minerva Boat Company** (☎ *03/779-6777* ⊕ *www.minervaboten.be*). Boats take four to five people and no special license is required. The embarkation and landing stage is at Coupure, on the corner of Lindenlei.

❼ **Sint-Baafskathedraal.** St. Bavo's Cathedral, begun in the austere 13th century but finished in the 16th century in the ornate Brabantine Gothic style, dramatically rises from a low, unimposing entryway. It contains one of the greatest treasures in Christendom: *De aanbidding van het Lam Gods* (The Adoration of the Mystic Lamb). Painted by brothers Jan and Hubert Van Eyk, this altarpiece is one of the most beautiful and influential paintings of the Middle Ages. One of its lower panels was stolen in 1934 and was never recovered, giving rise to numerous conspiracy theories and inspiring Albert Camus' novel, *The Fall.*

Fodor's Choice
★

The cathedral's ornate pulpit, made of white Italian marble and black Danish oak, was carved in the 18th century by the sculptor Laurent Delvaux. Angels, cherubs, massive trees, flowing robes, and tresses combine to create a masterwork. A Rubens masterpiece, *Saint Bavo's Entry into the Monastery,* hangs in one of the chapels. Other treasures include a baroque-style organ built in 1623 and a crypt crammed with tapestries, church paraphernalia, and 15th- and 16th-century frescoes. There are no visits during services. ⊠ *St-Baafsplein, Torenrij* 🎟 *Cathedral free, Mystic Lamb, €3* ☎ *09/269-2065* ⊕ *www.gent.be* ⏲ *Cathedral: Apr.–Oct., daily 8:30–6; Nov.–Mar., daily 8:30–5. Chapel: Apr.–Oct., Mon.–Sat. 9:30–4:45, Sun. 1–4:30; Nov.–Mar., Mon.–Sat. 10:30–3:45, Sun. 1–3:30.*

9

ALSO WORTH SEEING

❾ **De Wereld van Kina (Kind en Natuur).** This natural history museum shares an ancient abbey with the Kunsthal Sint-Pieters Abdij *(see below)*. Here you'll find "school subjects" on geology, the evolution of life, human biology and reproduction, and a diorama room of indigenous birds. There's an Internet station and a sound-and-light

> **BIKING**
>
> For cycling routes, pick up a bicycle map from the tourism office; it's in Flemish but easily deciphered. You can rent bikes at the train station or at **Biker** (⊠ *Sint-Michielsstraat 3* ☎ *09/224–2903*), open daily.

show about Gent and Emperor Charles V, featuring a large-scale model of 17th-century Gent. ⊠ *Sint-Pietersplein 14, Sint-Pietersplein* ☎ *09/244–7373* ⊕ *www.dewereldvankina.be* ☎ *€2.48* ☉ *Weekdays 9–5 and Sun. 2–5:30.*

🐚 ❶ **Het Huis van Alijn.** The Folklore Museum, the Kraanlei waterfront, and the ancient Patershol district behind it form an enchanting ensemble. The museum includes several settings, including 18 medieval almshouses surrounding a garden, reconstructed to offer an idea of life here 100 years ago. You'll also find a Gent version of Williamsburg, Virginia, with a grocer's shop, tavern, weaver's workshop, and washroom. The chemist's shop features 17th- to 19th-century pharmacy items, and the pipe and tobacco collection has a large selection of snuff, pouches, and tools. The visitors' route takes you from the houses to the chapel and out through the crypt. Children are often drawn to the giant pageant figures, board games, and frequent shows in the beamed-and-brick puppet theater. The star is "Pierke," the traditional Gent puppet. There are some English-language brochures available. ⊠ *Kraanlei 65, Gravensteen/Patershol* ☎ *09/269–2350* ⊕ *www.huisvanalijn.be* ☎ *Museum €2.50; puppet theater €2.50* ☉ *Tues.–Sun. 11–5.*

NEED A BREAK? Poesjkine (⊠ *Jan Breydelstraat 12, Gravensteen/Patershol* ☎ *09/224–2919*) is a popular spot for a caffeine fix—or a simple, sinful indulgence. Knowing locals recommend the cream and chocolate desserts. It's closed Wednesday and the first week of August.

⓬ **Klein Begijnhof.** Founded in 1234 by Countess Joanna of Constantinople, the Small Beguinage (a convent of Beguine nuns), is the best preserved of Gent's three beguinages. Protected by a wall and portal, the surrounding petite homes with individual yards were built in the 17th and 18th centuries, but are organized in medieval style. Each house has a statue of a saint and a spacious lawn; a few are still occupied by genuine Beguines leading the life stipulated by their founder 750 years ago. You can walk quietly through the main building and peek into the stone chapel—the houses, however, are private. ⊠ *Lange Violettestraat 71, Klein Begijnhof.*

NEED A BREAK? Drop by Het Groot Vleeshuis (Great Meat Hall) for coffee or lunch and a spot of toothsome shopping. The wood-beamed hall dates from the early 15th century and was used as a covered meat market. It's an impressive blend of ancient and modern; the metal-and-glass restaurant has been cleverly constructed without affecting the old hall itself. Both shop and restaurant focus on East Flemish specialties such as Ganda ham, local mustard, and O'de Flandres jenever. The hall is open from Tuesday to Sunday 10 to 6. ✉ *Groentenmarkt 7, Gravensteen/Patershol* ☎ *09/26–78–60)*

⑩ Kunsthal Sint-Pieters Abdij. There has been an abbey on this site since the seventh century, and during the Middle Ages it was one of the richest and most important Flemish abbeys. Most of the Baroque buildings you see today were built in the 17th century, however, and now house the St. Peter's Abbey Arts Center. You can walk around the abbey, the ruined gardens, and the cellars, where there is an exhibition about the checkered history of the abbey and its monks. ✉ *Sint-Pietersplein* ☎ *09/243–9730* ⊕ *www.gent.be/spa* ✉ *€3* ⊘ *Tues.–Sun. and public holidays 10–6.*

❽ Museum Arnold Vander Haeghen. Three of Gent's favorite locals are honored in this 18th-century former governor's home. Nobel prize–winning playwright and poet Maurice Maeterlinck (1862–1949) kept a library in this elegant, neoclassical building, and it still contains his personal objects, letters, and documents. A cabinet showcases work by the artist Stuyvaert, who illustrated Maeterlinck's publications, and the painter Doudelet. Look for the exceptional 18th-century silk wall decorations in the Chinese salon. There's no descriptive information in English. ✉ *Veldstraat 82, near Kouter* ☎ *09/269–8460* ✉ *Free* ⊘ *Weekdays 8–noon and 2–5.*

⑪ Museum voor Schone Kunsten. Built in 1902 at the edge of Citadelpark, the neoclassical Museum of Fine Arts is one of Belgium's best. The museum's holdings span the Middle Ages to the early 20th century, including works by Rubens, Gericault, Corot, Ensor, and Magritte. Its collection of Flemish Primitives is particularly noteworthy, with two paintings by Hieronymus Bosch, Saint Jerome and The Bearing of the Cross. It also has a fine collection of sculpture and French painting. The temporary exhibitions are usually exceptional. ✉ *Nicolaas de Liemaeckereplein 3, Citadelpark* ☎ *09/240–0700* ⊕ *www.mskgent.be* ⊘ *Tues.–Sun. 10–6.*

❹ Sint-Niklaaskerk. St. Nicholas's Church was built in the 11th century in Romanesque style, but was destroyed a century later after two disastrous fires; it was later rebuilt by prosperous merchants. The tower, one of the many soaring landmarks of this city's famed skyline, dates from about 1300 and was the first belfry in Gent. During the French Revolution the church was used as a stable, and its treasures were ransacked. The most recent restorations were completed in 2000, renewing Belgian's best example of Scheldt-Gothic once again. ✉ *Cataloniestraat, Torenrij* ✉ *Free* ⊘ *Mon. 2–5, Tues.–Sun. 10–5.*

❺ Stadhuis. The Town Hall is an early example of what raising taxes can do to a city. In 1516 Antwerp's Domien de Waghemakere and Mechelen's Rombout Keldermans, two prominent architects, were called in to build a town hall that would put all others to shame. However, before the building could be completed, Emperor Charles V imposed new taxes that drained the city's resources. The architecture thus reflects the changing fortunes of Gent: the side built in 1518–60 and facing Hoogpoort is in Flamboyant Gothic style; when work resumed in 1580, during the short-lived Protestant Republic, the Botermarkt side was completed in a stricter and more economical Renaissance style; and later additions include Baroque and rococo features. The tower on the corner of Hoogpoort and Botermarkt has a balcony specifically built for making announcements and proclamations; lacelike tracery embellishes the exterior. This civic landmark is not usually open to the public, but you can arrange a tour through the Gidsenbond van Genten *(see Tours in Gent Essentials)* or see it on a guided tour offered through the city's tourist office. Look for the glorious Gothic staircase, the throne room, and the spectacularly decorated halls—the Pacificatiezaal hall is where the Pacification Treaty of Gent between Catholics and Protestants was signed. ⊠*Botermarkt, Torenrij* ☎*09/266–5222* 🎫*€6* ☉*Guided visits only, May–Oct., Mon.–Thurs. at 3.*

WHERE TO EAT

$$$–$$$$ ✕**Jan van den Bon.** With room for 30, this distinguished restaurant is
Fodor'sChoice   a local favorite for French and classic Belgian dishes, particularly sea-
★   food and seasonal specialties. White asparagus, for instance, is cooked and sauced to perfection. Sip your aperitif on the terrace overlooking the garden, which supplies the herbs used in the kitchen. ⊠*Koning Leopold II Laan 43, Citadelpark 9000* ☎*09/221–9085* ⚠*Reservations essential. Jacket and tie* ▤*AE, DC, MC, V* ☉*Closed Sun. No lunch Sat.*

$$–$$$$ ✕**Belga Queen.** A magnificent restaurant in a magnificent location.
Fodor'sChoice   The former corn warehouse bordering the Leie has been redesigned by
★   the chef himself, Antoine Pinto. The large terrace leads to the ground floor's impressive bar, high tables, and cozy leather seats. The menu has daily fresh suggestions and a three-course lunch is €15. There's a cigar bar with occasional live jazz on the top floor. ⊠*Graslei 10, De Kuip 9000* ☎*09/280–0100* ⚠*Reservations essential* ▤*AE, DC, MC, V.*

$$–$$$ ✕**Pakhuis.** At peak times, this enormously popular brasserie in an old warehouse off the Korenmarkt crackles with energy. A giant Greek statue makes an incongruous counterpoint to the marble-top tables, parquet floors, and long oak bar. Locals rave about the seafood and the oyster bar; there's also more robust fare such as ham knuckle with sharp Gent mustard. You can choose the "market menu," based on what the chef picked up at the market that morning. ⊠*Schuurkenstraat 4, Torenrij* ☎*09/223–5555* ▤*AE, DC, MC, V* ☉*Closed Sun.*

$–$$$ ✕**Graaf van Egmond.** Gaze at the famed spires of Gent from this 13th-century riverside house, then turn your attention to the menu. (Ask for the special Charles V menu for the best selection.) Choose from such dishes as lobster salad, grilled lamb, or *Gentse Stoverij* (a traditional dish of beef stewed in beer). The restaurant's interior is lovely, with beamed ceilings, antique and reproduction pieces, and sparkling chandeliers. ⊠*Sint-Michielsplein 21, Torenrij* ☎*09/225–0727* ▤*AE, DC, MC, V.*

$-$$$ ✕ **Tête à Tête.** Though memorably good, this restaurant doesn't get a lot of press—locals must want to keep it for themselves. It's situated unassumingly on busy Jan Breydelstraat, so people tend to pass by without noticing. The kitchen draws on both French and Flemish cooking, with such specialties as bouillabaisse, salmon with a lime-inflected sauce, and duck in green-peppercorn sauce. Be sure to save room for one of the outstanding desserts. ⊠ *Jan Breydelstraat 32–34, Gravensteen/Patershol* ☎ *09/233–9500* ☐ *MC, V* ☉ *No lunch Mon.–Thurs.*

$$ ✕ **De 3 Biggetjes.** The name means "the three little pigs," and you'll definitely be tempted to wolf down the wonderful food at this tiny, stepgabled building set on the cobbled Zeugsteeg, or Sow Lane. Even if you huff and puff a bit to get there, the cooking makes the trip worthwhile. The menu combines Belgian, Vietnamese, and French influences. Seafood dishes are a highlight; chef Ly Chi Cuong relies on the daily market for turbot, sole, and the like, while other ingredients are flown in from all over the world, even the Seychelles. The set menus are a very good value. ⊠ *Zeugsteeg 7, Gravensteen/Patershol* ☎ *09/224–4648* ⚖ *Reservations essential* ☐ *MC, V* ☉ *Closed Wed. No lunch Sat. No dinner Sun.*

$-$$ ✕ **Brasserie Keizershof.** When you're looking for a change from the familiar waterzooi, but are still in the mood for comfort food, try this inexpensive tavern. Light meals and snacks are available all day— toasted sandwiches, spaghetti—but bring an appetite, because portions are huge. There's always a daily special, often the kind of food you would expect on a typical Flemish table. It can get quite busy, especially at noon, since the restaurant's size makes it a favorite of tour groups. ⊠ *Vrijdagmarkt 47, Vrijdagmarkt* ☎ *09/223–4446* ☐ *MC, V* ☉ *Closed Sun. and Mon.*

¢-$ ✕ **Avalon.** Head to this lunch spot near the Gravensteen for delicious organic, vegetarian meals—or, if you're peckish, soup or a snack. The menu features pasta, stews, and quiches. In good weather, try for a table on the terrace. Be sure to get here early, though—it's only open until 2 PM. ⊠ *32 Geldmunt, Gravensteen/Patershol* ☎ *09/224–3724* ☐ *AE, MC, V* ☉ *Closed Sun. No dinner.*

9

WHERE TO STAY

$$$$ ▦ **Sofitel Gent–Belfort.** In the heart of the old city, this grand hotel mirrors the elegance of the well-known international chain. Warmed with sandy beige colors and Art Nouveau style, it sticks to a business-friendly look. Spacious rooms are well-equipped; some are bi-level, with a second TV. The hotel also offers a family deal—children under 11 can stay free when adults pay full price. Pros: comfortable rooms, cozy bar, prime location for exploring the city. Cons: unremarkable service, impersonal atmosphere. ⊠ *Hoogpoort 63, Torenrij, B9000* ☎ *09/233–3331* ⊕ *www.sofitel.be* ⬳ *171 rooms, 8 suites* ⌖ *In-room: safe, refrigerator. In-hotel: restaurant, bar, gym, public Wi-Fi, parking (no fee)* ☐ *AE, DC, MC, V.*

$$ ▦ **Gravensteen.** Steps from its namesake, this handsome 19th-century mansion exudes atmosphere—at least, from most angles. The public areas are ornate with carved stucco, a marble staircase, and a cupola.

Hallways wind to small rooms with a more modern look; some have castle or canal views. Note that some rooms are in a newer, less attractive building at the back and that bathrooms are small, some with showers only. Pros: atmospheric building, great views from some rooms. Cons: some rooms have lumpy beds, public areas are often filled with smokers. ⊠*Jan Breydelstraat 35, Gravensteen/Patershol B9000* ☎*09/225–1150* ⊕*www.gravensteen.be* ↩*49 rooms* ♿*In-room: no a/c (some), refrigerators, Wi-Fi. In-hotel: bar, gym, parking (fee)* ☰*AE, DC, MC, V.*

$-$$ ☷ **The Boatel.** Get a different perspective on Gent by staying aboard this 1953 riverboat docked on the Leie since Portus Ganda opened. The rebuilt vessel shows off sections of the original woodwork. Cabins are large and bright, particularly the two master bedrooms above the sea line. The wood floor of the sunny breakfast room can double as the evening gathering spot or even a small meeting room. Free parking is available on the road nearby. Even though it is tightly roped to the shore, remember that boats tend to rock a bit. Pros: a taste of canal life, roomy cabins won't make you claustrophic. Cons: the seasick should steer well clear, a walk from the center. ⊠*Voorhoutkaai 44, Portus GandaB9000* ☎*09/267–1030* ⊕*www.theboatel.com* ↩*5 rooms* ♿*In-room: no a/c* ☰*AE, DC, MC, V.*

¢-$$ ☷ **Monasterium PoortAckere.** A complex comprising a former abbey, convent, and beguinage now provides a serene place to stay in a central neighborhood. Some sections date back to the 13th century; most of the buildings, though, are 19th-century Gothic Revival. There are large, comfortable rooms in the Monasterium, the former convent, while in the adjacent convent former cells have been transformed into small guest rooms with a washbasin, shared showers, and toilets. You can take breakfast in the chapter house and have a buffet dinner in the church. Pros: unique style, breakfasts are outstanding. Cons: a lot of stairs to climb, a maze of corridors. ⊠*Oude Houtlei 56, Torenrij B9000* ☎*09/269–2210* ⊕*www.monasterium.be* ↩*58 rooms, 45 with bath* ♿*In-room: no a/c, dial-up. In-hotel: restaurant, bar, parking (fee), no elevator.* ☰*AE, DC, MC, V* ⊚|*BP.*

★ $ ☷ **Erasmus.** From the flagstone and wood-beam library-lounge to the stone mantels in the individually decorated bedrooms, every inch of this noble 16th-century town house has been scrubbed, polished, and decked with period ornaments. Even the tiny garden has been carefully manicured. The couple that runs this distinctive hotel near the Korenlei takes care of everything from answering the bell pull at night to serving a delicious breakfast in the parlor. Pros: a huge amount of charm, extremely friendly owners, professional staff. Cons: lacks some modern conveniences, it's a hassle to arrive late or leave early. ⊠*Poel 25, Torenrij B9000* ☎*09/224–2195* ⊕*www.proximedia.com/web/hotel-erasmus.html* ↩*11 rooms* ♿*In-room: no a/c, refrigerator. In-hotel: bar* ☰*AE, MC, V* ☉*Closed mid-Dec.–mid-Jan.*

$ ☷ **Ibis Gent Centrum Kathedraal.** Location is this hotel's trump card: it's close to the cathedral. As in most branches of this no-frills chain, rooms have cookie-cutter modern decor and requisite amenities. This Ibis has a dependable level of service and comfort, but lacks local character. Triples are available. There's another branch, Ibis Gent Centrum Opera, close to the Flemish Opera building; some of its rooms are a tad cheaper. Pros: a great chain hotel, efficient service. Cons: no-frills focus, small rooms, few welcoming smiles from the staff. ⊠ *Limburgstraat 2, Torenrij B9000* ☎ *09/233–0000* ⊕ *www.ibishotel.com* ⇄ *120 rooms* ⌂ *In-room: no a/c, Wi-Fi. In-hotel: restaurant, bar, parking (no fee)* ⊟ *AE, DC, MC, V* ⦿⏐ *BP.*

¢–$ ⊞ **Astoria.** That this brick building with large, shuttered windows was once a home won't surprise you once you see the bright rooms, breezily comfortable with cane chairs and tables, colorful bedspreads, and large wooden wardrobes. Public areas are done in warm colors, with wall sconces and accents of polished wood. The hotel is in a clean but somewhat bland residential area near train and tram stations. Pros: good location for catching an early train and a cheerful enough place to spend a night. Cons: the rumble of trains can keep you awake, and it's too far from the center to allow you to explore on foot. ⊠ *Achilles Musschestraat 39, behind St-Pieters station, B9000* ☎ *09/222–8413* ⊕ *www.astoria.be* ⇄ *18 rooms* ⌂ *In-room: no a/c, DVD, Wi-Fi. In-hotel: parking (no fee)* ⊟ *AE, DC, MC, V.*

¢ ⊞ **De Draeke Youth Hostel.** With its location on the edge of the Lieve canal, near the Gravensteen, this hostel makes a terrific base for city explorations. Each room sleeping between two and five people has its own bathroom. You must pay an extra €3 per person if you're not a youth-hostel member. Pros: inexpensive rates, close to the action, safe. Cons: the reception is often unstaffed. ⊠ *Sint-Widostraat 11, Prinsenhof B9000* ☎ *09/233–7050* ⊕ *www.jeugdherbergen.be* ⇄ *27 rooms* ⌂ *In-room: no a/c, no phone, no TV. In-hotel: restaurant, bar, no elevator, public Internet* ⊟ *MC, V* ⦿⏐ *BP.*

NIGHTLIFE & THE ARTS

Check the "What's On" and "Other Towns" sections of the *Bulletin* to find schedules of the latest art shows and cultural events. You can find issues of the *Bulletin* in local newsstands and bookstores.

THE ARTS

CONCERTS **De Handelsbeurs** (⊠ *Kouter 29, Kouter* ☎ *09/265–9160* ⊕ *www.handelsbeurs.be*) is a concert hall for all kinds of music, from jazz, to folk, to world, to classical. **De Vlaamse Opera** (⊠ *Schouwburgstraat 3, Kouter* ☎ *09/225–2425* ⊕ *www.vlaamseopera.be*) shares its name—and many opera productions—with a sister company in Antwerp; if you go, note the splendid ceiling and chandelier. Head for the **Kunstencentrum Vooruit** (⊠ *Sint-Pietersnieuwstraat 23, Het Zuid* ☎ *09/267–2828* ⊕ *www.vooruit.be*) for top-quality dance, theater, and jazz programs; the venue also hosts rock and contemporary classical concerts. Grab a drink or quick meal in the cafeteria of this former cultural center of the Socialist Party.

NIGHTLIFE

As in most Belgian towns, nightlife in Gent centers around grazing and drinking and talking with friends through the wee hours. The student population generates a much busier, more varied nightlife than you'll find in Brugge or other towns in Flanders. The area around Oude Beestenmarkt and Vlasmarkt, near Portus Ganda, is mainly where young people gather for dancing and partying.

The **Town Crier** (☎ 09/222–6743 ⊕ *www.towncriers.be*), who spends his days walking the streets making announcements and tolling his bell, can also take you on a pub crawl. You'll need a reservation, though.

There are special dance nights, several gay bars, and lots of gay and lesbian organizations providing help and advice. The tourist office even provides a gay and lesbian city map. You can get more information at **Casa Rosa** (⊠ *Kammerstraat 22, Het Zuid* ☎ 09/269–2812 ⊕ *www.casarosa.be*).

BARS **De Dulle Griet** (⊠ *Vrijdagmarkt 50, Vrijdagmarkt* ☎ 09/224–2455) is a quintessential Gent pub. It has more than 250 kinds of drinks but specializes in the 1.2-liter *Kwak* beer, complete with a collector's stein and stand—ask for a "Max." If you brave this beer, though, you must leave one of your shoes as deposit when you order. The pub is open from noon until 1 or 2 AM, apart from Sunday evening when it closes early. To taste a potent Belgian specialty, head to **'t Dreupelkot** (⊠ *Groentenmarkt 12, Gravensteen/Patershol* ☎ 09/224–2120), which produces its own jenever in a multitude of different flavors, including vanilla and chocolate.

JAZZ CLUBS The busy late-night jazz café **Jazz Café Damberg** (⊠ *Korenmarkt 19, Gravensteen/Patershol* ☎ 09/329–5337) occupies one of the most historic pubs in Gent. Jazz musicians from all over the world play here. **Lazy River Jazz Café** (⊠ *Stadhuissteeg 5, Torenrij* ☎ 09/223–2301) is a friendly, intimate place beloved by locals and the older crowd. There are concerts as well as dance nights at **Muziekcafé Charlatan** (⊠ *Vlasmarkt 6, near Portus Ganda* ☎ 09/224–2311). It's open every day from 4 PM; music starts up at 10 or 11. Their lineup covers alt-rock, funk, and lots of DJ nights.

SHOPPING

Langemunt and **Veldstraat** are the major shopping streets, while the smart fashion boutiques cluster along **Voldersstraat**. Gent also has several exclusive shopping galleries where fancy boutiques are surrounded by upscale cafés and restaurants; try the **Bourdon Arcade** (Gouden Leeuwplein) and **Braempoort,** between Brabantdam and Vlaanderenstraat.

MARKETS

The largest market is the attractive and historic **Vrijdagmarkt,** held Friday 7–1 and Saturday 1–6. This is where leaders have rallied the people of Gent from the Middle Ages to the present day. The huge square is dominated by a turret that was part of the tanner's guild house, and the statue in the middle is of Jacob van Artevelde, who led a rebellion from here in 1338, defending the neutrality of the city and Flanders during the

Hundred Years' War. You can take home a supply of *Gentse mokken,* syrup-saturated biscuits available from any pastry shop, or famously strong Gent mustard. On Sunday mornings, also visit the **flower market** on the Kouter, where there is often a brass band playing, and sample oysters and a glass of champagne at **De Blauwe Kiosk,** a booth on the edge of the market at the corner of Kouter and Vogelmarkt.

GENT ESSENTIALS

BY AIR

Although Ostend-Bruges International may be the nearest airport, it doesn't have regular flights. It's far easier to fly to Brussels (Zaventem) and rent a car or travel by train from there to Gent, which is only 67 km (42 mi) away.

Airport **Ostend-Bruges International Airport** (⊠ *Nieuwpoortsesteenweg 889* ☎ *059/55–12–11* ⊕ *www.ost.aero*).

BY BUS OR TRAM

BUSES De Lijn has one trolley, three trams, and dozens of bus lines. There are stops all over town, and most buses run every 10 to 15 minutes. You can buy a ticket (€1.50) or a day pass (€6) at the bus terminal or on board. ■ TIP➔ **If you travel with at least five people, buy a group ticket: the fare will only be €80.** There are night buses on Friday and Saturday.

TRAMS If you arrive in Gent by train, take tram 1, 11, or 12 for the city center. The fare, which you can buy on the tram, costs €1.50. You can also buy a pass for a day's worth of tram travel for €6. Buy this day pass at the machines at the tram terminus by Gent Sint-Pieters train station; they only take small bills.

Line **De Lijn (Oost-Vlaanderen)** (☎ *09/210–9311 East Flanders* ⊕ *www.delijn.be*).

BY CAR

The main highways, situated to the south of the city, are easy to find from the city center. From Brussels, Gent is reached via the E40 highway, which continues to Brugge and the coast; get off at exit 9. From Antwerp, take the E17, which continues to Paris. Both the E40 and E17 take you very close to the city center, which is indicated by a white sign that reads Centrum. Traffic can be heavy on these roads during rush hour, and on summer weekends traffic on both highways can be bumper-to-bumper. Gent's parking lots are clearly indicated as you go into the city; ask which one your hotel is closest to when you make your reservation, and then drive in and follow the signs.

BY TRAIN

The Belgian national railway, NMBS/SNCB, sends two nonstop trains every hour to Gent from Brussels (27 minutes); they all pass through Brussels' three main stations. There's also a frequent direct train connection from Brussels airport to Gent that takes about an hour. Trains run twice an hour from Antwerp, as well. They take you to Gent in a little less than 50 minutes.

9

Stations **Brussels Gares du Midi, Central, and Nord** (☎ *02/528–2828*). **Gent Sint-Pieters** (✉ *Kon. Maria Hendrikaplein* ☎ *02/528–2828*).

Line **NMBS/SNCB** (☎ *02/528–2828* ⊕ *www.b-rail.be*).

CONTACTS & RESOURCES

EMERGENCIES

A duty doctor service is on call for nights, weekends, and holidays, and some pharmacies rotate night and weekend duty; calling the information hotline will give you the name and address of the current 24-hour or late-night pharmacy.

Emergency Contacts **Ambulance** (☎ *100*). **Duty doctors** (☎ *09/236–5000*). **Night pharmacies** (☎ *09/001–0500*). **Police** (☎ *101*).

MONEY MATTERS

ATMs are usually accessible 24 hours a day, but may run out of money by the weekend when the rush is on, so extract your funds early to be on the safe side.

VISITOR INFORMATION

Gent's tourist bureau has English-speaking staff and is open daily. Tours with the guide association Gidsenbond van Genten can be booked here. Another good resource for Gent is an online "urban dissection kit," **www.use-it.be**. This site (with English translations) is geared for students and other finger-on-the-pulse travelers..

City Tourist Bureau **Gent** (✉ *Botermarkt 17A, under the Belfry* ☎ *09/266–5650* ⊕ *www.visitgent.be*).

BRUGGE

204 km (122 mi) south of Amsterdam.

Wander through the tangled streets and enjoy the narrow canals, handsome squares, and charming old gabled houses. Brugge's historic center is encircled by a ring road that loosely follows the line of the city's medieval ramparts. In fact, the ancient gates—Smedenpoort, Ezelpoort, Kruispoort, and Gentpoort—still stand along this road. Most of Brugge's sights lie inside the center, which can easily be explored on foot.

TO & FROM

To reach Gent by car, take the A4 motorway to Antwerp, and then follow the E17 and then the E40, taking the Brugge exit. The journey takes around 2½ hours. By train, take a Thalys high-speed train to Brussels' Gare de Midi/Brussel Zuid station and then change to a Belgian Railways (SNCB/NMBS) train for Brugge. There are two an hour, and the trip takes less than an hour.

EXPLORING

MAIN ATTRACTIONS

★ ⑩ **Begijnhof.** This 13th-century beguinage is a pretty and serene cluster of small, whitewashed houses, a pigeon tower, and a church surrounding a pleasant green at the edge of a canal. The Begijnhof was founded in 1245 by Margaret, Countess of Constantinople, to bring together the Beguines—girls and widows from all social backgrounds who devoted themselves to charitable work but who were not bound by religious vows. Led by a superintendent known as the Grand Mistress, the congregation flourished for 600 years. The last of the Beguines died about 50 years ago; today the site is occupied by the Benedictine nuns, who still wear the Beguine habit. You may join them, discreetly, for vespers in their small church of St. Elizabeth. Although most of the present-day houses are from the 16th and 17th centuries, they have maintained the architectural style of the houses that preceded them. One house has been set aside as a small museum. Visitors are asked to respect the silence. The horse-and-carriage rides around the town have a 10-minute stop outside the beguinage—long enough for a quick look round. ⊠ *Oude Begijnhof, off Wijngaardstraat* ☎ *050/33–00–11* ⌨ *Free, house visit €2* ⊗ *Mar.–Nov., daily 10–noon and 1:45–5; Dec.–Feb., Mon., Tues., Fri. 10–noon, Wed. and Thurs. 2–4.*

⑤ **Burg.** A popular daytime meeting place and an enchanting, floodlit
Fodor'sChoice scene after dark, the Burg is flanked by striking civic buildings. Named
★ for the fortress built by Baldwin of the Iron Arm, the Burg was also the former site of the 10th-century Carolingian Cathedral of St. Donaas, which was destroyed by French Republicans in 1799. You can wander through the handsome, 18th-century law court, the Oude Gerechtshof, the Voormalige Civiele Griffie with its 15th-century front gable, the Stadhuis, and the Heilig Bloed Basiliek *(see below).* The Burg is not all historic splendor, though—in sharp contrast to these buildings stands a modern construction by Japanese artist Toyo Ito, added in 2002. Public opinion is sharply divided over Ito's pavilion over a shallow pool; you'll either love it or hate it. ⊠ *Hoogstraat and Breidelstraat.*

9

⑦ **Groeningemuseum.** The tremendous holdings of this gallery give you
Fodor'sChoice the makings for a crash course in the Flemish Primitives and their
★ successors. Petrus Christus, Hugo Van der Goes, Hieronymus Bosch, Rogier van der Weyden, Gerard David, Pieter Bruegel (both Elder and Younger), Pieter Pourbus—all are represented here. Here you can see Jan van Eyck's wonderfully realistic *Madonna with Canon Van der Paele,* in which van Eyck achieved texture and depth through multiple layers of oil and varnish. The painter's attention to detail is all-embracing; the canon's pouchy flesh and the nets of wrinkles around his eyes are as carefully depicted as the crimson folds of the Madonna's robe or her waving golden hair. There's also one of Hans Memling's greatest works, the *Moreel Triptych.* The namesake family is portrayed on the side panels, all with preternaturally blank expressions. As if this weren't enough, the museum also encompasses a strong display of 15th- to 21st-century Dutch and Belgian works, sweeping through to Surrealist and contemporary art. The Groeninge is set back from the

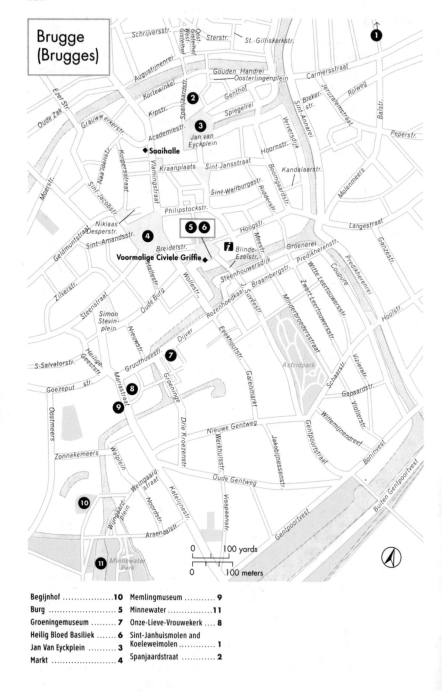

Brugge (Brugges)

street in a pocket-size park behind a medieval gate. Although it is blessedly small, its riches warrant a full morning or afternoon. Thoughtfully, there's a play area to keep antsy children busy. An audioguide is available in English. ⊠*Dijver 12* ☎*050/44–87–11* 💲*€8, €15 combo ticket includes Memling Museum* ☉*Tues.–Sun. 9:30–5.*

NEED A BREAK?

At the Taverne Groeninge (⊠*Dijver 13* ☎*050/34–41–54*) you can absorb even more art as you linger over a coffee, beer, or snack. The café is decorated with works by Frank Brangwyn, the Belgian-born painter, illustrator, and designer who became Britain's official war artist during World War I.

IF YOU ONLY HAVE 1 DAY

Get to Brugge as early as possible. Must-see spots include the Begijnhof near Minnewater, as well as the great buildings around Burg and Markt squares. Soak up the artwork, including the Groeninge and Memling museums, and Michelangelo's sculpture in the Onze-Lieve-Vrouwekerk. You might take an afternoon canal ride—or, after dinner, when crowds have thinned, you can wander alongside the water. Bear in mind that Brugge is one of Europe's top tourist destinations, and has prices to match.

❻ Heilig Bloed Basiliek. The Basilica of the Holy Blood manages to include both the austere and the ornate under one roof—not to mention one of Europe's most precious relics. The 12th-century Lower Chapel retains a stern, Romanesque character. Look for the poignant, 14th-century Pietà and the carved statue of Christ in the crypt. From this sober space, an elaborate, external Gothic stairway leads to the stunningly lavish Upper Chapel, which was twice destroyed—by Protestant iconoclasts in the 16th century and by French Republicans in the 18th—but both times rebuilt. (Note that the Upper Chapel is closed to visitors during Eucharistic Mass on Sunday 11 to noon.) The original stained-glass windows were replaced in 1845, and then again after an explosion in 1967, when they were restored by the Brugge painter De Loddere. The basilica's namesake treasure is a vial thought to contain a few drops of the blood of Christ, brought from Jerusalem to Brugge in 1149 by Derick of Alsace when he returned from the Second Crusade. It is exposed here every Friday in the Lower Chapel 8:30 to 10 and in the Upper Chapel 10 to 11 and 3 to 4. On Ascension Day, it becomes the centerpiece of the magnificent *De Heilig Bloedprocessie* (Procession of the Holy Blood), a major medieval-style pageant in which it is carried through the streets of Brugge. The small **museum** next to the basilica contains the 17th-century reliquary. ⊠*Burg* ☎*No phone* ⊕*www.holyblood.org* 💲*Museum: €1.50* ☉*Mar.–Sept., Thurs.–Tues. 9:30–noon and 2–6; Oct.–Mar., daily 10–noon and 2–4.*

❹ Markt. Used as a marketplace since 958, this square is still one of the FodorsChoice liveliest places in Brugge. In the center stands a memorial to the city's ★ medieval heroes, Jan Breydel and Pieter De Coninck, who led the commoners of Flanders to their short-lived victory over the aristocrats of France. On the east side of the Markt stand the provincial government house and the post office, an excellent pastiche of Burgundian Gothic. Old guild houses line the west and north sides of the square, their step-gabled facades overlooking the cafés spilling out onto the sidewalk. These buildings aren't always as old as they seem, though—often they're 19th-century reconstructions. The medieval **Belfort** (Belfry) on the south side of the Markt, however, is the genuine article. The tower dates to the 13th century, its crowning octagonal lantern to the 15th century. Altogether, it rises to a height of 270 feet, commanding the city and the surrounding countryside with more presence than grace. The valuables of Brugge were once kept in the second floor treasury; now the Belfort's riches are in its remarkable 47-bell carillon. (Impressing Belgians with a carillon is no mean feat, as Belgium has some of the best in the world.) If you haven't walked enough, you can climb 366 winding steps to the clock mechanism, and from the carillon enjoy a gorgeous panoramic view. Back down in the square, you may be tempted by the **horse-drawn carriages** that congregate here; a half-hour ride for up to four people, with a short stop at the Begijnhof, costs €30 plus "something for the horse." ⊠ *Intersection of Steenstraat, St-Amandstraat, Vlamingstraat, Philipstockstraat, Breidelstraat, and Wollestraat* ☎ *050/44–87–11* 🎟 *€5* ⏱ *Tues.–Sun., 9:30–5. Carillon concerts: Sun. 2:15–3. June 15–July 1 and Aug. 15–Sept., Mon., Wed., and Sat. 9 PM–10 PM. Oct.–June 14, Wed. and Sat. 2:15–3.*

★ ❾ **Memlingmuseum.** The collection contains six works, but they are of breathtaking quality and among the greatest—and certainly the most spiritual—of the Flemish Primitive school. Hans Memling (1440–94) was born in Germany, but spent the greater part of his life in Brugge. In *The Altarpiece of St. John the Baptist and St. John the Evangelist*, two leading personages of the Burgundian court are believed to be portrayed: Mary of Burgundy (buried in the Onze-Lieve-Vrouwekerk) as St. Catherine, and Margaret of York as St. Barbara. The "paintings within the painting" give details of the lives of the two saints. The miniature paintings that adorn the St. Ursula Shrine are likewise marvels of detail and poignancy; Memling's work gives recognizable iconographic details about cities, such as Brugge, Cologne, Basel, and Rome. The Memling Museum is housed in **Oud Sint-Janshospitaal**, one of the oldest surviving medieval hospitals in Europe. It was founded in the 12th century and remained in use until the early 20th century. Furniture, paintings, and hospital-related items are attractively displayed; the 13th-century middle ward, the oldest of three, was built in Romanesque style. A fascinating 18th-century painting shows patients arriving by sedan chair and being fed and ministered to by sisters and clerics. There is a short guide to the museum in English, and the audio-guide is in English, too. ⊠ *Mariastraat 38* ☎ *050/44–87–11* 🎟 *€8, €15 combo ticket includes Groeninge Museum* ⏱ *Tues.–Sun. 9:30–5.*

ALSO WORTH SEEING

❸ **Jan van Eyckplein.** This colorful yet low-key square lies at the center of Hanseatic Brugge, marked with a statue of the famed 15th-century painter. It includes the old **Tolhuis** (Customs House), built in 1477, where vehicles on their way to market had to stop while tolls were levied on goods brought from nearby ports. The building is now an information office for the province of West Flanders. The **Poorters-loge**, a late-Gothic building with a slender spire, was owned by the guild of porters and used as a meeting place for the burghers. Currently, it's used to store historic documents but is occasionally open for exhibitions. The bear occupying one niche represents the legendary creature speared by Baldwin of the Iron Arm and later became the symbol of the city. ⊠ *Intersection of Academiestraat, Spiegelrei, and Spanjaardstraat.*

8 **Onze-Lieve-Vrouwekerk.** The towering spire of the plain, Gothic Church of Our Lady, begun about 1220, rivals the Belfry as Brugge's symbol. It is 381 feet high, the tallest brick construction in the world. While brick can be built high, it cannot be sculpted like stone; hence the tower's somewhat severe look. Look for the small *Madonna and Child* statue, an early work by Michelangelo. The great sculptor sold it to a merchant from Brugge when the original client failed to pay. It was stolen by Napoléon, and during World War II by Nazi leader Hermann Göring; now the white-marble figure sits in a black-marble niche behind an altar at the end of the south aisle. The choir contains many 13th- and 14th-century polychrome tombs, as well as two mausoleums: that of Mary of Burgundy, who died in 1482 at the age of 25 after a fall from her horse; and that of her father, Charles the Bold, killed in 1477 while laying siege to Nancy in France. Mary was as well loved in Brugge as her husband, Maximilian of Austria, was loathed. Her finely chiseled effigy captures her beauty. ⊠ *Dijver and Mariastraat* ☎ *No phone* ✆ *€2.50* ⊙ *Weekdays 9–12:30 and 1:30–5, Sat. 9–12:30 and 1:30–4, Sun. 2–5.*

1 **Sint-Janshuismolen and Koeleweimolen.** The outer ramparts of the medieval city of Brugge used to be dotted with windmills; now four remain along the ring road. Of these, two can be visited and are still used to grind flour: the St-Janshuismolen (1770) and the Koeleweimolen (1765). The wooden steps leading up to them are quite steep and not for the faint-hearted. ⊠ *Kruisvest, Sint-Anna* ☎ *050/44–87–64* ✆ *€2* ⊙ *Sint-Janshuismolen: May–Sept., daily 9:30–12:30 and 1:30–5. Koeleweimolen: June–Sept., daily 9:30–12:30 and 1:30–5.*

2 **Spanjaardstraat.** The street leads up to the quay where goods from Spain were unloaded. The house at No. 9 was where St. Ignatius of Loyola stayed when he came to Flanders on holidays from his studies in Paris. Directly ahead are the three arches of the **Augustijnenbrug.** Dating from 1391, it's the oldest bridge in Brugge. On the other side of the canal, **Augustijnenrei** is one of the loveliest quays.

WHERE TO EAT

$$$$ ✕**De Karmeliet.** This stately, 18th-century house with a graceful English garden is a world-renowned culinary landmark. Owner-chef Geert Van Hecke's inventive kitchen changes the menu every two months; you might be offered goose liver with truffled potatoes or cod carpaccio with asparagus. The waitstaff perfectly choreographs each course

Fodor's Choice ★

with a cool professionalism in keeping with the restaurant's formal ambience. The wine cave plumbs the best of international vintages. ⊠*Langestraat 198000* ☎*050/33–82–59* ⚓*Reservations essential. Jacket required* ☰*AE, DC, MC, V* ⊗*Closed Mon. Closed Sun. June– Sept. No dinner Sun. and no lunch Tues. Oct.–May.*

$$$–$$$$ ✕**Chez Olivier.** Set above a quiet canal, with white swans gliding below, this French charmer is purely romantic. Chef Olivier Foucad uses impeccably fresh ingredients for "light food," such as scallops in ginger and herbs, duck in rosemary honey, and lightly marbled Charolais beef. Lunches are a bargain and the staff is flexible—if you want one main course or two starters instead of the full prix fixe menu, just ask. For the best views, request a window seat next to the water. ⊠*Meestraat 9* ☎*050/33–36–59* ☰*AE, MC, V* ⊗*Closed Thurs. and Sun. No lunch Sat.*

★ $$$–$$$$ ✕**De Visscherie.** To find this popular seafood restaurant overlooking the Vismarkt, look for the modern sculpture of a fisherman and the large fish hanging from its balcony. Business at the busy, outdoor terrace has been going strong for more than 25 years. Try one of the turbot variations, monkfish with Ganda ham and melon, or the langoustines with mozzarella, herbs, and sun-dried tomatoes. If you can't decide, order the restaurant's signature dish: waterzooi with saffron. ⊠*Vismarkt 8* ☎*050/33–02–12* ☰*AE, MC, V* ⊗*Closed Tues. and first half of Dec.*

$$$–$$$$ ✕**Spinola.** This canal-house restaurant by the Jan van Eyck statue is a real charmer. From an intimate main dining room an iron staircase leads to the upper tables; the open kitchen is in back. Here, chef-owners Sam and Vicky Storme cook up rich Burgundian cuisine: fresh game, goose liver, shellfish, and pigeon with truffles. Dinner by candlelight is the ultimate extravagance, with a choice of some 300 wines. ⊠*Spinolarei 1* ☎*050/34–17–85* ☰*DC, MC, V* ⊗*Closed Sun. No lunch Mon.*

$$–$$$ ✕**De Torre.** For traditional Belgian food at honest prices, this is the place. From noon until 10 PM, Flemish stew, tomato with shrimp, mussels, or fillet of sole are served as they are in many Flemish homes. The 18th-century house is decorated in Art Deco style and the sunny terrace has a lovely view of the Reien. ⊠*Langestraat 8* ☎*050/33–35–43* ☰*MC, V* ⊗*Closed Wed. in July and Aug.; Tues. and Wed. Sept.–June.*

$–$$$ ✕**'t Paardje.** Surely one of the few restaurants in Brugge that doesn't serve mussels, this small, family-owned place concentrates on all kinds of other Belgian specialties, many with beer-based sauces. Instead of the ubiquitous shellfish, you can choose from dishes such as eel with Lambic beer, fish with brown Rodenbach beer, even frogs' legs. The dining room's terra-cotta–and–lace decor is crisp and unpretentious. The lunch menus are an excellent value. ⊠*Langestraat 20* ☎*050/33– 40–09* ☰*MC, V* ⊗*Closed Mon. No dinner Tues.*

$$ ✕**Beethoven.** Chef Chantal Mortier built up a substantial local following over the years; she now serves them at her intimate Flemish restaurant off the Markt, with her husband at the front of the house. In winter a fire warms up the dining room and the menu offers comforting favorites like steak (fillet, tournedos, or rib-eye) with frieten. In summer the street-front tables become a prime spot for people-watching. The menu

Mussels & More

The backbone of Flanders food is the local produce that's served fresh and presented simply—you won't find painted plates or veggies sculpted beyond recognition. Naturally, this is seafood country, with fresh fish shipped in daily to Brugge; the coastal towns serve authentic North Sea delicacies at terrace restaurants whipped by sand and salt air. Even in landlocked Gent, some 50 km (30 mi) from the coast, locals snack on whelks and *winkles* (sea snails) as if they were popcorn. Flemings are mad about *mosselen* (mussels)—try them steamed, curried, or bathed in a white-wine broth accented with celery, onions, and parsley. Main courses are inevitably accompanied by a mountain of *frieten* (french fries), fried twice, making them especially crisp and delicious. For death by fries, buy them piping hot and salty from a stall, as the Belgians do, and dip them in the big dollop of accompanying mayo.

Paling (eels) are one of the region's specialties. The flesh is firm, fatty, and sweet, and served in long cross-sections with a removable backbone. *Paling in t'groen* is eel served in a green herb sauce, a heady mix of sorrel, tarragon, sage, mint, and parsley. Sole and turbot are also popular main courses, served broiled, poached with a light mousseline sauce, or grilled with a rich béarnaise or mustard sauce. Herring is eaten *maatjes* (raw) in the spring. To sound like a local, try these tongue-twisters when you order: *oostduinkerkse paardevissersoep* (fish soup) and *dronken rog op Nieuwpoortse wijze* (ray).

When the Flemish aren't eating their fish straight or in a blanket of golden sauce, they consume it in the region's most famous dish, *waterzooi* (a thick broth rich with cream and vegetables). The citizens of Gent have a chicken version, as well as *Gentse hutsepot* (a casserole with carrots, onions, potatoes, and meat). For a hearty dish, look for *vlaamse stoverij* (beef or pork stew with onions, braised in beer). *Paardenvlees* (horse meat), with its sweet flavor and beefy texture, is considered a delicacy.

If you visit Flanders in springtime, look for memorably delicious vegetables, such as the tender white *asperge* (asparagus), served either in mousseline sauce or with a garnish of chopped hard-boiled egg and melted butter. These pale stalks are sweeter than the familiar green ones and are called "white gold" because the Flemings snap them up as fast as they arrive during their short season. In March and April, seek out the rare, expensive *jets de houblon* (delicate shoots of the hops plant).

A cheese course is often served before—or in place of—dessert, and there are hundreds of delicious local choices, many runny and pungent. Chocolate and whipped cream are favorite dessert ingredients, and homemade ice cream turns up on all kinds of menus in warm months. Local pastries include *Gentse mokken* (hard sugar cookies), *lierse vlaaikens* (plum tarts), and *speculoos* (sugary ginger cookies), all of which are often accompanied by coffee. Warm pancakes and Belgian *waffelen* (waffles) topped with fruit or syrup are available everywhere from sidewalk stalls to fancy restaurants. The famous crisp waffles, which have a vanilla flavor, are formed in cast-iron molds with pre-sweetened dough.

9

lightens up accordingly, with salads such as goat cheese and honey or shrimp and smoked salmon. Though reservations aren't mandatory, they're highly recommended. ⊠ *Sint-Amandstraat 6* ☎ *050/33–50–06* ⊟ *MC, V* ⊙ *Closed Tues. and Wed.*

¢ ✕**Lotus.** The neat dining room, with its lines of flower-topped tables, fills up quickly at this popular vegetarian café. The menu changes weekly but always has small and large plates; you might try a four-cheese quiche, a basil and beetroot salad, or curried veggies. Whatever the combination, it's delicious and well presented. Don't miss the desserts; the lemon pie is particularly good. ⊠ *Wapenmakersstraat 5* ☎ *050/33–10–78* ⊟ *No credit cards* ⊙ *Closed Sun. and last 2 wks in July. No dinner.*

WHERE TO STAY

Brugge is a popular weekend escape, full as it is of romantic suites and secluded hideaways. You'll find old-fashioned accents at most hotels in the "City of Swans." The tourist office can help you make reservations for lodgings in Brugge and the surrounding countryside.

★ $$$–$$$$ ⛾**Oud Huis Amsterdam.** Two noble, 17th-century houses in the elegant Hanseatic district combine the grace of another era with the polish of a modern, first-class property. Parts of this town house date to the 1300s, and owners Philip and Caroline Train have preserved such antique details as tooled Cordoba leather wallpaper, rough-hewn rafters, and Delft tiles. Rooms with canal views overlook the busy street; back rooms with red rooftop views are quieter. Summer concerts are held in the courtyard terrace. Pros: great 17th-century exteriors, eye-popping antiques, pleasant bar. Cons: parts of hotel can be musty, some travelers have complained of poor housekeeping. ⊠ *Spiegelrei 3, B8000* ☎ *050/34–18–10* ⊕ *www.oha.be* ⇆ *44 rooms* ⛬ *In-room: no a/c (some), dial-up. In-hotel: bar, parking (no fee)* ⊟ *AE, DC, MC, V* ⊙*BP.*

$$$–$$$$ ⛾**Relais Bourgondisch Cruyce.** This truly magnificent hotel is situated in
Fodor'sChoice   one of the most romantic corners of Brugge. Some rooms overlook the
★   Reien and all of them, whether with classic or modern furnishings, live up to the highest expectations. Bathrooms are large and well equipped; all rooms have a large flat-screen TV. Pros: a fairy-tale setting, great views of the water, lovely decor throughout. Cons: lack of a bar mars the feeling of indulgence. ⊠ *Wollestraat 41, B8000* ☎ *050/33–79–26* ⊕ *www.relaisbourgondischcruyce.be* ⇆ *16 rooms* ⛬ *In-hotel: restaurant, airport shuttle* ⊟ *AE, MC, V.*

$$–$$$$ ⛾**Hotel Heritage.** Once a private mansion, this 19th-century building has been converted into a hotel. Guest rooms are in keeping with the building's heritage—elegant, with chandeliers, reproduction antique furniture, and warm fabrics in reds and golds. It's a few minutes' walk from the Markt. Pros: Helpful staff, high ceilings, near good restaurants. Cons: The extras are pricey compared to similar hotels. ⊠ *Niklaas Desparsstraat 11, B8000* ☎ *050/44–44–44* ⊕ *www.hotel-heritage.be* ⇆ *19 rooms, 5 suites* ⛬ *In-room: safe, dial-up. In-hotel: bar* ⊟ *AE, DC, MC, V* ⊙*BP.*

★ $$–$$$$ ▦ **De Tuileriëen.** Patrician tastes suffuse this 15th-century mansion. The decor is genteel, with reproduction antique furniture, Venetian glass windows, and weathered marble complemented by mixed-print fabrics and wall coverings in celadon, slate, and cream. Rooms are romantic, with marble-accented bathrooms, although those with canal views receive some traffic noise; courtyard rooms are quieter. The fire-lit bar is filled with cozy tartan wing chairs, and the neo-Baroque breakfast salon features a coffered ceiling. When the weather holds, breakfast is served on the terrace alongside the canal. Pros: turndown service includes chocolates, well-equipped spa. Cons: some rooms are dark. ⊠*Dijver 7, B8000* ☎*050/34–36–91* ⊕*www.hoteltuilerieen. com* ⇗*22 rooms, 23 suites* ⚴*In-room: safe, refrigerator, dial-up. In-hotel: bar, pool, bicycles, laundry service, spa, parking (fee)* ▤*AE, DC, MC, V* ⏍*BP.*

$$–$$$ ▦ **Walburg.** One of Brugge's grandest 19th-century town houses is now a hotel, only a few blocks from the Burg. It was built by Isidoor Alderwerelt, the same architect who finished the Palais de Justice in Brussels, and most of its original features were kept when the house was renovated in 1997. The lovely rooms, tastefully decorated in different color schemes with antique furniture and marble bathrooms, are a generous 750 square feet. Classical music welcomes you in the marble lobby and you can easily imagine Viennese-style balls taking place in the dining room. Pros: exceptionally large rooms, speedy room service, excellent breakfasts. Cons: views from the lower floors are disappointing, some room locks should be replaced. ⊠*Boomgaardstraat 13–15, B8000* ☎*050/34–94–14* ⇗*12 rooms, 1 suite* ⚴*In-room: safe, refrigerator, Wi-Fi. In-hotel: restaurant, bar* ▤*AE, DC, MC, V* ⊙*Closed Jan.* ⏍*BP.*

$–$$ ▦ **Bryghia.** This restored German–Austrian trade center is a handsome 15th-century landmark. Outside, the brick walls are lined with paned windows and flower boxes; inside, the hotel is warmed by pastel floral fabrics and beech cabinets. Bedrooms are simple yet comfortable, and the public rooms include small sitting areas and a beamed, slate-floor breakfast salon. Pros: efficient service, excellent buffet breakfast. Cons: anonymous decor inside doesn't live up to the striking exterior. ⊠*Oosterlingenplein 4, B8000* ☎*050/33–80–59* ⊕*www.bryghiahotel. be* ⇗*18 rooms* ⚴*In-room: safe, refrigerator. In-hotel: bar, parking (fee)* ▤*AE, DC, V* ⏍*BP.*

★ $ ▦ **Egmond.** Play lord of the manor at this refurbished 18th-century house near the Begijnhof. Public rooms have hearths and chimneypieces, beamed ceilings, and dark-wood moldings. Breakfast is served in an oak-beam hall with a Delft-tile fireplace. Each room has a special period feature or two, and all are airy, with garden views. You can stroll the perimeter of the Minnewater park; the hotel is only 10 minutes' walk from the bustle of central Brugge. Pros: nonsmoking hotel, pretty garden. Cons: rooms book up quickly. ⊠*Minnewater 15, B8000* ☎*050/34–14–45* ⊕*www.egmond.be* ⇗*8 rooms* ⚴*In-room: safe, Wi-Fi. In-hotel: parking (no fee)* ▤*No credit cards* ⏍*BP.*

$ ▦ **De Tassche.** It would be hard to beat the price for this location, behind the Belfort. While the building dates to the 17th century, the interiors are contemporary. Guest rooms have warm yellow-and-peach furnishings; some have sloped, beamed ceilings. The restaurant ($$) hews to classic Flemish dishes such as rabbit cooked in beer. The chef is committed to detail—the fries, for instance, are hand-cut—and cruises the dining room like a true gastronome. Pros: great location, staff really knows the area. Cons: street noise can be a problem, walls are rather thin. ⊠ *Oude Burg 11, B8000* 🕾 *050/33–03–19* ⊕ *www.tassche.com* 💤 *20 rooms* 🖒 *In-hotel: restaurant, bar* ▤ *MC, V* ⊗ *Restaurant closed Tues.*

🕙 ¢–$ 🏨 **Fevery.** This child-friendly hotel is part of a comfortable family home in a quiet corner of Brugge. There's enough clutter to make you feel like you never left your own house, and even a baby monitor so parents can relax with a drink downstairs after putting a child to bed. Rooms are small and basic, but provide anything a modest traveler needs. Families of four should ask for the double room for €125. Pros: family-friendly atmosphere, owner knows the best local attractions. Cons: some rooms are located in an adjacent apartment building. ⊠ *Collaert Mansionstraat 3, B8000* 🕾 *050/33–12–69* ⊕ *www.hotelfevery.be* 💤 *10 rooms* 🖒 *In-room: Wi-Fi. In-hotel: bar, parking (no fee)* ▤ *AE, DC, MC, V* 🍽 *BP.*

★ ¢ 🏨 **De Pauw.** From the ivy-covered brick exterior to the fresh flowers and doilies in the breakfast parlor, this is a welcoming little inn, set in a square opposite Sint-Gillis church. Rooms have names rather than numbers to give them a homier feel, and needlepoint cushions and old framed prints add to the warmth. Breakfast, which includes cold cuts, cheese, and six kinds of bread, is served on pretty china. Pros: good value, cozy atmosphere. Cons: tiny bathrooms, very steep stairs. ⊠ *Sint-Gilliskerkhof 8, B8000* 🕾 *050/33–71–18* ⊕ *www.hoteldepauw.be* 💤 *8 rooms, 6 with bath* 🖒 *In-hotel: parking (no fee), no elevator* ▤ *MC, V* 🍽 *BP.*

NIGHTLIFE & THE ARTS

The West Flanders Cultural Service hosts a helpful Web site, **www.tinck.be,** that lists upcoming arts events, museum exhibits, concerts, and the like.

THE ARTS

The monthly *Agenda Brugge,* available in English, gives details of all events in the city; you can get a copy at the tourist office. Listings for events and movie screenings are also published in the local Flemish newspaper *Exit,* available at bookstores and in the public library. Movies are invariably screened in their original language with Flemish subtitles, and there are plenty of English-language films on the local screens.

NIGHTLIFE

Brugge is not the liveliest city at night, but there are a handful of good hangouts.

Pubs, mostly catering to an under-30 clientele, are clustered around the Eiermarkt, at the back of the Markt. There are also several at 't Zand, such as **Ma Rica Rokk** (⊠ *'t Zand 7–8* 🕾 *050/33–83–58*), where dance beats pound all through the night. A chic, older crowd gravitates toward the clubs at the Kraanplein and the bars on Langestraat. The **Cactus Club** (⊠ *Magdalenastraat 27* 🕾 *050/33–20–14*) is the original Brugge venue for pop, rock, folk, and blues acts. It also hosts some comedy nights, occasionally in English. A somewhat older crowd gathers in **De Stoepa** (✉*Oostmeers 124* ☎*050/33–04–54*), a pub and restaurant with a slight Eastern touch in its setting as well as on its menu. Here you can enjoy couscous, beef teriyaki, and several spicy dishes. There are several gay-friendly bars in Brugge. Two well-known spots are **Bar Bolero** (✉*Garenmarkt 32*), which is closed on Thursday, and the **Psyclops** (✉*St-Pietersgroenstraat 13*), a dance club that opens at 8 PM from Friday to Monday. More information can be found on ⊕*www.gaybruges.be.*

SHOPPING

Most shops in Brugge are open Monday to Saturday 9 or 10 AM to 6; some souvenir shops are also open on Sunday. Although there are a couple of tacky tourist stores, Brugge has many trendy boutiques and shops, especially along Nordzandstraat, as well as Steenstraat and Vlamingstraat, both of which branch off from the Markt. Ter Steeghere mall, which links the Burg with Wollestraat, deftly integrates a modern development into the historic center. The largest and most pleasant mall is the Zilverpand off Zilverstraat, where 30-odd shops cluster in Flemish gable houses around two courtyards fringed with sidewalk cafés.

MARKETS

The Markt is the setting for the weekly **Woensdag Markt** (Wednesday Market), with vegetables, fruit, flowers, specialty cheeses, and hams. (Occasionally, if there is a major event taking place on the Markt, the market moves to the Burg.) Brugge's biggest market is the **Zaterdag Markt** (Saturday Market) on 't Zand, selling all kinds of cheeses, hams, and cooked meats, as well as some clothing and household items. The **Vismarkt** (Fish Market) is held, appropriately, on the Vismarkt, daily except Sunday and Monday. All three markets are morning events, from 8 to approximately 12:30. On weekends from March 15 through November 15 there's a **flea market** open throughout the day along the Dijver.

9

BRUGGE ESSENTIALS

BY AIR

Ostend-Bruges International Airport is slowly expanding into regular passenger service. However, most flights are still charters, so your best bet is to fly to Brussels and drive or take the train from there.

Airport Ostend-Bruges International Airport (✉*Nieuwpoortsesteenweg 889* ☎*059/55–12–11* ⊕*www.ost.aero*).

BY BUS

The De Lijn bus company provides bus, tram, and trolley service throughout Flanders. In Brugge most buses run every four minutes (less often on Sundays); minibuses are designed to navigate the narrow streets. Bus stops are clearly marked and dotted frequently around the town; the railway station is the main terminus. Several buslines take you from the station to the city center. Buy your tickets (€1.50) on board or from ticket machines at the terminus. Buses to surrounding towns and the coast also leave from the railway station.

Line **De Lijn** (☎ *070/220–200* ⊕ *www.delijn.be*).

BY CAR
Roads in this region are well maintained, with good signage. Be sure to watch out for cyclists.

CITY DRIVING   Brugge is 5 km (3 mi) north of the E40 motorway, which links Brussels with Gent and Oostende. It is 126 km (76 mi) from the Le Shuttle terminus at Calais. Access for cars and coaches into Brugge's center is severely restricted. The historic streets are narrow and often one way. There are huge parking lots at the railway station and near the exits from the ring road, plus underground parking at 't Zand. For those brave enough to face tackling the center's tricky one-way system, there is also underground parking at the Biekorf (behind the public library), Zilverpand, and Pandreitje, as well as parking at the Begijnhof.

BY TAXI
Brugge has large taxi stands at the railway station and at the Markt. Taxis are metered and the rates are reasonable, but public transport, only €1.50, is always a cheaper way of getting around.

BY TRAIN
The Belgian national railway, NMBS/SNCB, sends two trains each hour to Brugge from Brussels (52 minutes) and three trains an hour from Gent (25 minutes) and from Oostende (15 minutes).

Station **Brugge** (✉ *Stationsplein* ☎ *050/38–23–82*).

Line **NMBS/SNCB** (☎ *02/528–2828* ⊕ *www.b-rail.be*).

CONTACTS & RESOURCES

EMERGENCIES
A duty doctor service is on call for nights, weekends, and holidays. Some pharmacies rotate night and weekend duty; calling the information hotline will give you the name and address of the current 24-hour or late-night pharmacy.

Emergency Contacts **Ambulance** (☎ *100*). **Duty doctors** (☎ *050/36–40–10*). **Night pharmacies** (☎ *050/40–61–62*). **Police** (☎ *101*).

MONEY MATTERS
ATMs are usually accessible 24 hours a day, but may run out of money on weekends when the rush is on, so extract your funds early to be on the safe side.

VISITOR INFORMATION
Brugge's visitor information bureau is open daily year-round, though it closes for lunch breaks on weekends. In addition to its guides and services, it has a set of lockers where you can store your bags; buy a locker token at the desk for €1. A small branch office, also with lockers, is in the train station.

Tourist Bureau **Brugge** (✉ *Burg 11* ☎ *050/44–86–86* ⊕ *www.brugge.be*).

Holland By Bike & Barge

I recommend taking the train to Zaandvort-on-Zee (about 40 mins from Amsterdam via Haarlem) then renting a bike and riding the fabulous bike paths south through the dunes for as far as you want—first skirting the nude beach area and then several popular beaches—you can tell by the passel of bikes tied up on the bike path at the sandy walks to the beach. On nice day literally thousands of Dutch bike out here from nearby towns. The Dunes path goes all the way to Den Hague—rent a bike in Amsterdam, put it on a train to Zaandvort, and bike the 20 miles to Den Haag and take the train back.

—PalenQ

Updated by
Neil Carlson

TO EXPERIENCE THE NETHERLANDS THROUGH the eyes of a local, consider a trip that combines biking and barging: A national cult-like obsession with the bicycle, and a rich seafaring tradition that has been passed down through the ages in the form of a near-universal passion for boating, means that biking and barging give new meaning to "going Dutch." Need further convincing? Not only are biking and barging time-honored ways of seeing the country, they might be the easiest: The Netherlands' extensive network of lakes, rivers, and canals means that few cities aren't reachable by water, though to really boat tour like a Dutchman means to head away from the crowded cities and into the country's more pastoral regions.

While other European destinations share a tradition of barging, no nation rivals the Dutch enthusiasm for bicycles and no country comes close to providing cyclists with the astonishing amount of infrastructure that Holland does. And in case you don't consider yourself to be a closet Lance Armstrong, don't be dismayed: By virtue of the Netherlands' flat-as-a-pancake topography, bicycle tours are geared for leisure and place few physical demands on participants.

TRAVELING BY BARGE

A staggering number of waterways and a wealth of companies facilitating barging trips in the Netherlands ensure that there are a myriad of trips available, though most can be divided into two categories—self-guided trips and hotel barge tours.

Self-guided trips offer the freedom to pull anchor whenever you want and to customize your itinerary, but you are your own tour guide and the captain of your own ship—a responsibility which may seem daunting to landlubbers. Hotel barges are largely carefree affairs with a half-day spent on the boat and a half-day of sightseeing daily. Opt for a hotel barge experience and you will be committed to a set itinerary as well as a week spent in the company of strangers, as all hotel barge trips are group excursions conducted by an experienced captain on the water and by tour guides on land.

While many boaters elect to spend their entire holiday in the Netherlands, it is possible to combine a trip through the Dutch waterways with a foray into German, Belgian, or French waters. If you want to charter your own boat for a trip that takes in more than one country, make sure that the company you choose permits international voyages. Many hotel barge operators include multi-country trips.

PLANNING YOUR TRIP

Barging is an exceptionally popular way to tour the Netherlands and the season is relatively short. During the summer (June–August) vessels are in high demand. Repeat customers will book up to a year in advance to secure prime boats during high season, so you'll want to plan your trip long in advance. Most operators close shop from October through March, during the cold and rainy fall and winter.

HOTEL BARGE EXCURSIONS

Top of the line hotel barge excursions are all-inclusive affairs that cost about $3,000 per person for a voyage of six days and seven nights. If that price seems steep, remember that you'll sleep in luxurious digs—gourmet meals, shore excursions and entrance fees, an open bar, and the use of a bicycle are also included.

For a less expensive option, anticipate paying around $1,200 for a weeklong barge and bike trip that should include breakfast and dinner, a daily packed lunch, and capable guides. Incidentals like museum admissions, bicycle insurance, and alcoholic drinks will carry an extra cost, you won't have the benefit of a support van, and your shipboard sleeping quarters won't be as posh.

SELF-GUIDED BOATS

If you hire a self-guided boat, your rental agency should provide advice with itineraries. A weeklong trip is recommended for first-timers though discounts are offered for longer periods of time. Expect to pay $4,000 weekly per boat during high season—for a barge that sleeps four to six passengers—and roughly half that amount during the low season.

Boat rentals typically include a fully-equipped galley (allowing you to prepare meals on board), sets of linen, a boat driving demonstration and orientation, towels, life jackets, river and canal maps, and perhaps most importantly, round-the-clock technical support. You will be responsible for travel to and from the boat, fuel, a security deposit, personal holiday insurance, cancellation insurance, and the cost of a damage waiver covering collision or loss. Extras can include such items as bicycles, fishing licenses, and a surcharge for pets. On request, most boat rental agencies can stock the boat with preordered groceries; expect to pay the going rate for the groceries plus a 10% surcharge.

WHAT TO PACK

Reputable operators will send you a pre-trip information kit which outlines any specific items that you are expected to pack, but as a rule, you can plan for a barge trip as you would any vacation to the Netherlands. Bring a warm windbreaker for evenings on deck, and if you plan to combine your barge trip with some cycling, bring layers of activewear that can be removed as weather demands. Comfortable walking shoes are a must for exploring and rain gear is always a good idea.

10

WHAT TO EXPECT

There are hundreds of watery routes that one can take when traveling by boat. Springtime trips take advantage of the famous tulip fields in full bloom. Itineraries will typically include a visit to the Keukenhof, as well as a trip to the windmills at the Kinderdijk and the fishing villages on the Ijsselmeer. Alkmaar and Gouda, cities renown for their cheese, are also itinerary favorites. For the rest of the season, the pastoral region of Friesland, the quaint villages of the Ijsselmeer—Monnickedam, Hoorn, Enkhuizen, Zaandam, Edam—and urban centers like Amsterdam, Delft, and The Hague continue to attract their share of traffic. Those wishing to take the canal less traveled shouldn't have much trouble crafting a suitable itinerary. Most Dutch operators offer trips to the more off-the-beaten path areas of Holland: the Wadden Sea Islands, the northern province of Gronigen, and the southern province of Zeeland.

Should you opt for a hotel barge excursion, you can expect to cruise between three to five hours each day before disembarking to visit a major sight or city or to bike through an area of natural beauty. Hotel boats generally never travel while the guests are sleeping—watching the countryside slip by is part of the charm of barging. Most group barge trips include guided walking or biking shore excursions.

TYPES OF BOATS

Depending on your budget, hotel barges can range in luxury from spartan to stately, with most offering accommodations in the range of a four-star hotel. Some hotel boats are modern vessels but many are refurbished antique barges of mahogany and teak, complete with brass fitting, period furniture, paintings, and possibly even a piano. Cabins typically have a double- or twin-bedded layout, and a little window. Sharing a washroom with other guests can be commonplace, but luxury trips usually have an en-suite bathroom with shower.

Hotel barges come in a huge variety of sizes. The smallest captained boats will carry up to six passengers and the largest will accommodate nearly 40 people per voyage. The smaller boats offer the same standards of luxury as the larger ships, but larger boats do have more common spaces—and more breathing room.

Given the narrow Dutch canals and the frequency of encountering low bridges, many self-guided bargers elect to strike a compromise between small, low, and narrow boats which allow access to even the tiniest waterways, and the creature comforts that come with larger, modern, family cruise boats. It is possible to find long, slender, and low antique vessels for hire, but most boats will be modern versions of the classic canal boat. Typically 32–40 feet (10–12 meters) long, they have at least one shower, air-conditioning, a saloon which can be converted into additional sleeping space, a microwave, CD player, lockable safe, two steering positions—one outdoors on deck and one inside—a spacious sundeck, and a bathing platform at the stern.

TRAVELING BY BIKE

Touring the Netherlands by bike is arguably the finest way to see the country. Holland's bike-friendly cities and endless supply of charming villages can easily be visited under pedal-power as extensive *fietspads* (bike paths), a flat landscape, and a very cycle-friendly culture make this country the ideal place to enter the world of bike touring. You'll meet more locals, see more of the countryside, and do your part for the environment; working off the cheese and pancakes has never felt so good!

Given the ease of touring the country by bike, it's only a slight exaggeration to say that the most difficult part will be choosing to join up with an organized trip or to go it alone. Intrepid travelers wanting to self-plan and self-guide a bike tour can find a wealth of maps, books, and Web resources, and can rest assured that from the most basic campsites to the country's most luxurious hotels, the staff has experience accommodating those touring the country by bicycle.

Those wishing to join an organized group tour will find countless options designed to accommodate all imaginable itineraries and budgets. Bike tours are organized to visit nearly every nook and cranny of the Netherlands, and no region is too remote or obscure to escape the vision of Holland's many enterprising bike tour providers. Trips which take in the colorful tulip fields are popular in the spring, and city-to-city trips that take in villages and rural areas are tremendously popular anytime between late spring and early autumn. July and August represent the high season, so conveniently located budget campsites and lodgings can fill up quickly.

PLANNING YOUR TRIP

Tour operators will try to accommodate last minute plans, but cycle tours are popular and booking between four to six months in advance is highly recommended. Count on a weeklong trip and expect a wide range of options and budgets.

High-end luxury trips that provide accommodation in premier hotels start out at nearly $3,000 per person. If you're traveling solo, anticipate a single supplement as high as $800. The next price category offers a similar tour, but in two- and three-star hotels and some—but not all meals—for around $1,900.

For more detailed information on planning your trip, bike path maps, route descriptions, and public transportation information, check out Anja de Graaf and Paul van Roekel's excellent resource page at ⊕ *holland.cyclingaroundtheworld.nl.*

10

WHAT TO PACK
Bike tour operators will be happy to provide you with a list of clothing and personal effects that you'll want to bring, but a pre-trip visit to a local bike shop for a few biking-specific articles of clothing is a good idea. Plan on dressing in layers that can be taken on and off according to the weather. Peddling is surprisingly tough on feet, so stiffer-soled purpose-built cycling shoes are a good idea. A couple of pairs of padded cycling shorts are absolutely necessary. Sunglasses and a hat will prove invaluable when the sun shines brightly, and a pair of gloves, even in summer months, is recommended.

WHAT TO EXPECT

Depending on your itinerary and company, your trip could start virtually anywhere in the Netherlands. The coastline (including the Wadden Sea Islands), national parks "De Hoge Veluwe" and "De Veluwezoom," and the hills in Limburg offer the most attractive natural landscapes, though most bike tours and independent cyclists aim to strike a balance between nature, cities, and villages.

Count on cycling four to five hours daily with a break for lunch; that way you'll be able to cover between 40–60 km (25–37 mi) per day, stop to take in the must-see sights, and do a little exploring should something catch your eye. The best organized excursions will provide a support van that distributes refreshments throughout the day and that will give you a lift if you get tired. Many companies have trips that move on to a new hotel nightly; some tours return to the same hotel, using it as a home base to explore the nearby sights before moving on.

For the utmost in comfort consider booking with a company specializing in active-lifestyle luxury vacations. Both Backroads and Butterfield & Robinson have a long history of guiding bike tours in Holland, and both companies offer competitively priced packages. You'll enjoy four- to five-star twin or double accommodation, most—if not all—meals, and guides that take care of the behind-the-scenes logistics of the trip in addition to leading the ride. Also included are maps, admission to all events and attractions, baggage transport between destinations, use of high-quality bicycles, all gratuities, all transportation during the trip, and the use of a support van. More modest trips will include two- to three-star accommodation, luggage transport between hotels, and most meals. Admission to museums and gratuities may be extra and you might have to forgo the benefit of a support van.

If you decide to plan and book your own itinerary, your imagination will be your only constraint. You'll be free to cycle as much or as little as you wish on any given day, to take random days off when you're tired of peddling, and to make your own dining and lodging choices—from campsites or hostels to the most luxurious digs in town. The trade-off is that you'll forfeit the benefit of an experienced guide, and you will need either to carry your own gear for the duration of the trip or make costly arrangements to have it ferried to your next destination.

TYPES OF BIKES

Bikes provided on self-guided barge trips and hotel barges tend to fall into two categories—comfort bikes and hybrids. Comfort bikes or city bikes will typically feature a well-padded seat, a small rack for your "carry-on luggage," and few, if any, gears. While efficiency is slightly compromised, an upright seating position affords maximum comfort on a casual ride. Hybrid bicycles blend the characteristics of road bikes with the ruggedness of mountain bikes, making them a versatile option suitable for use on paved as well as dirt roads. They can handle light off-road duty, have lots of gears, and the riding position is a balanced compromise between efficiency and comfort. If you book a guided bike tour that includes a support van, you'll probably be provided with a hybrid bicycle. If you are carrying your own gear—either on a group tour or a self-supported journey—you'll want to use a touring bike. Touring bicycles are rugged, built for riding long distances, and they can easily accommodate panniers (fork-mounted bags used to transport your luggage). Touring bikes have a nice big selection of gears as well.

BARGING & BIKING TOUR OPERATORS

While by no means a definitive list, each of the tour providers mentioned below has a proven track record of guiding active visitors around the Netherlands. **Backroads** offers luxury cycling trips through the Dutch countryside, which take in the windmills at Kinderdijk, De Hoge Veluwe National Park, and the country's *Groene Hart* (Green Heart). The same itinerary can also be visited as part of a luxury family tour. ☎*800/462–2848* ⊕*www.backroads.com.*

Butterfield & Robinson offers a luxury tour that visits The Hague and Leiden, then Gouda before heading into the great heart of the country where canals, windmills, and cheese farms provide charm. Butterfield's tour wraps up in coastal Zeeland where gourmands can turn their attention to mussels. ☎*866/551–9090* ⊕*www.butterfield.com.*

Cycletours Holland is an Amsterdam-based company providing numerous tours that combine biking and barging. Some—like the "Tulip Tour," "Castles and Estates," and the Frisian "Eleven Cities Tour"—focus on exclusively Dutch themes, while others combine a trip to the Netherlands with a foray into Belgium. ☎*020/5521–8490* ⊕*www.cycletours. com.* **Euro-Bike and Walking Tours** offers two tours with three levels of service—budget, comfort, and luxury. "Highlights of Holland" is a four-day tour that visits classical draws like the Keukenhof, Haarlem, and The Hague, while "The Dutch Touch" heads north to Gronigen after taking in the fishing villages of the Ijsselmeer. ☎*800/321–6060* ⊕*www.euro-bike.com.* **Le Boat** can provide luxurious barge and bike tours, but is best known for chartering modern, luxury canal boats for visitors interested in a self-guided holiday. The Northern towns of Sneek and Strandhorst serve as their home ports in Holland. ☎*800/992–02911400* ⊕*www.leboat.com.*

10

Amsterdam &
the Netherlands
Essentials

PLANNING TOOLS, EXPERT INSIGHT,
GREAT CONTACTS

There are planners and there are those who, excuse the pun, fly by the seat of their pants. We happily place ourselves among the planners. Our writers and editors try to anticipate all the issues you may face before and during any journey, and then they do their research. This section is the product of their efforts. Use it to get excited about your trip to Amsterdam, to inform your travel planning, or to guide you on the road should the seat of your pants start to feel threadbare.

GETTING STARTED

We're really proud of our Web site: Fodors.com is a great place to begin any journey. Scan Travel Wire for suggested itineraries, travel deals, restaurant and hotel openings, and other up-to-the-minute info. Check out Booking to research prices and book plane tickets, hotel rooms, rental cars, and vacation packages. Head to Talk for on-the-ground pointers from travelers who frequent our message boards. You can also link to loads of other travel-related resources.

ONLINE TRAVEL TOOLS

Amsterdam and the Netherlands For a guide to what's happening in Holland, the official site for the Netherlands Board of Tourism is ⊕us.holland.com. The official Amsterdam site is ⊕www.amsterdam.nl. More information is found at ⊕www.visitamsterdam.nl. For Amsterdam maps, check out ⊕hipplanet.com/amsterdam. Another general site is ⊕www.amsterdamhotspots.nl. ⊕www.channels.nl is a Web site that guides you through the city with the help of many colorful photographs. For more information on the Netherlands, visit ⊕www.goholland.com. The American Society of Travel Agents is at ⊕www.astanet.com. For rail information and schedules, go to ⊕www.ns.nl. For airport information, go to ⊕www.schiphol.nl. For flight information and reservations on KLM/Northwest, the national carrier, go to ⊕www.klm.com; check out the low tariffs on ⊕www.easyjet.com, ⊕www.ryanair.com, and, for budget travelers, ⊕www.airfair.nl.

ALL ABOUT AMSTERDAM, THE NETHERLANDS & BELGIUM

Currency Conversion Google (⊕www.google.com) does currency conversion. Just type in the amount you want to convert and an explanation of how you want it converted (e.g., "14 Swiss francs in dollars"), and then voilà. **Oanda.com** (⊕www.oanda.com) also allows you to print out a handy table with the current day's conversion rates. **XE.com** (⊕www.xe.com) is a good currency conversion Web site.

VISITOR INFORMATION

AMSTERDAM AND BEYOND

The VVV (Netherlands Board of Tourism) has several offices around Amsterdam. The office in Centraal Station is open daily 8–8; the one on Stationsplein, opposite Centraal Station, is open daily 9–5; on Leidseplein, daily 9–5; and at Schiphol Airport, daily 7–10. Each VVV (Netherlands Board of Tourism) within Holland has information principally on its own region.

Every town in Belgium has an official tourist office with key visitor's information, maps, and calendars of events. The helpful staff is usually trilingual (English, French, and Flemish). The offices might close for an hour at lunchtime, but during the high season they might stay open past 6. Offices in the main destinations are open on weekends as well as weekdays.

Amsterdam and the Netherlands Tourist Information VVV—**Netherlands Board of Tourism** (⊕www.holland.com/amsterdam ⊠Spoor 2/Platform 2, Centraal Station, Centrum ⊠Stationsplein 10, Centraal Station ⊠Leidseplein 1, at Leidsestraat, Leidseplein ⊠Schiphol Airport, Badhoevedorp ☎020/551–2525 ⊠Wagenstraat 193, The Hague ☎070/402–3336 regional specialists ⊠Coolsingel 5, 3012 ACRotterdam ☎010/271–0120 regional specialists).

Belgian National Tourist Office Belgian Office of Tourism (⊠Rue Marché aux Herbes 61–63, Brussels B1000 ☎02/504–0300 🖷02/504–0377). **In the U.S.** (⊠220 E

42nd St., Suite 3402, New York, NY 10017 ☎212/758-8130 📠212/355-7675).

GEAR

When coming to the Netherlands or Belgium, be flexible: pack an umbrella (or two—the topography results in a blustery wind, which makes short work of a lightweight frame); bring a raincoat, with a thick liner in winter; and always have a sweater or jacket handy. For daytime wear and casual evenings, turtlenecks and thicker shirts are ideal for winter, under a sweater. Unpredictable summer weather means that a long-sleeved cotton shirt and jacket could be perfect one day, whereas the next, a T-shirt or vest top is as much as you can wear, making it hard to pack lightly. Bring a little something for all eventualities and you shouldn't get stuck.

Essentially, laid-back is the norm. Stylewise, anything goes. Men aren't required to wear ties or jackets anywhere, except in some smarter hotels and exclusive restaurants; jeans are very popular and worn to the office. Cobblestone streets make walking in high heels perilous— you don't want a wrenched ankle—and white sneakers are a dead giveaway that you are an American tourist; a better choice is a pair of dark-color, comfortable walking shoes.

Women wear skirts more frequently than do women in the United States, especially those over 35. Men only need include a jacket and tie if you're planning to visit one of the upper-echelon restaurants.

PASSPORTS & VISAS

All U.S., Canadian, and U.K. citizens, even infants, need only a valid passport to enter the Netherlands or Belgium for stays of up to 90 days.

It's a good idea to always carry your passport with you, even if think you don't need one, for example if traveling between the Netherlands and other countries within the European Schengen agreement (which includes Belgium, France, and Germany, but not the United Kingdom). You are required to carry valid ID at all times in both the Netherlands and Belgium, and although it's unlikely that you'll be asked for it, it's better to be safe than risk a fine.

PASSPORTS

A passport verifies both your identity and nationality—a great reason to have one. Another reason is that you need a passport now more than ever. At this writing, U.S. citizens must have a passport when traveling by air between the United States and several destinations for which other forms of identification (e.g., a driver's license and a birth certificate) were once sufficient. These destinations include Mexico, Canada, Bermuda, and all countries in Central America and the Caribbean (except the territories of Puerto Rico and the U.S. Virgin Islands). Soon enough you'll need a passport when traveling between the United States and such destinations by land and sea, too.

U.S. passports are valid for 10 years. You must apply in person if you're getting a passport for the first time; if your previous passport was lost, stolen, or damaged; or if your previous passport has expired and was issued more than 15 years ago or when you were under 16. All children under 18 must appear in person to apply for or renew a passport. Both parents must accompany any child under 14 (or send a notarized statement with their permission) and provide proof of their relationship to the child.

■TIP→**Before your trip, make two copies of your passport's data page (one for someone at home and another for you to carry separately). Or scan the page and e-mail it to someone at home and/or yourself.**

There are 13 regional passport offices, as well as 7,000 passport acceptance facilities in post offices, public libraries, and other governmental offices. If you're renewing a passport, you can do so by mail. Forms are available at passport acceptance facilities and online.

The cost to apply for a new passport is $97 for adults, $82 for children under 16; renewals are $67. Allow six weeks for processing, both for first-time passports and renewals. For an expediting fee of $60 you can reduce this time to about two weeks. If your trip is less than two weeks away, you can get a passport even more rapidly by going to a passport office with the necessary documentation. Private expediters can get things done in as little as 48 hours, but charge hefty fees for their services.

VISAS

A visa is essentially formal permission to enter a country. Visas allow countries to keep track of you and other visitors—and generate revenue (from application fees). You *always* need a visa to enter a foreign country; however, many countries routinely issue tourist visas on arrival, particularly to U.S. citizens. When your passport is stamped or scanned in the immigration line, you're actually being issued a visa. Sometimes you have to stand in a separate line and pay a small fee to get your stamp before going through immigration, but you can still do this at the airport on arrival.

If you must apply for a visa in advance, you can usually do it in person or by mail. When you apply by mail, you send your passport to a designated consulate, where your passport will be examined and the visa issued. Expediters—usually the same ones who handle expedited passport applications—can do all the work of obtaining your visa for you; however, there's always an additional cost (often more than $50 per visa).

Most visas limit you to a single trip—basically during the actual dates of your planned vacation. Other visas allow you to visit as many times as you wish for a specific period of time. Remember that requirements change, sometimes at the drop of a hat, and the burden is on you to make sure that you have the appropriate visas. Otherwise, you'll be turned away at the airport or, worse, deported after you arrive in the country. No company or travel insurer gives refunds if your travel plans are disrupted because you didn't have the correct visa.

U.S. Passport Information U.S. Department of State (☎877/487–2778 ⊕travel.state. gov/passport).

U.S. Passport & Visa Expediters A. Briggs Passport & Visa Expeditors (☎800/806–0581 or 202/338–0111 ⊕www. abriggs.com). **American Passport Express** (☎800/455–5166 or 800/841–6778 ⊕www. americanpassport.com). **Passport Express** (☎800/362–8196 ⊕www.passport express.com). **Travel Document Systems** (☎800/874–5100 or 202/638–3800 ⊕www. traveldocs.com). **Travel the World Visas** (☎866/886–8472 or 301/495–7700 ⊕www. world-visa.com).

SHOTS & MEDICATIONS

Standards of health in Belgium and the Netherlands are generally very good. You won't need any immunizations and you are unlikely to get sick. Older visitors however may wish to consider immunization against influenza if traveling over the winter months. If you do fall ill, you've picked the right place, as Belgian healthcare is generally acknowledged as the best in the world, and the Netherlands isn't far behind. *For more information see Health below.*

Health Warnings National Centers for Disease Control & Prevention (CDC; ☎877/394–8747 international travelers' health line ⊕www.cdc.gov/travel). **World Health Organization** (WHO; ⊕www.who.int).

BOOKING YOUR TRIP

ONLINE

You really have to shop around. A travel wholesaler such as Hotels.com or Hotel-Club.net can be a source of good rates, as can discounters such as Hotwire or Priceline, particularly if you can bid for your hotel room or airfare. Indeed, such sites sometimes have deals that are unavailable elsewhere. They do, however, tend to work only with hotel chains (which makes them just plain useless for getting hotel reservations outside of major cities) or big airlines (so that often leaves out upstarts like jetBlue and some foreign carriers like Air India).

Also, with discounters and wholesalers you must generally prepay, and everything is nonrefundable. And before you fork over the dough, be sure to check the terms and conditions, so you know what a given company will do for you if there's a problem and what you'll have to deal with on your own.

■TIP➜To be absolutely sure everything was processed correctly, confirm reservations made through online travel agents, discounters, and wholesalers directly with your hotel before leaving home.

Booking engines like Expedia, Travelocity, and Orbitz are actually travel agents, albeit high-volume, online ones. And airline travel packagers like American Airlines Vacations and Virgin Vacations—well, they're travel agents, too. But they may still not work with all the world's hotels.

WITH A TRAVEL AGENT

If you use an agent—brick-and-mortar or virtual—you'll pay a fee for the service. And know that the service you get from some online agents isn't comprehensive. For example Expedia and Travelocity don't search for prices on budget airlines like jetBlue, Southwest, or small foreign carriers. That said, some agents (online or not) *do* have access to fares that are difficult to find otherwise, and the savings can more than make up for any surcharge.

A knowledgeable brick-and-mortar travel agent can be a godsend if you're booking a cruise, a package trip that's not available to you directly, an air pass, or a complicated itinerary including several overseas flights. What's more, travel agents that specialize in a destination may have exclusive access to certain deals and insider information on things such as charter flights. Agents who specialize in types of travelers (senior citizens, gays and lesbians, naturists) or types of trips (cruises, luxury travel, safaris) can also be invaluable.

Agent Resources American Society of Travel Agents (☎703/739–2782 ⊕www.travelsense.org).

Amsterdam, the Netherlands & Belgium Travel Agents American Express Travel (☎212/640–5130 ⊕www.americanexpress.com).

ACCOMMODATIONS

Both the Netherlands and Belgium offer a range of options, from the major international hotel chains and small, modern local hotels to family-run restored inns and historic houses. Accommodations in Amsterdam are at a particular premium at any time of year, so you should book well in advance. Should you arrive without a hotel room, head for one of the city's four VVV (Netherlands Board of Tourism) offices, which have a same-day hotel booking service and can help you find a room.

The hotel situation elsewhere in the Netherlands and in Belgium is less tight outside of the summer months, but hotels in larger cities often fill with business customers during the week. Most hotels that do cater to business travelers sometimes grant substantial weekend rebates. These discounted rates are often available during the week as well in July and August, when business travelers are thin on the ground. Wherever you go, you will have a wider choice if you plan ahead.

Properties indicated by a ✕🏠are lodging establishments whose restaurants warrant a special trip.

■**TIP→**Assume that hotels operate on the European Plan (EP, no meals) unless we specify that they use the Breakfast Plan (**BP**, with full breakfast), Continental Plan (**CP**, Continental breakfast), Full American Plan (**FAP**, all meals), Modified American Plan (**MAP**, breakfast and dinner) or are all-inclusive (**AI**, all meals and most activities).

APARTMENT & HOUSE RENTALS

In Amsterdam, **City Mundo** has an excellent network, and whatever your requirements, this creative city specialist directory will try to hook you up to your ideal spot, whether that's a windmill or a houseboat. The price drops the longer you stay, up to the maximum of 21 nights, with a minimum of two nights. Book online, at the group's Web site *(⇨ Web Sites)*, where visuals and descriptions are constantly updated as new facilities come in.

It's also worth contacting **Holiday Link,** an agency that provides contacts and addresses for home-exchange holidays and house-sitting during holiday periods; bed-and-breakfasts; rentals of private houses in Holland; and budget accommodations. The company is part of **HomeLink International,** the worldwide vacation organization in more than 50 countries, so it knows what's what.

The VVVs (tourist information offices) in each region you plan to visit all have extensive accommodations listings. They can book reservations for you, according to your specific requirements. Call the number below for the local office in the area you plan to visit.

In Belgium, apartment rentals and *gîtes* (farmhouse rentals) are easy to find in popular vacation areas. Rentals from private individuals are usually for a one- or two-week minimum. Sheets and towels are not provided. You can also rent vacation villas within the Dutch and Belgian vacation parks. These self-contained parks, in rural or seaside settings, consist of residences and facilities such as swimming pools, hiking and bicycling trails, restaurants, and activities for children. There is usually a one-week minimum, although it is often possible to rent for shorter periods during the winter months. Center Parcs has eight such locations in the Netherlands and two in Belgium.

Local Agents in the Netherlands Center Parcs (☎ Admiraliteitskade 40, 3063ED Rotterdam ☎010/498–9898, 0900/660–6600 [€0.50 per min] ⊕www.centerparcs.com). **City Mundo** (✉ Schinkelkade 47 II, 1075VK Amsterdam ☎020/676–5270 ⊕www.citymundo.com). **Landal Green Parks** (☎ Box 910, 2270AX Voorburg ☎070/300–3506 🖶070/300–3515 ⊕www.landalgreenparks.com). **VVV tourist offices** (☎0900/400–4040 [€0.55 per min]).

Local Agents in Belgium Gîtes de Wallonie (✉ av. Prince de Liège 1, Namur B5100 ☎081/31–18–00 🖶081/31–02–00 ⊕www.gitesdewallonie.net). **Vacation Villas** (⊕www.vacationvillas.net).

BED & BREAKFASTS

A pleasant alternative to getting accommodations in a hotel is to stay at a bed-and-breakfast (B&B). You'll find a large choice scattered throughout the Netherlands. The best way to track down B&Bs in Amsterdam is either through creative city accommodations specialist City Mundo or Holiday Link, both of which deal with private houses and longer stays. Prices vary widely from €20 to €40 per person.

Bed-and-breakfast accommodations are less common in Belgium; the ones you do find usually need to be reserved in advance and, although clean, are very simple, often without private bathrooms. Listings are available at local tourist information centers, but you must make your own reservations directly with the proprietor. *Taxistop,* a company that promotes inexpensive lodging and travel deals, sells a B&B guide to Belgium and makes reservations.

Reservation Services in the Netherlands
Bed & Breakfast Holland (☎020/615-7527 ⊕www.bbholland.com). **Bed and Breakfast Service Nederland** (✉Hallenstraat 12a, 5531 AB Bladel ☎0497/330-300 🖷0497/330-811 ⊕www.bedandbreakfast.nl). **City Mundo** (✉Schinkelkade 47 II, 1075 VK Amsterdam ☎020/676-5270 ⊕www.citymundo.com).

Reservation Services in Belgium
Taxistop (✉Rue Fossé-aux-Loups 28, Brussels B1000 ☎070/222-292 ⊕www.taxistop.be).

HOME EXCHANGES
With a direct home exchange you stay in someone else's home while they stay in yours. Some outfits also deal with vacation homes, so you're not actually staying in someone's full-time residence, just their vacant weekend place.

Exchange Clubs

Home Exchange.com (☎800/877-8723 ⊕www.homeexchange.com); $59.95 for a 1-year online listing. **HomeLink International** (☎800/638-3841 ⊕www.homelink.org); $90 yearly for Web-only membership; $140 includes Web access and two catalogs. **Intervac U.S.** (☎800/756-4663 ⊕www.intervacus.com); $78.88 for Web-only membership; $126 includes Web access and a catalog.

HOSTELS
Hostels offer bare-bones lodging at low, low prices—often in shared dorm rooms with shared baths—to people of all ages, though the primary market is young travelers, especially students. Most hostels serve breakfast; dinner and/or shared cooking facilities may also be available. In some hostels you aren't allowed to be in your room during the day, and there

may be a curfew at night. Nevertheless, hostels provide a sense of community, with public rooms where travelers often gather to share stories. Many hostels are affiliated with Hostelling International (HI), an umbrella group of hostel associations with some 4,500 member properties in more than 70 countries. Other hostels are completely independent and may be nothing more than a really cheap hotel.

Dutch Organizations
Stayokay (Nederlandse Jeugdherberg Centrale) (☎020/551-3155 ⊕www.stayokay.com).

Belgian Organizations
Auberges de Jeunesse de la Belgique Francophone (✉Rue de la Sablonnière 28, 1000 Brussels ☎02/219-5676 🖷02/219-1451 ⊕www.laj.be). **Vlaamse Jeugdherbergen** (✉Van Stralenstraat 40, B2060 Antwerp ☎03/232-7218 🖷03/231-8126 ⊕www.vjh.be).

Information
Hostelling International—USA (☎301/495-1240 ⊕www.hiusa.org).

HOTELS
In line with the international system, Dutch and Belgian hotels are awarded stars (one to five) by the Benelux Hotel Classification System, an independent agency that inspects properties based on their facilities and services. Those with three or more stars feature en suite bathrooms where a shower is standard, whereas a tub is a four-star standard. Rooms in lodgings listed in this guide have a shower unless otherwise indicated.

One Dutch peculiarity to watch out for is having twin beds pushed together instead of having one double. If you want a double bed (or *tweepersoonsbed*), you may have to pay more. Keep in mind that the star ratings are general indications and that a charming three-star might make for a better stay than a more expensive four-star. During low season, usually November to March (excluding Christmas and the New Year) when a hotel is not full, it is sometimes possible to negotiate a discounted rate, if one is not already offered. Prices in Amsterdam are higher over the peak summer period, while those in less touristed cities may actually fall at this time when the core business trade tails off. Room rates for deluxe and four-star rooms are on a par with those in other European cities, so in these categories, ask for one of the better rooms, since less desirable rooms—and there occasionally are some—don't measure up to what you are paying for. Most cheaper hotels quote room rates including breakfast, while for those at the top end it usually costs extra. When you book a room and are in any doubt, specifically ask whether the rate includes breakfast.

Check out your hotel's location, and ask your hotelier about availability of a room with a view, if you're not worried about the extra expense: hotels in the historic center with a pretty canal view are highly sought after. Always ask if there is an elevator (called a "lift") or whether guests need to climb any stairs. Even if you are fairly fit, you may find traditional Dutch staircases in older buildings intimidating and difficult to negotiate. It's worth considering if you plan to stay in a listed monument, such as a historic canal-side town house. The alternative is to request a ground-floor room. In older hotels, the quality of the rooms may vary; if you don't like the room you're given, request another. This applies to noise, too. Front rooms may be larger or have a view, but they may also have a lot of street noise—so if you're a light sleeper, request a quiet room when making reservations. Remember to specify whether you care to have a bath or shower, since many bathrooms do not have tubs. It is always a good idea to have your reservation, dates, and rate confirmed by fax.

Taking meals at a hotel's restaurant sometimes provides you with a discount. Some restaurants, especially country inns in Belgium, require that guests take half board (*demi-pension* in French, *half-pension* in Flemish), at least lunch or dinner, at the hotel. Full pension (*pension* *complet* in French, *volledig pension* in Flemish) entitles guests to both lunch and dinner. Guests taking either half or full board also receive breakfast. If you take a *pension*, you pay per person, regardless of the number of rooms.

Many hotels in Amsterdam appear to be permanently full, and throughout the year conventions can fill up business hotels in Brussels, so book as far in advance as you can to be sure of getting what you want.

Aside from going directly to the hotels or booking a travel and hotel package with your travel agent, there are several ways of making reservations. The **Nederlands Reserverings Centrum** (the Dutch hoteliers' reservation service) handles bookings for the whole of the Netherlands on its Web site for cancellations and reservations; bookings are made online. The VVV (Netherlands Board of Tourism) offers the same services; branches of the VVV can be found in Schiphol Airport, Amsterdam Centraal Station, and at Leidseplein. Contact the VVV's office, or go to their Web site (⇨ *Web Sites*). Most agencies charge a booking fee, which starts at €9 per person. Among the reservations services in Belgium are Belgian Tourist Reservations, a free service for booking hotel rooms, and Toerisme Stad Antwerpen, which makes hotel and B&B reservations in Antwerp. Hotels in both countries will sometimes ask you to confirm your reservation by fax or e-mail. If you are having an extended stay, the property may request a deposit either in the local currency or billed to your credit card.

Reservation Services in Amsterdam

Nederlands Reserverings Centrum (Dutch hoteliers' reservation service ☎029/968–9144 ⊕www.hotelres.nl). **VVV Netherlands Board of Tourism Switchboard** (☎0900/400–4040 calls cost €0.55per minute)

Reservations Services in Belgium **Belgian Tourist Reservations** (BTR; ✉Blvd. Ans-

pach 111, Brussels B1000 ☎02/513–7484 ☎02/513–9277).

Toerisme Stad Antwerpen (✉Grote Markt 13, Antwerp B2000 ☎03/232–0103 ☎03/231–1937 ⊕www.visitantwerpen.be).

▮ AIRLINE TICKETS

Most domestic airline tickets are electronic; international tickets may be either electronic or paper. With an e-ticket the only thing you receive is an e-mailed receipt citing your itinerary and reservation and ticket numbers.

The sole advantage of a paper ticket is that it may be easier to endorse over to another airline if your flight is canceled and the airline with which you booked can't accommodate you on another flight.

▮**TIP**➔ Discount air passes that let you travel economically in a country or region must often be purchased before you leave home. In some cases you can only get them through a travel agent.

The least expensive airfares to the Netherlands originate from the UK and other European countries, are priced for round-trip travel, and must usually be purchased in advance online. Airlines generally allow you to change your return date for a fee; most-low fare tickets, however, are nonrefundable.

EasyJet has low fares to Amsterdam flying in from Belfast, Edinburgh, Geneva, Glasgow, Liverpool, London (Gatwick and Luton), and Nice. BasiqAir flies to Amsterdam and Rotterdam from Barcelona and Nice. Ryanair flies to the southern Dutch city of Eindhoven from London Stansted. BMIBaby flies to Amsterdam from its hub in Nottingham and from Cardiff.

Consolidators & Low-cost Airlines BasiqAir (☎0900/0737 in Holland). **BMIBaby** (⊕www. bmibaby.com). **EasyJet** (☎023/568–4880 in the Netherlands ⊕www.easyjet.com). **Ryanair** (⊕www.ryanair.com).

Air Pass Info All Europe Airpass (☎800/639–3590 ⊕www.allairpass.com). **Discover Europe Airpass** (☎800/788–0555 ⊕www.flybmi-canada.com). **FlightPass** (EuropebyAir ☎888/321–4737 ⊕www.europebyair. com). **oneworld visitor pass** (⊕www.oneworld.com). **Passport to Europe** (☎800/447–4747 ⊕www.nwa.com). **SkyTeam European Airpass** (☎800/223–5730 ⊕www.alitalia. com). **Star Alliance European Airpass** (☎800/864–8331 ⊕www.staralliance.com).

▮ RENTAL CARS

When you reserve a car, ask about cancellation penalties, taxes, drop-off charges (if you're planning to pick up the car in one city and leave it in another), and surcharges (for being under or over a certain age, for additional drivers, or for driving across state or country borders or beyond a specific distance from your point of rental). All these things can add substantially to your costs. Request car seats and extras such as GPS when you book.

Most major American rental-car companies have offices or affiliates in the Netherlands, but the rates are generally better if you make an advance reservation from abroad rather than from within Holland. Rates vary from company to company; daily rates start at approximately €30 for a one-day rental, €60 for a three-day rental, and €150 for a week. This may not include collision insurance or airport fee. Tax is included and weekly rates often include unlimited mileage. Most cars in Europe are stick shift. An automatic transmission will cost a little extra. Rental cars are European brands and range from economy, such as a Ford Ka, to luxury, such as a Mercedes. They will always be in good condition. It is also possible to rent minivans.

Autoverhuur (car rental) in Holland is best for exploring the center, north, or east of the country, but is to be avoided in the heavily urbanized northwest, known as the Randstad, where the public transport infrastructure is excellent. Signage on country roads is usually pretty good, but be prepared to patiently trail behind cyclists blithely riding two abreast (which is illegal), even when the road is not wide enough for you to pass.

Your driver's license may not be recognized outside your home country. You may not be able to rent a car without an International Driving Permit (IDP), which can be used only in conjunction with a valid driver's license and which translates your license into 10 languages. Check the AAA Web site for more info as well as for IDPs ($10) themselves.

CAR-RENTAL INSURANCE

Everyone who rents a car wonders whether the insurance that the rental companies offer is worth the expense. No one—including us—has a simple answer. It all depends on how much regular insurance you have, how comfortable you are with risk, and whether or not money is an issue.

If you own a car, your personal auto insurance may cover a rental to some degree, though not all policies protect you abroad; always read your policy's fine print. If you don't have auto insurance, then seriously consider buying the collision- or loss-damage waiver (CDW or LDW) from the car-rental company, which eliminates your liability for damage to the car. Some credit cards offer CDW coverage, but it's usually supplemental to your own insurance and rarely covers SUVs, minivans, luxury models, and the like. If your coverage is secondary, you may still be liable for loss-of-use costs from the car-rental company. But no credit-card insurance is valid unless you use that card for *all* transactions, from reserving to paying the final bill. All companies exclude car rental in some countries, so be sure to find out about the destination to which you are traveling.

■TIP➔ You can decline the insurance from the rental company and purchase it through a third-party provider such as Travel Guard (www.travelguard.com)—$9 per day for $35,000 of coverage. That's sometimes just under half the price of the CDW offered by some car-rental companies.

■ VACATION PACKAGES

Packages *are not* guided excursions. Packages combine airfare, accommodations, and perhaps a rental car or other extras (theater tickets, guided excursions, boat trips, reserved entry to popular museums, transit passes), but they let you do your own thing. During busy periods packages may be your only option, as flights and rooms may be sold out otherwise.

The Netherlands and Belgium are easy places to get around, and you don't really need an organized package to see everything. Language is rarely a problem as so many people speak good English, and many hotels offer online booking services that allow you to have everything arranged in advance. However, if your time is limited, having a prearranged package tour may allow you to pack more in while you are on the ground.

Independent vacation packages are available from major tour operators and airlines. The companies listed below offer vacation packages.

Air/Hotel **Central Holidays** (⇨ *Group Tours, above*). **Delta Vacations** (☎ 800/654–6559). **TWA Getaway Vacations** (☎ 800/438–2929). **US Airways Vacations** (☎ 800/455–0123).

Organizations **American Society of Travel Agents** (ASTA ☎ 703/739–2782 or 800/965–2782 ⊕ www.astanet.com). **United States Tour Operators Association** (USTOA ☎ 212/599–6599 ⊕ www.ustoa.com).

■TIP➔ Local tourism boards can provide information about lesser-known and small-niche operators that sell packages to only a few destinations.

▌GUIDED TOURS

Guided tours are a good option when you don't want to do it all yourself. You travel along with a group (sometimes large, sometimes small), stay in prebooked hotels, eat with your fellow travelers (the cost of meals sometimes included in the price of your tour, sometimes not), and follow a schedule.

But not all guided tours are an if-it's-Tuesday-this-must-be-Belgium experience. A knowledgeable guide can take you places that you might never discover on your own, and you may be pushed to see more than you would have otherwise. Tours aren't for everyone, but they can be just the thing for trips to places where making travel arrangements is difficult or time-consuming (particularly when you don't speak the language).

Whenever you book a guided tour, find out what's included and what isn't. A "land-only" tour includes all your travel (by bus, in most cases) in the destination, but not necessarily your flights to and from or even within it. Also, in most cases prices in tour brochures don't include fees and taxes. And remember that you'll be expected to tip your guide (in cash) at the end of the tour.

Among companies that sell tours to the Netherlands and Belgium from the United States, the following are nationally known, have a proven reputation, and offer plenty of options. The classifications used below represent different price categories, and you'll probably encounter these terms when talking to a travel agent or tour operator. The key difference is usually in accommodations, which run from budget to better, and better-yet to best.

RECOMMENDED COMPANIES

Super-Deluxe **Abercrombie & Kent** (✉1520 Kensington Rd., Suite 212, Oak Brook, IL 60523-2156 ☎630/954–2944 or 800/554–7016 🖷630/954–3324 ⊕www.abercrombiekent.com).

Deluxe **Globus** (✉5301 S. Federal Circle, Littleton, CO 80123-2980 ☎866/755–8581 ⊕www.globusjourneys.com).

First-Class **Brendan Worldwide Vacations** (✉21625 Prairie St., Chatsworth, CA 91311-5833 ☎800/421–8446 🖷818/772–6492 ⊕www.brendanvacations.com). **Trafalgar Tours** (✉11 E. 26th St., New York, NY 10010 ☎866/544–4434 🖷800/457–6644 ⊕www.trafalgartours.com).

SPECIAL-INTEREST TOURS

ART & ARCHITECTURE

From quaint to grandiose, Golden Age to Modernism, art and architecture in the Netherlands has never been anything less than visionary.

Contacts **Academic Arrangements Abroad** (✉1040 Ave. of the Americas, New York, NY 10018-3721 ☎212/514–8921 or 800/221–1944 🖷212/344–7493 ⊕www.arrangementsabroad.com).

BEER

One of Belgium's biggest draws is the extraordinary range of diverse beers it produces. It's reason enough to visit for many people.

Contacts **Beer Trips.com** (✉Box 7892, Missoula, MT 59807 ☎406/531–9109 🖷419/791–9425 ⊕www.beertrips.com).

TRANSPORTATION

With a history as venerable as Holland's, it's no surprise many of the country's *straten,* or streets take their name from its famous sons and daughters. In Amsterdam, for one example, Hugo de Grootstraat honors Delft's noted lawyer-philosopher (*straat* is "street"). In addition, you get all the variations: Hugo de Grootkade (*kade* is a street running parallel to a canal), Hugo de Grootplein (*plein* is "square"), ad infinitum. In Amsterdam, there's even an Eerste, Tweede, and Derde (first, second, and third) Hugo de Grootstraat. Of course, kings and queens feature too: Wilhelminastraat is named after Queen Wilhelmina, the grandmother of the current queen, Beatrix.

Other geographical terms to keep in mind are a *dwarsstraat,* which runs perpendicular to another street or canal, such as Leidsestraat and Leidsedwarsstraat. A *straatje* is a small street; a *weg* is a road; a *gracht* a canal; a *steeg* a very small street; a *laan* is a lane or avenue. *Baan* is another name for a road, not quite a highway, but busier than an average street. Note that in the Netherlands, the house number always comes after the street name on addresses.

The Dutch also have an infinite range of names for bodies of water, from *gracht* to *singel* to *kanaal* (all meaning "canal"). The difference between a singel and a gracht is hard to define, even for a Dutch person. In fact, the names can be doubly confusing because sometimes there is *no* water at all—many grachten have been filled in by developers to make room for houses, roads, and so on. Near harbor areas you'll notice *havens* (harbors), named after the goods that ships used to bring in, like in Rotterdam, *Wijnhaven* (Wine Harbor) and *Vishaven* (Fish Harbor).

Amsterdam streets radiate outward from Centraal Station; in general, street numbers go up as you move away from the station. Don't let common address abbreviations confuse you. BG stands for *Begane Grond* (ground floor); SOUT for *Soutterrain* (basement); HS for *Huis* (a ground-floor apartment or main entry). Common geographical abbreviations include *str.* for *straat* (street); *gr.* for *gracht* (canal); and *pl.* for *plein* (square). For example: Leidsestr., or Koningspl.

Addresses in Belgium are segregated by language throughout the country; they hew to the official language of each destination. The only place where the street names are in both French and Flemish is the officially bilingual capital, Brussels. Addresses are written with the street name first, followed by the number. Some common terms include: for street, *straat* in Flemish and *rue* in French; for square, *plein* or *place. Laan* or *avenue* means avenue as do *dreef* or *drève. Grote markt* or *grand place* indicates a market square, usually the historic center of town.

▍BY AIR

Flying time to Amsterdam is 7 hours from New York, 8 hours from Chicago, 10½ hours from Los Angeles, 9 hours from Dallas, 6½ hours from Montreal, 9½ hours from Vancouver, and 20 hours from Sydney.

Always ask your carrier about its check-in policy. Plan to arrive at the airport about two hours before your scheduled departure time—and don't forget your passport. If you are flying within Europe, check the airline whether food is served on the flight. If you have dietary concerns, request special meals when booking. Low-cost airlines don't provide a complimentary in-flight service, but snacks and drinks can be purchased on board. For help picking the most comfortable seats, check out SeatGuru.com, which has information about specific seat configurations for different types of aircraft.

Smoking is prohibited on flights to or from Amsterdam. You are not required to reconfirm flights, but you should confirm the departure time by telephone if you made your reservation considerably in advance, as flight schedules are subject to change without notice.

Airlines & Airports **Airline and Airport Links.com** (⊕www.airlineandairportlinks. com) has links to many of the world's airlines and airports.

Airline Security Issues **Transportation Security Administration** (⊕www.tsa.gov) has answers for almost every question that might come up.

A 2004 European Union regulation standardized the rights of passengers to compensation in the event of flight cancellations or long delays. The law covers all passengers departing from an airport within the European Union, and all passengers traveling into the EU on an EU carrier, unless they received assistance in the country of departure. Full details are available from the airlines, and are posted prominently in all EU airports.

AIRPORTS

Located 17 km (11 mi) southeast of Amsterdam, **Luchthaven Schiphol** (pronounced "Shh-kip-hole") is the main passenger airport for Holland. With the annual number of passengers using Schiphol approaching 40 million, it is ranked among the world's top five best-connected airports. A hotel, a service to aid passengers with disabilities, parking lots, and a main office of the Netherlands tourist board (in Schiphol Plaza and known as "HTi"—Holland Tourist Information) can prove most useful. The comprehensive Schiphol telephone service, charged at €0.10 per minute, provides information about flight arrivals and departures as well as all transport and parking facilities.

Rotterdam is the biggest of the regional airport options and provides daily service to many European cities; another regional airport is **Eindhoven**. An increasing number of international charter flights and some budget carriers choose these airports, as benefits include shorter check-in times and ample parking. However, there are no rail links that connect such regional airports with nearby cities, so passengers must resort to taking buses or taxis.

The major international airport serving Belgium is **Brussels Airport** at Zaventem, 14 km (9 mi) northeast of Brussels. It's sometimes called Zaventem for short. Brussels Airport has nonstop flights from the United States and Canada. It also has a wide range of amenities such as airport hotels, rental car agencies, travel agencies, and communications centers where you can either connect to the Internet via your own laptop or log on with a complimentary PC. Budget carrier Ryanair uses the smaller Brussels South Charleroi Airport, 46 km (29 mi) south of Brussels, as a hub. Though farther out of the city, it's connected to Brussels by a regular bus service.

Airport Information Holland **Amsterdam Luchthaven (Airport) Schiphol** (✉17 km [11 mi] southwest of Amsterdam ☎0900/0141 ⊕www.schiphol.nl). **Rotterdam Luchthaven (Airport)** (✉17 km [11 mi] northwest of Rotterdam ☎010/446-3444 ⊕www.rotterdam-airport.nl).

Airport Information Belgium **Brussels Airport** (☎02/753-7753 ⊕www. brusselsairport.be). **Brussels South Charleroi Airport** (☎071/25-12-29 ⊕www.charleroi-airport.com).

GROUND TRANSPORTATION

The Schiphol Rail Link operates between the airport and the city 24 hours a day, with service to Amsterdam Centraal Station (usually abbreviated to Amsterdam CS), and to stations in the south of the city. From 6:30 AM to 12:30 AM, there are four trains each hour to Centraal;

other hours, there is one train every hour. The trip takes about 15–20 minutes and costs €3.60. Schiphol Station is beneath Schiphol Plaza. From Centraal Station, Trams 1 and 2 go to Leidseplein and the Museum Quarter. Keep in mind that Schiphol Station is one of Holland's busiest—make sure you catch the shuttle to Amsterdam and not a train heading to The Hague! As always, when arriving at Amsterdam's Centraal Station, keep an eye out for pickpockets. Other than taxis, you may wish to hop aboard a tram or bus to get to your hotel, so go to one of the **Gemeentevervoerbedrijf (GVB) Amsterdam Municipal Transport** booths found in front of the Centraal Station. Here you can find directions, fare information, and schedules.

Connexxion Schiphol Hotel Shuttle operates a shuttle bus service between Amsterdam Schiphol Airport and all of the city's major hotels. The trip takes about a half hour and costs €12 one-way, or €19 return. Hours for this shuttle bus are 6:30 AM to 9 PM, every half hour.

Finally, there is a taxi stand directly in front of the arrival hall at Amsterdam Schiphol Airport. A service charge is included, but small additional tips are not unwelcome. New laws determine that taxi fares are now fixed from Schiphol to Amsterdam; depending on the neighborhood, a trip will cost around €40. When you're returning home, a ride to Schiphol from Amsterdam center city area, the Centrum, will cost around €22. A new service that might be convenient for budget travelers who count every euro is the Schiphol Travel Taxi. The taxi needs to be booked at least 24 hours in advance and rides are shared, so the trip will take a bit longer as the taxi stops to pick up/drop off passengers. Make bookings via the Schiphol Web site.

Contacts Connexxion Schiphol Hotel Shuttle (☎038/339–4741 ⊕www.schipholhotelshuttle.nl). **Schiphol Rail Link** (☎0900/9292 ⊕www.9292ov.nl). **Schiphol Travel Taxi** (⊕www.schiphol.nl).

FLIGHTS

When flying internationally to the Netherlands, you usually choose between a domestic carrier, the national flag carrier of the country, and a foreign carrier from a third country. You may, for example, choose to fly KLM Royal Dutch Airlines to the Netherlands for the basic reason that, as the national flag carrier, it has the greatest number of nonstop flights. Domestic carriers offer connections to smaller destinations. Third-party carriers may have a price advantage.

KLM and its global alliance partner Northwest—together with their regional partner airlines—fly from Amsterdam's Schiphol Airport to more than 400 destinations in more than 80 countries worldwide. Nearly 100 of those are European destinations, with three to four daily flights to most airports and up to 17 flights a day to London alone. Northwest Airlines now handles all reservations and ticket office activities on behalf of KLM in the United States and Canada, with KLM's biggest North American hubs in Detroit and Minneapolis, and Memphis, New York, and Washington D.C. among its gateways. KLM's direct flights connect Amsterdam to Atlanta, Los Angeles, and Miami, and numerous others. Including connections via KLM's hubs, the airline flies to more than 100 destinations in the United States from Amsterdam. In Canada, KLM/Northwest serves Montreal, Toronto, and Vancouver. For more information, contact the airline at one of the reservation numbers below. For further information about schedules and special fare promotions, go to KLM/Northwest's Web site.

Other international carriers include American Airlines, Continental Airlines, Delta Airlines, United Airlines, and US Airways. Dutch charter airline MartinAir has direct flights to Amsterdam from Orlando and Miami. None of these carriers makes a transatlantic flight to any of the Netherlands' regional airports. If your carrier offers Rotterdam as a final destination, for example, you fly into Amsterdam, then transfer. KLM City-hopper offers flights connecting Amsterdam with the smaller regional airports. Transavia Airlines flies from Amsterdam and Rotterdam to a number of European destinations, and many other carriers link European capitals with Amsterdam. Easy-Jet has budget flights to Amsterdam from several European destinations; Ryanair offers a similar service out of Eindhoven Airport. Check online or with your travel agent for details.

After the bankruptcy of Sabena, Belgium's national airline, SN Brussels Airlines became the country's foremost carrier, with routes to the United States, Africa, and all over Europe. Low-cost carrier Ryanair operates an ever-expanding network of routes out of its hub at Brussels South Charleroi Airport. This can be a very economical way of getting around Europe, and you'll get the best deals if you book well ahead.

Airline Contacts **Air Canada** (☎888/247–2262 in U.S. and Canada, 020/346–9539 in Holland ⊕www.aircanada.com). **American Airlines** (☎800/433–7300, 02/711–9969 in Belgium for service in Flemish, 02/711–9977 for service in French, 207/365–0777 in U.K. within London, 8457/789–789 outside London ⊕www.aa.com). **British Airways** (☎800/247–9297 in U.S., 0870/850–9850 in U.K., 02/717–3217 in Belgium, 020/346–9559 in the Netherlands ⊕www.britishairways.com). **Continental Airlines** (☎800/523–3273 for U.S. and Mexico reservations, 800/231–0856 for international reservations, 02/643–3939 in Belgium, 0845/607–6760 in U.K., 020/346–9381 in Holland ⊕www.continental.com). **Delta Airlines** (☎800/221–1212 for U.S. reservations, 800/241–4141 for international reservations, 02/711–9799 in Belgium, 0800/414–767 in U.K., 020/201–3536 in Holland ⊕www.delta.com). **EasyJet** (☎0900/265–8022 in the Netherlands ⊕www.easyjet.com). **KLM Royal Dutch Airlines** (☎070/222–747 in Belgium, 300/303–747 in Australia, 020/474–7747 in the Netherlands, 09/309–1792 in New Zealand, 0870/507–4074 in U.K. ☎800/447–4747 for Northwest/KLM sales office in U.S. and Canada ⊕www.klm.com). **MartinAir Holland** (☎800/627–8462 in U.S., 020/601–1767 in Holland ⊕www.martinair.com). **Northwest Airlines** (☎800/225–2525 ⊕www.nwa.com). **Ryanair** (☎0906/270–5656 in U.K., 0902/88007 in Belgium for service in French, 0902/88009 for service in Flemish ⊕www.ryanair.com). **SN Brussels Airlines** (☎516/622–2248 in U.S., 0870/735–2345 in U.K., 070/351–111 in Belgium ⊕www.flysn.com). **Transavia Airlines** (☎020/406–0406 in the Netherlands ⊕www.transavia.nl). **United Airlines** (☎800/864–8331 for U.S. reservations, 800/538–2929 for international reservations, 02/713–3600 in Belgium, 020/201–3708 in Holland ⊕www.united.com). **USAirways** (☎800/428–4322 for U.S. and Canada reservations, 800/622–1015 for international reservations, 020/201–3550 in Holland ⊕www.usairways.com).

▌ BY BOAT

International ferries link Holland with the United Kingdom. There are two daily Stena line crossings between the **Hoek van Holland** (Corner of Holland, an industrial shipping area west of Rotterdam) and Harwich, on the fast car ferry, taking approximately three hours. The overnight crossing takes about seven hours. These are the only ferry crossings that can be booked at the international travel window in large railway stations. There is one PO North Sea overnight crossing between the Europoort in Rotterdam and Hull, which takes about 14 hours, and one DFDS Seaways overnight crossing from Newcastle to IJmuiden, in Amsterdam, taking 15 hours.

An extensive domestic ferry system serves Holland. DFDS Seaways is a leading carrier. Ferries run from several locations, linking the mainland to the Frisian Islands. Ferries also cross the IJsselmeer.

Hire your own boat or take a guided city canal tour of Amsterdam, Leiden, or Delft; alternatively, take a harbor tour to **check out Rotterdam's extensive Europoort,** the world's biggest harbor, and the flood barrier. There are pedestrian ferries behind Amsterdam's Centraal Station across the IJ. *For more specific information about guided tours, see individual regional chapters.*

In Belgium, Hoverspeed LTD has services between Dover and Oostende, with up to eight daily round-trips. P & O North Sea Ferries operates overnight ferry services once daily from Hull to Zeebrugge. Schedules and fares fluctuate between low (winter) and high (summer) season. Travel agencies in the United Kingdom and in Belgium sell tickets and provide exact fares and schedules. Five-day excursion fares are significantly less expensive than last-minute bookings. These must be booked at least seven days in advance.

▌BY BUS

The bus and tram systems within Holland provide excellent transport links within cities. Frequent bus services are available in all towns and cities; trams run in Amsterdam, The Hague, between Delft and The Hague, and in Rotterdam. Amsterdam and Rotterdam also have subways, referred to as the metro. Amsterdam's metro system has lines running southeast and southwest; Rotterdam's metro system also has only two lines (east to west and north to south), which extend into the suburbs and cross in the city center for easy transfers.

Several large companies provide bus and tram services across the country, including Connexxion, BBA, and Arriva. GVB provides additional services in Amsterdam; HTM in The Hague; GVU in Utrecht; and RET in Rotterdam. There are maps of each city's network in most shelters. Buses are clean and easy to use, and bus lanes (shared only with taxis) remain uncongested, ensuring that you travel more swiftly than other traffic in rush hour.

Each city is divided into zones, and the fare you pay depends on the number of zones you travel through. A small city is one zone (two strips), but to travel across The Hague takes you through four (five strips) zones. These zones are displayed on transport maps. Each journey you make costs one strip plus the number of zones you travel through. When you get on a bus, you show the driver your strippenkaart and simply say where your final destination is, or the number of zones you plan to travel through, and let him or her stamp the strips.

In a metro you have to stamp your ticket yourself in the small yellow machines found near the doors. Count the number of strips you need (note that most tourists will be traveling within a one-zone area and therefore the tickets they buy directly from the driver only contain two or three strips), fold your ticket at the bottom of the last strip required, and stamp the final strip in the machine. A stamp on a strip uses that strip, and the strips above it. Two or more people can travel on the same strippenkaart, but the appropriate number of units must be stamped for each person. Trams in Amsterdam have ticket control booths in the center of the tram. You may only board the tram there, unless you already have a valid stamp on your ticket, in which case you may board at the front and show your ticket to the driver.

The stamp indicates the zone where the journey started, and the time, and remains valid for one hour, so you can travel within the zones you have stamped until the hour is up. Teams of ticket inspectors occasionally make spot checks. This doesn't happen often, but if you are checked and you don't have a stamped strippenkaart, you face a fine.

To get around by bus, tram, or metro in Rotterdam you'll need an OV-chipkaart (public transport chip card)—a new electronic payment system that's being tested in the city. These credit card-sized tickets can be loaded up with credit from machines in the railway and metro stations, and are debited as you board and leave trains and buses. There are information and sales points in the Beurs and Centraal Station metro stations, as well as in the main bus station. Or call the help desk ☎0900/500–6010 for more information. From 2009 the OV-chipkaart will be rolled out nationally across the Netherlands, and the strippenkaart will be phased out. Belgium has an extensive network of reasonably priced urban and intercity buses. STIB/MIVB (Société des Transports Intercommunaux de Bruxelles/Maatschappij voor het Intercommunaal Vervoer te Brussel) covers service around Brussels and to other towns in the region. De Lijn runs buses in Flanders, including Antwerp, Brugge, and Gent. Fares and schedules are available at the STIB and De Lijn sales offices or at local travel agencies. Buy tickets from the bus driver as you board.

Bus Information for the Netherlands and Belgium Information on all public transportation, including schedules, fares for **trains, buses, trams, and ferries** in the Netherlands (☎0900/9292 [€0.70 per min] ⊕www.9292ov.nl). **De Lijn** (☎070/220–200 ⊕www.delijn.be). **STIB/MIVB** (☎0900/10–310 ⊕www.stib.irisnet.be).

▌BY CAR

A network of well-maintained highways and other roads covers the Netherlands, making car travel convenient, although traffic is exceptionally heavy around the bigger cities, especially on the roads in the Randstad, and those approaching the North Sea beaches on summer weekends. There are no tolls on roads or highways. Major European highways leading into Amsterdam from the borders are E19 from western Belgium; E25 from eastern Belgium; and E22, E30, and E35 from Germany. Follow the signs for *Centrum* to reach the center of the city. At rush hour, traffic is dense but not so dense as to become stationary.

In Canada Canadian Automobile Association (CAA; ☎613/247–0117).

In the U.S. American Automobile Association (☎800/564–6222).

GASOLINE
Many of the gas stations in the Netherlands (especially those on the high-traffic motorways) are open 24 hours. Those that aren't open 24 hours generally open early in the morning, around 6 or 7 AM, and close late at night, around 10 or 11 PM. Unleaded regular costs about €1.40 per liter, and major credit cards are widely accepted. If you pay with cash and need a receipt, ask for a *bon*.

Gas stations are also plentiful throughout Belgium. Major credit cards are widely accepted. If you pay with cash and need a receipt, ask for a *reçu* (French) or *ontvangstbewijs* (Flemish). Unleaded regular costs around €1.35 per liter—slightly less than in the Netherlands. Gas stations are usually self-service. Unless you have a debit card from a Belgian bank, you must pay an attendant. On Sundays and late at night, some stations may be unmanned, so look for a gas station on a major highway, which should be open around the clock.

PARKING

Parking space is at a premium in Amsterdam as in most towns, especially in the Centrum (historic town center), which has narrow, one-way streets and large areas given over to pedestrians. Most neighborhoods are metered from 9 AM to 7 PM, so it is a good idea (if not the only option) to leave your car only in designated parking areas. *Parkeren* (parking lots) are indicated by a white P in a blue square. Illegally parked cars in Amsterdam get clamped by the **Dienst Parkheerbeheer** (Parking Authority) and, after 24 hours, if you haven't paid for the clamp to be removed, towed. You'll be towed immediately in some areas of the city. If you get clamped, a sticker on the windshield indicates where you should go to pay the fine (from €63 to more than €100).

ROAD CONDITIONS

Holland has an excellent road network, but there is a great deal of traffic using it every day, as you might expect from a country with a high population density. In cities, you will usually be driving on narrow one-way streets and sharing the road with other cars, buses, trams, and bicyclists, so remain alert at all times. When driving on smaller roads in cities, you must yield to traffic coming from the right. Traffic lights are located before intersections, rather than after intersections as in the United States. Traffic circles are very popular and come in all sizes. Driving outside of cities is very easy; roads are very smooth and clearly marked with signs. Traffic during peak hours (7 AM–9 AM and 4 PM–7 PM) is constantly plagued with *files* (traffic jams), especially in the western part of the country. If you are going to drive here, you must be assertive. Drivers are very aggressive; they tailgate

and change lanes at very high speeds. All road signs use the international driving symbols. Electronic message boards are used on some freeways to warn of traffic jams and to slow traffic down to 90, 70, or 50 km per hour.

A network of well-maintained, well-lit highways (*snelweg* in Flemish, *autoroute* in French) and other roads also covers Belgium, making car travel convenient. There are no tolls. Under good conditions, you should be able to travel on highways at an average of about 120 kph (75 mph), but congestion around Brussels and Antwerp can slow things considerably. If you are traveling in Belgium outside of Brussels, be prepared for signs to change language with alarming frequency. *Uitrit* is Flemish for exit; the French is *sortie*. City driving in Belgium is challenging because of chronic double parking and lack of street-side parking. Beware of trams in some cities, and of slick cobblestone streets in rainy weather.

ROADSIDE EMERGENCIES

If you haven't joined a motoring organization, the **ANWB** (Royal Dutch Touring Club) offers 24-hour road assistance in the Netherlands. If you aren't a member, you can call the ANWB after breaking down, but you must pay a €100 on-the-spot membership charge. Emergency crews may not accept credit cards or checks when they pick you up. If your automobile association is affiliated with the **Alliance International du Tourisme** (AIT), and you have proof of membership, you are entitled to free help. To call for assistance push the help button on any yellow ANWB phone located every kilometer (½ mi) on highways, and a dispatch operator immediately figures out where you are. Alternatively, ring their 24-hour emergency line or their information number for details about their road rescue service.

If you break down on the highway in Belgium, look for emergency telephones located at regular intervals. The emergency telephones are connected to an emergency control room that can send a tow truck. It is also possible to take out an emergency automobile insurance that covers all of your expenses in case of a breakdown on the road.

Contacts in Amsterdam and Holland ANWB **(Royal Dutch Touring Club)** (☎088/269–2888 emergency number, 088/269–2222 office number ⊕www.anwb.nl).

Contacts in Belgium Europ Assistance (☎02/533–7575). **Touring Secours** (☎02/233–2211).

RULES OF THE ROAD

Driving is on the right in the Netherlands and Belgium, and regulations are largely as in the United States. Speed limits are 120 kph (75 mph) on superhighways, 90 kph (62 mph) on other rural highways, and 50 kph (30 mph) on urban roads.

For safe driving, go with the flow, stay in the slow lane unless you want to pass, and make way for faster cars wanting to pass you. In cities and towns, approach crossings with care; local drivers may exercise the principle of priority for traffic from the right with some abandon. Although the majority of cyclists observe the stoplights and general road signs, many expect you, even as a driver, to give way. The latest ruling states that unless otherwise marked, all traffic coming from the right has priority, even bicycles. The driver and front seat passenger are required to wear seat belts, and other passengers are required to wear available seat belts.

Using a handheld mobile phone is illegal while driving, but you are allowed to drive while using a headset or earpiece. Turning right on a red light is not permitted. Fines for driving after drinking are heavy, including the suspension of license and the additional possibility of six months' imprisonment.

Fog can be a danger on highways in late fall and winter. In such cases, it is obligatory to use your fog lights.

▌BY PUBLIC TRANSPORTATION IN AMSTERDAM

METRO

Amsterdam has a full-fledged subway system, called the metro, but travelers will usually find trams and buses more convenient for getting around, as most metro stops are geared for city residents traveling to the outer suburbs. However, the Amsterdam metro can get you from point A to point C in a quantum leap— for instance, from Centraal Station (at the northern harbor edge of the city) to Amstel Station (a train station at the southeastern area of the city, with connections to many buses and trams)—much faster than a tram, which makes many stops along the way. A *strippenkaart,* or strip ticket, is used the same way as for other public transport.

Four metro lines, including the express tram (*sneltram*), serve Amsterdam and the surrounding suburbs. Although many stops on the metro will not be of use to the tourist, several stops can prove handy. Nieuwmarkt lets you off near the Red Light District and is near the famous sights of the Oude Zijde area. Waterlooplein is near the eastern edge of the Oude Zijde, stopping at the square where the Stadhuis-Muziektheater is located, and offers access to sights of the Jewish Quarter and the Plantage; a walk several blocks to the south leads you to the Eastern Canal Ring and its many historic houses. Wibautstraat is not too far from the Amstel River and provides access to the southern sectors of the city, including De Pijp. Amstel Station is a train station near the Amstel River in the southeastern area of the city, with connections to many buses and trams. Amsterdam Zuid/ WTC (South/World Trade Center) is at the southern edge of Amsterdam Zuid (South), and rarely used by any tourists. VU (Vrije Universiteit) is in the suburb of Buitenveldert. It's possible to transfer from the metro to trains at several shared stops, either by crossing the platform or merely going outside to an adjacent train station. Line 50 (Ringlijn) travels from Isolaterweg in the northeastern part of the city to Gein, a southeastern suburb. Lines 51, 53, and 54 all start at Centraal Station and follow the same routes until they head into the suburbs. They ride as a subway from Centraal Station to Amstel Station, then whiz along the rest of the routes above ground, parting ways at Spaklerweg. The No. 51 passes through Buitenveldert, stopping at the VU (Vrij Universiteit) and continuing south into Amstelveen. The 53 passes Diemen and ends up southeast in Gaasperplas. The 54 also travels southeast and shares the rest of its route with the 50, passing through Holendrecht and ending at Gein.

TRAMS & BUSES

Many tram and bus routes start from the hub at Centraal Station. A large bus depot is on the Marnixstraat, across from the main police station, and there's another one at Harlemmermeer station in the Overtoomseveld neighborhood of western Amsterdam. Trams and buses run from about 6 AM to midnight daily. The tram routes, with a network of 130 km (80 mi) of track, make this characteristic form of transport more useful than the bus for most tourists. Night owls can make use of the hourly night-bus services, with double frequency on Friday and Saturday night, but routes are restricted.

Between stops, trams brake only when absolutely necessary, so listen for warning bells if you are walking or cycling near tram lines. Taxis use tram lines, but other cars are allowed to venture onto them only when turning right. The newer fleets of buses are cleaner, and therefore nicer to use, and bus lanes (shared only with taxis) remain uncongested, ensuring that you travel more swiftly than the rest of the traffic in rush hour. If the bus is very crowded, you may have to stand, so hold on to a handrail, as the buses can travel quite fast; to **avoid rush hour**, don't

travel between 7:30 and 9 in the morning or between 4 and 6 in the afternoon. As with all urban systems of transportation, keep an eye out for pickpockets.

There are 16 tram lines servicing the city. Trams 1, 2, 4, 5, 9, 13, 16, 17, 24, and 25 all start and end their routes at Centraal Station. The most frequently used trams by visitors are the 1, 2, and 5, which stop at the big central Dam Square and, along with 6, 7, and 10, also stop at Leidseplein square. The numbers 2, 3, 5, and 12 will get you to Museumplein and the Museum District. Trams 5, 16, 24, and 25 travel through Amsterdam's chic Zuid district. The No. 4 tram stops at the RAI convention center and the No. 5 will take you to Station South/World Trade Center. The remaining lines pass through East and West Amsterdam and take you farther outside the center city Centrum to areas generally more off the beaten track for tourists.

More than 30 GVB buses cover all the city's neighborhoods and are a good way to get closer to specific addresses. The Conexxion bus company operates about 50 different buses that will take you from Amsterdam to all areas of Holland. Most of these depart from Centraal Station. Buses 110 to 117 travel to the "folkloric" area of North-Holland, just to the north of the city, where favorite tourist destinations include Volendam, Marken, Edam, Hoorn, and Broek in Waterland.

DE OPSTAPPER

A great new public transport option is the *Opstapper*, a transit van that traverses the elegant Prinsengracht—heart of the historic canal sector—between Centraal Station and the Music Theater. For a one-zone stamp on your strippenkaart, you can get on or off anywhere along the Prinsengracht. You can hail it on the street, or get on at its starting point in front of Centraal Station. There are no fixed stops. It passes within walking distance of the Anne Frank House, the Leidseplein, and maybe even your hotel. The buses run every 10 minutes from 7:30 AM to 6:30 PM. There are eight seats, and there is room for an additional eight standing passengers.

FERRIES

Four GVB ferry lines leave from Centraal Station, but only one is of any interest to tourists. The Buiksloterwegveer leaves from Pier 7 behind Centraal Station every eight to 15 minutes, day and night. The ferry transports pedestrians, cyclists, and motorcyclists across the IJ channel to North Amsterdam. There is no fee for the service. North Amsterdam may prove to be less interesting than the refreshing trip, which takes about five minutes.

TICKETS & STRIPPENKAART

Besides the national *strippenkaart* (strip ticket) system, covered above, in Amsterdam you can also buy 24, 48, 72, and 96 hour travel-anywhere tickets (€6.50 for one day; €10.50 for two days; €13.50 for three days), which cover all urban bus and streetcar routes. Fares are often reduced for children ages four to 11 and for people who are 65 years or older.

The All Amsterdam Transport Pass costs €23 and entitles you to a day of unlimited travel on tram, bus, metro, and Canal Bus plus coupons worth about €133 for major attractions, snacks, etc. This pass can be purchased at the GVB ticket office in front of Centraal Station and at the main Canal Bus office at Prins Hendrikkade. The electronic *I amsterdam Card*

(⇨ *Day Tours & Guides*), provides free or discounted admission to many top attractions, plus a free canal round-trip, and free use of public transport.

Contacts GVB (✉Prins Hendrikkade 108–114, Centrum ☎0900/9292 ⊕www.gvb.nl).

▌BY TAXI IN AMSTERDAM

Vacant taxis on the move through the streets are often on call to their dispatcher. Occasionally, if you get lucky, they'll stop for you if you hail them, but the regular practice is to wait by a taxi stand or phone them. Taxi stands are at the major squares and in front of the large hotels. You can also call Taxicentrale, the main dispatching office. A 5-km (3-mi) ride will cost about €20. A new initiative in the city is the *Wieler Taxi* (bike taxi), which resembles a larger version of a child's pedal car and isn't very practical in the rain.

A water taxi provides a novel, if pricey, means of getting about. Water taxis can be hailed anytime you see one cruising the canals of the city, or called by telephone. The boats are miniature versions of the large sightseeing canal boats, and each carries up to eight passengers. The cost is €75 for a half hour, including pickup charge, with a charge of €60 each half-hour period thereafter. The rate is per ride, regardless of the number of passengers.

Taxicentrale (☎020/677–7777). **Wielertaxi** (☎020/672–1149). **Water Taxi** (☎020/535–6363 ⊕www.water-taxi.nl).

▌BY TRAIN

Dutch trains are modern, and the quickest way to travel between city centers. Services are relatively frequent, with a minimum of two departures per hour for each route. Although many Dutch people complain about delays, the trains usually run roughly on time. Most staff speak English. Reserving a seat is not possible.

Intercity trains can come double-decker; they only stop at major stations. *Sneltreins* (express trains) also have two decks but take in more stops, so they are a little slower. *Stoptreins* (local trains) are the slowest. Smoking is not permitted on trains, and only permitted in designated zones in stations.

On the train you have the choice of first or second class. First-class travel costs 50% more, and on local trains gives you a slightly larger seat in a compartment that is less likely to be full. At peak travel times, first-class train travel is worth the difference.

Train tickets for travel within the country can be purchased at the last minute. Normal tickets are either *enkele reis* (one-way) or *retour* (round-trip). Round-trip tickets cost approximately 75% of two single tickets. They are valid only on the day you buy them, unless you ask specifically for a ticket with a different date. You can get on and off at will at stops in between your destinations until midnight.

You cannot buy domestic train tickets in the Netherlands with credit cards or traveler's checks. If you don't have euros, bureau de change GWK has a branch at Amsterdam Centraal Station and all major stations throughout the country. You can also buy tickets at the yellow touch-screen ticket machines in every railway station. These machines accept cards with a four-digit PIN code. Fares are slightly lower than if you visit a manned ticket desk. Note that you can't buy tickets aboard the trains, and you risk a hefty fine if you board and travel without one.

Train fares in Holland are lower than in most other European countries, but you can save money by looking into rail passes—there are a host of special saver tickets that make train travel even cheaper. Be aware, however, that if you don't plan to cover many miles, then you may as well buy individual tickets; a *dagkaart* (unlimited travel pass for one day) costs €40 second class, €60 first class, but it is almost impossible to rack up enough miles to make it worthwhile. If you're spending a long time in Holland and plan to do a lot of traveling, inquire about the *voordeelurenkaart* (discount hours card), available for all ages. It costs €49 and entitles the holder to a 40% discount on all first- and second-class tickets, when traveling after 9 AM, or at any time on weekends and in July and August. You need a residential address to apply for this card, as well ID. The card proper will take between four and six weeks to be processed and arrive on your doorstep, but you are issued a valid card for the interim time.

If you are visiting in July and August, and are traveling with one or two others, check out the Zomertoer, which allows second-class-only unlimited travel for two days within a 10-day period (€59 for two people, and €79 for three people).

Train is also the easiest mode of transportation within Belgium. Belgian National Railways (SNCB/NMBS) maintains an extensive network of prompt and frequent services. Intercity trains have rapid connections between the major towns and cities, while local and regional trains also stop at all smaller towns and villages in between. There are several connections every hour between the Brussels Airport and Brussels, from early morning until late evening. Tickets can be paid for using currency or a major credit card. Smoking is prohibited on all trains in Belgium.

Intercity trains link Amsterdam and Brussels in around 3 hours. Thalys high-speed trains link Brussels (in 1½ hours) and Amsterdam (4 hours) with Paris. Eurostar operates high-speed passenger trains between stations in London and Brussels (Midi) in 2½ hours. Check the Web sites for latest fares and schedules. Advance seat reservations are obligatory. Travel on both Thalys and Eurostar trains is available in first or second class. First-class seats are slightly more spacious, and first-class passengers are served complimentary beverages and a light meal.

Holland and Belgium are two of 18 countries in which you can use a Eurailpass, providing unlimited first-class travel in all 18 countries. If you plan to travel extensively, get a standard pass. Train travel is available for 15 or 21 days, or one, two, or three months. Children aged 4–11 receive a discount, and children under 4 travel for free. Order a free copy of the latest brochure, "Europe on Track," by calling **Eurail** (☎*888/382–7245*) in the United

States to compare prices and options, or obtain all the information on their Web site. Whichever pass you choose, remember to buy it before you leave for Europe. You can buy the passes in Holland but at a *15% hike-up* compared with buying at home.

Short of flying, taking the Channel Tunnel is the fastest way to cross the English Channel: 35 minutes from Folkestone to Calais, 60 minutes from motorway to motorway, or two hours and 15 minutes from London's St. Pancras Station to Paris's Gare du Nord. The Belgian border is just a short drive northeast of Calais. High-speed Eurostar trains use the same tunnels to connect London's St. Pancras Station directly with Midi Station in Brussels in around two hours.

Eurostar (☎0900/10–366 ⊕www.eurostar. com). **NS–Nederlandse Spoorwegen/Dutch Railways** (⊕www.ns.nl). **SNCB/NMBS** (☎02/528–2828 or 02/555–2525 ⊕www. b-rail.be). **Thalys** (☎0900/10–177 ⊕www. thalys.com).

Information & Passes **Eurail** (⊕www.eurail. com). **Rail Europe** (✉44 S. Broadway, No.

11, White Plains, NY 10601 ☎888/382–7245 in U.S., 800/361–7245 in Canada ⊕www. raileurope.com/us). **CIT North America, Ltd.** (✉15 W. 44th St., 10th fl., New York, NY 10036 ☎800/248–8687 ⊕www.cit-rail.com).

Train Information Holland-wide **Public Transport Information** (☎0900/9292 information officer), including schedules and fares. For **lost and found** (☎030/235–3923 hold the line for an operator) on train lines and in stations, ask for a form at the nearest station. **Nederlandse Spoorwegen** (Dutch Rail ☎0900/202–1163 calls cost 10¢ per minute) customer service.

Channel Tunnel Car Transport **Eurotunnel** (☎0870/535–3535 in the U.K., 070/223–210 in Belgium, 03–21–00–61–00 in France ⊕www.eurotunnel.com). **French Motorail/ Rail Europe** (☎0870/241–5415 ⊕www. raileurope.co.uk/frenchmotorail).

Channel Tunnel Passenger Service **Eurostar** (☎0870/518–6186, in the U.K. ⊕www.eurostar.co.uk). **Rail Europe** (☎888/382–7245 in the U.S., 0870/584–8848 in the U.K. inquiries and credit-card bookings ⊕www.raileurope.com).

ON THE GROUND

INTERNET

If you're traveling with a laptop, take a spare battery and an electrical-plug adapter with you, as new batteries and replacement adapters are expensive. Many hotels are equipped with jacks for computers with Internet connections, and most also have Wi-Fi hotspots. Some offer this service to hotel guests for free; others may charge up to €10 per hour for access. You will also find cybercafés in all major cities.

Contacts **Cybercafes** (⊕ www.cybercafes. com) lists over 4,000 Internet cafés worldwide.

PHONES

The good news is that you can now make a direct-dial telephone call from virtually any point on earth. The bad news? You can't always do so cheaply. Calling from a hotel is almost always the most expensive option; hotels usually add huge surcharges to all calls, particularly international ones. In some countries you can phone from call centers or even the post office. Calling cards usually keep costs to a minimum, but only if you purchase them locally. And then there are mobile phones *(⇨ below)*, which are sometimes more prevalent—particularly in the developing world—than landlines; as expensive as mobile phone calls can be, they are still usually a much cheaper option than calling from your hotel.

The country code for the Netherlands is 31. The area code for Amsterdam is 020. To call an Amsterdam number within Amsterdam, you don't need the city code: just dial the seven-digit number. To call Amsterdam from elsewhere in the Netherlands, dial 020 at the start of the number. In addition to the standard city codes, there are three other prefixes used: public information numbers starting with 0800 are free phone numbers, but be aware that information lines with the prefix 0900 are charged at premium rates (35¢ a minute and more). 06 numbers indicate mobile (cell) phones.

The area codes for other Dutch cities are: Delft, 015; Rotterdam, 010; Utrecht, 030; Haarlem, 023; The Hague, 070.

When dialing a Dutch number from abroad, drop the initial zero from the local area code, so someone calling from New York, for example, to Amsterdam would dial 011 + 31 + 20 + the seven-digit phone number. When dialing from the Netherlands overseas, the country code is 00–1 for the United States and Canada, 00–61 for Australia, and 00–44 for the United Kingdom. All mobile and landline phones in Holland are 10 digits long (although some help lines and information centers have fewer digits).

Since hotels tend to overcharge for international calls, it is best to use a public phone. When making a call, listen for the dial tone (a low-pitched hum), insert a credit card, then dial the number. Since the increase in cellular phones, the number of phone cells, or phone booths, is decreasing. At every railway station there are pay phones, either in the ticket hall or on the platforms.

The country code for Belgium is 32. Two- or three-digit area codes always begin with zero; the zero is dropped when calling from abroad. The city code for Brussels is 02; for Antwerp, 03; for Gent, 09; and for Brugge, 050. Toll-free numbers begin with 0800. Premium rate calls begin with 0900. For English-language telephone assistance, dial 1405. For international calls, dial 00, followed by the country code, followed by the area code and telephone number. All calls within the country must include the regional telephone code.

To ask directory assistance for telephone numbers outside the Netherlands, dial 0900/8418 (calls are charged at €0.90 per minute). For numbers within the Netherlands, dial 0900/8008 (calls are charged at €1.30 per call).

To reach an operator, make a collect call, or dial toll-free to a number outside the Netherlands, dial 0800/0101.

CALLING OUTSIDE

The country code for the United States is 1.

Access Codes in Holland AT&T Direct (☎0800/022–9111). **MCI WorldPhone** (☎0800/022–9122). **Sprint International Access** (☎0800/022–9119).

Access Codes in Belgium AT&T Direct (☎0800/100–10 in Belgium, 800/435–0812 other areas). **MCI WorldPhone** (☎0800/100–12 in Belgium, 800/444–4141 other areas). **Sprint International Access** (☎0800/100–14 Belgium, 800/877–7746 other areas).

CALLING CARDS

Telephone cards are no longer used in public phone booths in the Netherlands. They accept credit cards instead, or local chip-cards (only available with Dutch bank passes).

MOBILE PHONES

If you have a multiband phone (some countries use different frequencies than what's used in the United States) and your service provider uses the world-standard GSM network (as do T-Mobile, Cingular, and Verizon), you can probably use your phone abroad. Roaming fees can be steep, however: 99¢ a minute is considered reasonable. And overseas you normally pay the toll charges for incoming calls. It's almost always cheaper to send a text message than to make a call, since text messages have a very low set fee (often less than 5¢).

If you just want to make local calls, consider buying a new SIM card (note that your provider may have to unlock your phone for you to use a different SIM card) and a prepaid service plan in the destination. You'll then have a local number and can make local calls at local rates. If your trip is extensive, you could also simply buy a new cell phone in your destination, as the initial cost will be offset over time.

■TIP➜ If you travel internationally frequently, save one of your old mobile phones or buy a cheap one on the Internet; ask your cell phone company to unlock it for you, and take it with you as a travel phone, buying a new SIM card with pay-as-you-go service in each destination.

Cell phones are called GSMs, or mobiles. British standard cell phones work in the Netherlands and Belgium, but American and Canadian standard (non-satellite) cell phones do not. If you'd like to rent a cell phone while traveling, reserve one at least four days before your trip, as most companies will ship it to you before you travel. CellularAbroad rents cell phones packaged with prepaid SIM cards that give you a local cell phone number and calling rates. Planetfone rents GSM phones, which can be used in more than 100 countries. Cell phone telephone numbers in the Netherlands are preceded by 06, followed by eight digits.

Contacts Cellular Abroad (☎800/287–5072 ⊕www.cellularabroad.com) rents and sells GMS phones and sells SIM cards that work in many countries. **Locaphone** (☎32/2/2652–1414 ⊕www.locaphone.be). **Mobal** (☎888/888–9162 ⊕www.mobalrental.com) rents mobiles and sells GSM phones (starting at $49) that will operate in 140 countries. Per-call rates vary throughout the world. **Planet Fone** (☎888/988–4777 ⊕www.planetfone.com) rents cell phones, but the per-minute rates are expensive.

∎ CUSTOMS & DUTIES

You're always allowed to bring goods of a certain value back home without having to pay any duty or import tax. But there's a limit on the amount of tobacco and liquor you can bring back duty-free, and some countries have separate limits for perfumes; for exact figures, check with your customs department. The values of so-called "duty-free" goods are included in these amounts. When you shop abroad, save all your receipts, as customs inspectors may ask to see them as well as the items you purchased. If the total value of your goods is more than the duty-free limit, you'll have to pay a tax (most often a flat percentage) on the value of everything beyond that limit.

Visitors aged 17 or over arriving from countries outside the EU may bring in duty-free goods amounting to no more than 200 cigarettes or 50 cigars or 250 grams of tobacco, 1 liter of spirits or 2 liters of wine or sparkling wine, and 50 milliliters of perfume. Forbidden products include firearms, counterfeit goods, banned narcotic substances, protected animals and plants, and products made from these.

Duty-free shopping has been abolished when traveling within the EU. Arrivals from within the EU may bring in "a reasonable amount" of duty-paid goods for personal use.

Amsterdam Schiphol Airport Customs Office (☎020/405–8888).

Brussels Airport Customs Office (☎02/753–2920).

U.S. Information **U.S. Customs and Border Protection** (⊕www.cbp.gov).

▌DAY TOURS & GUIDES

The electronic *I amsterdam Card* provides free and discount admissions to many of Amsterdam's top museums, plus a free canal round-trip, free use of public transport, and a 25% discount on various attractions and restaurants; savings can amount to more than €100. A one-day pass costs €33, a two-day costs €43, and a three-day costs €53. The pass comes with a booklet in Dutch, English, French, and German. It can be purchased at branches of the VVV (Netherlands Board of Tourism), the GVB (City Transport Company), both at Centraal Station, and through some hotels and museums.

English-language sightseeing tours are routinely organized in all tourist cities. You can find information about reliable tours, guides, and schedules through national tourism offices (⇨ *Visitor Information*). Museums and special exhibits usually offer English-language guides or headphones with explanations in English.

Anyone planning to visit a lot of museums in the Netherlands should consider investing in a *Museum Jaarkaart* (Museum Year Card), or MJK. This gives you free entry to more than 440 museums throughout the country for a year, including all the top draws in Amsterdam. It is available on showing ID at VVV offices and participating museums for €25.

▌RECOMMENDED TOURS/GUIDES

BICYCLE TOURS
From April through October, guided 1½- to 3-hour bike trips through the central area of Amsterdam are available through Yellow Bike. Let's Go tours (contact the VVV for further details) takes you out of the city center by train before introducing you to the safer cycling of the surrounding countryside. Its tours include Edam and Volendam, Naarden and Muiden, and, in season, a Tulip Tour.

Let's Go (⊠ *VVV Netherlands Board of Tourism, Centraal Station, Centrum* ⊕*www.letsgo-amsterdam.com*).   **Yellow Bike** (⊠*Nieuwezijds Kolk 29, Centrum* ☎*020/620–6940* ⊕*www.yellowbike.nl*).

BOAT TOURS
The quickest, easiest, and (frankly) most delightful way to get your bearings in Amsterdam is to take a canal-boat cruise. Trips last from 1 to 1½ hours and cover the harbor as well as the main canal district; there is a taped or live commentary

available in four languages. Excursion boats leave from *rondvaart* (excursion) piers in various locations in the city every 15 minutes from March to October, and every 30 minutes in winter. Departures are frequent from Prins Hendrikkade near the Centraal Station, along the Damrak, and along the Rokin (near Muntplein), at Leidseplein, and Stadhouderskade (near the Rijksmuseum). For a tour lasting about an hour, the cost is around €11, but the student guides expect a small tip for their multilingual commentary. For a truly romantic view of Amsterdam, opt for one of the special dinner and candlelight cruises offered by some companies, notably Holland International. A candlelight dinner cruise costs upward of €27.50. Trips for all boat tours can also be booked through the tourist office.

Operators of canal cruises include Holland International, Meyers Rondvaarten, Rederij Lovers, Rederij P. Kooij, Rederij Noord/Zuid, and Rederij Plas.

A popular option for exploring the city's canals, and some of the attractions that lie along them, is to hop on board one of Canal Company's Canal Buses (actually ferry-like passenger boats). Canal Buses, which leave from Centraal Station and travel along the canals by three different routes, allow you to disembark at points of interest along the way. Stops along the Green Line include the Anne Frank House, Rembrandtplein, and Rembrandt's House; the Red Line stops at the Rijksmuseum, City Hall, and the Westerkerk; and the Blue Line stops at the Tropenmuseum, NEMO, and the Scheepvaartmuseum. A Canal Bus Day Pass, which costs €18, is valid from the time you buy it until noon the following day; you can hop on and off the boats as many times as you like within that time. Buying a day pass also gets you reduced entry rates at some museums along the routes.

Following a similar, but longer route is Museumboot Rederij Lovers, which makes seven stops near 20 different museums. The cost is €17 for a day ticket that entitles you to a 50% discount on admission to the museums.

The Canal Bike *Waterfiets* is a pedal-powered boat that seats up to four. You can tour the Grachtengordel ring of canals at your own pace. For one or two people, the hourly fee is €8 per person, and for three to four people, it costs €7 per person, per hour. Rental hours are between 10 and 6:30 daily. There are five landing stages throughout the city, with two of the most popular ones across from the Rijksmuseum and across from the Westerkerk.

Fees & Schedules Amsterdam Canal Cruises (⊠ Nicolaas Witsenkade, opposite the Heineken Brewery, De Pijp ☎ 020/626–5636). **Canal Bus** (⊠ Weteringschans 26–1, Leidseplein ☎ 020/623–9886 ⊕ www.canal.nl). **Holland International** (⊠ Prins Hendrikkade, opposite Centraal Station, Centrum ☎ 020/625–3035 ⊕ www.hir.nl). **Meyers Rondvaarten** (⊠ Damrak 4, Dam ☎ 020/623–4208 ⊕ www.meyersrondvaarten.nl). **Museumboot Rederij Lovers** (⊠ Prins Hendrikkade, opposite Centraal Station, Centrum ☎ 020/530–1092 ⊕ www.lovers.nl). **Rederij P. Kooij** (⊠ Rokin, near Spui, Centrum ☎ 020/623–3810 ⊕ www.rederijkooij.nl). **Rederij Plas** (⊠ Damrak, quays 1–3, Dam ☎ 020/624–5406 ⊕ www.rederijplas.nl).

BUS TOURS

Afternoon bus tours of Amsterdam operate daily. Itineraries vary, and prices range from €18 to €47. A 2½-hour city tour that includes a drive through the suburbs is offered by Key Tours. However, it must be said that this city of narrow alleys and canals is not best appreciated from the window of a coach. Also, a number of visitors feel unhappy that part of some tours involves a visit to a diamond factory, where they feel pressured into listening to a sales pitch. The same bus companies operate scenic trips to attractions outside the city.

Fees & Schedules Key Tours (✉Dam 19, Dam ☎020/200–0300 ⊕www.keytours.nl). **Lindbergh Excursions** (✉Damrak 26, Dam ☎020/622–2766 ⊕www.lindbergh.nl).

WALKING TOURS

The Netherlands Tourist Board (VVV) maintains lists of personal guides and guided walking and cycling tours for groups in and around Amsterdam and can advise you on making arrangements. You can also contact Guidor, Nederlandse Gidsen Organisatie (Dutch Guides Organization). The costs are from €152 for a half day to €250 for a full day. The tourist office also sells brochures outlining easy-to-follow self-guided theme tours through the central part of the city. Among them are "A Journey of Discovery Through Maritime Amsterdam," "A Walk Through the Jordaan," "Jewish Amsterdam," and "Rembrandt and Amsterdam."

Walking tours focusing on art and architecture are organized by Artifex, Stichting Arttra, and Archivisie. For walking tours of the Jewish Quarter, contact Joods Historisch Museum. Yellow Bike Tours organizes two-hour walking tours of the Jordaan and the Red Light District.

Probably the best deal in town is Mee in Mokum, which offers walking tours led by retired longtime residents. For a mere €4, you are given an entertaining three-hour educational tour of the inner city or the Jordaan, focusing on architecture and surprising facts. These tours are also popular with Amsterdammers who wish to discover new things about their city. The admission fee entitles you to reduced fees to a choice of museums and a reduction in the price of a pancake at a nearby restaurant. Tours are held daily and start promptly at 11 AM. You must reserve at least a day in advance. Tours are limited to eight people; private arrangements can also be made for other times of the day.

Fees & Schedules Archivisie (✑Postbus 14603, 1001 LC ☎020/625–8908). **Artifex** (✉Westeinde 20, 1017 ZP ☎020/620–8112). **Arttra Cultureel Orgburo** (✉Tweede Boomdwarsstraat 4, 1015 LK ☎020/625–9303 ⊕www.arttra.com). **Guidor, Nederlandse Gidsen Organisatie** (✉Wildenborch 6 ☎020/624–6072 ⊕www.guidor.nl). **Joods Historisch Museum** (✉Nieuwe Amstelstraat 1, Postbus 16737, 1001 RE, Plantage ☎020/531–0310 🖷020/531–0311 ⊕www.jhm.nl). **Mee in Mokum** (✉Hartenstraat 18, Jordaan ☎020/625–1390 call between 1 and 4). **Yellow Bike** (✉Nieuwezijds Kolk 29, Centrum ☎020/620–6940 ⊕www.yellowbike.nl).

▌ EATING OUT

For information on Dutch cuisine, mealtimes, reservations, what to wear, specific restaurants, and the price chart, please consult the individual chapters. The restaurants we list are the cream of the crop in each price category. Properties indicated by a ✕🏠 are lodging establishments whose restaurant warrants a special trip.

Most restaurants are open for lunch and dinner only. Cafés usually also have a snacks menu (*kleine kaart*), which is available all day. A set-price, three- or four- course menu for lunch is offered in many restaurants. Dinner menus are usually more elaborate and slightly more expensive.

Some top-end hotels serve buffet breakfast (*ontbijt* in Dutch) with cooked American fare. Smaller hotels and bed-and-breakfasts serve bread, rolls, butter, jam, ham and cheese with juice and coffee or tea and usually a hard-boiled egg.

Smoking in Dutch and Belgian restaurants, and cafés that serve food, is prohibited.

For information on food-related health issues, see Health below.

PAYING

Major credit cards are accepted in most restaurants. Visa and MasterCard are the most widely used; smaller establishments may not accept American Express or

Diners Club. Some bars and cafés won't accept credit cards, though most will. Don't rely on traveler's checks for paying restaurant bills.

Tipping 15% of the cost of a meal is not common practice in the Netherlands or in Belgium. Instead, it is customary to round off the total to a convenient figure, to reward good service. If paying with a credit card, pay the exact amount of the bill with your card, and leave a few euro in cash on the table for the waiting staff.

RESERVATIONS & DRESS

Regardless of where you are, it's a good idea to make a reservation if you can. In some places (Hong Kong, for example), it's expected. We only mention them specifically when reservations are essential (there's no other way you'll ever get a table) or when they are not accepted. For popular restaurants, book as far ahead as you can (often 30 days), and reconfirm as soon as you arrive. (Large parties should always call ahead to check the reservations policy.) We mention dress only when men are required to wear a jacket or a jacket and tie.

The Dutch and Belgians favor relatively casual dress when dining out; men in open-neck shirts are far more common than a dining room full of suits. Jackets and ties are a rarity, except in the very top establishments. If in any doubt, check ahead with the restaurant in question.

WINES, BEER & SPIRITS

When you ask for a beer in Holland, you will get a small (200 milliliters) glass of draft lager beer with 5% alcohol content, known as *pils*. There are a number of national breweries that turn out similar fare—in Amsterdam it will usually be Heineken, but you may also encounter Amstel, Oranjeboom, Grolsch, Bavaria, or a number of smaller outfits. The argument for serving beer in small glasses is that you can drink it before it gets warm, and that you can also drink more of them. Many bars will also serve you a pint (500

milliliters) if you ask them. There are a number of smaller artisanal breweries that attempt different beer styles with varying success—look out for the La Trappe and 't Ij names in particular—but in general specialist brewing is left to the Belgian experts. That country produces around 800 types of beer, and you will find several standards in most Dutch cafés, including Hoegaarden "white" beer, Leffe (which comes in brown and blond versions), Kriek, a fruit-flavored beer, and Duvel, a very strong blond beer. All the major cities also have a few specialist beer cafés, for real connoisseurs, with beer lists stretching into the hundreds. In Amsterdam, the In De Wildeman café is the best place to head on that score. Keep in mind that many Belgian beers have a high alcohol content; 8%–9% alcohol per volume is not unusual.

▮ ELECTRICITY

The electrical current in the Netherlands and Belgium is 220 volts, 50 cycles alternating current (AC); wall outlets take Continental-type plugs, with two round prongs.

Consider making a small investment in a universal adapter, which has several types of plugs in one lightweight, compact unit. Most laptops and mobile phone chargers are dual voltage (i.e., they operate equally well on 110 and 220 volts), so require only an adapter. These days the same is true of small appliances such as hair dryers. Always check labels and manufacturer instructions to be sure. Don't use 110-volt outlets marked FOR SHAVERS ONLY for high-wattage appliances such as hair dryers.

Contacts Steve Kropla's Help for World Traveler's (⊕ www.kropla.com) has information on electrical and telephone plugs around the world. Walkabout Travel Gear (⊕ www. walkabouttravelgear.com) has a good coverage of electricity under "adapters."

▌ EMERGENCIES

Police, ambulance, and fire (☎*112 toll-free 24-hour switchboard for emergencies*). The 24-hour help-line service **Afdeling Inlichtingen Apotheken** (☎*020/694–8709*) (*apotheken* means "pharmacy") can direct you to your nearest open pharmacy; there is a rotating schedule to cover evenings, nights, and weekends—details are also posted at your local *apotheken*, and in the city newspapers. The **Centraal Doktorsdienst/Atacom** (*Medical Center* ☎*020/592–3434*) offers a 24-hour English-speaking help line providing advice about medical symptoms. In the case of minor accidents, phone **directory inquiries** (☎*0900/8008*) to get the number for the outpatients' department at your nearest *ziekenhuis* (hospital). **TBB** (☎*020/570– 9595 or 0900/821–2230*) is a 24-hour dental service that refers callers to a dentist (or *tandarts*). Operators can also give details of pharmacies open outside normal hours.

For less urgent police matters, call the **central number** (☎*0900/8844*). Amsterdam's **police headquarters** is at the crossing Marnixstraat/Elandsgracht and can be reached with Tram line 3, 7, 12, or 17. For car breakdowns and other car-related emergencies call the big automobile agency in the Netherlands, the ANWB (⇨ *Car Travel, Emergency Services*).

Note that all numbers quoted above with the code 020 are for Amsterdam and surrounding area only, indicating that instead of a national central number for that service.

Contacts in Amsterdam and the Netherlands Medical emergencies, police, fire, accidents, ambulance (☎112).

Contacts in Belgium Police (☎101). Medical emergencies, fire, accidents, ambulance (☎100).

Hospitals in Amsterdam For emergency treatment, the AMC and Sint Lucas Andreas hospitals have first-aid departments. The largest, most modern hospital serving Amsterdam and surroundings is the **AMC (Academisch Medisch Centrum)** (✉Meibergdreef 9, 1105 AZ, Amsterdam Zuidoost ☎020/566–9111). It's outside the city proper, in the Holendrecht area. The **Sint Lucas Andreas Ziekenhuis** (✉Jan Tooropstraat 164, 1061 AE, Amsterdam ☎020/510–8911) is in the western part of the city, in Geuzenveld. **Slotervaart Ziekenhuis** (✉Louwesweg 6, 1066 EC, Amsterdam ☎020/512–9333) is in the southwestern part of the city. The **VU Medisch Centrum** (✉De Boelelaan 1117, 1081 HV, Amsterdam ☎020/444–4444) is a university teaching hospital in the Buitenveldert area.

▌ HEALTH

SPECIFIC ISSUES IN AMSTERDAM, THE NETHERLANDS & BELGIUM

While you are traveling in the Netherlands, the Centers for Disease Control and Prevention (CDC) in Atlanta recommends that you observe health precautions similar to those that would apply while traveling in the United States. The main Dutch health bureau is the GGD, which stands for Gemeentelijke Gezondheidsdienst (Communal Medical Health Service). English-speaking medical help is easy to find. Most doctors have a basic English vocabulary and are familiar with English medical terms. *Drogists* (drugstores) sell toiletries and nonprescription drugs *(see also Emergencies)*. For prescription drugs go to an *apotheek* (pharmacy).

OVER-THE-COUNTER REMEDIES

You will find most standard over-the-counter medications, such as aspirin and acetaminophen, in the *drogisterij* (drugstore). You will have difficulty finding antihistamines and cold medications, like Sudafed, without a prescription.

Medical Care in Holland For inquiries about medical care, contact the national health service agency: **GGD Nederland** (✉Nieuwe Achtergracht 100 ☎0900/9594 ⊕www.ggd.nl).

▮ HOURS OF OPERATION

Banks are open weekdays 9:30 to 4 or 5, with some extending their business hours to coordinate with late-night shopping. Some banks are closed Monday mornings.

The main post office is open weekdays 9 to 6, Saturday 10 to 1:30. In every post office you'll also find the Postbank, a money-changing facility, which has the same opening hours.

Apotheken (pharmacies) are open weekdays from 8 or 9 to 5:30 or 6. There are always pharmacies on-call during the weekend. The after-hours emergency pharmacy telephone number is ☎070/310–9499. Operators always speak English.

Most shops are open from 1 to 6 on Monday, 9 to 6 Tuesday through Saturday. Hairdressers are generally closed Sunday and Monday. If you really need a haircut on those days, try a salon at one of the larger hotels. Thursday or Friday (Thursday in Amsterdam) is a designated late-night shopping night—*Koopavond* (buying evenings)—with stores staying open until 9. *Markts* (markets) selling fruit, flowers, and other wares run from 10 to 4 or sometimes 5. Small *avondwinkels* (late-night shops) selling food, wine, and toiletries, are open from afternoon to midnight or later. Supermarkets are open weekdays until 8 or 10 PM and Saturday until 5 or 8 PM, with some (such as Albert Heijn on the Leidsestraat, Dam, and Museumplein) open on Sundays from 11 to 7.

Opening hours are similar in Belgium.

HOLIDAYS

In Holland, *nationale feestdagen* (national holidays) are New Year's Day (January 1); Easter Sunday and Monday; Koninginnedag (Queen's Day, April 30); Remembrance Day (May 4); Liberation Day (May 5); Ascension Day; Whitsunday (Pentecost) and Monday; and Christmas (December 25 and 26). During these holidays, banks and schools are closed; many shops, restaurants, and museums are closed as well. Some businesses close early for May 4, Remembrance Day. Throughout the Netherlands, there is a two-minute silent pause from 8–8:02 pm, and even traffic stops. Take note and please respect this custom. Although May 5 is technically a holiday, most establishments remain open and the country functions as normal. *For information on these and other holidays, see also "On the Calendar" in the front of this book.*

In Belgium, all government and post offices, banks, and most shops are closed on Belgium's national day, July 21. Businesses are also closed on Easter Monday, Labor Day (May 1), the Ascension, Pentecost, the Assumption (Aug. 15), All Saints' Day (Nov. 1), Armistice Day (Nov. 11), Christmas Day, and New Year's Day. If a holiday falls on a weekend, offices close the preceding Friday or following Monday.

▮ MONEY

The price tags in Amsterdam are considered reasonable in comparison with those in main cities in neighboring countries, although with the strength of the euro versus the dollar, they may feel expensive to North American visitors. Good value for the money can still be had in many places, and as a tourist in this Anglophile country you are a lot less likely to get ripped off in the Netherlands than in countries where English is less-widely embraced.

Here are some sample prices: admission to the Rijksmuseum is €10; the cheapest seats at the Stadsschouwbourg theater run €12 for plays, €20 for opera; €6.50–€9.50 for a ticket at a movie theater (depending on time of show). Going to a nightclub might set you back €5–€20. A daily English-language newspaper is €3–€5. A taxi ride (1⅓ km, or ¾ mi) costs about €8. An inexpensive hotel room for two, including breakfast, is about €65–€125, an inexpensive dinner is €20–€35 for two, and a half-liter carafe of house wine is €10. A simple sandwich item on the menu runs to about €2.50, a cup of coffee €1.50. A Coke is €2, and a half-liter of beer is €4.

Prices throughout this guide are given for adults. Substantially reduced fees are almost always available for children, students, and senior citizens.

■TIP➜ Banks never have every foreign currency on hand, and it may take as long as a week to order. If you're planning to exchange funds before leaving home, don't wait till the last minute.

ATMS & BANKS

Your own bank will probably charge a fee for using ATMs abroad; the foreign bank you use may also charge a fee. Nevertheless, you'll usually get a better rate of exchange at an ATM than you will at a currency-exchange office or even when changing money in a bank. And extracting funds as you need them is a safer option than carrying around a large amount of cash.

■TIP➜ PIN numbers with more than four digits are not recognized at ATMs in many countries. If yours has five or more, remember to change it before you leave.

The Dutch word for ATM is *Geld-automaat;* many locals call the machines simply "pin." They are widespread, and accessible 24 hours a day, seven days per week. The majority of machines work with Maestro, Cirrus, and Plus.

CREDIT CARDS

Throughout this guide, the following abbreviations are used: **AE,** American Express; **DC,** Diners Club; **MC,** Master-Card; and **V,** Visa.

It's a good idea to inform your credit-card company before you travel, especially if you're going abroad and don't travel internationally very often. Otherwise, the credit-card company might put a hold on your card owing to unusual activity—not a good thing halfway through your trip. Record all your credit-card numbers—as well as the phone numbers to call if your cards are lost or stolen—in a safe place, so you're prepared should something go wrong. Both MasterCard and Visa have general numbers you can call (collect if you're abroad) if your card is lost, but you're better off calling the number of your issuing bank, since MasterCard and Visa usually just transfer you to your bank; your bank's number is usually printed on your card.

If you plan to use your credit card for cash advances, you'll need to apply for a PIN at least two weeks before your trip. Although it's usually cheaper (and safer) to use a credit card abroad for large purchases (so you can cancel payments or be reimbursed if there's a problem), note that some credit-card companies *and* the banks that issue them add substantial percentages to all foreign transactions, whether they're in a foreign currency or not. Check on these fees before leaving home, so there won't be any surprises when you get the bill.

■TIP➜ Before you charge something, ask the merchant whether or not he or she plans to do a dynamic currency conversion (DCC). In such a transaction the credit-card *processor* (shop, restaurant, or hotel, not Visa or MasterCard) converts the currency and charges you in dollars. In most cases you'll pay the merchant a 3% fee for this service in addition to any credit-card company and issuing-bank foreign-transaction surcharges.

Dynamic currency conversion programs are becoming increasingly widespread. Merchants who participate in them are supposed to ask whether you want to be charged in dollars or the local currency, but they don't always do so. And even if they do offer you a choice, they may well avoid mentioning the additional surcharges. The good news is that you *do* have a choice. And if this practice really gets your goat, you can avoid it entirely thanks to American Express; with its cards, DCC simply isn't an option.

Major credit cards are accepted in most hotels, gas stations, restaurants, cafés, and shops. Be aware, however, that you cannot use credit cards to purchase train tickets in the Netherlands.

Reporting Lost Cards American Express (☎800/528-4800 in the U.S. or 336/393-1111 collect from abroad ⊕www.americanexpress.com). **Diners Club** (☎800/234-6377 in the U.S. or 303/799-1504 collect from abroad ⊕www.dinersclub.com). **MasterCard** (☎800/627-8372 in the U.S. or 636/722-7111 collect from abroad ⊕www.mastercard.com). **Visa** (☎800/847-2911 in the U.S. or 410/581-9994 collect from abroad ⊕www.visa.com).

Reporting Lost Cards in Amsterdam and the Netherlands: American Express (☎020/504-8666). **Diners Club** (☎020/557-3407). **MasterCard** (☎0800/022-5821). **Visa** (☎0800/022-3110).

Reporting Lost Cards in Belgium: American Express (☎02/676-2121). **Diners Club** (☎02/626-5004). **MasterCard** (☎070/344-344). **Visa** (☎0800/183-97).

CURRENCY & EXCHANGE

The single euro is the official currency of the Netherlands and Belgium. At press time, 1 euro = 1.33 US$. Shop around for the best exchange rates (and also check the rates before leaving home).

There are eight coins—1 and 2 euros, plus 1, 2, 5, 10, 20, and 50 cents—5, 10, 20, 50, 100, 200, and 500 euros. Note that because of counterfeiting concerns, few shops and restaurants will accept notes higher in value than 50 euro. If you do find yourself with higher denominations, change them in a bank. The Dutch also consider the 1 and 2 cent coins to be an irritation, and many shops round prices up or down to the nearest 5 cents.

These days, the easiest way to get euros is through an ATM, called a *geldautomaat* in the Netherlands. You can find them in airports, train stations, and throughout the cities. ATM rates are excellent because they are based on wholesale rates offered only by major banks. At exchange booths always confirm the rate with the teller before exchanging money—you won't do as well at exchange booths in airports, or in hotels, restaurants, or stores. To avoid lines at airport exchange booths, get some euros before you leave home.

GWK/Grenswisselkantoren is a nation-wide financial organization specializing in foreign currencies, where travelers can exchange cash and traveler's checks, receive cash against major credit cards, and receive Western Union money transfers. Many of the same services are available at banks.

■TIP➔ Even if a currency-exchange booth has a sign promising no commission, rest assured that there's some kind of huge, hidden fee. (Oh...that's right. The sign didn't say no *fee*.) And as for rates, you're almost always better off getting foreign currency at an ATM or exchanging money at a bank.

Exchange Services in Amsterdam GWK (bureau de change) (☎0900/0566) branches are in or near railway stations throughout the country. There's an office at **Amsterdam Schiphol Airport** (☎020/653-5121). You can find a **GWK** branch in the hall at **Centraal Station** (☎020/627-2731).

■ RESTROOMS

Restrooms (*toiletten* or *WC* in Dutch) in restaurants, bars, and other public places in the Netherlands are generally very clean, and most are free, although you may have to pay a few cents to an attendant in some cafés.

In Belgium, paying an attendant is more common, so carry some small change with you if you get caught short. A few older cafés and bars here may only have one unisex restroom. Women shouldn't be surprised to find a urinal, possibly in use, beside the washbasin in such establishments.

Find a Loo The Bathroom Diaries (⊕ www. thebathroomdiaries.com) is flush with unsanitized info on restrooms the world over—each one located, reviewed, and rated.

▍SAFETY

Amsterdam is unlike any other modern metropolis: although it has had certain problems with crime, and with abuse of legalized prostitution and soft drugs, the serious crime rate is exceptionally low, so having your bike stolen is the worst thing most likely to happen to you. Still, in crowded intersections and dark alleys, it is always best to be streetwise and take double safety precautions; it may be best to keep your money in a money belt and not flaunt your expensive camera. Be especially wary of pickpockets in crowds and while riding the tram. And use common sense when going out at night. Keep to well-lighted areas and take a taxi if you are going a long distance. Although it is easy to lose yourself in a romantic 18th-century haze taking a midnight stroll along the canals in Amsterdam, remember that muggings do very occasionally occur. Late at night, it may be best to keep to the main thoroughfares and not venture down deserted streets.

In Belgium, in popular tourist areas, beware of restaurant personnel beckoning tourists on the street and luring prospective diners with a complimentary glass of champagne. At the end of the meal, the "compliments" are reflected in the tab. Avoid highway rest stops and sparsely populated metro stations late at night. Although they aren't likely to assault, tramps and derelicts tend to make train stations unsavory at night.

▍TIP ➡ **Distribute your cash, credit cards, I.D.s, and other valuables between a deep front pocket, an inside jacket or vest pocket,** and a hidden money pouch. Don't reach for the money pouch once you're in public.

▍TAXES

Hotels in Holland always include the service charge, and the 6% VAT (BTW in Dutch), in the room rate. Tourist tax is never included and is a few euro extra. If in doubt, enquire when booking. In restaurants you pay 5% service charge, 6% VAT on food items, and 19% VAT on all beverages, all of which are included in the quoted menu prices. VAT is 19% on clothes and luxury goods, 6% on basic goods. On most consumer goods, it is already included in the amount on the price tag, so you can't actually see what percentage you're paying.

All hotels in Belgium charge a 6% Value-Added Tax (TVA), included in the room rate; in Brussels, there is also a 9% city tax. Belgian VAT ranges from 6% on food and clothing to 33% on luxury goods. Restaurants are in between; 21% is included in quoted prices.

When making a purchase, ask for a V.A.T. refund form and find out whether the merchant gives refunds—not all stores do, nor are they required to. Have the form stamped like any customs form by customs officials when you leave the country or, if you're visiting several European Union countries, when you leave the EU. After you're through passport control, take the form to a refund-service counter for an on-the-spot refund (which is usually the quickest and easiest option), or mail it to the address on the form (or the envelope with it) after you arrive home. You receive the total refund stated on the form, but the processing time can be long, especially if you request a credit-card adjustment.

Global Refund is a Europe-wide service with 225,000 affiliated stores and more than 700 refund counters at major airports and border crossings. Its refund form, called a Tax Free Check, is the most common across the European continent. The service issues refunds in the form of cash, check, or credit-card adjustment.

V.A.T. Refunds Global Refund (☎800/566–9828 ⊕www.globalrefund.com).

▌ TIME

The Netherlands and Belgium are on Central European Time (CET), one hour ahead of Greenwich Mean Time (GMT). Daylight saving time begins on the last Sunday in March, when clocks are set forward one hour; on the last Sunday in October, clocks are set back one hour. Both countries operate on a 24-hour clock, so AM hours are listed as in the United States and Britain, but PM hours continue through the cycle (1 PM is 13:00, 2 PM is 14:00, etc.). When it's 3 PM in Amsterdam, it is 2 PM in London, 9 AM in New York City, and 6 AM in Los Angeles. A telephone call will get you the **speaking clock** (☎*0900/8002*) in Dutch.

▌ TIPPING

In Dutch restaurants, a service charge of about 5% is included in menu prices. Round the bill up to a convenient figure, or leave a few euro extra, if you've really enjoyed the meal and you got good service, and leave the tip as change rather than putting it on your credit card. If you're not satisfied, don't leave anything. Though a service charge is also included in hotel, taxi, bar, and café bills, the Dutch mostly round up the change to the nearest two euros for large bills and to the nearest euro for smaller ones. Only consider tipping in bars if you were served at a table. Restroom attendants expect only change, €0.25, and a cloakroom attendant in an average bar expects €0.50 per coat (more in expensive hotels and restaurants).

In Belgium, a tip (*service compris* or *service inclusief*) may be included in restaurant and hotel bills; if it is, you'll see a clear indication on the bill. If service is not included, people often round up a bit when paying, but it isn't offensive to pay the exact amount. Taxi drivers also appreciate a rounding up of the bill, but again, paying the exact amount is perfectly acceptable. Railway porters expect €0.75 per item on weekdays and €1 on weekends. For bellhops and doormen at both hotels and nightspots, €2.50 is adequate. Bartenders are tipped only for notably good service; again, rounding off is sufficient.

INDEX

PHOTO CREDITS

NOTES

NOTES

NOTES

NOTES